Stratagems

Arguing Issues for Writers

Wayne Stein | Pam Washington | Deborah Israel | Candice McKee | Ona Lou Britton

University of Central Oklahoma

FOUNTAINHEAD
PRESS

Cover Design by Doris Bruey
Illustration by Alex Brodt
Book design by Ellie Moore

Books may be purchased for educational purposes.

For information, please call or write:

1-800-586-0330

Fountainhead Press
100 W. Southlake Blvd. Suite 142, #350
Southlake, TX 76092

Web site: www.fountainheadpress.com
Email: customerservice@fountainheadpress.com

Second Edition

ISBN: 978-1-59871-219-3

Printed in the United States of America

BRIEF CONTENTS

Preview of Stratagems: Interdependent Awareness xxiii

UNIT ONE: BUILDING A FOUNDATION FOR ARGUMENTS

Chapter 1: Stratagems for Arguing Issues: A WOVE Approach 3
Chapter 2: The Classical Elements of Arguments 17
Chapter 3: Reading and Annotating Arguments 33
Chapter 4: Written Arguments 43
Chapter 5: Oral Arguments 55
Chapter 6: Visual Arguments 89
Chapter 7: Electronic Arguments 131

UNIT TWO: RESEARCHING ARGUMENTS

Chapter 8: The Research Paper 169
Chapter 9: Research Strategies 185
Chapter 10: MLA Documentation Format 211
Chapter 11: APA Documentation Format 240

UNIT THREE: ARGUING ISSUES: THE READINGS

Chapter 12: Conspiracy Issues 273
Chapter 13: Gaming Issues 353
Chapter 14: Consumer and Capitalist Issues 397
Chapter 15: War Issues 435
Chapter 16: Environment Issues 513
Chapter 17: Immigration and Acculturation Issues 573

Glossary 621
Citations 627
Author Index 635
Index 641

CONTENTS

Preview of Stratagems: Interdependent Awareness xxiii

"Startling Story" (Cartoon) xxiii
by Travis Kelly
The PENROSE xxiv
Unit I Building a Foundation for Arguments xxv
WOVE Awareness xxvii
Unit II Researching Arguments xxviii
Unit III Arguing Issues: The Readings xxviii
The Issues: The Visuals, Songs, and Readings xxix
Chapter Introductions xxx
Headnotes xxx
Pre-Reading Prompts xxxi
Post-Reading Prompts xxxi
Student Awareness: Sample Student Papers xxxi
Activities for Responding to the Issues xxxi

UNIT ONE: BUILDING A FOUNDATION FOR ARGUMENTS

Chapter One: Stratagems for Arguing Issues: A WOVE Approach 3

"Joe Chemo" (Spoof Ad) 3
www.adbusters.org
Everything Has a Message 4
The Chaos of Messages 4
Creating Multimodal Messages: The WOVE Approach 5
Developing Multimodal Critical Awareness: Ask Questions 6
Analyzing the Hidden Arguments 7
Argument Examples: Thank You for Smoking! 7
Visual Arguments: Cartoons 8
"I Can Quit Anytime" (Political Cartoon) 8
by Mike Luckovich of the Atlanta Constitution
"The Nicotine or the Lying?" (Political Cartoon) 9
by Dan Wasserman, Los Angeles Times Syndicate
Oral Argument: Lyrics 10
"Another Puff" (Lyrics) 10
by Jerry Reed
Written Argument: Novel 12
"The Mod Squad: The Tobacco, Gun and Alcohol Clan" (Fiction) 12
by Christopher Buckley
The Seduction Factor 14

Chapter Two: The Classical Elements of Arguments 17

"Grand Theft Auto" (Political Cartoon) 17
by Mark Parisi
What Is Rhetoric? 18
The Rhetorical Elements of an Argument 18
The Claim: The Position 18
The Issue: Stasis Theory 19
The Evidence 20
Ethos: Claiming Authority 21
Pathos: Using Emotions 23
Logos: Using Logic 24
Example by Current Events 26
Example by History 26
Example by Personal Experience 26
Example by Literature and Personal Fiction 26
Logical Fallacies 29
Errors in Ethos 30
Errors in Pathos 30
Errors in Logos 31

Chapter Three: Reading and Annotating Arguments 33

"Then a Miracle" (Political Cartoon) 33
by S. Harris
Effective Reading Skills 34
Effective Annotating Skills 34
Marking Up: Critical Reading 34
Annotation Assignment 35
Kennedy Assassination: How About The Truth? 35
by Gerald R. Ford and David W. Belin
Marking Up Assignments: Kennedy Assassination 39
Uncover the Main Point: The Issue 39
Find the Claim: Use Stasis Theory 40
Evaluate the Evidence: Appeals 40
Look for Fallacies 41
Make Connections 41
Ask Questions 41
Conclusion 42
Checklist for Annotating Classical Arguments 42
The Key Points to Identify in any Reading 42
Marking Up: Physical Interaction 42

Chapter Four: Written Arguments 43

"My Little Angel" (Political Cartoon) 43
by Rob Smith Jr.

Persuasive Writing . . . 44
The Rhetorical Situation . . . 44
Why Are You Writing? . . . 45
Know Your Audience . . . 45
Find a Claim . . . 46
The Classical Method . . . 47
The Toulmin Method . . . 47
Improving the Syllogism . . . 48
Three Optional Components . . . 49
The Rogerian Method . . . 50
Common Ground . . . 50
Empathy in the Refutation . . . 50
The Gaming Model . . . 51
Refutation . . . 51
The Process of Arguing: The Process of Writing . . . 52
Classical Model . . . 53
Toulmin Model . . . 53
Rogerian Model . . . 53
Argument Writing Process Checklist . . . 54
Generating ideas . . . 54
Writing . . . 54
Strengthening . . . 54
Polishing . . . 54
Proofreading . . . 54

Chapter Five: Oral Arguments . . . 55

"The Kennedy/Nixon Presidential Debate" (Photograph) . . . 55
Poems, Song Lyrics and Political Speeches as Arguments . . . 56
Poems . . . 56
Sound . . . 56
Rhythm . . . 57
"How to Write a Political Poem" (Poem) . . . 58
by Taylor Mali
Lyrics . . . 60
Sound and Rhythm . . . 60
Genre Analysis . . . 60
"Give the People What They Want" (Lyrics) . . . 61
by Ray Davies of the Kinks
Advertising Techniques in Political Speeches . . . 62
Logos: Techniques of Logic . . . 62
Weasel Words . . . 62
Stating the Obvious . . . 63
Unfinished Comparison . . . 63
Scientific and Statistical Language . . . 64

Ethos: Techniques of Authority 64
You're Terrific. 64
Pathos: Techniques of Emotions 65
Meaningless Words. 65
Rhetorical Question 65
Speeches: The Content 66
"9/11 Speech" (Speech). 66
by President George W. Bush
Speech Analysis 68
Capturing Attention 68
Finding the Real Message 68
Identifying Appeals 68
Understanding the Conclusion 69
John F. Kennedy's Inaugural Address (Speech) 70
The Non-Verbal Aspects: Visual Delivery 73
Body Language: Stress Choices 73
Dress: Clothing Choices 74
Background: Environmental Choices 75
"Clinton-Obama Immigration Debate" (Debate) 76
"Johnnie Cochran's Closing Arguments" (Speech). 78
"Chewbacca Defense" (Teleplay) 80
by Trey Parker and Matt Stone
Simulations 82
"Stratagems: The Show" 82
Part I: Ice Breaker 83
Part II: Debate 83
Part III: Jacked into a Game. 83
"The CUBE of Rhetoric Adventure" 83
Conclusion: Cubicle of Deadly Words 85
"Meeting of the Minds Adventure" 85
"Post-Millennium Think Tank Adventure" 86
Teams of Three–Five Players 87
Research Paper 87
Duties 87

Chapter 6: Visual Arguments. 89

"Baby Loves McDonalds" (Advertisement) 89
Visual Discourse 90
Why Study Visual Discourse in an English Course? 91
Motivation 91
Enrichment. 91
Summation. 91
Presentation 92
Evaluation 92

What Do Advertising Companies Know about Their Audiences? ... 92
"The Nine American Lifestyles" (Essay) ... 92
by Arnold Mitchell
"Are You Army Strong?" (Advertisement) ... 94
"I Have Thunder Thighs" (Advertisement) ... 95
What Techniques Do Advertising Companies Use? ... 96
Logos Techniques ... 96
Weasel Words ... 96
"Prozac: Wash Your Blues Away" (Spoof Ad) ... 97
"Absolute Impotence" (Spoof Ad) ... 97
Obvious ... 98
Unfinished Comparison ... 98
"So What" ... 98
Vague ... 99
Scientific or Statistical ... 99
False Dilemma ... 100
"Go Ahead—Please Take Day Off" (World War II Propaganda Poster) ... 100
Ethos Techniques ... 100
Endorsement or Testimonial ... 100
"Compliment the Consumer" ... 101
"We Can Do It" (World War II Propaganda Poster) ... 101
"Nothing to Fear" ... 101
Pathos Techniques ... 101
Bandwagon ... 102
Snob ... 102
Patriotic ... 102
"Destroy This Mad Brute—Enlist" (World War I Recruitment Poster) ... 102
Rhetorical Question ... 102
Traditional Wisdom (ethos, pathos, and logic) ... 103
"He Fought for the Union of Our Lamb and Mint Jelly" (Advertisement) ... 103
What Visual Techniques Do Advertising Companies Use? ... 103
Abstract Visuals ... 104
Concrete Visuals ... 105
Understanding the Use of Colors in Visuals ... 105
Color Harmony ... 106
Malboro: "The New Frontier" (Spoof Ad) ... 107
Analogous Colors ... 107
Complementary Colors ... 108
Natural Colors ... 108
Color Context ... 108
Understanding the Use of Fonts in Visuals ... 109
Definition of Fonts ... 110
Personalities of Fonts ... 110
Size of Fonts ... 110
Problems with Understanding Visuals ... 111
"Busy" Visuals ... 111

- Cultural Perspectives ... 111
- Color, Color, Color ... 111
- Lack of Rules ... 112
- "A Dollar A Song?" (Advertisement) ... 113

Political Campaigns ... 114
- Campaign Piece ... 114
- "A Look at the Record" (Campaign Ad) ... 115

Cartoons ... 115
- "What Is the Secret of the Icon?" (Cartoon) ... 116
  excerpt from Scott McCloud's book Understanding Comics.
- Political Cartoons ... 123
- "Arms Payoff for Hostage Release" (Political Cartoon) ... 123
  by Herbert Block ... 123
- Regular Cartoons ... 124
- "Special Program for Writing Love Letters" (Cartoon) ... 124
  by Randy Glasbergen

CD Covers ... 125

Mock Advertisements ... 126
- "Utter Fool" (Spoof Ad) ... 127

Continuing Your Visual Studies ... 128

Responding to Visual Issues: Analyzing the Variables ... 128
- Written Rhetoric: Evaluating Publications ... 128
- Oral Rhetoric: Creating Your Own Advertisement ... 129
- Visual Rhetoric: Evaluating CD Covers ... 129
- Electronic Rhetoric: Evaluating DeviantArt.com ... 129
- WOVE Project: Analysis and Presentation ... 129

Suggested Readings ... 130

Chapter 7: Electronic Arguments ... 131

- "Permission to Enter?" (Cartoon) ... 131
  by G.B. Trudeau from Doonesbury

Converging Technologies Change Communication ... 132

The New Convergent CyberSites of Emergent Rhetoric ... 133
- Social Bookmarking ... 134
- del.icio.us (del.icio.us, wiki: del.icio.us/tag/wiki) ... 134
- Widgets ... 134
  - RSS (Feeds: Really Simple Syndication) ... 135
  - Mashable: Social Networking News (mashable.com) ... 135
  - Yahoo Widgets (widget.yahoo.com) ... 135
- Visual Networks ... 135
  - DeviantArt ... 136
- Social Networks ... 138
  - Facebook ... 138
  - WOVE Features of Facebook: ... 139

MySpace . . . 139
Twitter . . . 140
Virtual Worlds . . . 141
Second Life (www.secondlife.com, Wiki: wiki.secondlife.com) . . . 141
Wiki Collaborative Writing . . . 142
Writeboard (www.writeboard.com) . . . 143
Wikipedia (www.wikipedia.org) . . . 143
YouTube.com and the Rhetorical Appeals . . . 144
Finding the Message in Political Propaganda . . . 144
Tips for Watching Political Ads . . . 145
Using Logos to Persuade: Fooling the Mind . . . 145
Logos and Oversimplification: Rudy Giuliani's "Jumpstart" . . . 146
Logos and Glittering Generalities (Virtue Words): John McCain's "Service" . . . 147
Ethos and the Cult of Personality: Mike Huckabee's "Chuck Norris Approved" . . . 147
Using the Ethos of Persuasion . . . 148
Ethos and Scapegoating: Mitt Romney's "Momentum" (Washington is Broken) . . . 148
Ethos and Testimonials: Fred Thompson's "Substance" . . . 149
Ethos and Plain Folks: Hillary Clinton's "It's About People" . . . 150
Using Pathos to Persuade: Fooling the Heart . . . 150
Pathos and Fear Tactics: Dennis Kucinich's "No More Blood for Oil" . . . 150
Pathos and Emotional Transfer (like Patriotism): Rudy Giuliani's "Freedom" . . . 151
Pathos and the Fear of Control: "Anti-Hillary Ad" (Parody) . . . 152
A Call for Balance: The Booth Effect . . . 152
Gaming Theory and Emergent Rhetoric . . . 153
The New Rhetorical Situation: Games . . . 154
Show Them the Game Face . . . 154
The Five Classical Canons of Rhetoric . . . 155
Classical Aspects of Rhetoric for the Speaker . . . 155
Developing the Six Gaming Senses . . . 155
Game Theories Open New Ways to Explore Complex Issues . . . 156
Prisoner's Dilemma . . . 156
Chicken Fight . . . 156
Students' Dilemma . . . 157
Ineffective Rhetorical Rants and Raves . . . 157
Break the Spell . . . 158
John Nash and Gaming . . . 158
Gaming into Writing: Enhancing Communicative Learning . . . 158
Decision Making: Adjusting to Audiences . . . 159
Generating a Sense of Success within the Gaming Situation . . . 159
Gaming as Persuasion: A New Approach to Writing . . . 160
Appeals as Gaming Moves: Ask the Right Question . . . 160
Game Moves . . . 160
On-Line Video Games . . . 161
World of Warcraft (WoW) (www.warcraft.com, wikie: wowwiki.com) . . . 161
EverQuest (EQ) (everquest.com) . . . 161

Video Games . . . 162
Halo 3 and Xbox 360 . . . 163
Guitar Hero III: Legends of Rock . . . 164
Rock Band . . . 165
Wii: Super Mario . . . 165

UNIT TWO: RESEARCHING ARGUMENTS

Chapter 8: The Research Paper. . . 169

"I Used to Hate Writing" (Cartoon) . . . 169
by Bill Watterson from Calvin and Hobbes
Multitasking: Two Assignments as One . . . 170
Organizing the Argument . . . 171
The Sentence Outline: An Organizing Tool . . . 172
Sample Sentence Outline. . . . 173
Sentence Outline Form . . . 174
Organizing Research: Research Timeline. . . . 175
Sample Research Timeline Form. . . . 177
An Organizing Tool: A Working Bibliography . . . 178
Recording Bibliographic Information . . . 178
Checking for Variety of Sources . . . 179
Providing a Brief Summary about Your Source. . . . 179
Using and Documenting Sources Properly. . . . 179
Why use Sources in your Paper?. . . . 179
To Establish a Sense of Ethos . . . 180
To Construct Logos Arguments . . . 180
To Create a Sense of Pathos. . . . 180
How Should You Use Sources in Your Paper?. . . . 180
What Material Do You Need to Cite? . . . 181
Ways to Avoid Plagiarism. . . . 182

Chapter 9: Researching Strategies . . . 185

"Honey" (Cartoon) . . . 185
by Travis Kelly
Library Research. . . . 186
Searching within Electronic Databases: The Big Picture. . . . 187
Research in the Library or on the Web: What's the Difference?. . . . 188
Evaluating Resources. . . . 189
Focusing a Topic . . . 190
Keyword Searching with Boolean Logic. . . . 190
Boolean Operators . . . 191
Truncation. . . . 191
Synonyms . . . 192

Nested Searches . . . 193
More Boolean Command Words . . . 195
Subject Searching in Databases. . . . 196
Searching for Books, Articles, and Free Web Sites . . . 198
Searching for Books and Other Materials in the Library . . . 198
When a Book Is in Hand . . . 200
Searching Other Library Catalogs . . . 201
Searching for Articles: Why So Many Article Databases? . . . 201
Common Elements in Article Databases . . . 202
Limiting Results . . . 204
Searching "Visible" or Free Web Sites . . . 207
Criteria When Considering a Web Site . . . 208
Common Domains and Their Potential As Reliable Sources. . . . 208
More Internet Searching Tools . . . 209
Conclusion . . . 210

Chapter 10: MLA Documentation Format. . . . 211

The Modern Language Association. . . . 211
The Modern Language Association Format . . . 212
Page Header. . . . 212
Sections . . . 212
First Page and the Start of the Main Body. . . . 212
Title of Paper . . . 212
In-Text Citations: The Basics . . . 215
To Summarize . . . 215
For example: . . . 215
To Paraphrase . . . 215
To Quote . . . 216
Formal Quotations . . . 216
Informal Quotations . . . 217
Incorporated Quotations . . . 217
What Else Should You Keep in Mind? . . . 217
In-Text Citations: Author/Authors . . . 217
A Single Author. . . . 218
A Single Author Who Has Multiple Works. . . . 218
Two or Three Authors . . . 218
Four or More Authors . . . 218
Unknown or Anonymous Author . . . 219
Organization as Author . . . 219
Electronic Sources. . . . 219
Unknown Author and Unknown Page Number. . . . 220
Sources without Page Numbers. . . . 220
Interviews, Letters, E-Mails, and Other Person-To-Person Communications . . . 220
The Bible . . . 220

Works Cited Page Entries 221
- Single Author of Article 221
- Two and Three Authors of an Article 221
- Four Authors or More of an Article 221
- Two or More Works by the Same Author 222
- Article from an On-Line Periodical 222
- On-Line Scholarly Journal Article 222
- Article from a Database 222
- Nonperiodical Web Document, Web Page, or Report 223
- On-Line Forum or Discussion Board Posting 223
- Article in Journal Paginated by Volume 224
- Article in Journal Paginated by Issue 224
- Article in a Newspaper 224
- Article or Chapter in an Edited Book 224
- Government Document 224
- The Bible 225
- Personal Interview 225
- Speech or Lecture 225
- Advertisement 225
- Cartoon or Comic Strip 225
- Motion Picture in Movie Theaters 225
- Motion Picture on DVD or BlueRay 226
- Broadcast or Radio Program 226
- Single Episode of a Television Series 226
- Entire Albums 226
- Individual Songs 226
- Sample Student Paper 227

Practicing MLA 236

Chapter 11: APA Documentation Format 239

- American Psychological Association 239

The American Psychological Association Format 240
- Page Header 240
- Sections 240
  - Title Page 240
  - Abstract 242
  - Body Pages 243
  - Reference Page 244

In-Text Citations: The Basics 245
- In-Text Citation Capitalization, Quotes, and Italics 245
- Short Quotations 245
- Long Quotations 246
- Summary or Paraphrase 246

In-Text Citations: Author/Authors 247
- A Single Author 247

Two Authors . . . 247
Three to Five Authors . . . 248
Six or More Authors . . . 248
Unknown Author . . . 248
Organization as Author . . . 249
Electronic Sources . . . 249
Unknown Author and Unknown Date . . . 249
Sources Without Page Numbers . . . 249
Interviews, Letters, E-Mails, and Other Person-To-Person Communications . . . 250
Two or More Works Used to Support a Single Entry . . . 250
Authors with the Same Last Name but Different First Names . . . 250
References Page Entries . . . 251
Single Author of Article . . . 251
Two Authors of Article . . . 251
Three to Six Authors of Article . . . 251
More Than Six Authors . . . 251
Two or More works by the Same Author . . . 252
Article in Journal Paginated by Volume . . . 252
Article in Journal Paginated by Issue . . . 252
Article in a Newspaper . . . 252
Article or Chapter in an Edited Book . . . 253
Government Document . . . 253
Motion Picture . . . 253
Television Broadcast or Series Episode . . . 253
A Television Series . . . 253
Single Episode of a Television Series . . . 253
Music Recording . . . 254
Article From an On-Line Periodical . . . 254
On-Line Scholarly Journal Article . . . 254
Article From a Database . . . 254
Nonperiodical Web Document, Web Page, or Report . . . 254
On-Line Forum or Discussion Board Posting . . . 255
Computer Software . . . 255
Sample Student Essay . . . 256
Practicing APA . . . 269

UNIT THREE: ARGUING ISSUES: THE READINGS

Chapter 12: Conspiracy Issues . . . 273

"Magic Bullet" (Cartoon) . . . 273
by Cary Stringfield
"Brotherhood of the Magic Bullet" (Cartoon) . . . 274
by Kirk-Albert Etienne
The Issues . . . 276
The Rising Popularity of Conspiracy Theories . . . 276

What is a Conspiracy Theory? 277
Ask the Right Questions 277
Logos 278
Ethos 278
Pathos 278
Annotate the Text 278
How Does a Conspiracy Theory Work? 278
"The President Was Murdered by a Conspiracy" (Screenplay) 280
from JFK, *by Oliver Stone*
Conspiracy As Inductive Argument 282
Logical Fallacies in Conspiracies 283
Logos 283
Ethos 284
Pathos 284
The Readings 285
"It's Paul McCartney" (Cartoon) 285
by Jim Borgman
"The JFK Assassination—What About The Evidence?" (Essay) 286
by Oliver Stone
"Political Paranoia as Cinematic Motif: Stone's ***JFK***" (Essay) 292
by Robert S. Robins and Jerrold M. Post
"16 Questions on the Assassination" (Essay) 300
by Bertrand Russell
"The Principles of Newspeak" (Essay) 309
by George Orwell
"The Great Conspiracy: We Will Not Walk in Fear" (Screenplay) 318
by George Clooney and Grant Heslov
Issues of Liberty 323
"Freedom From Fear" (Essay) 323
by Aung San Suu Kyi
"V's Speech: Something Terribly Wrong" (Screenplay) 328
by the Wachowski Brothers
"V's Speech: Good Evening London" (Graphic Novel) 338
by Alan Moore and David Lloyd
Sample Student Paper 345
The Prince of Propaganda (Essay) 345
by Jeff Coldwell
Responding to the Conspiracy Issues 349
Written Rhetoric: Opinion Papers, Arguments, and Research 349
Oral Rhetoric: Speeches, Lyrics, and Simulations 349
Visual Rhetoric: Advertisements, Visuals, and Cinema 350
Electronic Rhetoric: Emergent Media and Gaming 350
WOVE Project 351
Song Lyrics 351
Cinematic List 351
Anime List 351
Television Shows 352

Comix List . . . 352
Video Games . . . 352
Xbox 360 . . . 352
Playstation 3 . . . 352
Wii . . . 352

Chapter 13: Gaming Issues . . . 353

"Bureaucrats" (Cartoon) . . . 353
by Ali Farzat
The Issues . . . 354
Ask the Right Questions . . . 354
Logos . . . 355
Ethos . . . 355
Pathos . . . 355
The Ratings System for Video Games . . . 355
Entertainment Software Rating Board (ESRB) . . . 355
www.esrb.org . . . 355
"You Play World of Warcraft? You're Hired!" (Essay) . . . 357
by John Seely Brown and Douglas Thomas
"Violence in Media Entertainment" (Essay) . . . 360
by Media Awareness Network (MNet) 2008
"Were Video Games to Blame for Massacre?" (Essay) . . . 366
by Winda Benedetti
"Violent Media is Good for Kids" (Essay) . . . 370
by Gerard Jones
"Dining with Cannibals" (Essay) . . . 374
by Pop
"Are You Human? The Test" (Screenplay) . . . 377
by Hampton Fancher and David Webb Peoples
"The Deliverator" (Fiction) . . . 383
by Neal Stephenson
Sample Student Paper . . . 391
Fun vs. Family: Mind-Numbing Deviltry (Essay) . . . 391
by Will Waldroup
Responding to Gaming Issues . . . 393
Written Rhetoric: Opinion Papers, Arguments, and Research . . . 393
Oral Rhetoric: Speeches, Lyrics, and Simulations . . . 394
Visual Rhetoric: Advertisements, Visuals, and Cinema . . . 394
Electronic Rhetoric: Emergent Media and Gaming . . . 394
WOVE Projects . . . 394
Cinematic List . . . 395
Television . . . 396
Reality TV . . . 396
Game List . . . 396
On-Line . . . 396
Video Games . . . 396

Chapter 14: Consumer and Capitalist Issues 397

Calvin Klein Underwear Ad (Advertisement). 397
The Issues 398
Ask the Right Questions 398
Logos 398
Ethos. 399
Pathos 399
Annotate the Text 399
Comparing Ads: Obsession Ads 399
"Obsession for Women" (Advertisement). 399
"Obsession for Men" (Advertisement) 400
"A Backlash to Advertising in an Age of Anything Goes" (Essay) 402
by Alexandra Marks
Comparing Ads: War Posters. 405
"I Gave a Man: War Bonds" (War Poster). 405
"Save Waste Fats for Explosives" (War Poster) 406
"Californication" (Lyrics) 406
by The Red Hot Chili Peppers
"Super Size Me" (Lyrics) 409
by Toothpick
"Why McDonald's Fries Taste Good" (Essay) 412
by Eric Schlosser
"The Selling Of Rebellion" (Essay) 418
by John Leo
"Some Hated Commercials Inspire Violent Fantasies" (Essay) 421
by Dave Barry
Sample Student Papers 424
"Does This Ad Make Me Look Fat?" (Essay). 424
by Sarah Bailey
Advertising Sex: Company Bias (Essay). 429
by Kimberly Williams
Responding to Consumer and Capitalist Issues 432
Written Rhetoric: Opinion Papers, Arguments, and Research 432
Oral Rhetoric: Speeches, Lyrics, and Simulations 432
Visual Rhetoric: Advertisement, Visuals, and Cinema 433
WOVE Projects 433
Electronic Rhetoric: The Emergent Media with Gaming 433
Cinematic List 434
Reality TV 434

Chapter 15: War Issues 435

"Welcome to the Suck" (Film Poster) 435
"Leave No Man Behind" (Film Poster). 436
"There Was a Time…" (Film Poster) 436
Jarhead, Black Hawk Down, and Band of Brothers 436

The Issues 437
Ask the Right Questions 438
Logos 438
Ethos 438
Pathos 438
Annotate the Text 438
Civilian Viewpoint 439
"Born in Hiroshima" (Graphic Novel) 439
by Keiji Nakazawa (translated by Project Gen)
"Born in the U.S.A." (Lyrics) 447
by Bruce Springsteen
"Dwight's Speech" (Teleplay) 449
by Paul Lieberstein
"The War Prayer" (Fiction) 450
by Mark Twain
"My Heart's Content: Thirty Years of One Man's Truth are Up for Reconsideration" (Memoir) 454
by Pat Conroy
"Time Flies" (Graphic Novel) 458
by Art Spiegelman
Soldier's Viewpoint 463
"We Band of Brothers" St. Crispin's Day Speech (Drama) 463
by William Shakespeare
General George S. Patton's "Blood and Guts Speech" (Speech) 466
"The Things They Carried" (Fiction) 468
by Tim O'Brien
"Why I Went to the War" (Essay) 482
by Terry Farish
"Vietnam War Films as War Porn" (Memoir) 484
by Anthony Swofford
Political Viewpoint 487
"America Should Not Enter the War" (Essay) 487
by Charles Lindbergh
"We Must Defeat Hitler" (Essay) 492
by James B. Conant
"Why Iraq Was a Mistake" (Essay) 495
by Lt. General Greg Newbold (Ret.)
"Our Troops Must Stay" (Essay) 498
by Joe Lieberman
Sample Student Papers 503
Media and the Mind War (Essay) 503
by Saad S. Muhammad
A Soldier's Manifesto (Essay) 506
by Cory Washington
Responding to War Issues 508
Written Rhetoric: Opinion Papers, Arguments, and Research 508

Oral Rhetoric: Speeches, Lyrics, and Simulations 508
Visual Rhetoric: Advertisements, Visuals, and Cinema 509
Electronic Rhetoric: Emergent Media and Gaming 509
WOVE Project 510
Song Lyrics 510
Civil War. 510
World War I 510
World War II. 510
Vietnam Conflict 510
Middle East Conflicts. 510
Cinematic List 511
World War II. 511
Vietnam Conflict 511
Middle East. 511
Video Games 511
Playstation3 511
Xbox 360 511
Wii 512
Online 512

Chapter 16: Environment Issues 513

"Plastic, again?!" (Cartoon). 513
by John Pritchett
The Issues 514
Ask the Right Questions 514
Logos 514
Ethos. 514
Pathos 515
Annotate the Text 515
"Anywhere But Here" (Lyrics) 515
by Rise Against
I Heart Huckabees (Screenplay) 518
by Jeff Baena
"Environmental Illness" (Screenplay). 526
by Todd Haynes
"Before They Got Thick" (Essay) 533
by Percy Bigmouth
"The Indians Grew Very Inquisitive" (Essay). 535
by John Winthrop
"How Can One Sell the Air? A Manifesto for the Earth" (Manifesto). 536
by Chief Seattle
"Mexican American Women Grassroots Community Activists:
'Mothers of East Los Angeles'" (Essay) 540
by Mary Pardo

"The Dumping Ground: Big Utilities Look to Native Lands to House Nuclear Waste" (Essay) 547
by Winona LaDuke
"The Eco-tist: Gore as Green" (Essay) 552
by Ronald Bailey
An Inconvenient Truth: "The Politicization of Global Warming" (Essay) 555
by Al Gore
"Better Living Through French Fries: Is Biodiesel the Fuel of the Future?" (Essay) 559
by Hal Clifford
Sample Student Paper 563
Global Warming: Fact or Fiction? (Essay) 563
by Lauren Kobernus
Responding to Environmental Issues 569
Written Rhetoric: Opinion Papers, Arguments, and Research 569
Oral Rhetoric: Speeches, Lyrics, and Simulations 569
Visual Rhetoric: Advertisements, Visuals, and Cinema 570
Electronic Rhetoric: Emergent Media and Gaming 570
WOVE Project 571
Cinematic List 571
Television 572
Video Games 572
On-Line Games 572
Fun and Games 572
PowerUp, the Game. IBM. 572

Chapter 17: Immigration and Acculturation Issues 573

"Nintendo Controls U.S.-Mexico Borders" (Cartoon) 573
by Cary Stringfield
"Nuestro Himno" ("Star-Spangled Banner") (Lyrics) 574
The Issues 575
Ask the Right Questions 576
Logos 576
Ethos 576
Pathos 576
Annotate the Text 576
"It's My Yardman" (Cartoon) 577
by John Branch
"Minute Men" (Cartoon) 577
by Steve Breen
"The Vegetable" (Graphic Novel) 578
by Marjane Satrapi
"No Leniency for Illegal Aliens" (Essay) 588
by Ian De Silva
"Conspiracy Against Assimilation" (Essay) 591
by Robert J. Samuelson

"Immigration: 'Neither Preference Nor Prejudice'" (Essay) 594
by Tim Kane and Kirk Johnson
"Mexicans Begin Jogging" (Poem) 597
by Gary Soto
President Bush's Speech on Immigration Policy (Speech) 598
A Day Without a Mexican (Screenplay) 604
by Sergio Arau
Issues of Language 607
"Why Fear Spanish?" (Essay) 607
by Carlos Alberto Montaner
Sample Student Paper 610
Illegal Immigrants' Access to Medical Care (Essay) 610
by Stephanie Egert
Responding to the Immigration and Acculturation Issues 617
Written Rhetoric: Opinion Papers, Arguments, and Research 617
Oral Rhetoric: Speeches, Lyrics, and Simulations 617
Visual Rhetoric: Advertisements, Visuals, and Cinema 618
Electronic Rhetoric: Emergent Media and Gaming 618
WOVE Project 619
Song Lyrics 619
Cinematic List 619
Comix 620

GLOSSARY 621
CITATIONS 627
AUTHOR INDEX 635
INDEX 641

"Startling Story"

by Travis Kelly

http://www.traviskelly.com/cartoon/index.html

The Rhetorical Situation: Thinking Critically

THE WOVE APPROACH

Written Rhetoric	→	Reading and Writing Critically
Oral Rhetoric	→	Speaking and Listening Critically
Visual Rhetoric	→	Seeing and Perceiving Critically
Electronic Rhetoric	→	Interacting and Gaming Critically

Some colleges and universities teach argument in composition-focused classes, while others teach it in literature classes. This reader integrates many genres into the argument class, asking students to uncover the arguments in a variety of communication forms.

Stratagems
The art and the means of obtaining or maintaining a rhetorical command over a situation.

A variety of **stratagems** will allow you to decode the arguments embedded in all sorts of genres, from cartoons to essays, lyrics to screenplays. We connect this multi-genre approach to WOVE—written, oral, visual, and electronic rhetorics that provide the different stratagems you can examine and then employ as you create your own texts. The text moves you through these stratagems, providing examples and exercises throughout for you to actively engage in to develop your argument skills.

The PENROSE

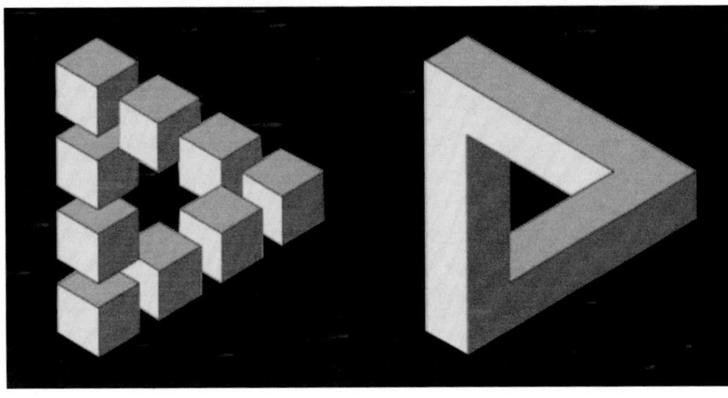

One of the key issues we examine in this book is conspiracies. Who knew what and when? The **penrose** is the symbolic image for this book because if you follow along the edge of the triangle, you may think you are making progress, but you will soon find out that you have only returned to the start. For the most part, this is symbolic of the problem with conspiracy theories that offer everything but actually give nothing. Don't just accept what people say or write. Be critical and thoughtful and research the topic. Stand back and see the penrose and the conspiracy for what they are, circular arguments offering the truth but only providing deceit.

> The Penrose Triangle
> Named after Roger Penrose (1931–) who made the tribar figure famous, and modeled on the Möbius strip, a mathematical geometrical circular fold symbolizing a continuous or indefinite plane where one can move along forever as it merges with its other side. M.C. Escher (1898–1972) used the mechanics of such a mathematical arrangement in his images to create the illusion of interconnectivity, infinity, or impossibility.

Unit I Building a Foundation for Arguments

Processing Awareness. In addition to the WOVE approach, this text takes a process approach to responding to the various readings and visuals. Such an approach requires that you fully interact with the text so as to get the most out of its contents. To further the process of arriving at consciously reasoned responses to issues, you will also have to do further research on the topics you become involved with.

Once you begin to write, you will continue to interact with your own text, making notes to yourself and commenting on your own writing after you let it cool. You will work to organize your writing organically to achieve the effect you desire, considering who your audience is and how you want to move them. It will help to examine the writing of other students to see how they approached the issues; critiquing what others have done will keep you from making the same mistakes. What follows are the components of this process approach.

> Meta-Awareness
> A sensitive mindfulness of your own rhetorical processes. By overtly understanding how you write, you are able to identify weaknesses and effect positive change.

Meta-Awareness. Another key process this text urges is being meta-aware of your own reading and writing processes. That is, you must step outside of yourself and observe yourself as a thinker and writer. Watch the watcher, write about the writer, and awaken within. Once you understand what you are doing and how, as well as the rhetorical choices you are making, you can analyze your own process and improve. The rewards of a skillful rhetor await the person who is mindful of the effects that rhetorical choices create.

Chapter 1: Stratagems for Arguing Issues: WOVE. Begins by explaining the WOVE approach, experiencing issues through written, oral, visual, and electronic rhetorics. This chapter also focuses on a process approach to reading and writing.

A WOVE Approach

Written Approach: Reading and writing about the issues.

Oral Approach: Speaking and hearing the issues.

Visual Approach: Seeing the issues and analyzing visual cues.

Electronic Approach: Integrating reading, writing, seeing, and hearing the issues in an interactive format.

Chapter 2: The Classical Elements of Arguments. Explains in detail the rhetorical elements of argument. This chapter takes a classical approach to provide you with a vocabulary for discussing the elements of argument.

Audience Awareness. When explaining an argument, many writers focus on the format, striving to write to a form instead of concentrating on effective content for readers, which will then lead to an effective format. The problem with placing form over content is that the overall effect may be greatly lessened. For example, the chapter of this text on political speeches demonstrates that effective speeches do not follow one particular form; they are more concerned with the effect that the message has on its audience than on the form of the speech. Likewise, essays should be organically created based on keen audience awareness. You must ask yourself: What is my message? What is my purpose? What is the best way to be effective in communicating that message?

Argument that is audience driven is more effective than argument that is form driven. In this text, you will examine Toulmin, Rogerian, and Classical Approaches to argument, but you must realize that these are only approaches. You may use them for guidelines, but realize that balancing the various elements of the rhetorical situation—subject, audience, and purpose—as well as the appeals—logos, pathos, and ethos—is a better approach.

Chapter 3: Reading and Annotating Arguments. Requires you to annotate written texts in order to decode the arguments they present, thus providing strategies of effectively reading essays.

Annotating Awareness. This text encourages you to begin the process by annotating what you read and see. Annotating is a key means of interacting with the complex information any text contains to better understand it. Chapter 3 provides detailed instruction on how to annotate a text. This activity pushes you to stay focused on what the author of the text is saying, noting both the strong points and the problems you see in the content. As this book moves through the various components of WOVE, it provides annotation tips for each of these different forms of rhetoric.

You will continue to use annotation skills during peer review, when you will annotate your classmates' essays to point out their strengths and weaknesses. Even when you revise your own work, you will continue annotating, adjusting your content based on your own observations after you let the work cool to get a more objective view of what you have written.

WOVE Awareness

Chapter 4: Written Arguments. Moves from reading to writing, focusing on the writing process. This chapter begins with audience analysis, examines different types of claims, and moves to different methods of developing arguments based on audience and claims.

Chapter 5: Oral Arguments. Examines the appeals found in famous speeches, by approaching speeches as items to be consumed just as ads and commercials try to persuade their audiences. The chapter offers a section on how to approach poems and lyrics. It also includes a sample of the famous Kennedy/Nixon debate and asks you to compare the written version to the spoken. Nixon quotes well when you read the debate. He does not do as well when you watch it. Visual rhetoric has a huge impact on how we interpret discourse.

Chapter 6: Visual Arguments. Explores how the appeals of pathos, logos, and ethos are persuasive in visual discourse such as advertisements, war posters, presidential campaign posters, cartoons, and images in our capitalistic world. Scott McCloud even examines how cartoons are iconic.

Chapter 7: Electronic Arguments. Approaches electronic formats that mash, merge, and emerge where rhetoric can potentially combine into various elements inherent in written, oral, and visual arguments. As you move through these convergent media, you will become more aware of the variety of arguments that surround you in your daily life.

Unit II Researching Arguments

Research Awareness. While this text contains many readings and visuals that explore the issues, you will be encouraged to do your own research to further your understanding of those issues.

Research today takes many avenues: in college libraries, through interviews, and on the Internet. With so many sources out there in this information age, you will need strategies for validating sources and integrating them within your own writing and projects. This is no easy task, given the many means individuals have of posting their own often biased or jumbled thoughts on the Internet. This text will help you find appropriate sources and navigate the many questionable sources available on-line.

Chapter 8: The Research Paper. Gives an overview of writing a research paper. Provides methods for organizing a research paper while emphasizing the importance of time management. Shares ways to avoid plagiarism.

Chapter 9: Research Strategies. Written by a university librarian, explains how to best create searches to get the most out of the electronic databases available through college and university libraries. This chapter also explores other Internet sources and discusses the reliability of those sources.

Chapter 10: MLA Documentation Format. Examines how to write in-text citations paraphrasing and quoting from sources, according to the Modern Language Association. Provides ample examples of how to document sources in the "Works Cited." Also provides a sample student paper.

Chapter 11: APA Document Format. Provides examples of how to write in-text citations. Also gives examples of paraphrasing and quoting from sources, according to the American Psychological Association. Provides ample examples of how to document sources in the "References" page. Also provides a sample student paper.

Unit III Arguing Issues: The Readings

Unit III provides a wide variety of readings, written, oral, visual, and electronic. These works examine some of today's major issues.

The Issues: The Visuals, Songs, and Readings

Chapter 12: Conspiracy Issues. This chapter examines conspiracy theory as a way to better understand arguments. Conspiracies often overlook key aspects of an argument in an effort to prove almost by faith that something is wrong. Or are there some valid conspiracies? Anyway that you approach conspiracies, you must be critical. Conspiracies test our ability to be objective. Again the JFK assassination theory is examined, mainly because much has been written on this, so you can examine more evidence than for some of the more current conspiracy theories. A series of readings—a screenplay excerpt, cartoons, and essays—are provided.

Chapter 13: Gaming Issues. This chapter examines gaming theories—such as the Prisoner's Dilemma, Chicken Fights, and the Stag Hunts—as a way to approach writing and thinking. To further understand the power of choice, read Johnnie Cochran's famous speech and the "Chewbacca Defense" from *South Park.* Compare those to the real excerpts from the O.J. Simpson case. Finally, the chapter focuses on role playing games (RPGs) as a way to approach writing in a more communicative manner through interaction and debate.

Chapter 14: Consumer and Capitalist Issues. We are what we see. This chapter examines how we are affected by advertisements, like those by Calvin Klein. We are what we eat. So eat lyrics like "Super Size Me" and readings like "Why Fries Taste Good" from *Fast Food Nation.* We are what we buy. Read these entries about the invasion of persuasion through consumerism. Dave Barry also gives his opinion about what commercials we love to hate.

Chapter 15: War Issues. From war posters to movie posters, this chapter examines the culture of conflict. From the Holocaust to Hiroshima, you will look at graphic novels that impart the visual impact of these acts of violence. From Vietnam to the Middle East, military conflicts continue to define who we are. We have a variety of powerful readings, for example, "The Things They Carry" by Tim O'Brien. We also have a variety of opinions on war. Hear the power of rhetorical pathos in Mark Twain's "The War Prayer," Bruce Springsteen's "Born in the USA," and Anthony Swofford's "Vietnam War Film as War Porn." We have classical calls to battle from Shakespeare's "We Band of Brothers" and Patton's "Blood and

Guts" speech to more modern cries, such as Dwight's famous speech for salesmen, "Blood Alone" from *The Office.* We end with speeches pro and con to wars past and present. Note the enduring similarities.

Chapter 16: Environment Issues. With the rise of oil prices, calls for new forms of energy have emerged. Al Gore claims that there is global warming while some politicians and scientists think the concern is a "hoax." Who is right? This chapter examines such issues from a variety of perspectives from Chief Seattle to women activists. The various genres of cartoons, lyrics, screenplays, and essays are offered as differing perspectives.

Chapter 17: Immigration and Acculturation Issues. Why would hearing the *Star Spangled Banner* in Spanish make some people angry? Americans continue to note the problems we have with immigration laws, but immigration problems happen to every country. We also examine the acculturation problems of an Iranian teenager becoming a woman in Europe.

Chapter Introductions

The Issues. Each chapter opens with a brief introduction that acquaints you with the complexities of the issue and the questions you must ask in order to fully explore the issue.

Rhetorical Appeals. The introductions also contain suggestions for approaching the issues based on the rhetorical appeals: logos, ethos, pathos.

Suggestions for Annotating the Text. Finally, you will find suggestions for annotating the texts so that you read analytically and critically.

Headnotes

Before each reading, a headnote provides information about the author. You should use these headnotes to determine the ethos of the writer and to find clues to the approach or perspective that the work will offer.

Pre-Reading Prompts

AS YOU READ: Annotate. After the headnotes, you will find specific annotation questions that focus on the important aspects of the text to follow. You should feel free, however, to comment in other ways as well, on what you find interesting, disturbing, or even boring. Anytime you interact with the text, you gain more from the reading experience.

Post-Reading Prompts

AFTER YOU READ: Analyze the Issues. These questions focus on the content of the specific readings. They ask you to think more deeply about the messages found within the readings.

AFTER YOU READ: Analyze the Rhetoric. These questions examine the rhetorical choices that the author used. They ask about style, emphasis, and other aspects of rhetoric that create the meaning of the text and affect the audience.

Sample Student Papers: Peer Review

Read the sample student papers at the end of each chapter. **Annotation prompts** are provided. Since annotating remains a form of thinking, review what was written. A peer review outline is provided after each paper for review of the rhetorical appeal of *logos, ethos,* and *pathos.* Such peer review outlines can be used for reviewing student papers in class.

Activities for Responding to the Issues

At the end of each chapter, you will find a variety of composition options related to the issue in each chapter. In keeping with the WOVE emphasis of the text, each chapter contains suggestions for all WOVE elements.

Written Rhetoric: Opinion Papers, Arguments, and Research. These are suggestions for you to give your opinion on topics of the day. Your opinion counts. Be sure to be critical. Learning to research critically is necessary in this information age. These are items that you might want to investigate in more detail. You will also find a list of suggested research topics related to the chapter.

Oral Rhetoric: Speeches, Lyrics, and Simulations. These are suggestions for writing about speeches and lyrics. The power of oral rhetoric is examined in your writings. Learning to speak critically is important for students. These dramatic debate settings provide a specific forum that the group or class can examine as a way to understand the complexities of issues in a more manageable way.

Visual Rhetoric: Advertisements, Visuals, and Cinema. Learn to see critically, and value this ability as a way to confront the rhetoric of desire that bombards us. Be more critical of the visual discourses that exist in various forms, such as commercials and ads.

Electronic Rhetoric: Emergent Media and Gaming. This chapter provides a list of suggested gaming activities and/or video games as related to the chapter.

WOVE Project. This project combines elements of written, oral, and visual rhetoric into a series of assignments.

Cinematic List. Some chapters have a list of films related to the topics of the chapter.

Song Lyrics. Some chapters have lyrics listed.

Games. Some chapters have on-line and video games listed.

Building a Foundation for Arguments

Chapter 1 . . . Stratagems for Arguing Issues

Chapter 2 . . . The Classical Elements of Arguments

Chapter 3 . . . Reading and Annotating Arguments

Chapter 4 . . . Written Arguments

Chapter 5 . . . Oral Arguments

Chapter 6 . . . Visual Arguments

Chapter 7 . . . Electronic Arguments

"JOE CHEMO"

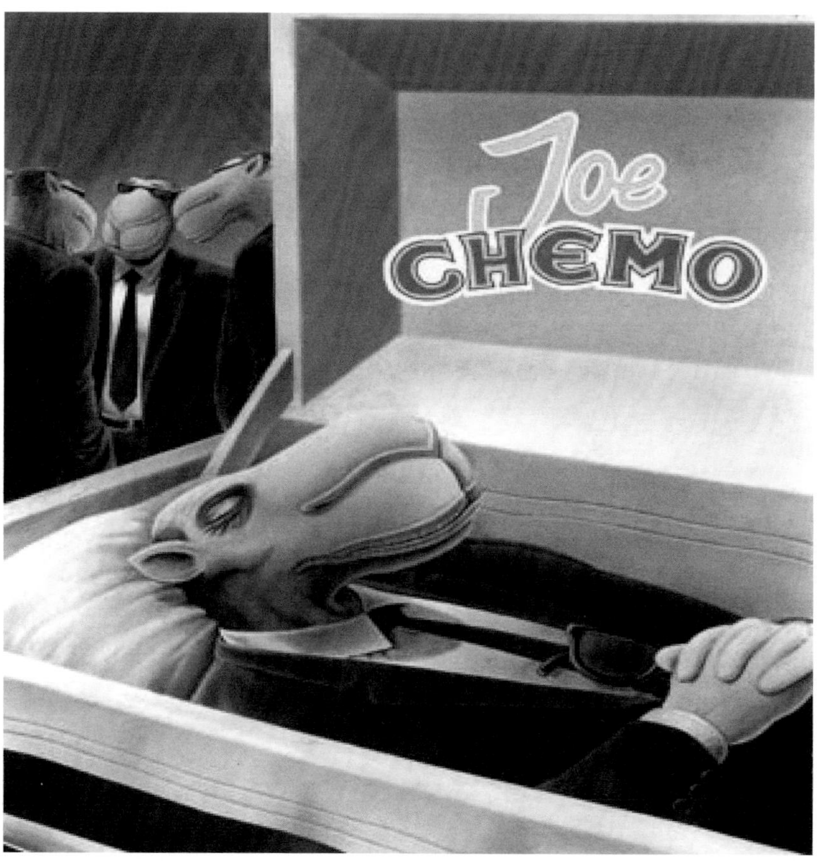

www.adbusters.org

Everything Has a Message

Indeed, we are surrounded by a multitude of messages in a variety of forms. How do we manage to sort through the messages to come to a reasoned understanding of important issues? Examine the cartoon on the previous page to begin to understand how we analyze communications.

1. What is the message of this advertisement?
2. What is it spoofing?
3. What brand is the ad making fun of?
4. Why isn't the dead camel wearing sunglasses?
5. What emotions does the ad appeal to?
6. Now go on-line and find more tobacco ads. Comment on their effectiveness.

Such ads are effective because we are able to be critical. Furthermore, we are able to laugh or smile because such a spoof can make fun of the rhetorical weaknesses of the original ad campaigns. Ultimately, humor is a type of intelligence or wisdom that we all have.

The Chaos of Messages

Some of us are awakened by music when our alarms go off, the words of which greet us with our first message of the day. Next, we may turn on the TV, only to get one person's version of the latest news followed by a barrage of commercials, or we may check our e-mail or Facebook for messages from friends.

As we drive to work or school, we continue to hear various messages over the radio while billboards add to the cacophony. At our destination, we must make sense of various readings, spreadsheets, images, Internet sites, and lectures, while items on bulletin boards beckon as well.

You name it; it "speaks" to us, encouraging us to believe certain assertions, buy a whole spectrum of products, vote for specific candidates, volunteer, attend a function, the list goes on and on.

In today's multimedia, multitasking world, we need stratagems for dealing with this daily onslaught.

As 21st century students, you have grown accustomed to this overwhelming volume of communication, taking it in stride as you maneuver through your daily routines. However, we need to take note of this volume and turn it down. We need to question the messenger and the multimodal characteristics of each message:

1. How do you come to terms with the messages so as to better deal with the issues of the day?
2. How do you decide which messages to pay attention to?
3. Which messages should you ignore?
4. Which should you believe?

You probably laughed at the "Joe Chemo" cartoon because Joe has obviously lost his cool, but not all messages are as clear; in fact, most are rather complex, requiring logical analysis to determine credibility. This textbook provides you with stratagems for interpreting messages in a variety of genres, new and old, so that you can come to reasoned conclusions about the issues they discuss and then argue your conclusions effectively.

WOVE Approach. Created by Iowa State University's communication-across-the-curriculum initiative as a form of "multimodal communication" where "teachers provide all students with the kind of communication instruction that prepares them to communicate with expertise in multiple settings and with multiple media" <http://isucomm.iastate.edu/about>. Such an approach prepares students for today's working environment that incorporates the varieties of new media which are emerging.

Creating Multimodal Messages: The WOVE Approach

You have probably been asked in other classes to respond to issues primarily in writing, the form of communication that predominated from the invention of movable type in the fifteenth century to the invention of the Web in the late twentieth century. This class will be different. You will create written, oral, visual, and electronic messages—the WOVE approach to communication.

The Interdependency of Rhetorics

Multiple Issues, Multiple Genres, Multiple Rhetorics

W Written Rhetoric: articles, essays, fiction, drama, & poems
O Oral Rhetoric: speeches, lyrics, congressional records, & screenplays
V Visual Rhetoric: photographs, posters, ads, cartoons, & graphic novels
E Electronic Rhetoric: gaming, blogs, wikis, Web sites, & e-mail

Because of the many types of messages that abound in our lives, this text provides a multitude of approaches to the issues it examines. You will not only read articles on these issues, but you will also read and hear lyrics and speeches, examine cartoons and other images, and explore Internet sites and other electronic formats. Each of these arguments has its own rhetoric.

In other words, you will experience the issues through written, oral, visual, and electronic arguments. They offer you a multitude of perspectives on any given subject and thus enrich your understanding of the issues of the day.

Each form of **rhetoric** employs its own method of communicating ideas. While as students you are most often asked to analyze written rhetoric, you have also been analyzing oral, visual, and electronic rhetorics your entire life.

> Rhetoric
> Using the most effective means of influencing or persuading audiences.

Developing Multimodal Critical Awareness: Ask Questions

Just as you have acquired an understanding of visual cues and can decode them, so have you developed an awareness of many types of oral communications. Turn your radio to a station playing a song. Ask yourself:

- What types of rhythm and beats occur?
- How do they complement the lyrics, the text?

You have also developed an awareness of electronic communications. Go to a random person's MySpace page. Ask yourself:

- What can I tell about the person who designed the page?
- Would I want to be that person's friend? Why?

Chances are, the design of the page, including colors, images, and music, as well as the person's photographs and the messages friends have sent, gave you the cues that helped you reach your conclusion.

The point is, you already know a lot about different kinds of arguments and their rhetorics.

Analyzing the Hidden Arguments

Yet we don't always focus on analyzing the multitude of arguments around us. Instead, we sometimes allow them to manipulate us to do things we would not have done or to believe ideas we might not have accepted had we taken the time to think about how these messages work to affect us.

As we eat junk food and more junk food, buy even more junk, and move our growing tons of junk into storage, we need to stop and ask why we respond as we do. We are the great consumers of goods and rhetoric. Ask yourself:

- How have these rhetorics seduced us?
- What is the purpose of each message?
- What is the weakness of each message?

The colors, the bright lights, the famous stars, the attractive voices, the scientific sounding statistics, and the dazzling entertainment are all part of the seduction.

Argument Examples: Thank You for Smoking!

Logically, we all know that smoking is bad for us. People die every day from lung cancer and other serious diseases because they smoked. So, why do people smoke? The answer is certainly complex, with no one simple answer. In fact, few issues are simple. Maybe their parents smoked, so it seemed natural for them to smoke as well. Perhaps they started smoking while they were anxious and found smoking had a calming effect, and then they could not stop. Or very possibly they wanted peer acceptance. Indeed, we have literally been persuaded to kill ourselves in the name of being "cool."

Whatever the reason, people continue to smoke. Rhetorically, words can kill, as demonstrated by the tobacco industry's effective manipulation of the media in all its forms. What follows are written, oral, visual, and electronic examples of communications focused on smoking. First examine the communication. As you answer the questions after each, you will begin to examine the arguments being made, each in its own way. Asking and answering questions puts you in touch with the argument inherent in each example.

Visual Arguments: Cartoons

Examine the visual aspects of the cartoons. Read the text silently and then read it aloud.

"I Can Quit Anytime"

by Mike Luckovich of the Atlanta Constitution

http://www.pulitzer.org/year/2004/editorial-cartooning/works/cartoon9.html

AFTER YOU READ: Answer These Questions

1. Who is the person in this cartoon?
2. What do the visual cues indicate about this person?
3. What makes this cartoon funny?
4. Who is the audience?
5. What argument does the cartoon make?
6. What emotions does this cartoon appeal to?

"The Nicotine or the Lying?"

by Dan Wasserman, Los Angeles Times Syndicate

AFTER YOU READ: Answer These Questions

1. Compare this cartoon to the previous one. How is it visually different?
2. Is the representative of the tobacco industry more or less appealing? Why?
3. Why does this cartoon have four frames while the first has only one?
4. What makes this cartoon funny?
5. What argument does the cartoon make?
6. How do you respond to the cartoon?

Oral Argument: Lyrics

Read the following lyrics. Note what they say about smoking. Read them aloud at one point to feel their oral power.

"Another Puff"

by Jerry Reed

I know there's a lotta talk going around today
About cigarette smoking whittling your life away
I've seen it and I've heard it so many times
That finally it just started to prey on my mind
I guess it scared me a little bit
That's why I decided I was gonna quit
So while I was sitting here forming my battle plan
I took another puff and turned on the fan
I just sat there in my easy chair
And thought of all the money I'd wasted on cigarettes all these years
I thought how I'd spend the rest of my days
After I kick this habit my body craves
Said to myself this ain't gonna be so tough
With that little bit of assurance
I took another puff

I took a puff, a puff, then I ripped off another puff
I decided I'd about had about enough
That breaking this habit won't be too tough

Now I've give a lot of thought to this thing
If I didn't smoke cigarettes I'd feel just like a king
Besides with the price going up every day
I knew I was just throwing all my good money away
You know I ain't lit one in an hour or so?
Just wanted to make sure I could quit you know
I was thinking maybe I oughta write all this down
Put it in a song kinda circulate it around

Can't ever tell it might make a hit
And that redneck Hall did a little bit

Can you imagine me a hit songwriter!
Now where's… where'd I put that cigarette lighter?
After all it's a habit and a habit you can break
Just a little bit of willpower son that's all it takes
I said to myself you got to be tough!
And with that little bit of wisdom
I took another puff

I took a puff, and then a puff, then I finally ripped off another puff
And I decided boy this ain't gonna be tough
Besides I'd just about had enough
I'm about ready to quit this rotten habit anyway

Oh I think they ought to take it off of television
It looks too good! Ow!
I like them skinny ones with the filter
Oh give it to me! Give it to me!
Cigarettes… I say if I quit smoking what'll I do?
Maybe I'll eat
Yeah I'll eat cigarettes
Ahh, I love it I love it I love it I love it I love it I love it
Chester B don't smoke, he smokes logs!
Makes you laugh funny too
Oh my throat's scratchin', oh
I wish I could think of something bad to say about cigarettes
Boo on cigarettes, don't smoke don't smoke don't smoke
You quit smoking that'll leave more for me!
I love it I love it, no I don't love cigarettes ya know
Don't misunderstand me I hate cigarettes
Makes ya cough, and when ya don't smoke it makes ya shake
I don't know what's worse, the shake or the cough
I think I'll make me a coughshake, oh!
Son did you ever smoke?
Oh I remember one time I quit smoking
I quit for three months
My wife left me
So did my children
She took my house and left
It was a mobile home

AFTER YOU READ: Answer These Questions

1. What is the main message of these lyrics?
2. What makes the lyrics humorous?
3. How effective is the humor?
4. Visit YouTube and watch the video. How does the video add to the humor?
5. What images in the video were most effective?
6. How do you respond to these lyrics? Does being a smoker or a nonsmoker make a difference in your response?
7. Did you anticipate the music that accompanied these lyrics in the video? How?

Written Argument: Novel

In this novel, professional representatives of the companies being sued meet regularly. They refer to themselves as the *Mod Squad*, a 1970's television show: Nick (Tobacco Company), Bobby Jay (Gun Company), and Polly (Alcohol Company). Read the following excerpt from the novel, *Thank You For Smoking,* pp. 127–129. Be sure to read sections of the excerpt aloud to feel its full rhetorical power.

"The Mod Squad: The Tobacco, Gun and Alcohol Clan"

by Christopher Buckley

"Polly," said Nick condescendingly, in tones suggesting that security matters were beyond women, "good bodyguards don't get lost by the people they're supposed to be protecting." He sighed. "Jesus. Look at me. *Bodyguards*."

"We're *all* going to need bodyguards soon," Polly said, "the way things are going. Did you *see* the coverage the fetal-alcohol people got themselves over the weekend?"

"Pathetic," Bobby Jay said.

"Don't you think the *Sun* sort of debased itself giving that kind of space to those people? I spoke to Dean Jardel over at S and B. They distribute two-thirds of the liquor in the D.C. area, and he says the *Washington Sun* is going to find itself without *any* liquor advertising for the next month."

"I wish we had that kind of leverage," Bobby Jay said, "but they don't take gun ads. Not that you *can* buy a gun in D.C."

"They made it sound like we encourage pregnant mothers to drink. It was so… PC I wanted to…"

"Throw up."

"I'm surprised *I* didn't get kidnapped on the way to work this morning."

Nick, taking all this in, brooding over the woman on the street, felt suddenly that his nicotine patch of courage was being co-opted. "Polly," he broke in, "I don't think people who work for the alcoholic beverage industry have to worry about being kidnapped, just yet."

Awkward silence. He'd made *alcoholic beverage* sound like *laxative* or *pet supplies*. Polly did a slow burn, blew a deep lungful of smoke out the side of her mouth in a cool, focused way, her eyes never leaving his, tapped her toe against the floor a few times. "Aren't we unholier than thou, today."

"Look," Nick said, "nothing personal, but tobacco generates a little more heat than alcohol."

"Oh?" Polly said. "This is news."

"Whoa," Nick said. "I'll put my numbers up against your numbers any day. My product puts away 475,000 people a year. That's 1,300 a day—"

"Waait a minute," Polly said. "*You're* the one who's always saying that 475,000 is bull—"

"Okay, 435,000. Twelve hundred a day. So how many alcohol-related deaths a year? A hundred thousand, tops. Two hundred and seventy something a day. Well wow-wee. Two hundred and seventy. That's probably how many people die every day from slipping on bars of soap in the bathtub. So I don't see terrorists getting excited enough to kidnap anyone from the alcohol industry."

Bobby Jay said, "You two sound like McNamara, all this talk about body counts. Let's just chill out here."

Nick turned to him. "How many gun deaths a year in the U.S.?"

"Thirty thousand," Bobby Jay said, "but that's gross."

"Eighty a day," Nick snorted. "Less than passenger car mortalities."

"It nets out to even less," Bobby Jay said mildly. "Fifty-five percent of those are suicides, and another eight percent are justifiable homicides, so we're really only talking eleven thousand one hundred."

"Thirty a day," Nick said. "Hardly worth counting. No terrorist would bother with either of you."

"Would you like to see some of *my* hate mail," Polly said, flushing. Nick hadn't seen her look this *up* since she went on *Geraldo* with the parents of an entire school bus that had been wiped out by a drunk driver.

"Hate mail? *Hate* mail?" Nick laughed sarcastically. "*All* of my mail is hate mail. I don't even open my mail anymore. I just assume it's a letter bomb. My mail goes directly to the FBI lab. Technicians in lead suits steam-open it. Please, don't even try to one-up me on the subject of *mail*."

"Why don't we put away the gloves and order," Bobby Jay said. "I'm starved."

"Fine," Nick said, grinding his teeth. *Expect a little sympathy…wait, she was being sympathetic until you told her she sounded like a get-well card.* There was that awful taste in his mouth again, like there was a cigarette butt under his tongue. The doctors had told him that his system was going to be flushing nicotine for the next three months. Food wasn't tasting very good these days, and spices made it taste like Drano.

Nick forced himself to say, "I wasn't *trying* to be unholier than thou."

AFTER YOU READ: Answer These Questions

1. What are these three reps arguing over?
2. How do you respond to their arguments?
3. How would you characterize the humor in this excerpt?
4. How does the humor affect you?
5. What argument does this excerpt make?
6. Do these characters have a strong sense of ethos?
7. While the content of this excerpt differs from that of the screenplay excerpt, what makes the two similar?

The Seduction Factor

Now we must become more aware of the tactics of the rhetoricians who created the messages so that we can respond more logically. To gain control in this "[dis]information age" in which we are bombarded with sound bites, images, ads, political debates, newspapers, journals, and Internet options, we must look for the hidden argument buried in every message.

Not only must you learn to decode these various rhetorics, but you must also work to integrate them into your own communications. This text will ask you to argue your position in WOVE projects that call for written, oral, visual and electronic components.

By creating your own WOVE components, you will learn to use different methods to your own advantage to convince your audience of your points. In other words, you will become effective communicators using a wide spectrum of methods and genres.

Are you ready?

EXERCISE: Evaluating WOVE Techniques

In this chapter you examined a number of communications dealing with smoking. Write an essay in which you compare and contrast the kinds of arguments—written, oral, visual, or electronic—by which these pieces commented on the issue. Focus your essay on the kinds of arguments rather than on the content of the pieces. Which kinds of arguments are most effective? Which are not very effective? If you were to create your own project on smoking, which WOVE components would you use?

"Grand Theft Auto"

by Mark Parisi

http://www.offthemark.com

What Is Rhetoric?

Rhetoric is the study of how we construct effective written, visual, or oral discourse. The discipline of rhetoric studies how we can best inform, persuade, entertain, or move our audiences. Although you may not realize it, you are a rhetorician.

You use rhetoric every day to decide what to say and how to say it. Persuading your friends to go eat at the restaurant you want to go to, telling your favorite story to a new acquaintance, or writing an e-mail to mom or dad to ask for money are all rhetorical acts. Most of your rhetorical skills you picked up by listening to others and through trial and error. You tried various arguments until you persuaded others to agree with you. For example, when you wanted to stay out after your normal curfew you picked your audience carefully—is mom or dad a more sympathetic audience? Then you might have tried a variety of arguments to persuade them to let you stay out late. Maybe you appealed to mom's sense of fairness (it's not fair that my brother, who is only two years older than me, gets to stay out an hour later than I do), or tried to get dad to feel sorry for you (it is so embarrassing that all my friends can stay out later than I can, it makes me look like a baby). If you are a normal young adult, you continued to try various arguments until the parent finally gave in and let you stay out. Most children are very effective rhetoricians when their parents are the audience.

As you move into the world of work and friends, your arguments need to become more sophisticated to be effective, and studying rhetoric will help you be more successful at getting raises, presenting information, and gaining agreement for your ideas. Life is rhetorical in nature. Consider, for example, the cartoon on the previous page. What rhetorical argument is it making?

The Rhetorical Elements of an Argument

> Claim
> The side of an issue about which the writer will argue.
>
> Issue
> An idea or belief about which there is debate.

The basic structure of an argument is simple. You make a **claim** about an **issue** and present evidence to support it. An issue is the point of a controversy or an idea about which people disagree.

The Claim: The Position

The claim states the position of a writer or a speaker on an issue. The tricky part of the claim is that it must be arguable—someone must be able to argue the opposite side of the claim or be able to construct a **counterclaim.**

Counterclaim
The side of an issue the writer will not argue, but should consider as the argument is constructed.

 **EXERCISE: Making a Claim**

Look at the following sentences that appear to be claims about whether violent video games cause harm. On a separate sheet of paper, write a counterclaim.

Example:

Claim: *Violent video games do not desensitize the players to violence.*
Counterclaim: *Violent video games do desensitize the players to violence.*

Claim: Playing violent video games is a harmless pastime.

Claim: Playing violent video games causes teens to act violently.

Claim: Playing violent video games exposes players to graphic violence.

If you cannot construct a counterclaim that makes sense, then the sentence is a *statement* and not a **claim**.

The Issue: Stasis Theory

There are several ways of looking at an issue and constructing a claim. Classical rhetoricians developed a series of questions to help them construct claims. This method for finding a claim was called **Stasis Theory.** The questions were developed to help the ancient Greeks find the right arguments for law cases. The following questions are an adaptation of the original stasis theory questions:

Stasis Theory
A methodology of four questions developed by the ancient Greeks to discover the appropriate claim to argue for any given law case.

Classical Method
Developed by ancient Greek rhetoric and used in Roman rhetoric. It has remained one of the most popular ways to arrange an argument or paper throughout the ages. It is composed of five parts: introduction (with thesis), a statement of fact (narration), evidence (confirmation), refutation (with concessions), and summation.

1. Did something happen?
   Yes, violent video games contain violence, so you could not claim that they do not.
2. What is the nature of the act?

We are exposed to violence every day. Is the violence in the video game "graphic" or "disturbing" or "acceptable"?

3. What is the quality of the act?
   Is the violence in video games more graphic or more disturbing than the violence that is seen on TV or in movies? You could argue no, it is not. But you could also argue that video games have the players participate in the violence whereas the TV or movie violence is only viewed.
4. What should be done?
   You could argue that so little evidence exists that the violence in video games affects the attitudes and behaviors of the players that nothing should be done. However, you could also argue that even the few cases where teens have committed crimes similar to the ones that they enacted in the video games point to a need to censor or ban violent video games.

Each question focuses attention on a different aspect of the issue while the claims generated by each question need different types of evidence or support.

Question 1 "Did something happen?" needs factual support such as data, but Question 2 "What is the nature of the act?" asks for a definition.

Question 3 "What is the quality of the act?" asks for an evaluation, and Question 4 "What should be done?" asks if the issue is so critical, then what action should be taken.

The Evidence

The type of **evidence** given to support an argument depends on what aspect of the issue the claim addresses and what types of evidence might best persuade your audience. Evidence falls into three types of **appeals:**

1. **Ethos**—using the authority of the writer, an expert, or a culture.
2. **Pathos**—using language to affect the emotions of an audience.
3. **Logos**—constructing arguments based on reason and logic.

> **Evidence**
> The points presented to prove the claim. Evidence can be based on logos, pathos, or ethos.
>
> **Appeals**
> Rhetorical strategies which improve the persuasive effectiveness of an argument. The three major types are ethos, pathos, and logos.
>
> **Ethos**
> Using the character of the writer or speaker or using effective sources with writers of expertise to make the discourse more appealing to the audience.

Ethos: Claiming Authority

Although most beginning writers think that an argument based on ethos is an "ethical" argument, in rhetoric, the argument based on ethos is an argument based on the testimony of an authority or the strength of personality of the writer. Advertisers use this type of argument when they have a famous basketball player endorse their product. Just as there are different types of examples, there are different types of ethical arguments:

- Expert testimony
- Popular testimony
- Personal testimony
- Cultural preference

Pathos
Creating elements within the text that move the emotions of the audience to make the discourse more appealing to the audience.

Logos
Using logic effectively to make the discourse seem more rational to the audience.

Expert testimony is the most persuasive. If you are an expert in a particular field, you can write using your own reputation with others in the field as your ethos. However, writers are often required to write on topics about which they are not experts. In those cases, writers use expert testimony and quote from another author who is well-respected in the field. When you write a research paper and use quotes from other scholarly sources to support your points, you are using expert testimony. Attorneys use expert witnesses to persuade the jury that what they are arguing was possible and probable. If you are writing on a topic on which you are not considered an expert, you will probably quote from an expert to make your points more persuasive. For example, in your argument against violent video games, you might call experts in the following fields: child psychology, criminology, or sociology. Another type of expert might be a teenager who has committed a violent crime and claims that violent video games made him do it.

Popular testimony is the type used most by advertisers. Getting rock stars or popular athletes to say that a product makes them perform better might persuade an audience who likes those particular stars or athletes to buy the product. This type of testimony is particularly persuasive if you understand your audience well enough to know whom they might admire and want to emulate. To create popular testimony for your video games argument, you might cite a television personality who is admired and who has had a personal experience with violent video games.

Personal testimony is persuasive only if you are well respected by your audience or if your audience considers you a part of their group. Writers must avoid telling their audience what they should do or believe because the audience could have the response, "Who are you to tell me what to do or think?"

Cultural preference relates to the social structures we live in. We all belong to various "cultures"—our peer groups, our school, our church, and our state, our country, etc. This argument only works if the group you are trying to persuade wants to be part of the culture you cite in your argument.

This argument might try to persuade the audience to do something "because everyone else is doing it." Does that argument sound familiar? Now you know why it didn't work on your parents—they didn't want to belong to your culture.

EXERCISE: Ranking Ethos

Thinking about your video violence argument, on a sheet of paper rank the following sources from 1–6 with 1 (one) being the most persuasive and 6 (six) being the least persuasive.

Senator Joseph Lieberman sponsored legislation against violent video games.

John Doe, President of the student government on your campus, says he plays *Grand Theft Auto* all the time and is not violent.

Dr. Craig Anderson is cited on the American Psychological Association Web site for his ten year study of the connection of video games and teen violence. (He believes there is a connection).

Boz Poz is a hip-hop artist whose work stresses non-violence because his father was killed by a video game player.

Lt. David Grossman, professor at the Air Force Academy, testified in the United States vs. Timothy McVeigh as an expert witness on violence and aggression.

Dr. David Walch, child psychologist, is cited on www.CBSnews.com as an expert on violence and children.

When trying to rank these experts, did you consider who your audience would be? What would your ranking be if you were writing to an audience of senior citizens? Parents of teenagers? To teenagers themselves? When you write you have limited space to argue your point, so you will have to choose from many possible sources of testimony.

Always consider who your audience will respect or will want to emulate.

Pathos: Using Emotions

Have you given money to a charity because you felt sorry for the people they were trying to help? Have you ever done something because a speaker made you feel angry about an injustice or problem? In both cases, you were persuaded to do something because your emotions were aroused. The pathetic appeal is based on creating a specific emotion in your audience. Like popular testimony, the pathetic appeal is used extensively in advertising. To sell products and services, advertising frequently plays on the audience's fears of losing status or desire for success. However, rhetoricians have identified other emotions that can move audiences to action—anger, love/hate, shame, compassion, pity, envy, and hope. These are a few that we see invoked today.

To use the pathetic appeals well, you must decide which emotion will best move your audience to do what you want them to do. To know what will move an audience you must know what emotions or state of mind an audience brings to the rhetorical situation.

For example, to move an audience to throw away *Grand Theft Auto*, you might want to invoke anger about the crimes that have been committed by teenagers after playing the game. A better argument would be to play on the pity the audience already feels and argue that the teenagers were victims of the greedy video game manufacturers. There are two techniques for creating an emotional response in an audience:

1. Enargeia
2. Honorific/Pejorative language

Enargeia is a type of description in which the writer tries to literally "recreate" a scene for the reader so that the reader experiences the same emotion as the main character of the scene. The most effective use of enargeia is narration—telling a story. Writers most often use this device in the introduction of a piece to hook reader interest. If the readers identify with and pity the main character of the narration, then they are likely to agree with any other pathetic arguments you might present.

Honorific/Pejorative language is used by sophisticated writers to subtly influence the way readers perceive the people they include in their articles. Of course, it is never effective to call names or use racial slurs. Pejorative language must be used carefully. For example, you might describe a university professor whose research is counter to your argument as an "ivory-tower" researcher to imply that the research is not applicable in the "real" world. An example of using honorific language might be calling a scholar who is arguing on your side a "well-respected" or "world-renowned" scholar.

EXERCISE: Using Pathos

Review the different possible audience emotions and/or states of mind below. Then write a brief note as to what pathetic appeal might work to convince them that playing violent video games DOES NOT cause teenage violence.

1. Families who have been victims of violent crime and are fearful.
2. Parents who are angry about the teenagers playing video games for hours.
3. Jury members at a trial where the defense is that the accused was influenced by *Grand Theft Auto*. Create appeals for the defense and the prosecution.
4. High school students in the "Teenagers Against Violence" group.

Of the three types of appeals, pathetic appeals are the most difficult to do well. In fact, many rhetoricians advise that writers use pathetic appeals only in introductions or conclusions. If you decide to use a pathetic appeal, be sure to have several people from your target audience read your paper and make any revisions that they suggest.

Logos: Using Logic

There are two types of logical appeals:

1. Deductive
2. Inductive

Deductive Appeal

> Deductive Appeal
> An argument made up of a major premise, a minor premise and a conclusion. A deductive appeal argues from general to specific.

When using **deductive appeal,** a writer connects generalities that the audience knows with specifics that the audience may not know. Rhetoricians often use deduction to show that the specific topic they are arguing about falls within a category or class that the audience is already familiar with. Deductive logic can argue that the specific example is an example of the commonly held belief or that the specific example is a reason for the commonly held belief.

Such an argument is made up of a **Major Premise,** a **Minor Premise,** and a **Conclusion**.

In rhetoric, the major premise is often based on a strongly held general societal belief. For your argument to work, your audience MUST agree with your major and minor premises. If you wanted to argue that violent video games were bad, you might construct the following argument:

Violence should be eliminated from our society. **Major Premise**

Grand Theft Auto (and similar games) contains violence. **Minor Premise**

Thus, *Grand Theft Auto* should be eliminated. **Conclusion**

This deduction argues that *Grand Theft Auto* is an example of the violence that should be eliminated; however, you could also construct a deductive argument that the violence in *Grand Theft Auto* causes the violence that should be eliminated:

Violence should be eliminated from our society. **Major Premise**

The violence in *Grand Theft Auto* (and similar games) can cause teenagers to commit violent acts. **Minor Premise**

Thus, *Grand Theft Auto* should be eliminated. **Conclusion**

If you believe that your audience supports your major premise that violence should be eliminated from our society, then this argument has a high probability of convincing your readers. To construct a major premise that your readers will agree with, you should complete a thorough audience analysis.

EXERCISE: Creating a Deductive Argument

On a sheet of paper, make a list of potential problems with this deductive argument.

All murder is wrong. **Major Premise**

Hunting animals is a type of murder. **Minor Premise**

Thus, hunting animals is wrong. **Conclusion**

Now try creating a deductive argument of your own. You are going to argue for more drug testing of professional athletes. Be sure to include a **major premise**, **minor premise**, and a **conclusion**. Then answer the following questions.

Which part of the argument was the hardest for you to construct?

What are the potential problems with your major premise?

With what type of audience would this argument be effective?

What will your audience need to believe to accept your major premise?

> **Inductive Appeal**
> An argument based on specific examples from which the writer draws a general conclusion.

Inductive Appeal

The opposite of deduction is **induction**: arguing from specifics to make a generality.

The most common form of an inductive argument is the **example**. By providing specific examples, the writer shows the audience that what he or she is arguing is possible and reasonable. There are several types of examples you can use to make your point:

Current events
History
Personal experience
Literature
Personal fiction that you make up

Example by Current Events

Rhetoricians believe that examples from current events are the most persuasive because your audience would be familiar with the examples and could see how they apply to your argument more readily than with other examples. Are current events reported accurately?

Example by History

Historical examples are the second most persuasive type of evidence. We are so persuaded by the facts and details of history. Are such examples accurate?

Example by Personal Experience

Why aren't personal examples more persuasive? Think about it. How persuaded would you be to change your beliefs if all a writer could offer was a personal example? A simple rebuttal to the argument would be "that would never happen in my life." Think about how many times you have ignored the advice of your parents, family, and friends because you didn't believe that their personal example applied to you?

Example by Literature and Personal Fiction

Examples from literature and examples you make up are the least persuasive because they are not based on actual events or people.

To use examples most effectively, choose a variety of examples that will defend most of the major points of the argument and show that the examples you cite are not isolated cases but are truly representative.

EXERCISE: Ranking Examples

Which of these types of examples do you think would be most persuasive? On a sheet of paper, rank the examples below from 1–5 with 1 (one) being the most effective and 5 (five) being the least. Which would be the most effective to help you argue that violence in video games is harmful?

An adult you know played a lot of violent video games. He also abused his wife.
Devin Thompson shot two police officers in 2003 after playing *Grand Theft Auto.*
Police found violent video games in Dylan Klebold and Eric Harris' houses after the Columbine shootings in 1999.
A hypothetical teen played violent video games and became a serial killer.
A violent teenager is a character from a short story about video games.

Be ready to defend your ranking in class discussion.

Extrinsic Proofs: Data

A specific type of example that ancient rhetoricians treat not as an appeal, but as an **extrinsic proof** (i.e., a proof that does not have to be invented), is **data**. In today's society that highly values scientific evidence, data is one of the most convincing arguments a writer can use. But be aware that statistics can be misleading. You must always look carefully at the source, method, and date of any data that you use. What was a meaningful percentage in 1960 probably doesn't mean much today. Writers who present data from polls and surveys should include the following information:

> Extrinsic Proof
> Any evidence brought to the argument such as scientific evidence, survey results, or statistics.

1. How were the respondents contacted?
2. How many total respondents were there?
3. What is the reliability rating of the poll or survey? (Accuracy to within plus or minus 3 percentage points is viewed as reliable.)

If you cite data from an academic article or study, you should include the following information:

1. Who did the study?
2. Where can the reader go to see the complete study?
3. Where does the borrowed material begin and end?

Be sure to give credit to anyone from whom you use data.

Specific numbers and statistics add authority to an argument. Look at the following two sentences:

> *Only a few teenagers who commit crimes played* Grand Theft Auto *before committing their crimes.*
> *Only 0.5% of the teenagers who commit crimes said that they played* Grand Theft Auto *before committing their crimes.*

Which sentence is more convincing? It depends on the reader's definition of "a few." Some readers might think that "a few" could mean about 1/4 or 1/3 of all teenagers who commit crimes played *Grand Theft Auto*. On the other hand, a reader might interpret "a few" as only one or two teenagers. By being vague, the writer runs the risk of the reader adding to or deleting from a population. Since you cannot guess which way the reader will define "a few," you should always be specific when you present data.

One of the ways humans learn is by testing actions in specific situations, then applying what was learned to all similar situations. If we did not have the ability to generalize, we would look at each situation as if we had never experienced it before. Inductive arguments work with readers' desire to generalize. By constructing a series of specific instances, the writer can lead the reader to agree with a generalization. Induction uses the example to its fullest advantage. Piling up case after case to prove your point can wear readers down, or it can bore them so that they quit reading your work; thus, it is important to choose your examples carefully.

For example, if you want to construct an inductive argument that video violence caused violence in society, you might use the following specific examples:

> An 18-year-old in Fayette, Alabama kills three policemen after playing *Grand Theft Auto* night and day for months. **Most current real life case.**
> A gang of six teenagers in Oakland, California, rob and kill six people. **Next current real life case.**
> Harvard undergraduates loot town after playing a new game called football. **Historical example.**
> "Game," *Law and Order Special Victims Unit* episode number 130, first aired February 8, 2005. (Two teenagers kick a woman to death after playing violent video games with the same scenario). **Fictional example.**

Your argument would look something like this:

After playing violent video games, X did Y and X did Y. **Major Premise**
Historically playing violent games causes X to do Y. **Minor Premise**
And even on television, X did Y. **Minor Premise**
Thus, playing violent video games can cause anyone to commit violence.

You can often find examples by browsing the Internet, **but be sure to cite your sources**! Check out www.tvtome.com for television shows, episode summaries, and airing dates. You can search this site to find episodes with the theme you are writing about.

EXERCISE: Creating Examples

Glance back and review the section on examples; then brainstorm some examples you could use in an argument against hunting and write them on a sheet of paper.

Based on what you know about the effectiveness of examples, rank yours with 1 (one) being the most effective. Next, write out your argument, labeling your major and minor premises and your conclusion.

Logical Fallacies

Not all arguments are well constructed. Often in trying to persuade, writers will use arguments that are not logical or well-constructed but sound good.

For example, how often have you heard someone say, "Don't take Professor X for history. Everyone knows he is too hard"? Did you ever stop to ask, "Who is everyone?"

The person speaking was trying to persuade you to do what he wants you to do by using a logical fallacy called **Bandwagon**. The person is not presenting you with examples of how the professor is hard. He is trying to persuade you by getting you to go along with what he says is "everyone." A **logical fallacy** is an error in the construction of an argument.

> Logical Fallacy
> Rational arguments that contain weak, deceptive or false rhetorical patterns.

The following is a list of some of the most common fallacies. You need to mark this list for future reference in annotating texts and for avoiding these errors in your own writing.

Errors in Ethos

Stacking the deck occurs when evidence is constructed or slanted specifically to support the author's opinion. Example: Eighteen of the twenty college students surveyed stated that playing violent video games never gave them violent thoughts.

> **Analysis:** Who are these college students? Do they play video games regularly? For long periods of time? Or are they the close friends of the author and not a representative sample? If the twenty college students are not a representative sample of the general population of video game playing college students, then the author has stacked the deck.

False authority occurs when an author presents someone as an authority on a subject who is not. Example: Talk show host Bob Smith has stated on his program that children who play video games are prone to violence.

> **Analysis:** Is a talk show host a valid authority on teen psychology? Maybe Dr. Phil who actually is a psychologist could be quoted, but who is Bob Smith? People often give celebrities authority that they don't deserve and so are often used as false authorities.

Errors in Pathos

Either-Or occurs when the author presents only two options for looking at an issue or problem when there are actually many options. Example: To solve the problem of teen violence caused by video game playing, we can either do nothing, and watch society crumble, or we can ban all violent video games.

> **Analysis:** There is also some middle ground. How about educating parents and teens about the effects of video games? How about modifying the types of violence in the games? By presenting only two extreme choices the author is presenting the audience with an either-or choice where one of the choices is obviously ridiculous.

Ad hominem occurs when the author attacks the person who is representing the opposite opinion, and not critiquing the opinion. Example: Anyone who believes that video games cause teens to be violent is an idiot.

> **Analysis:** Can everyone who holds this position really be an idiot? NO. This argument is really little more than name-calling. The author using the ad hominem argument is not thinking critically but just trying to arouse an emotion about the other person.

Errors in Logos

Non sequitur occurs when the author's conclusion does not logically follow from the evidence presented. Example: Because hunting is a form of violence, people who play violent video games are likely to become hunters.

> **Analysis:** Just because one plays video games does not mean he or she is likely to become a hunter. Even if there is a link between these two activities, the author has not provided it in his argument.

False cause (*post hoc, ergo propter hoc*) occurs when the author assumes that because two events follow each other in time, the first caused the second. Example: John played video games for two years, then became a hunter.

> **Analysis:** There could be many causes for John becoming a hunter. The author needs to prove that video games was the only or the main cause.

Red herring occurs when the author throws in an element unrelated to the argument to try to change the subject of the argument. Example: So what if violent video games cause teens to act violently? Aren't we really a violent society anyway?

> **Analysis:** The author is trying to move the focus from the effect of the games to the state of society.

Hasty generalization occurs when the author makes a broad statement based on only a few examples. Example: Last year two defendants in two court cases used the effect of violent video games as a defense for aggravated assault; thus the legal system has recognized that video games influence behavior.

> **Analysis:** Two cases out of the hundreds of assault cases a year are not sufficient evidence of a legal trend.

What are some other examples of logical fallacies?

Logical fallacies will be discussed again in the chapter on the Argument of Conspiracy.

UNIT ONE
CHAPTER THREE
Reading and . . .
Annotating Arguments

"Then a Miracle"

by S. Harris

THEN A MIRACLE OCCURS . . .
S. Harris
"I THINK YOU SHOULD BE MORE EXPLICIT HERE IN STEP TWO."

Effective Reading Skills

As a college student, and later as part of your job or to help you be informed about current affairs, you will be reading arguments. Newspapers and magazines are full of arguments—textual and visual. How will you decide what to believe? If you are persuaded by everything you read, or the opposite, never let yourself consider new points of view, you will never be able to make sense of our complex and rapidly changing world. To be an effective reader, you need to have a strategy for understanding the sometimes subtle arguments writers will use to try to persuade you.

Effective Annotating Skills

Reading critically means annotating. It is important to write on a text you are analyzing. Writing notes in the margins and highlighting important points will help you sort through all of the material and make it easier for you to discuss the piece in class and explain why you agree or disagree with the argument. This type of analysis is called **annotation**.

You can annotate any type of text by using a pen or highlighter to make written comments on the text while you read.

Annotation
The interaction with the text by writing critical commentaries in the margins.

Marking up
Annotating by writing as a way of interacting with the text in a way to understand the text.

Marking Up: Critical Reading

Be sure to annotate and note:

- **Connections.** Note how points connect with other points in the text or connect with issues outside the text.
- **Questions.** Write questions you have about the text.

Identifying the Elements of Argument

You should identify at least four elements of the argument as explained in the previous chapter.

- **Issue.** Mark the main point by writing the word "Issue."
- **Claim.** Use **Stasis Theory.**
- **Evidence.** Note the **Logical, Ethical, and Pathetic Appeals** in the text.
- **Logical Fallacies.** Note the faulty reason used.

NOTE: If you are doing readings for an on-line course, you will need to find an annotation system that works for you. One of the best ways to annotate an on-line reading is to copy and paste it into a Word file and then use the font color and highlighting tool to comment and highlight text.

Annotation Assignment

The following section will walk you through a process of critically reading and annotating the *Washington Post* Op-Ed piece, "Kennedy Assassination: How About the Truth?" by Gerald R. Ford and David W Belin.

Read this piece through once before you make any annotations on the text.

Kennedy Assassination: How About The Truth?

by Gerald R. Ford and David W. Belin

The media treatment of the Kennedy assassination tragedy and the Warren Commission Report is a microcosm of one of the central problems facing our democratic society: False sensationalist claims are given wide dissemination, the truth is submerged, and the responsible press usually does not undertake sufficient effort to expose the fraud that is being perpetrated. Two vivid examples are the recent series of five one-hour A&E television programs about the Kennedy assassination called "The Men Who Killed Kennedy" and the new Oliver Stone-Kevin Costner film, *JFK.*

The common denominator of these commercial productions is the big lie—the assertion that the top echelons of our government were conspiratorially involved in the assassination and that Lee Harvey Oswald was not the lone gunman who killed President Kennedy and Dallas Police Officer J.D. Tippit.

In *JFK* the big lie is disseminated through Kevin Costner, who portrays New Orleans District Attorney Jim Garrison. Repeatedly, he asserts the assassination was a coup d'etat—a "public execution" with a cover-up "all the way" to the top, including Lyndon Johnson, whom he calls an accessory after the fact. In the A&E series, the big lie is disseminated through key interviewees who are portrayed as purported experts, such as Col. Fletcher Prouty (a consultant to Oliver Stone in the production of *JFK*) who asserts: "You see, you're dealing with a very high echelon of power...otherwise, how could you have gotten people like the chief justice of the Supreme Court to participate in the cover-up?"

False charges of this kind are a desecration to the memory of President Kennedy, a desecration to the memory of Earl Warren and a fraudulent misrepresentation of the truth to the American public.

The basic format underlying the dissemination of lies is to cover up the overwhelming weight of the evidence and instead paste together scraps of testimony to form a case for conspiracy and an attempt to cover up the guilt of Lee Harvey Oswald. For instance, approximately 20 doctors have examined the autopsy photographs and X-rays of President Kennedy as members of formal panels. Nineteen of these experts have concluded that all of the shots that struck President Kennedy came from the rear. The 20th asserts that there was supposedly a simultaneous fourth shot that struck President Kennedy in the head and disintegrated, leaving no physical evidence of the bullet. This odd-man-out appeared repeatedly on the A&E network in a number of the sequences.

Nowhere does any one of the overwhelming majority of 19 experts appear in the telecast or in *JFK.* Nowhere is there any mention of the fact that they concluded that all of the shots came from the rear and that this conclusion is confirmed by the unequivocal ballistic evidence which shows that the bullet that passed through President Kennedy's neck and struck Gov. Connally were fired from Oswald's rifle found at the Texas School Book Depository Building. Instead *JFK* and the television production emphasize the backward movement of President Kennedy's head when he was struck, without telling the audience that wound ballistic experts unequivocally testified that the movement was not caused by the impact of the bullet but was rather caused by a massive neuromuscular reaction that occurs when there is major damage inflicted to nerve centers of the brain.

The A&E network is owned one-third by NBC and one-third by Capital Cities/ABC. When Michael Millardi, president of the broadcast group of Capital Cities/ABC, Inc., was asked about the A&E network's misrepresentations, he side-stepped the issue and instead replied that "it is our judgment that the extreme interest in the subject matter" and "the international perspective…all warranted A&E's decision to telecast the program."

Robert Wright, president of NBC, when contacted about the misrepresentations in the A&E program, chose to have Brooke Bailey Johnson, an A&E executive, reply. Johnson refused to comment about why none of the majority of 19 medical experts was ever shown on A&E. Instead, Johnson wrote, "We elected to purchase and telecast these programs for a number of reasons. The ongoing interest in the subject matter was a factor, as was belief that the multi-channel environment in which we operate is a highly appropriate one for the debate of controversial issues."

But so far as the public is concerned, there is no debate because the other side—which happens to be the truth—is almost never shown to the public. Certainly it is not shown in the Oliver Stone-Kevin Costner film, reputedly produced at a cost approaching $40 million.

Like the A&E series, *JFK* alleges a conspiracy supposedly including elements of the CIA, with the ultimate proof of the conspiracy supposedly being the killing of Oswald by Jack Ruby on Nov. 24, 1963. Oliver Stone's fantasy involves what Garrison calls "triangulation"—three separate gunmen firing a total of six shots, with Oswald as the "patsy" who is killed by the conspirators' hit man, Jack Ruby. But nowhere in the movie do viewers see anything about the overwhelming evidence that disproves the conspiracy claims, including central witnesses to these events such as Postal Inspector Harry Holmes.

On Sunday morning, Nov. 24, 1963, Holmes was on his way to church with his wife. At the last minute, he decided instead to go to the Dallas police station to see if he could help his friend, Capt. Fritz. Holmes had been assisting Fritz in the investigation of the murder of President Kennedy and the murder of Officer Tippit, the Dallas policeman who was killed by Oswald about 45 minutes after the Kennedy assassination and whose murder is really the Rosetta Stone to understanding the truth about the assassination. Holmes entered Capt. Fritz's office, where Oswald was being interrogated by Fritz and representatives of the Secret Service and the F.B.I. After they finished their interrogation, Fritz turned to Holmes and gave him the opportunity to ask questions, and the session was extended for approximately another half-hour.

Jack Ruby meanwhile had come downtown to the Western Union office to send a money order to one of his employees. The time stamp on the money order showed that he was at the Western Union office at 11:17 a.m. If Harry Holmes had just continued on to church that morning, the interrogation session would have ended a half hour earlier, and Oswald would have been transferred long before Jack Ruby ever got to the Western Union office. Obviously, if Jack Ruby were part of a conspiracy, he would have been downtown at least a half hour earlier. Of course, common sense would also dictate that a would-be conspiratorial "hit man" would not kill his target in the middle of a police station, where he would be certain to be apprehended for murder.

But nowhere do the movie audiences seeing *JFK* or A&E's television audience ever learn about Postal Inspector Holmes, whose testimony is one of many elements showing that Jack Ruby was not conspiratorially involved. Nor does *JFK* or A&E include any portion of the testimony of Rabbi Hillel Silverman, who saw Jack Ruby many times in Ruby's cell and who is convinced that Ruby was truthful when he said that he was not conspiratorially involved. Nor do viewers of the movie of the A&E television series learn about Jack Ruby's request for a lie detector test and the results of that test, which although not 100 percent accurate, confirmed that Jack Ruby was not part of any conspiracy.

Nowhere does the A&E telecast or the movie show the vivid testimony of the single most important witness to the assassination—Howard Brennan, who actually saw the gunman fire from the south-east corner of the window of the Texas School Book Depository Building—the window where cartridge cases were found, which ballistically were shown to have come from Oswald's rifles. It was Brennan who notified the police of the source of the shots and who described the assassin as slender, about 5 feet, 10 inches, 150 to 160 pounds, white—a description remarkably close to Oswald.

Nowhere do the viewers learn that the most probable time span of Oswald's three shots was around 10 seconds, in light of the fact that one of Oswald's shots missed—most likely the first or the last. Instead, Garrison speaks only of three shots being fired within 5.6 seconds, when most likely the 5.6-second time span was between the two shots that struck the president.

Nowhere in *JFK* (or in the A&E television script) does the viewer ever learn that six eye-witnesses, including cabdriver William Scoggins, who saw Oswald from as close a range as 12 feet, saw Oswald at the Tippit murder scene or running away from the Tippit murder scene with gun in hand, and positively identified Oswald as the gunman. Oswald was apprehended in the Texas Theater because an alert Dallas citizen, Johnny Calvin Brewer, became suspicious when he saw Oswald duck into Brewer's shoe store as police sirens were heard coming down the street. Brewer trailed Oswald to the Texas Theater and had the cashier call the police. When they approached Oswald, he pulled out his revolver, and ballistic evidence proved that this was the Tippit murder weapon.

The viewers of *JFK* and "The Men Who Killed Kennedy" never learn about these facts, nor do they ever learn about all of the other massive body of evidence which conclusively proves beyond a reasonable doubt that Oswald was the lone gunman who killed President Kennedy and Officer Tippit and that there was no cover-up by Earl Warren or by the Warren Commission.

When will Hollywood produce a movie that tells the truth? When will the A&E network—when will NBC and Capital Cities/ABC produce five hours of commercial television that presents the truth? When will the responsible leaders of our free press, who owe so much to Earl Warren, stand up for the truth, expose the techniques that have been used to disseminate the big lie and fully defend Earl Warren's name from the slanderous charges that have been made against him and the Warren Commission?

There are some who assert in the face of this conspiracy barrage by the mass media, particularly movies and television, that we will never know the truth. That simply is not accurate. The truth is known: Lee Harvey Oswald was the lone gunman who killed President Kennedy and Dallas Police Officer J.D. Tippit. Those of us who served on the Warren Commission and those lawyers on the staff who examined the evidence in depth know that to be the truth—beyond a reasonable doubt. And if the press were ever to approach this with the kind of diligence and with the kind of fairness that the American people have the right to expect, then the overwhelming majority of Americans will not only eventually understand the truth but will also understand the techniques of the perpetration of the big lie so that the kind of deceptive techniques used by the producer of *JFK* and the A&E series "The Men Who Killed Kennedy" will be exposed for all to see. The press owes that obligation to the memory of President Kennedy, to the memory of Earl Warren and, indeed, to the American people.

Former President Gerald R. Ford was a member of the Warren Commission. David W. Belin was counsel to the commission.

Marking Up Assignments: Kennedy Assassination

Now re-read the article and try to identify the following elements of their argument:

- The main point: the issue
- The claim
- The evidence, the appeals
- And the fallacies

Also make other comments and connections and ask other questions.

When you find these elements, you are ***marking up*** the paper.

Uncover the Main Point: The Issue

Students often think that the topic of an article is the issue the writer is exploring. Sometimes the argument being made is that obvious, but usually the topic is only a vehicle the writer uses to explore the issue, and often there is more than one issue in an argument. The topic of this article appears to be the A & E series "The Men Who Killed Kennedy" and the film *JFK*. But is this the issue of the argument? What did you think was the issue that Ford and Belin were exploring? Whether or not there was a conspiracy to kill Kennedy? Whether or not the media is presenting a biased view? Whether or not the Warren Commission findings were correct?

To find the issue in the article, think about the entire piece—***what was the main point***? What do you think was the ONE message the writers wanted you to remember? The main point of the argument is that there was NOT a conspiracy to kill Kennedy. The issue of the piece is the JFK conspiracy theory.

ON-LINE

As an on-line student, you can type the issue at the top of your cut and pasted document. You might want to use a different font, a color instead of black, or a larger font size so that your comments stand out from the text.

EXERCISE: Let's Annotate

At the top of the article, write the word "issue," then state the issue in your own words.

Find the Claim: Use Stasis Theory

The claim must be arguable. It is what the writer will be presenting evidence to support. Remember stasis theory, the questions that rhetoricians can use to construct claims?

- Did something happen?
- What is the nature of the act?
- What is the quality of the act?
- What should be done?

ON-LINE

As an on-line student, use the highlighter tool in your tool bar to highlight the claim. Then use a different color font to insert the stasis claim into the text.

EXERCISE: Let's Annotate

Re-read the article and find the claim. Underline the claim and write in the margin which question the claim is going to answer.

Evaluate the Evidence: Appeals

Most authors are going to use logical, ethical, and pathetic arguments, so it is important for you to ***note each type of argument***. As you re-read the article, you will need to identify what type of evidence is being presented, and whether the evidence is valid and the source of the evidence is reliable. Remember, it is relatively easy for a writer to find a "witness" that will give a statement consistent with the claim the writer is trying to support. It is also relatively easy to configure data to make it say what supports the claim, so evaluate the validity of the evidence carefully.

EXERCISE: Let's Annotate

Re-read the section on "The Evidence" in Chapter 2 to remind yourself of the elements of ethos, pathos, and logos. Then, as you go through the article, highlight the different pieces of evidence presented and label them as ethos, pathos, or logos. If you are not sure what type of argument is being presented, or if the evidence brings up a question, write that question in the margin.

Look for Fallacies

As you are finding and evaluating evidence, you can also look for logical fallacies. Review those found at the end of Chapter 2. It should be easy to find **hasty generalization** and **ad hominem.**

ON-LINE

On-line students can use the highlight tool and a colored font to insert comments and questions. Use different colors for comments and questions.

EXERCISE: Let's Annotate

Can you find other logical fallacies? If the evidence is a logical fallacy, place the word "fallacy" in brackets beside it.

Make Connections

Another step in annotating an argument is to ***make written notes about connections this text might have with others***. If you have seen the film *JFK* or have read other articles discussing the various conspiracy theories, then you should note places that this article supports or contradicts what you knew before you read the article. This textbook contains chapters with many articles on the same subject which frame the argument in different ways or present arguments from opposing sides. It will help you work through the arguments if you note in the margins where arguments agree or disagree. Be sure to cite the author's name by the notation so that you can find the piece again. You don't want to waste time re-reading several articles to find one point!

ON-LINE

On-line students, pick yet another color to insert your connections. When you look at your annotated text, you should be able to pick out your comments and identify whether they are questions, comments or connections by the color.

EXERCISE: Let's Annotate

Skim through the text and note in the margin evidence or arguments that you have seen before or that contradict evidence or arguments in other texts. Be sure to cite the source of the argument with an author's name or the title of the text.

Ask Questions

What doesn't make sense? What seems weak? What was not developed? It is important to write questions.

EXERCISE: Let's Annotate

As you are re-reading the article evaluating the evidence, it is a good time to write in the margin any questions the evidence brings to mind.

Conclusion

This chapter used a classical approach to reading and annotating an argument. The next chapter will introduce other methods to read and write an argument. You can use these other approaches as annotation variations. Read the next chapter to learn about these different approaches.

Checklist for Annotating Classical Arguments

The Key Points to Identify in any Reading

The Key Elements of the Argument

1. Issue, the topic
2. Claim, the position (may be implied)
    - Stasis theory
      Did something happen?
      What is the nature of the act?
      What is the quality of the act?
      What should be done?
3. Evidence, the support
    - Appeals
      Logos, logical
      Pathos, emotional
      Ethos, authority
4. Logical fallacies, faulty persuasive elements

Marking Up: Physical Interaction

- **Connections.** Make connections to other texts or issues.
- **Questions.** Ask questions about the text.

"My Little Angel"

by Rob Smith Jr.

http://www.robsmithjr.com/editorial/wp-content/uploads/2007/10/2007-0925-halo3-blog.jpg

AFTER YOU READ: Analyze the Issues

1. What is the message of the cartoon?
2. Do you agree with the message?
3. Have you played violent video games?

AFTER YOU READ: Analyze the Rhetoric

1. How did the text parallel the drawings?
2. Is humor used effectively?
3. Who is the audience for this?

Persuasive Writing

Almost all writing has an element of persuasion. Informative writing might convince a reader to buy a certain product; expressive writing might persuade an audience to adopt the writer's idea; entertaining writing encourages the reader to see the world through a particular lens. If you are writing specifically to persuade, you might be writing to move someone to do something you want, to join you in a cause, or to accept your belief about a controversial subject.

> Persuasive Writing
> The power to excite, engage, and arouse emotional, intellectual, or even moral awareness of an audience though textual discourse.

Persuasive writing focuses on providing evidence, logical arguments, authority testimony, and emotional appeals to move the reader to agree with you. When you try to persuade others, it is important that you know what your audience's beliefs and values are so that you do not offend them with your arguments. To write persuasively, you will need to find points of agreement with your audience and consider which types of arguments will most appeal to your specific audience.

The Rhetorical Situation

To be a good writer requires you to understand what is called the **rhetorical situation**: you must understand why and for whom you are writing and what claim you will support, as well as how the form of your writing affects the audience. If you don't take the time to work through these questions before you begin writing, you will either spend unnecessary time in the writing and editing stages, or have a piece of writing that may or may not accomplish what you want it to.

Rhetorical Situation
A context involving a communicator, an issue, and an audience. The communicator (writer or speaker) will strive to use effective communication to discuss/analyze the issue so as to affect the audience in a specific way.

Why Are You Writing?

If you do not know why you are constructing your argument, you will not construct an effective argument. Before you start picking evidence, decide whether you are going to try to persuade your audience to agree with your position, to do something to change the situation, or to feel differently about the issue or situation. This decision works with the knowledge you need about your audience to help you choose the best claim and form for your argument.

Know Your Audience

Before you begin a first draft of your argument, you need to consider who will be reading your essay. Obviously, your instructor will be reading it, but often you will have another audience. Sometimes, an instructor will require you to write for an alternate audience. If this audience is considerably different from you in age, gender, ethnicity, authority, religious or political beliefs, you need to spend some time thinking about what information the audience will need to grasp your idea, to be properly informed, to be persuaded, or to be entertained. To be an effective writer, you must always remember that you are writing for an audience.

Beginning writers often believe that they are writing for "the general audience," which usually means for no one in particular. The general audience is, in fact, a myth. No matter what you write, there is a specific audience for your piece of writing, even if you think that your instructor is your only audience. Take a moment to think about your instructor as your audience. What do you know about your instructor? Is your instructor male or female? How old is your instructor? Have you heard your instructor mention any causes or activist groups he/she might be involved in? What seem to be your instructor's favorite topics? What does your instructor value in a piece of writing? If you can answer any of these questions, you will be closer to writing a paper that is effective for your instructor.

The same questions need to be asked when you are writing for other audiences. Consider who will be reading your work—your boss? Your co-workers? Someone you want to hire you? Before you begin generating ideas about your topic, take a few minutes to answer the following questions:

1. What demographic information do I know about my audience?
2. What values and beliefs might my audience have?
3. What expectations does my audience have for this piece of writing?
4. What does my audience already know about my topic?

Write down the answers to these questions and refer to them as you generate ideas and draft your paper.

When you get to the editing stage of your process, try to find someone with similar characteristics to read your paper so that you can get his or her response. Listen to everything your reader tells you and make revisions based on what you are told. Taking the time to get an audience response will make you a more effective writer.

Refer back to the exercise where you were asked to list potential problems in the deductive argument on hunting. After reading this section, do you see some new potential problems?

Here are a few:

1. Would the audience consider hunting animals wrong?
2. Are people in my audience hunters?
3. Are people in my audience members of the NRA, or are they vegans?
4. How would my audience define "murder"?
5. Would my audience consider ALL murder wrong? What about self-defense?

Find a Claim

A claim acts as the thesis of your argument. In fact, the two words are often used interchangeably in other texts. As you construct your claim, you must make sure it is arguable. If you cannot write an opposite statement that makes sense, even if you don't agree with it, then you do not have an arguable thesis. For example, "Hunting kills animals: therefore, it is wrong," is not an arguable claim because the opposite statement, "Hunting doesn't kill animals; therefore, it is not wrong," doesn't make sense. A good claim would be "Hunting is a form of murder; therefore, it is wrong" because the opposite makes sense also, "Hunting is not a form of murder; therefore, it is not wrong." If you are constructing an argument where you believe there is a right and wrong answer or where you want to lead the audience to a certain conclusion, then you should consider the ***Classical Method***. The classical method for finding a claim is discussed thoroughly at the beginning of Chapter 2, so this section will only briefly review the material.

The Classical Method

The ***Classical Method*** of finding a claim uses the four questions of the stasis theory.

- Did something happen?
- What is the nature of the act?
- What is the quality of the act?
- What should be done?

Look back to our first reading, "Seeing Arguments" for a fuller explanation of each of these questions. In addition, the Classical Method relies on deductive and inductive reasoning. This method works very well if you know that your audience will agree with the general principle of your major premise. Let's use our previous example about hunting.

> All murder is wrong. **Major premise**
> Hunting animals is a type of murder. **Minor premise**
> Thus, hunting animals is wrong. **Conclusion**

This argument is based on the question "What is the nature of the act?" and defines "hunting" as "murder." Your claim could be worded like this:

> Hunting animals is wrong because it is a form of murder and all murder is wrong.

The Toulmin Method

Another method for finding a claim to argue was developed by Stephen Toulmin, a twentieth century British philosopher. Toulmin developed a new approach to argument based on what he felt were simple principles found in how people actually argue instead of the classical methods that people ought to use when arguing.

The necessary components to this model: **claim, data**, and **warrant.**

Let's return to the violence in video game argument to examine the Toulmin Model.

> **Claim: the point to make**
> Violent video games like *Grand Theft Auto* should be eliminated.

> Toulmin Method
> A way to analyze an argument, breaking it into its parts so that we can judge how effective the argument is, how well the parts work together. Writers using the Toulmin method identify the claims, the reasons, and the evidence in order to determine whether or not the argument "works."

Data: the support for the claim
Grand Theft Auto (and similar games) contains violence that influences teens to act violently.

Warrant : the underlying assumption of the claim
Violence should be eliminated from our society.

The Toulmin Method lets writers construct claims and argue positions for which the evidence is not certain. In this method, the claim is constructed from the evidence or data the writer has gathered and is based on an unstated **warrant**. A warrant is the belief, value, or principle that allows the writer to construct the claim based on evidence that doesn't fully support it. Unlike the Classical Method that begins by looking at the evidence and then constructing a claim based on that evidence, the Toulmin Method begins with the writer constructing the claim.

Improving the Syllogism

For the most part these three elements of the Toulmin Model parallel the syllogism that made up the classical argument though in a differing order and with a differing emphasis:

Major Premise *(Toulmin: Warrant)*
Violence should be eliminated from our society.

Minor Premise *(Toulmin: Data)*
Grand Theft Auto (and similar games) contains violence that influences teens to act violently.

Conclusion *(Toulmin: Claim)*
Violent video games like *Grand Theft Auto* should be eliminated.

Because it would be almost impossible to prove that violence should be eliminated from our society, your claim relies on the warrant for support, but it is never part of the actual claim. The writer should be sure that the warrant is a belief that will be held by the audience. Thus, your claim would look like this:

> Claim
> The side of an issue about which the writer will argue.
>
> Data
> In the classical method, extrinsic proofs such as scientific evidence, survey results, or statistics. In the Toulman method, data is any evidence that supports the claim.
>
> Warrant
> In the Toulman method, any underlying assumption the audience would have about the issue being argued.
>
> Syllogism
> A way to build a proof by providing two true statements (a major premise and a minor premise) which then direct the listener or reader to a "logical" third statement or conclusion. The biggest problem with a syllogism remains that the conclusion is not always valid. "All A are B. All C are A. Therefore, all C are B."

Violent video games like *Grand Theft Auto* should be eliminated because they contain violence that influences teens to act violently.

Three Optional Components

Three supporting elements that help to develop the arguments are **rebuttal, backing**, and the **qualifiers.**

1. Rebuttal: What will the opponents to your claim say?
   The Claim: Violent video games like *Grand Theft Auto* should be eliminated.
   Simulated violence can be an effective way to let go of natural aggression.

2. Backing: How can you defend the warrant with evidence?
   The Warrant: Violence should be eliminated from our society.
   Studies have shown the negative effects of video games…

3. Qualifier: Do you need to limit your warrant?
   The Warrant: Violence should be eliminated from our society.
   Perhaps in some cases, such video games are not harmful.

How effective were you in developing these components? How much of each of these optional elements is needed? Where do you place these components in the argument? What are the effects that these components will have in persuading the audience? What if the argument does not work on the audience?

Rebuttal
The point in the argument when the writer tries to refute or show as untrue the main points of the counterclaim.

Backing
In the Toulman method, the evidence to support the warrant; i.e., the evidence that the audience does indeed hold the assumptions necessary for the warrant.

Qualifier
In the Toulman method, the narrowing of the claim or warrant to be more specific or to limit the claim or warrant to a specific group of people.

The Rogerian Method

What if you know your audience is not going to agree with your claim? This is an audience you might not ever fully persuade to your point of view, but your argument might get them to start thinking differently about your topic. However, you never can win an argument by being openly confrontational. When you know your audience will disagree with your claim, try the Rogerian Model to rework your claim to one of compromise. Two key components needed in a Rogerian argument: 1) finding a common ground, and 2) skillfully using refutation or rebuttal.

> Rogerian Method
> Based on psychologist Carl Rogers (1902-1987), a type of argument that finds the middle ground of agreement instead of focusing on error and blame against the viewpoints of opponents.

Common Ground

What would the common ground be between two sides of the argument about video games violence?

> "Violent video games like *Grand Theft Auto* should be eliminated" and
> "Violent video games like *Grand Theft Auto* should be allowed"?

What concessions can be made to appease both sides? Let's look at the statement:

> Violence should be eliminated for our society.

Both sides might agree to this. Those who do not like violent video games don't like violence in society. Perhaps you can argue that simulated violence may be a way to get rid of violence in society. Look at the data. Violent crime rates have gone down since the introduction of violent video games. In Japan, the origin of most violent video games, crime is very low compared to America. If violent video games influence violence in our society, then crime rates should be up, especially in Japan.

Empathy in the Refutation

The writer must show empathy for the dissenting voices in refutation of the argument.

> For example,
> Violence is wrong in society, but violence in entertainment might allow one to relieve stress and ultimately cause there to be less violence in society. Perhaps what is needed is a better ratings system and parental guidance, not the elimination of violent video games.

In some ways, the Rogerian Model is less effective when examining topics like gun control or abortion or gay marriage because it becomes more difficult to persuade people that there is a common ground. The effectiveness of the essay is measured by how empathetic the writer appears to the reader.

The Gaming Model

Gaming Model
Based on game theories and asks that arguments be played out as a game, not a winner take all or zero-sum game, but as a negotiation between players as a way to find solutions as joint collaborations: win-win games.

The Toulmin Model may not be effective because of the zero-sum or either/or polarity of the argument:

> "Violent video games like *Grand Theft Auto* should be eliminated" or
> "Violent video games like *Grand Theft Auto* should be allowed"?

Gaming theory is about the consequences of the choices we make. The Rogerian Model uses the ideas from the Nash Equilibrium where both sides work together to win and come up with a solution. Gaming theory allows players to be more meta-aware, for they must know the psychology and philosophy behind winning. Gaming theory is the decision science of cause and effect. Whatever you write down has an effect on the other players (audience) of the game. Gaming theory is about style and attitude when creating a gaming mind (ethos). Whether you use Classical, Toulmin, Rogerian or some other model or a mixture of models, gaming theory can make you mindful of the effects of your rhetorical moves. Read more in this book about how to create the interactive rhetoric of gaming into your class efforts and essays. Gaming is not so much about playing. In addition to playing, question, and note the interdependencies between minds, lives, and issues.

Refutation

Refutation
An important strategy for arguments, where you object to the main arguments presented by the opposition.

An argument has many of the same elements as any other essay: an introduction, body paragraphs, and a conclusion. These elements have the same function in argument as they do in other types of essays. However, arguments include an additional element that might not be familiar to you: a **refutation**.

In your refutation, you will present the strongest arguments from the opposite side and then show why they are not valid. You don't need to answer every possible opposing argument, but you should address the most common and the strongest. If you cannot or do not refute the opposing arguments, the audience can easily ignore your argument by citing one of the opposite positions.

In your refutation, you should do the following:

1. Begin by acknowledging that there are valid opposing arguments. Example: Although the evidence that the JFK assassination was a conspiracy is strong, the official government position, stated in the Warren Commission, and believed by many individuals is that a lone gunman, Oswald, was responsible for the assassination.
2. Cite the strongest opposing argument, and if possible, its author. It is best if you can directly quote the argument. If that is not possible, you should paraphrase the argument and cite the document from which you have paraphrased. Example: Ford and Belin in their *Washington Post* editorial, "Kennedy Assassination: How About the Truth?" state that "Nineteen of these experts [doctors who have reviewed the autopsy photographs and X-rays} have concluded that all of the shots that struck President Kennedy came from the rear" (2).
3. Cite evidence that refutes the argument. Example: Oliver Stone in his *Washington Post* editorial refuting Ford and Belin states "…26 trained medical personnel—doctors, nurses, technicians—who treated the president at Parkland Hospital testified to the Warren Commission that they saw an exit-type wound in the back of the head…" (2).
4. State why your evidence should be believed over the opposition's. Example: I believe that the testimony of the medical personnel who treated Kennedy is more credible than doctors who looked only at autopsy photographs because photographs can be manipulated and doctored.
5. Conclude your paragraph with a transition statement. Example: Thus, even when considering the strongest pieces of evidence supporting the lone gunman theory, there is a strong case for a conspiracy.

Your approach to your refutation will depend on which method of argumentation you choose. If you choose the Toulmin Model, you will need to consider and refute the warrants of the opposing arguments as well as the actual argument. The Rogerian Method will require you to be more conciliatory and respectful of the opposing arguments. If you take a Gaming Method approach, you must think about which opposing arguments will be most advantageous to refute and which should be left unopposed.

No only do arguments add specific elements to the essay form, arguments arrange material in very specific ways in order to persuade the audience most effectively. Depending on which method you chose to construct your claim, you will follow that method's organizational pattern.

The Process of Arguing: The Process of Writing

Keep in mind that no method provides you with a fill-in-the-blank model for organization. Just because you have all the elements listed, you still may have a poorly

Classical Model

Classical rhetoricians developed an organizational pattern based on how arguments proceed in a law court. This is the organizational pattern you should follow if your purpose is to persuade your audience to think the way you do, and you think the audience is generally predisposed to think favorably about your claim.

Introduction—interest the reader in what you have to say; prepare them for your claim.
Statement of Fact—state your claim.
Evidence—present the facts to support your claim.
Refutation—address the strongest arguments from the other side.
Conclusion—restate in a summary way your facts and arguments while leaving the reader with a good impression of you.

Toulmin Model

Introduction—interest the readers in what you have to say; prepare them for your claim.
Claim—state your thesis.
Warrant—state the belief or value on which your claim is based.
Backing—provide evidence to support your claim.
Rebuttal—address the strongest arguments from the other side.
Conclusion—end with something that the readers will remember.

Rogerian Model

Introduction—start with something surprising or interesting.
Point of common ground—find a point that both sides will agree with.
Claim—state your thesis that both sides will agree with.
Evidence—prove your point with support.
Empathetic refutation—address the arguments that may go against your claim, but do so with sensitivity.
Conclusion—end with something that the audience will remember.

constructed argument. There are two keys to constructing an effective argument: audience awareness and following the writing process. The following is a brief writing process checklist.

Argument Writing Process Checklist

Generating ideas

Have you determined your claim?
Do you have adequate sources to support your claim?
Do you know what the other side thinks?
Have you determined the demographics of your audience?
Have you determined what your purpose is for writing?

Writing

Have you followed the organizational pattern of the method you used to construct your claim?
Do you have something written for each of the required sections in your method?
Have you supported each of your main points with evidence?
Have you documented all of your source material?

Strengthening

Is your evidence in the best order to convince your audience?
Is your introduction interesting?
Does your conclusion do more than summarize your main points?
Does your refutation address the strongest opposing arguments?
Have you considered and incorporated your peer editors' comments?
Have you considered and incorporated comments from your sample audience?
Have you checked your documentation to avoid plagiarism?

Polishing

Is your work grammatically correct?
Have you checked for errors like homophones that grammar check will not flag?
Have you read your piece out loud to catch errors?
Do you have a variety of sentence lengths and types?
Do you have effective transitions between main points and pieces of evidence?
Have you eliminated offensive words and tone?

Proofreading

Have you read your piece out loud to catch typing errors?
Have you checked for the types of errors you generally commit?

“The Kennedy/Nixon Presidential Debate”

AFTER YOU READ: Analyze the Issues

1. What is the message in the photograph?
2. Who is the audience?
3. Can you analyze the photo without knowing its historical context?

AFTER YOU READ: Analyze the Rhetoric

1. How are the men dressed?
2. Where are the lights?
3. Why is the flag present?

Poems, Song Lyrics and Political Speeches as Arguments

Some arguments are mostly aural. Whether you're listening to the radio, your iPod, a speech, or a lecture, you must pay attention to detect possible arguments implicit in the messages you receive. In a sense, oral arguments are forms of advertisement. They exist because the speakers or performing artists have a message they want you to "buy." In this chapter, we will examine different forms of oral communications, analyzing them as arguments in order to understand how they work to get their points across.

Poems

Poems are a form of discourse with an aural component that enhances the argument they present.

Sound

Poets strive to use sound to complement the meaning of their writing. For example, if a poem is sad, it probably will contain many long vowel sounds and soft consonant sounds that enhance the feeling of sadness. A happier poem would contain short vowel sounds and, perhaps, crisper consonant sounds.

Read these lines of poetry:

> Sound (poem)
> Has its own effect on those who hear it. An "s," for example, is soft and sensuous, while a "k" is harsh and crisp.

Deep into that darkness peering, long I stood there wondering, fearing,
Doubting, dreaming dreams no mortal ever dared to dream before;
But the silence was unbroken, and the darkness gave no token,
And the only word there spoken was the whispered word, "Lenore!"
This I whispered, and an echo murmured back the word, "Lenore!"—
Merely this, and nothing more.
("The Raven," Edgar Allan Poe)

What sounds does Poe emphasize in this verse of "The Raven"? Notice all the d's and the long e's in the first two lines, and the w's and the long o's in the last few lines. The repetition of these sounds helps to create the mysterious, melancholy mood of the poem. In a sense, Poe wishes his readers to believe that the narrator of this poem is in a glum situation, and so to emphasize this feeling, he artfully uses the sounds of the words to reinforce the mood.

Rhythm

Another aspect of sound in poetry is **rhythm.** Many poems follow a set rhythm, created by repeating specific stress patterns; that is, certain syllables are stressed when they are read, while others lack stress. The more stressed syllables in a line, the more emphatic the verse; conversely, the fewer stressed syllables in a line, the more soothing or mysterious the verse.

> Rhythm (poem)
> The regular or irregular pattern of beats or accents in a line of poetry.

Compare the following sets of lines of poetry:

Soft is the strain when Zephyr gently blows,
And the smooth stream in smoother numbers flows;
(*An Essay on Criticism,* Alexander Pope)

He clasps the crag with crooked hands;
Close to the sun in lonely lands,
Ringed with the azure world, he stands.
("The Eagle," Alfred, Lord Tennyson)

Pope's lines contain many more unstressed syllables than Tennyson's. Pope's lines are soothing, while Tennyson's create a stronger sound, in part because every other syllable is stressed. Notice, too, that the repeated sounds work hand in hand with the stresses. Pope's line, with many unstressed syllables, is dominated by the "s" sound, which adds to the soothing nature of the lines. Tennyson repeats the "c" sound, a hard sound that complements the many stresses.

TIP

Always read a poem out loud after reading it silently. You will have a different reading experience, for you will hear the sounds as they work to augment the meaning the poet is striving to convey.

EXERCISE: Annotating a Poem

Look at the following poem. Read it silently and then aloud several times.

1. In the margin, mark any sound devices you find. Look for repeated sounds, rhymes, and rhythms.
2. What is the genre of the poem?
3. How does the sound of the genre and the actual text work together? Once you've identified these devices, write a statement that explains how the sound devices in the work enhance the message.

"How to Write a Political Poem"

by Taylor Mali

However it begins, it's gotta be loud
and then it's gotta get a little bit louder.
Because this is how you write a political poem
and how you deliver it with power.

Mix current events with platitudes of empowerment.
Wrap up in rhyme or rhyme it up in rap until it sounds true.

Glare until it sinks in.

Because somewhere in Florida, votes are still being counted.
I said somewhere in Florida, votes are still being counted!

See, that's the Hook, and you gotta' have a Hook.
More than the look, it's the hook that is the most important part.
The hook has to hit and the hook's gotta fit.
Hook's gotta hit hard in the heart.

Because somewhere in Florida, votes are still being counted.

And Dick Cheney is peeing all over himself in spasmodic delight.
Make fun of politicians, it's easy, especially with Republicans
like Rudy Giuliani, Colin Powell, and … Al Gore.
Create fatuous juxtapositions of personalities and political philosophies
as if communism were the opposite of democracy,
as if we needed Darth Vader, not Ralph Nader.

Peep this: When I say "Call,"
you all say, "Response."

Call! Response! Call! Response! Call!

Amazing Grace, how sweet the—

Stop in the middle of a song that everyone knows and loves.
This will give your poem a sense of urgency.
Because there is always a sense of urgency in a political poem.
There is no time to waste!
Corruption doesn't have a curfew,
greed doesn't care what color you are
and the New York City Police Department
is filled with people who wear guns on their hips
and carry metal badges pinned over their hearts.
Injustice isn't injustice it's just in us as we are just in ice.
That's the only alienation of this alien nation
in which you either fight for freedom
or else you are free and dumb!

And even as I say this somewhere in Florida, votes are still being counted.

And it makes me wanna beat box!

Because I have seen the disintegration of gentrification
and can speak with great articulation
about cosmic constellations, and atomic radiation.
I've seen D. W. Griffith's *Birth of a Nation*
but preferred *101 Dalmations*.
Like a cross examination, I will give you the explanation
of why SlamNation is the ultimate manifestation
of poetic masturbation and egotistical ejaculation.

And maybe they are still counting votes somewhere in Florida,
but by the time you get to the end of the poem it won't matter anymore.

Because all you have to do is close your eyes,
lower your voice, and end by saying:

the same line three times,
the same line three times,
the same line three times.

AFTER YOU READ

Write your own political poem.

Lyrics

Lyrics are perhaps even more aural than poems, since they are meant to be set to music, which emphasizes the rhythm of the work. This text contains many song lyrics. Whenever they are assigned, see if you can find a recording of the lyrics and listen to them. Your listening experience will most likely enhance your response to the lyrics.

Sound and Rhythm

Be sure to examine the sound and rhythm of the aural elements just as you would in a poem.

Genre Analysis

The rhythms of lyrics often derive from the genre of music of the lyrics. A genre is a category of music, such as rap, gospel, country, and blues. When lyricists write in a particular genre, they identify their music with common associations with that genre. So, when someone writes with a punk-type beat, the music sounds rebellious, in part because of the stated message, but also because most associate punk with rebellion. Likewise, when music has a bluesy sound, listeners immediately associate it with sadness and depression. In this way, lyricists employ known genres as a means of establishing their message.

EXERCISE: Annotating a Song

Look at the following song. Read it silently and aloud several times.

1. Mark any sound devices you find. Look for repeated sounds, rhymes, and rhythms.
2. If you have access to a recording of the lyrics, listen to it as you read the lyrics. You might be able to find a video on YouTube.com.
3. What is the genre of the song?
4. How does the sound of the genre and the actual text work together?
5. Once you've identified these devices, write a statement that explains how the sound devices in the song enhance the message.

"Give the People What They Want"

by Ray Davies of the Kinks

Hey, hey, hey…
Give the people what they want

Well, it's been said before, the world is a stage
A different performance with every age.
Open the history book to any old page
Bring on the lions and open the cage.

Give the people what they want
You gotta give the people what they want
The more they get, the more they need
And every time they get harder and harder to please

The Roman promoters really did things right.
They needed a show that would clearly excite.
The attendance was sparse so they put on a fight
Threw the Christians to the lions, sold out every night

Give the people what they want
You gotta give the people what they want
The more they get, the more they need
And every time they get harder and harder to please

Give 'em lots of sex, perversion and rape
Give 'em lots of violence, and plenty to hate
Give the people what they want
Give the people what they want

When Oswald shot Kennedy, he was insane
But still we watch the re-runs again and again
We all sit glued while the killer takes aim
Hey mom, there goes a piece of the president's brain!

Give the people what they want
You gotta give the people what they want
Blow out your brains, and do it right
Make sure its prime time and on a Saturday night.

You gotta give the people what they want
You gotta give the people what they want
Give the people what they want
Give the people what they want
Give the people what they want

Advertising Techniques in Political Speeches

Advertisers spend billions of dollars every year to develop ads that will sell their products. And they sell big! If you understand how advertisements work and apply your knowledge to your own arguments, you will most likely be able to argue more effectively. Because of the visual nature of most advertisements, the techniques advertisers use to move their audiences will be discussed in more detail in Chapter 6, Visual Arguments.

For now, realize that all who work to persuade are effectively "advertisers"; they have a message (product) they want their audience to accept (buy), and they construct their communications to appeal as best they can to the needs of their audience. In addition, they use language in sometimes devious ways to create a specific impression. Here is a brief overview of some of these language-based techniques. Although such techniques are generally linked to advertising, the examples provided show that speakers employ them as well.

Such techniques are organized according to the Rhetorical Appeals:

Logos
Ethos
Pathos

Logos: Techniques of Logic

Weasel Words

What are weasels known for? Being devious! This conception comes from their ability to suck an egg dry without breaking its shell, which becomes hollow. **Weasel words** are words used deviously without stating an outright lie to make people think that

> Weasel Words
> Words that are ambiguous and not supported by facts. While their meaning may appear to be clear, in fact they tend to mislead readers into believing something that has no real proof.

something is true that is not necessarily so. So, the claim is hollow. Usually such a word implies a result without promising that result.

For example,

"Listerine fights bad breath."

This does not promise to stop bad breath, only "fight" it. In a speech about ending the war in Vietnam, President Richard Nixon stated, "I pledged in my campaign for the Presidency to end the war in a way that we could win the peace. I have initiated a plan of action which will enable me to keep that pledge." What is he saying here? Had he done anything? He had "initiated a plan" that would "enable" him to fulfill his promise. But he hadn't won the peace, nor did he ever do so. During the 2008 presidential primary, Hillary Clinton kept asserting in her stump speech that she would be "ready on day one." But what does "ready" mean? Ready for what? The word implies that she would be able to deal with America's problems, but does it promise that she will do anything specific? Not really.

Stating the Obvious

When an advertisement states the obvious, it seems to affirm the reader's belief. But what has it really affirmed?

For example,

"Shrank's water is really wet."

Duh! Much of what politicians tell us in their speeches is obvious: gas prices are high, people don't have health insurance, and global warming will destroy the planet if unchecked. They get us nodding our heads because we know these problems exist, and perhaps the fact that they acknowledge these conditions makes us feel that they understand our problems. But the real question is, what exactly will they do about these problems?

Unfinished Comparison

This type of language indicates a comparison but never clarifies what is really being compared.

For example,

Bounty paper towels are "the quicker picker-upper."

But what are they "quicker" than? Another well-known brand of paper towels? The store brand? A rag? Laura Bush, speaking at the Republican National Convention in 2004 asserted, "Our future will be better because of our actions today." In what way would our future be better, do you think? Perhaps *her* future would be better if her husband was elected to a second term, but in what way would the average American's future be better? This claim sounds hopeful, but is it really?

Scientific and Statistical Language

Many people who argue use lofty scientific terms and numbers to impress their audience. But we always must ask ourselves, what do those terms mean? Are those statistics meaningful? Often they are not.

For example,

"Wonderbread helps build strong bodies 12 ways."

This says little. And it even contains a weasel word (helps) along with a statistic (12). When President George W. Bush told the World Economic Forum in Egypt, "Since 2004, economic growth in the region has averaged more than 5%," what exactly was he saying? How did he measure economic growth, and who exactly benefited from the increase? Did big business earn more, or did the average person on the street experience this growth? He did not follow up to explain the details; he simply left his audience with a positive impression.

Ethos: Techniques of Authority

We're Different and Unique

Sometimes advertisers claim that there's nothing like the item being advertised, but is the difference important?

For example,

"Cougar is like nobody else's car."

This may be true; it's designed in a certain identifiable way. But does that mean it's better? Even though Barack Obama and Hillary Clinton often agreed that their proposed policies were similar, one of the key points of Obama's primary campaign speeches was that he was different because he would "change how business is done in Washington." The implication was that Clinton was a part of the old political machine and he was new and different. But if they agreed on so much, how different would he really be?

You're Terrific.

Often advertisers and speakers compliment you to make you feel special. Watch out for false flattery.

For example,

"The lady has taste!"

But does that mean their product or message is good? When Nancy Pelosi stated in a speech at the National League of Cities' annual conference, "Local leaders are the unsung heroes of America's communities," she was engaging in this kind of flattery.

Pathos: Techniques of Emotions

Meaningless Words

Some words are quite colorful, but also quite meaningless in advertising language.

For example,

"Its deep rich lather makes hair feel good again."

This may sound good, but what is it really saying? That the shampoo will clean your hair? When John McCain told Hispanic voters his plan called for "pro-innovation immigration policies," what exactly did he mean? What types of "innovation"? What does "pro-innovation" mean? Is it a meaningful term?

Rhetorical Question

Sometimes an ad or a speaker poses a question that really isn't a question at all. Instead, it implicitly provides the "right" answer.

For example,

"Shouldn't your family be drinking Hawaiian Punch?"

Are you supposed to answer, "No"? It's doubtful that's the answer the advertiser had in mind! When a presidential candidate asks if you want to pay more taxes, does he expect you to say, "Yes"? Clearly not!

Speeches: The Content

When was the last time you listened to someone giving a speech? Was it at school, when the president of the university welcomed you, or was it during the political season when candidates attempted to line out their policies and values? Or perhaps you attended a rally in which a speaker articulated the cause the rally represented. Whatever the occasion, the speaker certainly had some message he or she wanted you to agree with. The president of the university most likely wanted you to walk away feeling good about attending the university—in part, the message was that your chosen school is a fine one. Certainly the political candidate strove to get you to believe that he or she was the best candidate for the job, and the speaker at the rally encouraged you to feel even more strongly about the cause. In essence, each speaker had something to sell, and the speech was constructed to encourage you to "buy" the message. Whether or not you buy what the speaker offers depends on how skilled the speaker is at selling the "product." Sound like an advertisement?

Let's examine a speech to better understand how it acts as an advertisement. As you read the speech, try to figure out what Bush wanted his audience to "buy" and write the possibilities in the margin.

"9/11 Speech"

by President George W. Bush
Address to the Nation September 11, 2001

Good evening. Today, our fellow citizens, our way of life, our very freedom came under attack in a series of deliberate and deadly terrorist acts. The victims were in airplanes, or in their offices; secretaries, businessmen and women, military and federal workers; moms and dads, friends and neighbors. Thousands of lives were suddenly ended by evil, despicable acts of terror.

The pictures of airplanes flying into buildings, fires burning, huge structures collapsing, have filled us with disbelief, terrible sadness, and a quiet, unyielding anger. These acts of mass murder were intended to frighten our nation into chaos and retreat. But they have failed; our country is strong.

A great people has been moved to defend a great nation. Terrorist attacks can shake the foundations of our biggest buildings, but they cannot touch the foundation of America. These acts shattered steel, but they cannot dent the steel of American resolve.

America was targeted for attack because we're the brightest beacon for freedom and opportunity in the world. And no one will keep that light from shining.

Today, our nation saw evil, the very worst of human nature. And we responded with the best of America—with the daring of our rescue workers, with the caring for strangers and neighbors who came to give blood and help in any way they could.

Immediately following the first attack, I implemented our government's emergency response plans. Our military is powerful, and it's prepared. Our emergency teams are working in New York City and Washington, D.C. to help with local rescue efforts.

Our first priority is to get help to those who have been injured, and to take every precaution to protect our citizens at home and around the world from further attacks.

The functions of our government continue without interruption. Federal agencies in Washington which had to be evacuated today are reopening for essential personnel tonight, and will be open for business tomorrow. Our financial institutions remain strong, and the American economy will be open for business, as well. The search is underway for those who are behind these evil acts. I've directed the full resources of our intelligence and law enforcement communities to find those responsible and to bring them to justice. We will make no distinction between the terrorists who committed these acts and those who harbor them.

I appreciate so very much the members of Congress who have joined me in strongly condemning these attacks. And on behalf of the American people, I thank the many world leaders who have called to offer their condolences and assistance.

America and our friends and allies join with all those who want peace and security in the world, and we stand together to win the war against terrorism. Tonight, I ask for your prayers for all those who grieve, for the children whose worlds have been shattered, for all whose sense of safety and security has been threatened. And I pray they will be comforted by a power greater than any of us, spoken through the ages in Psalm 23: "Even though I walk through the valley of the shadow of death, I fear no evil, for You are with me."

This is a day when all Americans from every walk of life unite in our resolve for justice and peace. America has stood down enemies before, and we will do so this time. None of us will ever forget this day. Yet, we go forward to defend freedom and all that is good and just in our world.

Speech Analysis

In order to analyze this speech, we must ask ourselves a number of questions:

Capturing Attention

- Audience is a primary consideration for advertisers, speakers, and anyone else composing a message. If the presentation does not appeal to the audience, the message will not be effective. In what ways does President Bush attempt to capture his audience's attention?
- In this speech, the president emphasizes visuals to appeal to his audience and capture their interest. Notice the descriptions of the people and the attack. Visuals such as "airplanes flying into buildings, fires burning, huge structures collapsing" bring to mind the images of the Twin Towers caving in that the president's listeners had probably seen recently on television; such images connect emotionally with the listeners, stirring their feelings about the event. Not all speeches contain such visuals, but when they do, they provide an image for listeners that captures their imagination and attention. When you read the speeches later on in this book, look for ways in which the speakers attempt to stir their listeners' emotions and capture their attention. Remember that such appeals to emotions are generally subtle.

Finding the Real Message

- What is President Bush's message in this speech? Was he informing the nation that we had been attacked? Certainly people watching the president on television on September 11 already knew about the attacks on the World Trade Center and the Pentagon. And most certainly, the people considered the attacks to be evil. So, what was the president really doing in giving this speech? What did he want listeners to "buy"? Let's examine the content and the language of the speech to strive to answer this question.

Identifying Appeals

- Go back over the speech and underline all descriptions of America. Count the number of times Bush refers to America as free, strong, and the best. In what way are these words weasel words? How do they work together in the speech? How did the president want listeners to come away from his speech feeling? How did he want them to view their government? Certainly the president is striving to reassure Americans that they still live in a strong nation with an effective government. He appeals to Americans' patriotism and their pride in their belief that they live in the best nation in the world, one which is strong and free.

- We've already established that Bush believes his audience is patriotic and values a strong, free country. Does he appeal to any other values? Next to each paragraph, identify the value(s) he appeals to. Speakers must understand their listeners' values if they are to be effective.
- Why did Bush quote Psalm 23? Why quote the Bible in his speech? Bush recognizes the importance of religion in the lives of Americans and subtly connects with the religious nature of his audience through this quotation. Does this technique have its counterpart in advertising? Perhaps the Bible becomes a sort of endorsement for his speech; if God is with Americans, then surely we are being protected.
- Does the president use any other means of selling his message that might be viewed as advertising techniques? Notice how he compliments Americans, stressing their integrity and their love of peace and justice. Review the language-based advertising techniques discussed earlier in this chapter. Has the president employed any others?
- How does Bush employ pathos, ethos, and logos? Review these terms from Chapter 1. In this speech the president appeals to many emotions—fear, pride, the need for security—while at the same time providing logical responses to these feelings, indicating that the government is in control of the situation. The many details in paragraph seven specify the detailed, logical response the government will take, providing both ethos and logos, which Bush expects his audience to respond to.

Understanding the Conclusion

- Reread the final paragraph of this speech. What do you think Bush's goal was in this paragraph? Why does he continue to use the pronoun "we"? Realize that the conclusion of a speech must drive home the speaker's point; it is the final "sell," the last push to get listeners to "buy." In this case, Bush emphasizes American values, bringing all Americans together for a common cause, the cause of freedom which is the foundation of our life in this country.

After answering the questions above, you can see that President Bush wanted to "sell" his audience, "fellow citizens," on the idea that America is still a strong nation, that it will continue to be a strong nation, and that the government of our nation will continue to function well, despite the attempts of the terrorists to throw it into disarray. He appeals to our need to feel safe, our desire to believe that we live in the best nation in the world, our religious nature, and our sense of being a humane people. By analyzing the content of the speech as well as the language and advertising techniques used, we have determined what the president was "selling" when he addressed the nation.

EXERCISE: Annotating a Speech

Read and annotate the following speech, President Kennedy's famous inaugural address. Your goal is to determine what Kennedy wants to sell in his speech. As you annotate, make note of the following:

1. How does Kennedy go about capturing the listeners' attention?
2. What techniques does Kennedy use to sell his "product"?
   - What weasel words does he use?
   - What connotations of words does he depend on?
   - What values does he appeal to?
   - How does he use pathos, logos, and ethos?
   - What advertising techniques does he use?
3. How does Kennedy drive home the "sell" in the conclusion?

Be prepared to discuss your analysis of this speech with your class.

John F. Kennedy's Inaugural Address

We observe today not a victory of party but a celebration of freedom—symbolizing an end as well as a beginning—signifying renewal as well as change. For I have sworn before you and Almighty God the same solemn oath our forebears prescribed nearly a century and three-quarters ago.

The world is very different now. For man holds in his mortal hands the power to abolish all forms of human poverty and all forms of human life. And yet the same revolutionary beliefs for which our forebears fought are still at issue around the globe—the belief that the rights of man come not from the generosity of the state but from the hand of God.

We dare not forget today that we are the heirs of that first revolution. Let the word go forth from this time and place, to friend and foe alike, that the torch has been passed to a new generation of Americans—born in this century, tempered by war, disciplined by a hard and bitter peace, proud of our ancient heritage—and unwilling to witness or permit the slow undoing of those human rights to which this nation has always been committed, and to which we are committed today at home and around the world.

Let every nation know, whether it wishes us well or ill, that we shall pay any price, bear any burden, meet any hardship, support any friend, oppose any foe to assure the survival and the success of liberty.

This much we pledge—and more.

To those old allies whose cultural and spiritual origins we share, we pledge the loyalty of faithful friends. United, there is little we cannot do in a host of cooperative ventures. Divided, there is little we can do—for we dare not meet a powerful challenge at odds and split asunder.

To those new states whom we welcome to the ranks of the free, we pledge our word that one form of colonial control shall not have passed away merely to be replaced by a far more iron tyranny. We shall not always expect to find them supporting our view. But we shall always hope to find them strongly supporting their own freedom—and to remember that, in the past, those who foolishly sought power by riding the back of the tiger ended up inside.

To those peoples in the huts and villages of half the globe struggling to break the bonds of mass misery, we pledge our best efforts to help them help themselves, for whatever period is required—not because the Communists may be doing it, not because we seek their votes, but because it is right. If a free society cannot help the many who are poor, it cannot save the few who are rich.

To our sister republics south of our border, we offer a special pledge—to convert our good words into good deeds—in a new alliance for progress—to assist free men and free governments in casting off the chains of poverty. But this peaceful revolution of hope cannot become the prey of hostile powers. Let all our neighbors know that we shall join with them to oppose aggression or subversion anywhere in the Americas. And let every other power know that this hemisphere intends to remain the master of its own house.

To that world assembly of sovereign states, the United Nations, our last best hope in an age where the instruments of war have far outpaced the instruments of peace, we renew our pledge of support—to prevent it from becoming merely a forum for invective—to strengthen its shield of the new and the weak—and to enlarge the area in which its writ may run.

Finally, to those nations who would make themselves our adversary, we offer not a pledge but a request: that both sides begin anew the quest for peace, before the dark powers of destruction unleashed by science engulf all humanity in planned or accidental self-destruction.

We dare not tempt them with weakness. For only when our arms are sufficient beyond doubt can we be certain beyond doubt that they will never be employed.

But neither can two great and powerful groups of nations take comfort from our present course—both sides overburdened by the cost of modern weapons, both rightly alarmed by the steady spread of the deadly atom, yet both racing to alter that uncertain balance of terror that stays the hand of mankind's final war.

So let us begin anew—remembering on both sides that civility is not a sign of weakness, and sincerity is always subject to proof. Let us never negotiate out of fear. But let us never fear to negotiate.

Let both sides explore what problems unite us instead of belaboring those problems which divide us.

Let both sides, for the first time, formulate serious and precise proposals for the inspection and control of arms—and bring the absolute power to destroy other nations under the absolute control of all nations.

Let both sides seek to invoke the wonders of science instead of its terrors. Together let us explore the stars, conquer the deserts, eradicate disease, tap the ocean depths and encourage the arts and commerce.

Let both sides unite to heed in all corners of the earth the command of Isaiah—to "undo the heavy burdens … [and] let the oppressed go free."

And if a beachhead of cooperation may push back the jungles of suspicion, let both sides join in a new endeavor—not a new balance of power, but a new world of law, where the strong are just and the weak secure and the peace preserved.

All this will not be finished in the first 100 days. Nor will it be finished in the first 1,000 days, nor in the life of this administration, nor even perhaps in our lifetime on this planet. But let us begin.

In your hands, my fellow citizens, more than mine, will rest the final success or failure of our course. Since this country was founded, each generation of Americans has been summoned to give testimony to its national loyalty. The graves of young Americans who answered the call to service surround the globe.

Now the trumpet summons us again—not as a call to bear arms, though arms we need—not as a call to battle, though embattled we are—but a call to bear the burden of a long twilight struggle year in and year out, "rejoicing in hope, patient in tribulation"—a struggle against the common enemies of man: tyranny, poverty, disease and war itself.

Can we forge against these enemies a grand and global alliance, north and south, east and west, that can assure a more fruitful life for all mankind? Will you join in that historic effort?

In the long history of the world, only a few generations have been granted the role of defending freedom in its hour of maximum danger. I do not shrink from this responsibility—I welcome it. I do not believe that any of us would exchange places with any other people or any other generation. The energy, the faith, the devotion which we bring to this endeavor will light our country and all who serve it—and the glow from that fire can truly light the world.

And so, my fellow Americans: ask not what your country can do for you—ask what you can do for your country.

My fellow citizens of the world: ask not what America will do for you, but what together we can do for the freedom of man.

Finally, whether you are citizens of America or citizens of the world, ask of us here the same high standards of strength and sacrifice which we ask of you. With a good conscience our only sure reward, with history the final judge of our deeds, let us go forth to lead the land we love, asking His blessing and His help, but knowing that here on earth God's work must truly be our own.

The Non-Verbal Aspects: Visual Delivery

So far, we have been stressing the content of speeches. But we must recognize that most speeches are given in front of an audience and thus have a **nonverbal** component as well.

> Nonverbal Language
> Refers to communication that does not derive from words. People communicate using their bodies—posture, gestures, and facial expressions; objects—clothing, hair styles, furnishings, or anything else people choose to surround themselves with; or even the nonverbal elements of speech—tone, emotional response such as crying, and the level of sound that accompanies their words.

Body Language: Stress Choices

The visual aspects of the speech like body language bring it even more into the realm of advertising, contributing to the speech's persuasive nature.

The significance of the visual aspect of oral presentations becomes clear when examining the presentations of the competitors in the Kennedy-Nixon debate, perhaps the most analyzed oral presentation in terms of its visuals. This was the first televised presidential debate, and many believe Kennedy won the presidency because of how the two candidates looked on television. While Kennedy seemed composed, Nixon perspired and looked anxious. Kennedy appeared taller, more muscular, and more handsome; Nixon paled visually compared to his opponent. Kennedy appeared to be in control of his presentation, gesturing forcefully and effectively throughout; Nixon seemed to lack this control.

To see aspects of this debate, watch the video at:

http://www.unitedstreaming.com/videos/21232/chp911019_256k.asf

Always pay attention to the body language of a speaker. Body language refers to the postures, gestures, and facial expressions of the speaker that serve as nonverbal communication. Strong body language is a means of creating good ethos. When speakers seem open, caring, forceful at appropriate times, and at ease, then they are using their bodies to complement and drive home their message. Any deviation from good body language—lack of eye contact, for example—will detract from the effectiveness of the speaker's message.

We generally pick up on aspects of body language without thinking about them, but as you analyze speeches, pay particular attention to these nonverbal cues since you may acquire more insights into what the speaker is attempting to achieve through the speech. When does the speaker pause and look beseechingly at the audience? When does the speaker use the most forceful gestures? When does the speaker smile? The answers to these questions and others like them can enable us to better analyze speeches.

Dress: Clothing Choices

Another way speakers work to establish ethos is through clothing choices. You've probably heard the expression, "Clothes make the man (and the woman)." What exactly does this expression mean? The way people dress tells us a great deal about them. And when people choose what clothes to wear to give a speech, they are using that choice to complement what they will say. If, for example, a speaker wants to appeal to youth, he or she will work to appear youthful, wearing up-to-date styles in colors that are "in." People who wish to appeal to the opposite sex may even consider the sex-appeal aspect of their look. The colors people choose to wear also provide insights. Blue is the most receptive color to humans. Its hues and shades relax us and create a sense of well-being. Most politicians wear blue when they speak.

Don't assume that people are simply being themselves. Remember how Professor Higgins turned Eliza Doolittle, the street urchin, into a lady fit for court in *My Fair Lady?* Practiced speakers know Professor Higgins' tricks and use them to their advantage. As you watch someone speak, ask yourself: Why is he wearing that tie, that shirt, that suit? Or, why isn't he wearing a tie? Why did he choose to wear that color? Actively read clothing cues.

Background: Environmental Choices

When speakers have control over the environment in which they will be speaking, they will take the opportunity to construct their surroundings to their advantage. Notice the colors of the background, the objects surrounding the speaker, even the people who are present. Ask these questions:

- Are the colors neutral, relaxing, or stimulating?
- How might those colors complement the speech?
- What objects do you see?
- Is there a flag or some other symbolic object that establishes the speaker's values?
- Is the speaker's spouse present? If so, what is the unstated message about family and its importance to the speaker?
- Who else is present? Always ask *why* those people are there.

EXERCISE: Annotating a Debate

Debates continue to keep Americans riveted to their televisions during political campaigns.

More recently, Americans watched numerous debates between Democratic candidates Hillary Clinton and Barak Obama to determine whom they should vote for during the 2008 presidential primaries. Interestingly, these two candidates had very similar positions on many issues. What follows is an excerpt from their debate held at the University of Texas concerning immigration policy.

CNN's Campbell Brown moderated the debate, and Jorge Ramos of Univision and John King of CNN asked the questions. As you read this excerpt, note in the margin how each candidate attempts to distinguish his or her viewpoint. What points does each candidate make? What audience is each point directed at? Why does each make the points he or she does?

"Clinton-Obama Immigration Debate" (February 21, 2008)

RAMOS: (SPEAKING IN SPANISH) Federal raids by immigration enforcement officials on homes and businesses have generated a great deal of fear and anxiety in the Hispanic community and have divided the family of some of the 3 million U.S.-born children who have at least one undocumented parent.

Would you consider stopping these raids once you take office until comprehensive immigration reform can be passed?

CLINTON: I would consider that, except in egregious situations where it would be appropriate to take the actions you're referring to.

But when we see what's been happening, with literally babies being left with no one to take care of them, children coming home from school, no responsible adult left, that is not the America that I know.

(APPLAUSE)

CLINTON: That is against American values. And it is...

(APPLAUSE)

And it is a stark admission of failure by the federal government. We need comprehensive immigration reform. I have been for this. I signed onto the first comprehensive bill back in 2004. I've been advocating for it: tougher, more secure borders, of course, but let's do it the right way, cracking down on employers, especially once we get to comprehensive immigration reform, who exploit undocumented workers and drive down wages for everyone else.

I'd like to see more federal help for communities like Austin and others like Laredo, where I was this morning, that absorb the health care, education, and law enforcement costs.

And I personally, as president, would work with our neighbors to the south, to help them create more jobs for their own people.

Finally, we need a path to legalization, to bring the immigrants out of the shadows, give them the conditions that we expect them to meet, paying a fine for coming here illegally, trying to pay back taxes, over time, and learning English.

If they had committed a crime in our country or the country they came from, then they should be deported. But for everyone else, there must be a path to legalization. I would introduce that in the first 100 days of my presidency.

(APPLAUSE)

BROWN: Senator Obama, is your position the same as Hillary Clinton's?

OBAMA: There are a couple of things I would add. Comprehensive immigration reform is something that I have worked on extensively.

Two years ago, we were able to get a bill out of the Senate. I was one of the group of senators that helped to move it through, but it died in the House this year. Because it was used as a political football instead of a way of solving a problem, nothing happened.

And so there are a couple of things that I would just add to what Senator Clinton said.

Number one, it is absolutely critical that we tone down the rhetoric when it comes to the immigration debate, because there has been an undertone that has been ugly.

Oftentimes, it has been directed at the Hispanic community. We have seen hate crimes skyrocket in the wake of the immigration debate as it has been conducted in Washington, and that is unacceptable.

We are a nation of laws and we are a nation of immigrants, and we can reconcile those two things. So we need comprehensive reform...

(APPLAUSE)

... we need comprehensive reform, and that means stronger border security. It means that we are cracking down on employers that are taking advantage of undocumented workers because they can't complain if they're not paid a minimum wage.

They can't complain if they're not getting overtime. Worker safety laws are not being observed.

We have to crack down on those employers, although we also have to make sure that we do it in a way that doesn't lead to people with Spanish surnames being discriminated against, so there's got to be a safeguard there.

We have to require that undocumented workers, who are provided a pathway to citizenship, not only learn English, pay back taxes and pay a significant fine, but also that they're going to the back of the line, so that they are not getting citizenship before those who have applied legally, which raises two last points.

Number one, it is important that we fix the legal immigration system, because right now we've got a backlog that means years for people to apply legally.

(APPLAUSE)

And what's worse is, we keep on increasing the fees, so that if you've got a hard working immigrant family, they've got to hire a lawyer; they've got to pay thousands of dollars in fees. They just can't afford it. And it's discriminatory against people who have good character, we should want in this country, but don't have the money. So we've got to fix that.

The second thing is, we have to improve our relationship with Mexico and work with the Mexican government so that their economy is producing jobs on that side of the border.

And the problem that we have...

(APPLAUSE)

The problem that we have is that we have had an administration that came in promising all sorts of leadership on creating a U.S.-Mexican relationship. And, frankly, President Bush dropped the ball. He has been so obsessed with Iraq that we have not seen the kinds of outreach and cooperative work that would ensure that the Mexican economy is working not just for the very wealthy in Mexico, but for all people. And that's a policy that I'm going to change when I'm president of the United States.

(APPLAUSE)

"Johnnie Cochran's Closing Arguments"

September 27, 1995 O.J. Simpson Murder Case

Born in Shreveport, Louisiana, Johnnie Cochran (1937–2005) graduated from Loyola University School of Law (1962). In 1977, he was awarded the "Criminal Trial Lawyer of the Year" by the LA Criminal Courts Bar Association of Law. In 1993, he became a member of the elite organization called the American College of Trial Lawyers. He has defended high profile cases such as O.J. Simpson and Michael Jackson.

"Johnnie Cochran's Closing Arguments" excerpt from Criminal Murder Case, LA District Court. September 27, 1995.

AS YOU READ: Annotate

1. Note in the margins which words or phrases are repeated.
2. Place a star by any section you feel is effective.
3. Circle any words you do not know and write their meaning in the margins.

Background to the Murder Trial of O.J. Simpson. On June 12, 1994, Nicole Brown Simpson and Ronald Goldman were stabbed to death. O.J. Simpson was arrested for their murders. Judge Ito presided over the case. On October 3, 1995, the jury found Simpson not guilty. Perhaps one of the key reasons for the verdict was Cochran's closing speech. O.J. did not do so well in the civil suit where he was found liable for $8.5 million in compensatory damages.

MR. COCHRAN: The Defendant, Mr. Orenthal James Simpson, is now afforded an opportunity to argue the case, if you will, but I'm not going to argue with you, ladies and gentlemen. What I'm going to do is to try and discuss the reasonable inferences which I feel can be drawn from this evidence....

And when you are back there deliberating on this case, you're never going to be ever able to reconcile this time line and the fact there's no blood back there and O.J. Simpson would run into an air conditioner on his own property and then under her scenario, he still has the knife and the clothes. But what does she tell you yesterday? Well, he still has the knife and he's in these bloody clothes and presumably in bloody shoes, and what does he do? He goes in the house. Now, thank heaven, Judge Ito took us on a jury view. You've seen this house. You've seen this carpet.

If he went in that house with bloody shoes, with bloody clothes, with his bloody hands as they say, where's the blood on the doorknob, where's the blood on the light switch, where's the blood on the banister, where's the blood on the carpet? That's like almost white carpet going up those stairs. Where is all that blood trail they've been ranting about in this mountain of evidence? You will see it's little more than a river or a stream. They don't have any mountain or ocean of evidence. It's not so because they say so. That's just rhetoric. We this afternoon are talking about the facts. And so it doesn't make any sense. It just doesn't fit. If it doesn't fit, you must acquit.

Just before we break for our break, I was thinking—I was thinking last night about this case and their theory and how it didn't make any sense and how it didn't fit and how something is wrong. It occurred to me how they were going to come here, stand up here and tell you how O.J. Simpson was going to disguise himself. He was going to put on a knit cap and some dark clothes, and he was going to get in his white Bronco, this recognizable person, and go over and kill his wife. That's what they want you to believe. That's how silly their argument is. And I said to myself, maybe I can demonstrate this graphically.

Let me show you something. This is a knit cap. Let me put this knit cap on (Indicating). You have seen me for a year. If I put this knit cap on, who am I? I'm still Johnnie Cochran with a knit cap. And if you looked at O.J. Simpson over there—and he has a rather large head—O.J. Simpson in a knit cap from two blocks away is still O.J. Simpson. It's no disguise. It's no disguise. It makes no sense. It doesn't fit. If it doesn't fit, you must acquit.

AFTER YOU READ: Analyze the Issues

1. What does Cochran say about the "mountain of evidence"?
2. What is Cochran saying about the knit cap?
3. How effective is this excerpt of Cochran's closing statements?

AFTER YOU READ: Analyze the Rhetoric

1. Why repeat blood so many times?
2. What is the effect of repeating, "It just doesn't fit. If it doesn't fit, you must acquit."?
3. Go to YouTube.com or another on-line video site and see if you can watch the closing statement. Or read the closing statement aloud and note how powerful the speech becomes. Comment on this.

"Chewbacca Defense"

by Trey Parker and Matt Stone

TELEPLAY "Chewbacca Defense" by Trey Parker and Matt Stone, excerpt from *South Park* episode Season 2, episode 14 "Chef Aid," originally aired 7 Oct. 1998.

Trey Parker (1969–) and Matt Stone (1971–) both attended the University of Colorado. Parker majored in music while Matt majored in film. Parker and Stone made a brief animation series called *The Spirit of Christmas: Jesus vs. Santa* (1995) for Comedy Central. In 1997, *South Park* was created. The show is nearing some 200 episodes. It continues to be both successful and controversial. They also made films such as *Team America: World Police* and *Orgazmo!*

Background. *Chef is angry that a record company is profiting from a song he wrote over 20 years ago. He needs two million dollars to hire Johnnie Cochran to defend him. The following scene is a parody of Johnnie Cochran from the O.J. Simpson criminal trial.*

Ladies and gentlemen of the supposed jury, I have one final thing I want you to consider: (pulling out a drawing) this is Chewbacca. Chewbacca is a Wookiee from the planet Kashyyyk, but Chewbacca lives on the planet Endor. Now, think about that. That does not make sense! (The jury is confused!)

Why would a Wookiee—an eight foot tall Wookiee—want to live on Endor with a bunch of two foot tall Ewoks? That does not make sense!

But more importantly, you have to ask yourself: what does that have to do with this case? Nothing. Ladies and gentlemen, it has nothing to do with this case! It does not make sense!

Look at me, I'm a lawyer defending a major record company, and I'm talkin' about Chewbacca. Does that make sense? Ladies and gentlemen, I am not making any sense. None of this makes sense.

And so you have to remember, when you're in that jury room deliberating and conjugating the Emancipation Proclamation… does it make sense? No! Ladies and gentlemen of this supposed jury, it does not make sense.

If Chewbacca lives on Endor, you must acquit! The defense rests.

AFTER YOU READ: Analyze the Issues

1. Why are references to *Star Wars* being made in this speech?
2. What is the point that the creators of *South Park* are making with this speech?
3. Compare this parody to excerpts from the original.

AFTER YOU READ: Analyze the Rhetoric

1. What is the funniest part of this excerpt?
2. Read this aloud or try to watch the scene at YouTube.com. Comment on the effect of reading it aloud or seeing it.
3. Comment on the effect of repetition.

Simulations

"Stratagems: The Show"

Avatar

A visual representation of a person in the virtual or gaming world. Originally, the term is from Hinduism meaning an incarnation that various deities are able to manifest. The term was popularized by Neal Stephenson (1959–) in his post-cyberpunk classic, *Snow Crash* (1992).

Violence and Gaming. Does playing video games make teenagers more violent? What do you think? Gather a group of experts to debate this on the popular new show *Stratagems.* Be sure to read "Were Video Games to Blame for the Massacre?" by Winda Benedetti.

Background. See this recent timeline of school violence: www.infoplease.com/ipa/A0777958.html.

Also read the rating system for video games created by the Entertainment Software Rating Board: www.esrb.org/ratings.

Use these **avatars** from the reading or create others. Be sure to pick a host or GM to do the questioning. Break up into opposing teams.

Anti-gaming Avatars	Pro-gaming Avatars
Jack Thompson	**Jason Della Rocca**, International Game Association
Dr. Phil McGraw	**Isaiah Triforce Johnson**, New York Gaming Advocacy Group
	Dr. Karen Sternheimer, sociologist
	Hal Halpin, Entertainment Consumer Association

Part I: Ice Breaker

On *Stratagems: The Show*, introduce each other. Discuss the tragedy at Virginia Tech. Discuss other incidences of school violence. (5 minutes)

Part II: Debate

The various players debate their points. (10 minutes)

Make a transition (Commercial Break). Regroup into your team and discuss some quick strategies. (1–2 minutes)

Continue the debate. The various players again debate their points. (10 minutes)

Part III: Jacked into a Game

Make a transition (Commercial Break). Regroup into your team and discuss some quick strategies. (1–2 minutes)

This time the avatars find themselves in a videogame like "Counter Strike." Who will win? Use the die to decide. (5–10 minutes)

"The CUBE of Rhetoric Adventure"

This is loosely based on the science fiction film, *Cube* (Vincenzo Natali, 1997).

Four or five players find themselves lost in a strange maze. All the players woke up together in some sort of white room or cubicle. They are able to break out of the cubicle but only find themselves in another cubicle. They are trying to figure out how to get out. Each time as they break into another cubicle, they become damaged, either wounded or ill. Strangely, words can heal the damage as they try to solve the problems about issues they discuss.

Choose your character or avatar to play and feel free to alter the avatar. Keep in mind that you are in a science fiction or cyberpunk story. Review the readings related to science fiction in Chapter 13:

- "Dining with Cannibals," p. 374
- "Are You Human? The Test" *Blade Runner* excerpt, p 377
- "The Deliverator" *Snow Crash* excerpt, p. 383

Visit these sites for more background information:

- Information about Cyberpunk: project.cyberpunk.ru/idb
- Fan Site about *Blade Runner*: bladezone.com

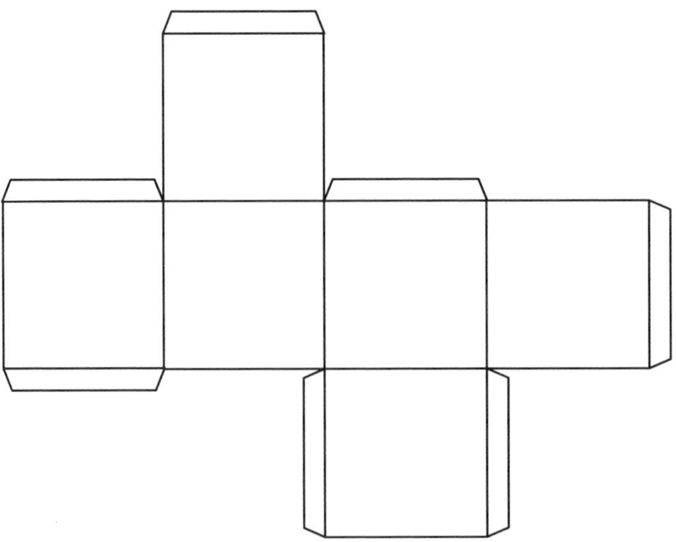

Masters or Leaders Powerful people who run the world	**Slaves or Revolutionaries (Hackers)** Workers or misfits
CEO Big Nose (High Tech Corporate Head from "Dining with Cannibals")	**Pop**, worker ("Dining with Cannibals")
Uncle Enzo, Pizza (Mafia boss from *Snow Crash*)	**Deliverator**, African American/ Korean Hacker (from *Snow Crash*)
Good Old Boy or Girl (Politician)	**Monkey Boy**, worker (from "Dining with Cannibals")
	Leon, (Replicant from *Blade Runner*)

First, they introduce themselves and tell the others what they did before going to sleep last night trying to figure out why they are all together. There is no food or water in the first cubicle, so they must try to escape to live. (Ice Breaker, 5 minutes)

Second, they break into another cubicle or room. Some are wounded or become ill. Role the die to find out what wound occurred. (2–3 minutes)

Bored, they begin to attack each other verbally; after all, these are people who don't like each other. However, as they talk, trying to recover, their voices have the power to heal. They run out of food, water, and other needed things. (10 minutes)

Third, as they again break out, they find yet another cubicle in the giant cube. Some are wounded or become ill. Role the die to find out what wound occurred. (2–3 minutes)

Bored, they begin to attack each other again verbally in an effort to heal. They again run out of food, water, and other needed things. (10 minutes)

Conclusion: Cubicle of Deadly Words

The class is ending and the players enter the Cubicle of Deadly Words, the final cubicle. Here as they debate, they are wounded by words or phrases. The GM will roll at certain times to see what happens.

"Meeting of the Minds Adventure"

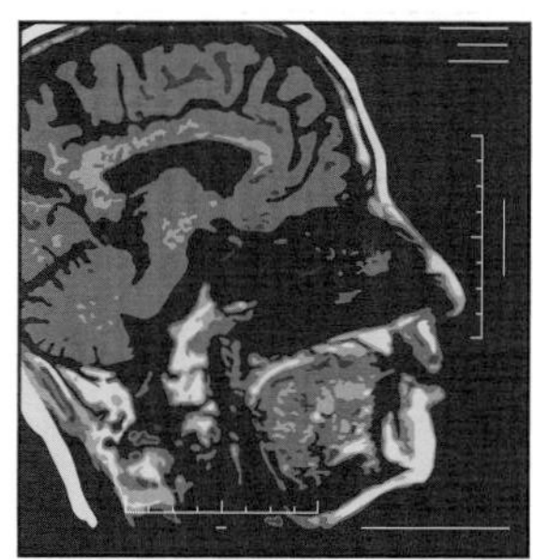

Historical characters from various times come together to debate on a current issue. Or you can pick a time and have other avatars only from one period interact with each other. Or you can use a character or figure from the readings. For example, you could have people from the first Gulf War debate someone from the current Gulf War about the causes of the war.

GM or Mediator

Choose your mediator or game master for this adventure.

Real Historical Persona

You could have Plato debating the Dalai Lama or the Pope about some topics.

Fictional Persona

Take characters from film or fiction and have them act out a situation. Characters from a Shakespeare play could debate.

Mixture

Both real historical and fictitious characters interact in an adventure. Be creative in how you set up your adventure.

Ways to Conclude

Spend about 3–5 minutes ending the adventure.

GM Decision

The GM decides who wins and has to tell why he or she thinks which side won. The GM may roll the die to decide which side wins but the GM still has to defend the outcome with explanations.

Audience Decision

The audience decides which side provided the best answers in a vote and have some audience members share why they voted the way they did. Again the GM should come up with a concluding statement.

Alternate Ending

Melee: Create some sort of fictional altercation, a Jerry Springer-like fiasco, celebrity championship wrestling, or mixed martial arts fight. The GM will use die to decide outcomes of fights.

"Post-Millennium Think Tank Adventure"

Game World: It is now the twenty-first century, and America is changing. America is becoming a microcosm of a complex, diverse, multicultural world, not the melting pot as was once predicted. For this new America to work, diverse views on complex issues will have to be understood in a new context. Social imbalances may permanently disrupt and dissolve America. Among the various types of fear is the fear that radical fringe groups to the left and right might be planning terrorist actions.

Civil unrest has begun due to misunderstandings of some contemporary issues. The Waco tragedy, the Oklahoma City bombing, the 9-11 attack, and wars may have been signs of that disruption. Abortion bombings are other examples of fringe actions based on strong belief. Because of scientific, religious, and political changes, more tragedies might be on their way. Experts feel that such tragedies might be avoided if more information gathering and an understanding of social problems become in tune with the new America. Protecting the borders and worrying about immigrants are among the many topics raised by Americans.

The **president** (your instructor) has set up Post-Millennium Think Tanks to try to understand some of these new social problems.

Each player is a member of its own Post-Millennium Think Tank, where some of the best minds in the world from different backgrounds join together to rethink and debate about complex issues in order to understand them.

Teams of Three-Five Players

The president will divide the class into smaller Think Tank units, composed of at least three to five individuals, who will together propose a topic, research all aspects of the topic, and provide a written analysis (research paper) of the issue. Each Think Tank Unit must choose one topic, a different topic from the other groups' choices. Within the groups, different opinions must be expressed.

Research Paper

An important part of the Think Tank will be researching and creating the research paper. It involves knowing how to use the Internet and library, comprehending how to validate sources and understanding what objective, academic writing requires.

This analysis of the issue will be in the form of an argument. Then, each individual within the unit will write his or her own viewpoint on that issue in the form of a research paper.

Duties

Two players will defend a specific aspect of the issue while the other two will write on the opposing aspects of the issue.

The GM will defend a viewpoint that tries to reconcile the two opposing viewpoints in a synthesis, proposing a compromise, or in an argument paper.

Defense of an Issue Viewpoint	**1–2 players**
Opposing Viewpoints	**1–2 players**
Synthesis/Solution or Argue a Position	**GM**

Create other adventures to examine controversial issues!

"Baby Loves McDonalds"

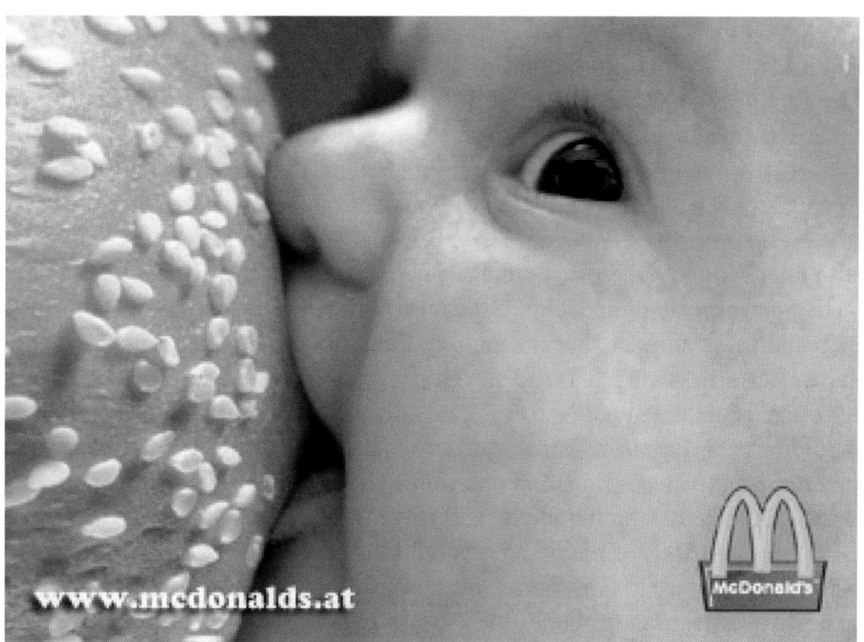

AFTER YOU READ: Analyze the Issues

1. What is the message of the ad?
2. Is the ad sending the wrong message?
3. Do kids love McDonalds? Are the ads partially responsible?

AFTER YOU READ: Analyze the Rhetoric

1. Which of the appeals is the ad using more: logos, pathos, ethos?
2. How is the ad using humor?
3. Who is the audience?

Visual Discourse

Traditionally rhetoric is thought of as the discipline that uses an extended, formal, thoroughly thought out discourse to inform or persuade or motivate an audience, either through the written or spoken word. Rhetoricians have carefully developed a set of parameters to help students understand rhetoric in what they consider its purest form. They often agree that it does not include gossip, jokes, directives, and other short snippets of speech. However, this approach addresses only a small part of the definition of rhetoric—an extended, formal discourse.

Some snippets of speech are meant to inform or persuade or motivate an audience and these snippets are thoroughly thought out. Imagine how long it takes the Budweiser advertising team to develop a concept for a Superbowl ad. While the discourse is not extended or formal, it is definitely intended to persuade or motivate an audience. Advertisers know that to persuade or motivate an American audience they must motivate, enrich, and entertain. They also know they must adapt, quickly, to the methods by which audiences receive information.

As newer forms of media emerged during the 20th century, the types of rhetoric, specifically persuasive discourse, needed to adapt to meet the new types of presentation. Advertising is probably the most ever-present form of persuasive discourse. It pervades every media type, including but not limited to TV, radio, magazines, journals, newspapers, billboards, and the Internet. Advertising, like other forms of rhetoric, relies on the basic elements of argument discussed in previous chapters of this book. Advertisements make assertions, provide evidence, and draw conclusions (though often subtly). Unlike speeches and other types of rhetoric, advertising often relies heavily on visuals as well as written or spoken words. The visuals support the written or spoken words, often providing tangible evidence. Furthermore, visuals retain a certain level of viewer control—that is, the person viewing the visual can, and does, use her or his own level of reasoning and understanding. But this control is not as pervasive as a viewer might think. Advertisers spend a lot of time and money understanding how individuals reason and understand. What advertisers know is one of the primary focuses of this chapter. This chapter examines **visual discourse** from a rhetorical approach, as well as the other techniques used to develop advertising, political campaigns, and cartoons.

Visual Discourse
The way people communicate through visual cues and other aspects of seeing. For example, your mother might give you "the look," and you know exactly what that look means. In fact, we have grown accustomed to many forms of visual communications in the 21st century—film, posters, advertisements, the visual arts, and anything else around us that sends a visual message.

Why Study Visual Discourse in an English Course?

Visuals are useful in a variety of ways, not only to you, a college student, but also to corporations, associations, and organizations. For now we will look at five ways visuals help you and other audiences to learn, to explain, to persuade, and to evaluate.

Motivation

Visuals grab a person's attention and create complex connections in a short amount of time. They are a great way to motivate people. Visuals persuade you every day. How many advertisements have you seen today? Will you see today? How many of the announcements do you read on the bulletin boards? Do you read the ones with visuals or the ones without?

Enrichment

Visuals often elaborate on the text they accompany. Have you ever read a course textbook describing a complex process? Did you look for a visual to help you understand? Did that visual confirm your understanding or even expand it?

Summation

Visuals, such as flowcharts and diagrams, often help you summarize a large set of information. If presented first, it might help your audience see the big picture before you delve into the smaller details.

Presentation

Visuals can help present information in a small space and help people understand complex information in small segments that can be connected easily.

Evaluation

Visuals often help people evaluate new ideas and make decisions about how new ideas relate to current ideas. Political campaign commercials offer connections between how the candidate believes the audience feels about current political processes and how the candidate hopes to change the processes if elected. Another example of visual evaluation occurs in pharmaceutical commercials. Current commercials for bipolar disorder medications use visuals that promote peace and happiness, two emotions not typically associated with the disorder.

As you can see, visuals offer you and others the opportunity to better understand the world around you.

What Do Advertising Companies Know about Their Audiences?

Audience analysis is key—not only in advertising but also in all situations that involve persuasion or argumentation. This type of analysis is not new. It has been around since Adam and Eve. Satan watched them in the Garden of Eden to see how best to persuade them to both eat from the tree of life.

Audience analysis has grown, strategically, of course, as opportunities for individuals to persuade others have grown. Many books, articles, and studies on people from different cultures and lifestyles exist. One of the most famous is *The Nine American Lifestyles* by Arnold Mitchell. Mitchell describes nine types of Americans that can be categorized into four broad groups.

"The Nine American Lifestyles"

by Arnold Mitchell

The need driven groups

> Survivors—Old, intensely poor, fearful, far removed from the cultural mainstream (4% of the U.S. adult population).
>
> Sustainers—Angry, resentful, street-wise, living on the edge of poverty, involved in the underground economy (7% of the U.S. adult population).

The outer-directed groups

> Belongers—Aging, conventional, content, intensely patriotic, traditional Middle Americans (35% of the U.S. adult population).
>
> Emulators—Young, ambitious, flashy, trying to break into the system (9% of the U.S. adult population).
>
> Achievers—Middle-aged, prosperous, self-assured; the leaders and builders of the American dream (22% of the U.S. adult population).

The inner-directed groups

> I-am-me—Very young, narcissistic, impulsive, exhibitionist; a transitional state to Outer-Direction (5% of the U.S. adult population).
>
> Experiential—Youthful, seeking direct experience, artistic, intensely oriented toward inner growth (7% of the U.S. adult population).
>
> Societally conscious—Mission-oriented, mature, successful, out to change the world (8% of the U.S. adult population).

The combined outer- and inner-directed group

> Intergrated—Psychologically mature, tolerant, understanding, flexible, able to see "the big picture" (2% of the U.S. adult population).

Advertisers take this information and develop a comprehensive understanding of the goals and needs of each audience type. Then they develop written scripts, visuals, and media tools that help them persuade the audience that the product or idea the advertiser is selling meets or exceeds the goals and needs of the audience.

Once an advertising company finds its target lifestyle group, it has to develop a concept that will persuade people within the group to purchase the product or to accept the assertion it is promoting. Most of the persuasive strategy lies within the words found in the ad.

To better understand how this works, let's pick a particular audience type: the outer-directed group. Some of the characteristics of this group are "patriotic," "ambitious," and "leaders." These characteristics match, almost directly, with the type of characteristics the Armed Services seek in new recruits. Ad campaigns for the Armed Services target these characteristics, which are valued by members of that audience type. By targeting these characteristics, the Armed Services increase their chances of persuading young, patriotic, ambitious, leaders to join their forces. How are the characteristics of outer-directed audiences targeted in this ad?

"Are You Army Strong?"

The primary characteristic targeted in this ad is "ambitious." People who are ambitious consider themselves "strong." They believe they have an emotional and physical strength that will allow them to be successful. The ad also challenges the audience to prove this belief: Are you Army Strong?

Finally, it also seeks outer-directed individuals who want to be "ambitious" and who want to be "leaders" by challenging them to "find [their] strength." The word "Army," of course, is patriotic all unto itself.

What other audience type is this ad targeting? The inner-directed group. How? Write a brief evaluation.

Now let's evaluate another ad to determine the type of audience targeted by the advertising consultants.

Look closely at the ad below. First look at the visuals. Second, look at the text.

"I Have Thunder Thighs"

I HAVE
THUNDER THIGHS.
AND THAT'S A COMPLIMENT
BECAUSE THEY ARE STRONG
AND TONED
AND MUSCULAR
AND THOUGH THEY ARE UNWELCOME
IN THE PETITE SECTION
THEY ARE CHEERED ON IN MARATHONS.
FIFTY YEARS FROM NOW
I'LL BOUNCE A GRANDCHILD ON MY THUNDER THIGHS
AND THEN I'LL GO OUT FOR A RUN.
JUST DO IT.
NIKEWOMEN.COM

AFTER YOU READ: Answer These Questions

1. Who is the target audience for this ad? What was your first clue?
2. Consider only the visual for a moment. What does the advertiser want the consumer to associate with Nike? Does the visual risk any of the problems often associated with the visuals?
3. Which language technique does the advertiser use to reach the target audience? Give examples from the copy.
4. What type of rhetorical appeal does the copy use to reach the target audience? Logos? Pathos? Ethos?
5. Does this ad seek to change any common misconceptions? If so, will it succeed?

What Techniques Do Advertising Companies Use?

Advertising, like other rhetorical forms, relies on the basic elements of persuasion: the rhetorical appeals. Many audience types can be further broken down into persuasive styles. Some people within each group can be persuaded by logos; others can be persuaded by ethos; and still others can be persuaded by pathos. No one area of the triangle is considered the best technique because you are most often flooded with advertising about basic needs: gasoline, beer, soft drinks, jeans, hair color, deodorant, and various medical products. These products are not so easily mapped out in terms of differences (usually presented through logos) because they are **parity products or ideas**. This means that the products or ideas are so closely related that differences are either non-existent or too small in detail to actually persuade an audience one way or another.

> Parity products or ideas
> Product categories where the several brands within the category have equivalent functional attributes. Users can select any item from the category and have basically the same options for use. For example, you can purchase an MP3 player from any number of companies (i.e., Apple or Sony) and all of them will store, play, and shuffle MP3s.

Parity products or ideas are so similar that advertisers must use advertising techniques to create the illusion that one is superior to others. The challenge, of course, is to not make false claims. How can advertisers handle this? They use one or more advertising techniques. Hundreds of books about how to write successful advertisements exist—as well as books on how to persuade and to command attention from people.

These techniques can be divided into different rhetorical appeals and are most often used in sets (using more than one appeal). More importantly, you need to remember that most of these strategies suffer from the various types of fallacies you studied in previous chapters. Because Americans believe they are protected on some level from being "lied" to about products or ideas, they often fail to see the fallacies present in visual discourse.

Logos Techniques

These techniques help advertisers distinguish the differences between products and ideas. By using logos, advertising companies can demonstrate facts or pseudo-facts for you to evaluate.

Weasel Words

Almost all ads use weasel words, modifiers that completely or almost negate the claim of the ad. These words initially appear to be substantial; however, with careful analysis the words collapse. Why? Because all of the words are used as modifiers of claims they often cannot support. These words often help advertisers avoid making false claims.

Examples of these words are: "helps," "like," "virtual," "bigger," "better," "fights," "fresher," "refreshes," "#1," "body," "flavor."

Let's look at some examples from around the house. Notice that the assertions are based on facts—sort of. Look at the spoof ad parodying household products, Prozac, the Mood Brightener, which claims it is "fresher" and cleaner" and "Better than Ever!"

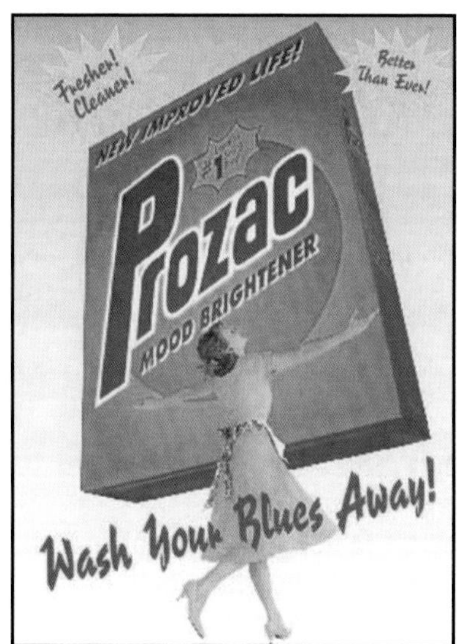

Spoof ad: adbusters.org

- **"Cage Free Eggs."** The chickens may not be in cages but they probably did not see the light of day (they are kept in large metal buildings).
- **"ADT is the #1 security company in America."** The listener or reader is to assume the company means #1 in service. In reality, "#1" means the company has more customers than any other security company in America. But, does having more customers mean the best? Maybe they are the only security company in larger populated areas.
- **"Bacos, the crispy garnish that tastes just like its name."** It does taste just like a "Baco"—but what exactly is a "Baco"?
- **"…and Smart Technology to help you brush your best."** Research indicates that electric toothbrushes do clean teeth better—but which type is still up for debate.
- **"Cheer helps protect against fading."** Cheer is intended to clean your clothes, not fade them.
- **"Cascade. Leaves dishes virtually spotless."** The idea is that if you see a spot, or two, the claim is not false.
- **"Oust. Eliminates odors by killing odor-causing airborne bacteria."** In other words, if Oust doesn't eliminate the odor, you can assume what caused the odor wasn't "odor-causing airborne bacteria."
- **"Absolut[e] Vodka."** Far from being "free from imperfections" which absolute implies. This Absolut Impotence spoof ad makes fun of perfection. It also has a quote from Shakespeare on the bottom com-

Spoof ad: adbusters.org

menting on the potency myth that alcohol ads often push: "Drink provokes the desire but takes away the performance."

Obvious

This type of claim states the obvious. It doesn't seek any real advantage over other products because it is a statement of fact. As long as advertisers state the obvious, they simply support current assumptions. Some examples include:

- **"Rheingold, the natural beer."** Made from water and grains—both natural ingredients.
- **"ADT. The alarm scared them off."** Don't all alarms intend to scare "them" off.
- **"Cheer cleans in any water temperature, even in cold water."** All detergents do. It's the chemicals in the detergent not the water temperature that breaks up dirt and kills bacteria.
- **"Gently exfoliates your skin every time you shave, leaving it smooth and luminous..."** When you shave you remove layers of skin (aka exfoliating).

Unfinished Comparison

This technique is often paired with the weasel claim. The "unfinished claim" begins a comparison but fails to finish it, leaving you to use inductive reasoning. The statement claims the product or idea is better than something else but never names the something else. Here the advertiser is relying on you to finish the comparison on your own. The chances are VERY high that you'll compare it to something you do not like. Let's look at some examples from around the house.

- **"Fabulash. 100% fuller lashes."** Fuller than what? My own lashes? Look closely at the visuals in these ads. See any other techniques?
- **"Scott makes it better for you."** Makes what better?
- "**Get more**" from Caltrate D. If you take calcium pills, you will get more calcium than you would otherwise. Does the ad mean more than if you don't take calcium pills or more than if you drink milk and eat other calcium enriched foods?

"So What"

The "So what" claim is similar to the obvious claim. Both state the obvious, but the "so what" claim asserts this fact makes the product better than other similar products. The idea here is to get you to believe that this simple obvious fact is the one fact that makes it different. It helps you choose between the parity products. Let's look at a few examples from around the house.

- **"...more than twice the calcium of other leading brands."** Is twice as much the most beneficial?
- **"...Keeps you up to 3Xs fresher than Secret or Dove solids when you're stressed.*" * In lab test using stress odor.** What other kind of odor is there? Relaxed odor?

Vague

These claims use colorful, yet meaningless, words. These claims often contain weasel words and are almost impossible, or at least difficult, to prove or disprove. Most of the facts in these claims are so grandiose that you would not test the accuracy or are so "obvious" that you would not see the need. Let's look at a few examples from around the house.

- **"Bounty White offers outstanding absorbency and strength and goes with any kitchen style."** Aren't all paper towels a one-size-fits-all? Are you willing to test this claim?
- **"Aussie shampoos and conditioners are designed to embrace and nurture the special needs of your hair."** Aren't all shampoos and conditioners designed to do so?
- **"Nobody doesn't like Sara Lee."** Does this mean just the people tested at the lab?

Scientific or Statistical

An ad that uses this technique will use statistics or scientific proof to support its claim. It might include experiments, specific numbers, or impressive mystery ingredients. Even though technology and science are more mainstream, most people are impressed by the jargon and language when it's used in advertising. Place this same language in a user's manual and it triggers the opposite effect.

Let's look at a few examples of scientific or statistical claims.

- **"Certs, with Retsyn."** And retsyn does what? Most consumers do not know. But it sounds pretty darn potent, doesn't it?
- **"...with 25% more staying power."** This claim is also an unfinished claim, isn't it? More staying power than? And how do they measure "staying power?"
- **"Significant relief in 5 minutes."** (Afrin) How do they measure "significant?"
- **"Developed After Years of Secret Research."** Secret research into what? With what? Why is the research secret?

False Dilemma

This type of claim attempts to make the reader or viewer think there are few choices, if any. It attempts to keep the reader or viewer from looking at other options. Here is an example:

WW II Propaganda Poster

- **Any Army or other military commercial.** These are especially useful during our time of renewed patriotism. If we don't fight today, we'll have to fight tomorrow. Maybe, maybe not. Some experts call these commercials "proactive" civil engagements.
- **"Go Ahead, Please—Take Day Off!"** This World War II poster presents a false dilemma, persuading people that taking time off from work is not an option. Perhaps such posters were so effective that Americans felt safer when all Japanese Americans were placed in internment camps. Note the Texaco logo on this government document.

Ethos Techniques

These techniques rely on ethos to connect with your idea of character or ethics. They are usually used in conjunction with logos because we believe that our ideas of character and ethics are based on logic. Furthermore, as the speaker, the advertisement will seek to develop your idea of its ethos.

Endorsement or Testimonial

This type of claim is probably the most recognizable. Famous people, celebrities or authorities, claim to use products. Many ads that use this strategy do so without words. Let's look at some examples:

- **"Passion—it's what drives me to wake up before dawn and head to the track while everyone else sleeps." —Ryan Shay, Pro Marathoner.** Which audience type does this ad target?
- **"Jeff Gordon likes his coffee steamin' hot and strong to the finish."** Strong to the finish of what?
- **"Look who we've got our Hanes on now."** Christina Applegate, Kevin Bacon, Michael Jordan, —heck, you name him or her, and he or she is wearing Hanes.

- **"Got Milk?"** Almost everybody has milk. How does a celebrity make milk special?

"Compliment the Consumer"

This claim offers flattery. In a world where vanity is almost a standard, this technique offers the "me" generation a lot of perceived power. With most Americans in the "Belongers" group, these techniques offer the advertiser a strategy for making certain each reader is part of the group and should be proud of it. Here are a few examples (some now considered classics):

- **"You've come a long way, baby."** This was very popular in the 70s during the feminist movement—but young, up-and-coming women still identify with it.
- **"Because you're worth it."** L'Oreal hair color.
- **"Beautiful. Colorful. You."** Bonne Bel cosmetics.
- **"We Can Do It!" (pictured at right)** J. Howard Miller, WWII (1942).

WW II Propaganda Poster

"Nothing to Fear"

This claim offers facts based on easing your fear—it focuses on the safety of the situation or product. This claim says that the company can be depended on because they are concerned about your safety. Here is an example from a car advertisement:

- **"The only five-star rating in its class."** Do they (the company) have cars that aren't five-star rated? More importantly, why aren't all cars required to meet a five-star rating?

Pathos Techniques

Most pathos techniques require you to respond based on your experiences and emotions. Some of the assertions clearly ask you to answer a question, while others encourage you to think about facts as they relate to your experiences or emotions.

Bandwagon

This type of claim asserts that everyone is doing it—whatever "it" is. This approach, along with the next two, are the most popular kinds of commercials and advertisements. Here is an example:

- "85% of consumers purchase IBM computers rather than Apple." All those people can't be wrong. IBM must make the best computers.

Snob

This type of claim asserts that all the BEST people are doing it—whatever "it" is. Here are two examples:

- **Mac computers.** Cool people use Mac computers; stuffy business nerds use PCs. This claim is seen mostly through the visuals.
- **Numerous car commercials.** Lexus, BMW, and other luxury car commercials make this claim.

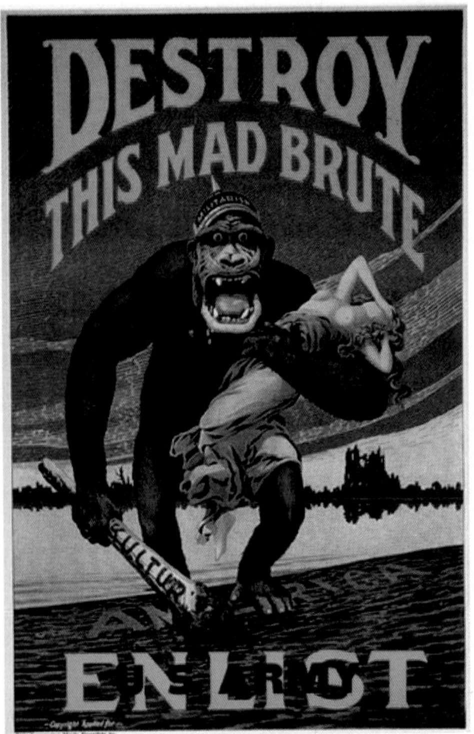

WWI US Army Recruitment Poster

Patriotic

This type of claim asserts that people who are patriotic are doing it—whatever "it" is. Here are a few examples:

- **Army and other military advertisements.** Notice these can also be listed under "False Dilemma." This example is from c. 1916, depicting Germans as "mad brute[s]." (H.R. Hopps)
- **Most beer commercials.** Budweiser and other "American" beer companies use "Made in America" in much of their advertising.

Rhetorical Question

This type of claim seeks to illicit a thoughtful response. The reader or listener's response reaffirms the product's or idea's goodness, uniqueness, etc. Here are a few examples:

- **"What would you do for love this Christmas?"** Jewelry commercial. The idea behind this question is that most people would do anything for the person she or he loves, especially at Christmas.

- **"What other kind is there?"** Quaker Oatmeal. What other brand name is associated with oatmeal? There isn't one. Quaker Oatmeal holds the name brand spot.

Traditional Wisdom (ethos, pathos, and logic)

This type of claim asserts that things were better in the past, ignoring the problems that were present in the past. Here is an example:

- **"He fought for the union of our lamb and mint jelly. "** An ad for the Golden Lamb. U.S. Grant had, to say the least, a troubled presidential term.

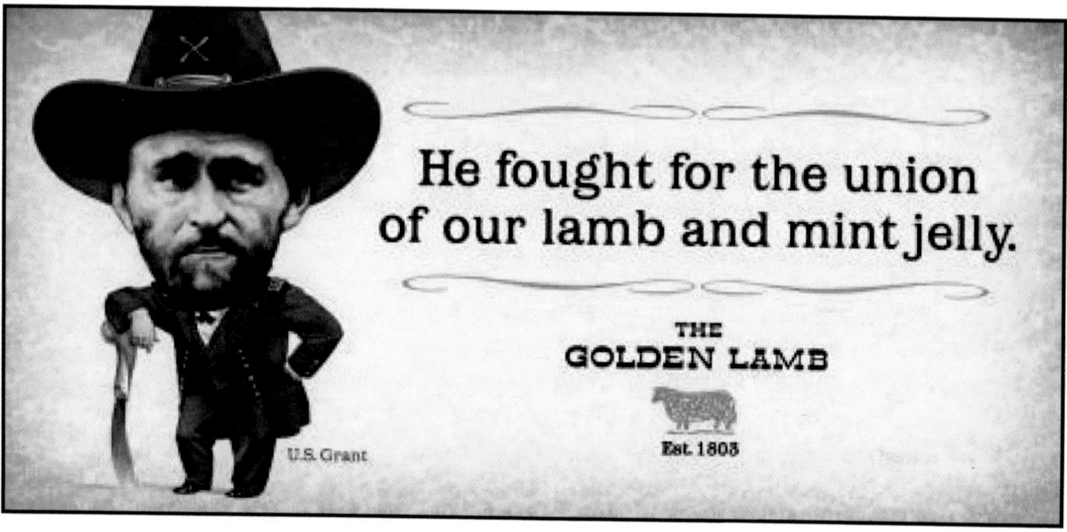

You may have noticed that most of these techniques focus on the use of words. You should not be surprised to learn that many books are dedicated to teaching you how to use words to persuade. Experts have developed their own words or phrases for these types of techniques, but all of the words or phrases indicate the same thing: humans can be persuaded.

What Visual Techniques Do Advertising Companies Use?

Advertising especially relies on visual techniques to support or provide evidence for the assertions made in the text. Sometimes the visual is quite subtle and at other times it is obvious. Visuals also help advertisers counteract any fallacies you might find in the text of the ad. Seeing is believing, correct?

You cannot understand visuals without relying heavily on resources used to interpret the real world. These resources include conceptual knowledge and images and examples, as well as your cultural context and experience. Conceptual knowledge is your knowledge of the world around you and how each part of it relates to the other parts. It is, then, the way you classify and organize everything you know about the world around you.

Abstract Visuals

Abstract visuals do not look like the things they represent but they appeal to knowledge on the conceptual level. Because the concept is not something we can see or touch, images for these types of visuals need to reflect as closely as possible something similar. They need to maintain a strong association with the concepts individuals and societies already use.

Consider your computer desktop. Microsoft Windows© and other software packages, whether PC or Mac versions, rely heavily on icons that represent abstract ideas. When you want to delete a file, you send it to the "Recycle Bin" or "Trash," just as you would an actual file folder if you had it in your hand. The icons for the "Recycle Bin" and "Trash" look like actual recycle bins or trash cans. These icons, then, represent an abstract concept by making a direct association with something you already understand.

> Abstract Visuals
>
> Represent something that cannot actually take place; they represent actions that are not touchable or that you cannot see someone doing. For example, on your computer you can put electronic files in a recycle bin (on the PC) or trashcan (on the MAC) but you are not actually putting them in a physical trash can. You are imitating the action.

Recycle Bin

Not all abstract thoughts can be so readily represented by an image. Consider the desktop publishing software you use most. If you look at the icon bar, you notice a lot of different icons. One of those icons might be a paint brush. What abstract concept does this icon represent? It represents painting, but painting what? This icon does not have a lot to do with painting pictures; instead, it has to do with painting attributes (bold, italics, underlining, etc.) of one text set to a different text set. Many users do not understand the actual purpose of this icon, but they do get the general idea. The visual still connects new information to information you already know; however, it does not clearly "describe" the actual concept.

Concrete Visuals

Concrete visuals look like the things they represent. These visuals are specific images or examples; however, the details represented vary. One of the most common types of concrete visuals you see is the "Pedestrian Crossing" sign.

> Concrete Visuals
> Visuals of or that relate to an actual, specific thing or instance. For example, if a visual wants you to put your trash in a trash can, it would have a person putting trash in a trash can. The visual represents, exactly, what takes place.

Pedestrian Crossing sign

Here is an "Illegal Immigrant Family" crossing sign placed on US highways.

Understanding the Use of Colors in Visuals

Colors are one of the most persuasive strategies used in visuals. Each person associates certain feelings and beliefs with colors. Take a moment and consider the colors of the local university. If you see someone wearing those colors, what do you assume? What colors can you think of that you associate with certain feelings or beliefs?

Does color ever serve a purpose? Research indicates that consumers make judgments within ninety seconds, and a large portion of those judgments is based on color. When classes began this semester, did you pick up a book, look at its cover, and say "Ugh. This book is going to stink"? And yet, another book on a similarly difficult subject looked "ok." Why? Think carefully for a moment. Did it have anything to do with the colors on the cover?

Just as with the textbooks, color can make or break any visuals.

Color theory is a vast topic that incorporates a lot of definitions, concepts, and applications. We simply seek to introduce you to the basics of color and its importance in the design of visuals. In this section we will look at two major areas of color: color harmony and color context.

Color Harmony

If you listen to music, read poetry, or eat, you are familiar with the idea of harmony. Eat? Yes, eat. Consider how you carefully combine spices and food items to get the perfect taste. You don't cook? Okay, consider how you carefully select food from a menu to make certain it tastes good to you. It must be pleasing to the palette.

In the visual experience, colors must be pleasing to the eye—they must be harmonious. The color or colors must engage the viewer and generate an experience of balance. If the colors do not create a sense of balance, they create a sense of chaos or boredom. The color spectrum has two extremes: at one end the colors do not engage the viewer and appear bland, and at the other end the colors are so "overdone" that the viewer cannot stand to look at the color combination. The human brain cannot process what does not make sense or what it cannot organize. Ultimately, the goal of using color is to create a sense of order for the consumer. Colors are one of the non-textual signals of a visual.

Do these non-textual signals really matter? Do they have any impact? Suppose your doctor sent you to a Web site to view your test results. When you access the site, you see the following colors: neon pink, black, and neon green. How would you react? Would you question the doctor's credibility? The credibility of the results? Would you retype the address to make certain that you accessed the correct site?

> **Color Harmony**
> Occurs when the colors on the page, in the visual, or on the screen are pleasing to the eye. The colors do not have too much contrast (differences) that prevent the eye from adjusting quickly to see the letters or picture and the background. The colors, also, do not have too little contrast, causing the eye to have difficulty in determining the difference in words or pictures, and the background, or any combination.

Malboro: "The New Frontier"

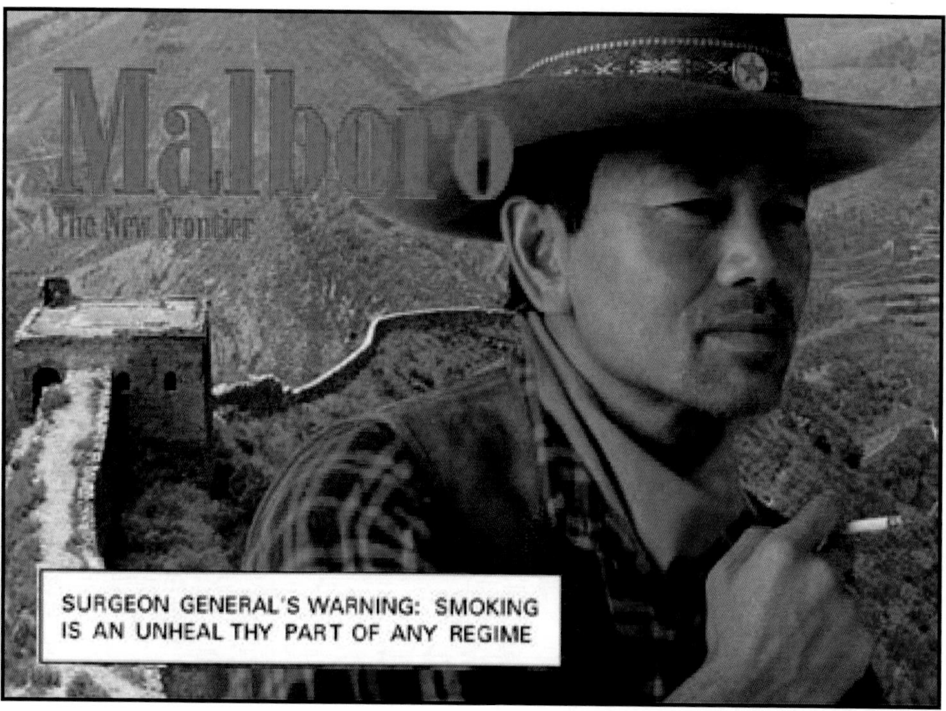

www.adbusters.org

There are a lot of theories for creating harmony and we cannot cover all of them in this course. We can, however, cover a few basic theories that are easy to remember and to use.

Analogous Colors

Analogous colors are any three colors which are side by side on a 12 part color wheel. Usually one of the colors dominates the others. Using a color wheel, you can develop a number of combinations.

- blue-green, yellow-green, and yellow
- blue-purple, blue, and blue-green
- red-orange, red, and red-purple

> Analogous Colors
> Colors that immediately follow one another on the color wheel. These colors are always in harmony, not having too much or too little contrast.

Complementary Colors

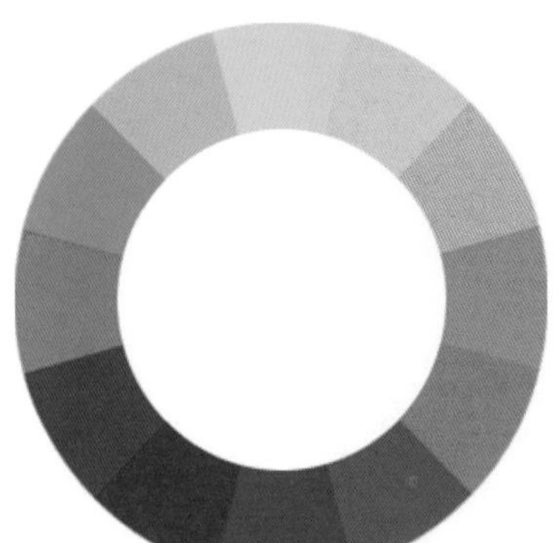

Complementary colors create maximum contrast and maximum stability. These colors are any two colors which are directly opposite each other on a color wheel. Using the color wheel, you can develop a number of combinations.

- yellow and blue
- red and green
- yellow-green and red-purple

These colors can enhance and strengthen the appearance of what you are trying to highlight. You can make a word or a bar in a chart look crisper by using complementary colors. You can even make potentially negative data look more positive.

Natural Colors

Natural colors are those that exist in combination in nature. Mother Nature (or whichever creator you see responsible) has a unique ability to combine colors in harmonious ways. Consider the colors of a sunset; the colors in a flower bed; the colors found on mountains. These color combinations can bring excitement, peace, or even desire. Natural colors are naturally harmonious to the human eye.

Color Context

Color context remains one of the most complex concepts of color. Color context is the way color behaves in relation to other colors and shapes. The same color can appear bright or dull depending on the other colors around it.

The contrast moves or shifts easily (see below). A square can appear larger in size or smaller in size based on the background. What are the differences? Does the difference in shape make any difference? Also notice that shades of the same color appear differ-

> **Complimentary Colors**
> Colors across the color wheel from each other. These colors are always in harmony, not having too much or too little contrast. Three pairs of complementary colors are: red and green, blue and orange, purple and yellow.
>
> **Natural Colors**
> Colors that occur together in nature. Examples of natural colors are white and light blue (as in the clouds in the sky) or orange, brown, and green (the color of fall leaves).
>
> **Color Context**
> How colors look (bright, dark, dull) when placed on different backgrounds or when seen with different levels of light intensity. For example, if you want a red MP3 player to look big and bright, you would place it on a white background. If you want that same red MP3 player to look small and dull, you would place it on a gray background.

ently on different backgrounds. The squares and circles are the same size but they do not appear to be so.

Color context, then, can be used to make something appear bigger, smaller, more significant, less significant, etc. than the object to which it is being compared.

Understanding the Use of Fonts in Visuals

Modern	
Jazz Let	Marker Felt
Comic Sans	Playbill
Traditional	
Garamond	Times New Roman
Courier	ENGRAVERS

Fonts are like clothing—they give an immediate impression. Fonts are a focal piece of any visual. The choice in fonts gives the audience an impression of how the designer feels about the subject matter of the visual and how the designer hopes the audience will feel about the visual. Fonts send the audience a non-verbal signal that once expressed cannot be taken back. If the designer has poorly selected fonts, she or he can lose the audience almost immediately—within 20 seconds. The audience will either mis-read or discredit the designer or product because the font choice is too difficult to read or inappropriate for the context. And, once the audience develops a first impression of the product, they will not change their mind easily, if at all.

Definition of Fonts

What are fonts? Fonts are the typefaces used in advertisements and visuals. What you are reading right now are fonts. Fonts come in all shapes and sizes, and a small variation in typeface, size, density, or spacing helps users identify how pieces of information are related to each other.

Personalities of Fonts

Advertisers and designers select fonts that are effective and emotive in the context for which they are using them. It is likely that you, the viewer, will begin to question why writers and designers select the fonts they do for certain visuals. You may even find yourself noticing the subtle control the writer or designer has on you, the viewer, through the font choice.

Believe it or not, there is a science and theory behind fonts. Here we will cover only the basics. All fonts have a visual personality. In other words, the look of the font expresses meaning, whether it is conservative, pop culture, traditional, archaic, etc. (see table).

Some fonts are associated with specific workplace activities, products, or people. You know when you see a Coke product because of the font choice. You probably do not even read the can to see if you pick up the right drink.

Typefaces come in many shapes and sizes. As noted before, they have specific "personalities" and often create the look and feel of a visual without the use of graphics or photos. Examine the typefaces in the table (see table). For what audience types might the designer use each one?

Size of Fonts

The size gives advertisers and designers the opportunity to emphasize words and ideas. They select specific words to place in larger text or smaller text. Have you ever seen a commercial or ad with teeny-tiny text across the bottom of the screen or page? Legally, the advertisers and designers must place certain information on the ad. By using teeny-tiny text, they meet their legal obligations and avoid the audience actually reading the text.

Problems with Understanding Visuals

Before we can begin to look at visuals and analyze them, we need to take a moment to consider some of the problems people have when trying to understand visuals. Visuals, whether concrete or abstract, cannot always be worth a thousand words.

"Busy" Visuals

Some visuals have too many or unnecessary details. The viewer cannot determine what is supposed to be communicated. You may have experienced this when you viewed a map on the Internet.

Cultural Perspectives

Another problem with visuals is that many different objects that might be represented, such as phones and eating utensils, come in different shapes and sizes. Often these differences are most important when using visuals across cultures. In America we use forks, spoons, and knives when eating a meal; in China they use chopsticks; in India they use their right hand. A visual of utensils to represent "restaurant" would not work in areas where the culture is diverse. It definitely would not work as a universal visual.

Visuals are not always iconic, as you know. Photos and line drawings also offer concrete visual information. Still, no matter how clear the photos or line drawings, cultural perspectives cannot be avoided. Companies that sell nursing equipment across the world might avoid using male nurses in their advertising because in some cultures, it is still only acceptable for women to be nurses.

Color, Color, Color

Color should serve a purpose—not just be added because it looks good. As you remember, the use of color can make something chaotic or boring. Another issue that should be considered is that color means something different to each individual. Financial advisers may see green as meaning profit, money, etc. Medical personnel (doctors, nurses, etc.) may dislike blue because it is associated with death (code-blue). Some cultures wear black to weddings and white to funerals. In some cases, the color assigned to information does not always represent the actual value of that information.

Anna Nicole Smith Funeral vs Nadaraja Raviraj Funeral

Lack of Rules

For the most part, the design of visuals, whether iconic or photographic, lacks a set of rules by which to be measured. The design of visuals simply needs to meet the goals of their producers. Advertisers and politicians have used the lack of rules to their advantage, as we will see later in this chapter.

"A Dollar A Song?"

Look closely at the ad below. First look at the visual. Second, look at the text.

from Alternative Press

The ad reads:

A Dollar a Song? We're not Buying It.
Some people just don't know the value of a dollar. With a Napster® Membership you get unlimited access to our library of over 1.5 million songs. Which you can download onto 3 computers and 2 MP3 players. You never need to own music again. Browse, make and share playlists, customize, whatever. It's just responsible music budgeting, freeing up cash for things like fireworks. Say it with us now: Own Nothing. Have Everything.

Try it for free at Napster.com

The target audiences for this ad fall within the inner-directed and outer-directed groups. Based on the visual, which appears to be quite "devilish," you might guess that it's directed mostly toward the inner-directed group. With the "devilish" look to the logo, Napster is creating an even stronger sense of rebellion. With the visual in the center of the ad, Napster does not risk having the ad too chaotic—it is instead just chaotic enough to draw attention from the youthful group. Color is absent from this ad, as it is with most Napster ads. The use of black and white creates just enough contrast and interest yet keeps the information dark and almost intentionally hidden. The text or copy of the ad focuses on pathos and ethos techniques, and often alludes to the idea that using Napster is "logical," even though it is also rebellious. Napster has a reputation for going against authority, so the copy (the words) and the visual supplement these ideas.

Political Campaigns

Many people think of political campaigns and advertising as being completely separate. But are they? Obviously the TV ads you see are similar to corporation advertising. What about campaign literature, such as posters and brochures? What are the visuals used in these types of media trying to do? How have these visuals changed over the years?

Campaign Piece

Let's look at a 1960 campaign piece for John F. Kennedy.

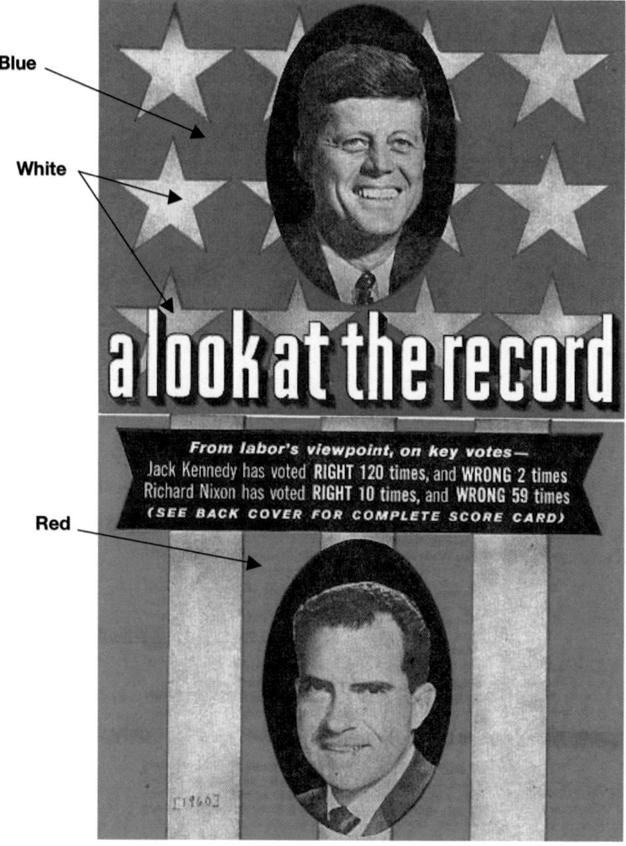

Notice that the colors used in the poster are red, white, and blue—patriotic colors—for a focus on the flag. Other than the fact that this is a political piece, why else might the Kennedy campaign have selected these colors? Kennedy was campaigning during the Cold War.

Both candidates, Kennedy and Nixon, are on the piece. How does the position of the candidates affect the perception? Why is Kennedy placed among the "stars?" Does the placement of his picture make an impact? What other visual cues do you get from this piece? Did you notice that Kennedy is facing your right and Nixon your left? What might this mean?

Cartoons

Cartoons are for kids, right? Actually, cartoons are such a part of our daily lives that we, as adults, often ignore the impact they have on us. In a variety of disciplines, cartoons are used to help pass-along information, especially safety information. When was the last time you received information on fire safety that did not have some type of cartoon character associated with it?

Political cartoons are especially important as you begin to develop your sense of social and political values. These cartoons appear in many magazine types (*The New Yorker*, *Playboy*, *Harper's Bazaar*, etc.) and often seek to mimic what the editors of the magazine believe to be the reader's (your) social and political values. Just as with campaign ads and regular product ads, political cartoons present an argument of some type. The artists use a variety of visual and textual techniques to develop the meaning of the message.

Regular (print) cartoons appear in weekly newspapers. These cartoons, like political cartoons, intend to make an argument about social and political ideas or issues. In addition, these cartoons often simply make fun of human nature—a skill many readers cannot employ without a visual prompt. Most cartoons communicate a single message in a short series of panels or single panel, as in "Family Circle." In some cases, cartoons (called serials) take months or years to develop the overall message the artist wishes to communicate ("Alley Oop," "Li'l Abner", "Jump Start," etc.).

TV cartoons seek to put action to the cartoon messages. Charles Schulz's cartoon "Peanuts" began as a newspaper cartoon but evolved into a premier TV cartoon. Both the print and TV versions offer similar messages, but TV cartoons afford the artist the opportunity to fully develop all sides to an argument.

"What Is the Secret of the Icon?"

excerpt from Scott McCloud's book Understanding Comics.

The following pages contain a revealing piece by Scott McCloud dissecting comics and iconography in order to reveal an underlying visual discourse even in the most basic of images, imagery that says much about who we are both as a culture and as individuals.

AS YOU READ: Annotate

1. Place a star by the panels that are effective.
2. Summarize key points in the margins.

IN THE NON-PICTORIAL ICONS, MEANING IS FIXED AND ABSOLUTE. THEIR APPEARANCE DOESN'T AFFECT THEIR MEANING BECAUSE THEY REPRESENT INVISIBLE IDEAS.
M
m
M
m
m
5
5
5
5
5

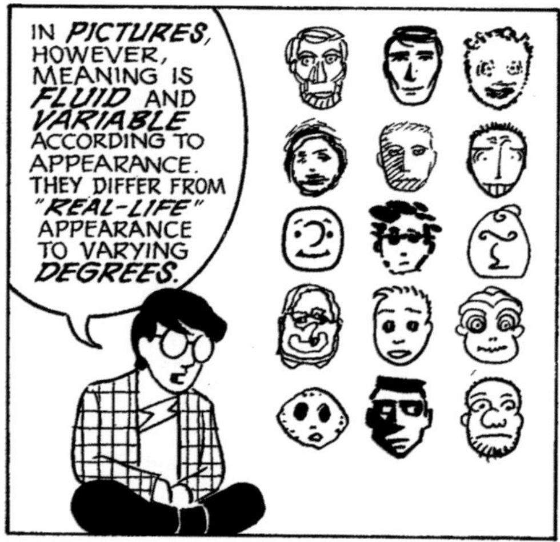
IN PICTURES, HOWEVER, MEANING IS FLUID AND VARIABLE ACCORDING TO APPEARANCE. THEY DIFFER FROM "REAL-LIFE" APPEARANCE TO VARYING DEGREES.

WORDS ARE TOTALLY ABSTRACT ICONS. THAT IS, THEY BEAR NO RESEMBLANCE AT ALL TO THE REAL McCOY.
EYE

BUT IN PICTURES THE LEVEL OF ABSTRACTION VARIES. SOME, LIKE THE FACE IN THE PREVIOUS PANEL, SO CLOSELY RESEMBLE THEIR REAL-LIFE COUNTERPARTS AS TO ALMOST TRICK THE EYE!

OTHERS, LIKE YOURS TRULY, ARE QUITE A BIT MORE ABSTRACT AND, IN FACT, ARE VERY MUCH UNLIKE ANY HUMAN FACE YOU'VE EVER SEEN!

LET'S SEE IF WE CAN PUT THESE PICTORIAL ICONS IN SOME SORT OF ORDER.

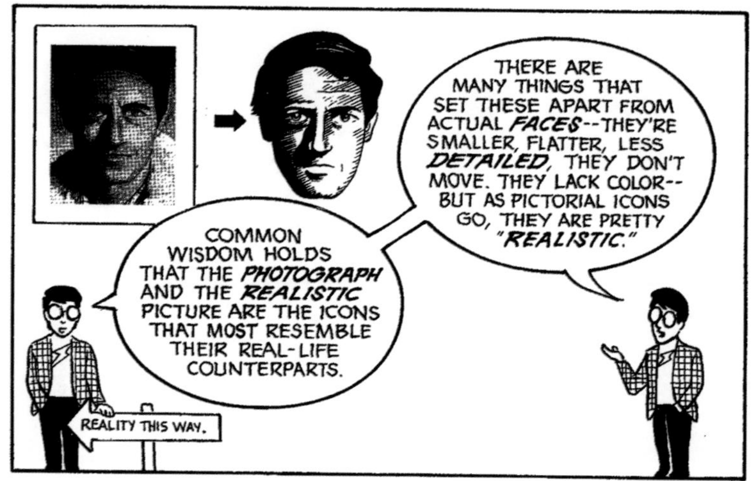
COMMON WISDOM HOLDS THAT THE PHOTOGRAPH AND THE REALISTIC PICTURE ARE THE ICONS THAT MOST RESEMBLE THEIR REAL-LIFE COUNTERPARTS.
THERE ARE MANY THINGS THAT SET THESE APART FROM ACTUAL FACES--THEY'RE SMALLER, FLATTER, LESS DETAILED, THEY DON'T MOVE. THEY LACK COLOR--BUT AS PICTORIAL ICONS GO, THEY ARE PRETTY "REALISTIC."
REALITY THIS WAY.

SOMEWHAT *MORE* ABSTRACT IS *THIS* STYLE OF DRAWING FOUND IN MANY ADVENTURE COMICS.
ONLY OUTLINES AND A HINT OF SHADING ARE STILL PRESENT, BUT WE EASILY RECOGNIZE THIS AS A *HUMAN FACE.*

THIS WAY.
AS WE CONTINUE TO ABSTRACT AND *SIMPLIFY* OUR IMAGE, WE ARE MOVING FURTHER AND FURTHER FROM THE *"REAL"* FACE OF THE PHOTO.
WHY, THEN, IS THE FACE ABOVE SO *ACCEPTABLE* TO OUR EYES? WHY DOES IT SEEM JUST AS *REAL* AS THE OTHERS?

WAY.
WHAT IS THE SECRET OF THE ICON WE CALL--
--THE *CARTOON?*

WHY--
--ARE--
--WE--
--SO--
--INVOLVED?

WHY WOULD ANYONE, YOUNG OR OLD, RESPOND TO A CARTOON AS MUCH OR MORE THAN A REALISTIC IMAGE?

WHY IS OUR CULTURE SO IN THRALL TO THE SIMPLIFIED REALITY OF THE CARTOON?

DEFINING THE CARTOON WOULD TAKE UP AS MUCH SPACE AS DEFINING COMICS, BUT FOR NOW, I'M GOING TO EXAMINE CARTOONING AS A FORM OF AMPLIFICATION THROUGH SIMPLIFICATION.

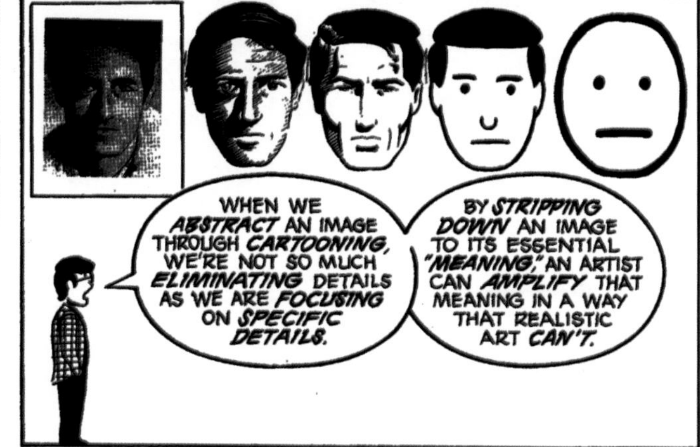
WHEN WE ABSTRACT AN IMAGE THROUGH CARTOONING, WE'RE NOT SO MUCH ELIMINATING DETAILS AS WE ARE FOCUSING ON SPECIFIC DETAILS.
BY STRIPPING DOWN AN IMAGE TO ITS ESSENTIAL "MEANING," AN ARTIST CAN AMPLIFY THAT MEANING IN A WAY THAT REALISTIC ART CAN'T.

FILM CRITICS WILL SOMETIMES DESCRIBE A LIVE-ACTION FILM AS A "CARTOON" TO ACKNOWLEDGE THE STRIPPED-DOWN INTENSITY OF A SIMPLE STORY OR VISUAL STYLE.

THOUGH THE TERM IS OFTEN USED DISPARAGINGLY, IT CAN BE EQUALLY WELL APPLIED TO MANY TIME-TESTED CLASSICS. SIMPLIFYING CHARACTERS AND IMAGES TOWARD A PURPOSE CAN BE AN EFFECTIVE TOOL FOR STORYTELLING IN ANY MEDIUM.
CARTOONING ISN'T JUST A WAY OF DRAWING, IT'S A WAY OF SEEING!
FOLLOW! FOLLOW!

THE ABILITY OF CARTOONS TO FOCUS OUR ATTENTION ON AN IDEA IS, I THINK, AN IMPORTANT PART OF THEIR SPECIAL POWER, BOTH IN COMICS AND IN DRAWING GENERALLY.

ONE
A FEW
THOUSANDS
MILLIONS
(NEARLY) ALL
ANOTHER IS THE UNIVERSALITY OF CARTOON IMAGERY. THE MORE CARTOONY A FACE IS, FOR INSTANCE, THE MORE PEOPLE IT COULD BE SAID TO DESCRIBE.

BUT I BELIEVE THERE'S SOMETHING MORE AT WORK IN OUR MINDS WHEN WE VIEW A CARTOON--ESPECIALLY OF A HUMAN FACE--WHICH WARRANTS FURTHER INVESTIGATION.

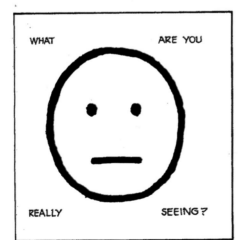

WHAT
ARE YOU
REALLY
SEEING?

THE FACT THAT YOUR MIND IS CAPABLE OF TAKING A CIRCLE, TWO DOTS AND A LINE AND TURNING THEM INTO A FACE IS NOTHING SHORT OF INCREDIBLE!

BUT STILL MORE INCREDIBLE IS THE FACT THAT YOU CANNOT AVOID SEEING A FACE HERE. YOUR MIND WON'T LET YOU!

ASK A FRIEND TO DRAW YOU SOME SHAPES ON A PIECE OF PAPER. THEY SHOULD BE CLOSED CURVES, BUT OTHERWISE CAN BE AS WEIRD AND IRREGULAR AS HE OR SHE WANTS.
LET'S SAY THE RESULTS LOOK SOMETHING LIKE THIS.

NOW-- YOU'LL FIND THAT NO MATTER WHAT THEY LOOK LIKE, EVERY SINGLE ONE OF THOSE SHAPES CAN BE MADE INTO A FACE WITH ONE SIMPLE ADDITION.

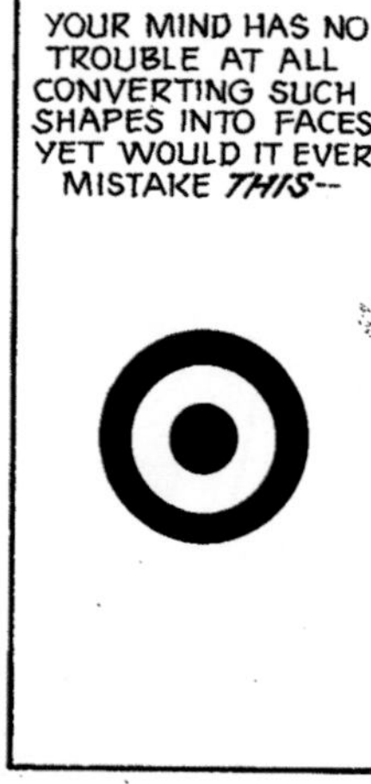
YOUR MIND HAS NO TROUBLE AT ALL CONVERTING SUCH SHAPES INTO FACES, YET WOULD IT EVER MISTAKE THIS--

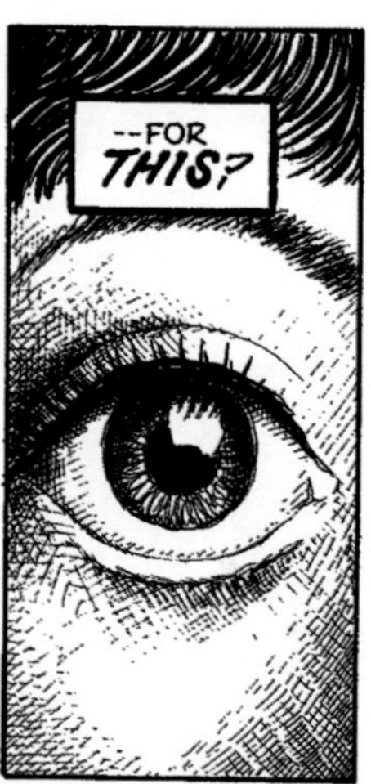
--FOR THIS?

WE HUMANS ARE A SELF-CENTERED RACE.

WE SEE OURSELVES IN EVERYTHING.

WE ASSIGN IDENTITIES AND EMOTIONS WHERE NONE EXIST.
KRAFT

AND WE MAKE THE WORLD OVER IN OUR IMAGE.

Political Cartoons

"Arms Payoff for Hostage Release"

by Herbert Block

http://www.loc.gov/rr/print/swann/herblock/images/s03287u.jpg

Most political cartoons are devoid of color. Why might the cartoonists keep the color scheme black and white—or, as discussed previously in this chapter, dull? This cartoon was published during the highly regarded presidency of Ronald Reagan. What rhetorical appeal does the cartoonist use? What is the main idea or argument of the cartoon? How does this cartoon relate to the situation the US faces in the 21st century?

Again, notice the position and actions of the two main people. How does Reagan's position impact or represent how the cartoonist believes the world views Americans and the American perspective?

Regular Cartoons

"Special Program for Writing Love Letters"

by Randy Glasbergen

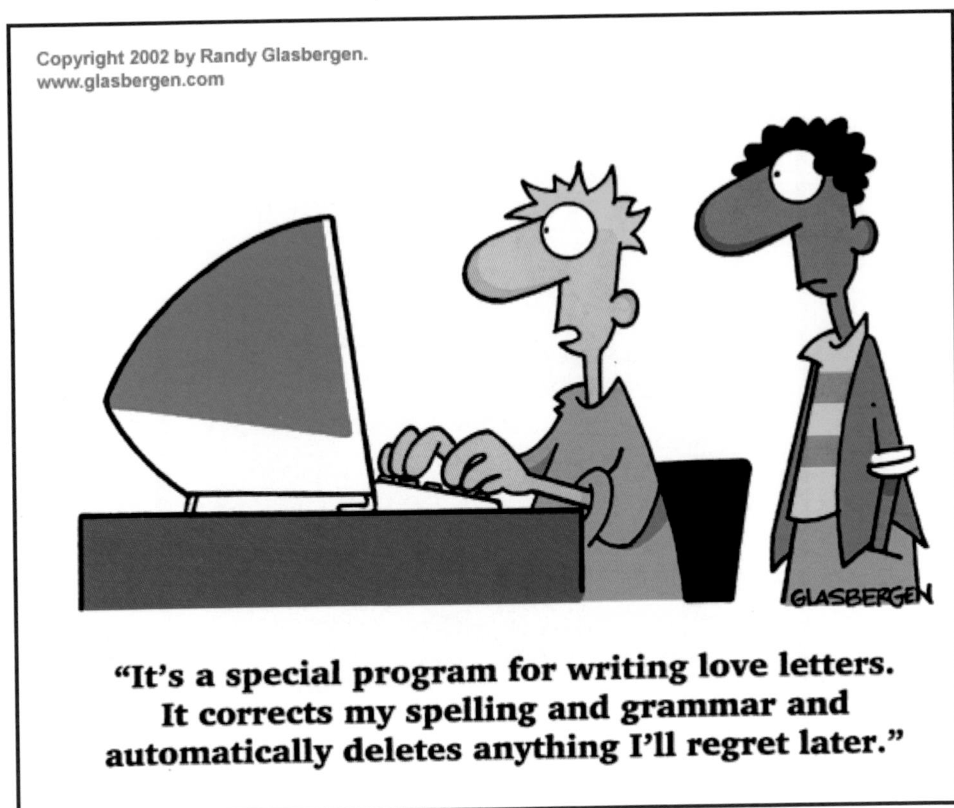

Unlike political cartoons, regular print cartoons employ a lot of color. Why might the cartoonists want to keep regular print cartoons full of color? This cartoon offers commentary on what users expect from software programs. What is the main idea

or argument of the cartoon? Why would this cartoon be funny to the 21st century computer user? To your English instructor?

Notice the race and position of the two characters. Why is the character who is sitting "white" and the character who is standing, behind, "black"? Is there any reason to question how the characters are positioned?

CD Covers

CD covers are representative of the types of music (genres) they represent. As you know there are many genres of music: classical, jazz, rock, country. And within these major genres, there are many sub-genres: acid jazz, hardcore, punk, indie, rockabilly, country pop, country rock. Each of these genres represents the identity with which the musicians want to be associated. Musicians want their CD covers, and not just their musical sound, to represent that identity as well. Some musicians create their own covers; others use artists to generate the cover.

Two Oklahoma bands, Little League Hero and Student Film, produced concept albums in 2006 and 2007. This means the albums have a unified theme that is presented through the lyrics and the musical composition, as well as the art used on the CD covers. Look closely at the two CD covers below.

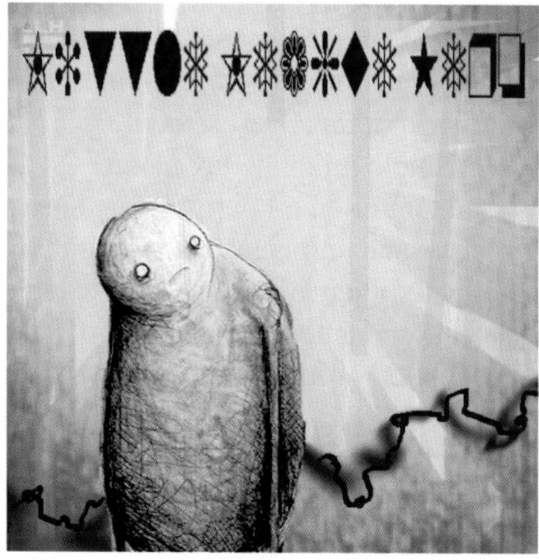

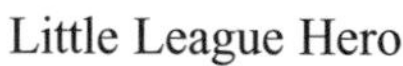
Little League Hero

Student Film

What concept is each artist representing? How easy or difficult is it to identify? What type of art is used, concrete or abstract? How does the color of each cover convey the concept? Of what genres or sub-genres do you think the groups are members? What emotion do the animal figures express? What mood do you expect from the lyrics and music based on this expression?

If possible, access the two groups on www.MySpace.com or at www.studentfilm-music.net. Listen to the lyrics of a few songs from each group. Is it easier to understand the visual concept after hearing the lyrics? Do you think the musicians found the artwork before they wrote the lyrics to the song—they fit the music and lyrics to the art—or they found the art after writing the music and lyrics—they fit the art to the music and lyrics?

Mock Advertisements

As noted earlier in this chapter, many products are so similar (parity products) that distinguishing them through advertising is difficult. Pharmaceutical and tobacco companies are especially susceptible to this dilemma. The advertising teams for pharmaceutical and tobacco companies have to use creative strategies to persuade their audiences that their brand is somehow better. In an effort to expose these "creative strategies," Web sites like Adbusters.org produce advertisements that mock the persuasive falsities that the ads promote.

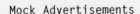

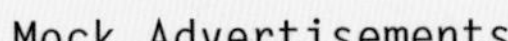

Mock Advertisements

Fake (false) advertisements meant to mimic actual advertisements. Often mock advertisements treat the subject of the ad with contempt or ridicule. Sometimes mock advertisements seek to improve the message of an advertisement considered to be frivolous or dangerous. An example might be taking an advertisement for an oil company that has a picture of an oil pump set against a beautiful, natural background with flowers, trees, and animals and making it an oil pump set against a gray, drab background with oil covered birds, trees, and flowers. The first advertisment indicates that oil production and nature are in harmony; the second advertisement indicates that oil production destroys nature.

"Utter Fool"

Adbusters.org.

AFTER YOU READ: Answer These Questions

- Which product is this ad mocking? Why?
- What argument is this visual making?
- How does the font choice work for or against the visual argument of this ad?
- Is the visual concrete or abstract? Is this ad informing you?
- Is the ad summarizing a concept?
- Is it asking you to evaluate current ideas with new ideas?

If possible, find the ad that "Utterfool" mocks.

- Which ad has more persuasive power? Why?

Continuing Your Visual Studies

You are inundated with visuals. As you look around through the day, you should continue to ask yourself the following questions:

1. What argument is the visual making?
2. What audience type does the visual target (outer-directed, inner-directed, etc.)?
3. Why are the colors so appeasing or repulsive?
4. What textual elements promote the overall argument of the visual?
5. What techniques are being used?
6. What can I learn about how visuals affect my emotions and behavior?

By answering these questions you can become an informed consumer, more of an individual, and a better persuader.

Responding to Visual Issues: Analyzing the Variables

Written Rhetoric: Evaluating Publications

As you make your way through the next few hours of the day, take notes on the type of visual discourse you see. What magazines, newspapers, and other publications convey information to you through visuals and visuals plus text? Consider classifying the visuals by type (concrete or abstract) and/or by purpose (motivation, evaluation, summation, presentation, enrichment). What claims are used?

Using the notes you take, write a reflective essay on the observations. Discuss the types of visuals and techniques you find most persuasive. Consider answering the following questions:

- Which visual(s) was the most subtle? How?
- Which visual(s) was the most surprising, upsetting, etc.? Why?
- Which visual(s) was the most persuasive? Why?
- How does your cultural experience affect the visuals you see? The visuals you find the most persuasive?
- Based on your analysis, in which of nine American lifestyles do you fit?

Oral Rhetoric: Creating Your Own Advertisement

Select a product you find completely unusable, ridiculous, or unnecessary. It must be an actual product. Decide on a target audience. Remember to consider age and interests. Create and enact an advertisement using three of the advertising techniques and the right type of weasel words for your target audience.

Visual Rhetoric: Evaluating CD Covers

In 2003, Johnny Cash recorded a cover of the 1994 Nine Inch Nails (NIN) song "Hurt." Cash's version was well received not only by country music fans but NIN fans as well. The video of Cash's version won a Grammy for Best Short Form Video and was nominated for seven MTV awards, of which it won Best Cinematography. Locate the following two CD covers on-line.

1. *The Downward Spiral* by Nine Inch Nails (NIN)
2. *American IV: A Man Comes Around* by Johnny Cash

Look closely at the color choice for the two CD covers. What rhetorical appeal does the NIN cover use? Does it give any indication of the focus of the songs it represents? What rhetorical appeal does the Cash album use? Does the use, or lack thereof, of color create a stronger or weaker presence for the singers?

Electronic Rhetoric: Evaluating DeviantArt.com

Do a search for a topic that interests you. See what visual images occur because of your search. Try to find three or four similar images. Create a blog examining the visual impact of such images.

WOVE Project: Analysis and Presentation

For this assignment you need to locate a **visual** (political cartoon, advertisement, brochure, covers on magazines and journals, etc.) that **presents an argument.** The key to selecting the visual is that it must present an argument. If you fail to select a visual that presents an argument, you cannot complete a rhetorical analysis. Maintain a blog recording your investigation.

After selecting the visual, you need to write a 2200 word essay in which you argue for the persuasiveness of the visual. Naturally, this means you must use persuasive strategies to persuade the reader. You might want to review chapter 2 in this text to make certain you fully understand the strategies of persuasion. In addition, your essay should have the following elements:

- Describe the visual, in as much detail as possible. Which elements are concrete? Abstract?
- What is the main argument of the visual? What is the overall purpose of the visual?
- Who is the audience (look at Mitchell's lifestyle groupings)?
- What is the context of the visual?
- How do colors affect the argument? What type of color harmony does it use? Is this harmony specific to the purpose of the visual?
- Is the visual busy? Culturally specific?
- What rhetorical appeals are used? Logos? Pathos? Ethos? Give examples.
- What effects do these appeals have? Be specific and give examples.
- How do the textual additions support or even create the argument?
- What type of claim does the text present?

Suggested Readings

Here are just a few books targeted at any one who wants to "sell" products, services, or even ideas or who wants to understand those who do:

Bayan, Richard. *Words that Sell*. Chicago: Contemporary Books, 1994.
Explains how to choose words that meet your end goal.

Beemer, C. Britt. *Predatory Marketing*. Broadway Publishers, 1998.
Uses a study of 3,000,000 people to determine what words persuade them to purchase products or accept ideas.

Girard, Joe. *How to Sell Anything to Anybody*. Warner Brothers Publishing, 1986.
Explains techniques for how to get people to accept your ideas or buy your products.

Packard, Vance. *The Status Seekers*. Pocket Books, 1959.
Explains how advertising focused on "keeping up with the Jones"— though an older book, the strategies still work.

"Permission to Enter?"

by G.B. Trudeau from Doonesbury

http://www.doonesbury.com

AFTER YOU READ: Analyze the Issues

1. What is the main message of the cartoon?
2. Why is the second frame in silhouette?
3. Can you relate to the cartoon strip?

AFTER YOU READ: Analyze the Rhetoric

1. How effective is the drawing in telling the story?
2. How does humor work in the strip?

"I want you to make a choice. . . . I want to play a game."
—*John Jigsaw from* Saw *(2004)*

Converging Technologies Change Communication

As television shows pop up on the Internet (YouTube.com), as phones become computers and cameras (iPhones), as gamers become filmmakers by creating short fan films (Halo 3 videos), and as new technologies continue to combine and procreate, these multiverses of new media emerge. As Walter Ong (1912–2003) would point out, our very consciousness is changing as the word is technologized in ever new forms. One example of how such changes are positive is that new technologies enable people with visual impairment to navigate through the world using sound, much like bats do in the dark. They in fact may "see" or "sound" better than people without visual impairment because their perceptions are heightened and the world may appear in more detail. Similarly, these new technologies enable all of us to heighten our senses and to gain new perspectives.

We live in what Jean Baudrillard (1929–2007) calls a hyperreality. Our new world is not a model of any place that we have ever known before nor a perfection of the beautiful natural environment that once surrounded us. Indeed, we basically are destroying nature with a rapidity never before seen. As we immerse ourselves into our entertainment vistas, our information overloads, and our mutant technologies, the simulations produced by our imaginations are starting to take over. These are seductive simulations with a persuasive rhetoric that we must begin to understand and conquer.

The word has been reborn in this emergent media. Writing is actually more important today than ever because although math, science, and technology can enhance and define these new electronic devices that converge into each other and into our consciousness at an alarming and dangerous rate, we now need new coders and spin masters to shape these fictional worlds we live in. The latest products are before us, but we need to control the process. Writing returns us to the control room, for it is our future that we write. Developing an understanding of electronic rhetoric will weave our various forms of rhetoric together: Written, Oral, Visual, and Electronic. WOVE!

The New Convergent CyberSites of Emergent Rhetoric

On the Internet, different types of sites are merging, mashing, and feeding into each other. Now it is possible to listen to music or watch a video from another site within your own blog or site. This convergence or combination of actions and locations is changing how we multitask as it expands the possibilities of the new emergent rhetorics.

Each site is starting to reproduce the characteristics and content of competing sites or allowing them to be integrated seamlessly into existing sites through widgets, chunks of code that can be embedded in any Web page to bring live content to that page and thus produce effortless interaction with other Web pages. A key factor for all of the following sites is their interactive, communal aspect. Business, social, and political interactions are changing as we change the way we think of our community because of virtual interactions.

Social Bookmarking

del.icio.us

Widgets

RSS (Feeds: Really Simple Syndication)
Mashable
Yahoo Widgets

Visual Networks

YouTube
deviantART

Social Networks

Facebook
MySpace
Twitter

Virtual Worlds

Second Life

Wiki

Writeboard
Wikipedia

One of the interesting trends for Web sites is the ability to import, subscribe and feed into features from other sites. Mashing, bookmarking, and navigating smart are important ways to stay ahead.

Social Bookmarking

As cyberpace continues to grow, participants need an indexing system to keep everything organized. The bookmarking features that come with your browser are not intricate enough.

> Social Bookmarking
> Instead of simply recording the location of a site of personal interest, social bookmarking allows you to share those locations with others who value the same sites. Such sites became a virtual gathering of people who share the same interests where friends and acquaintances can be stimulated.

del.icio.us (del.icio.us, wiki: del.icio.us/tag/wiki)

del.icio.us was created by Joshua Schachter in 2003. Yahoo bought del.icio.us in 2005. For the most part when you become a member of a site like YouTube, MySpace or Second Life, it has its own bookmarking features. The advantage of using del.icio.us is that it will maintain your bookmarks even if you use a different computer. An even greater value of such social bookmarking is that you can share your bookmarks with others and can learn about other bookmarks from people of similar interests.

So join del.icio.us to maintain a healthy Web appetite.

BOOKMARKING RESEARCH EXERCISE: A WOVE Approach

del.icio.us can be used to bookmark sites you will use for your research. Try a WOVE approach:

Written. Bookmark examples of textual information.
Oral. Bookmark music or speeches.
Visual. Bookmark film clips or art works.
Electronic. Bookmark sites liked by other users with similar interests.

Widgets

If, on your own site, you are watching a certain YouTube video and at the same time listening to a music theme, feeding updated NFL football scores, and viewing weather conditions, then you are using widgets to display these components. Such components allow you to use the WOVE approach. Creating a blog or a Web site for research assignments with **widgets** will allow you to explore issues from a variety of perspectives and rhetorical inputs.

> Widgets
> Allow information gathered at one site to be displayed or integrated into other sites. For example, the weather or time could be displayed at other sites. Music, art work, and other information can be shared at a variety of sites without the user being solely at that site.

RSS (Feeds: Really Simple Syndication)

This image with the dot and two radio-like waves represents the ability to access an RSS, or feed, at that Web site. You can download such feeds to your homepage or Web site. Go to Google to find a list of available feeds.

Mashable: Social Networking News (mashable.com)

This site also offers a list of sources that provide feeds. It also offers codes to use with sites like MySpace to allow feeds to work.

More importantly, it provides updates on the world of feeds, which is rapidly changing. In the future, instead of us visiting other Web sites because of social bookmarks and feeds, Web sites will come looking for our Web sites. Our future sites will morph and mash. Such types of media collaboration are already changing how sites operate.

Yahoo Widgets (widget.yahoo.com)

If you find yourself always visiting a site, why not just add aspects of that site to your homepage, blog, or social networking site, like MySpace? Instead of a link, embed elements of that site into your site.

There are about 5000 different widgets listed at this site that you can add to your own sites. You may want a special calendar, sport news of your favorite team, tips about being green, updates on the cheapest gas prices. There are a multitude of widgets you can add to your site. More are being added constantly. Such sites connect you to the sources you find most interesting.

Visual Networks

If your interests are more artistic, then finding a social network that has a deep richness for visual elements is a must. Try DeviantArt.com since such sites provide for interconnectivity with artists of similar interests.

Once upon a time during the early 1990's, the Internet was merely textual in nature and was called Gopher. Students, of course, thought it wondrous while spending countless hours "going for" information. Then something called Netscape came about in the mid 1990's and revolutionized the Internet because it allowed for images and later sound and videos to be easily shared. The Internet hasn't been the same. Such sites as YouTube and Deviant Art allows for all of us to access countless videos and images and share them with each other.

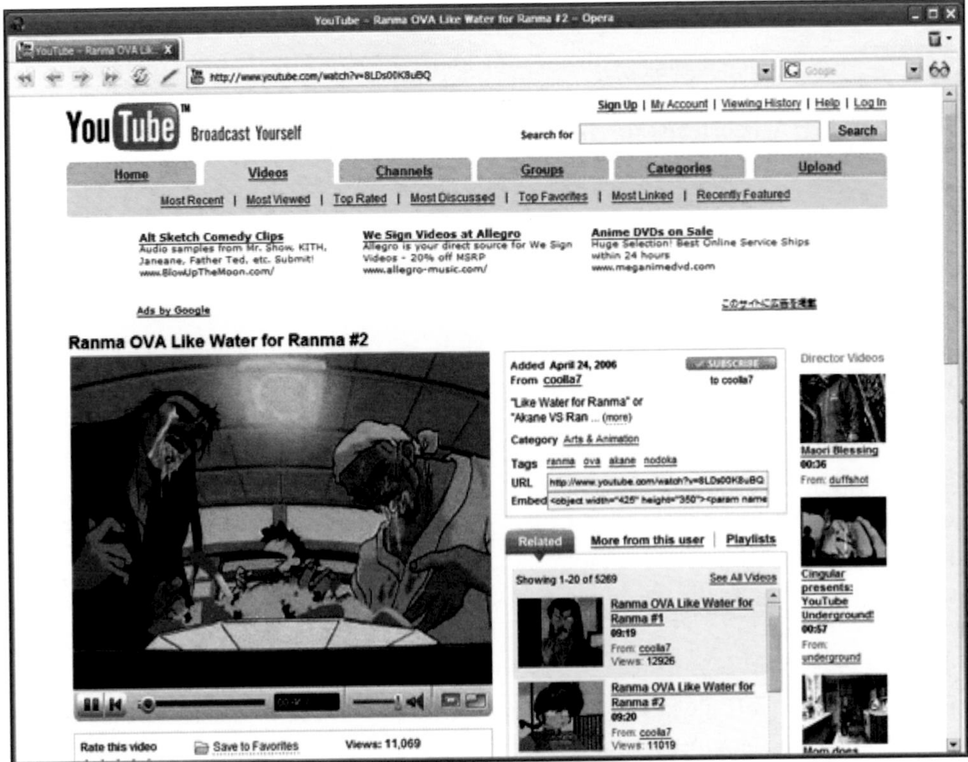

DeviantArt

This site focuses on art: fan art, digital art, cartoons, manga/anime, photography, traditional arts, designs, and literature of individuals who want to share their works.

Web Site: www.deviantart.com

You can have friends with similar artistic interests. Enjoy and browse around and discover amazing works. Sure you can find artworks and images in Google, but you also find so many things that you may not want. If you like the visual arts, then this is your visual network!

WOVE Features:

Written. Examine the poetry, fiction, and cartoons.
Oral. Read aloud the poems and other works. Comment aloud about images you see.
Visual. Note the richness of the digital photos, the drawing, and other art works.
Electronic. Use the bookmarking tools and chat features of the site

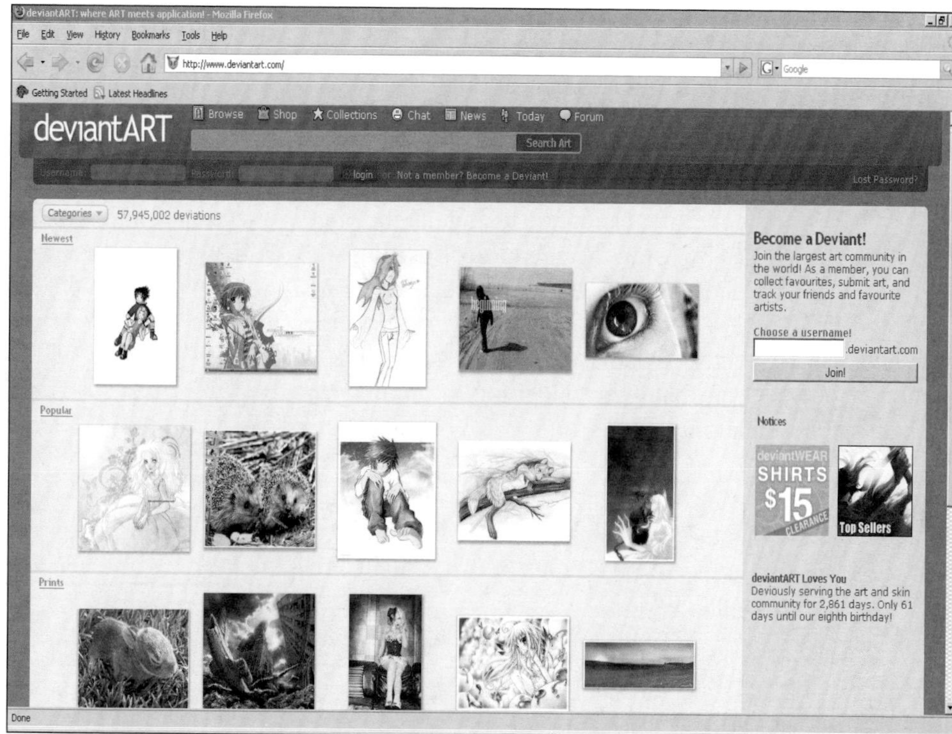

DeviantArt EXERCISE:

Do a search on one of the issues explored in this book:

- Conspiracy
- Gaming
- Consumerism
- War
- Environment
- Immigration.

Examine the images related to your topic or issues. Find a couple of images you think are intriguing, captivating, or disturbing. Keep in mind that a visual image also represents an argument or a message of persuasion. Answer these questions:

1. What appeals are being used?
2. What is the message or argument found in the image?
3. What is being sold?
4. Who is the audience?
5. How does it make you feel?

Social Networks

The power of the virtual world comes of age. As the Internet evolves into a more viable cultural, social, and political phenomenon, it gains momentum as a life altering entity with its principle of interdependency.

Barack Obama has revolutionized political campaigning and has become the first candidate to engage the youth to care about politics by using the s**ocial networking** sites they use. Chris Hughes, a co-founder of Facebook, helped to design the Obama Web site and made it more interactive and, consequently, Obama raised vast amounts of monies. He went from being an underdog to winning the Democratic nomination.

> Social Network
> Allows pictures, videos, words, music and a variety of information to be shared with friends, family, and anyone allowed access to the site. This virtual community grows in importance and extends the limits of how we define ourselves.

- my.barackobama.com
- www.facebook.com/barackobama
- my.barackobama.com/page/community/post/chrishughesatthecampaign/CZFL

Visit these sites and note how the political landscape is changing.

Facebook

Facebook was created in 2004 as a social network for students at Harvard University. Within a year it was open to all Ivy League universities as well as certain high schools. In 2006, it was open to everyone. As with MySpace, Facebook offers members the ability to network with other members who have the same interests. Members can join "friends" in their local city, university, and workplace, or they can join other interest groups. Universities, musicians, and other initiates can create profiles that connect them with members who may be interested in their events. Some Facebook users claim that it has a cleaner or more professional look than MySpace.

EXERCISE: If you do not have a Facebook account, create one. Then answer these questions:

The tagline for Facebook is:
Facebook is a social utility that connects you with the people around you.

- What rhetorical value does this tagline have for Facebook?
- Why does the tagline specifically use the word "utility"?

Other questions:

- Why is Facebook so popular with college students?
- What are some of the differences between MySpace and Facebook?

WOVE Features of Facebook:

- **Written.** Facebook provides the ability to blog. You can import other blog systems into Facebook.
- **Oral.** With the "iLike" feature, you can add music videos from YouTube.com and your own videos.
- **Visual.** People like to post their photo albums to share with others. Some Facebook users feel that it has a more professional and clean look compared to MySpace which is loud and clunky to some users.
- **Electronic.** Note the various widgets that are used.

MySpace

MySpace launched in 2003 as a site where indie musicians and indie music lovers from Los Angeles could learn about and promote music and events. Since then, tweens, teens, 20-, 30-, 40-, and 50-somethings have made it their own space to socialize and create identities. Tweens, teens, and 20-something members use it primarily as a socialization tool.

In order to socialize, the members must create a profile. A profile is the member's on-line "clothes." Just as clothing reflects the personality of the person wearing them, so does the look of a member's profile. Through the profile the user creates an impression of who he or she is—or who the user wants viewers to think he or she is. MySpace allows the member to create this impression with text, video, photos, and page design. In addition, it allows the member to receive feedback from friends (people the member invites to join his or her other circle) and/or from outsiders (people who can view the page even though they are not friends with the member). Visitation restrictions can be added.

MySpace is the parent media of several children. These media children include

- Videos: vids.myspace.com
- Karaoke: ksolo.myspace.com

Using these media, members can further specify their profiles. These spaces have a look that is similar to, yet different from, the original MySpace site.

Beware: Going job hunting? What have you been posting on-line? Just because you can post it doesn't mean you should. Such sites can cause people not to be considered as serious candidates because employers now look on-line to see how their applicants behave in such public spaces.

MYSPACE EXERCISE: Answer these Questions.

- What are people doing on MySpace?
- Why types of argument are being made?
- Is MySpace a private or public space, even when the member lists her/his page as "private"?

- What do the differing colors used mean to the average user who views it? Why were those colors selected by MySpace creators?
- Why do you think MySpace expanded its offerings to separate spaces for videos and karaoke?
- Many well-known musicians have MySpace sites. Find some. What rhetorical value does this space offer to an already well-known musician or group?

EXERCISE: User Specific Questions

Answer these questions about your own experiences. If you do not use MySpace, quickly create a site, and experiment with it, and then answer these questions:

- What type of impression are you making with your site?
- What rhetorical strategies are you using?
- What colors are you using and what impression do they make?
- Do you upload videos? Music? Karaoke?

Twitter (twitter.com)

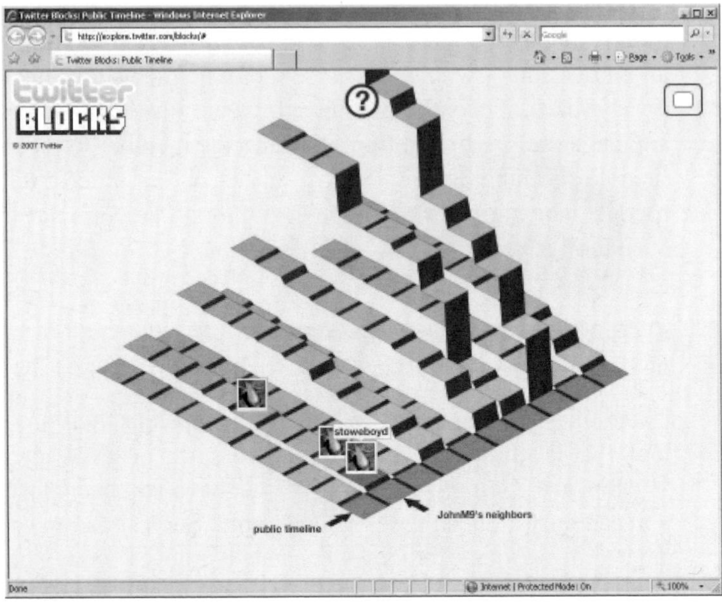

Do you "tweet"? If not, you may be a bit behind in terms of technology. Twitter is one of the fastest growing emergent media. It merges social networking and micro-blogging, allowing users to post up to 140-word micro-blogs, called "tweets," on twitter.com and other social networking sites.

Users can post the micro-blog via cell phones, instant messaging, Facebook, Twitterific, and other third party services. The micro-blogs post instantly to the user's Twitter account and are disseminated to members who have signed up to receive them. The micro-blogs can be viewed on the Twitter Web site, instant messaging, SMS, RSS, e-mail, or other applications.

The graphic demonstrates how Twitter connects its users. If you are a friend of JohnM9, you will see his "tweets" as well as others in his neighborhood. It also tells you the time the user "tweeted."

Tweeting is becoming ever popular among teens, 20-, 30-, and 40-somethings because of its accessibility. You can "tweet" from practically anywhere. It allows users to have an immediate "blog" instead of having to be behind the computer.

TWITTER EXERCISE: Answer These Questions:

- What impression are users of Twitter trying to make?
- What types of messages can be conveyed in 140 characters or less?
- How do users create a "personality" using Twitter?
- How does Twitter use its site design to develop Twitter's persona as an emergent media?
- CNN uses Twitter to broadcast news feeds. What is the rhetorical value of Twitter to such news feeds?
- John Edwards used Twitter in the campaign trail. What rhetorical value would messages sent by John Edwards have to his campaign supporters?

Virtual Worlds

Neal Stephenson in his cyberpunk farce *Snow Crash* (1992) envisioned a world called Metaverse where people would live vicariously and virtually as avatars. The term **avatar** that Stephenson created is now used when discussing characters in virtual worlds like Second Life, the most popular virtual world.

> Avatar
> A visual representation of a person in the virtual or gaming world. Originally, the term is from Hinduism meaning an incarnation that various deities are able to manifest. The term was popularized by Neal Stephenson (1959–) in his post-cyberpunk classic, *Snow Crash* (1992).

Second Life (www.secondlife.com, Wiki: wiki.secondlife.com)

If possible, access and join Second Life. Please be aware that the image in the center of the Web page changes each time you visit, so you will not see the same images as those in this book. After accessing the site, you should look closely at the visual design, including the color schemes, used on the main page as well as other pages. Most of the colors are subtle and use some shade of blue, the color most appeasing to the human psyche. Also notice how the site uses muted as well as bright colors to draw your attention or divert your attention.

Second Life was created in 2003 by Linden Lab. This Web site offers its patrons the ability to create an alternate second life—for most people a more exciting life. It is free, so join and participate in the virtual world. It has its own economy and its own money: Linden Dollars.

You can create your own island, for a price. You can buy things there that you want—a house, a car, or clothes. Whatever avatars make, they own or they can sell for Linden Dollars. You can dance to music, visit museums, take classes, and do anything else you do in real life.

WOVE Features of Second Life:

Written. Notice that your avatar interacts with chat features instead of oral voices, which seems to be a standard for on-line games and virtual worlds.
Oral. Listen to music and other sounds available at the site.
Visual. Immerse yourself in the rich 3D textures of Second Life.
Electronic. Experience the rich environment by flying around. Interact with others.

SECOND LIFE EXERCISE. Answer the following questions:

- Why would it be important for the visual design to demonstrate the excitement and varied abilities of the site?
- What rhetorical appeals do the colors imply at this site?
- What rhetorical appeals are being used with the text?
- Whom are the designers targeting?
- Does the target audience appear to be "interested"? How do you know?
- Why would it be important to list how many people are logged on, have joined, etc.?
- What overall argument does listing the number of people make?
- Why would flying be a normal feature for avatars in Second Life?

Wiki Collaborative Writing

Wikis allow participants to interact in writing projects. More importantly wikis allow users to share their knowledge and input. Instead of reacting, you can be proactive. It is this collaborative nature that makes wikis popular. The advantage is that writers can edit, change, or otherwise revisit old versions of a text as they interact with others. The disadvantage is that not everyone likes to interact with others.

Fortunately, wikis can be used in a non-collaborative format. As a writer you can maintain a wiki for every assignment as you draft it. Wikis can be used to create peer review assignments. Thus, wikis are perfect for writing classes. Social network sites like MySpace and gaming sites like World of Warcraft have their own wiki. Wikis have become indispensible.

Writeboard (www.writeboard.com)

Writeboard, like most wikis, is free and allows you to maintain control of the drafts. You can return to old versions. You can control who is in the group and allowed to participate. You don't need to save a draft because Writeboard will save it for you. As long as you have access to the Internet, you don't need Word or a flash drive.

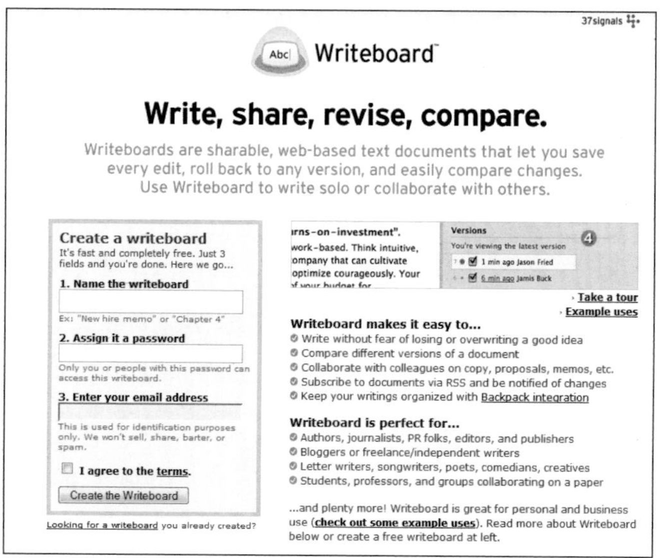

Wikipedia (www.wikipedia.org)

Established in 2001 and maintained by volunteers, Wikipedia has basically replaced in popularity the book format of the encyclopedia, with some 2 million articles and growing. As a general reference tool, it does contain useful information and links; however, beware of its accuracy, especially since anyone can edit it. Always double check sources, which is something researchers must constantly do.

Quoting only from Wikipedia as your main source will not impress anyone. Recently published articles may contain errors, and some have been vandalized. The biography of George W. Bush has been vandalized a multitude of times and filled with erroneous information. So be careful when you quote from Wikipedia.

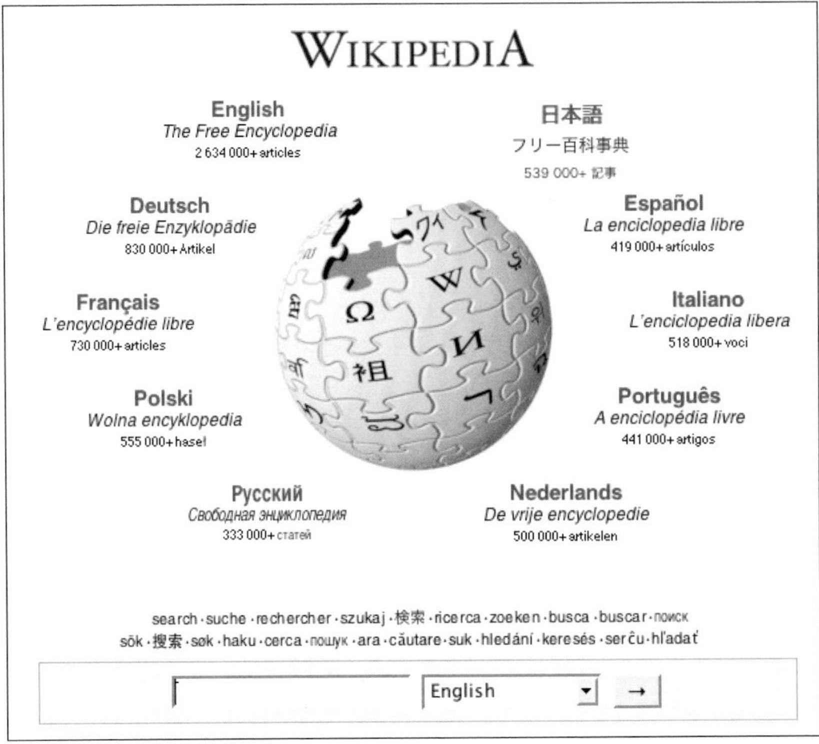

YouTube.com and the Rhetorical Appeals

Perhaps one of the most popular places to view the impact of the emergent media's use of rhetorical techniques is YouTube.com, which was founded in February 2005 by Chad Hurley and Steve Chen. In November of 2006, Google acquired YouTube.com.

According to YouTube.com, each day, some one million people visit the site where some 65, 000 new clips are added daily . YouTube.com has become part of the presidential election process. On July 23, 2007, it hosted the Democratic Debates, and on September 2007, it did the same for the Republican Debates.

Viewers can control the effect of the messages to a degree by selecting what they see and when they see them. This can empower candidates who cannot afford to pay for massive amounts of air time on television. Candidates can post a variety of commercials trying to sell their message. Viewers can post parodies of the messages and also comment on each video in a sort of blog format. This interaction differs from the way we are used to reacting to commercials on television. YouTube is also a depository of classical political messages.

Finding the Message in Political Propaganda

Let's look at these ads in YouTube from the 2008 presidential candidates, from both Republican and Democratic sides. Ads often combine the three elements of the classical appeals: logos, ethos, and pathos. However, most ads usually favor one appeal over the others in order to magnify the effectiveness.

Tips for Watching Political Ads

- Note how the music is used in the ads. Watch the ad without sound.
- Everything in the ad was placed or edited into the message for maximum effect. Take nothing for granted.
- Re-watch and re-think what you see.
- Disassociate the message from the candidate to be more objective.

Ask these questions:

- What is really being said?
- What is NOT being said?
- What is missing?
- How original is the ad?
- Is the ad really that effective?

Using Logos to Persuade: Fooling the Mind

By using logical and rational words complemented with well-placed images, logos can be an effective persuasive technique. Using numbers as evidence can also seem logical and rational. However, they can also obscure the issue.

Logos and the Number's Game: John Edwards' "Season"

By opening this ad with some statistics, John Edwards tries to bring two tragic realities into perspective—homeless veterans and poverty. With a Christmas tree in the background, he looks into the camera and says, "One out of every four homeless people is a veteran. Thirty seven million people live in poverty." Then he rhetorically asks, "Who speaks for them?" He then answers, of course, that he does. In his "Underdog" ad, he also mentions 200,000 homeless veterans who need attention. These numbers seem to provide rational support for his message.

However, no answers to the issues are actually provided. Even with ample answers and solutions, thirty seconds is not enough time to explore the problems in detail.

NUMBER'S GAME EXERCISE:
Watch the Ad and Answer these Questions:

- How effective are these numbers to the audience?
- Where did he get the numbers?
- What about the other homeless people, the three out of four roaming the streets? Should we care about them? Don't they count?
- What defines poverty?

Logos and Oversimplification: Rudy Giuliani's "Jumpstart"

Where do our candidates stand on the issues and what will they do when they rule? Here is a popular strategy used by many candidates who tell us what they will or can do: they promise the moon. A professionally paid voice states: "Taxes, insurance, housing, all a mess, but Rudy Giuliani knows how to fix those. He reformed welfare before others tried and delivered more tax relief than the other Republicans combined. Now Rudy will jumpstart our economy with the biggest tax cut in modern history, eliminate wasteful spending. And he is the only Republican candidate to fight for a national catastrophe fund to reduce insurance waste."

In sixty-four words, Rudy shares with the American public his plans to solve the economic and catastrophic problems. The ad also mentions the housing problem but never explains how to solve it. Though he is going to create the biggest tax cut in history, he wants to set up a national catastrophe fund. Where will the funds come from? More taxes? Because of the oversimplification of such issues, we don't really learn much here about how he plans to fix such problems.

OVERSIMPLIFICATION EXERCISE:
Watch the Ad and Answer these Questions:

- Why should we take him at his word?
- If he becomes president, will the public ever remember what he said he would do?
- Do elected officials ever keep their promises?
- Is this an effective ad?

Find other examples of oversimplification from other candidates.

Logos and Glittering Generalities (Virtue Words): John McCain's "Service"

This commercial was made for a specific audience, South Carolina. But it could easily have been written for any state. Virtue words, like "Freedom," "Family Values," and "Service," can't miss since they have positive and conservative connotations. Here is what McCain personally delivers to the camera: "I've served our country all my adult life. I have never lived a day in good times or bad I wasn't grateful for the privilege. Now I ask to serve as your president as thousands of South Carolinians risk their lives to defend us. Our purpose can't be ours alone. America is our cause: her greatness, our hope; her strength, our protection; her goodness, the hope of mankind. That's why I run for your president and ask for your support. I'm John McCain, I approve this message. "

GLITTERING GENERALITIES EXERCISE:
Watch the Ad and Answer these Questions:

- How many virtue words did you notice?
- What does he say that separates him from other candidates?
- How effective is the ad?

In one sense, if you didn't know this was John McCain speaking, you couldn't separate the message from the messenger since any party candidate could have read this and it would still work effectively. Such virtue words are more like empty platitudes, ultimately devoid of meaning and not very thought provoking. Of course, since McCain served in Vietnam, he is trying to say that the word "service" represents his unique virtue word. But such service didn't seem to work for past presidential candidate John Kerry.

Ethos and the Cult of Personality: Mike Huckabee's "Chuck Norris Approved"

Which candidates wouldn't want Chuck Norris to endorse them? There is a novelty to having Chuck covering your back, and Mick Huckabee welcomed the B movie star. In his ad with Chuck Norris by his side, Mike Huckabee asks the audience, "My plan to secure the border? Two words. Chuck Norris. . . . There is no chin behind Chuck Norris's beard, only another fist. When Chuck Norris does a push up, he

Mike Huckabee's "Chuck Norris Approved"

isn't lifting himself up, he is pushing the Earth down." Chuck Norris replies, "Mike Huckabee wants to put the IRS out of business." Intentionally, the ad becomes one of humor and less of substance.

CULT OF PERSONALITY EXERCISE: Watch the Ad and Answer these Questions:

- Does Chuck Norris help the cause?
- How effective is having Norris and even the Western music in the ad?
- Does the ad work for the political cause?

Using the Ethos of Persuasion

When Oprah openly endorsed Barak Obama, some felt that she should not have shown support in that manner because of the power she has. They may have felt she crossed an ethical line. However, candidates have always welcomed endorsements from powerful personalities. Nothing has changed. Character, authority, personality, or ethos remains a powerfully persuasive tool.

ETHOS EXERCISE: Answer These Questions:

- Do such endorsements matter?
- Does authority help or hinder the cause or message?
- Why do pictures of Ronald Reagan appear in Republican ads? Are they effective?

Ethos and Scapegoating: Mitt Romney's "Momentum" (Washington is Broken)

Scapegoating is a popular tool for politicians who want to fix something. First, they have to identify what is broken and who is responsible, and second, they have to offer their services to repair the damage. All too often, after elected, they simply merge into the problem and do not offer much of a solution.

In this ad, Mitt Romney uses an effective call and response technique—often used by preachers—to attack Washington as the scapegoat to all our problems. He starts the call with, "Washington told us they ___________________." The audience then responds: "But they haven't." He starts with "Washington told us they *would secure the borders*." Then he continues his calls:

- *would live by high ethical standards, . . .*
- *would fix social security, . . .*
- *would get better health care and better education, . . .*

- *would get us a tax break for middle income Americans, . . .*
- *would cut back on the earmarks and pork barrel spending, . . .*
- *would reduce our dependence on foreign oil, . . .*

The audience continues to respond, "But they haven't." He concludes by saying, "Who is going to get the job done? We are."

SCAPEGOATING EXERCISE:
Watch the Ad and Answer these Questions:

- How effective is the music?
- Does the call and response technique work for this ad?
- Why is repetition effective?
- How effective are the images in the ad?

Find the same speech at YouTube without the music and images. Comment on the effectiveness of the edited message of the ad when compared to the speech.

Ethos and Testimonials: Fred Thompson's "Substance"

This ad has a list of five sources who support Thompson: 1) *Wall Street Journal*, 2) a leading economic group, 3) *National Review*, 4) *Investor's Business Daily*, and 5) National Right to Life Committee. The ad ends by saying that the candidate is "The Clear Conservative Choice." Note the patriotic and conservative tone of the music. Of course, no hip hop sounds are used. Note the weakness of one of the sources. Watch the ad and comment on how effective it is.

Fred Thompson's "Substance"

TESTIMONIAL EXERCISE:
Watch the Ad and Answer These Questions:

- Who is the leading economic group?
- Why wasn't the name of that group mentioned?
- Why would we care about what others say?
- What if you read those complete articles or sources that these excerpts came from?
- How effective are such testimonials?
- What about the images used to support the testimonials?

Note that these testimonials are not exactly complete endorsements of the candidate. Indeed, they are only short excerpts of positive comments. Those same sources may have contained some critical, or even some strong negative statements. **The shortness of the testimonials calls into question the effectiveness of the comments.**

Ethos and Plain Folks: Hillary Clinton's "It's About People"

Everyone wants to feel she or he is part of the process. Ads that focus on the average Joe or Jane, the middle classes, or the common person can be effective ways to gain votes.

In the ad, Clinton begins a speech by saying, "I listened to you, and found my own voice. . . It's about people, about making a difference in your lives. It's time we had a president who stands up for all of you!" Note the use of images. Interestingly, John Edwards seemed to use this strategy of plain folks more in his campaign.

PLAIN FOLKS EXERCISE:
Watch the Ad and Answer these Questions:

- Who is standing behind Clinton when she speaks? Why?
- What types of people are in the video?
- How effective is the speech?

Find more examples of the Plain Folks strategy in ads by other candidates. Compare them to this advertisement.

- Which ads are more effective? Why?
- Which ads are the least effective? Why?

Using Pathos to Persuade: Fooling the Heart

Images alone can evoke powerful emotions. The youthful image of Barak Obama is no doubt helping him with the young voters. The good looks of John Edwards and Mitt Romney evoke positive emotions for some voters. Even the age of John McCain can work for him in states like Florida. Other emotions like fear and patriotism can be effective ways to work the hearts of the audience.

Pathos and Fear Tactics: Dennis Kucinich's "No More Blood for Oil"

Almost no spoken words are used in this commercial. We just hear the sound of a gas pump meter clicking away numbers like the cost of filling a gas tank, the number of dead US soldiers in Iraq, the number of wounded US soldiers in Iraq, the number of Iraqi civilians killed and wounded, the amount of oil company profits, and finally, the amount of tax money spent on the war. Interestingly, most candidates avoided the war issue or at least did not emphasize it as much. Perhaps they all agreed that it needs to end. Is Kucinich beating a dead horse?

FEAR TACTICS EXERCISE:
Watch the Ad and Answer these Questions:

- How effective is the sound used in this ad?
- Do the numbers presented evoke any emotions?
- What are other issues or things voters now fear?

Find other ads that use fear to win votes. How effective are these ads?

Pathos and Emotional Transfer (like Patriotism): Rudy Giuliani's "Freedom"

Of course, the former mayor of New York City would use patriotism for his campaign. He helped the city survive a bitter attack. Giuliani opens the ad by mentioning the book *The Greatest Generation* by Tom Brokaw about the sacrifices made during World War II. First we see the famous picture of the American flag at Iwo Jima and then the American flag put up by firefighters on ground zero in New York City. We are also provided an image of the American flag on the Moon.

Rudy Giuliani's "Freedom"

EMOTIONAL TRANSFER EXERCISE:
Watch the Ad and Answer these Questions:

- How many images of the American flag are shown?
- Is the comparison between World War II and the War against Terrorism valid? Does this work?
- How effective is using patriotism as the wars in Iraq and Afghanistan continue?
- Did the images work well for the ad? Why or why not?

Find more ads that use patriotism. Which ads are the most patriotic?

Pathos and the Fear of Control: "Anti-Hillary Ad" (Parody)

Though not created by the Obama people, this dystopian parody of George Orwell's *1984* mixes the original Apple Macintosh commercial (1985) released during the Super Bowl with Hillary Clinton giving a speech. Note the words Clinton is saying in the parody. Obama's name is written like an Apple logo. Try to find the original ad.

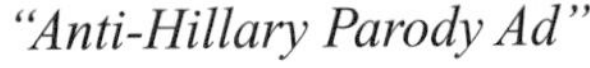
"Anti-Hillary Parody Ad"

PARODY EXERCISE:
Watch the Ad and Answer these Questions:

- How effective are the images in the parody?
- What does the parody say about Hillary Clinton?
- What does the ad imply about Barack Obama?

There are ample parody ads on-line, from *Saturday Night Live* versions to the many uploaded or created by YouTube viewers. This is the real excitement of YouTube as its audience become media savvy through installation, manipulation, and experimentation. Humor remains an effective way to deconstruct and reframe meaning.

A Call for Balance: The Booth Effect

Political ads for the most part seem to lack a balance of the three classical argumentative appeals: logos, ethos, and pathos. If a message contains too much of one appeal, it can be ineffective as rhetorician Wayne Booth explains how the appeals affect the stance of the message:

- **Pedant's Stance (mind):** With too much logos, the theme leans too much toward the message itself as the main power and becomes too dry.
- **Entertainer's Stance (body):** With too much ethos, the theme becomes an actor's spotlight to showcase his or her cleverness, and though the show may be entertaining, the effectiveness may be in question.
- **Advertiser's Stance (heart)**: With too much pathos, the theme pays too much attention to pleasing the emotions of the audience, and though it may have heart, it may have no point.

YouTube has now become ubiquitous since it allows people to post their videos at other sites like Facebook. At one point media companies were filing law suits as people posted videos from films, television, and music. The copyright issues are still being worked out. However, the motion picture, television, and music companies are now creating their own sites. You can now download clips from *South Park* from the Comedy Central site or from *American Dad* from the Hulu site. Many television shows can now be seen on-line after they are shown on television. These changes are all part of the converging media; however, more changes are on the way.

Gaming Theory and Emergent Rhetoric

With the introduction of new technologies, gaming as a whole, and role-playing games in particular have emerged from the backroom (or kitchen table) to become a much greater part of our everyday lives. From on-line Sudoku to total emersion fantasy games such as World of Warcraft, electronic games are becoming more and more popular and have largely supplanted more traditional forms of game playing.

The largest growth has occurred in role-playing games.

On-Line Gaming

Fantasy Games

- World of Warcraft (WoW)
- EverQuest (EQ)

Video Gaming

First-Person Shooter Game

- Xbox 360 and Halo 3

Music Video Performance Games

- Guitar Hero III
- Rock Band

New Kinetic Energy Games

- Wii and SuperMario

A variety of games exist, with the most basic being the zero-sum game, in which the winner takes all. This zero-sum design remains essentially Darwinian in form, with a survival of the fittest pattern paralleling our thirst to win. However, other varieties of games with more enlightened philosophies have emerged. These are called "non zero-sum" games.

The New Rhetorical Situation: Games

The game creates a rhetorical situation where we can re-see and re-think the motives, actions, and reactions that are to be presented (played). This extends our traditional discovery methodology, allowing us to explore non-linear solutions in real-world scenarios. The game becomes a metaphor of our mind and our world. As a game player we can now extend our abilities to think and to write critically.

The rhetorical situation is now the gaming situation.

Show Them the Game Face

In games, you are not merely regurgitating words. You are participating and acquiring life's lessons. Intelligence is not *what* we learn; rather it is our ability to *inquire and acquire* chunks of information.

Lev Vygotsky said that knowledge is not based on what we memorize or think by ourselves. Instead, knowledge is based on what we are able to come up with when working with others. Gaming can be more effective if it can be thought of as working with others instead of reacting or competing against each other. It becomes a key sequence of moves setting everyone up to win.

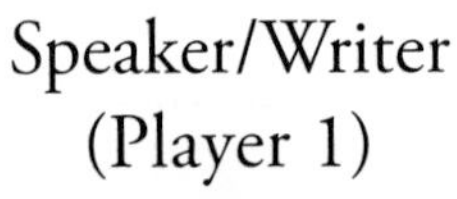

Gaming in the Context of the Rhetorical Triangle

Like gaming, writing isn't about being right and wrong. The audience is taken through a sequence of logical, ethical, and emotional moves. How does the audience react? For every action, there is a reaction.

In a game, these moves are evident, but in an essay, we can't always imagine the best moves. Gaming and adventures help us imagine those moves. Gaming tests thinking as it tests your ability to strategize, to learn.

The most effective rhetorical games are ones in which the goal is not mutual destruction, but an achievement of interdependence and reliance. In these gaming scenarios you are sharing personal "stories" and reaching a depth of narrative not examined in fights to the death. Storytelling becomes an exploration of a possible world in which to live, for we are not trying to prove that the other side is wrong. Instead, we are reacting to the situation with which we are presented and trying to solve a problem so the game advances. We listen to other's perspectives, we adjust, we learn, we analyze, and we persuade.

The Five Classical Canons of Rhetoric

During ancient Greek times Aristotle developed the classical components of rhetoric. During Roman times, Cicero adopted these **canons of rhetoric** which have been divided into the basic elements known as the five canons. These five canons have remained an invaluable way to understand the complexities of communication.

> Classical Canons of Rhetoric
> The basic elements of rhetoric that allow for speakers, writers or creators to become meta-aware of how such aspects can effect change or be persuasive.

Classical Aspects of Rhetoric for the Speaker

- **Invention**, how we discover the content or message.
- **Arrangement,** how we organize the message.
- **Style**, how we structure the parts of speech.
- **Delivery**, how we convey the content to the audience.
- **Memory,** how we remember the content.

Developing the Six Gaming Senses

A different way to see these components or canons is to think of them as the senses or limbs of a gamer or avatar. The senses or limbs physically interact with the game world. The most important interactor remains in our gut (the chi or inner energy zone), which can be called the motivator.

> Gaming Senses
> A super sensitivity to the audience, the game, and the plays or moves within a game that gamers must develop to be successful.

We must be motivated to interact, just as we must be motivated to learn. You can have skill, but heart is sometimes more important when you game. If you don't have a motivation to game or to write, nothing a teacher can do will work. Resistance is not futile; it kills any game. Attitude is everything.

The rhetorical canon becomes our measurement of the gaming interconnectivity. In order to move within a game successfully, we must immerse ourselves within the game space with these six senses.

1. **Invention,** how we move or counter move, predicting the impact.
2. **Arrangement,** how the game space is set up.
3. **Style,** how we interact within the gaming environment.
4. **Delivery,** how we activate the performances of the avatars.
5. **Memory**, how we learn to reshape the plasticity of the game.
6. **Motivation,** how we immerse ourselves in the greed of the moment.

Game Theories Open New Ways to Explore Complex Issues

Game theories are based on basic dilemmas. The following dilemmas identify certain gaming problems that often develop when players try to make decisions that have repercussions. These dilemmas are basically rhetorical choices that are part of the game.

Gaming theories can be applied to any genre and any issue.

Play on.

Prisoner's Dilemma

How do you get prisoners to confess or share vital information? The Geneva Convention does not condone using torture to obtain information. From popular television shows like *24* to the reality of Guantanamo Bay or Abu Ghraib, a popular technique used to make prisoners speak is rhetorical—not physical in nature—and is even approved by the Geneva Convention: deceit.

Imagine if you pick up two prisoners who know each other. The hope is that one of them will sell out the other one. Divide and conquer. If one prisoner tells on the other, then favors will be given to the prisoner who cooperates. In this psychological game where the two are competing against each other and one seemingly wins, you have what appears to be a zero-sum situation. However, the reality is often that both sides lose.

Chicken Fight

Another version of the zero-sum game is the Chicken Fight. The cold war is perhaps the greatest example of the application of the Chicken Fight. Two cars or countries race directly toward each other. Neither moves until the last minute, then one flinches: the chicken.

During the Cold War, the crazy idea of mutual mass destruction as a deterrent was used by the Soviet Union and the United States as each bluffed its way through a costly arms race. Sanity or brains was not part of this game. This game still continues while politicians modify it to fit current historical situations, maintaining the fear factor, machismo, and patriotism to fuel the Chicken Fight.

Students' Dilemma

For some students, the composition class may seem like a prison where you are forced to write an argumentative paper and show the power of your voice. You may employ the Chicken Fight strategy to compose your assignment, especially in a right vs. wrong paper.

Many argumentative essays are written with a **zero-sum** attitude, where one side is right and the other side is wrong. When we approach such issues as abortion, war, gun control, or same sex marriage with such a zero-sum methodology, we end up with a battle between good and evil. No matter how well you dance through the various aspects of the issue, such papers often just don't work.

Why do some of us have problems writing arguments? Both teachers and students in composition struggle with this writers' dilemma.

The key problem is that we are not good at negotiation or face-to-face confrontation, especially when it comes to important issues. We are not used to the dynamics needed for success.

Zero-Sum Situation
A gaming situation that is win or lose where the winner takes everything from the loser, like in the classic game of chess.

Ineffective Rhetorical Rants and Raves

If we merely approach such issues in a zero-sum manner, such papers are often doomed to fail because the audience is polarized and then becomes defensive. The probability of convincing the majority in an audience who opposes your viewpoints to change their views is slim at best.

In composition classes, we run the risk of writing argumentative essays that really have no effect. What is the point of thinking that I am right and you are wrong? How persuasive, if ever, is such a strategy?

When poorly constructed, such a strategy fails. Even when well constructed, such constructs are not arguments since the only audience that will be moved to agree are those who already agree. The audience of opposition simply maintains its anger. Such essays become ineffective rants.

In actuality, we are merely writing to an audience that already agrees with us. We are not really trying to persuade anyone but ourselves and that is not what an argument is supposed to do.

Conspiracy theories, though they may try to be reasonable in tone, often fall into this trap and become ineffective and emotional, although sometimes entertaining, rants.

Break the Spell

Let's approach gaming and writing in a non zero-sum manner. With issues being often more complex than presented, we need to return to a purer way of gaming and writing. We need to possess the original game face instead of being pulled into the prefabricated poser dogmatic faces. We need to have a beginner's mind. As we reframe issues, let's visit more game theories.

Ready to play?

John Nash and Gaming

John Nash, a famous mathematician, felt that in the real world, with more than two players, cooperation was key to make bargaining or life work. Nash explored the possibility of non zero-sum gaming. He wrote his 27-page dissertation on the "Nash Equilibrium" about strategic non-cooperative games. The number of players can be unlimited as this simulates events in our lives. To understand this more, let's examine the stag hunt scenario.

The Stag Hunt

Jean-Jacques Rousseau (1712-1778) used this game to ask a question about choice: imagine two people entering into a hunt for a stag. If successful, the payoff is greater for the lone hunter. However, the risk of failure is also greater. If the two hunters cooperate, they have a better chance to succeed even though the payoff is less.

The risk factor is balanced against the payoff factor. With cooperation, the social factor is emphasized. Both win and both eat. Interdependency becomes a vital part of gaming. What will it take to win? Whatever will work! Cooperation works best.

Instead of winner take all, the Stag Hunt shows that through cooperation, we both win. Our odds increase and the payoff is greater. Look at the Chicken Fight as Game of Mutual Mass Destruction; the end result is that we all lose.

Gaming into Writing: Enhancing Communicative Learning

For these adventures, you will work in groups of at least three to five members. Working in groups, you will have to perform in a "spontaneous" debate or a series of simulations over a given topic or various topics. This interaction is a form of cooperative learning.

Writing is a great way to come to know your subject. Writing can stimulate your mind as a way to maintain information better, which is more effective than just reading or memorizing. Because writing is a process and takes time, you come to know the topic in a deeper way and start to understand the complexities better. You have to interact with the information. You become better prepared for your simulations and will feel more relaxed about doing them. Thus, the research paper can be part of the pre-simulation or post-simulation activities.

What is my next move? How can I make my paper better?

Decision Making: Adjusting to Audiences

We, as writers, often have to imagine audiences. We don't have a strong sense of why a paper works well or is weak because we don't get a chance to test it orally with a real audience. What moves the audience?

Peer review sessions can seem pointless because we can disagree with what our peers think. Even as we increase our attention to the writing process with its rhetorical features, writing can become a bit too formulaic or out of touch. What is post-process—what happens after the initial writing is completed?

When we write an argument paper, we really need to hear the oppositional voices aloud. Otherwise, we tend to think of argument as nothing more than a highly defined series of logical explanations. However, even if we do our research, just presenting evidence with facts and data might not be enough.

A successful argument needs other elements to be effective. Without testing the effect that such reasoning might have, we may not know what will work. Gaming involves a variety of cognitive processes and integrates research, opposing viewpoints, and the testing of the argument's effectiveness.

Generating a Sense of Success within the Gaming Situation

Gaming allows us to test our hunches in the arena of play. Winning is not so much the point as is seeing how our text interacts or moves the gamers. When we play, we constantly re-adjust to the rhetorical gaming situation. By gaming more, we learn to understand the power of the probabilities offered in the game world.

Learning to write an effective argument paper presents special problems. Lawyers often create mock trial situations to plan for a real defense.

Performance becomes a key way to test ideas and rethink the issues. People in general often fear public speaking, so combining speech and writing alone may not work for many people. Gaming attacks the fear factor of speaking by making speaking fun.

Gaming is performance. For our purposes, game playing can re-invigorate the writer/player to notice rhetorical strategies that might have been missed in a regular approach to writing.

Gaming as Persuasion: A New Approach to Writing

Gaming theory allows you to regain a sense of audience, feedback, and interaction with others. This offers a new way to approach writing. You can become a player or character trying to predict the outcome of your next rhetorical move, and as you try to predict what others will do, your writing mind is activated as a gaming mind within the strategies of engagement.

The rhetorical act becomes alive within the contested battles of moves, counter-moves, and surprises. It becomes meaningful, complex, and invigorating!

Learning to learn is what gaming is about.

Gaming theory thrives within the realm of rhetoric. Rhetoric, the art of persuasion, is definitely about bargaining and negotiating. Games remain rhetorical in nature. Indeed, games are restricted, purely imagined rhetorical situations where the relationship between the audience, speaker, and the text are usually defined by its rules. On a larger scale, life is a game with a set of social rules that we live within. As in a game, you will do well by knowing the rules and learning life skills (strategies) to survive. Apply the "Nash Equilibrium" by thinking of games as cooperative events instead of competitive endeavors.

Appeals as Gaming Moves: Ask the Right Question

In any gaming situation, you must know how the Gaming Appeals apply. If the appeals are constructed correctly, the game will work well.

Game Moves

Balancing the appeals is the key to having harmony within a game or text.

Moves of Logos

Are the rules logical and simple?
What is the background?
How do the players seem logical?

Moves of Ethos

Do the players seem real to the audience?
What are some character flaws?
How do the players present themselves?

Moves of Pathos

Does the game have human aspirations?
How is humor a part of the game?
Is the game emotionally engaging?
Is the game fun?

On-Line Video Games

Combine the richness of video games and the interactive features of the Internet, and you have some players addicted to these communal cult-like activities, which continue to evolve.

World of Warcraft (WoW)
(www.warcraft.com, wikie: wowwiki.com)

The most successful and most popular massively multiplayer on-line role-playing game (MMORPG) is WoW, which was released in an earlier format in 1994. It has become an industry of its own.

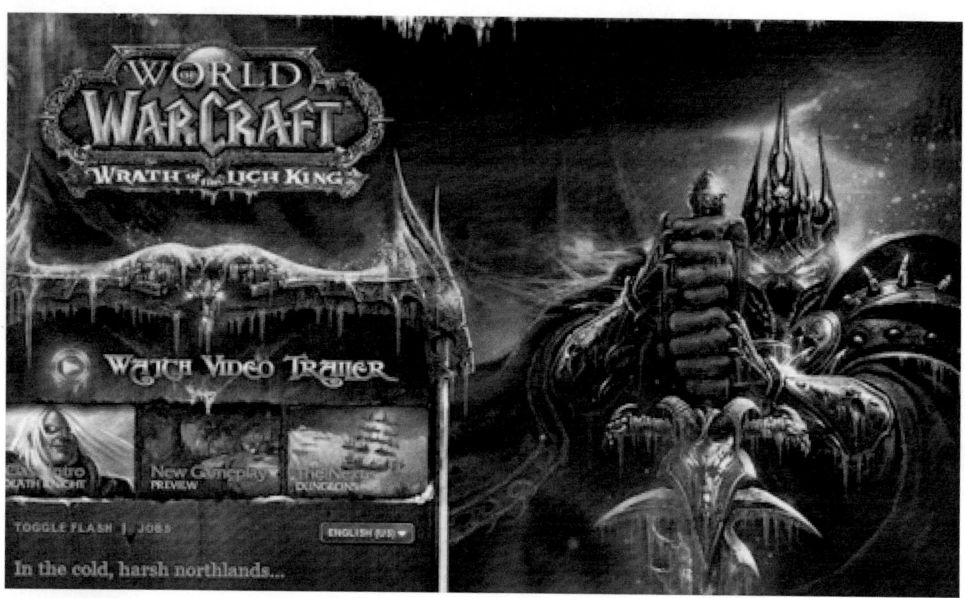

WoW was influenced by Dungeons and Dragons with its player characters (PCs) and its non-player characters (NPCs). In this fantasy realm, players become PCs and are part of a class system as they go through a series of adventures, duels, battles, and quests. True gamers will buy a special World of Warcraft keyboard. Be warned, it becomes highly addictive and expensive if you buy various extras that enhance the game.

EverQuest (EQ) (everquest.com)

EQ, a MMORPG, was released in 1999 by Sony Online Entertainment. The game, like World of Warcraft, was influenced by Dungeons and Dragons, the paper role-playing game.

Players become avatars like dwarfs, ogres, wizards, and clerics. Such avatars belong to certain classes of people who interact in a variety of battles, quests, and challenges. They search for rewards and experience points.

WOW AND EQ EXERCISE:

Both WoW and EQ allow new players to join temporarily for free. Join one or both and play for about a week, then answer the following questions:

- Why do you think that such fantasy games are so addictive or popular?
- Share with us some of the adventures you had.
- What do such games tell us about our society?
- Can such games be used for education? How?
- What can we learn from playing such games?
- Would playing such a game cause someone who is unstable to become violent in real life?

Video Games

Video games continue to be popular though games like Halo 3 also have Web sites that allow for interaction between players for a monthly fee although some players are able to create their own networks and play games like Halo 3 without using the Microsoft site

Halo 3 and Xbox 360

Without this first-person shooter science fiction video game, Microsoft and its Xbox would not be as popular as it has become. The United Space Command of the future, the 26th century, is fighting a war against various aliens, who fight under the command of the Covenant. What makes the game so popular is the multiplayer format, where many fighters can enter a battle either united or against each other. Indeed, there are Halo tournaments across the country on every campus.

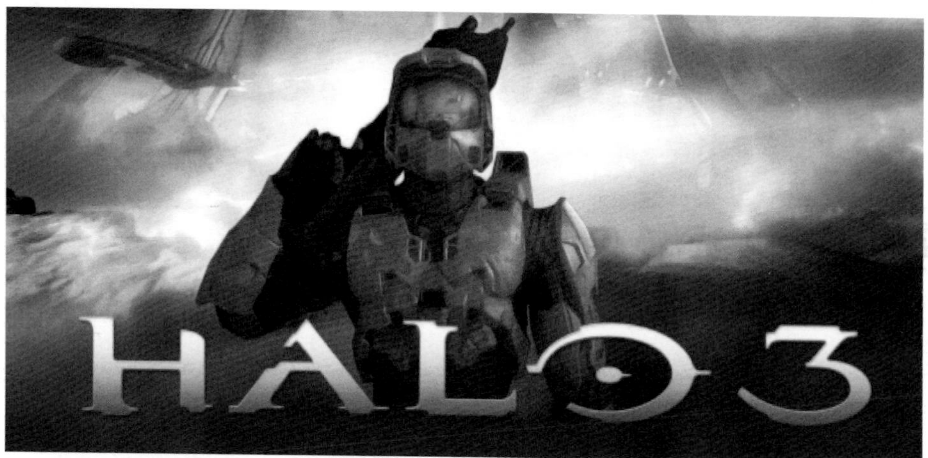

The first version of Halo was released in 2001. With each generation, the game becomes more cinematic, and indeed, fans create their own short films by capturing scenes from the game, redubbing them, and adding music. Perhaps because of the violent nature of the game, Halo 3 remains more popular with males. Halo is also on-line in Xbox Live.

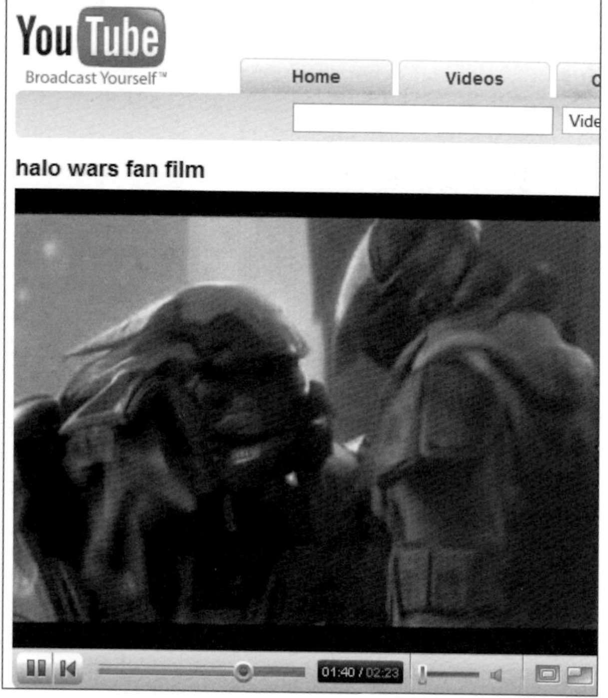

Fan films about Halo have become very popular. Indeed, Microsoft encourages this method of expression and even provides tips on how to create them.

HALO 3 EXERCISE:

Go to YouTube.com and watch a variety of Halo 3 fan films, and note how narration, music, and images are utilized. Some fan films are simply music videos. Identify a fan film you like and answer the following questions:

1. What is the name of the fan film?
2. How did the author/s use narration in the clip?
3. Why did you like it?
4. What are some weaknesses or ways to improve the clip?

Guitar Hero III: Legends of Rock

What happens when you mix the movements and creativity of air guitar, where performers pretend to be rock stars, and a gaming system? Guitar Hero, developed in 2005, has become a megahit with teenagers and college students.

As Hip Hop continues to be so popular, GH3 is helping to revive interest in the older rock classics for a new generation. Players can even download new songs online every month. The game is popular with both males and females.

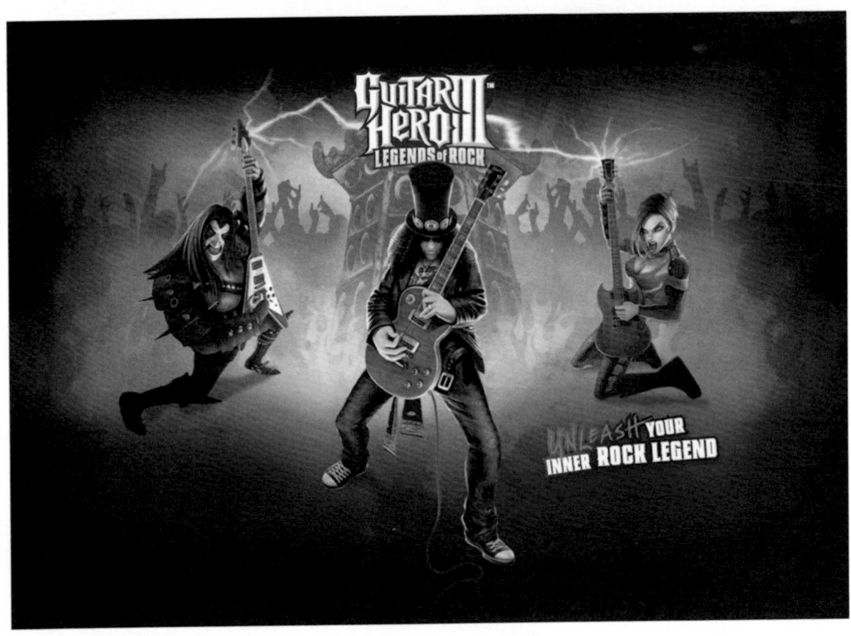

Perhaps it has become so popular because unlike air guitar contests which were performed in front of audiences, Guitar Hero III players become immersed in the virtual game without worrying about any audience that may be looking at them from behind, therefore avoiding stage fright. The players watch the video screen and concentrate on hitting the right notes at the right time, thus staying engaged while earning points.

One of the big reasons for its success is the guitar controller that allows players to strum to the beat.

Rock Band

Rock Band, a different music video game, goes one step further than Guitar Hero by allowing up to four players with its microphones, drum set, bass guitar, and regular electric guitar.

WOVE Features of Guitar Hero III and Rock Band:

Written. Read the written lyrics when you rock out.
Oral. Listen to music, and try to sing if you are the singer.
Visual. Pick a provocative avatar and immerse yourself in the audience.
Electronic. Experience the power and fame of being a star in a rock concert.

GUITAR HERO III AND ROCK BAND EXERCISE:

If you have not played Guitar Hero III or Rock Band, find someone who has it. It shouldn't be hard. Then play it. Answer the following questions:

1. Why is Guitar Hero III or Rock Band so popular?
2. Why is it so different from games like Halo 3 or World of Warcraft?
3. How does the game use ethos?
4. What did you like about playing it?

Wii: Super Mario

Just as sales for Nintendo games, especially GameCube, seemed to level off and lose to Xbox 360, Nintendo reinvented the video game with Wii in 2006. The innovation is in the virtual wireless consoles, where the movements of the players become the movements of the avatars in the game. This revolution in gaming is outselling Xbox 360 and Playstation 3. Wii versions of SuperMario are quite popular as participants go through various obstacles, races, or fights to gain points.

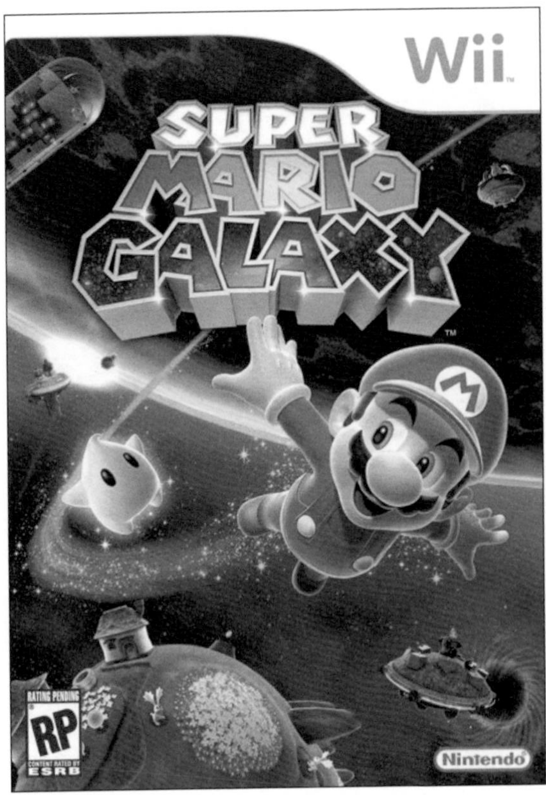

Perhaps one of the reasons for the sales is that Wii is more inclusive of the general public. The games it has created can be played by a large demographic. Super Mario games like Galaxy can be played with the entire family.

WII EXERCISE:

If you have not played a Wii, find someone who has it. Then play. Answer the following questions:

1. What Wii game did you play?
2. Why are Wii games so popular?
3. Why is it so different from gaming systems like Xbox 360 and Playstation 3?
4. How does the game use your movements?
5. Was the game fun? Do you want to play more?

Researching Arguments

Chapter 8 . . . The Research Paper

Chapter 9 . . . Research Strategies

Chapter 10 . . . MLA Documentation Format

Chapter 11 . . . APA Documentation Format

"I Used to Hate Writing"

by Bill Watterson from Calvin and Hobbes

AFTER YOU READ: Analyze the Issues

1. What idea about writing has Calvin internalized?
2. Why has this idea developed? Do you think "good" writing is hard to understand?

AFTER YOU READ: Analyze the Rhetoric

1. What is "funny" about the title of Calvin's paper? How many of the words did you not understand? Was it the individual words or the way they were strung together that led to a lack of meaning?
2. Does this cartoon use logos, ethos, or pathos?
3. How do the images contribute to the humor?

Multitasking: Two Assignments as One

When you are assigned a research paper, you are actually given two assignments: a writing assignment and a research assignment. To complete the writing assignment successfully, you will need to remember all of the steps of the writing process and all the techniques of successfully convincing your audience to agree with the position that you will present.

Research papers, like any good piece of argumentative writing, will have several parts:

- an introduction,
- detailed body paragraphs,
- a refutation, and
- a conclusion.

To complicate the process that you hopefully have become familiar with, a research paper adds a critical thinking component—you must present other scholars' research and ideas to build a frame for your ideas. Therefore, your second assignment is finding appropriate articles, books, web sources, and video pieces that will support your point of view. Thus an additional part of a research paper is the Bibliography (MLA: Works Cited; APA: References).

> MLA (Modern Language Association)
> Founded in 1883, a scholarly organization that promotes an annual conference, an extensive bibliography and a style manual.
>
> APA (American Psychological Association)
> Founded 1892, a scientific and professional organization that created its own style manual.

If you have done a documented essay, then you might be familiar with this element. However in a research paper, the Works Cited page is critical because it provides your reader with a complete listing of the sources you have used in your paper.

Organizing the Argument

Before you begin looking for sources, you should have a clear idea of the claim and main points you will be working to support.

Note: Don't make the mistake of finding sources and then putting together your paper by citing one source after another with only brief transitions in between.

This method leads to what teachers call a "cut and paste" paper where your ideas are either lost or minimally presented, or worse it leads to unintentional plagiarism.

To avoid the "cut and paste" syndrome, create the bones of your paper before you begin researching. Follow the steps outlined in the "Creating Written Arguments" section and finish a rough draft of your argument before you ever look for sources.

- Make sure you have a claim that is arguable.
- Outline your main arguments making sure that you explore possible **ethos, logos** and **pathos** arguments.
- Outline your refutation. What do you think are the main points of your opposition? How do you think you will refute them?
- Think out your introduction and conclusion. Note what strategies you will use for each of these important sections.

A rough draft will help you make the best use of your research time because you will know exactly what types of sources you will need.

For example,

Your topic is the environment. You narrow your topic to air pollution. You develop the following elements.

Your claim:

Air quality can be improved by more extensive use of bio-diesel fuel and hybrid cars.

Your warrant:

Car emissions contribute significantly to air pollution.

There are many types of sources that you could find to support your claim. A **logos** source might be a scientific report on car emissions. An **ethos** source might be an article by a high profile scientist, or a well-known public figure. A **pathos** argument might be an article that describes what our world will be like if air pollution isn't stopped.

SOURCES EXERCISE:

What types of sources do you need to find if your claim is "Air quality can be improved by the United States enforcing stricter environmental policies in trade agreements"?

1. For **ethos** arguments:
2. For **logos** arguments:
3. For **pathos** arguments:
4. To find out what your opposition is saying:

Now that you know what types of sources you will be looking for you need to create a research timeline to make sure that you will meet all your deadlines.

The Sentence Outline: An Organizing Tool

Sometimes before you write a full rough draft, creating a sentence outline will help you get your arguments together. Moving, cutting, and adding information is easier when you are dealing with sentences rather than paragraphs. Sentence outlines require that you not only identify your argumnts by topic, but also create the topic sentence that will guide you as you build your paragraphs. Thus, this type of outlining will help you identify any flaws in your arguments so that you can correct them before drafting.

Some instructors always require outlines so that they can review the structure of your argument before you begin writing; others assign them so that you can practice organization. Whether your instructor requires one or not, you might create an outline to help you organize your arguments before you begin to collect sources.

Note: You may use Classical, Toulmin, or Rogerian organization. This sample uses Classical arrangement:

> **Topic**: *Does watching violent video games cause teenage violence?*
> **Issue:** *What is the quality of the act? (Stasis theory question)*
> **Claim:** *Watching violent video games does not cause teenage violence.*

Below is a sample sentence outline. Your instructor may give you different instructions as to the content required for each element of the sentence outline. This example notes the type of argument and gives a summary of the argument.

Sample Sentence Outline

Title: Violence and Video Games: Making the Case for a Connection

I. Introduction: I will provide examples of teenagers who play violent video games and have been recognized for community service and/or volunteerism.

II. Statement of Fact: Watching violent video games does not cause teenage violence.

III. Evidence:
  - **a. Logos**—Provide the number of games sold a year/number of crimes committed by teenagers who use the violent video game defense and the legal precedent and case law which states that exposure to violence in a video game is less a predictor of teenage violence than exposure to physical abuse within the family unit. The nature of the violence can be a predictor, but it is being a victim of violence that is the true predictor, not the acting out of violence in a game.
  - **b. Ethos**—Use expert testimony and published findings that state that acting out the violence through video games is actually cathartic making teenagers less likely to be violent in real life.
  - **c. Pathos**—Compare violence in video games with violence in "slasher" movies to show that the nature of the violence is the same.

IV. Refutation:
  - a. There have been cases of teens imitating violence they played on video games but these teens have had severe psychological problems and thus the video games should not be considered the "cause" of the violence.
  - b. There is some evidence that a teen who is "saturated" with violence from playing video games could become angry and aggressive, but it is the quantity of exposure not the exposure itself that is the problem.

V. Conclusion: Call for Action. The nature of the violence in video games nor the fact that teenagers "act out" violence when playing the games is proven to cause teenagers to become violent. We should take action to educate parents about limiting the number of hours a teen plays such games and about the warning signs that a teen might be at risk for developing problems, but we should not ban games because of the false fear of these games causing the average teenager to become violent.

Sentence Outline Form

Name________________________ Date ________________________

Title: ________________________

____

Introduction: ________________________

____

Statement of Fact: ________________________

____

Evidence for Body Paragraphs:

Logos:________________________

____

Ethos:________________________

____

Pathos: ________________________

____

Refutation:________________________

____

Conclusion: ________________________

____

Organizing Research: Research Timeline

Research takes time. You need to set aside time to find sources, review those sources, and probably to find additional sources. A great time management tool is a research timeline.

You will find a sample research timeline on the next page. You should start with the due date of your final draft and work backward in time. Don't forget to allow yourself time to revise and proofread. Make sure that all parts of the assignment are included in your timeline. For example, if your teacher requires a working bibliography, it should appear as an item on your timeline.

In addition to the research timeline, you will need a system for keeping track of what databases you have searched, what search terms you have used, what sources you have requested, what you will look for next and what you have already discarded. The more research papers you write, the more refined your system will become and the more effective and efficient your process will become.

- **Complete a library orientation**. Most university libraries provide an orientation session, which teaches students how to use the various search engines and databases that the library subscribes to. Many libraries provide an on-line version of this orientation. Take advantage of an orientation and you will save yourself hours of frustration trying to figure out how your library's search engines work. This step is particularly important if your teacher wants you to use academic/scholarly sources.
- **Make a list of possible databases to search.** After you complete a library orientation, make a list of the databases you think will be best suited to your topic and claim. Keep in mind the requirements of your assignment. If your teacher wants you to use a variety of sources, make sure you include a search of your library's book catalog or *WorldCat,* a global search engine. If your teacher has said no internet sources, don't put Wikipedia on your list or use Google to search.
- **Keep a search log**. Designate a place in your course notebook as your search log. As you search for sources, write down which database you are searching, and note your search terms. If you write down your search terms, you can take your notes to a reference librarian, or e-mail them to your professor to get advice about more effective terms or sources. Also note what results you get. For example, did you get 1200 articles but none of them were really on your topic, or did you get 2 articles that were exactly what you were looking for? This information will help you know which terms to retry in other databases and which ones are useless.
- **Keep track of sources you have requested**. It is not unusual for a library not to have all the sources that look like they might be helpful. Interlibrary loan is a quick and easy way to obtain sources that exist in other libraries. When you

order a book or article, either print out your request, or make a note in your search log of what you have ordered and the date you ordered it. Keeping track of your requests will keep you from ordering the same sources over and over. You can also keep track of when items arrive so that you know when everything has arrived. Check your e-mail frequently since many articles will be sent as full text Adobe Acrobat files to your e-mail address. If you do not have Acrobat Reader on your computer, there is a free software download available.

- **Make notes about your sources to create the next search stage**. If you find a great source, make note of it. Signal yourself to find the sources listed in its bibliography or works cited page. Also write down the author's name so that you can search for other works by that author. Both of these search strategies will save you time and effort.
- **Write down sources you have discarded and why**. Nothing is more frustrating than picking up the same unusable article or book chapter over and over. Keep a list of articles you will not be using and note why they weren't helpful to you.
- **Note articles that present the opposite point of view**. You always need to keep an eye out for sources that you can use in your refutation. Write down the citation of these sources and what arguments they present. When you get ready to write this part of your paper, you will have already identified sources to quote.

Sample Research Timeline Form

Name______________________________ Assignment Due Date: ______________

Topic______________________________

Finish By

1. Decide on your claim and create rough draft ____________
2. Make a list of types of sources to look for ____________
3. Complete a library orientation ____________
4. Complete a preliminary search ____________
5. Request interlibrary loan items ____________
6. Complete working bibliography ____________
7. Complete annotated articles ____________
8. Add sources to first draft ____________
9. Revise and check in-page citation format ____________
10. Create Works Cited page ____________
11. Turn in final draft ____________

An Organizing Tool: A Working Bibliography

A **working bibliography** is a list of potential **sources** which you collect as you research. You will not include all of the sources from your working bibliography in your Works Cited page. Generally a working bibliography serves three functions:

> **Working Bibliography**
> A gathering of potential resources that a writer or speaker may use for a paper. Such a bibliography should have quality sources along with a larger quantity of sources or resources than are needed since many sources end up being un-useful to the paper. Developing a good working bibliography allows a writer to map out the research process and ascertain if more research is necessary.
>
> **Source**
> The original document, person, or reference that a passage or idea is derived from when you are writing, speaking or creating a work.

Recording Bibliographic Information

It helps you keep a record of the bibliographic information for the sources that you think have potential for your research. Nothing is more frustrating than to begin incorporating sources into your writing only to discover that you do not have the bibliographic information necessary to cite your source or to complete the Works Cited page. Going back to the electronic database or the library to track down this information wastes valuable revising time. As you find a source, take a couple of minutes to record as much bibliographic information as you can. Specifically you will need information about

1. the author(s)
2. the title(s)
3. how and/or where and/or by whom the source was published or disseminated
4. page numbers
5. date you found the source (especially important for on-line sources)

Be sure to have your documentation style sheet handy. This book gives you examples of MLA and APA style, but your instructor might want you to use another style (CMS, CSE or CGOS). Before you leave a source, look up the documentation model for that type of source and make sure you have all of the necessary information.

Information to include in citations:

Books—author's last name, first name, title, city of publication, publisher, copyright year
Articles—author's last name, first name, title, title of periodical, date of publication, volume and issue numbers, page numbers of article

On-line—author's last name, first name, title, name of database, name of Web site's sponsor, date of last revision, date you accessed the information, URL

Checking for Variety of Sources

As you collect sources, it is often difficult to see the big picture of the variety and authority of your sources because you are absorbed in what each source offers you in support for your argument. A well researched argument will use a variety of sources—books, academic journals, primary sources, secondary sources, popular magazines, TV programs, films, documentaries, etc. A working bibliography provides you a way of looking specifically at the list of sources to evaluate whether you have a variety of source material. If you have used chapters from 10 books, you will probably need to look for academic or popular articles or Web sites that will contain very recent information. A lot can happen in one year—the typical amount of time it takes for a book to go from manuscript to publication. In addition, if you have an abundance of on-line Web sites, you probably want to add some books and articles to your list.

Note: be sure to check your assignment guidelines as to how many and what kind of sources your instructor wants you to use.

Providing a Brief Summary about Your Source

A working bibliography is a perfect place to record information about the sources you are finding. It helps you keep your notes about what information is in a source, which side of the issue it is on, and where you found the source. Some instructors require students to compile an **annotated working bibliography**. In addition to the citation information, an annotated working bibliography usually includes at least a summary of the source, and sometimes an evaluation of the arguments in the source. Even if your instructor does not require this additional information, keep it for your own use as you work through your research process.

Using and Documenting Sources Properly

Why use Sources in your Paper?

When you write to persuade or to present a new interpretation of an event or issue, you will often use the words and ideas of others to support your main points. Even experts writing to experts will review the work of other researchers and writers before presenting their own ideas. Why?

To Establish a Sense of Ethos

To acknowledge the work of others. It is important that a writer present an ethos of reason and respect. When you acknowledge the work of others in the field, you are letting your audience know that you have read deeply in your subject area and have an opinion based on knowledge, not guess work. In fact, professionals in every field are very careful to show how their ideas relate to the ideas of others. A professional's reputation is on the line when he/she presents material and claims it is original.

To support the writer's ethos. Sometimes a writer might not be an expert in the field in which he/she is writing. For example, as a student, you will not be an expert in most of the fields in which you will be asked to write research papers. You can compensate for not being an acknowledged expert by citing the work of experts. Audiences are willing to listen to new ideas from non-experts if it is clear that work by experts in the field would support the idea.

To Construct Logos *Arguments*

Deductive arguments rely on facts and statistics to be successful. As you construct your research paper, you will need to find sources that contain very specific facts and pieces of data to construct your major and minor premises. Good writers find and acknowledge these sources of information to give their arguments persuasive detail.

Inductive arguments rely on examples to be successful. Popular and academic articles which provide good examples must be cited. If you are going to reference a TV news program or fictional sit-com, you must cite the program.

To Create a Sense of Pathos

Sometimes one of the examples you discover not only provides an important point in your logical argument, but creates emotion in your reader. Facts and statistics can create emotional moments also. As you research your topic, look for sources that can create in your reader an emotion that will help them see your side of the issue.

How Should You Use Sources in Your Paper?

1. Maintain your voice.
   The first, and most important, thing to remember is that it is YOUR paper, not a series of quotes and paraphrases from other sources. There should

always be more of your words than borrowed words in your work. The argument should be your argument, the idea, your idea; your work is supported by the work of others but is not just a compilation of others' ideas.

2. Choose elements that support your points.
   The quotes and paraphrases you use should contribute to the argument. Students sometimes get in a rush and quote any bit of material that they think sounds good. However, if the quote or paraphrase doesn't add to the reader's understanding of the argument or research, it is useless to the writer. In fact, it weakens the writer's work because readers are very good at finding "fluff."

3. Integrate your sources.
   Your sources should be seamlessly integrated into your work, not just stuck in to meet a requirement. Your readers should not have to stop reading because they don't understand a quote or paraphrase. If the wording is awkward or the verb tenses don't agree, readers stop reading to try to figure out what is "wrong" with the sentence or paragraph. You want the readers to be following your ideas, not working out your grammar issues. In the section below, you will be given some ideas about how to integrate sources seamlessly into your own words.

4. Be accurate.
   You should quote your sources so that you accurately represent the opinions and work of the original author. Resist the temptation to "twist" another author's words so that they appear to be supporting your point of view. Readers, particularly those who know something about your topic, will know you have misrepresented someone else's point of view and not see you as a reliable source of information. Your argument and ideas will not be seen as valid.

What Material Do You Need to Cite?

Any material that is original or unique must be properly cited. If you borrow someone's idea or words, you MUST cite the source or you have committed plagiarism. Below are some guidelines on what material must be cited:

1. **Facts do not need to be cited**. A fact is something verifiable. For example, someone's date of birth, the date of an event, or the place an event happened can all be verified and will be the same in every source you see. If there is controversy about something then the version you choose will need to be cited. For example, if one source says that an event happened at 10:00 a.m. on December 11, 2006 and a different source says it happened at 12:00 p.m. on December 13, 2006 then you will need to pick which source you think is most authoritative and cite the material. However, if every source you read states that the event

happened at 11:00 a.m. on December 12, 2006 then you can consider the time and date a fact and do not need to cite it.

2. **Opinions need to be cited**. Everyone has an interpretation of events. Scientific experiments can be interpreted differently. Opinions about how something happened or the meaning of something is not a fact that can be verified. When you "borrow" someone's interpretation or opinion you must give him/her credit for the idea. The material must be cited properly.
3. **Unique or new ideas, even if they might be considered a fact, must be cited.** Use what is called the rule of **common knowledge**. If an idea is so well known that you knew about it before you began researching, and if you believe most of the population understands the idea, then it might be common knowledge and doesn't need to be cited. For example, most people understand what germs are and that they can make us sick, but most people would not know exactly how a germ works. That germs can make us sick is common knowledge and doesn't need to be cited; the process of exactly how germs make us sick would need to be cited, even though it might be factual.

Ways to Avoid Plagiarism

The best way to avoid **plagiarism** is to write a complete **rough draft** before you begin researching sources. The rough draft can then serve as a touchstone throughout your writing and revising process. If it was in the rough draft that you created before researching, you can be pretty sure it is your idea and your words. Anything that does not appear in that rough draft should be carefully checked and cited properly.

> Plagiarism
> The intentional or unintentional copying of text or ideas from another person or source and presenting them without due credit.

Remember that even if you use one sentence from a source it must be cited. In some cases, **even distinctive phrases must be cited**. If you "borrow" someone's words because "they've written it really well," or "you like the way they phrased it" then you need to give proper credit to that author. Many plagiarism detection software programs such as Turnitin.com® will mark passages as short as three words as plagiarism.

Changing a few words in the sentence or paragraph does not make the material "yours." Students often think that if they "change every third word" or "every big word" then they have avoided plagiarizing. However, all you've done is change the wording of the idea. Plagiarizing the idea carries the same penalty as plagiarizing someone's words.

The best way to avoid this type of plagiarism is to **never write what you intend to be your ideas and words while you are looking at your sources.** Put your sources in a drawer and then write out what you are trying to say. If your passage is still close to the original source, cite the material.

As you proofread, make sure that readers can **clearly identify the beginning and ending of every summary, quote, and paraphrase.** Readers will NOT assume your borrowed material begins at the beginning of the paragraph or the beginning of the new sentence. It is your job to make the beginning clear to them. In addition, make sure that the reader clearly sees the end of the borrowed material. Too often students don't put ending quotation marks or in-page citations at the end of material because they want to go back to their source material and check something. They think,"I'll put that in when I revise," but then it just doesn't get added and the result is unintentional plagiarism.

When in doubt, cite the source. If you are not sure something could be considered common knowledge, cite it. No penalty attaches for over citing sources.

Your instructor can serve as a great reference person, so don't hesitate to ask if something needs to be cited. Take the original source and your text so that he/she can make an informed judgment.

"Honey"

by Travis Kelly

http://www.traviskelly.com/cartoon/editor.html

AFTER YOU READ: Analyze the Issues

1. Why are bees important to the ecology?
2. What is the message?
3. How would you do a search to determine the real facts behind this cartoon?
4. Do you think this message about bees might be true? Or do you disagree?

AFTER YOU READ: Analyze the Rhetoric

1. Who is the audience?
2. Though the bee population is decreasing, what other factors might be killing bees?
3. How effective is the humor in the cartoon?

Library Research

Library research is essential to formulating and writing a successful research paper. Some students find research about as interesting as reading the phone book. Others enjoy it, finding it as challenging as a game of poker—when to hold, and when to lay 'em down.

What all students come to realize is that research skills eventually become life skills. When you must know the side effects of a prescription drug, the laws regarding child custody, or the way to rebuild a transmission, you will be armed with the confidence and the know-how to find the information you need.

This chapter introduces strategies for research, making this increasingly complex world of information respond to reason and to human need.

This chapter discusses:

- How to choose an information source based on information need
- How to focus a topic

Check vocabulary boxes as you read if you come across an unfamiliar term.

Bibliography
A list of sources an author used when writing a book, article or essay, found at the end of written works.

Format
The form in which information is presented, such as a book, CD, computer file, or journal.

Information Source
A material beyond one's own thoughts in nearly any format from book to Web site.

Journal
Mostly scholarly periodicals but sometimes magazines and newspapers.

Reference Work
Works with brief overviews of a topic, key ideas, important concepts, or tables of primary information.

Searching within Electronic Databases: The Big Picture

Information sources are available in many **formats,** and choosing among them is a daunting task. However, you can simplify research by realizing that the sources you consult depend heavily on what kind of information you need to find.

For example,

Use:	**For:**	**But Not For:**
Books	In-depth analysis and discussion; history and background **Example:** History of photography	Events occurring in the last few months; recent research
Magazines, Newspapers, News Web sites	Current events; non-technical analysis; brief overviews **Example:** Popular articles or information on dating	In depth analysis, scholarly research, historical discussion, **bibliographies**
Journals	Scholarly research on particular aspects of a topic; in-depth analysis; bibliographies **Example:** Research on carbon dating	General overviews, historical background
Reference works	Brief facts, key ideas, dates, general overviews, bibliographies **Example:** An overview of how a vaccine works	In-depth analysis, recent research, current events
Government information	Statistics, government sponsored research and reports, primary sources **Example:** Statistics on employment by state	Appropriate for all types of research needs; use in conjunction with other sources

Sources vary most in their timeliness, depth of detail, and reliability. The above table illustrates the type of information found in different source formats. You'll have trouble, for example, finding books on an event that happened a few days ago, but you should find many relevant articles in magazines, newspapers, or on Web sites. You might have difficulty finding in-depth analysis of an historical event on a Web site, but you should find many books and journal articles on the topic. To find the sources themselves, start by going to the library.

Research in the Library or on the Web: What's the Difference?

"Visible," or free Web sites, located with popular searching tools like Google or Hotbot, offer readily available and numerous results. Free Web sites are useful for current news and for general information of the type found in a brochure. However, free Web sites have pitfalls.

> **Visible or Public Web Sites**
> Web sites accessed for free using search engines such as Google.

Free Web sites:

- Are often lightweight, repetitive, and unreliable
- Require extensive evaluation since the internet has no standardized quality control
- Are impermanent and change frequently, making returning to a source difficult or impossible
- Are inefficient to search because the searching tools are weak

A library's primary function is to organize information for easy retrieval, making the library a better starting point for finding the most useful sources quickly. The library has other advantages:

- Libraries select authoritative, reliable, and relevant resources.
- Libraries subscribe to many resources that are free for students or registered patrons to use.
- Libraries have friendly professionals trained in searching for sources.
- Libraries have permanent collections that do not disappear as Web sites often do.

> **Invisible Web Sites**
> Web sites with restricted access, usually requiring a subscription; not searchable with public web searching tools.

Most libraries have extensive Web sources that are part of the **"invisible" Web.** These invisible, subscription-based sources do not appear in searches using the tools of the free Web. Instead, you go to the library's Web site to search for them. You have access to these sources as a student of the university you attend. Library sources are often more reliable than sources found on the visible Web, and the tools available for searching are more powerful. Starting your research at the library or at the library's Web site gives immediate access to reliable, stable, and more in-depth sources.

NOTE: As a rule of thumb, the more detailed or scholarly your research the less you should rely on visible Web sources.

Evaluating Resources

Any source you consider must undergo an evaluation process. While most library sources are reliable, you should evaluate them. Some sources contain biased or inaccurate information regardless of whether you access them through the visible Web or through the library. Free Web sites need more evaluation than others.

Consider the following criteria for any source, particularly any source from the visible Web:

Accuracy	Are the facts verifiable? Where did the author get his/her information? Could you find it yourself?
Authority	Who is the author or Web site sponsor? What makes you trust this author?
Currency	When was the source created or published? If a Web site, is it updated regularly?
Objectivity	Are there logical errors such as biased viewpoint, lack of alternative explanations, generalizations, or personal attack?
Usefulness	Is the information sufficiently detailed and relevant?

Sources meeting these criteria are worthy of consideration for your information need.

Focusing a Topic

Students often start looking for information on topics that are too large to manage in the short space of a composition paper. Human cloning, the death penalty, and steroid use are typical examples of topics so large that you could write books about them rather than papers. Concentrating on one issue within a topic, or focusing, allows you to select and reject resources depending on whether or not they address the elements of the chosen topic.

One method for narrowing a topic is to start with a general topic and think about specific issues associated with that topic. Here are examples of issues associated with the broad topic of human cloning:

You could focus on one of these issues and select only sources dealing exclusively with that issue. A good strategy is to compose a question about the topic, such as this one:

> What are the ethical issues of human cloning in medicine?

This topic combines two of the issues listed above, cloning ethics and the use of cloning in medical treatment.

Other methods exist for deciding on and narrowing a topic. You might consult an encyclopedia, a news related Web site, or a popular magazine. These sources might suggest an interesting issue within the topic on which to focus your research.

Keyword Searching with Boolean Logic

You are now ready to begin searching for sources, and you will probably start your search in a library **database.** Databases vary widely in the sources and subject matter they cover, but they all tend to use similar searching techniques, called Boolean Logic. Based on the theories of mathematician George Boole, the effective elements of **Boolean Logic** are Boolean **Operators** and **Nested Searching**.

You can see how they function using the following sample topic:

Database
An on-line index of articles, books, Web sites, or other media.

Boolean Logic
Developed by George Boole (1815-1864), a way to organize library searches.

Operators
Words used to connect ideas in Boolean Logic; **and**, **or**, and **not** are common.

Nested Searching
Used in libraries or online queries, are provisions and/or phrases combined together in specific correlations using parentheses, quotation marks, and/or other symbols in order to make searches more effective.

What are the ethical issues of human cloning in medicine?

The following sections demonstrate how Boolean Logic works in conjunction with another searching strategy, **Truncation**.

Boolean Operators

The actual "operators" or connectors in Boolean Logic are the words **and**, **or**, and **not**. Combining these words with relevant keywords in a database retrieves relevant results. The above topic's main ideas are **human cloning** and **ethics** and **medicine**. A database search using these words looks like this:

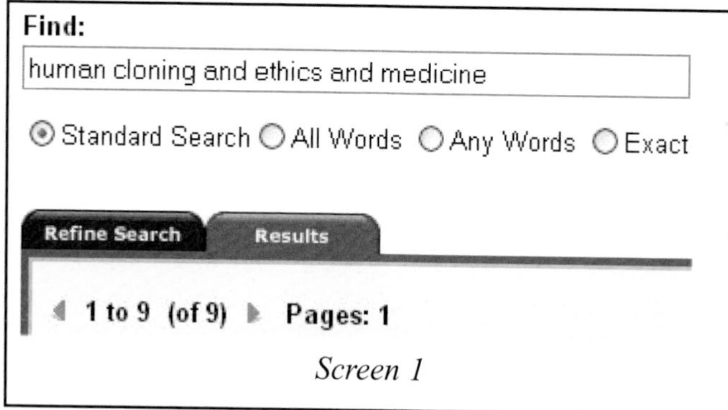

Screen 1

This search, connecting three ideas with the word **and**, retrieved 9 **records.** The phrase **human cloning** and the words **ethics** and **medicine** appear in all the results. While a good start, this list may contain too few records, depending on the information need.

> **Record**
> A description of a single source and often contains the necessary information to locate it.
>
> **Truncation**
> A symbol added to the stem of a word, most often an asterisk (*) but sometimes a question mark (?), pound symbol (#), or exclamation point (!). A search with a truncated term finds that stem plus anything that comes after it.

Truncation

Boolean Logic works well with another searching technique called Truncation, a useful search strategy for increasing results. The truncation symbol is often an asterisk (*). When you add it to the stem of a word it finds that stem plus any of the stem's endings. Putting a truncation symbol in the right place retrieves the following:

Original Keyword	Truncated Keyword	Words retrieved with truncation
cloning	clon*	clone, clones, cloned, cloning
ethics	ethic*	ethic, ethics, ethical, ethically
medicine	medic*	medicine, medical, medicinal, medication, medications, medicate, medicates, medicated, medicating

The truncation symbol assures a more thorough search including all of a word's various endings.

NOTE: Make sure you place the truncation symbol at the appropriate spot in a word. Too late (medicines*) and you will have no endings to replace, making the strategy useless; too early (med*) and you will retrieve results with irrelevant words.

Using truncation retrieves 73 results in the search below:

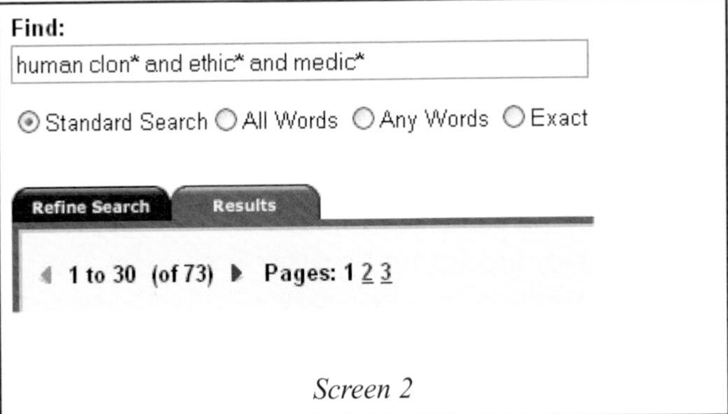

Screen 2

Synonyms

All words must appear in a record if you include them in a Boolean search using **and**, so the words you pick are crucial to retrieving relevant results. Using **synonyms** for your keywords can enhance your search.

> Synonym
> A word possessing the same meaning as another word.

Synonyms might include acronyms or broader or narrower terms for a topic. An example with the sample topic follows:

	Concept #1 **human cloning**	Concept #2 **ethical issues**	Concept #3 **medicine**
Keyword #1	human cloning	ethics	medicine
Keyword #2	genetic engineering	morals	therapy
Keyword #3	biotechnology	politics	treatment

Often one keyword retrieves more records than another, so trying different synonyms may increase the number of relevant records. You may try several searches on a topic by changing the keywords and connecting them with **and**.

A search using synonyms for the sample topic appears below:

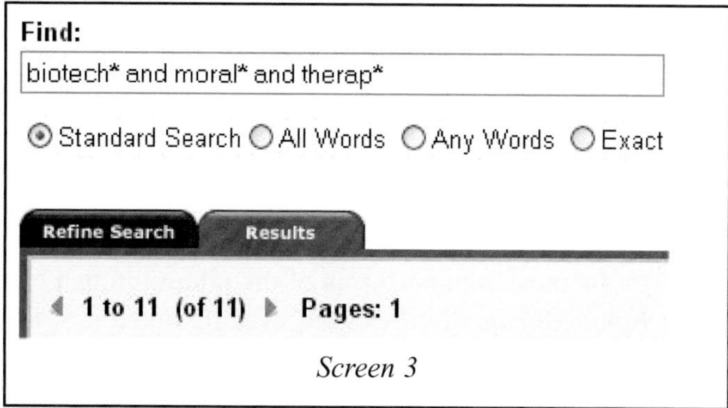

Screen 3

This combination of keywords retrieved 11 results, more results than the first combination of keywords.

Nested Searches

Nested searching employs another of the Boolean operator words, the word **or**. Using **or** in a search is exactly the opposite of using **and**. Connecting keywords with **or** retrieves results with any of the keywords, regardless of whether the keywords are in the same record. The result is a giant retrieval list.

The search below connects the keywords morals and ethics with the **or** operator:

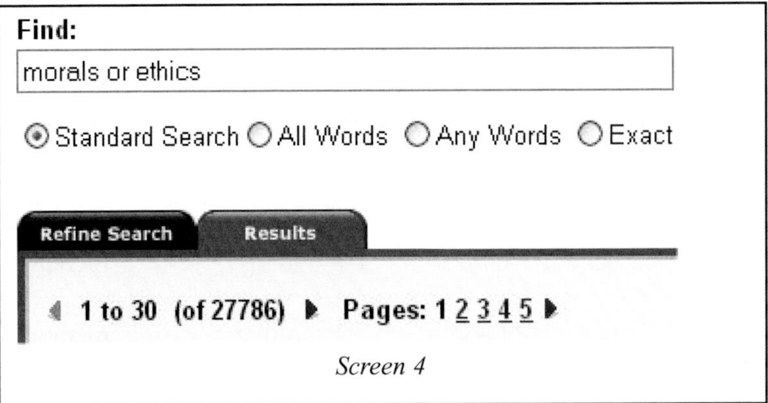

Screen 4

This search retrieved 27,786 results because it includes any result containing either keyword. Obviously, an **or** search by itself is rarely useful. However, putting an **or** search in parentheses creates an effective nested search.

Nesting allows you to use two or more synonyms in one search. You simply put parentheses around the **or** part of the search, like this:

Human clon* and (moral* or ethic*) and medic*

Putting parentheses around a keyword search using **or** allows you to search for all synonyms simultaneously. However, you must use **and** to connect the part of the search in parentheses with another keyword or parentheses combination. In the search above, the results must contain forms of the phrase human cloning and the word medicine as well as forms of either the keywords morals or ethics. You can nest any part of the search.

For example,

(human clon* or biotech*) and (moral* or ethic*) and (medic* or therap*)

The above search retrieves:

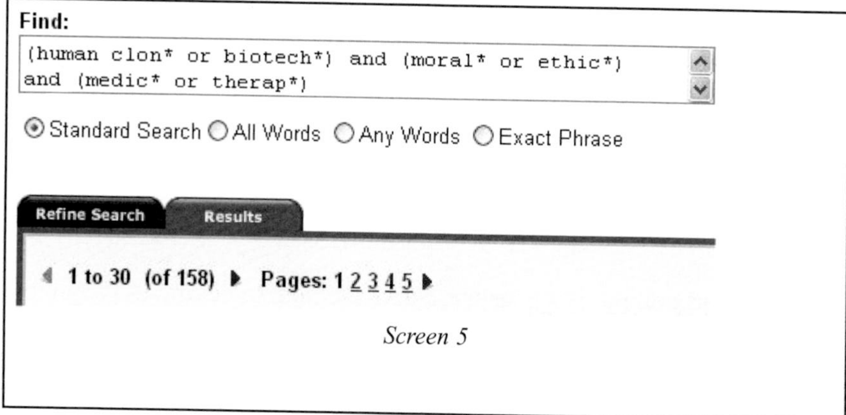

Screen 5

The search now contains 158 results, a substantial list of potentially relevant records.

More Boolean Command Words

And and **or** serve most searching needs, though other operators exist. After these, **not** is the most commonly used Boolean command word. Using **not** allows you to exclude keywords that retrieve irrelevant results. For example, the search below retrieves any results excluding forms of the keyword **cosmetic**:

(human clon* or biotech*) and (moral* or ethic*) and (medic* or therap*) not cosmetic*

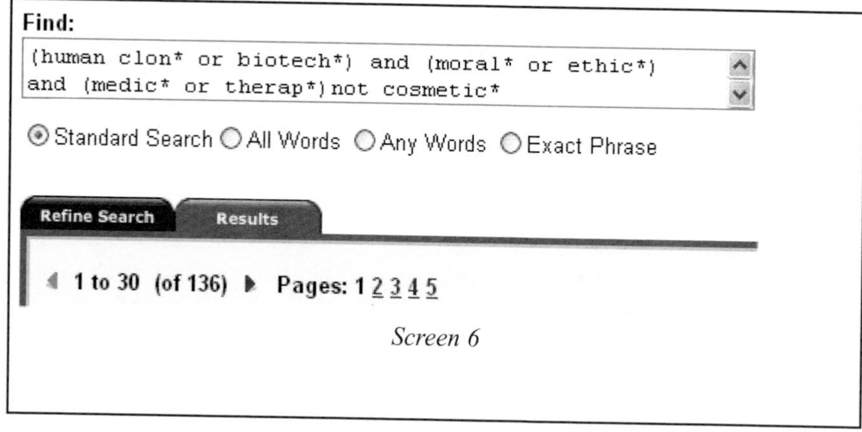

Screen 6

This search should only include records about using cloning technology for healing purposes rather than for cosmetic purposes. Not all databases use the same operators, though nearly all use **and**, **or**, and **not**. For other Boolean operators, check the help screens in the database you are using.

Subject Searching in Databases

While keyword searching is an easy search method to learn, it is not perfect. Sometimes, records from a keyword search mention the keyword only once; other times the record may refer to another topic entirely because a keyword has more than one meaning. Subject searching is a searching method which alleviates these problems.

Subject searching uses a standardized list of headings chosen by database providers to represent different topics. Thus, subject searching is more precise than keyword searching: any result with a relevant subject heading contains substantial information about the topic the subject heading represents. Many databases, especially databases searching library catalogs, use *Library of Congress Subject Headings*, and often you can click on a subject heading to look at all the results in the database with that subject heading. The catch with subject searching is that the standardized term chosen for the topic is sometimes not what you expect it to be.

For example,

Topic	Library of Congress Subject Heading
Vietnam war	Vietnamese conflict
Second hand smoke	Passive smoking
Generation gap	Conflict of generations

Also, some databases use other subject heading lists besides the Library of Congress headings, so the headings can vary from database to database for the same topic.

Many databases include subject headings in their records. To search using subject headings, start by doing a keyword search, find a relevant record, and click on any relevant subject heading in that record. You may find some databases use other terms for Subject Headings, such as “Descriptors” or merely “Subjects.” The concept, however, is the same from database to database.

EXERCISE: Focusing a Topic

On a separate sheet of paper, answer the following:

1. Write down a possible topic in one or two words.
2. Write three different topics within that topic.
3. Take the one you like best from above and rewrite it as a question.

EXERCISE: Truncated Keywords

On the same separate sheet of paper, make three columns. Pick three words from the question you wrote that you might use as keywords and write them in the first column, labeled "Original Keyword." Complete the grid by truncating the keyword at the best spot in the word to retrieve the most relevant words for the second column. Write those words retrieved from the truncation in the last column.

Original Keyword	Truncated Keyword	Words retrieved with truncation

EXERCISE: Synonyms

On a separate sheet of paper, create a grid like the one below. Write each separate concept in your topic in the large boxes across the top. Try to come up with at least two keywords to describe each concept. You may include the words from the large boxes as keywords.

	Concept #1	Concept #2	Concept #3
Keyword #1			
Keyword #2			
Keyword #3			

- On the same sheet of paper, combine keywords from the grid you filled out above to create a simple search and a nested search and write them down. You may truncate the words as necessary.

> Library Catalog
> A database that inventories all materials the library owns.

EXERCISE:
Finding Sources in a Library Catalog

On a separate sheet of paper, answer the following:

1. Go to your library's catalog and type in a keyword search you created in the exercises earlier in the chapter. Use fewer keywords to retrieve more records.
2. Write down the title of a source retrieved from the library catalog that you might consult.
3. What is the format of the source (book, video, government document)?

Searching for Books, Articles, and Free Web Sites

The previous section discussed general search strategies for databases. This section focuses on searching for particular sources in databases: books, articles, and free Web sites.

Searching for Books and Other Materials in the Library

> Index
> A list of records searchable by various fields such as author or subject.

Most libraries have a library catalog, a database to **index** their materials. The library catalog allows you to search for any resources the library owns in its collection, including:

- Circulating books. These can be checked out.
- Reference works. These cannot be checked out.
- Journal, magazine and newspaper titles (not the actual articles contained in these sources)
- Archives—rare and historical items
- Government documents
- Films
- Music and musical scores

- Books on tape
- Maps and atlases
- Curriculum materials for public schools

Many types of sources mentioned in the table at the beginning of the chapter are searchable in a library's catalog. An example of a library catalog search screen appears below. The search box contains a keyword search. The truncating symbol is a question mark:

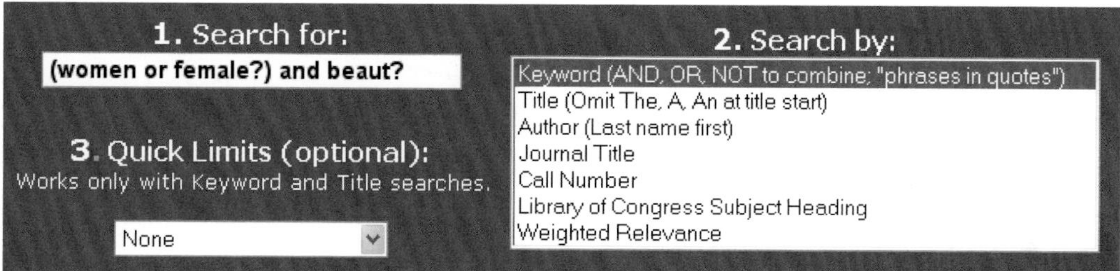

Screen 7

A keyword search using Boolean Logic retrieves a list of results from the library's collection.

Below is a typical book record for *The Beauty Myth: How Images of Beauty Are Used Against Women*, by Naomi Wolf:

Main Author:	Wolf, Naomi.
Title:	The beauty myth : how images of beauty are used against women / Naomi Wolf.
Subjects(s):	Feminine beauty (Aesthetics) Femininity. Sex role.
Publisher:	New York : Anchor Books, 1992.
Description:	Book 1st Anchor Books ed. 348 p. ; 21 cm.
Location:	3rd floor
Call Number:	HQ1219 .W65 1992
Status:	Not Checked out

> Call Number
> A combination of letters and numbers indicating a source's location in a library.

The record includes a good deal of information about the book, including whether or not it is available for checkout. The **Call Number,** listed at the bottom of the record above, leads you to the physical copy of the book. The call number classifies the book into a broad subject and then further classifies it into a particular subheading. On the following page you can see the breakdown of *The Beauty Myth*'s call number:

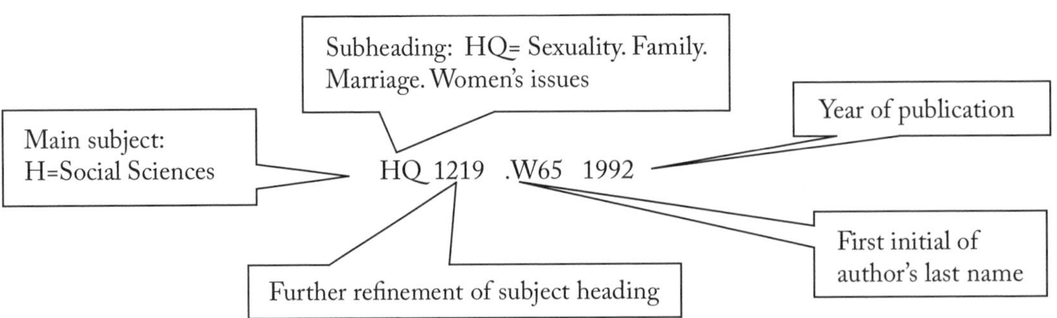

Consult a map of the library you're using to find out where the library shelves the book.

In the example above, you can click on the call number and see a list of other books shelved near this one. This strategy works well; libraries classify and shelve books by subject, and the books shelved near a needed book may also be useful sources.

When a Book Is in Hand

You may shy away from using book sources because you fear you won't have time to read several long books before your project is due. Sometimes an entire book is important to a topic, and you do need to read it all. Often only parts of the book are useful for your information need. Try the following strategies to find the pertinent elements in a book:

- Read the table of contents to pick out the chapters most relevant to your topic.
- Scan the index for the terms pertinent to your topic and consult relevant pages or sections.
- Read or skim the book's introductory chapter. Authors often summarize the book's content there.
- Read the first paragraph or two of each chapter. These paragraphs usually give some indication of the chapter's content.

Also, check to see if the book has a bibliography at the end of the book or at the end of each chapter. Bibliographies can lead you to other resources about your topic.

Searching Other Library Catalogs

You may want to consult the catalogs of other libraries if you do not find enough sources at your university library. Many states have catalogs which list the library contents of an entire state, a useful option if you want to look for sources at libraries nearby. Also, most libraries can access *WorldCat*, a database searching library catalogs nationally and internationally. The databases for these catalogs look different from your university's library catalog, but nearly all use Boolean Logic and **subject headings** for searching.

You may use **interlibrary loan** to request materials your library does not own, and a lending library will send the sources to your library for your use. You must allow extra time for interlibrary loan since processing the request and sending the material takes a few days or even weeks.

Subject Headings
A standardized list of terms representing particular topics. Library of Congress Subject Headings are commonly used, though not universally.

Interlibrary Loan
Refers to libraries borrowing materials from other libraries.

Citation
Information needed to locate an item; includes title, author, and publication information depending on item format.

Searching for Articles: Why So Many Article Databases?

Unlike library catalogs that cover sources in all disciplines, article databases cover only selected journals in an academic discipline. Therefore, university libraries subscribe to many article databases to serve the information needs of all academic programs.

Most databases differ in the following characteristics:

General — Covers many topics **Example:** *Academic Search Elite*	OR	**Specific** — Covers one subject **Example:** *PsycInfo*
Full Text—Full text articles **Example:** *Project Muse*	OR	**Citation** — Only citations **Example:** *Art Abstracts*
Journals and More — Covers books, reports or reference works **Example:** *PsycInfo*	OR	**Journals Only** — Covers journal articles **Example:** *Business Source Elite*
Popular — For general readers **Example:** *MasterFILE Premier*	OR	**Scholarly**—For researchers **Example:** *Medline*

Your choice of database depends on your information need. General databases work well for a short composition paper, but you might need a more specialized database for an in-depth paper in a specific academic discipline. Your library should have a guide to pertinent databases for your field of study. Check with a librarian if you are uncertain about what databases to use.

Common Elements in Article Databases

While databases differ in the topics they cover and in how they look, they tend to share some elements. Take a look at the opening screen of the database below:

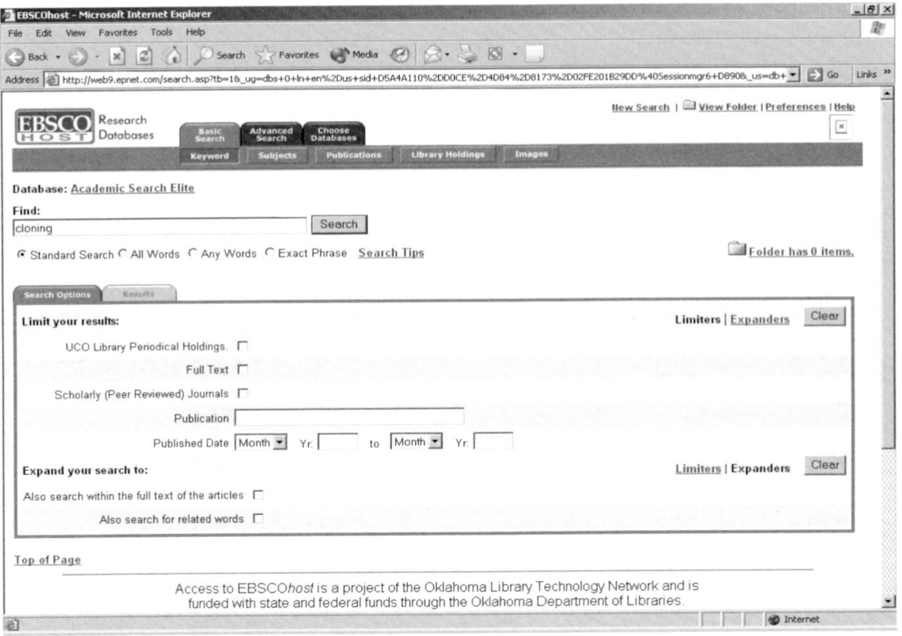

Like most databases, this one has a place to type in keywords, the **Find** box in this case. This sample has the word "cloning" typed in the **Find** box. The screen with records retrieved from this search looks like this:

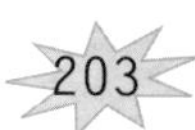

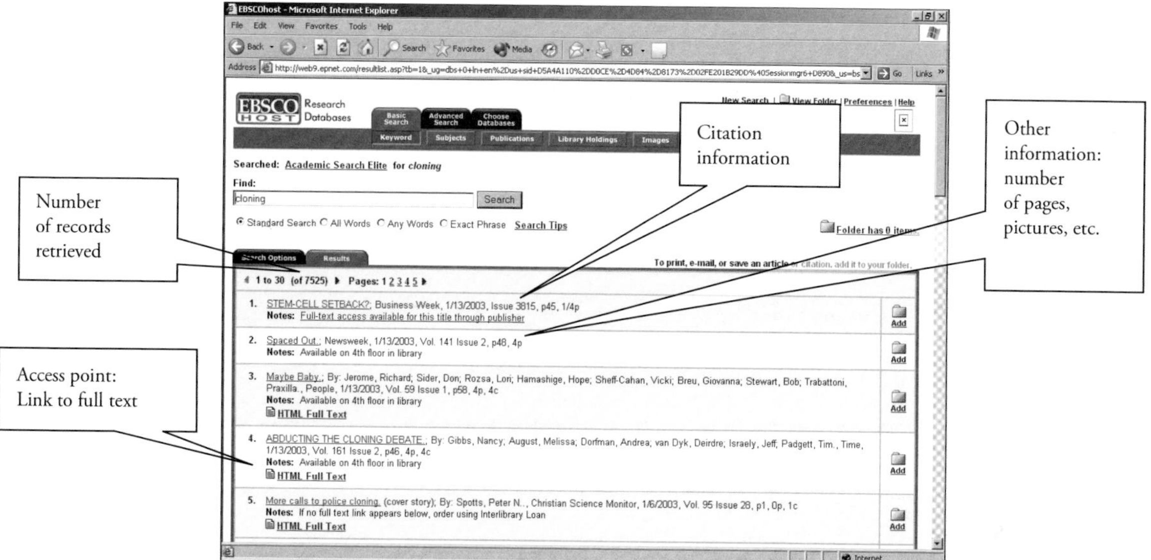

The results this database retrieves are articles from various **periodicals** in many academic disciplines. This database, like most, lists results with the most current articles first. This screen contains a good deal of information including:

> **Fields**
> Parts of a record: the author, title, periodical name, or abstract.
>
> **Full Text**
> The complete electronic text of a source.
>
> **Periodicals**
> Journals, magazines, newspapers.

- **Number of records retrieved.** Located just above the first result, this search retrieved 7525 results.
- **Citation information.** Includes the article's title, author, journal title, volume, issue, page number, and publication date. This information is crucial for crediting, or citing, the sources used in the project.
- **Other information.** Indicates the article's length and whether it has pictures or graphs.
- **Access points.** Indicates whether the article is available full text on the screen, available in the library in print, or only available through interlibrary loan. Full text articles have a link from this page to the full text.

While information a database includes varies, most display a number of records retrieved and citation information. Clicking on the title from the result screen above retrieves a record screen like the one below. It contains additional information about the article:

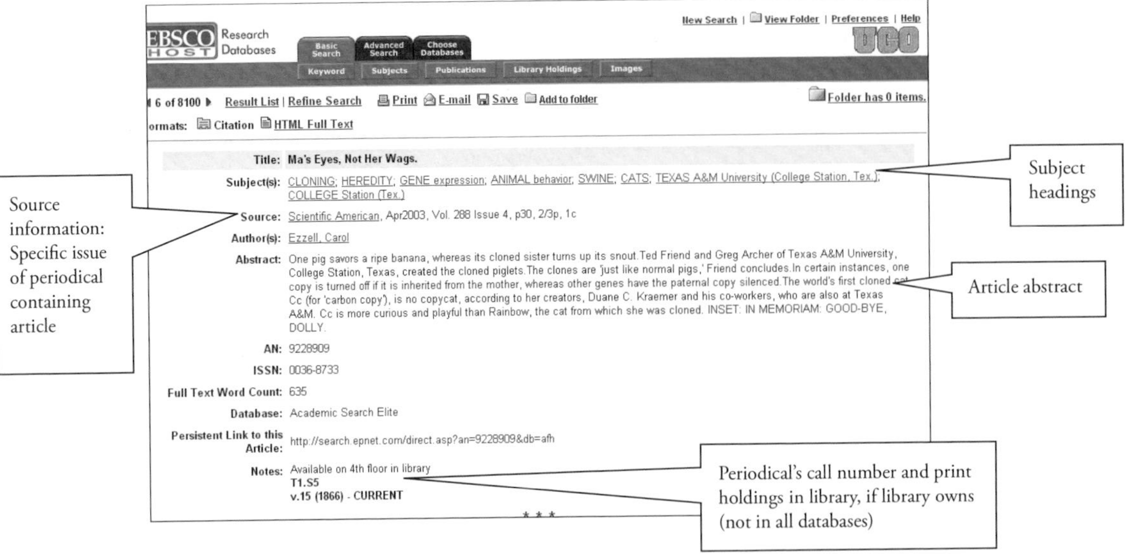

- **Subject headings** The words chosen by the database provider to represent the topic. Clicking on one displays a new result list of all the records containing that subject heading.
- **Source information** Specific issue of the periodical containing this article.
- **Abstract of article** Brief summary of the article. Very useful if article is lengthy or not available full text electronically.
- **Periodical call number and holdings information** Contains periodical's call number and print holdings in the library, if the library subscribes to it. Useful if the article is not available full text. Not all databases include this feature.

Abstract
A brief summary of an article's contents.

This information can help you decide whether or not you want to use the article before you read the entire article.

Limiting Results

Many databases offer various options for limiting a search. A typical search limit screen appears below with several limiting possibilities:

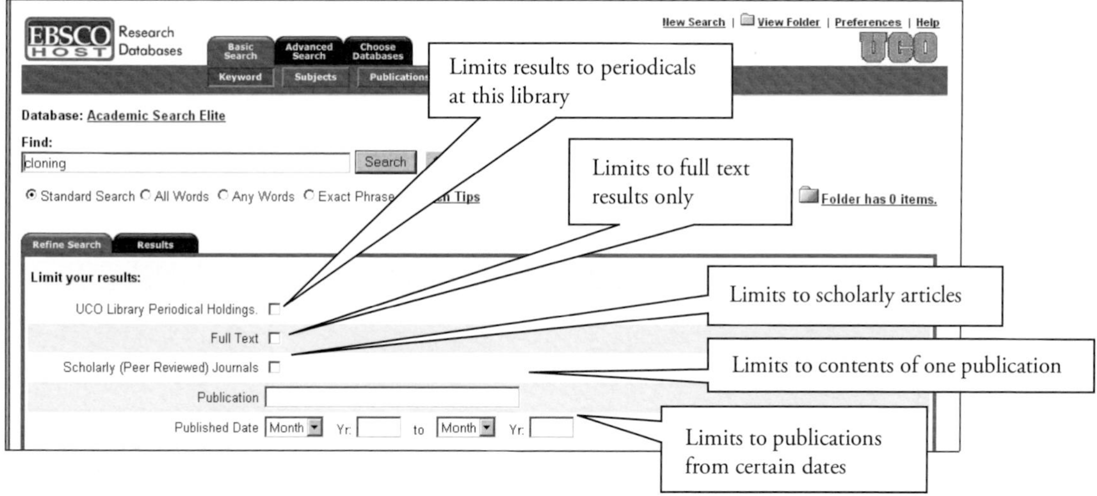

Limiters vary from database to database; some contain more options than shown above and some contain fewer. Regardless, limiters are an effective tool to restrict the result list, such as to a particular date range or publication. However, you must use limits wisely! Limiting to full text can remove many pertinent articles, for example.

Scholarly or Popular?

The limiting screen above contains a limit for "scholarly **(peer-reviewed)** journals." This limit warrants more discussion since instructors regularly require students to use scholarly journals, and understanding the differences between different types of journals is important.

All journals are not created equal, and scholars consider some more reliable than others.

The Various Types of Journals Indexed in Article Databases

	Magazines	Trade Journals	Scholarly Journals	Refereed or Peer-Reviewed Journals
Audience	general public	professionals	academics	academics
Reading level	high school or lower	high school–college	college or graduate	upper-level college–graduate
Documentation	none or minimal	some, not consistent	fully documented	fully documented
Examples	*Newsweek, Ladies Home Journal*	*Library Journal, Progressive Grocer*	*Journal of Economic Issues, Lancet*	*JAMA, History of Education Review*

Documentation
Recognition of outside sources used by authors, often in the form of a works cited list or other reference list.

Peer-Reviewed or Refereed Journals
Journals containing articles reviewed and critiqued by noted experts ("peers") in the same profession.

Popular Magazine
Publications for a general audience. Usually do not include Works Cited or references to other sources used.

Scholarly Journals
Journals published on an academic topic, assuming prior knowledge of the topic. Sometimes peer-reviewed but not always.

Trade Journals
Journals with content about a particular profession.

In general, popular journals or magazines are written for a general reading audience, and they do not document their sources. Trade journals are often no more scholarly than general magazines, but they only contain articles about a specific profession. Scholarly journals usually cover only a particular element of a larger topic, and the publishers assume readers already know something about the topic. More importantly, authors of scholarly articles document the sources they use in their articles. A reader can trace the author's source material through the works cited. Refereed or peer-reviewed journals are also scholarly journals, but they draw their editors from experts in that academic discipline, or "peers." As you advance in your field of study, you will probably use scholarly sources exclusively for your projects.

What If the Database Doesn't Allow Limiting to Scholarly Sources?

Databases with a variety of scholarly, popular, and trade journals often contain a limiting option for scholarly sources. Though generally accurate, these limiters sometimes include journals that instructors do not consider scholarly. Conversely, many specialized databases contain citations or text only from scholarly periodicals and so do not need a limit for scholarly journals. Other databases contain scholarly or trade journals but no limiting options. How can you determine whether a journal is scholarly or not?

Two methods work well for verifying a journal's publication type. First, the editorial information at the beginning of a journal issue usually lists the journal type. However, you may not be able to find this information readily, especially when using electronic sources. Try consulting *Ulrich's Periodicals Directory*, a source listing most periodicals in publication, if the journal's publication information is unavailable to you. *Ulrich's* indicates whether a journal is scholarly or peer-reviewed, popular, or trade. Most libraries subscribe to either a print or electronic version.

Searching "Visible" or Free Web Sites

The search process for the free Web is similar to subscription databases: Boolean Logic, truncation, and nested searching generally apply. However, the unmonitored nature of the free Web calls its validity into question. Books and articles from established journals have editors to monitor their content. Since the Internet has no such monitor, you must assess a Web site's validity before using it as a resource.

Criteria When Considering a Web Site

Authority	Author's credentials and contact information
Content	Web site's purpose
Currency	Update information
Documentation	Author's information sources

You should be able to locate this information easily on a Web site. Question using a Web site if this information is difficult to find or if you cannot find it at all!

One way to start assessing a site's accuracy is to look at the domain of the Web site's URL: the last three or four letters of the Web site address.

Common Domains and Their Potential As Reliable Sources

Domain	Type of Information	Authority
.com — commercial site **Example:** www.espn.com	Ads, business information, shopping	***
.edu — education site **Example:** www.ucok.edu	school info, links to libraries and academic departments	****
.gov — US government site **Example:** www.fitness.gov	Federal databases, statistics, public information	*****
.ok.us — state sponsored site **Example:** www.state.ok.us	State agency databases, statistics, public information	*****
.org — organization site **Example:** www.plannedparenthood.org	Non-profit information; interest-group agendas	***
.net — Internet service provider **Example:** www.free-ed.net	Often sponsors personal sites	**

Government and education Web sites are the most reliable though they too must meet assessment criteria. You can limit a search to a particular URL in many Internet search tools, usually from the advanced search screen.

You can see such a limiting option below in the advanced search screen of Google:

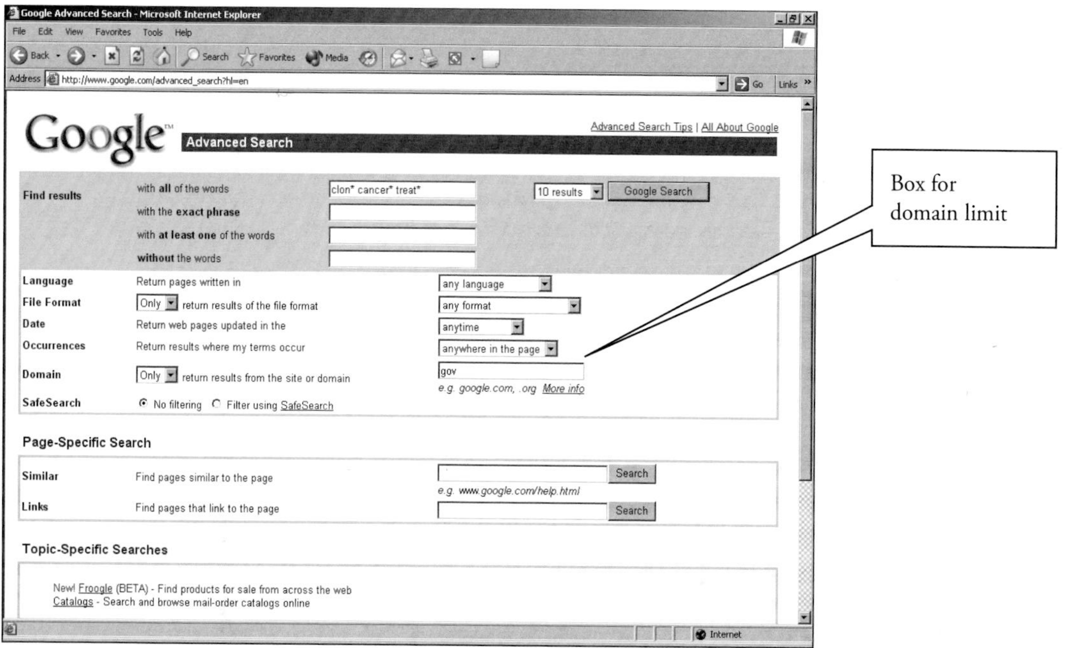

Using a domain limiter removes many of the more questionable Web sites from a search.

More Internet Searching Tools

Search engines like Google are well known and popular, but many other free Internet tools exist for pinpointing reliable Web sites. The Librarian's Index to the Internet (www.lii.org) is an example of one such tool. Librarians maintain it and decide what Web sites to include, thus serving as editors for the index. Such tools do not retrieve as many results, but the sites included should be of higher quality. Consult a librarian for other high quality free Internet tools.

Conclusion

Sources and resources vary, but the search techniques you use for searching them are remarkably similar. When you need to search for information, think about:

Your information need
This determines the kinds of sources to look for and what databases to consult.

Depth of analysis you need
This determines whether to go to popular or more scholarly resources.

Always consult a librarian if you are in doubt about what sources to use.

EXERCISE: Finding Free Web Sites with Google

1. Go to the search engine Google (http://www.google.com) and try keywords from your topic without limits.
2. On a separate sheet of paper, write down the number of results you retrieved.
3. Then, on a scale from 1-5, rate the quality of the results retrieved overall. Explain your rating in 2 sentences.
4. Go to the advanced search screen Google and limit the domain to .gov.
5. Write down the number of results you retrieved.
6. On a scale of 1-5 rate the quality of the results. Explain your rating in 2 or more sentences.

EXERCISE: Finding Articles Part I — Reading Database Records

1. Go to a general library article database. Ask a librarian if you need help finding one. Type in a nested search you created in the exercises from Chapter 7.
2. On a separate sheet of paper, write down the number of records you retrieved.
3. Next, scan the list of articles. Write down the title of an article you might consult for your topic.
4. How many pages does the article contain?
5. Is it available full text or in print only?

EXERCISE: Finding Articles Part II—Scholarly Journals

1. Using a general database, limit the search you used in Part I to scholarly journals.
2. On a separate sheet of paper, write down the number of results retrieved.
3. Scan the titles of the articles on the result list. Explain in two or more sentences the differences between these results and the results retrieved when you do not limit the search to scholarly journals.

The Modern Language Association

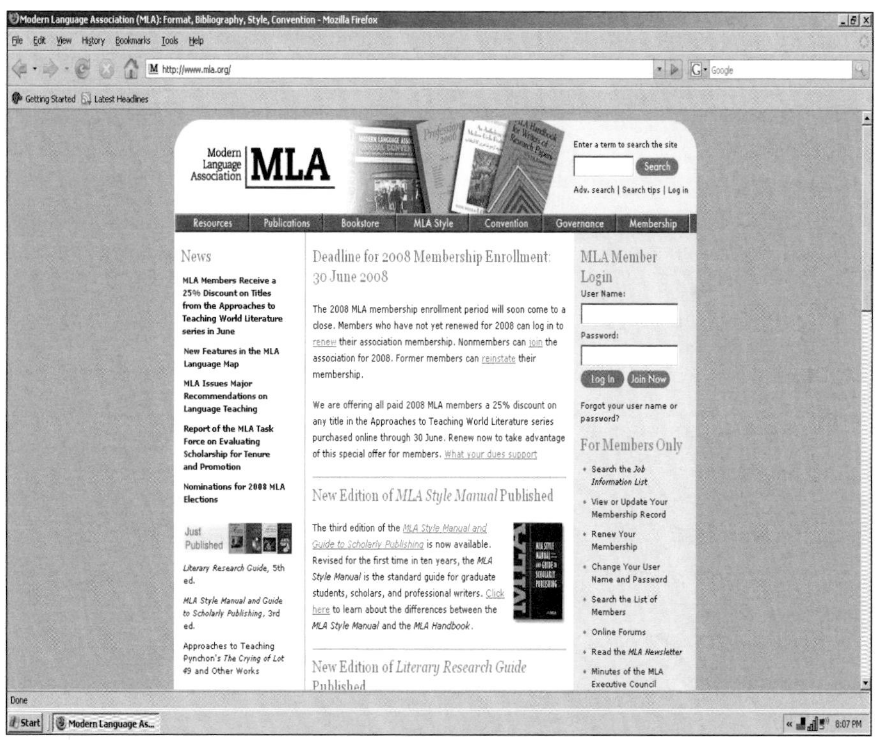

www.mla.org

The Modern Language Association Format

MLA requires that academic works should be typed, double-spaced with 1-inch margins on all sides. Usually, students should use 12 pt. Times New Roman or Garamond. However, individual professors may have a preference as to font type and size, so be sure to ask what you will be required to use. For the complete guidelines, see the *MLA Handbook for Writers of Research Papers*, 6th edition.

Page Header

Each page of the research paper contains:

- Writer's last name with page number in top right hand corner, ½ inch from the top

The first page header is in the left hand corner, 1 inch from the top:

- Your name
- Your professor's name
- Class title
- Date of the assignment

> **Works Cited**
> When mentioning or quoting from sources, this type of bibliography is required for the Modern Language Association (MLA) format.

Sections

MLA papers include three major sections:

- First page
- Main body
- Works Cited page

First Page and the Start of the Main Body

- Page number
- Page header
- Title of the research paper, centered
- The introduction and the start of the body of the essay

Title of Paper

- Do not place the entire title in quotation marks. *
- Do not underline the entire title *
- Do not italicize the entire title.*

** Unless you are referring to a work that needs to be in quotation marks, underlined or italicized.*

Kunkle 1

Abigail Kunkle

Professor Smith

English 1213, Section 24528

12 April 2005

To Spank or Not to Spank: That is the Question

The use of corporal punishment as a form of childhood discipline . . .

Works Cited

The names are listed alphabetically not numerically.

Last name of the student.

Page Number

Kunkle 10

Works Cited

Dobson, James C. Dare to Discipline. Carol Stream: Tyndale House, 1981.

Dodson, Fitzhugh. How to Discipline With Love (From Crib to College). New York: Rawson and Wade, 1978.

Kaye, Kenneth. Family Rules. New York: Walker, 1984.

Kazdin, Alan E., and Corina Benjet. "Spanking Children: Evidence and Issues." Current Directions in Psychological Science 56.4 (2003): 99–103.

Meyerhoff, Michael K. "A Different Slant on Spanking." Pediatrics for Parents 19.6 (2001): 8–10.

The New Revised Standard Version Bible: Catholic Edition. Nashville: Catholic Bible, 1990.

Straus, Murray A., and Denise A. Donnelly. Beating the Devil Out of Them. New Brunswick: Transaction, 2001.

Vockell, Edward P. Whatever Happened to Punishment. Muncie: Accelerated Development, 1977.

Wilson, John. "Corporal Punishment Revisited." Cambridge Journal of Education 32.3 (2002): 409–417.

Double-spaced!

In-Text Citations: The Basics

There are three main ways to cite material:

1. to summarize
2. to paraphrase
3. to quote

To Summarize

Take a long and complicated passage and simplify it for the reader. You will want to summarize if the idea you want to cite is embedded in a long passage full of examples or explanation. A summary is significantly shorter than the original and is written in your own words.

For example:

> In their article, "Kennedy Assassination: How About The Truth?" Gerald Ford and David Belin state that Oliver Stone's movie *JFK* misrepresents the truth and insults the memory of those involved in the official investigation.

To Paraphrase

State the idea of a short passage in the writer's own words. NOTE: Simply replacing some of the main words in a passage with your words while leaving the original sentence structure intact is NOT **paraphrasing.**

> Paraphrase
> Rewording a quote from a source using different or original words instead of a verbatim word for word version.

Original excerpt from Gerald Ford and David Belin's article "Kennedy Assassination: How About the Truth?"

> The media treatment of the Kennedy assassination tragedy and the Warren Commission Report is a microcosm of one of the central problems facing our democratic society: False sensationalist claims are given wide dissemination, the truth is submerged, and the responsible press usually does not undertake sufficient effort to expose the fraud that is being perpetrated. Two vivid examples are the recent series of five one-hour A&E television programs about the Kennedy assassination called *The Men Who Killed Kennedy* and the new Oliver Stone-Kevin Costner film, *JFK*.

Paraphrase:

> Gerald Ford and David Belin have stated in their article "Kennedy Assassination: How About the Truth?" that our society feeds on sensationalism and that false information, if it is sensational, is often not refuted. Oliver Stone's movie *JFK* and A & E's five-hour series *The Men Who Killed Kennedy* are examples of the media's lack of regard for the truth (1).

NOTE: This example states the ideas in the paragraph but has unique sentence structure and word choice. Also note that it is clear where the paraphrase begins and where it ends.

When paraphrasing, it is always important to begin the borrowed material with an introductory phrase that alerts the reader to the beginning of the borrowing. You should end the borrowed material with the page number in parentheses, then a period.

To Quote

Direct quotes are used when the unique wording of a selection conveys a specific tone or message that the writer wants to incorporate into his or her writing. There are three types of quotations:

1. Formal
2. Informal
3. Incorporated

Formal Quotations

Create an introductory sentence which provides a context for the quote. After this sentence, there is a colon, followed by the quotation:

Gerald Ford and David Belin believe that current media productions misrepresent the truth of the Kennedy assassination:

> The common denominator of these commercial productions is the big lie—the assertion that the top echelons of our government were conspiratorially involved in the assassination and that Lee Harvey Oswald was not the lone gunman who killed President Kennedy and the Dallas Police Officer J.D. Tippit. (1)

Note: Since this quote is longer than three (3) typed lines it is indented five (5) spaces from the left and there are no quotation marks. The indention serves to mark the beginning and ending of the quote. Also note that the period—for long quotes only—goes before the citation parentheses.

This sentence makes a good direct quote because the of the unique words "the big lie" and the phrase "the top echelons of our government were conspiratorially involved." If this sentence were paraphrased, it would lose some of its rhetorical power.

Informal Quotations

Start with an introductory phrase or clause that assists the reader in understanding the quote. The introductory phrase or clause is followed by a comma:

> In speaking of the evidence misused or left out, Ford and Belin state, ". . . nowhere do the movie audiences seeing *JFK* or A&E's television audience ever learn about Postal Inspector Holmes. . ." (4).

Incorporated Quotations

Incorporate a small number of the source's words into a longer sentence created by you. Thus, the quoted words and the writer's original words form one complete sentence:

> Ford and Belin would like us to believe that there is a "massive body of evidence which conclusively proves beyond a reasonable doubt" that there was no conspiracy, only a lone-gunman (5).

What Else Should You Keep in Mind?

1. There should always be more of your words than words from source material. It is your paper, not a compilation of others' words.
2. Always use an introductory tag so that your reader knows where borrowed material begins.
3. Always conclude a piece of borrowed material with a citation. If you have two borrowed pieces back to back from the same source but from different sections of the source, end the first one and introduce the second so that it is clear to the reader that the material you borrowed is from separate sections of the source.
4. Keep long quotes to a minimum.

In-Text Citations: Author/Authors

As with all formatting styles, MLA has specific rules for citing sources. In this section you will find only the most common. If you do not find what you need, you should access www.mla.org. Remember: if you do not cite your information correctly, it is plagiarism or academic dishonesty—both of which earn an "F" on assignments and perhaps even expulsion from the university.

A Single Author

To cite a single author, use the author's last name and the page number.

> George Alexander asserts that students need to read newspaper articles to understand the expectations of employers (32).
> or
>
> Students need to read newspaper articles to understand the expectations of employers (Alexander 32).

A Single Author Who Has Multiple Works

Some authors are well known in their fields and produce multiple works on the same subject. If you want to use two works in one sentence and the author's last name in the phrase, you need to include a shortened title in quotation marks and the page number.

> George Alexander asserts that students need to read newspaper articles to understand the expectations of employers, ("What Students Need" 32) as well as speak to HR Directors and hiring agencies ("What HR Directors Know" 10).

Two or Three Authors

When a work has two authors, use the names of both authors in the phrase or in the parentheses each time you cite the work. In addition, you must use the word "and" between the authors' names.

> In the study completed by John Maddison and Erma Koche, the authors demonstrated that professors spend significant time teaching students how to write (14).
>
> The authors demonstrated that professors spend significant time teaching students how to write (Maddison and Koche 14).

Four or More Authors

You can name all of the authors, or you can include the first author's last name followed by the Latin term "et al." which means "and others."

> One research study indicates that professors should consider having managers, HR Directors, and other hiring personnel speak to freshman composition classes (Maddison, Koche, Alexander, and Maxel 832).
>
> or
>
> One research study indicates that professors should consider having managers, HR Directors, and other hiring personnel speak to freshman composition classes (Maddison et al. 832).

Unknown or Anonymous Author

If you are using the Internet, you may find more often than not that works do not have a specified author or are listed as "anonymous." In this case, you need to cite the source by its title in the phrase or use the first word or two of the title in the parentheses. Titles of books and reports are italicized; titles of articles and chapters are in quotation marks.

> An article posted on Yahoo! News notes that poor communication, both verbal and written, is the primary reason employees are dismissed ("Writing In" 32).

Organization as Author

When an organization, government agency, or corporation authors a piece, mention the name of it in the phrase or in the parenthetical citation the **first time** you cite the source.

> According to the National Institute of Mental Health, Hispanics suffer depression primarily within the first six months of the acculturation phase (32–36).

Electronic Sources

When possible, cite an electronic document the same as any other document by using the author-page number style.

> Mackery asserted that in the past two decades, students' writing skills have become less focused and meaningful (89).

When it's not possible, you will use one of the following:

Unknown Author and Unknown Page Number

Often electronic sources do not have an author or page number. When this occurs, use the title in your phrase or use the first word or two of the title in the parentheses.

> Professors might consider having students complete a small assignment where the students research how important employers consider verbal and written communication ("What Employers").

Sources without Page Numbers

Note: Never use the page numbers of Web pages you print because the way the printer reads the code sent from the computer differs based on the printer and the computer.

In MLA, use only the information you have: the author or the title of the article or Web page.

> According to Candice McKee, students will not understand the importance of writing until they enter the workplace.
>
> Students will not understand the importance of writing until they enter the workplace (McKee).

Interviews, Letters, E-Mails, and Other Person-To-Person Communications

Personal communications are an important part of research. When you want to cite one in a paper, use the communicator's name(s).

> Bill Gates agrees with Robert Maxel that employers are seeking employees with strong verbal and written skills.
>
> Employers are seeking employees with strong verbal and written skills (Gates).

The Bible

When you cite the Bible, use the name of the specific edition, followed by an abbreviation of the book and chapter: verse(s).

> (Holy Bible King James Version, John 3:16)

Works Cited Page Entries

When you create the Works Cited page entries, keep the following formatting guidelines in mind:

- Capitalize the "W" in "Web site" and keep the two words separate (not Website).
- Italicize or underline the names of Web sites, journal titles, magazine titles, etc.
- Place article names and Web page titles in quotations marks.
- Simplify long URLs. <http://www.truthdig.com/report/item/20080529_the_unsung_victims_of_the_emerald_city/?ln> becomes <http://www.truthdig.com>.
- Do not list the URL for the articles that you access from an Electronic Subscription Service, such as EBSCOhost.

Single Author of Article

When you have a work with a single author, list the last name first, followed by author's first name.

> Gordan, Daryl. "I'm Tired. You Clean And Cook. Shifting Gender Identities and Second Language Socialization." TESOL Quarterly 38.3 (2004): 437–457.

Two and Three Authors of an Article

When you have two authors, reverse the name of the first author only.

> Garrett, Paul, and Patricia Baquedero-Lopez. "Language Socialization: Reproduction and Continuity, Transformation, and Change." Annual Review of Anthropology 31 (2002): 339–361.

Four Authors or More of an Article

If there are more than three authors, list the first author and then "et al."

> Masters, Amy, et al. "Writing In The Technical Writing Classroom." Journal of Technical Writing 23.2 (1998): 223–229.

Two or More Works by the Same Author

Use the author's name for all entries and then list the entries in alphabetical order. List the author's single works before shared works (see below). If there are entries with the same author(s), use three hyphens in place of the author's name for every entry after the first.

Schieffellin, Bambi. The Give and Take of Everyday Life: Language Socialization of Kaluli Children. New York: Cambridge University Press, 1990.

Schieffellin, Bambi, and Elinor Ochs. Language Socialization Across Cultures. New York: Cambridge University Press, 1986.

—. "Language Socialization." Annual Review of Anthropology 15 (1988): 163–191.

Article from an On-Line Periodical

The only difference between a print article and an on-line article is the way in which you access it. When citing an on-line periodical, include **all** of the information the on-line host makes available, including an issue number and the number of paragraphs when known.

Dillon, Sam. "What Corporate America Can't Build: A Sentence." The New York Times 149. 07 December 2004. 3 March 2008 <http://www.nytimes.com/2004/12/07/business/07write.html>.

On-Line Scholarly Journal Article

Katz, Susan. "Assessing a Hybrid Format." Journal of Business and Technical Communication 22 (2008): 15 pars. 25 February 2008 <http://jbt.sagepub.com/content/vol22/issue1>.

Article from a Database

When referencing material obtained from an on-line database—EBSCOhost, etc.—you must provide appropriate print citation information. In addition, also add information that gives the date of retrieval and the proper name of the database. You must do both because some people may need to retrieve the information without the use of the database.

Wallace, James. "Warning! Poor Writing Skills May Be Hazardous To Your Career." Public Relations: Tactics 11:4 (2004). Business Source Elite. EBSCOhost. University of Central Oklahoma Lib., Edmond, OK. 4 March 2006.

Barrera, Rebeca María. "A Case for Bilingual Education." Scholastic Parent and Child Nov.–Dec. 2004: 72–73. Academic Search Premier. EBSCOhost. St. Johns River Community Coll. Lib., Palatka, FL. 1 Feb. 2005 <http://search.epnet.com>.

Nonperiodical Web Document, Web Page, or Report

These types of resources are popular but risky. When you use these sources, list as much of the following information as possible. This means you cannot be lazy—you must hunt for information and you must be aware of the information you retrieve. Furthermore, if you locate a page with an address with a bunch of gobbledygook, delete all of the gobbledygook up to http://www.theWebsitename.com/):

Bissonnette, Zac. "Employers Say Young Workers Can't Write." Blogging Stocks. 27 August 2007. 8 March 2008 <http://www.bloggingstocks.com /2007/08/27/employers-say-young-workers-cant-write/>.

"How To Cure A Hangover." Howstuffworks.com. 8 March 2008 <http://health.howstuffworks.com/hangover6.htm>.

Note: When an Internet document is *more than one Web page*, provide a URL that links to the home page or entry page for the document. MySpace and Facebook postings follow this format.

On-Line Forum or Discussion Board Posting

Two popular sources are on-line forums or discussion boards. For these sources, list the title of the message and the URL of the newsgroup or discussion board. MySpace and Facebook postings follow this format.

Anderson, Cami. "Environmentalism Becoming A Trend." On-line posting. 31 Jan. 2008. Oklahoma Sustainability. 5 May 2008 <http://lists.oksustainability.org/>.

Note: When available, use the author's real name. If only the screen name is available for the author, then use the screen name.

Note: Be sure to provide the exact date of the posting.

Article in Journal Paginated by Volume

Journals that are paginated by volume begin with page one in issue one, and continue numbering issue two where issue one ended, etc. Note the word "volume" is NOT included.

Schieffellin, Bambi, and Elinor Ochs. "Language Socialization." Annual Review of Anthropology 15 (1988): 163–191.

Article in Journal Paginated by Issue

Journals paginated by issue begin with page one every issue; therefore, the issue number is indicated by separating the issue number from the volume number with a period.

Gordan, Daryl. "I'm Tired. You Clean and Cook. Shifting Gender Identities And Second Language Socialization." TESOL Quarterly 38.3 (2004): 437–457.

Article in a Newspaper

Do not use p. or pp. to precede page numbers for a newspaper source. Simply give the page number.

Dillon, Sam. "What Corporate America Can't Build: A Sentence." The New York Times 7 December 2004: 23B.

Article or Chapter in an Edited Book

Tannen, Deborah. "A Comparative Analysis of Oral Narrative Strategies: Athenian Greek and American English." The Pear Stories: Cognitive, Cultural, and Linguistic Aspects of Production. Ed. W.L. Chafe. Norwood, N.J.: Ablex Publishing Corporation, 1980. 51–87.

Government Document

Government documents are listed just as you would a book without an author.

Depresion: Lo Que Toda Mujer Debe Saber. Washington, DC: U.S. Government Printing Office, 2001.

The Bible

You need to list the name of the specific edition, any editor(s) associated with the edition, and the publication information, including the date.

The Holy Bible: King James Version. Peabody, MA: Hendrickson Publishers, 2004.

Personal Interview

McKee, Candice. Personal Interview. 2 May 2008.

Speech or Lecture

Obama, Barack. "Renewing the American Economy." Keynote Address. New York, NY. 27 March 2008.

Advertisement

List the company, business, or organization; the publication, broadcast network, or Web address where the advertisement appeared.

L'Oreal. Advertisement. <u>More Magazine</u> 20 Oct. 2007: 75.

Cartoon or Comic Strip

List the artist, the title of the cartoon in quotations, and the publication.

Schultz, Charles. "Peanuts." Comic Strip. <u>The Daily Oklahoman</u> [Oklahoma City] 20 Oct. 2007: 5.

Motion Picture in Movie Theaters

<u>Garden State</u>. Dir. Zack Braff. Perf. Zack Braff, Natalie Portman. Camelot Pictures, 2004.

Or, if you reference it by director in the body of your paper:

Braff, Zack, dir. <u>Garden State</u>. Camelot Pictures, 2004.

Motion Picture on DVD or BlueRay

Garden State. Dir. Zack Braff. Perf. Zack Braff, Natalie Portman. 2004. DVD. 20th Century Fox, 2004.

Television Broadcast or Radio Program

"Six Degrees Could Change The World." National Geographic. Washington D.C. 17 December 2007.

Single Episode of a Television Series

"Family 8108." Cold Case. TNT. Atlanta. 21 May 2008.

Entire Albums

Rilo Kiley. Under the Black Light. Warner Bros., 2007.

Individual Songs

Rilo Kiley. "Silver Lining." Under the Black Light. Warner Bros., 2007.

Sample Student Paper

Kunkle 1

Abigail Kunkle

Professor Smith

English 1213, Section 24528

12 April 2005

To Spank or Not to Spank: That Is the Question

The use of corporal punishment as a form of childhood discipline has been, especially most recently, a topic of great controversy. Many agree that spanking a child is an act of barbarism, yet various studies have shown that it is very much a part of today's parenting methods. Some professionals have even proposed that children should have the same legal rights as adults under the circumstance of being attacked or beaten. So, is corporal punishment an acceptable way to discipline children? Shakespeare touched on the issue quite well in his play *Troilus and Cressida* when Ulysses said, "Take but degree away, untune that string, And hark what discord follows… Strength should be lord of imbecility, And the rude son should strike his father dead: Force should be right…" (qtd. in Wilson 413). Shakespeare, as well as a number of today's professionals, do agree that corporal punishment is beneficial, if not sometimes essential, in the rearing of a child. Spanking has many advantages for both the children and the parents involved and has been proven to have positive outcomes. Therefore, corporal punishment is an acceptable and productive form of childhood discipline in the twenty-first century.

The definition of corporal punishment, though widely varied, is most commonly stated as hitting a child with an open hand on the buttocks with the intent to discipline, without causing physical harm (Kazdin and Benjet 99). The buttocks is the preferred region to smack the child since it inflicts the least amount of physical pain upon the child but stings just enough to get the child's attention. That is the ultimate goal of spanking. Any type of corporal punishment that causes more than a smack into reality, such as bruising or bleeding of any sort, may be considered abuse. Though spanking can ultimately be very helpful to a child, it must be used warily and within limitations, as with any form of punishment.

Michael K. Meyerhoff, the executive director of "The Education for Parenthood Information Center," affirmed that "in order to teach a child to be personally safe and respectful of others, it is necessary to 'speak' to the child in a 'language' he truly understands. And given the limited cognitive capacities of a toddler, a small spanking often results in a considerably better 'education' than a prolonged discussion" (9). This is obviously why spanking can be of such benefit to the child. For instance, most studies have found that when spanking immediately follows misbehavior, it almost always results in the compliance of the child (Kazdin and Benjet 100). From this compliance, it can be determined that the child was cognitively able to correlate his actions to the negative consequence that followed and conclude that his action must also have been negative, or wrong. So essentially, the child is learning to discern right from wrong on a level that he is able to understand.

Kunkle 3

One factor that is important in the effectiveness of corporal punishment is the attitude of the parents. As long as parents incorporate a genuine expression of love in connection with a firm discipline strategy, the child will not be hurt emotionally. Edward L. Vockell, a former associate professor at Purdue University, Calumet Campus, stated that parents must be careful to administer the spanking to the specific behavior that was performed by the child and not communicate a general hatred toward the child (106). This can obviously have negative effects, even into adulthood, and is where many parents err. By sticking with a positive spanking method, while also using a system of rewards to congratulate the child when he has done right, many parents have achieved a great deal through the use of corporal punishment (108).

Dr. James C. Dobson, an Associate Clinical Professor of Pediatrics at the University of Southern California School of Medicine, is another who agrees that spanking is a healthy form of discipline. Dobson contends that when a child consistently and defiantly challenges his parent, the parent should not give in to the challenge but should rather stand up and win. This does not mean (which some parents may view it as) going to war with the child and beating him senseless. It is examples of parents like that who take corporal punishment to the level of abusiveness. Dobson meant that parents need to be firm with their children and gently let them know who is boss (50). There is an alarming increase in the number of parents today who literally bombard their children with adoration and then feel

Kunkle 4

as if their children hate them when they must punish them, since the children are rarely, if ever, punished. As an example, one day after dinner, little Bobby's mother gives him a piece of candy to eat. Bobby discovers that he likes the sweet taste of it and asks his mother for the same candy the following night for dinner. His mother says no, because he has not eaten his dinner yet. But little Bobby does not understand and begins to cry and scream for candy as he rolls on the floor. Of course, Bobby's mother wants him to stop throwing a tantrum and eat his dinner, so she gives in and gives him a piece of the candy. Bobby eats it triumphantly and then sits down for dinner like his mother wanted him to. The next evening, Bobby does the same thing and screams for more candy. His mother again tries to calm him down but ultimately provides him with the piece of candy, since she discovered that last time it had produced the effect she had wanted. This time he eats it, wants more candy, and will not eat his dinner. This process continues for days, until finally Bobby's mother can take it no longer. She puts Bobby in a time-out, where he only continues his tantrum. She ignores him for a while, hoping that he will begin to calm down. Finally, using a method she had never before used on Bobby, she spanks him on the buttocks. She feels horrible for hitting her son but soon realizes that little Bobby was so astounded that he had stopped fussing. Then, asking Bobby if he was ready to eat, his mother sat him at the table, and he began to eat. The following night, Bobby threw the same tantrum, but his mother was ready and swiftly gave him a spanking, to which Bobby reacted desirably, and sat him down for dinner. Bobby was soon out of the candy

Kunkle 5

habit. Not only had he learned that candy is not an acceptable dinner food, but he was also able to understand that negative actions (throwing a tantrum to get what he wanted) are likewise rewarded negatively (spanking). Though this story is fiction and was made to use as an example, Dobson explains many similar situations in his book Dare to Discipline.

The story about Bobby illustrates two important points on the views on corporal punishment. As stated earlier, it first provides the child with a sense of determining between right and wrong. Secondly, it assists the parent in sticking with a consistent form of discipline. If the parent is not consistent in the punishment that is used, the child may become confused on what he can or cannot do, especially during the younger childhood years. It is also very helpful to the parent, since it can be used in nearly any situation. For instance, one day Bobby and his mother are at the grocery store, and Bobby sees the candy that he loves so much and begins to cry for it. Bobby's mother can calmly threaten Bobby that he cannot have any right now, and if he continues to cry, he will receive a spanking. This can be used as a motivator to Bobby, since he will recall the shame of his previous spanking and will be less motivated to make the same mistake again (Wilson 411). This is in no way scarring the child emotionally, as long as his mother reprimands him caringly. The threat merely lets him know that there are times when he cannot always have his way and cautioning him that acting out of line will have its consequences.

Corporal punishment also works well in helping parents maintain the rules (and the chaos level) of their household. Kenneth Kaye, a developmental psychologist at Northwestern University Medical School, observed, "our society seems to be suffering from an illusion of helplessness, particularly among parents, in the face of increasingly out-of-control behavior by children" (119). Why is this out-of-control behavior becoming so prominent in children today? Many parents are too timid to step up, set limits and potential goals for their children, and, most importantly, enforce rules should those limits be broken. Parents are increasingly trying to befriend their children, when in reality their children need guidance and discipline, especially in the early years. In Kaye's book, <u>Family Rules</u>, he stresses the importance of parents having power over their children (119–127). This does not imply that parents have the right to torture their misbehaving children, though. It simply means that children must have limitations, even if they consciously struggle to overcome them. In Bobby's case, if his mother had never taken that step to spank him, he may have never responded to time-outs or lectures, depending upon his cognitive capacity, and therefore continue his outrageous tantrums until he got what he wanted. Had his mother taken this route, Bobby would not only have been labeled "out-of-control" but also "spoiled," since he would probably be eating candy every evening for dinner. Thanks to his mother's take-charge attitude, Bobby learned an important lesson, not through lecturing or time-out, but through a punishment that he was able to understand.

Kunkle 7

In the other spectrum of the spanking rainbow lie the anti-corporal punishment supporters. Those who do not condone the use of spanking are likely to claim that "spanking [is] associated with decreased internalization of morals, diminished quality of parent-child relations, poorer child and adult mental health, increased delinquency and antisocial behavior for adults…" and so on (Kazdin and Benjet 101). These claims, though, are quite difficult to prove. Most completed studies on adult outcomes of corporal punishment have been found to be relatively biased and the groups are often specifically chosen. Meyerhoff, who has actually completed research at Harvard Medical School, has found that, while research suggests that nearly eighty-five percent of death-row inmates were spanked as children, the exact same percent of graduates from Harvard Medical School were also spanked as children (8). After coming to these two conclusions, it is seemingly useless to declare spanking as the reason that the inmates are where they are now. If spanking is so cruel and inhumane, as some claim it to be, how did the eighty-five percent of Harvard graduates who were also spanked as children get to where they are now? Why are they, too, not in prison?

One of the chief arguments found within the controversy of corporal punishment is, again, the supposedly damaging and depressing effects to the spanked child. Many anti-corporal punishment supporters are not only pushing parents to stop spanking, but to also spread the word of the "detrimental" effects of spanking. One way they claimed that this could be done is to print a notice on all birth certificates stating, "Warning: Spanking has been determined to be dangerous to the health and well being of your child. Do not, under any circumstances, spank or hit your child" (Straus and Donnelly 211). Yet, even Dr. Fitzhugh Dodson, author of How to Discipline with Love (From Crib to College), who believes that parenting can be accomplished without smacking a child, wrote that any parent who has never spanked his children must be quite "saintly" in order to not give them a good "wallop" every so often (48). Should those "wallops" become a frequent form of discipline, it does not have to produce emotional distress upon the child, as long as the parent continually and openly expresses the love that is felt for the child. It has been proven to work best when the child can interpret that familial love and separate it from the discipline that his parents have conveyed to him as part of life and growing up. If this method is applied correctly, there is no evidence that the child will grow into a violent or depressed individual.

In the Bible, Hebrews 12:5-6, it is stated, "My child, do not regard lightly the discipline of the Lord, or lose heart when you are punished by him; for the Lord disciplines those whom he loves…" (226). This summarizes the significance of corporal punishment and the care that must accompany it. In this respect, God can be compared to a parent who must lovingly instruct his children in the differences of right and wrong. It is imperative, in today's fast-paced and changing world, that children be given limits and appropriate punishments to be administered if those limits are broken. Through love and compassion, parents can convey to their children a sturdy sense of what is acceptable behavior and what is not, with the aid of corporal punishment.

Kunkle 9

Works Cited

Dobson, James C. Dare to Discipline. Carol Stream: Tyndale House, 1981.

Dodson, Fitzhugh. How to Discipline With Love (From Crib to College). New York: Rawson and Wade, 1978.

Kaye, Kenneth. Family Rules. New York: Walker, 1984.

Kazdin, Alan E., and Corina Benjet. "Spanking Children: Evidence and Issues." Current Directions in Psychological Science 56.4 (2003): 99–103.

Meyerhoff, Michael K. "A Different Slant on Spanking." Pediatrics for Parents 19.6 (2001): 8–10.

The New Revised Standard Version Bible: Catholic Edition. Nashville: Catholic Bible, 1990.

Straus, Murray A., and Denise A. Donnelly. Beating the Devil Out of Them. New Brunswick: Transaction, 2001.

Vockell, Edward P. Whatever Happened to Punishment. Muncie: Accelerated Development, 1977.

Wilson, John. "Corporal Punishment Revisited." Cambridge Journal of Education 32.3 (2002): 409–417.

Practicing MLA

EXERCISE: Creating a "Works Cited" Page

Create a "Works Cited" page using the following sources listed in a student's notes.

William Beach. Inviting collaborations in stories about a woman. Language in Society, Volume 39, pages 379 to 407. 2000.

Polanyi, L. "So what's the point?" Semiotica, 25 Volume. 3 issue 4 pages 207 to 241. 1979.

Deborah Tannen 1982 Oral and literate strategies in spoken and written texts. Language, 58 (1), 1-21. Retrieved from that JSTOR thing on November 11, 2008.

In A. Durenti (Ed.). Linguanthropology: A reader. (263-307). Oxford, England: Blackwell.Schieffellin, B. & E. Ochs. (2001). "Language acquisition and socialization: Three developmental stories and their implications."

Candice McKee. Interview. UCO. March 2, 2008.

EXERCISE: Working With In-Text Citations, part 1

Using the sources above, list the proper in-text citation for each.

1. Write an in-text citation where the author's name is used in the sentence.
2. Write an in-text citation as though you paraphrase two paragraphs from the source.
3. Write an in-text citation where the author's name and the date of publication are unknown.

EXERCISE: Working With In-Text Citations, part 2

Label the following as "C" for "Correct" and "NC" for "Not Correct."

1. Tannen asserts…(Tannen 65).
2. The Interviewee noted …(McKee).
3. In Durenti (2001), the author states…(Durenti 33).
4. Beach demonstrates the need…(987)

Rewrite the ones you labeled as "NC" for "Not Correct."

EXERCISE: Formatting Entries for the "Works Cited" Page of the Major Assignment

Locate four sources for your major assignment. Correctly format the entries.

American Psychological Association

www.apa.org

The American Psychological Association Format

APA essays should be typed, double-spaced with 1-inch margins on all sides. You should use 10–12 pt. (depending on your instructor's individual preferences) Times New Roman font or a similar font, such as Cambria or Garamond. For the complete guidelines, see the *Publication Manual of the American Psychological Association*, 5th edition.

Page Header

Each essay needs to include a page header in the upper right-hand corner of every page. A page header has the first 2 to 3 words of the title of your essay. To create a page header:

1. Open the header in the document.
2. Type the first 2–3 words of the title of the paper
3. Insert five spaces
4. Insert the page number

Sections

APA style essays include four major sections:

1. Title Page
2. Abstract
3. Main Body
4. References

Title Page

The title page includes the page header (described previously), as will all of the susequent pages. On the first line of the title page flush-left, add a running head (see Figure 1). To add a running head:

1. Begin the running head with the words "Running Head" followed by a colon.
2. Give an abbreviated title of your paper in 50 characters or less in all CAPS.

Note: The "Running Head" is only on the title page. You do not include it on other pages.

3. Press the "Return" key twice, so that you are in the middle upper half of the page.
4. Set the alignment to center.
5. Type the full title.

   Note: The title may wrap several lines.

6. Press the "Return" key once, and type your name and/or names of the authors of the essay.
7. Press the "Return" key once and type the name of your university.

Formatting an Essay 1

Running head: FORMATTING AN ESSAY

Formatting an Essay or Paper in APA Style

Jason Thompson

University of Central Oklahoma

Figure 1: Example of a Title Page in APA Style

Abstract

The **abstract** is a summary of the entire paper. It should be a single, double-spaced paragraph of less than 120 words (see figure 2 below). To create the abstract complete the following:

> **Abstract**
> A summary of a paper highlighting the key aspects of that paper in a brief overview.

1. Begin a new page. Your abstract page should already include the page header (described previously).
2. Set the alignment to center.
3. Type the word "Abstract."

   Note: Leave the word unformatted; do not use bold, italics, underlining, or quotation marks.

4. Press the "Return" key once.
5. Write a concise summary of the key points of your research.

   Note: Do not indent.

> Formatting an Essay 2
>
> Abstract
>
> I am an abstract. I am an abstract. I am not any longer than 120 words but I summarize all of the important points within the essay or paper. My purpose is to demonstrate the purpose and main points of the essay or paper. I summarize the ENTIRE paper.

Figure 2: Example of an "Abstract" in APA Style

Body Pages

All body pages have the same page header as the title page and abstract (see Figure 3).

1. Begin a new page.
2. Type the title of the paper centered at the top of the page and then double space.
3. Indent the first paragraph and begin typing.

   Note: Make certain to use double-spacing, size 10 or 12 font.

Formatting an Essay 3

The Title of the Paper

I am the first page of the paper. This first paragraph is the "Introduction." In this paragraph you should make certain to have a thesis statement. Failure to have a thesis statement will lead to an "F" on the assignment.

Figure 3: Example of body pages in APA Style

Reference Page

The **"Reference Page"** is the final page in the document (see Figure 4). This is where you list ALL sources you use in your paper, including paraphrases, summaries, and long and short direct quotes.

> Reference Page
> A specific type of bibliography used by the American Psychological Association (APA).

1. Begin a new page.
2. Set the alignment to center.
3. Type the word "References."
4. Press the "Return" key and begin entering the sources.

Note: Sources are entered alphabetically by the author's last name or first word of the title of the article when the author is unknown.

Formatting an Essay 23

References

Baake, K. (2003). Metaphor and knowledge: The challenges of writing science. Albany, NY: SUNY Press.

Battalio, J. (Ed.). (1998). Essays in the study of scientific discourse: Methods, practice, and pedagogy. Stanford, CT: Ablex.

Bazerman, C. (1998). Shaping written knowledge: The genre and activity of the experimental article in science. Madison: U of Wisconsin Press.

Ceccarelli, L. (2001). Shaping science with rhetoric: The cases of Dobzhansky, Schrodinger, and Wilson. Chicago: University of Chicago Press.

Ding, D. (2002). The passive voice and social values in science. Journal of Technical Communication *32*(2), 137–154.

Figure 4: Example of a "References" page in APA Style

In-Text Citations: The Basics

When you use information from a source, any source, in the body of your essay or paper, you MUST include in-text citations or you are committing plagiarism, which may result in your expulsion from the university.

Writing Style: APA style requires you to use the past tense or present perfect tense when using introductory phrases to describe earlier research. For example, an in-text citation might look like:

Alexander (2005) **asserted...**
or
Alexander (2005) **has asserted...**

An introductory phrase is a phrase that begins with the author's name (see above).

In-Text Citation Capitalization, Quotes, and Italics

- Always capitalize proper nouns, including author names and initials: D. Jones.
- If you refer to the title of a source within your paper, capitalize all words that are four letters long or greater within the title of a source, as well as proper nouns: APA Style. Exceptions apply to short words that are verbs, nouns, pronouns, adjectives, and adverbs.

Note: When you create the References page, only the first word of a title will be capitalized; for example, Writing essays in APA style.

- When capitalizing titles, capitalize both words in a hyphenated compound word.
- Capitalize the first word after a dash or colon.
- Italicize or underline the titles of longer works such as books, edited collections, movies, television series, documentaries, or albums.
- Put quotation marks around the titles of shorter works such as journal articles, articles from edited collections, television series episodes, and song titles.

Short Quotations

If you are **directly quoting** from a work, you will need to include the author, year of publication, and the page number for the reference (preceded by "p."). Introduce the quotation with a phrase that includes the author's last name followed by the date of publication in parentheses.

> According to Alexander (2005), "Students do not see a need to cite information when developing documents in the workplace" (p. 3). Alexander (2005) found that students believe that once they leave the academic environment all intellectual knowledge is available without consequence. The students noted "employers do not care where we get information as long as the company gets credit for the idea so the company can get paid" (p. 6). Maxel states, firmly, this is "an incorrect assumption that can cost the students their jobs" (p. 343).

Long Quotations

When you use long quotes—that is quotes that are 40 words or longer—you need to place them in a freestanding block of typewritten lines. You also need to omit quotation marks.

1. Start the quotation on a new line, indented five spaces from the left margin.
2. Type the entire quotation on the new margin.
3. Indent the first line of any following paragraph within the quotation five spaces from the new margin.
4. Continue to use double-spacing throughout.

The parenthetical citation should come after the closing punctuation mark.

Note: You should seldom, if ever, use long quotes. You should only do so when not using the information word-for-word will change the meaning or emphasis. You should, instead, use summarizing or paraphrasing when including your sources.

> Alexander's (2005) study found the following: Students do not believe professors or professionals when told that citing sources is a copyright issue. Students, instead, believe the professors are simply trying to maintain authority even after the student leaves the university. The professionals are believed to be ex-students who volunteer to speak on behalf of the professor (p. 7).

Summary or Paraphrase

Page numbers are not required if you are paraphrasing. You only have to make reference to the author and year of publication in your in-text reference. APA guidelines do encourage you to use the page number to better assist the reader if she or he wants to access the particular information.

> According to Maxel (2008), employers, especially Fortune 500 companies and major government agencies, find lack of citations to be indicative of poor writing abilities. Employers have found that most entry-level employees have poor writing skills, as well as a poor understanding of business ethics. Citations are a clear marker of copyright authority, which in the business world means money (Maxel, 2008, p. 347).

In-Text Citations: Author/Authors

As with all formatting styles, APA has specific rules for citing sources. In this section you will find only the most common. If you do not find what you need, you need to access www.apa.org. Remember: if you do not cite your information correctly, it is plagiarism or academic dishonesty—both of which earn an "F" on assignments and perhaps even expulsion from the university.

A Single Author

To cite a single author, use the author's last name and the date of the publication.

> Alexander (2005) asserts that students need to read newspaper articles to understand the expectations of employers.
>
> or
>
> Students need to read newspaper articles to understand the expectations of employers (Alexander, 2005).

Two Authors

When you have a work with two authors, use the names of both authors in the phrase or in the parentheses each time you cite the work. In addition, use the word "and" between the authors' names within the text BUT use the ampersand in the parentheses.

> In the study completed by Maddison and Koche (1999), the authors demonstrated that professors spend significant time teaching students how to write (14).
>
> The authors demonstrated that professors spend significant time teaching students how to write (Maddison & Koche, 1999).

Three to Five Authors

The **first time you list a work** with three to five authors, you list all the authors in the single phrase or in parentheses.

> (Maddison, Koche, Alexander, & Maxel, 2000)

In all subsequent citations from the work, use the first author's last name followed by "et al." Notice that there is a period after "et al." and a comma after the period.

> (Maddison et al., 2000)

Six or More Authors

Use the first author's name followed by et al. in the phrase or in parentheses.

> Maddison et al. (2000) indicates that professors should consider having managers, HR Directors, and other hiring personnel speak to freshman composition classes.
>
> or
>
> One research study indicates that professors should consider having managers, HR Directors, and other hiring personnel speak to freshman composition classes (Maddison et al., 2000).

Unknown Author

If you are using the Internet, you may find more often than not that works do not have a specified author. In this case, cite the source by its title in the phrase or use the first word or two in the parentheses. Titles of books and reports are italicized; titles of articles and chapters are in quotation marks.

> In an article posted on Yahoo! News, it is noted that poor communication, both verbal and written, is the primary reason employees are dismissed ("Writing In," 2007).

Note: At times "Anonymous" is listed for the author. When this occurs, use it as the author's name (Anonymous, 2007). Then in the reference list, use the name Anonymous as the author.

Organization as Author

When an organization or government agency authors a piece, mention the organization in the phrase or in the parenthetical citation the **first time** you cite the source.

> According to the National Institute of Mental Health (2003),...

If the organization has an abbreviation that is used by most people or as its most common reference, include the abbreviation in brackets the **first time** the source is cited and then use only the abbreviation in later citations.

> *First citation:* (National Institute of Mental Health [NIMH], 2003)
>
> *Second citation:* (NIMH, 2003)

Electronic Sources

When possible, you should cite an electronic document the same as any other document by using the author-date style.

> Mackery (2000) asserted...

When it's not possible, you will use one of the following:

Unknown Author and Unknown Date

Often electronic sources do not have an author or date listed. When this occurs, use the title in your phrase or use the first word or two of the title in the parentheses and use the abbreviation "n.d." (for "no date").

> Professors might consider having students complete a small assignment where the students research how important employers consider verbal and written communication ("What Employers," n.d.).

Sources Without Page Numbers

Note: Never use the page numbers of Web pages you print because the way the printer reads the code sent from the computer differs based on the printer and the computer.

When electronic sources lack page numbers, try to include information that will help readers find the passage being cited. You can do this several ways:

- You can use the abbreviation for paragraph (para.) followed by the paragraph number (Mackery, 2000, para. 23).
- When an electronic document has numbered paragraphs, use the ¶ symbol (Mackery, 2000, ¶ 23). You do not count the paragraphs. The paragraphs should be numbered in the original source.
- If *the paragraphs are not numbered and the document includes headings*, provide the appropriate heading and specify the paragraph under that heading.

> According to McKee (2008), ... (Why Headings Matter section, para. 2).

Interviews, Letters, E-Mails, and Other Person-To-Person Communications

Personal communications are an important part of research. When you want to cite one in a paper, you use the communicator's name(s), indicate it was a personal communication, and provide the date of the communication.

Note: *Do not* include personal communication in the reference list.

> (B. Gates, personal communication, April 2, 2008).

> B. Gates agrees with Maxel that employers are seeking employees with strong verbal and written skills (personal communication, April 2, 2008).

Two or More Works Used to Support a Single Entry

When your citation includes two or more works, put them in the order they appear in the reference list, separated by a semi-colon.

> (Maxel, 2008; Montgomery et al., 2006)

Authors with the Same Last Name but Different First Names

Use the first initials with the last names when you have authors with the same last name.

> (K. Maxel, 2008; J. Maxel, 1992)

References Page Entries

Single Author of Article

When you have a work with a single author, list the last name first, followed by author initials. List both the first and middle initials if known.

Gordan, D. (2004). I'm tired. You clean and cook. Shifting gender identities and second language socialization. TESOL Quarterly, 38(3), 437–457.

Two Authors of Article

When you have two authors, list the entry by their last names and initials. In addition, use the ampersand instead of "and."

Garrett, P., & Baquedero-Lopez, P. (2002). Language socialization: Reproduction and continuity, transformation, and change. Annual Review of Anthropology, 31, 339–361.

Three to Six Authors of Article

Even when articles have three to six authors, you list the entry by last names and initials. Use commas to separate author names, while the last author name is preceded again by an ampersand.

Cantrell, B., Gibbons, S., Brown, A., Atteberry, N., & Ward, B. (2005). The importance of academic counselors in the success of student graduation rates. Journal of Education, 78, 332–356.

More Than Six Authors

If there are more than six authors, list the first six as above and then "et al."

Masters, A., McDonald, L., Ryan, S., Rogers, M., Tomlinson, J., Rowe, T., et al. (1998). Writing in the technical writing classroom. Journal of Technical Writing, 23(2), 223–229.

Two or More works by the Same Author

Use the author's name for all entries and then list the entries by the year. List in reverse chronological order. List the author's single works before shared works (see below).

Schieffellin, B. (1990). <u>The give and take of everyday life: Language socialization of Kaluli children</u>. New York: Cambridge University Press.

Schieffellin, B. & Ochs, E. (1986). <u>Language socialization across cultures</u>. New York: Cambridge University Press.

Schieffellin, B. & Ochs, E. (1988). Language Socialization. <u>Annual Review of Anthropology</u>, 15, 163–191.

Article in Journal Paginated by Volume

Journals that are paginated by volume begin with page one in issue one, and continue numbering issue two where issue one ended, etc.

Schieffellin, B., & Ochs, E. (1988). Language Socialization. <u>Annual Review of Anthropology</u>, 15, 163–191.

Article in Journal Paginated by Issue

Journals paginated by issue begin with page one every issue; therefore, the issue number gets indicated in parentheses after the volume. The parentheses and issue number are not italicized or underlined.

Gordan, D. (2004). I'm tired. You clean and cook. Shifting gender identities and second language socialization. <u>TESOL Quarterly</u>, 38(3), 437–457.

Article in a Newspaper

Unlike other types of entries, p. or pp. precede page numbers for a newspaper source. Single pages take p., and multiple pages take pp.

Dillon, S. (2004, December 7). What corporate America can't build: A sentence. <u>The New York Times</u>, p. 23B.

Article or Chapter in an Edited Book

Note that in this type of entry, you use the p. or pp. before page numbers.

Tannen, D. (1980). A comparative analysis of oral narrative strategies: Athenian Greek and American English. In W.L. Chafe (Ed.), The Pear Stories: Cognitive, Cultural, and Linguistic Aspects of Production. (pp. 51–87). Norwood, N.J.: Ablex Publishing Corporation.

Government Document

Government documents are listed by the agency that produces them.

National Institute of Mental Health. (2001). Depresion: Lo Que Toda Mujer Debe Saber (DHHS Publication No. 01-4794 (SP)). Washington, DC: U.S. Government Printing Office.

Motion Picture

DeVito, D. (Producer), & Braff, Z. (Director). (2004). Garden State [Motion picture]. United States: Camelot Pictures.

Television Broadcast or Series Episode

Bowman, R. (Producer). (December, 2007). Six Degrees Could Change The World [Television broadcast]. Washington D.C.: National Geographic Channel.

A Television Series

D'Esposito, A. (Producer). (2003). Cold Case [Television series]. Hollywood: CBS Paramount Network Television.

Single Episode of a Television Series

Randall, E., & Garrett, K. (Writers). (2007). Family 8108 [Television series episode]. In M. Stehm, J. Bruckheirmer, J. Littman (Producers), Cold Case. Hollywood: CBS Paramount Network Television.

Music Recording

Lewis, J. (2007). Under the black light [Recorded by Rilo Kiley]. Under the Black Light [CD]. Burbank, CA: Warner Bros.

Article From an On-Line Periodical

The only difference between a print article and an on-line article is the way in which you access it. When citing an on-line periodical, include **all** of the information the on-line host makes available, including an issue number in parentheses.

Author, A. A., & Author, B. B. (Date of publication). Title of article. Title of Online Periodical, volume number (issue number if available). Retrieved month day, year, from http://www.theWebsitename.com/url/

Dillon, S. (December 7, 2004). What corporate America can't build: A sentence. The New York Times, 149. Retrieved March 3, 2008, from http://www.nytimes.com/2004/12/07/business/07write.html

On-Line Scholarly Journal Article

Katz, S. (2008). Assessing a hybrid format. Journal of Business and Technical Communication, 22. Retrieved February 25, 2008 from http://jbt.sagepub.com/content/vol22/issue1

Article From a Database

When referencing material obtained from an on-line database—EBSCOhost, etc.—you must provide appropriate print citation information. In addition, also add information that gives the date of retrieval and the proper name of the database. You must do both because some people may need to retrieve the information without the use of the database.

Wallace, J. (2004). Warning! Poor writing skills may be hazardous to your career. Public Relations: Tactics, 11(4). Retrieved March 8, 2006, from Business Source Elite database.

Nonperiodical Web Document, Web Page, or Report

These types of resources are popular but risky. When you use these sources, you must list as much of the following information as possible. This means you cannot be lazy—you must hunt for information and you must be aware of the information you retrieve. Furthermore, if you locate a page with an address with a bunch of gobbledygook, delete all of the gobbledygook up to http://www.theWeb sitename.com/):

Bissonnette, Z. (August 27, 2007). Employers say young workers can't write. Retrieved March 8, 2008, from http://www.bloggingstocks.com /2007/08/27/employers-say-young-workers-cant-write/

Note: When an Internet document is *more than one Web page*, provide a URL that links to the home page or entry page for the document.

Note: If there isn't a date available for the document, use (n.d.) for no date.

On-Line Forum or Discussion Board Posting

Two popular sources are on-line forums or discussion boards. For these sources, list the title of the message and the URL of the newsgroup or discussion board. MySpace and Facebook postings follow this format.

Anderson, C. (2008, January 31). Environmentalism becoming a trend. [Msg 12]. Message posted to http://lists.oksustainability.org/

Note: When available, use the author's real name. If only the screen name is available for the author, then use the screen name.

Note: Be sure to provide the exact date of the posting.

Computer Software

Obvious, LLC. (2006). Twitter [computer software]. California: San Francisco.

Sample Student Essay

Waterproofing New Orleans

Karen Nelson

ENG 1213 English Composition

Professor Janeen Myers

March 15, 2008

Abstract

Though the tragedy of the flooding of New Orleans in 2005 had real human consequences, the reasons for the flooding had less to do with a tragic environmental event and more to do with poor political and economic choices made which avoided the scientific warnings. It was never a question of "if" but "when" the levees would break. This paper examines how science had warned that prevention was an option that was overlooked. Furthermore, the paper examines some of the tragic political choices made concerning the levees. Finally, the real tragedy of New Orleans remains that the loss of human lives and property could have been avoided.

Waterproofing New Orleans

On August 29, 2005, America experienced the worst disaster in its history when Hurricane Katrina slammed into the Gulf Coast, annihilating everything in its path and killing approximately 1500 people (Reid, 2006). Most of those deaths occurred in New Orleans. Dead bodies are still being discovered in the rubble eighteen months later (Reid, 2006). Much of the city still looks like a weapon of mass destruction was dropped on it. The property damage is estimated to be billions of dollars. In a mass exodus, hundreds of thousands of citizens either evacuated or were rescued from rooftops and are now dispersed throughout the country. Some may never be able to return. The road home to recovery is going to be a long, hard, painful, expensive journey.

There is a great debate raging on whether or not the city of New Orleans should be rebuilt and exactly what steps should be taken to prevent this from ever happening again. There are even some who say New Orleans should not be rebuilt at all. Instead, they propose to relocate everyone to higher ground (Kusky, 2006). It is sad that people can be so cruel, yet seriously thinking they are helping people. Thanks, but no thanks. No one needs that kind of help.

New Orleans is a very old historic city, full of great people, and a very unique blending of cultures. It has a thriving fishing industry. Everyone loves Mardi Gras. Nobody can beat the food by chefs who are the world's best. Oh! Do not forget about the "unforgettable" jazz music. There is no place on earth that can compare to it. There is so much to love about it. It is home to over a million people, many of whom can trace their heritage back many generations even before the United States of America existed. Many native New Orleanians would rather gamble with losing all their worldly possessions than to leave their homeland forever. There is something there for everyone. New Orleans is a great place to live or visit. It is well worth saving, for some things are priceless. New Orleans is one of them, a city with an eternal spirit that cannot be broken.

The truth of the matter is that the mass destruction and deaths were not caused directly by Hurricane Katrina or by the fact that much of the city is below sea level. Much of the flooding did not occur until the next day when the levees, flood walls, and water pumping systems failed. The dirty little secret is that the massive flooding in New Orleans was not caused by nature, but rather a man-made disaster of poor workmanship, bad planning, gross negligence, and possibly corruption and embezzlement by the United States Army Corps of Engineers who were in charge of the massive project since its inception. They were given federal money in the 1970s to beef up the levees to a specific standard. Supposedly, they were still building the system at the time of Katrina. After investigating the matter, the Corps of Engineers concluded that the levees were obviously and tragically not built up to code. Then, and only then, did the Corps finally confess its incompetence and negligence of duty in regards to the breakdown of the flood protection system. There is also evidence that the Corps knew about these deficiencies as far back as 1980 ("Levee Verdict" 2006). Another investigation, conducted by the Louisiana State University, discovered that pilings in the breached levees were only 10 feet deep. The Corps insisted that they installed them at the required depth of 17 feet (Stromberg, 2006).

Many viable options to successfully implement a flood control system would prevent and defend against catastrophic flooding in the greater New Orleans metropolitan and surrounding areas. First and foremost, the new system would have a strong foundation built on accountability and an airtight system of checks and balances to govern all those involved in planning and carrying out plans for disaster preparation, flood control planning, and the coordination of all emergency first response systems. A drastic need for a clearly laid out, all-inclusive plan would simplify procedures, define protocol, and cut red-tape, thus bridging the communication gaps between all necessary levels of government, engineers, planners, responders, and residents. The antiquated systems would be brought up to date and modernized. High technology and state of the art materials would be used, including sensors that would detect and warn of any failure or erosion within the structure (Lougheed, 2006). The state of Louisiana should be required to award contracts to highly reputable, experienced private corporations to take over the planning and maintenance of their flood control systems, given the government's past track record of utter failure.

New Orleans could learn from the Netherlands. Much like New Orleans, the Netherlands sits well below sea level and is in a dangerous position on the North Sea if a storm strikes. In 1953, a winter storm breached the system of dikes in the Netherlands, killing almost 2,000 people. Another similarity with New Orleans is that their dikes were also in antiquated condition. After this tragedy, the Dutch people united with their government to build an intricate system of barriers to protect themselves from future flood disasters; their success has been unprecedented worldwide (Lougheed, 2006).

Over a thirty year time span, they built huge dams, connecting them with earthen dikes (levees) which enclosed the vulnerable land, much like a fortress or walled city. This vast system in its entirety is called the Delta Works. Gigantic flood gates, called sluice gates, stretch across the delta and the mouths of the Rhine, Mass, Waal, and Schelde Rivers. Another storm surge barrier, the Oosterschelde, is ecology friendly, providing protection for the sanctuary that surrounds it by allowing the tides to ebb and rise naturally through openings in the barrier (Lougheed, 2006).

This same idea could be used in Louisiana to promote the restoration of eroding wetlands that provide a natural barrier against hurricanes and are home to many species of wildlife and plant life (Biever, 2006). The wetlands along Louisiana's Gulf Coast are eroding and sinking at an alarming rate. Each year, Louisiana experiences a loss in land mass the size of the city of Manhattan (Kusky, 2006). New Orleans is already ten feet below sea level and still sinking at a rate of approximately one inch per year (Reid, 2006). Some explanations for this loss are land subsidence (sinking), rising sea levels, extraction of oil and gas, and channel dredging (Finkl, 2006).

The Oosterschelde is 5 miles wide and has 65, 100-foot-high concrete piers. These piers were placed on large, steel mesh, sand and gravel filled "mattresses." The purpose of these mattresses is to prevent erosion that could cause the concrete piers to shift (Lougheed, 2006). This type of shifting contributed to the failure of flood gates and walls, and levee breaches after Katrina tore through the Gulf Region. Obviously, this is a technique that would be extremely useful in rebuilding the New Orleans flood protection system. Overtopping of the levees also occurred, causing waterfalls that created holes which further weakened the levees. This could have been prevented by installing huge concrete aprons at strategic locations on the levees ("Levee Verdict" 2006).

Materials used to build flood control structures are very important. There are several new developments in these types of materials that can provide underground support and erosion prevention for levees, gates, and floodwalls: geosynthetic fabrics, impenetrable textiles, geomembrane, and geogrid. In addition, there are many innovative materials, and electronic and optic sensors that can be utilized to monitor structural stability and detect leaks (Lougheed, 2006).

The Maeslant flood barrier is the newest of the Dutch innovations. These gigantic, hollow, arched gates float dormant along the sides of the channel until they are needed. Then the gates are rolled into position on large ball joints where they meet each other in the middle, fill with water, and sink onto a concrete pad, effectively stopping the storm water from erupting full force onto the land. The United States Army Corps of Engineers in Louisiana is currently researching a project to build gates similar to the Maeslant ones at the Industrial Canal entrance into Lake Pontchartrain. These immense gates, 50 feet tall and 150 feet wide, can swing open and close as the need arises. Other plans are also being formulated to build similar gates for the M.R.G.O., Gulf Intracoastal Waterway, Orleans Canal, London Avenue Canal, and the 17th Street Canal. The estimated operational date is set for the year 2010.

M.R.G.O. is the initials for the Mississippi River Gulf Outlet. It is a very controversial issue concerning hurricane protection. It was originally constructed as a shortcut for commercial shipping. The ships enter the man-made canal

from the Gulf of Mexico and from there it is a straight shot into the Port of New Orleans via the Industrial Canal. It saves a lot of time and money because the Mississippi River snakes around for miles. There is only one slight problem. When a hurricane approaches, the canal becomes like a funnel cloud, sucking the water straight up the canal and into Saint Bernard Parish and the infamous Lower 9th Ward ("Ship Canal was Storm Funnel," 2005). M.R.G.O. has been notoriously nicknamed "hurricane alley." It is also blamed for the high rate of erosion of the wetlands. Congress has "deauthorized deep draft navigation" on M.R.G.O. (Reid, 2006). There has been a lot of talk about closure or channel reduction, but as of yet, no real changes have been made because the large shipping magnates hold the purse strings to Congress, making change difficult.

Another area considered to be part of this funnel is Lake Borgne which is located just below Lake Pontchartrain with only a thin piece of land separating the two lakes. The Corps is considering a system of flood gates called the "leaky levee." The gates would close during a storm and remain open the rest of the time, allowing natural tides to nourish the marshes (Reid, 2006).

Ivor Van Heerden, a highly esteemed specialist in his area of expertise at the Louisiana State University Hurricane Center ("Levee Verdict," 2006), has introduced a proposition to build a series of flood gates and locks into the Interstate-10 Twin Span Bridge that crosses Lake Pontchartrain. His plan would reduce the need for other flood gates in some of the city's canals because the water would be stopped before it reached them. His idea originated from the Dutch models (Reid, 2006).

The Corps is trying to redeem itself, working hard to repair the levees. By June 2006, they had repaired 220 miles of damaged levees and flood walls; 25 of those miles were totally rebuilt. They claim to be using better materials. The junctions between different materials where flood walls and levees meet are now being reinforced with rocks and other hard substances. Some levees have been strengthened, while others are being raised. The "I" walls are being replaced with "T" walls. "The ultimate goal is to provide 100-year flood protection by the year 2010." In the meantime, temporary gates and pumping stations will be installed (Reid, 2006).

One of the biggest obstacles in the fight to save and rebuild New Orleans is government officials getting organized and on the same page. They love to appoint all kinds of committees to conduct endless research to make a plan, to make a plan, to… Well, you get the picture. The problem is they spend so much money on the research there is nothing left to get the job done. Hans Vrijling, a famous Dutch engineer, said "…can't understand what the Corps is going to study for so long. The technology already exists and has been tested over decades in the Netherlands…Dutch and American engineers, working together, would need only a couple of months to draw up a detailed plan" (qtd. in Hosenball, 2006).

Now, the second obstacle is, of course, the almighty dollar. According to expert Vrijling, the cost of complete protection for New Orleans would be $10

Waterproofing New Orleans 10

billion, and that includes even the lowest areas. He says the high risk flood areas do not need to be abandoned (Hosenball, 2006). Where do we get all the money, you ask? "If we had the will and one month's money from Iraq, we could do all the levees and restore the coast. We can save Louisiana. It is very doable," says Ivor Van Heerden (qtd. in Hosenball, 2006). If that is not enough money, there is still another source to generate a constant flow of income. The Senate passed a bill this past summer increasing Louisiana's royalties from 2% to 25% and possibly even up to 63%. Gee, that was nice of them to give them back a percentage of their own profits from the state's natural resources.

There is one common ground most experts are in agreement about. A whole new approach must be taken. The man-made and natural defenses must be restored in conjunction with one another. Some level of harmony between man and nature must be struck for the sake of survival. This improved approach would involve extending the "battle line of defense" much further away from the population. It calls for multi-level defense systems. Some of the other levels would include restoring marshes, barrier islands, and wetlands. When this occurs, the hurricanes are stopped from traveling so far inland. There is a plan being considered that would use sand from an old underwater island to rebuild the barrier islands. Another possibility involves sinking old ships to form reefs to block the storm surge. A deal is being considered to purchase huge amounts of sediments from Illinois and ship it down river by barge to use as fill for the eroding marshlands. In the past, the hurricane protection system was compartmentalized into distinctly different and separate areas. Now, it is becoming clear that shipping, flood control, nature, and the environment have to be coordinated to work in unity with each other. Previously, nature was ignored, and men sought to dominate their environment with short-sighted solutions to their problems. We must learn from our mistakes before the damage becomes irreversible (Reid, 2006).

There is a great need for strong, highly skilled, dedicated, "take the bull by the horns" kind of leadership in New Orleans. All of the "allocated" funding needs to be distributed. God knows this problem has been researched and talked to death. Now is the time for action, serious action.

The Big Easy is having a real hard time. The city that care forgot is now on the critical care list, wishing she could forget, forgotten by the millions who come to taste her pleasures only to return to the comfort of their home, abandoning her in the hour of her greatest need. She is like the woman scorned by all her lovers. It has left a hole in the soul of America and it stinks. It is beyond sad. It is a huge, gaping, festering wound. Some are still throwing salt into it. Yes, there is a big crime problem in New Orleans. Does that mean only perfect people are worthy of help, or that the good have to suffer because of the bad? Others say people in new Orleans are stupid for living below sea level, implying that they deserved what happened to them, using that as an excuse not to help. Tell me, where is it 100% safe to live? The very nature of all life involves risk.

New Orleans is such a great place. It does not deserve to die. The citizens of New Orleans have a constitutional right to be able to go back home where they were born and raised, surrounded by their families. Family and a sense of belonging are basic and essential to human stability and happiness. In this high tech world, there are so many ways to make the city totally safe from hurricanes and floods. Yes, it costs lots of money, but so does everything. Some things are worth more than money, like life. New Orleans lives and breathes. She is alive. It is a worthwhile investment to resuscitate her. New Orleans is so rare and her people so genuine. America, rally around your fellow countrymen; rebuild this great city and restore the spirit of her people. The horror shows about Katrina with all the gut wrenching scenes no longer flash across the television daily, but do not let that fool you. Many parts of the city are still a ghost town. Others are piled high with rubble. In many places, time stands eerily still, frozen on August 29, 2005. Many of her people are still orphans; they have no home. A house is the building you live in whereas a home is where your soul lives and flourishes.

Waterproofing New Orleans 13

References

Biever, C. (2006). Why splitting the Mississippi won't save the wetlands. New Scientist 191(2571), 10–11. Retrieved March 13, 2007, from Academic Search Premier Database.

Finkl, C. W., et al. (2006). Fluvial sand sources for Barrier Island restoration in Louisiana:

Geotechnical investigations in the Mississippi River. Journal of Coastal Research 22(4), 773–787. Retrieved March 13, 2007, from Academic Search Premier Database.

Hosenball, M. (2006). It's cheaper to go Dutch. Newsweek 148(10), 36. Retrieved March 13, 2007, from Academic Search Premier Database.

Kusky, T. (2006). View point. Planning 72(4), 62. Retrieved March 13, 2007, from Academic Search Premier Database.

Levee verdict. (2006). New Scientist 189(2543), 6. Retrieved March 13, 2007, from Academic Search Premier Database.

Lougheed, T. (2006). Raising the bar for the levees. Environmental Health Perspectives 114(1), A44. Retrieved March 13, 2007, from Academic Search Premier Database.

Reid, R. (2006). The big uneasy. Civil Engineering 76(10), 46–86. Retrieved March 13, 2007, from Academic Search Premier Database.

Ship canal was storm funnel. (2005). New Scientist 188(2524), 5. Retrieved March 13, 2007 from Academic Search Premier Database.

Stromberg, M. (2006). Little good news on levees and wetlands. Planning 72(1), 40–41. Retrieved March 13, 2007, from Academic Search Premier Database.

Practicing APA

EXERCISE: Creating a "References" Page

Create a "References" page using the following sources.

> William Beach. Inviting collaborations in stories about a woman. Language in Society, Volume 39, pages 379 to 407. 2000.
>
> Polanyi, L. "So what's the point?" Semiotica, 25 Volume. 3/4 issue pages 207 to 241. 1979.
>
> Deborah Tannen 1982 Oral and literate strategies in spoken and written texts. Language, 58 (1), 1-21. Retrieved from that JSTOR thing on November 11, 2008.
>
> In A. Durenti (Ed.). Linguanthropology: A reader. (263-307). Oxford, England: Blackwell.Schieffellin, B. & E. Ochs. (2001). "Language acquisition and socialization: Three developmental stories and their implications."
>
> Candice McKee. Interview. UCO. March 2, 2008.

EXERCISE: Working With In-text Citations, Part 1

Using the sources above, list the proper in-text citation for each.

1. Write an in-text citation where the author's name is used in the sentence.
2. Write an in-text citation as though you paraphrased two paragraphs from the source.
3. Write an in-text citation where the author's name and the date of publication are unknown.

EXERCISE: Working With In-text Citations, Part 2

Which of the following are correct? Rewrite the ones you labeled as incorrect.

1. Tannen asserts…(Tannen, 1982).
2. The Interviewee noted …(McKee, 2008).

3. In Durenti (2001), the author states…(Durenti, 2001).
4. Beach (2000) demonstrates the need…

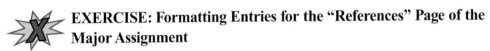

EXERCISE: Formatting Entries for the "References" Page of the Major Assignment

Locate four sources for your major assignment. Correctly format the entries.

Arguing Issues: The Readings

Chapter 12 . . . Conspiracy Issues

Chapter 13 . . . Gaming Issues

Chapter 14 . . . Consumer and Capitalist Issues

Chapter 15 . . . War Issues

Chapter 16 . . .Environment Issues

Chapter 17 . . . Immigration and Acculturation Issues

"Magic Bullet"

by Cary Stringfield

AFTER YOU READ: Analyze the Issues

1. What is the main purpose of this cartoon?
2. Why are the other assassinations mentioned?

AFTER YOU READ: Analyze the Rhetoric

1. What is funny about this cartoon?
2. Why place Oswald in the final panel?

"Brotherhood of the Magic Bullet"

by Kirk-Albert Etienne
from the Big Book of Conspiracies. *Paradox Press.*

AS YOU READ: Annotate

1. Place a star by the panels that are effective.
2. Summarize key points in the margins.
3. Comment on the Masonic symbol in the background that is repeated.

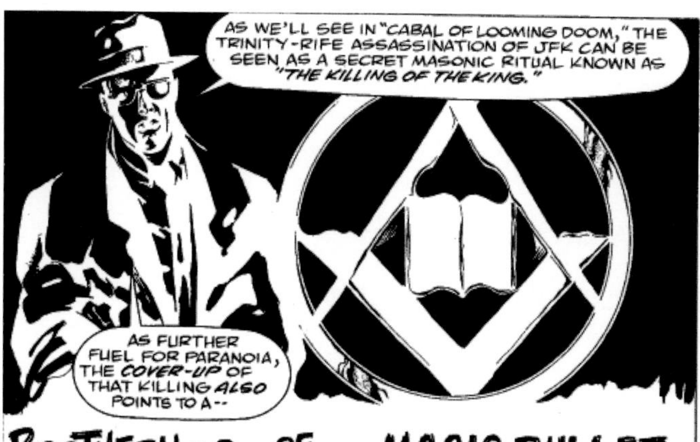

AS WE'LL SEE IN "CABAL OF LOOMING DOOM," THE TRINITY-RIFE ASSASSINATION OF JFK CAN BE SEEN AS A SECRET MASONIC RITUAL KNOWN AS "THE KILLING OF THE KING."
AS FURTHER FUEL FOR PARANOIA, THE COVER-UP OF THAT KILLING ALSO POINTS TO A--
BROTHERHOOD OF THE MAGIC BULLET

THE "TRIPLE UNDERPASS" OF DEALEY PLAZA ITSELF, SITE OF THE ASSASSINATION, LITERALLY FORMS THE OCCULT SYMBOL OF A TRIDENT.
IT WAS ALSO THE SITE OF THE FIRST MASONIC TEMPLE IN DALLAS.

LYNDON JOHNSON, MASONIC HEIR OF THE ASSASSINATION, SQUELCHED ALL INDEPENDENT INVESTIGATIONS BY CREATING THE WARREN COMMISSION.
THESE RUMORS OF CONSPIRACY MUST BE STOPPED.

33RD DEGREE MASONIC COMMISSION MEMBER (AND FBI SPY) GERALD FORD SUMMED UP THE "FINDINGS":
OSWALD WAS A LONE NUT-- J. EDGAR TOLD US SO.

FELLOW 33RD DEGREE MASON, FBI DIRECTOR J. EDGAR HOOVER, FED THE COMMISSION ITS CONCLUSIONS:
THE THING I AM CONCERNED ABOUT IS HAVING SOMETHING ISSUED SO WE CAN CONVINCE THE PUBLIC THAT OSWALD IS THE REAL ASSASSIN.

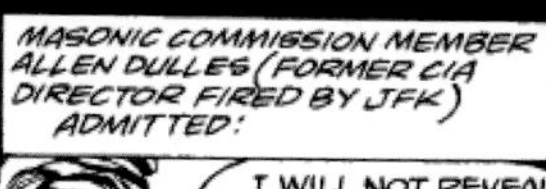

MASONIC COMMISSION MEMBER ALLEN DULLES (FORMER CIA DIRECTOR FIRED BY JFK) ADMITTED:

I WILL NOT REVEAL CIA BUSINESS TO ANY-ONE EXCEPT THE PRESIDENT.
THEN HE HINTED THAT DECEIVING EVEN THE PRESIDENT WOULD NOT BE UNUSUAL.

MASONIC HEAD OF THE "TRUTH-FINDING" COMMISSION, EARL WARREN, HAD THIS TO SAY ABOUT THE RELEASE OF DOCUMENTATION:

IT MAY NOT BE IN YOUR LIFETIME. THERE MAY BE SOME THINGS THAT WOULD INVOLVE SECURITY. THIS WOULD NOT BE MADE PUBLIC.

AND AS A FINAL TIDBIT, THE NEW ORLEANS CIA STATION HOUSE -- LINKED TO DAVID FERRIE, CLAY SHAW, AND LEE HARVEY OSWALD-- WAS LOCATED IN NOTHING LESS THAN A MASONIC TEMPLE.
BOOGA-BOOGA, FOLKS!

Brotherhood of the Magic Bullet

AFTER YOU READ: Analyze the Issues

1. What is the main purpose of the comic strip?
2. What was Hoover's role?

AFTER YOU READ: Analyze the Rhetoric

1. Why is the opening panel bigger than the other panels?
2. Did the comic need action? Why or why not?

The Issues

One of the first conspiracies to overtake the imagination of the public was the assassination of John F. Kennedy. What are the arguments being made? What are the arguments not being made? Read more. Explore more. Ask more. So to achieve a more complete story or picture, research the other voices. Be mindful of the world of conspiracies that surrounds us. Watch *JFK* by Oliver Stone and ask what is true and what is fabricated. Question such approaches to history.

The Rising Popularity of Conspiracy Theories

- Rogue members of the CIA and the U.S. "military-industrial complex" masterminded the assassination of President Kennedy.
- The Catholic Church has covered up the existence of a holy bloodline.
- The Freemasons have a covert plot to control American politics.
- The government has a secret warehouse full of alien spacecraft and technology.

Hidden truths or the imaginings of fanatics? The list above highlights only a few of the theories that are circulated through alternative newsletters, Internet sites, and even popular novels and movies. They fascinate us, and they are all considered conspiracy theories.

The obvious question is why are we discussing conspiracy theories in a textbook designed to teach you how to analyze and construct arguments. The primary reason is that all conspiracy theories are weak arguments. Proponents of these theories want others to view an event or series of events in a different way from the accepted version. If you can work your way through the often convoluted and circumstantial evidence presented to support the claim of a conspiracy theory, then you should be able to work your way through a more straightforward argument.

What is a Conspiracy Theory?

Let's look at the popular conspiracies mentioned above. What aspects of the claims are similar? Here are some to consider:

- They offer alternate explanations of important historical and/or current events.
- The conspirators are powerful.
- The activity is covert rather than overt.

These three commonalities form the basis for a definition of **"conspiracy theory."** Although you won't find a formal definition of "conspiracy theory" in the dictionary, many less formal on-line sources have tried to establish a definition. ***Wikipedia***, the on-line encyclopedia, states "a conspiracy theory attempts to explain the cause of an event as a secret, and often deceptive, plot by a covert alliance rather than an overt activity or as a natural occurrence" (accessed 6-10-06). ***Reference.com*** defines a conspiracy theory as "a theory that claims an event or series of events is the result of secret manipulations by two or more individuals or an organization, rather than the result of a single perpetrator or natural occurrence. Conspiracy theories often defy an official or dominant understanding of events, and proponents sometimes substitute zeal for logic" (accessed 6-10-06). Both of these definitions incorporate the three elements that we identified in our example theories, but there needs to be something more. Groups of people work covertly all the time. Business men often work in secret to gain an advantage over their competitors. Political parties work covertly to win elections. But neither of these activities is considered a conspiracy. This type of secret activity is accepted as part of social and political culture.

> Conspiracy Theory
> Narratives or theories about critical events such as the Kennedy assassination, Area 51, 9/11 and so on developed by the public when a lack in confidence occurs in official investigative institutions either due to corruption and/or incompetency.

Ask the Right Questions

What should we ask when examining the issues at hand and when reading about them?

Logos

What type of reasoning is provided?
Is the argument logical?
What is illogical about the reading?

Ethos

Who are the sources that provide the information?
Who is the author trying to please?
What bias does the author show?
Who is the audience?
What are the motives of the author/s?

Pathos

What emotions does the issue bring up?
Does the reading make you mad? Why?
Would this reading offend anyone?

Annotate the Text

In addition to paying attention to the text's use of logos, ethos, and pathos, annotate the readings as follows:

- Who is the writer's intended audience?
- Underline the main argument or summarize the key point in the margin.
- After reading a selection, write a brief overview commenting on the effectiveness of the organization of the message.
- Comment on the evidence provided. Is the evidence effective? Can you trust the source?
- Circle the weasel or buzz words.

How Does a Conspiracy Theory Work?

A conspiracy theory gains its power by suggesting rather than proving. Often the actual explanations and timelines that theorists construct are almost impossible to follow. The chain of events seems filled with what might be "coincidences," and/or there is no corroborating evidence. However, if the theorist can make an alternate explanation ***sound*** plausible, then others might at least take a moment to consider it. To make a theory sound plausible or possible, the theory must have the following elements:

1. The conspirators must have the power and resources to have carried out the action.
2. There must be a clear benefit for the conspirators.
3. There should be at least some circumstantial or partial evidence.
4. The theory should speak to broader concerns or fears.

Let's look at our example conspiracy theory to see if these four elements are present.

> Rogue members of the CIA and the U.S. "military-industrial complex" covertly masterminded the assassination of President Kennedy.

The CIA would certainly have the money and power to plan a presidential assassination, and according to this theory, the members would benefit from the assassination by putting Lyndon Johnson in power thus halting Kennedy's dismantling of the CIA and withdrawal of troops from Vietnam. There has long been disbelief that Oswald could have fired all the shots that injured Governor Connelly and killed the President. The Zapruder film contains shadowy figures that even with our modern enhancement techniques cannot be ruled out as gunmen. Jack Ruby, who shot Oswald, stated early on that he was part of a "conspiracy" but would not elaborate. This particular conspiracy theory plays on our fears that the "covert" branches of our government frequently carry out initiatives that involve the running of our government.

This theory also plays on the deeply held belief that good is more powerful than evil. It is hard to accept that all the hope and promise that JFK represented for the nation could be destroyed by one disturbed individual. It would be more comforting to believe that it took a large, powerful, well-organized, group like the CIA to kill such an important person and symbol.

The example above contains all four elements of a good conspiracy theory.

On a separate sheet of paper, write down another theory about the JFK assassination, or if you haven't heard an alternate theory, make up one.

Take time to look at the theory and then note how it contains or does not contain the four essential elements.

Conspiracy theories are very formulaic and once you have constructed one, it is easy to come up with a conspiracy theory about most major world events. Have some fun and fill in the blanks to create your own conspiracy theory about your favorite topic using the form found at www.cjnetworks.com/~cubsfan/old_conspiracy.html.

The Oliver Stone movie *JFK* suggests that President Kennedy was killed by a secret group of people who were connected to the CIA and the military. These people were opposed to Kennedy's policies concerning Vietnam and Cuba. The film is based on Jim Garrison's trial of Clay Shaw and on several books that Garrison has written on his theory of Kennedy's assassination. In the film, Garrison makes the following arguments for a CIA conspiracy.

"The President Was Murdered by a Conspiracy"

from JFK, *by Oliver Stone*

AS YOU READ: Annotate

As you read this excerpt from *JFK*, note the following elements of a conspiracy theory:

1. The conspiracy is connected to broader concerns or fears.
2. Covert activity is covered up.
3. Conspirators benefited.
4. Conspirators must have the power and resources to have carried out the action.

Be prepared to discuss your findings in class.

JIM GARRISON:

"Treason doth never prosper," wrote an English poet, "What's the reason? For if it prosper, none dare call it treason." The generals who sent Dreyfus to Devils Island were among the most honorable men in France, the men who killed Caesar were among the most honorable men in Rome. And the men who killed Kennedy, no doubt, were honorable men. I believe we have reached a time in our country, similar to what life must've been like under Hitler in the 30's, except we don't realize it because Fascism in our country takes the benign disguise of liberal democracy. There won't be such familiar signs as swastikas. We won't build Dachaus and Auschwitzes. We're not going to wake up one morning and suddenly find ourselves in gray uniforms goose-stepping off to work... "Fascism will come," Huey Long once said, "in the name of anti-fascism"—it will come in the name of your security—they call it "National Security," it will come with the mass media manipulating a clever concentration camp of the mind. The super state will provide you tranquility above the truth, the super state will make you believe you are living in the best of all possible worlds, and in order to do so will rewrite history as it sees fit. George Orwell's Ministry of Truth warned us, "Who controls the past, controls the future." The American people have yet to see the Zapruder film. Why? The American people have yet to see the real photographs and X-rays of the autopsy. Why? There are hundreds of documents that could help prove this conspiracy. Why have they been withheld or burned by the Government? Each time my office or you the people have asked those questions, demanded crucial evidence, the answer from on high has been "national security." What kind of "national security" do we have when we have been robbed of our leaders? Who determines our "national security"? What "national security" permits the removal of fundamental power from the hands of the American people and validates the ascendancy of invisible government in the United States? That kind of "national security," gentlemen of the jury, is when it smells like it, feels like it, and looks like it, you call it what it is—it's Fascism! I submit to you that what took place on November 22, 1963 was a coup d'etat. Its most direct and tragic result was a reversal of President Kennedy's commitment to withdraw from Vietnam. War is the biggest business in America worth $80 billion a year. The President was murdered by a conspiracy planned in advance at the highest levels of the United States government and carried out by fanatical and disciplined Cold Warriors in the Pentagon and CIA's covert operations apparatus—among them Clay Shaw here before you. It was a public execution, and it was covered up by like-minded individuals in the Dallas Police Department, the Secret Service, the FBI, and the White House—all the way up to and including J. Edgar Hoover and Lyndon Johnson, whom I consider accomplices after the fact.

JIM GARRISON: (his voice cracking)

There is a very simple way to determine if I am being paranoid here. (laughter) Let's ask the two men who have profited the most from the assassination—your former President Lyndon Baines Johnson and your new President, Richard Nixon—to release 51 CIA documents pertaining to Lee Oswald and Jack Ruby, or the secret CIA memo on Oswald's activities in Russia that was "destroyed" while being photocopied. All these documents are *yours*—the people's property—you pay for it, but because the government considers you children who might be too disturbed to face this reality, because you might lynch those involved, you cannot see these documents for another 75 years. I'm in my 40's so I'll have shuffled off this mortal coil by then, but I'm already telling my 8-year-old son to keep himself physically fit so that one glorious September morning in 2038 he can walk into the National Archives and find out what the CIA and FBI knew. They may even push it back then. It may become a generational affair, with questions passed down from father to son, mother to daughter, in the manner of the ancient runic bards. Someday, somewhere, someone might find out the damned Truth. Or we might just build ourselves a new Government like the Declaration of Independence says we should do when the old one ain't working—maybe a little farther out West.

Conspiracy As Inductive Argument

All conspiracy theories operate through inference. Theorists cite specific examples and then make generalizations based on those examples. For example, one argument for CIA involvement in Kennedy's assassination could be based on past CIA involvement in assassinations. By citing examples from the past, the theorist leaves the audience to draw its own conclusion about how past action reflects how the CIA would have behaved in this circumstance. Garrison uses this type of inductive argument in his closing statement you just read above. Garrison's closing argument only points to what might be possible, and leaves the rest of the argument to the audience.

Let's analyze how Garrison builds his argument in the closing statement above:

1. Garrison uses examples to infer that groups of insiders have killed political leaders in the past to support his argument that the CIA planned the Kennedy assassination.
2. Garrison uses analogy to imply the United States government is operating similarly to Hitler's fascism.
3. Garrison cites examples of documents and evidence that are being suppressed and infers that the suppression is part of the plot.

However, Garrison never says *how* his supposed insider group is like the ones he presents as historical examples, never defines fascism or shows clear points of comparison to our government's suppression of documents for "national security" and fascist actions, and he never states exactly what he thinks those 51 CIA documents might have proved.

Conspiracy theories work to build a causal argument to prove that the effect/event was ***caused*** by something other than the official cause. Like all inductive arguments, conspiracy theories rely on inferences the audience is required to make about the causal links, examples or facts compiled to support the theory. Theorists present two events that happened one after the other or two facts that might have a connection, but they can never prove that one event caused the other or that the connection really exists.

For example, look at some of the pieces of evidence that Garrison presented at Clay Shaw's trial, which are visually portrayed in *JFK*. After each, list what Garrison asks the audience to assume or infer.

1. Oswald might have had an office at 544 Camp Street in New Orleans since this was the address stamped on the Fair Play for Cuba pamphlets he distributed.

The same address occupied by Guy Banister's detective agency. Banister was connected to the anti-Castro Cubans.

2. As a teenager, Oswald was in the Civil Air Patrol in New Orleans. David Ferrie was Captain of the unit. Ferrie later worked for the anti-Castro Cubans and bragged of CIA connections.
3. New Orleans lawyer Dean Andrews told the Warren Commission that a man who identified himself as Clay Bertrand called him the day after the assassination and asked that he represent Oswald. Garrison claimed that Clay Bertrand was Clay Shaw who witnesses say was seen with David Ferrie and Guy Banister.
4. The man who had an epileptic seizure in Dealey Plaza, who never checked into the hospital, was a planned diversion for security posted in the spot.

Logical Fallacies in Conspiracies

Each of these pieces of evidence above and Garrison's closing argument contain problems in the structure or content of the argument called **logical fallacies**.

Logos

Faulty Causality, or Post Hoc Ergo Procter Hoc: Just because one thing follows another in time does not mean that the first event caused the second event. Faulty causality claims that there is a relationship between two events just because they occurred one after another or simultaneously. Garrison's argument that the epileptic seizure was a diversion planned by the conspirators to distract security is faulty causality because there is no evidence to connect the two events.

Hasty Generalization: "Steve did not wave at me when he passed me in the hall, so he must be mad at me." The previous sentence is an excellent example of a hasty generalization. The conclusion that Steve is mad is based on inadequate evidence. Steve might not have seen you or might not have recognized you in time to wave. Garrison's theory that Oswald and Ferrie were in the same Civil Air Patrol Unit, so they must have been co-conspirators, is a hasty generalization. They might have only been acquaintances, or they might have been enemies. There is no evidence to support that they had any kind of relationship.

Faulty Analogy: This fallacy occurs when two things are brought into a comparison that are not comparable or when the two elements being compared are irrelevant. Garrison's comparison of America in the 1960's and Fascist Germany is a faulty analogy. Garrison says that the government's suppression of evidence about the assassination is the same as Hitler's suppression of information from the German people.

Ethos

False Authority: This fallacy occurs when the argument relies on an unreliable or un-authoritative source for information. When Garrison mentions the Zapruder film—at that point, the validity of the film has not been proven.

Ad Hominem: "I can't believe you won't let me stay out past curfew—You are so mean!" You probably didn't know it at the time, but this was a logical fallacy. When you quit presenting evidence to support your argument and attack the person representing the other side of the argument, you have resorted to an *Ad Hominem* fallacy. At the end of the Garrison speech, he attacks a list of people without showing evidence. He attacks J. Edgar Hoover, but does not offer proof that Hoover is responsible.

Pathos

Either/or: Also called "black and white syndrome," this fallacy occurs when only two options are offered as explanations, causes, or effects. Most complex issues have many explanations and complicated causes and effects. This fallacy plays on the audience's emotions by presenting extreme choices. When Garrison says that we have to believe that either the assassination was carried out by one person or was carried out by "fanatical and disciplined Cold Warriors in the Pentagon and CIA's covert operations apparatus," he has presented an either/or fallacy.

Scare Tactics: "All of these documents are yours—the people's property—you pay for it, but because the government considers you children who might be too disturbed to face this reality, because you might lynch those involved, you cannot see these documents for another 75 years." This sentence from Garrison's closing argument is a perfect example of subtle scare tactics. This argument plays with the audience's emotions by implying that the truth about the assassination is so horrible that we can't handle it.

The Readings

"It's Paul McCartney"

by Jim Borgman

LEE
HARVEY
OSWALD
"GOOD GLORY, GENTLEMEN! IT'S PAUL McCARTNEY!"

May 19, 2006
Cincinnati Enquirer

AFTER YOU READ: Analyze the Issue

1. What is the message of the political cartoon?
2. How does the text support the image?
3. Where is the humor?

AFTER YOU READ: Analyze the Rhetoric

1. Comment on the effectiveness of the humor.
2. Why use the ethos of Paul McCartney's name?

"The JFK Assassination— What About The Evidence?"

by Oliver Stone
Response letter to the editor of the Washington Post

Oliver Stone was born in 1946 and studied at Yale University and the New York University Film School. In 1967, Stone did a tour of duty in Vietnam, which he says changed his worldview. Stone's filmography includes *Any Given Sunday*, *Nixon*, *Born on the Fourth of July*, *Platoon*, and *Wall Street*. His films focus on his characters' trials and triumphs and show us our own humanity. The film *JFK* was made in 1991 and stirred a debate throughout most major newspapers as to its accuracy.

AS YOU READ: Annotate

1. Look back at how you annotated the Belin and Ford article and review which arguments convinced you. Note in the margins whether Stone's responses to Belin and Ford's arguments convince you.
2. Underline any conspiracy theory elements.
3. After you finish the article, write a brief sentence about whether you were convinced by Stone's argument or not, and tell why or why not.

One day after prominently displaying a "news" story in which David Belin—the ultimate frustrated losing prosecutor as almost the lone defender of the Warren Commission's version of the assassination of President Kennedy—called me a "prostitute" and my unreleased film, *JFK* a lie worthy of Adolf Hitler, *The Washington Post* was fit last Tuesday to give him nearly half its op-ed page to continue his intemperate assault.

Belin and former president Gerald Ford are the last of a dying breed:

Warren Commission apologists. Today, not even the government itself contends the Warren Commission investigation into the assassination of President Kennedy was an adequate one. The 1976-79 House Select Committee on Assassinations (HSCA) concluded that the CIA, the F.B.I. and military intelligence withheld information from the Warren Commission, and these agencies and the commission never thoroughly investigated even the possibility of conspiracy.

Belin and Ford make their case by using a combination of ignorance of new evidence and a selective presentation of Warren Commission material. As the reader will see from this presentation of their bald assertions versus the evidence, it is not a very good case.

BELIN AND FORD: Nineteen medical experts have examined the autopsy photographs and x-rays of President Kennedy and concluded that all the shots struck Kennedy from the rear.

EVIDENCE: While the "official" autopsy photos and x-rays do show that all shots came from the rear, the 26 trained medical personnel—doctors, nurses, technicians—who treated the president at Parkland Hospital testified to the Warren Commission that they saw an exit-type wound in the back of the head, a wound that is inconsistent with the photos and x-rays. Neither the Warren Commission nor the HSCA showed the photos and x-rays to the Dallas doctors. Until this happens the medical evidence proves absolutely nothing.

BELIN AND FORD: Unequivocal ballistics evidence shows that the bullet that struck the president in the head and the bullet that passed through President Kennedy's neck and struck Gov. Connally were fired from Oswald's rifle.

EVIDENCE: The evidence is far from unequivocal. The Warren Commission tests reported "minor variations" in the various bullet fragments, making the results at best inconclusive. More sophisticated analysis by the HSCA came to the same non-conclusion—that it was "highly likely" but not certain that the fragments matched each other in composition.

Belin still believes (as of his 1988 book, *Final Disclosure*) that Kennedy was shot in the back of the neck. The autopsy photographs show that the wound was in his *upper back*, making it even more unlikely that the "magic bullet" exited through his throat and struck Gov. Connally. Moreover, Belin and Ford are obviously unaware of the declassified F.B.I. document stating the bullet in the back penetrated only about two inches and did not exit—proving that the "single bullet" scenario could not have happened at all.

Taking Exception

BELIN AND FORD: A "massive neuromuscular reaction" caused the president's head to move backward when struck from the rear by a bullet.

EVIDENCE: A "massive neuromuscular reaction," according to Messrs. Ford and Belin, occurs when there is "massive damage inflicted to nerve centers of the brain." The nerve centers of the brain are the pons, the medulla, the cerebellum—all located in the rear of the brain. According to the Warren Commission and the HSCA, the head shot damaged the right cerebral hemisphere of Kennedy's brain—not a nerve coordination center, not capable of causing a "massive neuro-muscular reaction."

BELIN AND FORD: Postal Inspector Holmes delayed Oswald's transfer, thus proving Ruby was not part of any conspiracy.

EVIDENCE: If Ruby was part of a conspiracy and Ruby was allowed into the police station by a contact there, then the Holmes excuse is nonsense. The conspirators would make sure Ruby was there for the transfer. Ford and Belin argue that no would-be hit man would kill his target in a police station. No, of course not, unless he had help.

BELIN AND FORD: Rabbi Hillel Silverman said he is convinced Ruby was telling him the truth when he says he wasn't conspiratorially involved.

EVIDENCE: Ruby told the Warren Commission he couldn't tell the truth in Dallas and begged to be taken to Washington. He also gave press conferences in 1966 saying he would like to tell the truth. By then Ruby was no longer in contact with Silverman. The rabbi left the Dallas area in 1965. Why Belin thinks we should take Silverman's word over Ruby's is unclear.

BELIN AND FORD: Jack Ruby's lie detector test results—although not 100 percent accurate, confirmed that Ruby was not part of any conspiracy.

EVIDENCE: While the polygraph results show Ruby was not lying when he said he acted alone, Belin and Ford conveniently leave out J. Edgar Hoover's comment in Appendix XVII of the Warren Report that, based on a psychiatrist's diagnosis of Ruby as a "psychotic depressive," the polygraph results should be considered "non-conclusive."

BELIN AND FORD: Witness Howard Brennan saw the gunman fire out the sixth-floor window and gave his description to the police.

EVIDENCE: Warren Commission counsel Joseph A Ball questioned Brennan and found several reasons to doubt his credibility:

- Brennan's account had several glaring inaccuracies with respect to the gunman's clothing and his shooting position.
- Brennan could not identify Oswald as the gunman when he first viewed the police lineup. Two months later, Brennan repeated to the F.B.I. that he wasn't able to identify Oswald at the lineup. But in March 1964 Brennan told the Warren Commission that he could have identified Oswald as the gunman but *he lied to protect himself and his family.*

BELIN AND FORD: The most probable time span of Oswald's three shots was around 10 seconds.

EVIDENCE: *Nowhere* is there evidence of 10 seconds. The Warren Commissioner concluded the time frame was from 4.8 to 7.9 seconds, depending on which of the three shots missed the car completely. The HSCA set a *maximum* time span of 8.3 seconds—but based on four shots and two gunmen. Most serious research agrees on the 5.6 seconds indicated by the Zapruder film.

BELIN AND FORD: Cabdriver William Scoggins saw Tippit's killer from within 12 feet and identified him as Oswald.

EVIDENCE: Although Scoggins did identify Oswald as the culprit, we know the lineups Scoggins viewed were heavily biased. Fellow cabbie William Whaley saw the lineups at the same time as Scoggins and told the Warren Commission:

> "… you could have picked Oswald without identifying him just by listening to them because he was bawling out the policemen, telling them it wasn't right to put him in with these teenagers . . he told them they were trying to railroad him and he wanted his lawyer . . "

Scoggins saw the lineup on Saturday, long after Oswald's name and occupation had been broadcast widely. Unlike the other men in the lineups, Oswald gave his correct name and place of work.

What Belin and Ford never mention is that Scoggins (as well as another credible witness) reported that Tippit's killer was walking *west* on 10th street—the wrong direction for Oswald to be walking.

BELIN AND FORD: Ballistics evidence proved that Oswald's revolver was the Tippit murder weapon.

EVIDENCE: There is no chain of evidence for the four cartridge cases found at the scene. Both policemen who handled them marked them with their initials, but neither could identify the cases as the ones they turned in when they testified to the Warren Commission—they couldn't find their initials. *Furthermore, the cartridge cases—two Western-Winchester and two Remington-Peters—don't match the bullets—three Western-Winchester, one Remington-Peters—recovered from Tippit's body.*

BELIN AND FORD: Those of us who served on the Warren Commission and its staff know it to be the truth—beyond a reasonable doubt—that Lee Harvey Oswald was the lone gunman who killed President Kennedy and Officer Tippit.

EVIDENCE: Apparently Ford and Belin didn't keep in touch with their colleagues. Commissioners Hale Boggs, Richard Russell and John Sherman Cooper had grave doubts from the start about the "single bullet" theory. In later years they went public with their dissatisfaction with the commission's finding. "I had strong doubts," Boggs said. Cooper was "unconvinced" by the single-bullet theory. In a 1970 *Washington Post* article, Russell said he believed President Kennedy was killed as the result of a criminal conspiracy and joined forces with researcher Harold Weisberg in an effort to declassify commission transcripts.

Conveniently, Ford and Belin wrap up their presentation by referring to the "other massive body of evidence which conclusively proves beyond a reasonable doubt that Oswald was the one gunman." They decline to present this massive body of evidence to the readers. Should we take these men at their word? Probably not.

Former President Ford's actions have been called into question more than once in the JFK case. For example, Ford seems to have reported on the Warren Commission to the F.B.I. A Dec. 12, 1963, internal F.B.I. memo from Hoover aide Cartha DeLoach noted:

> Ford indicated he would keep me thoroughly advised as to the activities of the commission. He stated this would have to be done on a confidential basis, however, he thought it had to be done. He also asked if he could call me from time to time and straighten out questions in his mind concerning our investigation.

With regard to Belin, there is overwhelming evidence that he was less than truthful in taking Charles Givens' testimony for the Warren Commission. Givens, a co-worker of Oswald's at the Book Depository, originally told Dallas police he saw Oswald on the *first* floor shortly before noon on the day of the assassinations. Later, he told the Warren Commission he had seen Oswald all alone on the *sixth* floor at that same time. In a memo written before he spoke to Givens, Belin made note of the statement, yet he did not mention it when Givens told him the new "sixth floor" version.

An F.B.I. document found at the National Archives—available to the commission—put Givens' credibility in doubt. The document quoted Dallas policeman Jack Revill as saying Givens "would probably change his testimony for money." In his books and articles, Belin champions Givens as the man who placed Oswald on the sixth floor shortly before the shooting. Researchers have asked Belin about this on many occasions; he has yet to provide an answer.

In earlier tandem performance, Belin appeared as Ford's counsel when the former president testified before the HSCA. During a break in the hearing, Ford, obviously thinking the microphones were turned off, leaned over to Belin and asked, "Have I compromised anything yet?"—a rather curious statement under the circumstances.

All of Ford and Belin's "evidence" comes from the commission volumes and report—they ignore all of the Commission Documents (not published within the volumes), all of the evidence turned up by the Jim Garrison investigation, the 1975 Senate Intelligence (Church) Committee hearings, the House Select Committee on Assassinations investigation and all of the evidence brought to light over the years by private researchers and scholars through Freedom of Information Act suits and rigorous document analaysis. The reason is simple: None of this evidence strengthens their dog-eared conclusions. Most of it contradicts them.

The Ford/Belin piece is tired, obsolete, highly selective information, printed many times before over the past 28 years, not believed by 75 percent of the American people or even supported by the conservative findings of the HSCA that JFK was killed as the result of a "probable" conspiracy.

It is disappointing that prominent men like Belin and Ford are so narrow and vindictive in their rendering of history and their ugly condemnation of me and my film. It is more disappointing *The Washington Post* gives them a forum for their discredited views.

AFTER YOU READ: Analyze the Issues

1. Why would a filmmaker so adamantly defend the historical accuracy of his film? Why wouldn't he just say it was a fictional account?
2. What points of Stone's rebuttal are most controversial? Which ones are most convincing?
3. Review your notes comparing Stone's responses to Belin and Ford's arguments. How would you determine what was the truth?
4. Compare Stone's arguments to Garrison's closing argument in the film *JFK* quoted earlier in the book. How are they alike? How are they different?

AFTER YOU READ: Analyze the Rhetoric

1. Review your notes on how Stone's argument in the *Washington Post* is different from Garrison's closing arguments in the film. How is spoken rhetoric different from written rhetoric?

2. In the margin, note Stone's use of logical, ethical, and pathetic appeals. Also note which are the most effective. Does Stone's attack on Ford's ethos seem harsh now that former President Ford is dead? Does Ford's death affect how you read this piece?
3. Note the places that Stone uses connotative words. How does he try to influence the reader?
4. How is Stone's argument organized? Is it effective?

"Political Paranoia as Cinematic Motif: Stone's *JFK*"

by Robert S. Robins and Jerrold M. Post
(Essay)

Robins and Post collaborated on this academic paper, which was presented at the 1997 American Political Science Association Conference in Washington, D.C. Dr. Robins taught at Tulane University from 1965 to 2004 and is now a Professor Emeritus. Dr. Post began teaching in the Psychology Department at George Washington University after 21 years with the CIA. This paper can be accessed at http://mcadams.posc.mu.edu/rogins.htm.

AS YOU READ: Annotate

1. Academic writing tends to be very formal. Underline passages that use formal language and put parallel lines next to paragraphs that have a formal structure.
2. Highlight the claim of the essay. In the margin, rewrite the claim in your own words.
3. In the margins, mark the arguments presented as ethical, pathetic, or logical. Note whether you agree or disagree with the point being made.

Paranoia in Political Context

paranoia, n.

> mental disorder characterized by systematized delusions and the projection of personal conflicts, which are ascribed to the supposed hostility of others; chronic functional psychosis of insidious development, characterized by persistent, unalterable, logically reasoned delusions, commonly of persecution and grandeur

paranoid, n.

suffering from paranoia

a. morbidly or excessively suspicious

paranoid style.

[Qualities] of heated exaggeration, suspiciousness, and conspiratorial fantasy. Hofstadter, "The Paranoid Style in American Politics."

The paranoid personality disorder is characterized by a pervasive distrust and suspiciousness of others such that their motives are interpreted as malevolent. Individuals with the paranoid personality disorder

- suspect, without sufficient basis, that others are exploiting, harming, or deceiving them;
- are preoccupied with unjustified doubts about the loyalty, or untrustworthiness, of friends or associates;
- are reluctant to confide in others because of unwarranted fear that the information will be used maliciously against them;
- read hidden demeaning or threatening meanings into benign remarks or events;
- persistently bear grudges, i.e., are unforgiving of insults, injuries, or slights;
- perceive attacks on their character or reputation that are not apparent to others and are quick to react angrily, or to counterattack;
- have recurrent suspicions, without justification, regarding fidelity of spouse or sexual partner.

At its most malignant, the paranoid response is associated with serious mental illnesses, both functional and organic. Severe paranoid symptoms are associated with paranoid schizophrenia, manic-depressive disorders, the late stages of substance-abuse diseases, and organic psychoses.

Increasingly the term paranoia has been used more broadly to refer not only to this specific diagnostic entity but also to a personality trait and a personality style, characterized by guardedness, suspiciousness, hypersensitivity, and isolation. An important aspect of this style is a pattern of disowning uncomfortable personal feelings and attributing them to others, the psychological defense mechanism known as projection.

With the understanding that the paranoid response springs from diverse sources and varies in consistency and intensity, throughout this essay we will interchangeably use the terms paranoid and paranoia in this broader sense, to subsume both clinical paranoid illnesses as well as paranoid style and paranoid outlook.

Although the paranoid outlook affects many areas of human affairs, it is most evident in the adversarial world of politics where it is a constant feature. At its extreme, the paranoid style is more destructive than any other political style. Paranoids do not have adversaries or rivals or opponents; they have enemies, and enemies are not to be simply defeated and certainly not to be compromised with or won over. Enemies are to be destroyed. As Huey Long, governor of Louisiana, would say to those who opposed him: "I'm not just going to beat you. I'm going to ruin you!"

What makes paranoia so difficult to define and to understand is that it begins as a distortion of a healthy political response— suspicion—but then far overshoots the mark. The paranoid message is not restricted to government leaders like Hitler and Stalin or to paranoid agitators like David Duke and Louis Farrakhan. Because it is so deep within the human condition, and because it so resonates with politics, it readily appears in the popular culture of political cinema.

Paranoia in Popular Cinema

> The Event was so great; its consequences threatened to be so dangerous, that it seemed almost blasphemous to attribute so world-shaking a crime to a young, highly unstable, badly educated, semi-literate partisan of what he called "Marxism." The event deserved a greater cause, to amend Horace.
>
> *D. W. Brogan, "Death in Dallas."*

> When they killed our president.
>
> *Caller to C-SPAN referring to Kennedy Assassination. September 11, 1992*

> Always leave them asking for more.
>
> *Old show business maxim*

The paranoid message will give more and more, and then it will give even more. The entertainment resources of the paranoid message are unrivaled. It offers puzzles, drama, passion, heroes, villains, and struggle. If the story-line can be tied to an historical event, especially one that involves romantic characters and unexpected death, then fiction, history, and popular delusion can be joined in the pursuit of profit. The story, moreover, need never end. If evidence appears that refutes the conspiracy, the suppliers of the discrediting material will themselves be accused of being part of the conspiracy. The paranoid explanatory system is a closed one. Only confirmatory evidence is accepted. Contradictions are dismissed as being naive or, more likely, part of the conspiracy itself.

The death of Marilyn Monroe and the assassination of John F. Kennedy have engendered films, television programs, books, and articles. The Kennedy assassination has even produced study groups and an annual convention in Dallas. One of the most remarkable examples of conspiracy portrayed as entertainment is the film *JFK*, directed by Oliver Stone (Warner Brothers, 1992). Our purpose is not to review the controversy concerning the circumstances surrounding President Kennedy's assassination (although we do reject the idea that the assassination was part of a conspiracy). Nor is our purpose to review the film (although we will evaluate the film within an aesthetic and literary tradition). Rather we intend to show how the paranoid theme added narrative power and commercial value to the film, to illuminate the part that the paranoid message plays in popular entertainment.

Films are not simply entertainment, they are also cultural, intellectual, and political influences. Research demonstrates the influence on beliefs, attitudes, emotions, and behavior of such films as the anti-nuclear *The Day After*, the anti-Soviet *Amerika*, *Holocaust*, and the multigenerational saga of a black family, *Roots*. The effect, however, is not so much to change people's minds as to solidify and exaggerate beliefs and attitudes already held. Films do not create cultural trends, but they do accelerate and exaggerate them. A survey and analysis of viewer reaction to *JFK* demonstrated that this film and others like it can produce "markedly altered emotional states, belief changes spread across specific political issues, and … an impact on politically relevant behavioral changes. [*JFK* viewers] reported emotional changes, [became] significantly more angry and less hopeful…Those who had seen the movie were significantly more likely to believe [the various conspiracies depicted in the film]."

JFK is not a historical film in the way that William Makepeace Thackeray's *Henry Esmond*, Alexandre Dumas's *Three Musketeers*, and Margaret Mitchell's *Gone with the Wind* are historical novels. Stone does not take fictional characters and put them in an historical context, as the fictional Scarlett O'Hara and Rhett Butler are placed in civil-war Georgia. Stone takes genuine historical characters—New Orleans District Attorney James Garrison and civic activist Clay Shaw, for example—and presents his version of what happened. Films of this sort are called docudramas because they dramatize historical events and historical characters and for the screen. A film like *Gone with the Wind* attempts to tell the viewer what things were like, what sorts of things happened in a past historical period. In contrast, a docudrama like *JFK* attempts to convey a particular version of history; the film does not simply lay out the director's version of history; it seeks to persuade the viewer that the version is the truth.

Film as media presents opportunities and limitations that are absent in a written work. These strengths and restrictions were first demonstrated in D. W. Griffith's seminal American film, *The Birth of a Nation* (Epic, 1915). This film, which set the "grammar and syntax" of cinema as narrative entertainment, carried a powerful racist message. It idealized the Old South, praised slavery, described Klansmen as heroic saviors of the white South from bestial blacks and their Northern white allies, and opposed racial "pollution." Financially it was very successful. Politically it facilitated the revival of the Ku Klux Klan. Its racism was so simplistic and offensive that, even in an era tolerant of racism, it was banned in several cities and became the object of small riots. Griffith saw himself as the victim of the forces (blacks and their Northern sympathizers) that he "exposed" in the film.

From *The Birth of a Nation*'s release in 1915 to the appearance of *JFK* in 1992 American historical films developed a cinematic pattern with the following characteristics:

- The story is presented in a filmic style of a seamless visual and aural pattern; the viewer seems to be looking directly at reality;
- The story has a strong moral message;
- The story is simple and definitive. Alternate versions are rarely suggested; if suggested, they are dismissed or mocked;
- The story is about individuals, usually heroic ones, fighting for good in the interest of humanity (that is, the audience);
- The story has a strong emotional tone.

JFK adds several other techniques. It seamlessly interweaves newsreel footage from the assassination with fictional material, so that the boundary between historical fact and the director's or writer's fictional elaborations are progressively blurred. It is crammed with information, presented in words and suggested in pictures. It contains not only many short speeches and several long orations but much dialogue. More important, it includes many scenes without dialog, some seemingly only one or two seconds long, which impart or suggest information. Not one locus of conspiracy is suggested but eight: the CIA, weapons manufacturers, the Dallas police, the armed forces, the White House, the establishment press, renegade anti-Castro Cubans, and the Mafia. The persuasive value of such an onslaught is to leave the viewer, if not convinced, at least believing that "there has to be something to it." One viewer said that she and her companion "walked out of the movie feeling like we had just undergone a powerful 'paranoia induction.'"

These facts, inventions, and insinuations do not necessarily come from the director's private beliefs. They are driven by the commercial and narrative needs of the form. Popular art requires continuity and order, elements generally lacking in genuine events. The film depiction of events must grab the viewer's attention, keep him fixed in his seat, make him identify with the action and principal characters, and induce him to tell his neighbors to buy a ticket for the next performance. The paranoid perspective advances these commercial and artistic ambitions:

- It too gives a simplified view of reality. Indeed, the paranoid world-view is one that demands coherence, even when such consistency is lacking.
- It too takes a moral stand: us against them, good against evil, openness against conspiracy.
- It too presents the "truth" as simple in essence but highly complex in details.
- It too describes a struggle, not between abstract forces, but between individuals and groups.
- It too brings powerful emotions to the narration.

Thus, the paranoid message is uniquely suited to the form of a historical film drama, or docudrama. This message is seen most powerfully in *JFK* but also in other paranoid films: *Silkwood*, *Missing*, and *The Parallax View*.

The paranoid theme complements another influence: deconstruction, a prominent feature of late twentieth century criticism and art. The most important part of the deconstructive position for our purposes is its contention that "texts" (novels, films, poems) have no meaning apart from how they are perceived. If the audience receives the "true" story, then the "facts" in the text are true. Truth is itself a shifting concept whereby the political interests of the creator and the audience (generally expressed in terms of race, gender, and economic position) define what is true. If what is presented persuades people that it is true and if this truth is "politically progressive," then the events presented in the text are true.

The political commentator Ronald Steel identifies this dynamic in *JFK*:

> Because of the director's ability to cut, splice, fuse, restage, and invent, it is virtually impossible for a viewer of his film to tell if he is seeing a real or a phony event. Stone mixes real black-and-white footage, such as the Zapruder film of Kennedy's murder, with restaged black-and-white episodes that may or may not have happened. The result is a deconstructionist's heaven. Every event becomes a pseudo-event, fictions become fact, imagination becomes reality, and the whole tangible world disappears.

Stone acknowledges that what he shows as happening need not ever have happened. Asked whether he has a responsibility to historical fact, Stone replied that the questioner was getting "into the area of censorship" and that it is "up to the artist himself to determine his own ethics by his own conscience." In any event, Stone argues that he was creating a myth that "represents the inner spiritual meaning of an event."

Stone's reference to myth as central to the film is an appropriate one. Myths are meta-explanations: they explain beyond what we can see or understand. A paranoid message can also have a great role in developing and enhancing a myth.

The life of John F. Kennedy has become an American myth, symbolizing youth, vigor, progress, and glamour. In fact, the historical Kennedy was quite different from the mythic Kennedy, but for the most part the public has set aside the facts in favor of the symbols. There are many reasons for the generation of this myth in the face of the facts. The Kennedy family (and Kennedy himself when he was alive) and their partisans fostered it: they presented Kennedy as associated with other mythic figures (Lincoln, Jefferson, Roosevelt), and they have made use of mythic archetypes (New Frontier, Camelot). Most important, however, were the timing and circumstances of Kennedy's death. Had Kennedy lived, he might be remembered as a successful or an unsuccessful president, but not as a legendary hero. His untimely death and the dramatic conditions surrounding it gave rise to his legend: in mythic style a young king promising a new world was killed in a public place in the presence of his beautiful queen, and his realm changed forever.

What is required in the myth-creating circumstances is a destructive force proportional to the event. A nerdish left wing sympathizer who manages to fire a couple of lucky shots from a cheap mail-order rifle is not a suitable instrument for the destruction of a mythic hero. In real life such things happen. In myth and film, never.

Only two destructive forces are suitable for creating the Kennedy myth. An occurrence that could be interpreted in supernatural terms would be appropriate to ending Kennedy's life and beginning the legend. An earthquake, a meteor, a tornado, the sudden collapse of an ancient bridge, or a heart attack or stroke during an historic event would all give mythic color to his death. The other possibility is that some great human source of evil was responsible.

Here we return to our initial point, the effectiveness of the paranoid message as a means of completing, or fulfilling, an artistic statement. The paranoid message is a dramatically strong one, like adultery or murder. In the case of Kennedy, it perfects the myth. Because the public has committed itself to believing the rest of the Kennedy myth, there is a natural inclination to believe in a conspiracy. It completes the story and fulfills the audience's desire for understanding. People cling to this belief with remarkable tenacity. For example, Gerald Posner, who wrote the well-reviewed anti-conspiracist *Case Closed*, was the object of threatening telephone calls and picketing by demonstrators carrying signs saying "Case Not Closed." Some conspiracists even advocated a day of national resistance to the book.

Thus, the great strength of the paranoid message in docudrama lies in its capacity to add an element that both explains an event and testifies to its importance. The technique, moreover, adds drama to a film. It also makes for a more profitable film. But such a film is not simply entertainment. As it entertains, it persuades. In fact, if the audience is not persuaded it will lose interest. The social harm that the film commits goes beyond the distortion of history. It creates a broader intellectual pollution. Each paranoid film gives weight to a popular mentality of paranoid belief. If event after event is "shown to be" the product of a malign conspiracy, then the public will accept that that is how the world works.

References

Brogan, D. W. "Death in Dallas." *Encounter* (December, 1964): 20–26.

Boorstin, D. *The Creators*. New York: Random House, 1992.

Butler, L., C. Koopman, and P. Zimbardo. "The Psychological Impact of Viewing the Film *JFK*." *Political Psychology*. 16 (1995): 237–258.

de Bock, H., and J. van Lil. "'Holocaust' in the Netherlands." In G. C. Wilhoit and H. de Bock (eds.), *Mass Communication Review Yearbook*. vol.2. Newbury Park, Calif.: Sage, 1981, pp. 639–646.

Diagnostic and Statistical Manual of Mental Disorders: DSM-IV. Washington, D.C.: American Psychiatric Association, 1994.

Felkins, P. K., and I. Goldman. "Political Myth as Subjective Narrative." *Political Psychology*. 14 (1993): 447–467.

Hofstadter, R. "The Paranoid Style in American Politics." In R. Hofstadter, *The Paranoid Style in American Politics and Other Essays*. New York: Vintage, 1967. 3–40.

Lenart, S., and K. M. H. McGraw, "America Watches 'Amerika.'" *Journal of Politics*. 51, no. 3 (1989): 697–712.

Morrow, L. and M. Smilgis. "Plunging into the Labyrinth." *Time*. December 23, 1991, pp. 74–76.

Rosentone, R. A. "*JFK*: Historical fact/historical film. *American Historical Review*." 97 (1992): 506–511.

Schofield, J. and M. Pavelchak. "'The Day After': The Impact of a Media Event." *American Psychologist*. 40 (1985): 542–548.

Steel, R. "Mr. Smith Goes to the Twilight Zone." *New Republic*. February 3, 1992, pp.30–32. Surlin, S. H. "'Roots' Research: A Summary of Findings. *Journal of Broadcasting*. 22 (1978): 309-320.

Zelizer, B. *Covering the Body*. Chicago: University of Chicago Press. 1992.

AFTER YOU READ: Analyze the Issues

1. Although the authors said they were not going to argue for or against a Kennedy conspiracy, does the essay persuade you one way or the other?
2. According to Robins and Post, what are "myths"? How was John F. Kennedy mythic? Can you remember a president who was "mythic"? What prevents this process?
3. Why is the "paranoid message" effective?
4. What are the logical, ethical and/or pathetic arguments that the authors use to support their claim about the film?

AFTER YOU READ: Analyze the Rhetoric

1. Robins and Post list several filmic elements that Stone uses to convince the audience that *JFK* is "historical." What are they? How would such techniques be persuasive?
2. Did the formal language and structure give the theory more or less authority? Note places the language made you feel the argument was correct.
3. How was this essay organized? Can you construct an alternate organization that would also be effective?

"16 Questions on the Assassination"

by Bertrand Russell
(Essay)

Bertrand Russell was born May 18, 1872 in Wales. He studied mathematics at Trinity College at Cambridge University and published several books on mathematical theory. In addition, Russell was a political activist and wrote many essays supporting freedom of thought and his book *A History of Western Philosophy* (1945) became an instant best seller and helped to win him a Nobel Prize in Literature in 1950. In 1938, Russell moved to the U.S. and taught at the University of Chicago until returning to England in the early sixties. Russell was vocally opposed to the U.S. invasion of Vietnam and accused the U.S. of genocide. The following essay first appeared in *The Minority of One*, 6 September 1964, pp. 6–8.

AS YOU READ: Annotate

1. Note places that the author's logical training comes into view. Particularly look for enthymemes.
2. Russell is a trained philosopher and his writing tends to be very academic. Highlight words that you don't know and underline phrases that you don't understand.
3. In the margins, try to answer each question as Russell asks it. Put the answer in your own words.

The official version of the assassination of President Kennedy has been so riddled with contradictions that it has been abandoned and rewritten no less than three times. Blatant fabrications have received very widespread coverage by the mass media, but denials of these same lies have gone unpublished. Photographs, evidence and affidavits have been doctored out of recognition. Some of the most important aspects of the case against Lee Harvey Oswald have been completely blacked out. Meanwhile, the F.B.I., the police and the Secret Service have tried to silence key witnesses or instruct them what evidence to give. Others involved have disappeared or died in extraordinary circumstances.

It is facts such as these that demand attention, and which the Warren Commission should have regarded as vital. Although I am writing before the publication of the Warren Commission's report, leaks to the press have made much of its contents predictable. Because of the high office of its members and the fact of its establishment by President Johnson, the Commission has been widely regarded as a body of holy men appointed to pronounce the truth. An impartial examination of the composition and conduct of the Commission suggests quite otherwise.

The Warren Commission has been utterly unrepresentative of the American people. It consisted of two Democrats, Senator Russell of Georgia and Congressman Boggs of Louisiana, both of whose racist views have brought shame on the United States; two Republicans, Senator Cooper of Kentucky and Congressman Gerald R. Ford of Michigan, the latter of whom is a leader of his local Goldwater movement and an associate of the F.B.I.; Allen Dulles, former director of the Central Intelligence Agency, and Mr. McCloy, who has been referred to as the spokesman for the business community. Leadership of the filibuster in the Senate against the Civil Rights Bill prevented Senator Russell from attending hearings during the period. The Chief Justice of the United States Supreme Court, Earl Warren, who rightly commands respect, was finally persuaded, much against his will, to preside over the Commission, and it was his involvement above all else that helped lend the Commission an aura of legality and authority. Yet many of its members were also members of those very groups which have done so much to distort and suppress the facts about the assassination. Because of their connection with the Government, not one member would have been permitted under U.S. law to serve on a jury had Oswald faced trial. It is small wonder that the Chief Justice himself remarked that the release of some of the Commission's information "might not be in your lifetime" Here, then, is my first question: *Why were all the members of the Warren Commission closely connected with the U.S. Government?*

If the composition of the Commission was suspect, its conduct confirmed one's worst fears. No counsel was permitted to act for Oswald, so that cross-examination was barred. Later, under pressure, the Commission appointed the President of the American Bar Association, Walter Craig, one of the supporters of the Goldwater movement in Arizona, to represent Oswald. To my knowledge, he did not attend hearings, but satisfied himself with representation by observers.

In the name of national security, the Commission's hearings were held in secret, thereby continuing the policy which has marked the entire course of the case. This prompts my second question: *If, as we are told, Oswald was the lone assassin, where is the issue of national security?* Indeed, precisely the same question must be put here as was posed in France during the Dreyfus case: *If the Government is so certain of its case, why has it conducted all its inquiries in the strictest secrecy?*

****

At the outset the Commission appointed six panels through which it would conduct its enquiry. They considered: (1) What did Oswald do on November 22, 1963? (2) What was Oswald's background? (3) What did Oswald do in the U.S. Marine Corps, and in the Soviet Union? (4) How did Ruby kill Oswald? (5) What is Ruby's background? (6) What efforts were taken to protect the President on November 22? This raises my fourth question: *Why did the Warren Commission not establish a panel to deal with the question of who killed President Kennedy?*

All the evidence given to the Commission has been classified "Top Secret," including even a request that hearings be held in public. Despite this the Commission itself leaked much of the evidence to the press, though only if the evidence tended to prove Oswald the lone assassin. Thus, Chief Justice Warren held a press conference after Oswald's wife, Marina, had testified. He said that she believed her husband was the assassin. Before Oswald's brother Robert testified, he gained the Commission's agreement not to comment on what he said. After he had testified for two days, the newspapers were full of stories that "a member of the Commission" had told the press that Robert Oswald had just testified that he believed that his brother was an agent of the Soviet Union. Robert Oswald was outraged by this, and he said that he could not remain silent while lies were told about his testimony. He had never said this and he had never believed it. All that he had told the Commission was that he believed his brother was innocent and was in no way involved in the assassination.

The methods adopted by the Commission have indeed been deplorable, but it is important to challenge the entire role of the Warren Commission. It stated that it would not conduct its own investigation, but rely instead on the existing governmental agencies—the F.B.I., the Secret Service and the Dallas police. Confidence in the Warren Commission thus presupposes confidence in these three institutions. *Why have so many liberals abandoned their own responsibility to a Commission whose circumstances they refuse to examine?*

It is known that the strictest and most elaborate security precautions ever taken for a President of the United States were ordered for November 22 in Dallas. The city had a reputation for violence and was the home of some of the most extreme right-wing fanatics in America. Mr. and Mrs. Lyndon Johnson had been assailed there in 1960 when he was a candidate for the Vice-Presidency. Adlai Stevenson had been physically attacked when he spoke in the city only a month before Kennedy's visit. On the morning of November 22, the Dallas *Morning News* carried a full-page advertisement associating the President with Communism. The city was covered with posters showing the President's picture and headed "Wanted for Treason." The Dallas list of subversives comprised 23 names, of which Oswald's was the first. All of them were followed that day, except Oswald. *Why did the authorities follow many persons as potential assassins and fail to observe Oswald's entry into the book depository building while allegedly carrying a rifle over three feet long?*

The President's route for his drive through Dallas was widely known and was printed in the Dallas *Morning News* on November 22. At the last minute the Secret Service changed a small part of their plans so that the President left Main Street and turned into Houston and Elm Streets. This alteration took the President past the book depository building from which it is alleged that Oswald shot him. How Oswald is supposed to have known of this change has never been explained. *Why was the President's route changed at the last minute to take him past Oswald's place of work?*

After the assassination and Oswald's arrest, judgment was pronounced swiftly: Oswald was the assassin, and he had acted alone. No attempt was made to arrest others, no road blocks were set up round the area, and every piece of evidence which tended to incriminate Oswald was announced to the press by the Dallas District Attorney, Mr. Wade. In such a way millions of people were prejudiced against Oswald before there was any opportunity for him to be brought to trial. The first theory announced by the authorities was that the President's car was in Houston Street, approaching the book depository building, when Oswald opened fire. When available photographs and eyewitnesses had shown this to be quite untrue, the theory was abandoned and a new one formulated which placed the vehicle in its correct position. Meanwhile, however, D.A. Wade had announced that three days after Oswald's room in Dallas had been searched, a map had been found there on which the book depository building had been circled and dotted lines drawn from the building to a vehicle on Houston Street, showing the alleged bullet trajectory had been planned in advance. After the first theory was proved false, the Associated Press put out the following story on November 27: "Dallas authorities announced today that there never was a map."

The second theory correctly placed the President's car on Elm Street, 50 to 75 yards past the book depository, but had to contend with the difficulty that the President was shot from the front, in the throat. How did Oswald manage to shoot the President in the front from behind? The F.B.I. held a series of background briefing sessions for *Life* magazine, which in its issue of December 6 explained that the President had turned completely round just at the time he was shot. This too, was soon shown to be entirely false. It was denied by several witnesses and films, and the previous issue of *Life* itself had shown the President looking forward as he was hit. Theory number two was abandoned.

In order to retain the basis of all official thinking, that Oswald was the lone assassin, it now became necessary to construct a third theory with the medical evidence altered to fit it. For the first month no Secret Service agent had ever spoken to the three doctors who had tried to save Kennedy's life in the Parkland Memorial Hospital. Now two agents spent three hours with the doctors and persuaded them that they were all misinformed: the entrance wound in the President's throat had been an exit wound, and the bullet had not ranged down towards the lungs. Asked by the press how they could have been so mistaken, Dr. McClelland advanced two reasons: they had not seen the autopsy report—and they had not known that Oswald was behind the President! The autopsy report, they had been told by the Secret Service, showed that Kennedy had been shot from behind. The agents, however, had refused to show the report to the doctors, who were entirely dependent on the word of the Secret Service for this suggestion. The doctors made it clear that they were not permitted to discuss the case. The third theory, with the medical evidence rewritten, remains the basis of the case against Oswald at this moment. *Why has the medical evidence concerning the President's death been altered out of recognition?*

****

Although Oswald is alleged to have shot the President from behind, there are many witnesses who are confident that the shots came from the front. Among them are two reporters from the Forth Worth *Star Telegram*, four from the Dallas *Morning News*, and two people who were standing in front of the book depository building itself, the director of the book depository and the vice-president of the firm. It appears that only two people immediately entered the building: the director, Mr. Roy S. Truly, and a Dallas police officer, Seymour Weitzman. Both thought that the shots had come from in front of the President's vehicle. On first running in that direction, Weitzman was informed by "someone" that he thought the shots had come from the building, so he rushed back there. Truly entered with him in order to assist with his knowledge of the building. Mr. Jesse Curry, the Chief of Police in Dallas, has stated that he was immediately convinced that the shots came from the building. If anyone else believes this, he has been reluctant to say so to date. It is also known that the first bulletin to go out on Dallas police radios stated that "the shots came from a triple overpass in front of the presidential automobile." In addition, there is the consideration that after the first shot the vehicle was brought almost to a halt by the trained Secret Service driver, an unlikely response if the shots had indeed come from behind. Certainly Mr. Roy Kellerman, who was in charge of the Secret Service operation in Dallas that day, and traveled in the presidential car, looked to the front as the shots were fired. The Secret Service has had all the evidence removed from the car, so it is no longer possible to examine it. *What is the evidence to substantiate the allegation that the President was shot from behind?*

Photographs taken at the scene of the crime could be most helpful. One young lady standing just to the left of the presidential car as the shots were fired took photographs of the vehicle just before and during the shooting, and was thus able to get into her picture the entire front of the book depository building. Two F.B.I. agents immediately took the film which she took. *Why has the F.B.I. refused to publish what could be the most reliable piece of evidence in the whole case?*

In this connection it is noteworthy also that it is impossible to obtain the originals of photographs bearing upon the case. When *Time* magazine published a photograph of Oswald's arrest—the only one ever seen—the entire background was blacked out for reasons which have never been explained. It is difficult to recall an occasion for so much falsification of photographs as has happened in the Oswald case.

The affidavit by Police Office Weitzman, who entered the book depository building, stated that he found the alleged murder rifle on the sixth floor. (It was first announced that the rifle had been found on the fifth floor, but this was soon altered.) It was a German 7.65 mm Mauser. Late the following day, the F.B.I. issued its first proclamation. Oswald had purchased in March 1963 an Italian 6.5 mm Mannlicher-Carcano. D.A. Wade immediately altered the nationality and size of the weapon to conform to the F.B.I. statement.

Several photographs have been published of the alleged murder weapon. On February 21, *Life* magazine carried on its cover a picture of "Lee Oswald with the weapons he used to kill President Kennedy and Officer Tippitt [sic]." On page 80, *Life* explained that the photograph was taken during March or April of 1963.

According to the F.B.I., Oswald purchased his pistol in September 1963. *The New York Times* carried a picture of the alleged murder weapon being taken by police into the Dallas police station. The rifle is quite different. Experts have stated that no rifle resembling the one in the *Life* picture has even been manufactured. *The New York Times* also carried the same photograph as *Life*, but left out the telescopic sights. On March 2, *Newsweek* used the same photograph but painted in an entirely new rifle. Then on April 13 the Latin American edition of *Life* carried the same picture on its cover as the U.S. edition had on February 21, but in the same issue on page 18 it had the same picture with the rifle altered. *How is it that millions of people have been misled by complete forgeries in the press?*

The authorities interrogated Oswald for nearly 48 hours without allowing him to contact a lawyer, despite his repeated requests to do so. The director of the F.B.I. in Dallas was a man with considerable experience. American Civil Liberties Union lawyers were in Dallas requesting to see Oswald and were not allowed to do so. By interrogating Oswald for 48 hours without access to lawyers, the F.B.I. created conditions which made a trial of Oswald more difficult. A confession or evidence obtained from a man held 48 hours in custody is likely to be inadmissible in a U.S. court of law. The F.B.I. director conducted his interrogation in a manner which made the use of material secured in such a fashion worthless to him. This raises the question of whether he expected the trial to take place.

Another falsehood concerning the shooting was a story circulated by the Associated Press on November 23 from Los Angeles. This reported Oswald's former superior officer in the Marine Corps as saying that Oswald was a crack shot and a hot-head. The story was published widely. Three hours later AP sent out a correction deleting the entire story from Los Angeles. The officer had checked his records and it had turned out that he was talking about another man. He had never known Oswald. To my knowledge the correction has yet to be published by a single major publication.

The Dallas police took a paraffin test on Oswald's face and hands to try to establish that he had fired a weapon on November 22. The Chief of the Dallas Police, Jesse Curry, announced on November 23 that the result of the test "proves Oswald is the assassin." The Director of the F.B.I. in the Dallas-Fort Worth area in charge of the investigation stated: "I have seen the paraffin test. The paraffin test proves that Oswald had nitrates and gunpowder on his hands and face. It proves he fired a rifle on November 22." Not only does this unreliable test not prove any such thing, it was later discovered that the test on Oswald's face was in fact negative, suggesting that it was unlikely he fired a rifle that day. *Why was the result of the paraffin test altered before being announced by the authorities?*

****

Oswald, it will be recalled, was originally arrested and charged with the murder of Patrolman Tippitt [sic]. Tippitt was killed at 1:06 p.m. on November 22 by a man who first engaged him in conversation, then caused him to get out of the stationary police car in which he was sitting and shot him with a pistol. Miss Helen L. Markham, who states that she is the sole eye-witness to this crime, gave the Dallas police a description of the assailant. After signing her affidavit, she was instructed by the F.B.I., the Secret Service and many police officers that she was not permitted to discuss the case with anyone. The affidavit's only description of the killer was that he was a "young white man." Miss Markham later revealed that the killer had run right up to her and past her, brandishing the pistol, and she repeated the description of the murderer which she had given to the police. He was, she said, "short, a little heavy, and had somewhat bushy hair." (The police description of Oswald was that he was of average height, or a little taller, was slim and had receding fair hair.) Miss Markham's affidavit is the entire case against Oswald for the murder of Patrolman Tippitt, yet District Attorney Wade asserted: "We have more evidence to prove Oswald killed Tippit than we have to show he killed the President." The case against Oswald for the murder of Tippitt, he continued, was an absolutely strong case. *Why was the only description of Tippitt's killer deliberately omitted by the police from the affidavit of the sole eye-witness?*

Oswald's description was broadcast by the Dallas police only 12 minutes after the President was shot. This raises one of the most extraordinary questions ever posed in a murder case: *Why was Oswald's description in connection with the murder of Patrolman Tippitt broadcast over Dallas police radio at 12:43 p.m. on November 22, when Tippitt was not shot until 1:06 p.m.?*

According to Mr. Bob Considine, writing in the New York *Journal American*, there had been another person who had heard the shots that were fired at Tippitt. Warren Reynolds had heard shooting in the street from a nearby room and had rushed to the window to see the murderer run off. Reynolds himself was later shot through the head by a rifleman. A man was arrested for this crime but produced an alibi. His girl-friend, Betty Mooney McDonald, told the police she had been with him at the time Reynolds was shot, according to Mr. Considine. The Dallas police immediately dropped the charges, even before Reynolds had time to recover consciousness, and attempt to identify his assailant. The man at once disappeared, and two days later the police arrested Betty Mooney McDonald on a minor charge and it was announced that she had hanged herself in the police cell. She had been a striptease artist in Jack Ruby's nightclub, according to Mr. Considine.

Another witness to receive extraordinary treatment in the Oswald case was his wife, Marina. She was taken to the jail while her husband was still alive and shown a rifle by Chief of Police Jesse Curry. Asked if it were Oswald's, she replied that she believed Oswald had a rifle but that it didn't look like that. She and her mother-in-law were in great danger following the assassination because of the threat of public revenge on them. At this time they were unable to obtain a single police officer to protect them. Immediately after Oswald was killed, however, the Secret service illegally held both women against their will. After three days they were separated and Marina has never again been accessible to the public. Held in custody for nine weeks and questioned almost daily by the F.B.I. and Secret Service, she finally testified to the Warren Commission and, according to Earl Warren, said that she believed her husband was the assassin. The Chief Justice added that the next day they intended to show Mrs. Oswald the murder weapon and the Commission was fairly confident that she would identify it as her husband's. The following day it was announced that this had indeed happened. Mrs. Oswald, we are informed, is still in the custody of the Secret Service. To isolate a witness for nine weeks and to subject her to repeated questioning by the Secret Service in this manner is reminiscent of police behavior in other countries, where it is called brainwashing. The only witness produced to show that Oswald carried a rifle before the assassination stated that he saw a brown paper parcel about two feet long in the back seat of Oswald's car. The rifle which the police "produced" was almost 3½ feet long. *How was it possible for Earl Warren to forecast that Marina Oswald's evidence would be exactly the reverse of what she had previously testified?*

After Ruby had killed Oswald, D.A. Wade made a statement about Oswald's movements following the assassination. He explained that Oswald had taken a bus, but he described the point at which Oswald had entered the vehicle as seven blocks away from the point located by the bus driver in his affidavit. Oswald, Wade continued, then took a taxi driven by a Daryll Click, who had signed an affidavit. An inquiry at the City Transportation Company revealed that no such taxi driver had ever existed in Dallas. Presented with this evidence, Wade altered the driver's name to William Whaley. The driver's log book showed that a man answering Oswald's description had been picked up at 12:30. The President was shot at 12:31. D.A. Wade made no mention of this. Wade has been D.A. in Dallas for 14 years and before that was an F.B.I. agent. *How does a District Attorney of Wade's great experience account for all the extraordinary changes in evidence and testimony which he has announced during the Oswald case?*

These are only a few of the questions raised by the official versions of the assassination and by the way in which the entire case against Oswald has been conducted. Sixteen questions are no substitute for a full examination of all the factors in this case, but I hope that they indicate the importance of such an investigation. I am indebted to Mr. Mark Lane, the New York criminal lawyer who was appointed counsel for Oswald by his mother, for much of the information in this article. Mr. Lane's enquiries, which are continuing, deserve widespread support. A Citizen's Committee of Inquiry has been established in New York, at Room 422, 156 Fifth Avenue, New York. N.Y. (telephone YU9-6850) for such a purpose, and comparable committees are being set up in Europe.

In Britain, I invited people eminent in the intellectual life of the country to join a "Who Killed Kennedy Committee," which at the moment of writing consists of the following people: Mr. John Arden, playwright; Mrs. Carolyn Wedgwood Benn, from Cincinnati, wife of Anthony Wedgwood Benn, M.P.; Lord Boyd-Orr, former director-general of the U.N. Food and Agricultural Organization and a Nobel Peace Prize winner; Mr. John Calder, publisher; Professor William Empsom, Professor of English Literature at Sheffield University; Mr. Victor Golancz, publisher; Mr. Michael Foot, Member of Parliament; Mr. Kingsley Martin, former editor of the *New Statesman*; Sir Compton Mackenzie, writer; Mr. J.B. Priestley, playwright and author; Sir Herbert Read, art critic; Mr. Tony Richardson, film director; Dr. Mervyn Stockwood, Bishop of Southwark; Professor Hugh Trevor-Roper, Regius Professor of Modern History at Oxford University; Mr. Kenneth Tynan, Literary Manager of the National Theatre; and myself.

We view the problem with the utmost seriousness. U.S. Embassies have long ago reported to Washington world-wide disbelief in the official charges against Oswald, but this has scarcely been reflected by the American press. No U.S. television program or mass circulation newspaper has challenged the permanent basis of all the allegations—that Oswald was the assassin, and that he acted alone. It is a task which is left to the American people.

AFTER YOU READ: Analyze the Issues

1. Russell was a lifelong believer in Ockham's Razor, a philosophical position that the simplest solution is usually the correct solution. Do Russell's questions pare down the issues or confuse them? According to Russell, what is the solution to the assassination questions?
2. What is your impression of Russell's sources of information? Are they reliable? Why or why not?
3. Which of the 16 questions was most troubling? Why? Could it be answered now?
4. What is your impression of the people on the "Who Killed Kennedy Committee"? Are these people in positions that would give them access to information? Why did Russell list these people?

AFTER YOUR READ: Analyze the Rhetoric

1. What is the effect of the very specific details that Russell includes? Does it help or hurt his argument?
2. Review the words and passages you highlighted because they were unfamiliar to you. What is the effect of Russell's elevated language? Does it give him more or less authority?
3. This article was published right before the Warren Commission Report was published, and is one of the earliest conspiracy theory pieces we have. Which of the arguments seems most current? Which seem old or have already been conclusively answered?

"The Principles of Newspeak"

by George Orwell
Appendix to Nineteen Eighty-four *(1948)*
(Essay)

Eric Blair or George Orwell is most famous for his two novels *Animal Farm* (1946) and *Nineteen Eighty-four* (1948). Both works warn against the fascism that can arise in democratic countries. For some, his works have become a prophetic note of the evils that may be found in our own times.

"Principles of Newspeak" Appendix (essay) excerpt from *Nineteen Eighty-four* by George Orwell. Harcourt Brace. Centennial Edition, 2003. 309–323.

AS YOU READ: Annotate

1. Place a star in the margin by sections you like.
2. Circle the following words, and any others you don't know, and write their meanings in the margins: *provisional, superfluous, unorthodox, etymological, staccato, rendering, euphony, panegyric,* and *utilitarian.*

Newspeak was the official language of Oceania, and had been devised to meet the ideological needs of Ingoc, or English Socialism. In the year 1984 there was not as yet anyone who used Newspeak as his sole means of communication, either in speech or writing. The leading articles of the *Times* were written in it, but this was a tour de force which could only be carried out by a specialist. It was expected that Newspeak would have finally superseded Oldspeak (or standard English, as we should call it) by about the year 2050. Meanwhile, it gained ground steadily, all party members tending to use Newspeak words and grammatical constructions more and more in their everyday speech. The version in 1984, and embodied in the Ninth and Tenth Editions of Newspeak dictionary, was a provisional one, and contained many superfluous words and archaic formations which were due to be suppressed later. It is with the final, perfected version, as embodied in the Eleventh Edition of the dictionary, that we are concerned here.

The purpose of Newspeak was not only to provide a medium of expression for the world-view and mental habits proper to the devotees of IngSoc, but to make all other modes of thought impossible. It was intended that when Newspeak had been adopted once and for all and Oldspeak forgotten, a heretical thought—that is, a thought diverging from the principles of IngSoc—should be literally unthinkable, at least so far as thought is dependent on words. Its vocabulary was so constructed as to give exact and often very subtle expression to every meaning that a Party member could properly wish to express, while excluding all other meaning and also the possibility of arriving at them by indirect methods. This was done partly by the invention of new words, but chiefly by eliminating undesirable words and stripping such words as remained of unorthodox meanings, and so far as possible of all secondary meaning whatever. To give a single example—the word *free* still existed in Newspeak, but could only be used in such statements as "The dog is *free* from lice" or "This field is *free* from weeds." It could not be used in its old sense of "politically free" or "intellectually free," since political and intellectual freedom no longer existed even as concepts, and were therefore of necessity nameless. Quite apart from the suppression of definitely heretical words, reduction of vocabulary was regarded as an end in itself, and no word that could be dispensed with was allowed to survive. Newspeak was designed not to extend but to *diminish* the range of thought, and this purpose was indirectly assisted by cutting the choice of words down to a minimum. Newspeak was founded on the English language as we now know it, though many Newspeak sentences, even when not containing newly created words, would be barely intelligible to an English-speaker of our own day. Newspeak words were divided into three distinct classes, known as the A vocabulary, the B vocabulary, and the C vocabulary. It would be simpler to discuss each class separately, but the grammatical peculiarities of the language can be dealt with in the section devoted to the A vocabulary, since the same rules held good for all three categories.

The A Vocabulary. The A vocabulary consisted of words needed for the business of everyday life—for such things as eating, drinking, working, putting on one's clothes, going up and down stairs, riding in vehicles, gardening, cooking, and the like. It was composed almost entirely of words that we already possess—words like *hit, run, dog, tree, sugar, house, field*—but in comparison with the present-day English vocabulary, their number was extremely small, while their meanings were far more rigidly defined. All ambiguities and shades of meaning had been purged out of them. So far as it could be achieved, a Newspeak word of this class was simply a staccato sound expressing *one* clearly understood concept. It would have been quite impossible to use the A vocabulary for literary purposes or for political or philosophical discussion. It was intended only to express simple, purposive thoughts, usually involving concrete objects or physical actions.

The grammar of Newspeak has two outstanding peculiarities. The first of these was an almost complete interchangeability between different parts of speech. Any word in the language (in principle this applied even to very abstract words such as *if* or *when*) could be used either as verb, noun, adjective, or adverb. Between the verb and noun form, when of the same root, there was never any variation, this rule of itself involving the destruction of many archaic forms. The word *thought*, for example, did not exist in Newspeak. Its place was taken by *think*, which did duty for both noun and verb. No etymological principle was involved here; in some cases it was the original noun that was chosen for retention, in other cases the verb. Even where a noun and a verb of kindred meanings were not etymologically connected, one or other of them was frequently suppressed. There was, for example, no such word as *cut*, its meaning being sufficiently covered by the noun-verb *knife*. Adjectives were formed by adding the suffix *-ful* to the noun verb, and adverbs by adding *-wise*. Thus, for example, *speedful* meant "rapid" and *speedwise* meant "quickly." Certain of our present-day adjectives, such as *good, strong, big, black, soft,* were retained, but their total number was very small. There was little need for them, since almost any adjectival meaning could be arrived at by adding *-ful* to a noun-verb. None of the now-existing adverbs was retained, except for a few already ending in *-wise*; the *-wise* termination was invariable. the word *well*, for example, was replaced by *goodwise*.

In addition, any word—this again applied in principle to every word in the language—could be negative by adding the affix *un-*, or could be strengthened by the affix *plus-*, or, for still greater emphasis *doubleplus-*. Thus, for example, uncold meant "warm" while *pluscold* and *doublepluscold* meant, respectively, "very cold" and "superlatively cold." It was also possible, as in present-day English, to modify the meaning of almost any word by prepositional affixes such as *ante-, post-, up-, down-*, etc. By such methods it was possible to bring about an enormous diminution of vocabulary. Given, for instance, the word *good*, there was no need for such a word as *bad*, since the required meaning was equally well —indeed better— expressed by *ungood*. All that was necessary, in any case where two words formed a natural pair of opposites, was to decide which of them to suppress. *Dark*, for example, could be replaced by *Unlight*, or *light* by *undark*, according to preference.

The second distinguishing mark of Newspeak grammar was its regularity. Subject to a few exceptions which are mentioned below, all inflections followed the same rules. Thus in all verbs the preterite and the past participle were the same and ended in *-ed*. The preterite of *steal* was *stealed*, the preterite of *think* was *thinked*, and so on throughout the language, all such forms as *swam, gave, brought, spoke, taken,* etc., being abolished. All plurals were made by adding *-s* or *-es* as the case might be. The plurals of *man, ox, life,* were *mans, oxes, lifes*. Comparison of adjectives was invariably made by adding *-er, -est* (*good, gooder, goodest*), irregular forms and the *more, most* formation being suppressed.

The only classes of words that were still allowed to inflect irregularly were the pronouns, the relatives, the demonstrative adjectives, and the auxiliary verbs. All of these followed their ancient usage, except that whom had been scrapped as unnecessary, and the *shall, should* tenses had been dropped, all their uses being covered by *will* and *would*. There were also certain irregularities in word-formation arising out of the need for rapid and easy speech. A word which was difficult to utter, or was liable to be incorrectly heard, was held to be ipso facto a bad word: occasionally therefore, for the sake of euphony, extra letters were inserted into a word or an archaic formation was retained. But this need made itself felt chiefly in connexion with the B vocabulary. Why so great an importance was attached to ease of pronunciation will be made clear later in this essay.

The B Vocabulary. The B vocabulary consisted of words which had been deliberately constructed for political purposes: words, that is to say, which not only had in every case a political implication, but were intended to impose a desirable mental attitude upon the person using them. Without a full understanding of the principles of Ingsoc it was difficult to use these words correctly. In some cases they could be translated into Oldspeak, or even into words taken from the A vocabulary, but this usually demanded a long paraphrase and always involved the loss of certain overtones. The B words were a sort of verbal shorthand, often packing whole ranges of ideas into a few syllables, and at the same time more accurate and forcible than ordinary language.

The B words were in all cases compound words. They consisted of two or more words, or portions of words, welded together in an easily pronounceable form. The resulting amalgam was always a noun-verb, and inflected according to the ordinary rules. To take a single example: the word *goodthink*, meaning, very roughly, "orthodoxy", or, if one chose to regard it as a verb, "to think in an orthodox manner." This inflected as follows: noun-verb, *goodthink*; past tense and past participle, *goodthinked*; present participle, *goodthinking*; adjective, *goodthinkful*; adverb, *goodthinkwise*; verbal noun, *goodthinker*.

The *B words* were not constructed on any etymological plan. The words of which they were made up could be any parts of speech, and could be placed in any order and mutilated in any way which made them easy to pronounce while indicating their derivation. In the word *crimethink* (thoughtcrime), for instance, the *think* came second, whereas in *thinkpol* (Thought Police) it came first, and in the latter word *police* had lost its second syllable. Because of the great difficulty in securing euphony, irregular formations were commoner in the B vocabulary than in the A vocabulary. For example, the adjective forms of *Minitrue, Minipax,* and *Miniluv* were, respectively, *Minitruthful, Minipeaceful,* and *Minilovely*, simply because -*trueful,-paxful,* and -*loveful* were slightly awkward to pronounce. In principle, however, all B words could inflect, and all inflected in exactly the same way.

Some of the B words had highly subtilized meanings, barely intelligible to anyone who had not mastered the language as a whole. Consider, for example, such a typical sentence from a *Times* leading article as *Oldthinkers unbellyfeel Ingsoc*. The shortest rendering that one could make of this in Oldspeak would be: "Those whose ideas were formed before the Revolution cannot have a full emotional understanding of the principles of English Socialism." But this is not an adequate translation. To begin with, in order to grasp the full meaning of the Newspeak sentence quoted above, one would have to have a clear idea of what is meant by *Ingsoc*. And in addition, only a person thoroughly grounded in Ingsoc could appreciate the full force of the word *bellyfeel*, which implied a blind, enthusiastic acceptance difficult to imagine today; or of the word *oldthink*, which was inextricably mixed up with the idea of wickedness and decadence. But the special function of certain Newspeak words, of which *oldthink* was one, was not so much to express meanings as to destroy them.

These words, necessarily few in number, had had their meanings extended until they contained within themselves whole batteries of words which, as they were sufficiently covered by a single comprehensive term, could now be scrapped and forgotten. The greatest difficulty facing the compilers of the Newspeak Dictionary was not to invent new words, but, having invented them, to make sure what they meant: to make sure, that is to say, what ranges of words they cancelled by their existence.

* Compound words such as *speakwrite*, were of course to be found in the A vocabulary, but these were merely convenient abbreviations and had no special ideological colour.

As we have already seen in the case of the word *free*, words which had once borne a heretical meaning were sometimes retained for the sake of convenience, but only with the undesirable meanings purged out of them. Countless other words such as *honour, justice, morality, internationalism, democracy, science,* and *religion* had simply ceased to exist. A few blanket words covered them, and, in covering them, abolished them. All words grouping themselves round the concepts of liberty and equality, for instance, were contained in the single word *crimethink*, while all words grouping themselves round the concepts of objectivity and rationalism were contained in the single word *oldthink*. Greater precision would have been dangerous. What was required in a Party member was an outlook similar to that of the ancient Hebrew who knew, without knowing much else, that all nations other than his own worshipped "false gods." He did not need to know that these gods were called Baal, Osiris, Moloch, Ashtaroth, and the like: probably the less he knew about them the better for his orthodoxy. He knew Jehovah and the commandments of Jehovah: he knew, therefore, that all gods with other names or other attributes were false gods. In somewhat the same way, the party member knew what constituted right conduct, and in exceedingly vague, generalized terms he knew what kinds of departure from it were possible. His sexual life, for example, was entirely regulated by the two Newspeak words *sexcrime* (sexual immorality) and *goodsex* (chastity). *Sexcrime* covered all sexual misdeeds whatever. It covered fornication, adultery, homosexuality, and other perversions, and, in addition, normal intercourse practised for its own sake. There was no need to enumerate them separately, since they were all equally culpable, and, in principle, all punishable by death. In the C vocabulary, which consisted of scientific and technical words, it might be necessary to give specialized names to certain sexual aberrations, but the ordinary citizen had no need of them. He knew what was meant by *goodsex*—that is to say, normal intercourse between man and wife, for the sole purpose of begetting children, and without physical pleasure on the part of the woman: all else was *sexcrime*. In Newspeak it was seldom possible to follow a heretical thought further than the perception that it was heretical: beyond that point the necessary words were nonexistent.

No word in the B vocabulary was ideologically neutral. A great many were euphemisms. Such words, for instance, as *joycamp* (forced-labour camp) or *Minipax*

(Ministry of Peace, i. e. Ministry of War) meant almost the exact opposite of what they appeared to mean. Some words, on the other hand, displayed a frank and contemptuous understanding of the real nature of Oceanic society. An example was *prolefeed*, meaning the rubbishy entertainment and spurious news which the Party handed out to the masses. Other words, again, were ambivalent, having the connotation "good" when applied to the Party and "bad" when applied to its enemies. But in addition there were great numbers of words which at first sight appeared to be mere abbreviations and which derived their ideological colour not from their meaning, but from their structure.

So far as it could be contrived, everything that had or might have political significance of any kind was fitted into the B vocabulary. The name of every organization, or body of people, or doctrine, or country, or institution, or public building, was invariably cut down into the familiar shape; that is, a single easily pronounced word with the smallest number of syllables that would preserve the original derivation. In the *Ministry of Truth*, for example, the Records Department, in which Winston Smith worked, was called *Recdep*, the Fiction Department was called *Ficdep*, the Teleprogrammes Department was called *Teledep*, and so on. This was not done solely with the object of saving time. Even in the early decades of the twentieth century, telescoped words and phrases had been one of the characteristic features of political language; and it had been noticed that the tendency to use abbreviations of this kind was most marked in totalitarian countries and totalitarian organizations. Examples were such words as *Nazi, Gestapo, Comintern, Inprecorr, Agitprop*. In the beginning the practice had been adopted as it were instinctively, but in Newspeak it was used with a conscious purpose. It was perceived that in thus abbreviating a name one narrowed and subtly altered its meaning, by cutting out most of the associations that would otherwise cling to it. The words *Communist International*, for instance, call up a composite picture of universal human brotherhood, red flags, barricades, Karl Marx, and the Paris Commune. The word *Comintern*, on the other hand, suggests merely a tightly-knit organization and a well-defined body of doctrine. It refers to something almost as easily recognized, and as limited in purpose, as a chair or a table. *Comintern* is a word that can be uttered almost without taking thought, whereas *Communist International* is a phrase over which one is obliged to linger at least momentarily. In the same way, the associations called up by a word like *Minitrue* are fewer and more controllable than those called up by *Ministry of Truth*. This accounted not only for the habit of abbreviating whenever possible, but also for the almost exaggerated care that was taken to make every word easily pronounceable.

In Newspeak, euphony outweighed every consideration other than exactitude of meaning. Regularity of grammar was always sacrificed to it when it seemed necessary. And rightly so, since what was required, above all for political purposes, was short clipped words of unmistakable meaning which could be uttered rapidly and which roused the minimum of echoes in the speaker's mind. The words of the

B vocabulary even gained in force from the fact that nearly all of them were very much alike. Almost invariably these words—*goodthink, Minipax, prolefeed, sexcrime, joycamp, Ingsoc, bellyfeel, thinkpol*, and countless others—were words of two or three syllables, with the stress distributed equally between the first syllable and the last. The use of them encouraged a gabbling style of speech, at once staccato and monotonous. And this was exactly what was aimed at. The intention was to make speech, and especially speech on any subject not ideologically neutral, as nearly as possible independent of consciousness.

For the purposes of everyday life it was no doubt necessary, or sometimes necessary, to reflect before speaking, but a Party member called upon to make a political or ethical judgment should be able to spray forth the correct opinions as automatically as a machine gun spraying forth bullets. His training fitted him to do this, the language gave him an almost foolproof instrument, and the texture of the words, with their harsh sound and a certain willful ugliness which was in accord with the spirit of Ingsoc, assisted the process still further.

So did the fact of having very few words to choose from. Relative to our own, the Newspeak vocabulary was tiny, and new ways of reducing it were constantly being devised. Newspeak, indeed, differed from most all other languages in that its vocabulary grew smaller instead of larger every year. Each reduction was a gain, since the smaller the area of choice, the smaller the temptation to take thought. Ultimately it was hoped to make articulate speech issue from the larynx without involving the higher brain centers at all. This aim was frankly admitted in the Newspeak word *duckspeak*, meaning "to quack like a duck". Like various other words in the B vocabulary, *duckspeak* was ambivalent in meaning. Provided that the opinions which were quacked out were orthodox ones, it implied nothing but praise, and when *The Times* referred to one of the orators of the Party as a *doubleplusgood duckspeaker* it was paying a warm and valued compliment.

The C Vocabulary. The C vocabulary was supplementary to the others and consisted entirely of scientific and technical terms. These resembled the scientific terms in use today, and were constructed from the same roots, but the usual care was taken to define them rigidly and strip them of undesirable meanings. They followed the same grammatical rules as the words in the other two vocabularies. Very few of the C words had any currency either in everyday speech or in political speech. Any scientific worker or technician could find all the words he needed in the list devoted to his own speciality, but he seldom had more than a smattering of the words occurring in the other lists. Only a very few words were common to all lists, and there was no vocabulary expressing the function of Science as a habit of mind, or a method of thought, irrespective of its particular branches. There was, indeed, no word for "Science," any meaning that it could possibly bear being already sufficiently covered by the word *Ingsoc*.

From the foregoing account it will be seen that in Newspeak the expression of unorthodox opinions, above a very low level, was well-nigh impossible. It was of course possible to utter heresies of a very crude kind, a species of blasphemy. It would have been possible, for example, to say *Big Brother is ungood*. But this statement, which to an orthodox ear merely conveyed a self-evident absurdity, could not have been sustained by reasoned argument, because the necessary words were not available. Ideas inimical to *Ingsoc* could only be entertained in a vague wordless form, and could only be named in very broad terms which lumped together and condemned whole groups of heresies without defining them in doing so. One could, in fact, only use Newspeak for unorthodox purposes by illegitimately translating some of the words back into Oldspeak. For example, *All mans are equal* was a possible Newspeak sentence, but only in the same sense in which *All men are red-haired* is a possible Oldspeak sentence.

It did not contain a grammatical error, but it expressed a palpable untruth—i.e. that all men are of equal size, weight, or strength. The concept of political equality no longer existed, and this secondary meaning had accordingly been purged out of the word *equal*. In 1984, when Oldspeak was still the normal means of communication, the danger theoretically existed that in using Newspeak words one might remember their original meanings. In practice it was not difficult for any person well grounded in *doublethink* to avoid doing this, but within a couple of generations even the possibility of such a lapse would have vanished. A person growing up with Newspeak as his sole language would no more know that *equal* had once had the secondary meaning of "politically equal," or that *free* had once meant "intellectually free," than for instance, a person who had never heard of chess would be aware of the secondary meanings attaching to *queen* and *rook*. There would be many crimes and errors which it would be beyond his power to commit, simply because they were nameless and therefore unimaginable. And it was to be foreseen that with the passage of time the distinguishing characteristics of Newspeak would become more and more pronounced—its words growing fewer and fewer, their meanings more and more rigid, and the chance of putting them to improper uses always diminishing.

When Oldspeak had been once and for all superseded, the last link with the past would have been severed. History had already been rewritten, but fragments of the literature of the past survived here and there, imperfectly censored, and so long as one retained one's knowledge of Oldspeak it was possible to read them. In the future such fragments, even if they chanced to survive, would be unintelligible and untranslatable. It was impossible to translate any passage of Oldspeak into Newspeak unless it either referred to some technical process or some very simple everyday action, or was already orthodox (*goodthinkful* would be the Newspeak expression) in tendency. In practice this meant that no book written before approximately 1960 could be translated as a whole. Pre-revolutionary literature could only be subjected to ideological translation—that is, alteration in sense as well as language.

Take for example the well-known passage from the Declaration of Independence:

> We hold these truths to be self-evident, that all men are created equal, that they are endowed by their creator with certain inalienable rights, that among these are life, liberty, and the pursuit of happiness. That to secure these rights, Governments are instituted among men, deriving their powers from the consent of the governed. That whenever any form of Government becomes destructive of those ends, it is the right of the People to alter or abolish it, and to institute new Government…

It would have been quite impossible to render this into Newspeak while keeping to the sense of the original. The nearest one could come to doing so would be to swallow the whole passage up in the single word *crimethink*. A full translation could only be an ideological translation, whereby Jefferson's words would be changed into a panegyric on absolute government.

A good deal of the literature of the past was, indeed, already being transformed in this way. Considerations of prestige made it desirable to preserve the memory of certain historical figures, while at the same time bringing their achievements into line with the philosophy of Ingsoc. Various writers, such as Shakespeare, Milton, Swift, Byron, Dickens, and some others were therefore in process of translation: when the task had been completed, their original writings, with all else that survived of the literature of the past, would be destroyed. These translations were a slow and difficult business, and it was not expected that they would be finished before the first or second decade of the twenty-first century. There were also large quantities of merely utilitarian literature—indispensable technical manuals, and the like—that had to be treated in the same way. It was chiefly in order to allow time for the preliminary work of translation that the final adoption of Newspeak had been fixed for so late a date as 2050.

AFTER YOU READ: Analyze the Issues

1. Discuss the title. Do you like it? Can you write a better title? What is your improved title?
2. What is the main argument of the essay?
3. Do you agree with this? Why or why not?
4. Are there weaknesses to the argument? What are they?
5. What does it say about the "well-known passage" found in the Declaration of Independence?

AFTER YOU READ: Analyze the Rhetoric

1. Note the strong sense of logos. Why would a strong sense of logos be important for this type of essay?
2. His essay reads like a historical document. What are some of the characteristics of this genre of writing? How does it differ from other types of essays?
3. Is this style of writing too formal? If it was written in an informal manner, would the effect be the same? Why or why not?

"The Great Conspiracy: We Will Not Walk in Fear"

by George Clooney and Grant Heslov
(Screenplay 2006) excerpt from Good Night, and Good Luck

George Clooney was born on May 6, 1961 in Lexington, Kentucky, George Clooney was born to a family familiar with being in front of the camera. His father was Nick Clooney, a TV newscaster in Cincinnati. His uncle, Jose Ferrer won Best Actor for his role in *Cyrano de Bergerac*. His aunt Rosemary Clooney was a famous singer. He first gained fame starring on the TV show *ER*. Clooney was voted the Sexiest Man Alive by *People Magazine* in 1997. He won Best Supporting Actor for *Syriana* (2005). Besides writing and acting in *Good Night, and Good Luck*, he also directed the film.

Born on May 15, 1963 Grant Heslov has had a rather extensive acting career since the 1980's mostly as a guest star on various TV shows, such as *Baywatch* or *Seinfeld*. He co-wrote *Good Night, and Good Luck* with George Clooney and even started a production company Smoke House with Clooney.

"The Great Conspiracy: We Will Not Walk in Fear" (Screenplay) by George Clooney and Grant Heslov. *Good Night, and Good Luck* (Screenplay) New York: Newmarket Press, 2006. 147–151.

AS YOU READ: Annotate

1. Place a star by the section you like the most.
2. Circle words you do not know and write their meaning in the margins.

Background: Born in Greensboro, North Carolina, Edward R. Murrow (1908–1965), a broadcast journalist, started working for CBS in 1935. He first did well in radio as a journalist, and later he would break new ground in the fledgling field of television journalism. In 1953, he ran a show "The Case Against Lt. Milo Radulovich" defending the former WWII veteran against the "Red Scare" hysteria. This was one of the first instances of resistance against that hysteria. Radulovich had joined the Army Air Corps in 1944. On October 20, 1953, he had been dismissed because his father, a Serbian, had subscribed to a communist paper. Thus, the son was suspected of Red connections. Murrow felt that Radulovich had served his country and was not being treated right by Senator Joseph McCarthy. Some nine months later, Murrow in his most powerful and remembered moment, broadcasted the famous *See it Now,* March 9, 1954 attack against Senator Joseph McCarthy mostly using clips of the senator. That show would essentially end the power McCarthy had. In 1961, Murrow became the director of the United States Information Agency under the Kennedy administration.

INT. CONTROL ROOM

The show is already underway, you could cut the tension with a knife. MURROW continues his pre-recorded introduction on the monitor.

MURROW

Because a report on Senator McCarthy is by definition controversial, we want to say exactly what we mean to say and request your permission to read from a script whatever remarks Murrow and Friendly may make. If the Senator feels that we have done violence to his words or pictures and desires so to speak to answer himself, an opportunity will be afforded him on this program. Our working thesis tonight is this quotation: "If this fight against Communism has made a fight between America's two great political parties, the American people know that one of these parties will be destroyed ...

WILLIAMS

Ready two.

The phone rings, he answers.

WILLIAMS (CONT'D)

No, this is not the eleven o'clock news try forty-four —Operator, I tell you every week to shut off these phones. Now please, no calls 'til eleven.

(CONTINUED)

MURROW

And the Republic cannot endure very long as a one party system." ... We applaud that statement and we think Senator McCarthy ought to. He said it seventeen months ago in Milwaukee.

WILLIAMS

Take two... roll film

We now see McCarthy on camera.

MCCARTHY

The American people realize that this cannot be a fight between America's two great political parties. If this fight against communism is made a fight against America's two great political parties the American people know that one of those parties will be destroyed and the Republic can't endure very long as a one party system.

CUT TO:

INT. PALEY'S OFFICE

PALEY sits watching by himself

MURROW

On one thing the Senator had been consistent. Often operating as a one man committee, he has traveled far, interviewed many, terrorized some, accused civilian and military leaders of the past administration of a great conspiracy to turn over the country to communism.

CUT TO:

INT. "SEE IT NOW" SET

MURROW is seated in his chair. On the monitors is McCarthy.

(CONTINUED)

MCCARTHY

Well, may I say that I was extremely shocked when I heard that Secretary Stevens told two Army officers that they had to take part in the cover up of those who promoted and coddled communists. As I read this statement I thought of that quotation, "On what meat doth this our Caesar feed?"

INT. STAGE 44

DON HOLLENBECK sits at the news desk watching a monitor with great pride.

On the monitor is more footage of the REED HARRIS hearing.

SENATOR MCCLELLAN

Do you think this book that you wrote then did considerable harm? It's publication might have an adverse effect on the public by an expression of the views contained in it?

HARRIS

The sale of that book was so abysmally small, it was so unsuccessful, that the question of its influence, uh really, you can go back to the publisher, you'll see it was one of the most unsuccessful books ever put out. He's still sorry about it, just as I am.

SENATOR MCCLELLAN

Well, I think that's a compliment to American intelligence.

INT. JOE & SHIRLEY WERSHBA'S NY APT.

Shirley watches on the TV

MURROW

The Reed Harris hearing demonstrates one of the Senator's techniques. Twice he said, "The American Civil Liberties Union was listed as a subversive front." The Attorney General's list does not and never has listed the ACLU as subversive, nor does the FBI, or any other federal government agency. And, the ACLU holds in its files, letters of commendation from President Truman, President Eisenhower and General MacArthur.

(CONTINUED)

The rest of MORROW'S speech will be intercut with closeups of all our players. Sitting silently at home, in the control room, the newsroom, Paley's office, at home with Shirley Wershba.

MURROW (CONT'D)

Earlier, the Senator asked, "Upon what meat does this our Caesar feed?" Had he looked three lines earlier in Shakespeare's "Caesar" he would have found this line which is not altogether inappropriate: "The fault , dear Brutus, is not in our stars but in ourselves." No one familiar with the history of this country can deny that congressional committees are useful. It is necessary to investigate before legislating, but the line between investigating and persecuting is a very fine one; and the Junior Senator from Wisconsin has stepped over it repeatedly. We must not confuse dissent with disloyalty. We must remember always that accusation is not proof and that conviction depends upon evidence and due process of law. We will not be driven by fear into an age of unreason, if we dig deep in our history and our doctrine, and remember that we are not descended from fearful men, not from men who feared to write, to speak, to associate and to defend the causes that were for the moment unpopular.

We proclaim ourselves as indeed we are, the defenders of freedom wherever it continues to exist in the world; but we cannot defend freedom abroad by deserting it at home. The actions of the Junior Senator from Wisconsin have caused alarm and dismay amongst our allies abroad and given considerable comfort to our enemies. And, whose fault is that? Not really his. He didn't create this situation of fear, he merely exploited it, and rather successfully. Cassius was right. "The fault dear Brutus is not in our stars but in ourselves." Good night. And good luck.

AFTER YOU READ: Analyze the Issues

1. What is the main message of Murrow's speech?
2. What relevance does the speech have for today's American political situations? Explain.
3. Why does Murrow bring up history?

AFTER YOU READ: Analyze the Rhetoric

1. Discuss the effects of ethos. Do the quotes help the speech?
2. What aspects of pathos exist in the speech?
3. Why bring up the audience "American people"?

Issues of Liberty

"Freedom From Fear"

by Aung San Suu Kyi
(Essay)

Born in 1945 in Rangoon, Aung San Suu Kyi's father, Bogyoke Aung San (1914-1947), was one of the founding fathers of Burma and was instrumental in earning liberation from Britain though he was assassinated at a young age! Kyi would grow up to win the Nobel Peace Prize in 1991 for her efforts to speak against the government in Myamar (Burma) where she remains under house arrest with orders not to speak out against the government. She was educated at Oxford and married Michael Aris. In 1988, she traveled to Burma to take care of her ailing mother. General Ne Win, the military dictator of Burma, resigned. Popular unrest began and Aung San Suu Kyi found herself fighting for the people and speaking out against the military as it took over the country. This speech, her most popular, voices her concern and demand that people not live in fear.

"Freedom from Fear" by Aung San Suu Kyi From *Freedom from Fear*. Penguin Books, 1991. 180–185.

AS YOU READ: Annotate

1. Place a star by sections you like.
2. Circle any words you do not know, look up their meanings and write them in the margin. Also circle these words and define them, such as *a-gati, moga-gati, aberration, bhaya-gan, chanda-gati, dosa-gati, eking, avarice, precarious, iniquities, abhaya, insidious, miasma,* and *bulwarks.*

It is not power that corrupts but fear. Fear of losing power corrupts those who wield it and fear of the scourge of power corrupts those who are subject to it. Most Burmese are familiar with the four *a-gati*, the four kinds of corruption. *Chanda-gati,* corruption induced by desire, is deviation from the right path in pursuit of bribes or for the sake of those one loves. *Dosa-gati* is taking the wrong path to spite those against whom one bears ill will, and *moga-gati* is aberration due to ignorance. But perhaps the worst of the four is *bhaya-gati*, for not only does *bhaya*, fear, stifle and slowly destroy all sense of right and wrong, it so often lies at the root of the other three kinds of corruption. Just as *chanda-gati*, when not the result of sheer avarice, can be caused by fear of want or fear of losing the goodwill of those one loves, so fear of being surpassed, humiliated or injured in some way can provide the impetus for ill will. And it would be difficult to dispel ignorance unless there is freedom to pursue the truth unfettered by fear. With so close a relationship between fear and corruption it is little wonder that in any society where fear is rife corruption in all forms becomes deeply entrenched.

Public dissatisfaction with economic hardships has been seen as the chief cause of the movement for democracy in Burma, sparked off by the student demonstrations in 1988. It is true that years of incoherent policies, inept official measures, burgeoning inflation and falling real income had turned the country into an economic shambles. But it was more than the difficulties of eking out a barely acceptable standard of living that had eroded the patience of a traditionally good-natured, quiescent people—it was also the humiliation of a way of life disfigured by corruption and fear.

The students were protesting not just against the death of their comrades but against the denial of their right to life by a totalitarian regime which deprived the present of meaningfulness and held out no hope for the future. And because the students' protests articulated the frustrations of the people at large, the demonstrations quickly grew into a nationwide movement. Some of its keenest supporters were businessmen who had developed the skills and the contacts necessary not only to survive but to prosper within the system. But their affluence offered them no genuine sense of security or fulfillment, and they could not but see that if they and their fellow citizens, regardless of economic status, were to achieve a worthwhile existence, an accountable administration was at least a necessary if not a sufficient condition. The people of Burma had wearied of a precarious state of passive apprehension where they were "as water in the cupped hands" of the powers that be.

> Emerald cool we may be
> As water in cupped hands
> But oh that we might be
> As splinters of glass
> In cupped hands.

Glass splinters, the smallest with its sharp, glinting power to defend itself against hands that try to crush, could be seen as a vivid symbol of the spark of courage that is an essential attribute of those who would free themselves from the grip of oppression. Bogyoke Aung San regarded himself as a revolutionary and searched tirelessly for answers to the problems that beset Burma duri ng her times of trial. He exhorted the people to develop courage: "Don't just depend on the courage and intrepidity of others. Each and every one of you must make sacrifices to become a hero possessed of courage and intrepidity. Then only shall we all be able to enjoy true freedom."

The effort necessary to remain uncorrupted in an environment where fear is an integral part of everyday existence is not immediately apparent to those fortunate enough to live in states governed by the rule of law. Just laws do not merely prevent corruption by meting out impartial punishment to offenders. They also help to create a society in which people can fulfill the basic requirements necessary for the preservation of human dignity without recourse to corrupt practices. Where there are no such laws, the burden of upholding the principles of justice and common decency falls on the ordinary people. It is the cumulative effect on their sustained effort and steady endurance which will change a nation where reason and conscience are warped by fear into one where legal rules exist to promote man's desire for harmony and justice while restraining the less desirable destructive traits in his nature.

In an age when immense technological advances have created lethal weapons which could be, and are, used by the powerful and the unprincipled to dominate the weak and the helpless, there is a compelling need for a closer relationship between politics and ethics at both the national and international levels. The Universal Declaration of Human Rights of the United Nations proclaims that "every individual and every organ of society" should strive to promote the basic rights and freedoms to which all human beings regardless of race, nationality or religion are entitled. But as long as there are governments whose authority is founded on coercion rather than on the mandate of the people, and interest groups which place short-term profits above long-term peace and prosperity, concerted international action to protect and promote human rights will remain at best a partially realized struggle. There will continue to be arenas of struggle where victims of oppression have to draw on their own inner resources to defend their inalienable rights as members of the human family.

The quintessential revolution is that of the spirit, born of an intellectual conviction of the need for change in those mental attitudes and values which shape the course of a nation's development. A revolution which aims merely at changing official policies and institutions with a view to an improvement in material conditions has little chance of genuine success.

Without a revolution of the spirit, the forces which produced the iniquities of the old order would continue to be operative, posing a constant threat to the process of reform and regeneration. It is not enough merely to call for freedom, democracy and human rights. There has to be a united determination to persevere in the struggle, to make sacrifices in the name of enduring truths, to resist the corrupting influences of desire, ill will, ignorance and fear.

Saints, it has been said, are the sinners who go on trying. So free men are the oppressed who go on trying and who in the process make themselves fit to bear the responsibilities and to uphold the disciplines which will maintain a free society. Among the basic freedoms to which men aspire that their lives might be full and uncramped, freedom from fear stands out as both a means and an end. A people who would build a nation in which strong, democratic institutions are firmly established as a guarantee against state-induced power must first learn to liberate their own minds from apathy and fear.

Always one to practise what he preached, Aung San himself constantly demonstrated courage—not just the physical sort but the kind that enabled him to speak the truth, to stand by his word, to accept criticism, to admit his faults, to correct his mistakes, to respect the opposition, to parley with the enemy and to let people be the judge of his worthiness as a leader. It is for such moral courage that he will always be loved and respected in Burma—not merely as a warrior hero but as the inspiration and conscience of the nation. The words used by Jawaharlal Nehru to describe Mahatma Gandhi could well be applied to Aung San:

> "The essence of his teaching was fearlessness and truth, and action allied to these, always keeping the welfare of the masses in view."

Gandhi, that great apostle of non-violence, and Aung San, the founder of a national army, were very different personalities, but as there is an inevitable sameness about the challenges of authoritarian rule anywhere at any time, so there is a similarity in the intrinsic qualities of those who rise up to meet the challenge. Nehru, who considered the instillation of courage in the people of India one of Gandhi's greatest achievements, was a political modernist, but as he assessed the needs for a twentieth-century movement for independence, he found himself looking back to the philosophy of ancient India: "The greatest gift for an individual or a nation … was *abhaya*, fearlessness, not merely bodily courage but absence of fear from the mind."

Fearlessness may be a gift but perhaps more precious is the courage acquired through endeavour, courage that comes from cultivating the habit of refusing to let fear dictate one's actions, courage that could be described as "grace under pressure"—grace which is renewed repeatedly in the face of harsh, unremitting pressure.

Within a system which denies the existence of basic human rights, fear tends to be the order of the day. Fear of imprisonment, fear of torture, fear of death, fear of losing friends, family, property or means of livelihood, fear of poverty, fear of isolation, fear of failure. A most insidious form of fear is that which masquerades as common sense or even wisdom, condemning as foolish, reckless, insignificant or futile the small, daily acts of courage which help to preserve man's self-respect and inherent human dignity. It is not easy for a people conditioned by fear under the iron rule of the principle that might is right to free themselves from the enervating miasma of fear. Yet even under the most crushing state machinery courage rises up again and again, for fear is not the natural state of civilized man.

The wellspring of courage and endurance in the face of unbridled power is generally a firm belief in the sanctity of ethical principles combined with a historical sense that despite all setbacks the condition of man is set on an ultimate course for both spiritual and material advancement. It is his capacity for self-improvement and self-redemption which most distinguishes man from the mere brute. At the root of human responsibility is the concept of perfection, the urge to achieve it, the intelligence to find a path towards it, and the will to follow that path if not to the end at least the distance needed to rise above individual limitations and environmental impediments. It is man's vision of a world fit for rational, civilized humanity which leads him to dare and to suffer to build societies free from want and fear. Concepts such as truth, justice and compassion cannot be dismissed as trite when these are often the only bulwarks which stand against ruthless power.

*The British use of single quotation marks was modified to the American method of using double quotation marks.

AFTER YOU READ: Analyze the Issues

1. What is the main message of the essay? Do you agree with it?
2. Do you agree that non-violence is a way to fight for freedom in Burma?
3. How did non-violence work with race problems in America?

AFTER YOU READ: Analyze the Rhetoric

1. Does using the Burmese terms for corruption, *a-gati,* take away from the universality of the essay?
2. The author uses the word "man." Is this okay or is this sexist? Explain.
3. How effective is it to use a quote by Jawaharlal Nehru to describe Mahatma Gandhi? Explain.

"V's Speech: Something Terribly Wrong"

by the Wachowski Brothers
Excerpt from V for Vendetta
V for Vendetta *used courtesy of Warner Bros. Entertainment Inc.*
(Screenplay)

Born and raised in Chicago, the Wachowski Brothers have been working together for more than 30 years. Prior to writing and producing *V for Vendetta*, Andy and Larry Wachowski wrote, directed and executive produced the *Matrix* trilogy. In 1996, they wrote and directed their first feature film, *Bound*, a thriller starring Gina Gershon, Jennifer Tilly and Joe Pantoliano.

"V's Speech: Something Terribly Wrong" (screenplay) V for Vendetta: From Script to Film screenplay by the Wachowski Brothers, DC Comics, 2006, Dialogues 51-86, pages 35–42.

AS YOU READ: Annotate

1. Place a star by the section you like the most.
2. Circle words you do not know and write their meanings in the margins.

50 INT. MIDDLE CLASS HOME—DAY 50

The family sits poised around the television.

BOY
What's wrong with the telly?

51 INT. P.A. ROOM—DAY 51

The television winks at Evey as it suddenly fills with a close up of V.

V
Good evening, London.

Evey shrinks away.

52 INT. HALL—DAY 52

The security men are still trying to break down the door as Dascomb sees the "ON AIR" light turn on. V's voice can be heard everywhere.

V
Allow me to first apologize for this interruption.

DASCOMB
That's the emergency channel!

He bolts to find a television.

53 INT. WARDROBE DEPARTMENT—DAY 53

Finch, searching for Evey is stopped dead by the smiling mask on the television.

V
I do, like many of you—

FINCH
Bloody Hell.

54 INT. MIDDLE CLASS HOME—DAY 54

(CONTINUED)

They stare at the television.

V

Appreciate the comforts of the everyday routine—

BOY

Mama, who's that?

MAMA

Shhh.

55 INT. RETIREMENT HOME—DAY 55

The pensioners look blankly through their bifocals.

V

The security of the familiar—

56 INT. BAR—DAY 56

The alcohol-inured stare wordlessly.

V

The tranquility of repetition. I enjoy them as much as any bloke.

57 EXT. PICCADILLY CIRCUS—DAY 57

V's face looms over the urban landscape.

V

But in the spirit of commemoration, whereby those important events of the past, usually associated with someone's death or the end of some awful, bloody struggle, are celebrated with a nice holiday—

58 INT. VTV—DAY 58

V sits behind a generic desk. Behind him, we see the letter "V" in a circle spray-painted over the BTN logo.

(CONTINUED)

V
I thought we could mark this November fifth, a day that sadly is no longer remembered, by taking some time out of our daily lives to sit down and have a little chat.

59 INT. TELEVISION OFFICE—DAY 59

Several guards and Patricia stand waiting, watching the television and Dascomb, who is pacing in front of it.

V
There are of course, those who do not want us to speak.

DASCOMB
Let me think, let me think.

V
I suspect right now orders are being shouted into phones and men with guns will soon be on their way.

A cell phone rings and Patricia answers it.

PATRICIA
It's Chancellor Sutler.

DASCOMB
Goddamnit!

60 INT. HALL—DAY 60

V's voice echoes in the hall as two big cops try unsuccessfully to force open the door with a crow bar.

V (V.O.)
Anything and everything will be done to stop me from talking to you.

61 INT. TELEVISION SECURITY STATION—DAY 61

Finch stands alone watching the monitor in the corner as Dominic runs up.

(CONTINUED)

DOMINIC
We're going to need a torch.

Finch nods, listening more to V.

V
Why? Because while the truncheon may be used in lieu of conversation, words will always retain their power.

62 INT. P.A. ROOM—DAY 62

Evey remains transfixed, feeling as if he were talking directly to her.

V
Words offer the means to meaning and for those who will listen, the enunciation of truth.

62A INT. TELEVISION SECURITY STATION—DAY 62A

Finch stands as transfixed as Evey.

V
The truth is there is something terribly wrong with this country isn't there?

63 INT. TELEVISION OFFICE—DAY 63

Dascomb is on the phone.

DASCOMB
You designed it sir. You wanted it foolproof. You told me every television in London—

V
Cruelty and injustice—

64 EXT. FINGER HEADQUARTERS—DAY 64

Dozens of heavily armed men jump inside a tactical military transport.

V (V.O.)
—intolerance and oppression.

(CONTINUED)

65 INT. TELEVISION SECURITY STATION —DAY 65

Finch is hardly aware as policemen haul a large acetylene Torch from the elevator.

V

And where once you had the freedom to object, to think and speak as you saw fit—

66 INT. TELEVISION OFFICE—DAY 66

Dascomb stops pacing, suddenly aware of V's words.

V

You now have censors and systems Of surveillance, coercing your conformity and soliciting your submission.

DASCOMB

Cameras! We need cameras!

67 INT. VTV—DAY 67

He opens his hands as though asking the camera.

V

How did this happen? Who is to blame? Certainly there are those who are more responsible than others and they will be held accountable, but again, truth be told—

68 INT. P.A. ROOM—DAY 68

Evey's reflection can be seen in the screen of the television.

V

If you are looking for the guilty, You need only look into a mirror.

69 INT. MIDDLE CLASS HOME—DAY 69

The family stares back.

(CONTINUED)

V

I know why you did it.

70 INT. RETIREMENT HOME—DAY 70

The old people have put down their cards.

V

I know you were afraid.

71 INT. TENEMENT BUILDING—DAY 71

The Little Girl stares at V, mesmerized.

V

Who wouldn't be?

72 EXT. PICCADILLY CIRCUS—DAY 72

The square hangs suspended in time, no traffic, no movement, almost no sound except V's voice.

V

War. Terror. Disease. Food and water shortages. There were a myriad of problems.—

73 INT. BAR—DAY 73

The cigarette ash falls unnoticed.

V

Which conspired to corrupt your reason and rob you of your common sense.

74 INT. VTV—DAY 74

Even his mask cannot hide V's disappointment.

V

Fear got the best of you and in Your panic you turned to now High Chancellor, Adam Sutler, with his gleaming boots of polished leather and his garrison of goons.

(CONTINUED)

75 INT. CREEDY'S CAR—DAY—OMITTED 75

76 INT. MILITARY TRANSPORT—DAY 76

The military soldiers sit as cocked as their guns.

V (V.O.)
He promised you order. He promised you peace.

77 INT. TELEVISION SECURITY STATION—DAY 77

Dominic rushes in.

V
And all he demanded in return was your silent, obedient, consent.

DOMINIC
Inspector, they're almost through.

Finch nods uncertain, turning away from the monitor and following Dominic out.

78 INT. P.A. ROOM—DAY 78

V continues.

V
Last night, I sought to end the silence. Last night, I destroyed the Old Bailey to remind this country of what it has forgotten.

79 INT. HALL—DAY 79

The torch has eaten three-quarters of the way down the length of the door as Dascomb arrives with a small video crew.

V
More than four hundred years ago, a great citizen wished to embed the fifth of November forever in our memory.

Molten metal spits from the center of the fire-worked flame.

(CONTINUED)

80 INT. VTV—DAY 80

V leans forward.

V

His hope was to remind the world that fairness, justice and freedom were more than words. They are perspectives.

81 INT. MIDDLE CLASS HOME—DAY 81

V

So, if you have seen nothing, if the crimes of this government remain unknown to you, then I suggest that you allow the fifth of November to pass unmarked.

82 INT. BAR—DAY 82

V

But if you see what I see—

83 INT. RETIREMENT HOME—DAY 83

V

If you feel as I feel—

84 INT. TENEMENT—DAY 84

V

And if you would seek as I seek freedom from their tyranny and an end to this oppression—

85 EXT. PICCADILLY CIRCUS—DAY 85

V

Then I ask you to stand beside me, one year from tonight outside the gates of Parliament—

86 INT. P.A. ROOM —DAY 86

Evey remains as mesmerized as everyone else.

(CONTINUED)

V

And together, we shall give them a fifth of November
that shall never, ever be forgot.

The recording ends and V's face is lost to static. Evey snaps out of her trance and bolts from the room.

87 INT. HALL—DAY 87

The torch slices through the last of the heavy soundproofed door and the police kick it in. A thick cloud of fog belches into the hall. It is too much smoke to be caused by the torch.

AFTER YOU READ: Analyze the Issues

1. What is the main message of V's speech?
2. Does the speech have relevance to the American political system? Explain.

AFTER YOU READ: Analyze the Rhetoric

1. What effect does including the various reactions from the television audience have on the speech? Explain.
2. What motivational aspects exist in the speech?
3. Read the script aloud and compare the effect of oral reading. What did you notice when reading aloud?

"V's Speech: Good Evening London"

Excerpt from V for Vendetta
by Alan Moore and David Lloyd
V for Vendetta *used courtesy of Warner Bros. Entertainment Inc.*
(Graphic Novel)

Born in Northampton, Alan Moore (1953–) has become one of the most influential comic book writers. Working for DC Comics, Moore wrote such works as *Swamp Thing* (1970s), *Watchmen* (1986-87), and *From Hell* (1999). David Lloyd (1950–) has illustrated for Marvel: "Night Raven" and "House of Cards." Perhaps his greatest fame is illustrating *V for Vendetta.* Visit his Web site at www.lforlloyd.com.

AS YOU READ: Annotate

1. Place a star by the panel you think is the most effective.
2. Circle any words you do not know, look up their meanings and write them in the margin. Circle *bristling* and *wheedled* and define them.

Background for the graphic novel. The protagonist, V, in the book wears a Guy Fawkes mask to protect his identity. In 1605, Guy Fawkes tried to kill the King of England (James I) and blow up the House of Parliament in what became known as the Gunpowder Plot of 1605. Why? Basically, Guy represented dissatisfied Catholics getting back at an unjust Protestant rule. He later became a representative of individuals dissatisfied with government. Guy Fawkes failed, was captured, and executed. King James asked that the event not be forgotten and on the anniversary of the event which is now called the Bonfire Night, it continues to be remembered with fireworks. The event became a famous nursery rhyme:

Remember, Remember the Fifth of November
The Gunpowder Treason and Plot
I know of no reason why the Gunpowder Treason
Should ever be forgot

In the following sequence of scenes, V has managed to break into a television station and illegally broadcast a speech while police try to break in and arrest V for the speech.

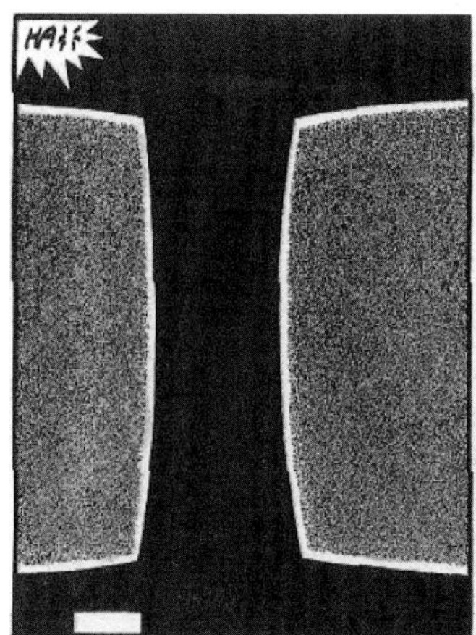
HA!

"PICTURE'S GONE..."
"SEE TO IT, FATHER."
"BLOODY PICTURE'S GONE.."
"DAD! TELLY'S PACKED UP!"

"IS IT THE AERIAL?"
"MUM? THE TELLY..."
"...PAY YOUR BLOODY LICENCE MONEY FOR?"

"WAIT A MINUTE.."
"THAT'S A BIT BETTER... HOLD IT THERE..."
"AHHH.."

GOOD EVENING, LONDON.
I THOUGHT IT TIME WE HAD A LITTLE TALK.
VTV

ARE YOU SITTING COMFORT-ABLY?

THEN I'LL BEGIN...

(07)

FEBRUARY 23RD, 1998: PEAK TIME.
VTV
I SUPPOSE YOU'RE WONDERING WHY I'VE CALLED YOU HERE THIS EVENING.

WELL, YOU SEE, I'M NOT ENTIRELY SATISFIED WITH YOUR PERFORMANCE LATELY... I'M AFRAID YOUR WORK'S BEEN SLIPPING, AND...
...AND, WELL, I'M AFRAID WE'VE BEEN THINKING ABOUT LETTING YOU GO.

OH, I KNOW, I KNOW. YOU'VE BEEN WITH THE COMPANY A LONG TIME NOW. ALMOST... LET ME SEE. ALMOST TEN THOUSAND YEARS! MY WORD, DOESN'T TIME FLY?
IT SEEMS LIKE ONLY YESTERDAY...

I REMEMBER THE DAY YOU COMMENCED YOUR EMPLOYMENT, SWINGING DOWN FROM THE TREES, FRESH-FACED AND NERVOUS, A BONE CLASPED IN YOUR BRISTLING FIST...
"WHERE DO I START, SIR?" YOU ASKED, PLAINTIVELY.

I RECALL MY EXACT WORDS: "THERE'S A PILE OF DINOSAUR EGGS OVER THERE, YOUNGSTER," I SAID, SMILING PATERNALLY THE WHILE.
"GET SUCKING."

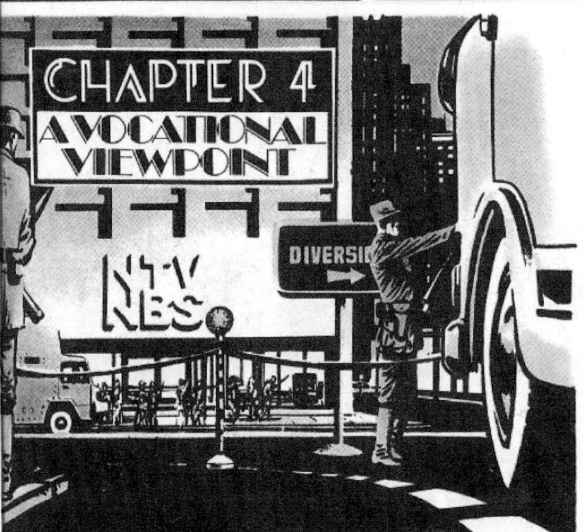
CHAPTER 4
A VOCATIONAL VIEWPOINT
DIVERSI
NTV
NBS

WELL, WE'VE CERTAINLY COME A LONG WAY SINCE *THEN*, HAVEN'T WE? AND YES, YES, YOU'RE RIGHT, IN ALL THAT TIME YOU HAVEN'T MISSED A DAY.

(07)

WELL DONE, THOU GOOD AND FAITHFUL SERVANT.

ALSO, PLEASE DON'T THINK I'VE FORGOTTEN ABOUT YOUR OUT-STANDING SERVICE RECORD, OR ABOUT ALL OF THE INVALUABLE CONTRIBUTIONS THAT YOU'VE MADE TO THE COMPANY...
FIRE, THE WHEEL, AGRICULTURE... IT'S AN IMPRESSIVE LIST, OLD-TIMER. A JOLLY IMPRESSIVE LIST. DON'T GET ME WRONG.

BUT...WELL, TO BE FRANK, WE'VE HAD OUR PROBLEMS, TOO. THERE'S NO GETTING AWAY FROM IT.
DO YOU KNOW WHAT I THINK A LOT OF IT STEMS FROM? I'LL TELL YOU...

IT'S YOUR BASIC UNWILLINGNESS TO GET ON WITHIN THE COMPANY. YOU DON'T SEEM TO WANT TO FACE UP TO ANY REAL RESPONSIBILITY, OR TO BE YOUR OWN BOSS.
LORD KNOWS, YOU'VE BEEN GIVEN PLENTY OF OPPORTUNITIES...

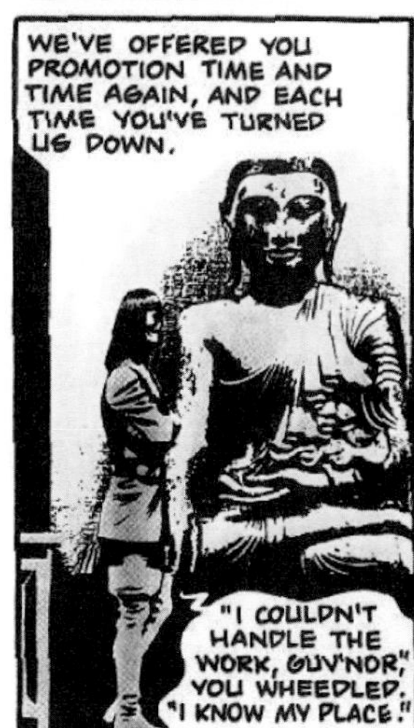
WE'VE OFFERED YOU PROMOTION TIME AND TIME AGAIN, AND EACH TIME YOU'VE TURNED US DOWN.
"I COULDN'T HANDLE THE WORK, GUV'NOR," YOU WHEEDLED. "I KNOW MY PLACE."

TO BE FRANK, YOU'RE NOT TRYING, ARE YOU?

YOU SEE, YOU'VE BEEN STANDING STILL FOR FAR TOO LONG, AND IT'S STARTING TO SHOW IN YOUR WORK...

(07)

AND, I MIGHT ADD, IN YOUR GENERAL STANDARD OF BEHAVIOUR.

THE CONSTANT BICKERING ON THE FACTORY FLOOR HAS NOT ESCAPED MY ATTENTION...

...NOR THE RECENT BOUTS OF ROWDINESS IN THE STAFF CANTEEN.

THEN OF COURSE THERE'S...
HMM. WELL, I DIDN'T REALLY WANT TO HAVE TO BRING THIS UP, BUT...

WELL, YOU SEE, I'VE BEEN HEARING SOME DISTURBING RUMOURS ABOUT YOUR PERSONAL LIFE.
NO, NEVER YOU MIND WHO TOLD ME. NO NAMES, NO PACK DRILL...

I UNDERSTAND THAT YOU ARE UNABLE TO GET ON WITH YOUR SPOUSE. I HEAR THAT YOU ARGUE. I AM TOLD THAT YOU SHOUT. VIOLENCE HAS BEEN MENTIONED.

I AM RELIABLY INFORMED THAT YOU ALWAYS HURT THE ONE YOU LOVE...
...THE ONE YOU SHOULDN'T HURT AT ALL.

(07)

IT WAS *YOU!* *YOU* WHO APPOINTED THESE PEOPLE! *YOU* WHO GAVE THEM THE POWER TO MAKE YOUR DECISIONS FOR YOU!

WHILE I'LL ADMIT THAT ANYONE CAN MAKE A MISTAKE ONCE, TO GO ON MAKING THE SAME LETHAL ERRORS CENTURY AFTER CENTURY SEEMS TO ME NOTHING SHORT OF DELIBERATE.
ON THE AIR

YOU HAVE *ENCOURAGED* THESE MALICIOUS INCOMPETENTS, WHO HAVE MADE YOUR WORKING LIFE A SHAMBLES.

YOU HAVE ACCEPTED WITHOUT QUESTION THEIR SENSELESS ORDERS.

YOU HAVE ALLOWED THEM TO FILL YOUR WORKSPACE WITH DANGEROUS AND UNPROVEN MACHINES.
YOU COULD HAVE *STOPPED* THEM.

ALL YOU HAD TO SAY WAS, *"NO."*
YOU HAVE NO SPINE. YOU HAVE NO PRIDE.
YOU ARE NO LONGER AN ASSET TO THE COMPANY.

I WILL, HOWEVER, BE GENEROUS.
YOU WILL BE GRANTED TWO YEARS TO SHOW ME SOME IMPROVEMENT IN YOUR WORK. IF AT THE END OF THAT TIME YOU ARE STILL UNWILLING TO MAKE A GO OF IT...

(07)

AND WHAT ABOUT THE CHILDREN? IT'S ALWAYS THE CHILDREN WHO SUFFER, AS YOU'RE WELL AWARE.
POOR LITTLE MITES. WHAT ARE THEY TO MAKE OF IT?

WHAT ARE THEY TO MAKE OF YOUR BULLYING, YOUR DESPAIR, YOUR COWARDICE AND ALL YOUR FONDLY NURTURED BIGOTRIES?

REALLY, IT'S NOT GOOD ENOUGH, IS IT?

AND IT'S NO GOOD BLAMING THE DROP IN WORK STANDARDS UPON BAD MANAGEMENT, EITHER...

..THOUGH, TO BE SURE, THE MANAGEMENT IS VERY BAD.
IN FACT, LET US NOT MINCE WORDS... THE MANAGEMENT IS TERRIBLE!

WE'VE HAD A STRING OF EMBEZZLERS, FRAUDS, LIARS AND LUNATICS MAKING A STRING OF CATASTROPHIC DECISIONS.
THIS IS PLAIN FACT.

BUT WHO ELECTED THEM?

AFTER YOU READ: Analyze the Issues

1. Who are the men behind V when he speaks of "a string of embezzlers, frauds, liars and lunatics"?
2. What are the "dangerous and unproven machines"?
3. What is the main message of the speech?

AFTER YOU READ: Analyze the Rhetoric

1. How effective are the images projected behind V as he speaks?
2. Have someone read the speech aloud without looking at the picture. Now compare the power of the speech with the power of the images. What do you notice?
3. What do the police who are trying to stop the speech add to this excerpt?

Sample Student Paper

The Prince of Propaganda

By Jeff Coldwell

AS YOU READ: Annotate

1. Place a star by the sections you like the most.
2. Place question marks by sections you have problems with or do not understand.
3. Place a [+] by sections that need to be developed more or that seem to be incomplete.
4. Write other comments in the margins as you see fit.

Although propaganda *is* an egregious practice, *it* remains the premier method of communication to the public by world leaders, and perhaps no entity is as adept at propaganda as the Bush administration. There are numerous instances of this administration's betrayal of Americans' trust that can be seen in two very pivotal speeches: President Bush's post *9/11* address to the nation and the 2003 State of the Union Address. Speeches are the lifeline of propaganda and politicians; therefore, speeches are essential to any prominent leader's success even if the virtues of the speeches do not reflect the truth. Even though propaganda is a tool used by most politicians, it does not make it an acceptable device to deceive the American people that gave the politicians the power to manage the government in the first place. Ultimately, the method to unveil the propaganda of the Bush administration is through the analysis of the words of its leader, George W. Bush.

An excellent example of *propaganda* is found in President Bush's 9/11 address that ushered in the most common theme of his subsequent speeches, terrorism. This was undoubtedly President Bush's finest hour as he finally found his voice, direction, and an approval rating of 88%; however, his momentum eventually waned as reality caught up with politics ("Bush's Approval Rating"). The method Bush used to propagate his doctrine and deliver a speech that would pierce the hearts of Americans was threefold.

He made sure to maintain short logical sentences in order to keep things as simplistic as possible, he used compelling imagery, and most importantly he used pathos, propagandas biggest ally, to coax the American people into buying his message ("George W. Bush's *Address to .....*"). The content of the speech was an immaculate display of propaganda as unity, resiliency, and freedom were constantly harped upon. "America was targeted for attack because we're the brightest beacon for freedom and opportunity in the world. And no one will keep that light from shining" is a quote from President Bush that was taken from his first address to the nation after 9/11 and encompassed all the things listed above ("Statement by the President…") Perhaps the most ominous and influential quote from George Bush's 8:30 pm 9/11 address to the nation was, "Today, our fellow citizens, our way of life, our very freedom came under attack in a series of deliberate and deadly terrorist acts" ("Statement by the President..."). This single quote helped foster a religion of fear that was shown in George Bush's future speeches and made a very questionable president unquestionable. Those like Democratic Senator Ted Kennedy who stood their ground and rebelled against the President's precarious policies such as the *Patriot Act* were blackballed, and almost no politician, even ardent Democratic Senators like Nancy Pelosi, thought of regarding Bush's actions with dubiousness due to the fear of being painted as unpatriotic and losing future elections (Kennedy). Bush's persuasive use of pathos was paramount in reaching the core of Americans. This was especially true when he evoked Psalm 23: "Even though I walk through the valley of the shadow of death, I fear no evil, for You are with me" ("Statement by the President..."). It remained clear that propaganda was an art that was not lost upon George W. Bush and his administration when at times his speeches would make even Joseph Goebbels blush.

The President's 2003 State of the Union Address was another great work in his history of propaganda, yet legitimacy in content continued to fail. He soundly convinced Americans that his tax cuts were a great boost to the economy even though in history tax cuts have never stimulated the growth rate of the GDP (Gross Domestic Product) and most importantly that the vast majority of the tax breaks went to those who needed it the least ("Responses to Bush's 2003 .. ."). People who made between 10,000 to 20,000 dollars received only $48 from the President's tax cut, but those who made over a million received 90,000 dollars; therefore, the bias in the tax breaks was very present ("Responses to Bush's 2003...").

George Bush spoke highly of his half-hearted poorly constructed health care plan that would stave off the "evils" of universal health care, and regardless of his plan's validity he has taken little to no measures in curbing the upward spiraling costs of health care. One would guess it doesn't matter immediately if the president actually improved something just as long as one thinks he improved something.

President Bush then moved on to a subject the commander-in-chief is not afraid to touch on, terrorism. He stated that "more than 3,000 suspected terrorists have been arrested,'" which is a very impressive number if one ignores the word "suspected" and the fact that many detainees who are released become so jaded by the ordeal they filter into terrorist groups ("Annan: Shut Guantanamo..."). Despite the integrity of the statement it still is an admirable piece of propaganda. The 2003 State of the Union Address ushered in the infamous "yellow-cake" uranium incident when Bush stated that Iraq recently sought *mass quantities* of uranium from Africa ("Responses to Bush's 2003..."). This is accurate if by recent he meant in 1982 during the period the United States backed and armed Iraq as they unsuccessfully sought uranium (Wilson). Perhaps the crowning moment of the address was when the President linked Saddam Hussein to the 9/11 terrorists saying, "Imagine those 19 hijackers with other weapons and other plans, this time armed by Saddam Hussein. It would take one vial, one canister, one crate slipped into this country to bring a day of horror like none we have ever known" ("Responses to Bush's 2003 ..."). There is no link between 9/11 and Saddam and certainly no healthy relationship between Saddam and Osama Bin Laden or the Taliban due to the fact they both are hard-headed ideologues who despise one another (Feldmann). Of course, after one absorbs this statement, they would surely make a connection between 9/11 and Saddam that would spur the initiative for war with Iraq. A poll taken immediately after 9/11 showed that 3% of Americans even mentioned Hussein or Iraq in the same breath as of September 11th but by January of the next year 44% of U.S. citizens believed that some or most of the hijackers were Iraqi when in reality none were (Feldmann). The sharp spike in the amount of Americans who believed that Iraq had a hand in 9/11 could be attributed to sources such as the media or the president, yet one must ask who had the most to gain? So, whether or not one agrees with his politics, President Bush is undoubtedly a master of propaganda.

Even though propaganda is an extremely irresponsible method of communication, it is to this day the most popular method of conveying information to masses by their government, and one of the greatest proponents of this practice is George W. Bush. His adeptness at delivering speeches that appeal to the pathos and ignore logos is almost unparalleled in today's world. The American people must become able to differentiate the truth from the propaganda in speeches and protect their best interests. The country as a whole often forgets that they are the body of this nation and their will, for the most part, must be carried out by the government to whom the electorate gives authority. The manipulation machine that is the Bush administration has lost touch with reality and frequently with the best interest of the American people. Possibly the best way to show George Bush's confidence in his own propaganda is to borrow one of his own quotes,"You can fool some of the people all the time, and those are the ones you want to concentrate on" (thinkexist.com).

Works Cited

"Annan: Shut Guantanamo Prison Camp." CNN. 17 Feb. 2006. 29 Mar. 2006 <http://www.cnn.com/2006>.

"Bush's Approval Rating." Wall Street Journal. 17 Nov. 2005. 18 Mar. 2006 <http://.wallstreetjournal.com>.

"George W. Bush's *Address to Congress On 9/11/2001 Terrorist Attack."* School-for-Champions. 8 Aug. 2005. 18 Mar. 2006 <http://www.school-for-champions.com/speeches/gwbush_21 sep01.htm>.

Kennedy, Edward M. "On Wiretapping, Bush Isn't Listening to the Constitution." Boston Globe. 22 Dec. 2005. 28 Mar. 2006 <http://www.baston.com>.

Feldmann, Linda. "The Impact of Bush Linking 9/11 and Iraq." Csmonitor.Com. 14 Mar. 2003. 29 Mar. 2006 <http://www.csmonitor.com/2003>.

"Responses to Bush's 2003 'State of the Union' Address." Accuracy.Org. 1 Mar. 2003. 18 Mar. 2006 <http://www.accuracy.org/article>.

"Statement by the President in His Address to the Nation." The White House. 11 Sept. 2001. 18 Mar. 2006 <http://www.whitehouse.gov/news/releases/2001/09/20010911-16.html>.

Thinkexist.Com. 2001. 18 Mar. 2006 <http://en.thinkexist.com/quotation>.

Wilson, Joseph C. "What I Didn't Find in Africa." New York Times. 06 July 2003. 29 Mar. 2006 <www.commondreams.orgiviewQ3>.

PRO PEER REVIEW OUTLINE

Directions. Asking the right questions: As you ask these questions and answer them, be specific in your comments so as to be more helpful to the author. Provide details.

1. **Logos.** Comment on the quality and amount of the evidence or research conducted. Is it balanced or enough? Does the author need more? Why or why not? Is the paper too logical or not logical enough? What else can you say about logos?
2. **Pathos.** Comment on the emotional appeals used in the paper. What can the author do to improve this appeal? Should there be less, more, or no emotions? Explain.

3. **Ethos.** Does the author use enough quality sources to improve the impact of the ethos of the paper? Is there a human element in the paper? What does the author need to do to improve the character aspect? Should the author add a personal story? Is the paper too personal? Should it be more logical?
4. **Call for Improvement.** Which aspects in the paper need to be revised or improved? Explain in detail.

Responding to the Conspiracy Issues

Written Rhetoric: Opinion Papers, Arguments, and Research

1. Which of the articles in this section is most persuasive? Make your case by discussing its use of ethos, logos, and pathos.
2. Compare and contrast conspiracy theories written soon after JFK's assassination such as "16 Questions on the Assassination," with a theory written more recently such as "What about the Evidence." Which arguments are still being used? Which no longer seem valid?
3. Write a paper analyzing the logical fallacies in one of the pieces you read. Which fallacies seem most logical? Which were most obvious?
4. Choose an event about which there are conspiracy theories that is not discussed in this chapter: Oklahoma City bombing; 9-11; anonymous attacks on Scientology; Masonic involvement in government; the price of gas, etc. Research the theory to find its main claims and then write a paper which supports or tries to disprove the theory.
5. Research the assassination of Bobby Kennedy, and write a paper comparing the conspiracy theories surrounding his and JFK's assassinations.
6. Your text contains Ford and Belin's response to Oliver Stone's film *JFK*. Research what other responses there were to the film, and then write a paper comparing and contrasting these responses. Which seem most accurate?

Oral Rhetoric: Speeches, Lyrics, and Simulations

1. Spend some time searching YouTube for videos of people expressing their beliefs about the JFK assassination. Which speeches are the most convincing? Why? Be sure to analyze both the text and the visual elements of the speech.
2. There have been some songs written about the JFK assassination and general distrust of the government. See the list below and choose two or three songs that express

paranoia or a conspiracy theory and analyze their lyrics for use of logos, ethos, and pathos. What rhetorical devices do song writers use to make their points?

3. Who really had the means and the motives to carry out the JFK assassination? Create a simulation where each of the people/organizations who have been accused of being behind the assassination tries to convince the others that they did NOT have the means or the motives.
4. How do conspiracy theories get started? Choose a current event and then create a simulation that constructs alternate explanations for the event. Be sure that your explanations contain the elements of an effective conspiracy theory.

Visual Rhetoric: Advertisements, Visuals, and Cinema

1. Do a Google image search for *JFK* movie posters. Choose a poster. Analyze the visual rhetoric of the poster. Does it visualize any of the elements of a good conspiracy theory?
2. Choose one aspect of the conspiracy theory of JFK's assassination that you think sounds believable. Create a 30–45 second video visualizing that aspect of the theory to try to persuade people that your interpretation of the event is the correct one. You can use voice-over to create the context and present your argument. Post your video on YouTube. Be prepared to discuss, either orally or in writing, how you used ethos, logos and/or pathos to be persuasive.
3. Watch Oliver Stone's *JFK* film. How do the visuals in the film illustrate Jim Garrison's speech found on pages 140–141? Do the visuals make the written text more or less believable?
4. Watch a film about a conspiracy theory. Write an essay about how the filmmaker connects the conspiracy to broader fears or concerns in the country.
5. Go to www.deviantart.com and search using the words "conspiracy" and "John F. Kennedy" or a topic you are interested in. Save the images that you find the most effective. Write an essay about the images. Include the images in your report.

Electronic Rhetoric: Emergent Media and Gaming

1. Through the "Groups" function on Facebook, explore what types of conspiracy theory groups have a presence there. Pick a group to research and then write a paper about the function of the group and the types of people who join these groups.
2. Explore the blog site www.abovetopsecret.com. Pick a conspiracy theory and read through several blogs on that theory. What rhetorical devices do these bloggers use to convince their readers? Or are they trying to convince their readers? Is the rhetoric in a blog different from or the same as the rhetoric in formal arguments?

WOVE Project

Choose an historic event which seems to have some mystery surrounding it. You might pick one that already has conspiracy theories about it. Create a 45–60 second video which presents a conspiracy theory about this event. Make sure that your theory contains all the elements of a good conspiracy theory. This video should incorporate oral as well as visual elements and should reference good source material such as newspaper articles, TV interviews, etc. Then, prepare an oral or written presentation of your video for your class explaining why you made the choices you did about the visual and oral elements of your video. Post it in YouTube.

Song Lyrics

"The Spirit of JFK," Devo
"The Conspiracy Song," Dead Milkmen
"Bush Killed Kennedy," The Strap-Ons
"The Day John Kennedy Died," Lou Reed
"The Ballad of Peter Pumpkinhead," XTC

Cinematic List

Arlington Road (Mark Pellinton, 1999)
Bent (Sean Mathias, 1997)
Capricorn One (Peter Hyams, 1978)
Conspiracy Theory (Richard Donner, 1997)
The Constant Gardener (Fernando Meirelles, 2005)
The Conversation (Francis Ford Coppola, 1974)
The Crucible (Nicholas Hytner, 1996)
The DaVinci Code (Ron Howard, 2006)
Fahrenheit 9/11 (Michael Moore, 2004)
Good Night, and Good Luck (George Clooney, 2005)
Manchurian Candidate (John Frankenheimer, 1962)
Manchurian Candidate (Jonathan Demme, 2004)
V for Vendetta (James McTeigue, 2005)
Wag the Dog (Barry Levinson, 1997)
Watchmen (*Zack Snyder,* 2009)
Winter Kills (William Richert, 1997)
The X-Files: The Movie (Rob Bowman, 1998)
The X-Files: I Want to Believe (Chris Carter, 2008)

Anime List

Akira (Katsuhiro Otomo, 1988)
Blood: The Last Vampire (Hiroyuki Kitakubo, 2000)

Jin Roh (Hiroyuki Okiura, 1998)
Ghost in the Shell (Mamoru Oshii, 1996)
Serial Experiments: Latin (Ryutaro Nakamura, 1998)

Television Shows

The 4400 (created by Scott Peters, Rene Echevarria, 2004–)
Alien Nation (created by Kenneth Johnson, 1989–1990)
American Dad (created by Seth McFarlane, Mike Barker, and Matt Weitzman 2005–)
The Lone Gunmen (created by Chris Carter, Vince Gilligan, and John Shiban, 2001)

Comix List

100 Bullets (Brian Azzarello)
Akira (Katsuhiro Otomo)
Big Book of Conspiracies (Doug Moench)
DMZ (Brian Wood)
Eagle: The Making Of An Asian-American President (Kaiji Kawaguchi)
Ghost in the Shell (Masamune Shirow)
Sin City (Frank Miller)
Transmetropolitan (Warren Ellis)
V for Vendetta (Alan Moore and David Lloyd)
Watchmen (Alan Moore and Dave Gibbons)

Video Games

Xbox 360

Robert Ludlum's The Bourne Conspiracy
Hitman: Blood Money
Lost Planet: Extreme Condition
Resident Evil 5

Playstation 3

Assassin's Creed (Crusades)
Fallout 3

Wii

Resident Evil 4

“Bureaucrats”

by Ali Farzat

from *A Pen of Damascus Steel: The Political Cartoons of an Arab Master*. Seattle: Cune Press , 2005 page 103.

AFTER YOU READ: Analyze the Issues

1. What are the rules of this game?
2. What sorts of stratagems are being used to win?
3. What is the endgame?

AFTER YOU READ: Analyze the Rhetoric

1. Since the author is from Syria, what do you think the cartoon is criticizing?
2. Comment on the humor in the cartoon.
3. If the author had written more information than the title "Bureaucrats," what might he add? What would you add?

The Issues

Do you play video games? Video games are now outselling DVDs and are becoming more cinematic in characteristics. Indeed, game writers and screen writers are starting to merge. The impact of games in education, in the military, in business, and in social contexts will only increase with each generation. This chapter will examine how gaming impacts our lives.

After the Columbine High shootings of 13 people on April 20, 1977, it was discovered that the two killers played violent video games, such as *Doom*. Players then started to defend first-person shooter games like *Grand Thief Auto*. Indeed, after the Korean American student killed 32 people and himself at Virginia Tech on April 16, 2007, some critics assumed that he was an addicted player who spent time doing violent video games. However, no evidence about any such connections could be made. Such arguments remain alive as gamers still continue to defend their right to play such forms of entertainment. Should video game makers take some of the blame and be responsible for such real acts of violence? Or are the causes of violence more complex than we think?

This chapter examines other social, psychological, legal, and economic impacts that games have. What interpersonal skills do we learn from gaming? Perhaps such games are providing helpful skills for the next generations of workers. Perhaps we should start putting that we play such games on our resumes. We might get hired.

We end the chapter with some science fiction: an excerpt from the screenplay of *Blade Runner* inspired by Philip K. Dick and an excerpt from *Snow Crash* by Neal Stephenson.

Ask the Right Questions

What should we ask when examining the issues at hand and when reading about them?

Logos

Are the claims used by the authors logical?
How rational are the arguments presented?
How does the evidence support the arguments presented?
Is the argument arranged logically?

Ethos

How is authority used in the works?
Does authority work in the arguments?
What types of sources are used to defend the messages?
How will the various audiences react to the message?
Does the voice of the author affect the reader?

Pathos

How do the authors use emotions to convey their messages?
Why do the gaming issues often evoke such powerful emotions?
What prejudices are involved in the arguments?
What attitudes do we have about games?

Annotate the Text

In addition to the text's use of logos, ethos, and pathos, annotate the readings as follows:

- Examine the warrants provided in the arguments.
- Make connections to other writers and works.
- Comment on the evidence provided in the readings.
- Write questions about the text in the margins.

The Ratings System for Video Games

Entertainment Software Rating Board (ESRB)

www.esrb.org

Video games continue to be criticized for their violence, language, and sexuality. Many critics don't really know about the rating system that exists for such games. As you read and look at the ESRB rating system, be critical of its content.

AS YOU READ: Annotate

1. Circle the age group mentioned for each rating.
2. Write “yes” in the margins if you agree with the description of what is suitable for the age group.
3. Write at least three other comments in the margin.

EARLY CHILDHOOD
Titles rated EC (Early Childhood) have content that may be suitable for ages 3 and older. Contains no material that parents would find inappropriate.

EVERYONE
Titles rated E (Everyone) have content that may be suitable for ages 6 and older. Titles in this category may contain minimal cartoon, fantasy or mild violence and/or infrequent use of mild language.

EVERYONE 10+
Titles rated E10+ (Everyone 10 and older) have content that may be suitable for ages 10 and older. Titles in this category may contain more cartoon, fantasy or mild violence, mild language and/or minimal suggestive themes.

TEEN
Titles rated T (Teen) have content that may be suitable for ages 13 and older. Titles in this category may contain violence, suggestive themes, crude humor, minimal blood, simulated gambling, and/or infrequent use of strong language.

MATURE
Titles rated M (Mature) have content that may be suitable for persons ages 17 and older. Titles in this category may contain intense violence, blood and gore, sexual content and/or strong language.

ADULTS ONLY
Titles rated AO (Adults Only) have content that should only be played by persons 18 years and older. Titles in this category may include prolonged scenes of intense violence and/or graphic sexual content and nudity.

AFTER YOU READ: Analyze the Issues

1. Did you know about these ratings?
2. How effective are these ratings?
3. Do people even care about these ratings?

AFTER YOU READ: Analyze the Rhetoric

1. Are the images effective symbols for the ratings? What changes would you suggest?
2. Are the right age groups picked for the suitability of the content mentioned?
3. Is such a rating system helpful for its audience: parents?

"You Play *World of Warcraft?* You're Hired!"

by John Seely Brown and Douglas Thomas
Wired *Issue 14.04—April 2006 http://www.wired.com/wired/archive/14.04/learn.html*
(Essay)

John Seely Brown was the past chief scientist for Xerox and its director of the Palo Alto Research Center (PARC). Today he calls himself "Chief of Confusion" because he helps confused people to "ask the right questions" as a way to solve their problems. Douglas Thomas, an associate professor, specializes in Critical Theory and Cultural Studies of Technology at University of Southern California's Annenberg School for Communication.

- John Seely Brown: www.johnseelybrown.com/
- Douglas Thomas: www-rcf.usc.edu/~douglast/bio1.shtml

AS YOU READ: Annotate

1. Write "agree" and "disagree" in the margins.
2. Place stars by sections you think are powerful.
3. Circle any words you do not know and look them up in the dictionary and write their meanings in the margins.

Why multiplayer games may be the best kind of job training.

In late 2004, Stephen Gillett was in the running for a choice job at Yahoo!—a senior management position in engineering. He was a strong contender. Gillett had been responsible for CNET's backend, and he had helped launch a number of successful startups. But he had an additional qualification his prospective employer wasn't aware of, one that gave him a decisive edge: He was one of the top guild masters in the on-line role-playing game *World of Warcraft*.

Gaming tends to be regarded as a harmless diversion at best, a vile corruptor of youth at worst. But the usual critiques fail to recognize its potential for experiential learning. Unlike education acquired through textbooks, lectures, and classroom instruction, what takes place in massively multiplayer on-line games is what we call accidental learning. It's *learning to be*—a natural byproduct of adjusting to a new culture—as opposed to *learning about*. Where traditional learning is based on the execution of carefully graded challenges, accidental learning relies on failure. Virtual environments are safe platforms for trial and error. The chance of failure is high, but the cost is low and the lessons learned are immediate.

Simulation games have proven excellent tools for training people in manual skills; for example, *X-Plane*, a flight simulator that runs on home computers, has been certified by the Federal Aviation Administration. But accidental learning transcends intentional training. When role-playing gamers team up to undertake a quest, they often need to attempt particularly difficult challenges repeatedly until they find a blend of skills, talents, and actions that allows them to succeed. This process brings about a profound shift in how they perceive and react to the world around them. They become more flexible in their thinking and more sensitive to social cues. The fact that they don't think of gameplay as training is crucial. Once the experience is explicitly educational, it becomes about developing compartmentalized skills and loses its power to permeate the player's behavior patterns and worldview.

In this way, the process of becoming an effective *World of Warcraft* guild master amounts to a total-immersion course in leadership. A guild is a collection of players who come together to share knowledge, resources, and manpower. To run a large one, a guild master must be adept at many skills: attracting, evaluating, and recruiting new members; creating apprenticeship programs; orchestrating group strategy; and adjudicating disputes. Guilds routinely splinter over petty squabbles and other basic failures of management; the master must resolve them without losing valuable members, who can easily quit and join a rival guild. Never mind the virtual surroundings; these conditions provide real-world training a manager can apply directly in the workplace.

And that's exactly what Gillett is doing. He accepted Yahoo!'s offer and now works there as senior director of engineering operations. "I used to worry about not having what I needed to get a job done," he says. "Now I think of it like a quest;

by being willing to improvise, I can usually find the people and resources I need to accomplish the task." His story—translating experience in the virtual world into success in the real one is bound to become more common as the gaming audience explodes and gameplay becomes more sophisticated. The day may not be far off when companies receive resumes that include a line reading "level 60 tauren shaman in *World of Warcraft*."

The savviest employers will get the message.

AFTER YOU READ: Analyze the Issues

1. Do you think putting on your resume that you game will help you get a job? Why or why not?
2. According to the article, playing games like *Warcraft* can make you a better leader. Do you agree? Why or why not?
3. What does the article say about learning?

AFTER YOU READ: Analyze the Rhetoric

1. Comment on the title of the essay? Can you come up with a better title? Share it.
2. Does the ethos of the authors help support the statements made in the article?
3. How effective is the last line of the article? Explain.

"Violence in Media Entertainment"

by Media Awareness Network (MNet) 2008
(Essay)

MNet is a Canadian non-profit organization established in 1996. "MNet focuses its efforts on equipping adults with information and tools to help young people to understand how the media work, how the media may affect their lifestyle choices and the extent to which they, as consumers and citizens, are being well informed." The organization is comprised of a variety of media experts from such fields as education, journalism, and mass communications.

http://www.media-awareness.ca/english/issues/violence/violence_entertainment.cfm

AS YOU READ: Annotate

1. Place stars by sections you think are important.
2. Circle sections that include the use of authority (ethos).
3. Underline words you do not know and look them up. Write their meanings in the margin.

Between 2000 B.C. and 44 A.D., the ancient Egyptians entertained themselves with plays re-enacting the murder of their god Osiris— and the spectacle, history tells us, led to a number of copycat killings. The ancient Romans were given to lethal spectator sports as well, and in 380 B.C. Saint Augustine lamented that his society was addicted to gladiator games and "drunk with the fascination of bloodshed."

Violence has always played a role in entertainment. But there's a growing consensus that, in recent years, something about media violence has changed.

For one thing, there's more of it. Laval University professors Guy Paquette and Jacques de Guise studied six major Canadian television networks over a seven-year period, examining films, situation comedies, dramatic series, and children's programming (though not cartoons). The study found that between 1993 and 2001, incidents of physical violence increased by 378 per cent. TV shows in 2001 averaged 40 acts of violence per hour.

Francophone viewers experienced the greatest increase. Although physical violence on the three anglophone networks in the study increased by 183 per cent, on their francophone counterparts it increased by 540 per cent. One network, TQS, accounted for just under half (49 per cent) of all the physical violence on the networks studied.

Paquette and de Guise also identified a disturbing increase in psychological violence, especially in the last two years. The study found that incidents of psychological violence remained relatively stable from 1993 to 1999, but increased 325 per cent from 1999 to 2001. Such incidents now occur more frequently than physical violence on both francophone and anglophone networks.

Canadians are also heavily influenced by American programming. Paquette and de Guise found that over 80 per cent of the TV violence aired in Canada originates in the U.S. They speculate that francophone networks and stations may have a higher incidence of violence because they broadcast more movies, and this, in turn may be due to lower production budgets. Canadian-made violence is most likely to appear on private networks, which broadcast three times as many violent acts as public networks do. Overall, 87.9 per cent of all violent acts appear before 9 p.m., and 39 per cent air before 8 p.m.—at a time when children are likely to be watching.

More Graphic, More Sexual, More Sadistic

> In 2001, only a quarter of the most violent television shows, and two-fifths of the most violent movies, were rated R. The majority were rated PG or PG-13.
>
> (Source: *Center for Media and Public Affairs*, 2001)

Other research indicates that media violence has not just increased in quantity; it has also become much more graphic, much more sexual, and much more sadistic.

Explicit pictures of slow-motion bullets exploding from people's chests, and dead bodies surrounded by pools of blood, are now commonplace fare. Millions of viewers worldwide, many of them children, watch female World Wrestling Entertainment wrestlers try to tear out each other's hair and rip off each other's clothing. And one of the top-selling video games in the world, *Grand Theft Auto*, is programmed so players can beat prostitutes to death with baseball bats after having sex with them.

The Globalization of Media

Concerns about media violence have grown as television and movies have acquired a global audience. When UNESCO surveyed children in 23 countries around the world in 1998, it discovered that 91 per cent of children had a television in their home— and not just in the U.S., Canada and Europe, but also in the Arab states, Latin America, Asia and Africa. More than half (51 per cent) of boys living in war zones and high-crime areas chose action heroes as role models, ahead of any other images; and a remarkable 88 per cent of the children surveyed could identify the Arnold Schwarzenegger character from the film *Terminator*. UNESCO reported that the *Terminator* "seems to represent the characteristics that children think are necessary to cope with difficult situations."

> On average, children in the 23 countries surveyed watch television three hours each day, and spend 50 per cent more time watching

> the small screen than they spend on any other activity outside of school.
>
> (Source: *UNESCO*, 1998)

Violence Without Consequences or Moral Judgment

The notion of violence as a means of problem solving is reinforced by entertainment in which both villains and heroes resort to violence on a continual basis. The Center for Media and Public Affairs (CMPA), which has studied violence in television, movies and music videos for a decade, reports that nearly half of all violence is committed by the "good guys." Less than 10 per cent of the TV shows, movies and music videos that were analyzed contextualized the violence or explored its human consequences. The violence was simply presented as justifiable, natural and inevitable— the most obvious way to solve the problem.

PG: Parental Guidance?

> Incidents of sexual violence and sadism doubled between 1989 and 1999, and the number of graphic depictions increased more than five-fold.
>
> (Source: *Parent Television Council*, 1999)

Busy parents who want to protect their children from media violence have a difficult task before them. The CMPA found that violence appears on all major television networks and cable stations, making it impossible for channel surfers to avoid it.

Nightly news coverage has become another concern. In spite of falling crime rates across North America, disturbing images of violent crime continue to dominate news broadcasting. As news shows compete with other media for audiences, many news producers have come to rely on the maxim: "If it bleeds, it leads." Violence and death, they say, keep the viewer numbers up. Good news doesn't.

As well, movie ratings are becoming less and less trustworthy in terms of giving parents real guidance on shows with unsuitable content. PG-13 movies tend to make more money than R-rated films, and as a result, the industry is experiencing a "ratings creep": shows that the Motion Picture Association of America would once have rated R are now being rated as PG-13, in order to increase box-office profits and rental sales.

In movie theatres, there is some control over who watches what. But at home, there's little to stop children from watching a restricted movie on one of the many emerging specialty channels. Kids may also have access to adult video games at the local video store. In December 2001, the U.S. Federal Trade Commission reported that retailers allowed 78 per cent of unaccompanied minors, ages 13 to 16, to purchase video games rated "mature."

To make supervision even more problematic, American children often have their own entertainment equipment. According to the Annenberg Public Policy Center, 57 per cent of kids aged 8 to 16 have TVs in their bedrooms, and 39 per cent have gaming equipment.

A Youth Subculture of Violence

While many parents are concerned about the graphic violence and put-down humour in many kids' shows, there's a growing subculture of violence that parental radar often misses.

Music and Music Videos

Music and music videos are pushing into new and increasingly violent territory. When singer Jordan Knight, formerly of the popular New Kids on the Block group, released a solo album in 1999, Canadian activists called for a boycott of the album because it included a song advocating date rape.

And when the controversial rap artist Eminem came to Toronto in 2000, politicians and activists unsuccessfully called for the government to bar him from the country, on the grounds that his violent lyrics promoted hatred against women. For instance, his song *Kim* graphically depicts him murdering his wife; and *Kill You* describes how he plans to rape and murder his mother.

> "Don't you get it, bitch? No one can hear you.
> Now shut the fuck up, and get what's comin' to you... You were supposed to love me!!!!! (Sound of Kim choking)
> NOW BLEED, BITCH, BLEED
> BLEED, BITCH, BLEED, BLEEEEEED!"
>
> (Source: From the song *Kim*, by Eminem)

In spite of (or perhaps because of) his promotion of violence, Eminem continues to be a commercial success. His *Marshall Mathers* release sold 679,567 copies in Canada in 2000, and was the year's best-selling album. And *The Eminem Show* topped Canadian charts for months in 2002, selling, at one point, approximately 18,000 copies a week.

Eminem's success is not exceptional. Extremely violent lyrics have moved into the mainstream of the music industry. The Universal Music Group, the world's largest music company, lists Eminem, Dr Dre and Limp Bizkit all of whom have been criticized for their violent and misogynist lyrics among its top-grossing artists. And Madonna's 2002 music video *What It Feels Like For a Girl* contained such graphic violence that even MTV refused to air it more than once.

Video Games

Violence in general, and sexual violence in particular, is also a staple of the video game industry. The current trend is for players to be the bad guys, acting out criminal fantasies and earning points for attacking and killing innocent bystanders. Although these games are rated M, for mature audiences, it's common knowledge that they are popular among pre-teens and teenaged boys.

> "As easy as killing babies with axes."
> (Source: Advertising copy for the game *Carmageddon*)

For example, players in *Grand Theft Auto 3* (the best-selling game ever for PlayStation2) earn points by carjacking, and stealing drugs from street people and pushers. In *Carmageddon*, players are rewarded for mowing down pedestrians—sounds of cracking bones add to the realistic effect. The first-person shooter in *Duke Nukem* hones his skills by using pornographic posters of women for target practice, and earns bonus points for shooting naked and bound prostitutes and strippers who beg, "Kill me." In the game *Postal*, players act out the part of the Postal Dude, who earns points by randomly shooting everyone who appears—including people walking out of church, and members of a high school band. Postal Dude is programmed to say, "Only my gun understands me."

The level of violence in the gaming habits of young people is disturbingly high. In MNet's 2001 study *Young Canadians In A Wired World* (which found that 32 per cent of kids 9 to 17 are playing video games "every day or almost every day"), 60 per cent cited action/combat as their favourite genre. Stephen Kline of Simon Fraser University reported similar findings in his 1998 study of over 600 B.C. teens. Twenty-five per cent of the teens he surveyed played between seven and 30 hours a week and when asked for their one favourite game, their choice was "overwhelmingly" in the action/adventure genre.

Web Sites

Virtual violence is also readily available on the World Wide Web. Children and young people can download violent lyrics (including lyrics that have been censored from retail versions of songs), and visit Web sites that feature violent images and video clips. Much of the violence is also sexual in nature.

For example, the site Who Would You Kill? allows players to select real-life stars of television shows, and then describe how they would kill them off in the series. The entries frequently include bizarre acts of degradation and sexual violence. Murder is also a staple of the Web site newgrounds.com, which features a number of Flash movies showing celebrities being degraded and killed. When MNet surveyed 5,682 Canadian young people in 2001, the newgrounds site ranked twelfth in popularity among 11- and 12-year-old boys.

Other popular sites such as gorezone.com and rotten.com feature real-life pictures of accident scenes, torture and mutilation. In 2000, rotten.com was investigated by the FBI for posting photographs depicting cannibalism.

Many kids view these sites as the on-line equivalent of harmless horror movies. But their pervasive combination of violence and sexual imagery is disturbing. Gorezone's front-page disclaimer describes the images on its site as "sexually oriented and of an erotic nature" and then warns viewers that they also contain scenes of death, mutilation and dismemberment. The disclaimer then normalizes this activity by stating, "my interest in scenes of death, horrifying photos and sexual matters, which is both healthy and normal, is generally shared by adults in my community."

Anecdotal evidence suggests that gore sites are well known to Canadian schoolchildren, although parents and teachers are often unaware of their existence. In MNet's 2001 survey, 70 per cent of high school boys said that they had visited such sites.

The presence of violence, degradation and cruelty in a range of media means that children are exposed to a continuum of violence, which ranges from the in-your-face attitude of shows like *South Park* to extreme depictions of misogyny and sadism. Young people generally take the lead when it comes to accessing new media but the MNet survey found that only 16 per cent of children say their parents know a great deal of what they do on-line. This is particularly problematic, given the results of a 1999 AOL survey that found on-line activities are emerging as a central facet of family life; and that a majority of parents believe that being on-line is better for their children than watching television.

AFTER YOU READ: Analyze the Issues

1. According to the article, what has changed in media violence?
2. What is the main message of the article? Do you agree?
3. What in the article do you disagree with? Why?
4. What did you find the most interesting and why?

AFTER YOU READ: Analyze the Rhetoric

1. Why does the article use statistics and surveys to defend its points (logos)? Is it effective or not? Why or why not?
2. How does the article use ethos to support its argument?
3. Comment on the academic voice of the paper. Do you feel it should have included a personal voice? Explain.

"Were Video Games to Blame for Massacre?"

by Winda Benedetti

Winda Benedetti is a Seattle-based freelance writer and an MSNBC contributor. Note the variety of sources that were used to create this article. Again the press and public enjoyed attacking video game makers and users. This article gives an overview of the blame game that went on immediately after the tragedy in Virginia Tech in 2007. Even before the facts were in judgments were made. Read and see why this continues.

MSNBC CT April 20, 2007. http://www.msnbc.msn.com/id/18220228/page/2/

AS YOU READ: Annotate

1. Write "agree" or "disagree" in the margins by the key sections of the argument.
2. Circle any words you do not know and write their meaning in the margin.

Pundits rushed to judge industry, gamers in the wake of shooting

The shooting on the Virginia Tech campus was only hours old, police hadn't even identified the gunman, and yet already the perpetrator had been fingered and was in the midst of being skewered in the media.

Video games. They were to blame for the dozens dead and wounded. They were behind the bloodiest massacre in U.S. history.

Or so Jack Thompson told Fox News and, in the days that followed, would continue to tell anyone who'd listen.

"These are real lives. These are real people that are in the ground now because of this game. I have no doubt about it," said Thompson, a Florida attorney and fervent critic of the video game industry.

The game he's talking about is "Counter-Strike," a massively popular team-based tactical shooting game that puts players in the heavily armed boots of either a counter-terrorist or terrorist.

But whether Seung-Hui Cho, the student who opened fire Monday, was an avid player of video games and whether he was a fan of "Counter-Strike" in particular remains, even now, uncertain at best.

Meanwhile, in the aftermath of the school shootings and the finger-pointing that followed, game players and industry advocates say they're outraged that the brutal acts of a deeply disturbed and depressed loner with a history of mental illness would be blamed so quickly on video and computer games. They say this is perhaps the most flagrant case of anti-game crusaders using a tragedy to promote their own personal causes.

"It's so sad. These massacre chasers—they're worse than ambulance chasers—they're waiting for these things to happen so they can jump on their soapbox," said Jason Della Rocca, executive director of the International Game Developers Association.

"It disgusts me," said Isaiah Triforce Johnson, a longtime gamer and founder of a New York-based gaming advocacy group that, in response to the accusations, is now planning what is the first ever gamer-driven peace rally.

"Mental masturbation"

When Jack Thompson gets worked up, he refers to gamers as "knuckleheads." He calls video games "mental masturbation."

When he's talking about himself and his crusade against violent games, he calls himself an "educator." He likes to use the word "pioneer."

Certainly Thompson has made a name for himself. After all, he knows a thing or two about publicity. He's spent no small bit of time in front of a camera.

On those rare occasions when a student opens fire on a school campus, Thompson is frequently the first and the loudest to declare games responsible. In recent years he's blamed games such as "Counter-Strike," "Doom" and "Grand Theft Auto III" for school shootings in Littleton, Colo., Red Lake, Minn. and Paducah, Ky.

He's blamed them for shootings beyond school grounds as well. In an attempt to hold game developers and publishers responsible for these spasms of violence, Thompson has launched several unsuccessful lawsuits.

But in the hours after the Virginia Tech massacre, Thompson wasn't the only one rushing to make a connection between the shootings and video games. Police were still struggling to piece together the nightmare that had unfolded on campus that morning when Dr. Phil McGraw appeared on Larry King Live and took aim at the usual suspect.

"The problem is we are programming these people as a society," he said. "You cannot tell me—common sense tells you that if these kids are playing video games, where they're on a mass killing spree in a video game, it's glamorized on the big screen, it's become part of the fiber of our society. You take that and mix it with a psychopath, a sociopath or someone suffering from mental illness and add in a dose of rage, the suggestibility is too high. And we're going to have to start dealing with that."

Meanwhile, by Tuesday, The Washington Post had posted a story on its Web site stating that several youths who knew Cho said that in high school he'd been a fan of violent video games, especially "Counter-Strike."

But a short time later, the newspaper removed that paragraph from the story without explanation. Meanwhile, authorities released a search warrant listing the items found in Cho's dorm room. Not a single video game, console or gaming gadget was on the list, though a computer was confiscated. And in an interview with Chris Matthews of "Hardball," Cho's university suite-mate said he had never seen Cho play video games.

None of this seems to matter to Thompson.

"This is not rocket science. When a kid who has never killed anyone in his life goes on a rampage and looks like the Terminator, he's a video gamer," he told MSNBC.com.

And in a letter sent to Bill Gates Wednesday, he wrote: "Mr. Gates, your company is potentially legally liable (for) the harm done at Virginia Tech. Your game, a killing simulator, according to the news that used to be in the *Post*, trained him to enjoy killing and how to kill."

(Microsoft did not create "Counter Strike" but did publish a version of it for the Xbox. The company's representatives declined to comment on Thompson's letter. MSNBC.com is a Microsoft-NBC Universal joint venture.)

While Thompson concedes that there are many elements that must have driven Cho to commit such a brutal act, he insists that without video games Cho wouldn't have had the skills to do what he did.

"He might have killed somebody but he wouldn't have killed 32 if he hadn't rehearsed it and trained himself like a warrior on virtual reality. It can't be done. It just doesn't happen."

Kids these days

Dr. Karen Sternheimer, a sociologist at the University of Southern California and author of the book *Kids These Days: Facts and Fictions About Today's Youth*, disagrees. She believes that it didn't require much skill for Cho to shoot as many people as he did. After all, eye witness accounts indicate many of the victims were shot at point-blank range.

And for all of Thompson's claims that violent video games are the cause of school shootings, Sternheimer points out that before this week's Virginia Tech massacre, the most deadly school shooting in history took place at the University of Texas in Austin… in 1966. Not even "Pong" had been invented at that time.

"One thing that people often don't realize is that in the years since video game sales have really exploded, not only have youth violence rates decreased but violence rates in the U.S. have declined precipitously," she added.

Meanwhile, Sternheimer says the rush to blame video games in these situations is disingenuous for yet another reason. Although it remains unclear whether Cho played games, it seems nobody will be surprised if it turns out he did. After all, what 23-year-old man living in America hasn't played video games?

"Especially if you're talking about young males, the odds are pretty good that any young male in any context will have played video games at some point," Sternheimer says.

"I think in our search to find some kind of answer as to why this happened, the video game explanation seems easy," she says. "It seems like there's an easy answer to preventing this from happening again and that feels good on some level."

The blame game

Jason Della Rocca agrees. "Everyone wants a simple solution for a massively complex problem. We want to get on with our lives."

As the leader of an organization that represents video game creators from all over the world, Della Rocca knows the routine all too well.

Someone opens fire on a school campus. Someone blames video games. His phone starts ringing. People start asking him questions like, "So how bad are these games anyway?"

Of course, he also knows that this is far from the first time in history that a young form of pop culture has been blamed for any number of society's ills. Rock and roll was the bad guy in the 1950s. Jazz was the bad guy in the 1930s. Movies, paintings, comic books, works of literature…they've all been there.

Still, Della Rocca believes that people like Thompson are "essentially feeding off the fears of those who don't understand games."

For those who didn't grow up playing video games, the appeal of a game like "Counter-Strike" can be hard to comprehend. It can be difficult to understand that the game promotes communication and team work. It can be hard to fathom how players who love to run around gunning down their virtual enemies do not have even the slightest desire to shoot a person in real life.

"It's the thing they don't understand," Della Rocca says. "It's a thing that's scary."

Fed up with the scapegoating and lack of understanding, gamer groups have begun to get increasingly organized in their attempts to change public perception of their favorite hobby.

Hal Halpin, president of the Entertainment Consumers Association, says there's more than 30 million gamers in the U.S. alone. He says the ECA, a nonprofit membership organization, was created last year specifically to represent the needs and interests of those who play computer and video games.

Meanwhile, the members of Empire Arcadia—a grassroots group dedicated to supporting the gaming community and culture—have been so incensed by the recent attempts to blame video games for the Virginia Tech shootings that they've begun planning a rally in New York City with the assistance of the ECA.

"There we will protest, mourn and show how real gamers play video games peacefully and responsibly," organizer Johnson wrote on the group's Web site. "This demonstration is to show that gamers will not take the blame of this tragic matter but we will do what we can to help put an end to terrible events like this."

Johnson says that, ultimately, he hopes the rally—scheduled for May 5—will help people better understand video game enthusiasts like him.

"We are normal people," he says. "We just play games."

AFTER YOU READ: Analyze the Issues

1. What are some of the arguments for those who blame video games for violence?
2. What are some of the arguments for those who say video games are not to blame?
3. Which side do you agree with? Why?

AFTER YOU READ: Analyze the Rhetoric

1. Did the author include enough quotes from both sides of the argument? Was the author biased?
2. Comment on the effectiveness of the concluding sentence.

"Violent Media is Good for Kids"

by Gerard Jones
June 28, 2000
(Essay)

A scene from Gerard Jones and Will Jacobs' comic

As an author who feels violent fantasies are healthy and promote cathartic mental growth, Jones has researched this topic extensively and writes about it and the history of popular culture, specifically about comics in such works as *Killing Monsters: Why Children Need Fantasy, Super Heroes, and Make-Believe Violence* and *Men of Tomorrow: Geeks, Gangsters, and the Birth of the Comic Book,* which won the Eisner Award, 2005. Read the essay. Do you agree?

- Homepage: www.gerardjones.com
- Gerard Jones's Blog://www.redroom.com/author/gerard-jones
- Blogspot: gerardjones.blogspot.com

www.motherjones.com/commentary/columns/2000/06/violent_media.html

AS YOU READ: Annotate

1. Place stars by the sections that you think represent the best part of the article.
2. Underline sections you think are weak and explain in the margins why.
3. Circle examples of ethos in the article.

At 13 I was alone and afraid. Taught by my well-meaning, progressive, English-teacher parents that violence was wrong, that rage was something to be overcome and cooperation was always better than conflict, I suffocated my deepest fears and desires under a nice-boy persona. Placed in a small, experimental school that was wrong for me, afraid to join my peers in their bumptious rush into adolescent boyhood, I withdrew into passivity and loneliness. My parents, not trusting the violent world of the late 1960s, built a wall between me and the crudest elements of American pop culture.

Then the Incredible Hulk smashed through it.

One of my mother's students convinced her that Marvel Comics, despite their apparent juvenility and violence, were in fact devoted to lofty messages of pacifism and tolerance. My mother borrowed some, thinking they'd be good for me. And so they were. But not because they preached lofty messages of benevolence. They were good for me because they were juvenile. And violent.

The character who caught me, and freed me, was the Hulk: overgendered and undersocialized, half-naked and half-witted, raging against a frightened world that misunderstood and persecuted him. Suddenly I had a fantasy self to carry my stifled rage and buried desire for power. I had a fantasy self who was a self: unafraid of his desires and the world's disapproval, unhesitating and effective in action. "Puny boy follow Hulk!" roared my fantasy self, and I followed.

I followed him to new friends—other sensitive geeks chasing their own inner brutes—and I followed him to the arrogant, self-exposing, self-assertive, superheroic decision to become a writer. Eventually, I left him behind, followed more sophisticated heroes, and finally my own lead along a twisting path to a career and an identity. In my 30s, I found myself writing action movies and comic books. I wrote some Hulk stories, and met the geek-geniuses who created him. I saw my own creations turned into action figures, cartoons, and computer games. I talked to the kids who read my stories. Across generations, genders, and ethnicities I kept seeing the same story: people pulling themselves out of emotional traps by immersing themselves in violent stories. People integrating the scariest, most fervently denied fragments of their psyches into fuller senses of selfhood through fantasies of superhuman combat and destruction.

I have watched my son living the same story—transforming himself into a bloodthirsty dinosaur to embolden himself for the plunge into preschool, a Power Ranger to muscle through a social competition in kindergarten. In the first grade, his friends started climbing a tree at school. But he was afraid: of falling, of the centipedes crawling on the trunk, of sharp branches, of his friends' derision. I took my cue from his own fantasies and read him old Tarzan comics, rich in combat and bright with flashing knives. For two weeks he lived in them. Then he put them aside. And he climbed the tree.

But all the while, especially in the wake of the recent burst of school shootings, I heard pop psychologists insisting that violent stories are harmful to kids, heard teachers begging parents to keep their kids away from "junk culture," heard a guilt-stricken friend with a son who loved Pokémon lament, "I've turned into the bad mom who lets her kid eat sugary cereal and watch cartoons!"

That's when I started the research.

"Fear, greed, power-hunger, rage: these are aspects of ourselves that we try not to experience in our lives but often want, even need, to experience vicariously through stories of others," writes Melanie Moore, Ph.D., a psychologist who works with urban teens. "Children need violent entertainment in order to explore the inescapable feelings that they've been taught to deny, and to reintegrate those feelings into a more whole, more complex, more resilient selfhood."

Moore consults to public chools and local governments, and is also raising a daughter. For the past three years she and I have been studying the ways in which children use violent stories to meet their emotional and developmental needs—and the ways in which adults can help them use those stories healthily. With her help I developed Power Play, a program for helping young people improve their self-knowledge and sense of potency through heroic, combative storytelling.

We've found that every aspect of even the trashiest pop-culture story can have its own developmental function. Pretending to have superhuman powers helps children conquer the feelings of powerlessness that inevitably come with being so young and small. The dual-identity concept at the heart of many superhero stories helps kids negotiate the conflicts between the inner self and the public self as they work through the early stages of socialization. Identification with a rebellious, even destructive, hero helps children learn to push back against a modern culture that cultivates fear and teaches dependency.

At its most fundamental level, what we call "creative violence"—head-bonking cartoons, bloody videogames, playground karate, toy guns—gives children a tool to master their rage. Children will feel rage. Even the sweetest and most civilized of them, even those whose parents read the better class of literary magazines, will feel rage. The world is uncontrollable and incomprehensible; mastering it is a terrifying, enraging task. Rage can be an energizing emotion, a shot of courage to push us to resist greater threats, take more control, than we ever thought we could. But rage is also the emotion our culture distrusts the most. Most of us are taught early on to fear our own. Through immersion in imaginary combat and identification with a violent protagonist, children engage the rage they've stifled, come to fear it less, and become more capable of utilizing it against life's challenges.

I knew one little girl who went around exploding with fantasies so violent that other moms would draw her mother aside to whisper, "I think you should know something about Emily...." Her parents were separating, and she was small, an only child, a tomboy at an age when her classmates were dividing sharply along gender lines. On the playground she acted out *Sailor Moon* fights, and in the classroom she wrote stories about people being stabbed with knives. The more adults tried to control her stories, the more she acted out the roles of her angry heroes: breaking rules, testing limits, roaring threats.

Then her mother and I started helping her tell her stories. She wrote them, performed them, drew them like comics: sometimes bloody, sometimes tender, always blending the images of pop culture with her own most private fantasies. She came out of it just as fiery and strong, but more self-controlled and socially competent: a leader among her peers, the one student in her class who could truly pull boys and girls together.

I worked with an older girl, a middle-class "nice girl," who held herself together through a chaotic family situation and a tumultuous adolescence with gangsta rap. In the mythologized street violence of Ice T, the rage and strutting of his music and lyrics, she found a theater of the mind in which she could be powerful, ruthless, invulnerable. She avoided the heavy drug use that sank many of her peers, and flowered in college as a writer and political activist.

I'm not going to argue that violent entertainment is harmless. I think it has helped inspire some people to real-life violence. I am going to argue that it's helped hundreds of people for every one it's hurt, and that it can help far more if we learn to use it well. I am going to argue that our fear of "youth violence" isn't well-founded on reality, and that the fear can do more harm than the reality. We act as though our highest priority is to prevent our children from growing up into murderous thugs—but modern kids are far more likely to grow up too passive, too distrustful of themselves, too easily manipulated.

We send the message to our children in a hundred ways that their craving for imaginary gun battles and symbolic killings is wrong, or at least dangerous. Even when we don't call for censorship or forbid "Mortal Kombat," we moan to other parents within our kids' earshot about the "awful violence" in the entertainment they love. We tell our kids that it isn't nice to play-fight, or we steer them from some monstrous action figure to a pro-social doll. Even in the most progressive households, where we make such a point of letting children feel what they feel, we rush to substitute an enlightened discussion for the raw material of rageful fantasy. In the process, we risk confusing them about their natural aggression in the same way the Victorians confused their children about their sexuality. When we try to protect our children from their own feelings and fantasies, we shelter them not against violence but against power and selfhood.

AFTER YOU READ: Analyze the Issues

1. Do you agree or disagree with the argument? Why?
2. How do the best sections of the paper support the argument?
3. How can the weak sections of the article be improved?

AFTER YOU READ: Analyze the Rhetoric

1. How does the author use authority (ethos) to defend his argument?
2. What examples of pathos are used in the article?
3. Which part of the article was better: the introduction or conclusion? Why?

"Dining with Cannibals"

by Pop
(Essay)

Note the tone of this letter. Pop is the pseudonym of the author who writes out of anger for the way he has been and is treated. Computer technicians are often glamorized or stereotyped as nerds in the media. This letter addresses some of the issues that are not examined. This letter has become quite popular on-line because of the lack of respect computer technicians often receive. Do you agree with the message? Read it and comment.

AS YOU READ: Annotate

1. Underline at least three interesting descriptions that you find.
2. Put boxes around any fragments that you come across.
3. Circle the following words and any others you do not know and write their meaning in the margins: *lackey, minions, viable,* and *yurt.*

"Soylent Green is people!"

— *Charlton Heston, Soylent Green*

The computer industry eats people, consumes them whole, and spits out bleached-white bones. While corpulent, sickly-white pre-public CEOs masturbate over their vested stock, their lackeys, their Dockers-and-button-down-clad minions, push and push and *push* the people who do the actual work until stomachs writhe in acid and sleep disappears and skin goes bad and teeth ache. The people who do the actual work rarely push back. Instead they snap. They freak out and they crumble like a freeway in an earthquake.

If only they could manage to crush those who are just along for the ride.

This industry is sick, sick to the core. Apps, games, the Web, all of it. People who work eight hours a day then go home to families and lives are derided as not being "team players." People who throw themselves into criminally unreasonable lumbermill schedules (part buzz-saw, part log jam) are rewarded with more work. People who point all this out are threatened with the loss of their jobs and labeled attitude problems.

If you think the blatant greed and stupidity that Wall Street has demonstrated where tech stocks are concerned is disgusting, try sneaking into the boardroom or CEO's office of a company that's about to go public. From the cubes in Development, you can hear oily hands being rubbed together and fat, dripping tongues smacking wet lips, just waiting for the cash to rain out of the sky. Human costs aren't considered, families don't exist, there is no Outside (only, perhaps, Outside). "Tell them they have to work weekends," the boss says to his winged monkey. "Tell them that they're not working hard enough."

And the winged monkey, just to show you what a wonderful guy he is, offers to buy you a burrito and a Coke because you're missing dinner at home. Josh, Brad, *thanks*.

The days when it was worth it are over. There used to be a time, long ago, when killing yourself for the company was worth it. I believe that. I read *Hackers* and *Show-stopper!* and fell for it, fell for it hard. I believed that you could eat shit and say it was porridge for a few years and come out of it with a huge number of neurons fried, but with enough lucre in the bank that you could spend the rest of your life working it out in a hillside bunker (or, better yet, a yurt filled with high-tech toys).

But that doesn't happen any more. Kill yourself now and the only thing you are is dead, and all you'll get is a gold-plated coffin. For the people who can make it through the entire vesting period, the shares almost never add up to anything significant: Yes, yours for just the cost of four years of your life—friends, sex, contentment, peace, and an apartment free of that sickly smell it gets when you haven't been there in a long time—a new car!

Whoop-de-fuckin'-do. The equivalent of, what? A ten percent raise? At the cost of a stomach lining? A decent night's sleep? A full head of hair? A *life*?

Never before in history have nerds, as a class, become economically viable. It was never worthwhile to exploit astronomers. But computer programmers can actually make something people want, something people will pay for. And they overfocus anyway! Convince them that The Product is somehow important to their lives, more important *than* their lives, and hang a turd from a stick and call it a carrot. And bang! Coding machines! "Machines" being the operative word.

It's sick and it's immoral. A friend of mine was beeped to work—they made him carry a beeper—on a weekend, on his wife's birthday, and he didn't return home until 2 A.M. The video game he was working on had a bug. The *video game*. The manager who called him in probably got a raise.

Something is desperately wrong, wrong and evil. Butchers and bakers and candlestick makers don't have to put up with this kind of shit, so why should we? Why is it expected? Demanded? Why is it given? Why is an eight-hour day a "good start"? When did the job become the end instead of the means?

Why should I make that evil bastard in the corner office rich? Why should he get a million dollars for the product I architected? For *my* product? The product he's too stupid to understand?

Because that's the way it is.

Fine. At least I don't have to watch.

I quit.

AFTER YOU READ: Analyze the Issues

1. Why do you think this letter has become quite popular?
2. What is the main message of the letter?
3. Do you agree with the writer? Why or why not?

AFTER YOU READ: Analyze the Rhetoric

1. Comment on the use of fragments.
2. Read the letter aloud. Is it more powerful or less effective?
3. Discuss the humor in the letter.

"Are You Human? The Test"

by Hampton Fancher and David Webb Peoples
excerpt from Blade Runner *(1982)*
(Screenplay)

Born July 18, 1938 in Los Angeles, California, Hampton Fancher, actor, producer and screenwriter, and director, is best known for writing the screenplay for *Blade Runner*. He was also the executive producer and had some creative differences with the director Ridley Scott. Recently, he directed and co-wrote the critically successful *The Minus Man* (1999) about a serial killer.

David Webb Peoples was born in 1940 in Middletown, Connecticut. He studied English at the University of California. He revised Hampton Fancher's original script for *Blade Runner*. He also co-wrote the screenplay for the science fiction film *Twelve Monkeys* with his wife, Janet Peoples. Perhaps his most famous screenplay was the Oscar nominated western *Unforgiven* (1992), directed by Clint Eastwood.

Born in Chicago, Philip K. Dick (1928–1982) was one of the most influential science fiction writers of his age. He received the Hugo award for *The Man in the High Castle* (1963). In 1974, he started to experience extra-ordinary events which became part of his fiction. Just before his death, his writings became more mystical, reflecting his own experiences. What is fiction and what is reality? His characters often asked these questions as Dick himself was also asking these questions. Though he did not get to see the final print of *Blade Runner*, he did see a cut that he was pleased with. He remained very apprehensive about what Hollywood would do to his works. Since his death, several short stories and novels have been made into films: *Total Recall* (1990), *Minority Report* (2002), and *A Scanner Darkly* (2006).

"Are You Human?" screenplay excerpt from *Blade Runner* © 1981 screenplay by Hampton Fancher and David Peoples.

AS YOU READ: Annotate

1. Place a star in the margin by any lines where the tension in the scene seems to increase.
2. Circle any words you do not know and write their meaning in the margin.

Background. What is the Intelligence and the Imitation Game? Can you determine who is a male or female simply by the text they create? What if both pretend to be a male? Can you decide who is male and who is female based on their writing? Remember both are pretending to be the same sex.

What about artificial intelligence? What if you made a machine so perfect it looked and sounded like a human? Will a human be able to figure out the difference between man and machine? In 1950, Alan Turing conceived of a test to determine if a machine can think like a human. Can a machine be clever enough to imitate a human? What is it that makes us human?

The following scene from the film *Blade Runner* tries to recreate the Turing Test as Holden who works for the Tyrell Corporation uses a Voight-Kampff Apparatus, a sort of lie detector test to determine if the captured person is a replicant (android), who has been killing humans. The tool measures subtle degrees of empathy, something that a machine can imitate but not really feel. The Turing Test would only measure rhetorical textual output. So the Voight-Kampff apparatus, like a lie detector test, is measuring physical response to a question. Based on Philip K. Dick's novel *Do Android's Dream of Electric Sheep?* the film is considered a science fiction film classic. Visit the official site: www.philipkdick.com.

android (an'droid) adj. Possessing human features —n.
A synthetic man created from biological materials.
Also called humanoid. (Late Greek androeides,
manlike: ANDR[O] —OID.)

The American Heritage
Dictionary of the English
Language (1976)

android (an'droid) n, Gk. humanoid automation. more at
robot./1. early version utilized for work too
boring, dangerous or unpleasant for humans.
2. second generation bio-engineered. Electronic
relay units and positronic brains. Used in space
to explore inhospitable environments. 3. third
generation synthogenetic. REPLICANT, constructed
of skin/flesh culture. Selected enogenic transfer
conversion. Capable of self perpetuating thought.
paraphysical abilities. Developed for emigration
program.

Webster's Dictionary
New International (2012)

(CONTINUED)

FADE IN:

EXT. HADES —DUSK

We are MOVING TOWARD the Tyrell Corporation across a vast plain of industrialization, menacing shapes on the horizon, stacks belching flames five hundred feet into the sky the color of cigar ash. The CAMERA MOVES INTO a window in the large pyramid-shaped building. A man is sitting at a table. Another man enters the room and sits down. The following scene is reflected in the eye until HOLDEN is seated.

INT. TYRELL CORPORATION INTERROGATION ROOM —DUSK

The eye is magnified and deeply revealed. Flecks of green and yellow in a field of milky blue. Icy filaments surround the undulating center.

The eye is brown in a tiny screen. On the metallic surface below, the words VOIGHT-KAMPFF are finely etched. There's a touch-light panel across the top and on the side of the screen, a dial that registers fluctuation of the iris.

The instrument is no bigger than a music box and sits on a table between two men. The man talking is big, looks like an overstuffed kid. LEON it says on his breast pocket. He's dressed in a warehouseman's uniform and his pudgy hands are folded expectantly in his lap. Despite the obvious heat, he looks very cool.

The man facing him is lean, hollow-cheeked, and dressed in grey. Detached and efficient, he looks like a cop or an accountant. His name is Holden and he's all business, except for the sweat on his face.

The room is large and humid. Rows of salvaged junk are stacked neatly against the walls. Two large FANS WHIRR above their heads.

LEON

Okay if I talk?

Holden doesn't answer. He's centering Leon's eye on the machine.

LEON

I kinda get nervous when I take tests.

HOLDEN

Don't move.

LEON

Sorry.

He tries not to move, but finally his lips can't help a sheepish smile.

LEON

I already had I.Q. test this year... but I don't think I never had a...

(CONTINUED)

HOLDEN
Reaction time is a factor in this so please pay attention. Answer as quickly as you can.

LEON
Uh… sure…

HOLDEN
One one eight seven at Hunterwasser…

LEON
Oh… that's the hotel.

HOLDEN
What?

LEON
Where I live.

HOLDEN
Nice place?

LEON
Huh? Sure. Yeah. I guess. Is that… part of the test?

Holden smiles a patronising smile.

HOLDEN
Warming you up, that's all.

LEON
Oh. It's—

HOLDEN
You're in a desert, walking along
in the sand when….

LEON
Is this the test now?

HOLDEN
Yes. You're in a desert, walking along in the sand when all of a sudden you look down and see a…..

LEON
What one?

(CONTINUED)

It was a timid interruption, hardly audible.

HOLDEN
What?

LEON
What desert?

HOLDEN
Doesn't make any difference what
desert… it's completely hypothetical.

LEON
But how come I'd be there?

HOLDEN
Maybe you're fed up, maybe you want to be by yourself… who knows.
So you look down and see a tortoise. It's crawling toward you….

LEON
A tortoise. What's that?

HOLDEN
Know what a turtle is?

LEON
Of course.

HOLDEN
Same thing.

LEON
I never seen a turtle.

He sees Holden's patience is wearing thin.

LEON
But I understand what you mean.

HOLDEN
You reach down and flip the tortoise over on its back, Leon.

Keeping an eye on his subject, Holden notes the dials in the Voight-Kampff. One of the needles quivers slightly.

LEON
You make these questions, Mr. Holden, or they write 'em down for you?

(CONTINUED)

Disregarding the question, Holden continues, picking up the pace.

HOLDEN

The tortoise lays on its back, its belly baking in the hot sun, beating its legs trying to turn itself over. But it can't. Not without your help. But you're not helping.

Leon's upper lip is quivering.

LEON

Whatya mean, I'm not helping?

HOLDEN

I mean you're not helping! Why is that, Leon?

Holden looks hard at Leon, piercing look.

Leon is flushed with anger, breathing hard, it's a bad moment, he might erupt.

Suddenly Holden grins disarmingly.

HOLDEN

They're just questions, Leon. In answer to your query, they're written down for me. It's a test, designed to provoke an emotional response.

Leon is glaring now, the blush subsides, his anger slightly defused.

Holden smiles cheerfully, very smooth.

HOLDEN

Shall we continue?

Leon nods, still frowning, suspiciously.

HOLDEN

Describe in single words. Only the good things that come into your mind. About your mother.

LEON

My….

Leon looks shocked, surprised. But the needles in the computer barely move. Holden goes for the inside of his coat. But big Leon is faster. His laser burns a hole the size of a nickel through Holden's stomach. Unlike a bullet, a laser causes no impact. It goes through Holden's shoulder and comes out his back, clean as a whistle. Like a rag doll he falls back into the seat. Big slow Leon is already walking away, but he stops, turns, and with a little smile of satisfaction fires through the back of the seat.

As Leon walks out of the room the Voight-Kampff begins to blink, faint but steady.

AFTER YOU READ: Analyze the Issues

1. Is it normal to be nervous about a test? Explain. At what point does the replicant seem even more nervous?
2. Why is the turtle important?
3. What happens in the end?

AFTER YOU READ: Analyze the Rhetoric

1. Discuss the effectiveness of the narratives in this screenplay.
2. Read the screenplay aloud or watch the scene from the film. What are the effects of this reading or viewing?
3. How is the tension increased in this scene?

"The Deliverator"

by Neal Stephenson
excerpt from Snow Crash, *Bantam Spectra Book, 1992, 1–10*

Born in Fort Meade, Maryland, 1959, Neal Stephenson majored in physics and geography at Boston University. *Snow Crash* is his third novel, a post-cyberpunk novel. The idea of virtual persona called avatar, now popular at such sites as Second Life, originated from this book. His other novels include: *Cryptonomicon*, *The Diamond Age* and his Baroque Cycle (*Quicksilver*, *The Confusion*, and *The System of the World*). Visit his site at www.nealstephenson.com.

AS YOU READ: Annotate

1. Place a star by any section you find interesting.
2. Write "humorous" next to sections you think are funny.
3. Circle the following words and any you do not know and write their meaning in the margins: *hallowed, wafts, napalmed, sintered, armogel, sphincters, Bedouin, sporadic,* and *congealing.*

The Deliverator belongs to an elite order, a hallowed subcategory. He's got esprit up to here. Right now, he is preparing to carry out his third mission of the night. His uniform is black as activated charcoal, filtering the very light out of the air. A bullet will bounce off its arachnofiber weave like a wren hitting a patio door, but excess perspiration wafts through it like a breeze through a freshly napalmed forest. Where his body has bony extremities, the suit has sintered armorgel: feels like gritty jello, protects like a stack of telephone books.

When they gave him the job, they gave him a gun. The Deliverator never deals in cash, but someone might come after him anyway—might want his car, or his cargo. The gun is tiny, aero-styled, lightweight, the kind of a gun a fashion designer would carry; it fires teensy darts that fly at five times the velocity of an SR-71 spy plane, and when you get done using it, you have to plug it into the cigarette lighter, because it runs on electricity.

The Deliverator never pulled that gun in anger, or in fear. He pulled it once in Gila Highlands. Some punks in Gila Highlands, a fancy Burbclave, wanted themselves a delivery, and they didn't want to pay for it. Thought they would impress the Deliverator with a baseball bat. The Deliverator took out his gun, centered its laser doo-hickey on that poised Louisville Slugger, fired it. The recoil was immense, as though the weapon had blown up in his hand. The middle third of the baseball bat turned into a column of burning sawdust accelerating in all directions like a bursting star. Punk ended up holding this bat handle with milky smoke pouring out the end. Stupid look on his face. Didn't get nothing but trouble from the Deliverator.

Since then the Deliverator has kept the gun in the glove compartment and relied, instead, on a matched set of samurai swords, which have always been his weapon of choice anyhow. The punks in Gila Highlands weren't afraid of the gun, so the Deliverator was forced to use it. But swords need no demonstrations.

The Deliverator's car has enough potential energy packed into its batteries to fire a pound of bacon into the Asteroid Belt. Unlike a bimbo box or a Burb beater, the Deliverator's car unloads that power through gaping, gleaming, polished sphincters. When the Deliverator puts the hammer down, shit happens. You want to talk contact patches? Your car's tires have tiny contact patches, talk to the asphalt in four places the size of your tongue. The Deliverator's car has big sticky tires with contact patches the size of a fat lady's thighs. The Deliverator is in touch with the road, starts like a bad day, stops on a peseta.

Why is the Deliverator so equipped? Because people rely on him. He is a role model. This is America. People do whatever the fuck they feel like doing, you got a problem with that? Because they have a right to. And because they have guns and no one can fucking stop them. As a result, this country has one of the worst economies in the world. When it gets down to it—talking trade balances here—once we've brain-drained all our technology into other countries, once things have evened out, they're making cars in Bolivia and microwave ovens in Tadzhikistan and selling them here—once our edge in natural resources has been made irrelevant by giant

Hong Kong ships and dirigibles that can ship North Dakota all the way to New Zealand for a nickel—once the Invisible Hand has taken all those historical inequities and smeared them out into a broad global layer of what a Pakistani brickmaker would consider to be prosperity—y'know what? There's only four things we do better than anyone else

- music
- movies
- microcode (software)
- high-speed pizza delivery

The Deliverator used to make software. Still does, sometimes. But if life were a mellow elementary school run by well-meaning education Ph.D.s, the Deliverator's report card would say: "Hiro is *so* bright and creative but needs to work harder on his cooperation skills."

So now he has this other job. No brightness or creativity involved—but no cooperation either. Just a single principle: The Deliverator stands tall, your pie in thirty minutes or you can have it free, shoot the driver, take his car, file a class-action suit. The Deliverator has been working this job for six months, a rich and lengthy tenure by his standards, and has never delivered a pizza in more than twenty-one minutes.

Oh, they used to argue over times, many corporate driver-years lost to it: homeowners, red-faced and sweaty with their own lies, stinking of Old Spice and job-related stress, standing in their glowing yellow doorways brandishing their Seikos and waving at the clock over the kitchen sink, I swear, can't you guys tell time?

Didn't happen anymore. Pizza delivery is a major industry. A managed industry. People went to CosaNostra Pizza University four years just to learn it. Came in its doors unable to write an English sentence, from Abkhazia, Rwanda, Guanajuato, South Jersey, and came out knowing more about pizza than a Bedouin knows about sand. And they had studied this problem. Graphed the frequency of doorway delivery-time disputes. Wired the early Deliverators to record, then analyze, the debating tactics, the voice-stress histograms, the distinctive grammatical structures employed by white middle-class Type A Burbclave occupants who against all logic had decided that this was the place to take their personal Custerian stand against all that was stale and deadening in their lives: they were going to lie, or delude themselves, about the time of their phone call and get themselves a free pizza; no, they deserved a free pizza along with their life, liberty, and pursuit of whatever, it was fucking inalienable. Sent psychologists out to these people's houses, gave them a free TV set to submit to an anonymous interview, hooked them to polygraphs, studied their brain waves as they showed them choppy, inexplicable movies of porn queens and late-night car crashes and Sammy Davis, Jr., put them in sweet-smelling, mauve-walled rooms and asked them questions about Ethics so perplexing that even a Jesuit couldn't respond without committing a venial sin.

The analysts at CosaNostra Pizza University concluded that it was just human nature and you couldn't fix it, and so they went for a quick cheap technical fix: smart boxes. The pizza box is a plastic carapace now, corrugated for stiffness, a little LED readout glowing on the side, telling the Deliverator how many trade imbalance-producing minutes have ticked away since the fateful phone call. There are chips and stuff in there. The pizzas rest, a short stack of them, in slots behind the Deliverator's head. Each pizza glides into a slot like a circuit board into a computer, clicks into place as the smart box interfaces with the onboard system of the Deliverator's car. The address of the caller has already been inferred from his phone number and poured into the smart box's built-in RAM. From there it is communicated to the car, which computes and projects the optimal route on a heads-up display, a glowing colored map traced out against the windshield so that the Deliverator does not even have to glance down.

If the thirty-minute deadline expires, news of the disaster is flashed to CosaNostra Pizza Headquarters and relayed from there to Uncle Enzo himself—the Sicilian Colonel Sanders, the Andy Griffith of Bensonhurst, the straight razor-swinging figment of many a Deliverator's nightmares, the Capo and prime figurehead of CosaNostra Pizza, Incorporated—who will be on the phone to the customer within five minutes, apologizing profusely. The next day, Uncle Enzo will land on the customer's yard in a jet helicopter and apologize some more and give him a free trip to Italy—all he has to do is sign a bunch of releases that make him a public figure and spokesperson for CosaNostra Pizza and basically end his private life as he knows it. He will come away from the whole thing feeling that, somehow, he owes the Mafia a favor.

The Deliverator does not know for sure what happens to the driver in such cases, but he has heard some rumors. Most pizza deliveries happen in the evening hours, which Uncle Enzo considers to be his private time. And how would you feel if you had to interrupt dinner with your family in order to call some obstreperous dork in a Burbclave and grovel for a late fucking pizza? Uncle Enzo has not put in fifty years serving his family and his country so that, at the age when most are playing golf and bobbling their granddaughters, he can get out of the bathtub dripping wet and lie down and kiss the feet of some sixteen-year-old skate punk whose pepperoni was thirty-one minutes in coming. Oh, God. It makes the Deliverator breathe a little shallower just to think of the idea.

But he wouldn't drive for CosaNostra Pizza any other way. You know why? Because there's something about having your life on the line. It's like being a kamikaze pilot. Your mind is clear. Other people—store clerks, burger flippers, software engineers, the whole vocabulary of meaningless jobs that make up Life in America—other people just rely on plain old competition. Better flip your burgers or debug your subroutines faster and better than your high school classmate two blocks down the strip is flipping or debugging, because we're in competition with those guys, and people notice these things.

What a fucking rat race that is. CosaNostra Pizza doesn't have any competition. Competition goes against the Mafia ethic. You don't work harder because you're competing against some identical operation down the street. You work harder because everything is on the line. Your name, your honor, your family, your life. Those burger flippers might have a better life expectancy—but what kind of life is it anyway, you have to ask yourself. That's why nobody, not even the Nipponese, can move pizzas faster than CosaNostra. The Deliverator is proud to wear the uniform, proud to drive the car, proud to march up the front walks of innumerable Burbclave homes, a grim vision in ninja black, a pizza on his shoulder, red LED digits blazing proud numbers into the night: 12:32 or 15:15 or the occasional 20:43.

The Deliverator is assigned to CosaNostra Pizza #3569 in the Valley. Southern California doesn't know whether to bustle or just strangle itself on the spot. Not enough roads for the number of people. Fairlanes, Inc. is laying new ones all the time. Have to bulldoze lots of neighborhoods to do it, but those seventies and eighties developments exist to be bulldozed, right? No sidewalks, no schools, no nothing. Don't have their own police force—no immigration control—undesirables can walk right in without being frisked or even harassed. Now a Burbclave, that's the place to live. A city-state with its own constitution, a border, laws, cops, everything.

The Deliverator was a corporal in the Farms of Merryvale State Security Force for a while once. Got himself fired for pulling a sword on an acknowledged perp. Slid it right through the fabric of the perp's shirt, gliding the flat of the blade along the base of his neck, and pinned him to a warped and bubbled expanse of vinyl siding on the wall of the house that the perp was trying to break into. Thought it was a pretty righteous bust. But they fired him anyway because the perp turned out to be the son of the vice-chancellor of the Farms of Merryvale. Oh, the weasels had an excuse: said that a thirty-six-inch samurai sword was not on their Weapons Protocol. Said that he had violated the SPAC, the Suspected Perpetrator Apprehension Code. Said that the perp had suffered psychological trauma. He was afraid of butter knives now; he had to spread his jelly with the back of a teaspoon. They said that he had exposed them to liability.

The Deliverator had to borrow some money to pay for it. Had to borrow it from the Mafia, in fact. So he's in their database now—retinal patterns, DNA, voice graph, fingerprints, footprints, palm prints, wrist prints, every fucking part of the body that had wrinkles on it—almost—those bastards rolled in ink and made a print and digitized it into their computer. But it's their money—sure they're careful about loaning it out. And when he applied for the Deliverator job they were happy to take him, because they knew him. When he got the loan, he had to deal personally with the assistant vice-capo of the Valley, who later recommended him for the Deliverator job. So it was like being in a family. A really scary, twisted, abusive family.

CosaNostra Pizza #3569 is on Vista Road just down from Kings Park Mall. Vista Road used to belong to the State of California and now is called Fairlanes, Inc. Rte. CSV-5. Its main competition used to be a U.S. highway and is now called

Cruiseways, Inc. Rte. Cal-12. Farther up the Valley, the two competing highways actually cross. Once there had been bitter disputes, the intersection closed by sporadic sniper fire. Finally, a big developer bought the entire intersection and turned it into a drive-through mall. Now the roads just feed into a parking system—not a lot, not a ramp, but a system—and lose their identity. Getting through the intersection involves tracing paths through the parking system, many braided filaments of direction like the Ho Chi Minh trail. CSV-5 has better throughput, but Cal-12 has better pavement. That is typical—Fairlanes roads emphasize getting you there, for Type A drivers, and Cruiseways emphasize the enjoyment of the ride, for Type B drivers.

The Deliverator is a Type A driver with rabies. He is zeroing in on his home base, CosaNostra Pizza #3569, cranking up the left lane of CSV-5 at a hundred and twenty kilometers. His car is an invisible black lozenge, just a dark place that reflects the tunnel of franchise signs—the loglo. A row of orange lights burbles and churns across the front, where the grille would be if this were an air-breathing car. The orange light looks like a gasoline fire. It comes in through people's rear windows, bounces off their rearview mirrors, projects a fiery mask across their eyes, reaches into their subconscious, and unearths terrible fears of being pinned, fully conscious, under a detonating gas tank, makes them want to pull over and let the Deliverator overtake them in his black chariot of pepperoni fire.

The loglo, overhead, marking out CSV-5 in twin contrails, is a body of electrical light made of innumerable cells, each cell designed in Manhattan by imageers who make more for designing a single logo than a Deliverator will make in his entire lifetime. Despite their efforts to stand out, they all smear together, especially at a hundred and twenty kilometers per hour. Still, it is easy to see CosaNostra Pizza #3569 because of the billboard, which is wide and tall even by current inflated standards. In fact, the squat franchise itself looks like nothing more than a low-slung base for the great aramid fiber pillars that thrust the billboard up into the trademark firmament. Marca Registrada, baby.

The billboard is a classic, a chestnut, not a figment of some fleeting Mafia promotional campaign. It is a statement, a monument built to endure. Simple and dignified. It shows Uncle Enzo in one of his spiffy Italian suits. The pinstripes glint and flex like sinews. The pocket square is luminous. His hair is perfect, slicked back with something that never comes off, each strand cut off straight and square at the end by Uncle Enzo's cousin, Art the Barber, who runs the second-largest chain of low-end haircutting establishments in the world. Uncle Enzo is standing there, not exactly smiling, an avuncular glint in his eye for sure, not posing like a model but standing there like your uncle would, and it says

The Mafia
You've got a friend in The Family!
Paid for by the Our Thing Foundation

The billboard serves as the Deliverator's polestar. He knows that when he gets to the place on CSV-5 where the bottom corner of the billboard is obscured by the pseudo-Gothic stained-glass arches of the local Reverend Wayne's Pearly Gates franchise, it's time for him to get over into the right lanes where the retards and the bimbo boxes poke along, random, indecisive, looking at each passing franchise's driveway like they don't know if it's a promise or a threat.

He cuts off a bimbo box—a family minivan—veers past the Buy 'n' Fly that is next door, and pulls into CosaNostra Pizza #3569. Those big fat contact patches complain, squeal a little bit, but they hold on to the patented Fairlanes, Inc. high-traction pavement and guide him into the chute. No other Deliverators are waiting in the chute. That is good, that means high turnover for him, fast action, keep moving that 'za. As he scrunches to a stop, the electromechanical hatch on the flank of his car is already opening to reveal his empty pizza slots, the door clicking and folding back in on itself like the wing of a beetle. The slots are waiting. Waiting for hot pizza.

And waiting. The Deliverator honks his horn. This is not a nominal outcome.

Window slides open. That should never happen. You can look at the three-ring binder from CosaNostra Pizza University, cross-reference the citation for *window, chute, dispatcher's,* and it will give you all the procedures for that window—and it should never be opened. Unless something has gone wrong.

The window slides open and—you sitting down?—*smoke* comes out of it. The Deliverator hears a discordant beetling over the metal hurricane of his sound system and realizes that it is a smoke alarm, coming from inside the franchise.

Mute button on the stereo. Oppressive silence—his eardrums uncringe—the window is buzzing with the cry of the smoke alarm. The car idles, waiting. The hatch has been open too long, atmospheric pollutants are congealing on the electrical contacts in the back of the pizza slots, he'll have to clean them ahead of schedule, everything is going exactly the way it shouldn't go in the three-ring binder that spells out all the rhythms of the pizza universe.

Inside, a football-shaped Abkhazian man is running to and fro, holding a three-ring binder open, using his spare tire as a ledge to keep it from collapsing shut; he runs with the gait of a man carrying an egg on a spoon. He is shouting in the Abkhazian dialect; all the people who run CosaNostra pizza franchises in this part of the Valley are Abkhazian immigrants.

It does not look like a serious fire. The Deliverator saw a real fire once, at the Farms of Merryvale, and you couldn't see anything for the smoke. That's all it was: smoke, burbling out of nowhere, occasional flashes of orange light down at the bottom, like heat lightning in tall clouds. This is not that kind of fire. It is the kind of fire that just barely puts out enough smoke to detonate the smoke alarms. And he is losing time for this shit.

The Deliverator holds the horn button down. The Abkhazian manager comes to the window. He is supposed to use the intercom to talk to drivers, he could say anything he wanted and it would be piped straight into the Deliverator's car, but no, he has to talk face to face, like the Deliverator is some kind of fucking ox cart driver. He is red-faced, sweating, his eyes roll as he tries to think of the English words.

"A fire, a little one," he says.

The Deliverator says nothing. Because he knows that all of this is going onto videotape. The tape is being pipelined, as it happens, to CosaNostra Pizza University, where it will be analyzed in a pizza management science laboratory. It will be shown to Pizza University students, perhaps to the very students who will replace this man when he gets fired, as a textbook example of how to screw up your life.

"New employee—put his dinner in the microwave—had foil in it—boom!" the manager says.

Abkhazia had been part of the Soviet fucking Union. A new immigrant from Abkhazia trying to operate a microwave was like a deep-sea tube worm doing brain surgery. Where did they get these guys? Weren't there any Americans who could bake a fucking pizza?

"Just give me one pie," the Deliverator says.

Talking about pies snaps the guy into the current century. He gets a grip. He slams the window shut, strangling the relentless keening of the smoke alarm.

A Nipponese robot arm shoves the pizza out and into the top slot. The hatch folds shut to protect it.

As the Deliverator is pulling out of the chute, building up speed, checking the address that is flashed across his windshield, deciding whether to turn right or left, it happens. His stereo cuts out again—on command of the onboard system. The cockpit lights go red. *Red.* A repetitive buzzer begins to sound. The LED readout on his windshield, which echoes the one on the pizza box, flashes up: 20:00.

They have just given the Deliverator a twenty-minute-old pizza. He checks the address; it is twelve miles away.

AFTER YOU READ: Analyze the Issues

1. Though this is about a strange future, how does this excerpt comment on our own times?
2. What are the four things Americans can do the best?
3. What was the best part of this work?

AFTER YOU READ: Analyze the Rhetoric

1. What are the multiple meanings of "Deliverator"?
2. Did you like the humor? What were some of the funniest parts?
3. Comment on the conclusion of this excerpt.

Sample Student Paper

Fun vs. Family: Mind-Numbing Deviltry

by Will Waldroup

AS YOU READ: Annotate

1. Place a star by the sections you like the most.
2. Place question marks by sections you have problems with or do not understand.
3. Place a [+] by sections that need to be developed more or that seem to be incomplete.
4. Write other comments in the margins as you see fit.

Plasma screens, DVDs, MP3 players: most people salivate at the mere mention of any part of the ghastly variety of technology in the United States that is devoted exclusively to entertainment. This mind-numbing deviltry results in people spending less time with their loved ones. Why would someone want to play catch in the park if they can sit in front of the television and watch someone else do it? If an individual had the choice of visiting grandparents or downloading music from the internet, chances are they would choose the latter. The ever-increasing advancement in entertainment technology has caused social distance in American families and led to a decrease in values.

The art of creating visual entertainment devices is moving at such an alarming pace that the latest plasma screen television is out of date as soon as it is released. As Orange Chief Executive Sanjiv Ahuja said, "Entertainment is the big thing in 2005" ("Phones"). The citizens of the United States are so completely obsessed with having the coolest new gadgets that they often lose sight of more important things. Also, Americans have a never-ending desire for more, as Stephane Maes, senior product manager of PalmOne, said, "Clearly there are new people coming to the category and people buying their third and fourth devices" (qtd. in Kuchinskas). No one is willing to walk the dog or go to the playground with their kids if they can plop down in front of the tube and watch "Friends" in high definition. This is a direct result of having too many distractions and is detrimental to society.

Music can be another great divide among family in the country. In past times, whole families would have a night out together and go see a concert, a symphony or perhaps a brass quintet performance. Now the symphony is all but dead. People seem content to spend their time downloading or burning music and never even consider what a thrill a live performance would be. The only place a new symphonic work can be found is in movies, yet another branch of the plethora of activities that dominate American life.

Families cannot even travel together without resorting to some sort of technological entertainment. As these devices become more advanced, they always seem to become smaller. This means now people can have the latest gadgets in their cars as well as at home. Too often when a family makes a trip do the members find themselves stuck to the television screen watching their new extended edition DVD. Honestly, do people ever just talk anymore?

The airlines are no better than automobiles. The one thing that everyone seems to know about air travel is that there is an in-flight movie. American airlines has recently released a new device that will give passengers the choice of movies, music, television sitcoms, audio books, and various card games all in a convenient handheld device. This may not lead directly to distance between families; however, it does provide a perfect example of how Americans have a constant need to take their mind from life. When people spend so much time in a world of fantasy, they are apt to lose touch with the finer things life has to offer, such as friends and family.

Possibly the most vivid example of how people reject family for technology is found in personal computers and the internet. What cannot be found on the internet? Americans find that it is too easy to shut themselves off from the outside world and surf the web at every waking hour. Sure this can be fun and there is a great deal to learn, but instead could not a parent read a classic story to their child or help them with their homework? This would, without a doubt, be more beneficial than playing the latest overrated computer game.

American families are being torn from each other by a never-ending increase in entertainment technology. From televisions to satellite radio and DVD's, the range of distraction is limitless. These devices are problematic to families, they are distracting to citizens, and they are often highly unnecessary. If people would just consider spending time together rather than on the couch, they would realize that life is comprised of more than Xbox and iPod. If only the technological addicts out there would discover that the greatest aspects of living are the simplest. The best things in life are free, and family does not cost a dime.

Works Cited

Evangelist, Benny. "PC-Makers Unveil Home Entertainment Devices." *San Francisco Chronicle*. 1 Oct. 2003. 13 Feb. 2005. <http://www.sfgate.com>.

Kuchinskas, Susan. "PDAs Flat; Other Devices to Shine." 29 July 2004. 15 February 2005. <http://www.internetnews.com/wireless>.

"Phones Will Be Entertainment Devices." 15 Feb. 2005 <http://www.reuters.com>.

PEER REVIEW OUTLINE

Directions. Asking the right questions: As you ask these questions and answer them, be specific in your comments so as to be more helpful to the author. Provide details.

1. **Logos.** Comment on the quality and amount of the evidence or research conducted. Is it balanced or enough? Does the author need more? Why or why not? Is the paper too logical or not logical enough? What else can you say about logos?
2. **Pathos.** Comment on the emotional appeals used in the paper. What can the author do to improve this appeal? Should there be less, more, or no emotions? Explain.
3. **Ethos.** Does the author use enough quality sources to improve the impact of the ethos of the paper? Is there a human element in the paper? What does the author need to do to improve the character aspect? Should the author add a personal story? Is the paper too personal? Should it be more logical?
4. **Call for Improvement.** Which aspects in the paper need to be revised or improved? Explain in detail.

Responding to Gaming Issues

Written Rhetoric: Opinion Papers, Arguments, and Research

1. Create a paper examining how writing is different and changing because of emergent media. Give examples. How should education address such changes?
2. Write an argument paper about the negative or provocative language used in cyberspace. Why are some people so rude on-line? What does that tell us about ourselves?
3. Should video game makers be responsible for tragic shootings like the one at Columbine High? Argue for or against and defend your points with evidence and support.
4. How serious is video game addiction? What are some of the solutions? Do some research and share your results in a paper.
5. What are some positive aspects of gaming? Focus your research on one aspect: education, dating, business, etc.
6. Come up with your own research project.

Oral Rhetoric: Speeches, Lyrics, and Simulations

1. Get into groups and argue about violence in gaming. Some participants will create a speech defending violence in video games while other participants create a speech against violence.
2. Create a simulation or drama about video game addiction. Have avatars or players in various stages of denial about their addictions.
3. You are in a job interview and you have a degree in hand from a university. However, you lack experience, but you know a lot about how to use the Internet, MySpace, and video or on-line games. First define the job, and then in an oral defense of the job, use such virtual experience to get your job.

Visual Rhetoric: Advertisements, Visuals, and Cinema

1. What are some of the worst Web sites you have visited? What are the characteristics of bad Web sites? What would improve them? Give suggestions.
2. Compare the visual effects found in video or on-line games. Why are such effects important? Which games are visually more stimulating? Why?
3. Visit artistic social networks like DeviantArt.com and examine how artists draw or imagine games. Write an essay about what such works of art have to say about gaming.
4. Watch a film or compare films and examine some of the issues associated with gaming and emergent media.

Electronic Rhetoric: Emergent Media and Gaming

1. Enter the virtual world and explore what you discover about its realities. You might try Second Life. Go to different places and observe. Focus on what you think is interesting.
2. Examine gender differences on-line. Act as the opposite gender from your own in Second Life or another virtual community and write about what you experienced. What did you learn?
3. Create a PowerPoint presentation or a Web site about some other virtual places that people should visit that were not mentioned in this chapter.

WOVE Projects

1. Brainstorm on your own opinion about violent video games. Play some violent video or on-line games. Create a simulation where the characters from the video games defend their art against those who disagree with such games. Be sure to comment on how the visual aspects of the games affect the psychology of the

participants. Create a blog where these characters interact with students who are against video games. Be sure to include research you have found and quote the sources in the blog and simulation.

2. Examine the social aspects of an on-line game like *Everquest* or a site like *MySpace.* Join the site and participate. Try to become an expert. Create a blog or wiki about the site with other members in your class. Be sure to examine the visual impact of the site. How is sound used in the site or game? How does the site affect the lives of the participants? Give advice on how the site could be improved and how participants can maximize the quality. Give a presentation about the project.
3. Create your own WOVE project. Be sure to outline and defend the project in detail. Obtain you instructor's approval of the various aspects of the project.

Cinematic List

3-Iron (Kim Ki Duk, 2004)
Battle Royale (Kinji Fukasaku, 2000)
A Beautiful Mind (Ron Howard, 2001)
The Blood of Heroes (David Webb Peoples, 1989)
The Cannonball Run (Hal Needham, 1981)
Cube (Vincenzo Natali, 1997)
Death Race 2000 (Paul Bartel, 1975)
Dr. Strangelove or How I Learned to Stop Worrying and Love the Bomb (Stanley Kubrick, 1964)
eXistenZ (David Cronenberg, 1999)
Fight Club (David Fincher, 1999)
Funny Games (Michael Haneke, 1997)
Gambling (J.P. Allen, 2004)
The Game (David Fincher, 1997)
Hard Target (John Woo, 1993)
It's a Mad Mad Mad Mad World (Stanley Kramer, 1963)
Nothing (Vincenzo Natali, 2003)
Ocean's Eleven (Steven Soderbergh, 2001)
Old Boy (Chan-wook Park, 2003)
Papillon (Franklin J. Schaff ner, 1973)
Rollerball (Norman Jewison, 1975)
Rosencrantz & Guildenstern Are Dead (Tom Stoppard, 1990)
The Resurrection of the Little Match Girl (Sun-Woo Jang, 2002)
Saw (James Wan, 2004)
Saw II—Saw V (Darren Lynn Bousman 2005, 2006, 2007; David Hackl, 2008)
Soylent Green (Richard Fleischer, 1973)

Shaolin Soccer (Stephen Chow, 2001)
The Sting (George Roy Hill, 1973)

Television

24 (Joel Surnow, 2001–)
Alias (J.J. Abrams, 2001–2006)
The X-Files (Chris Carter, 1993–2002)

Reality TV

13 Weeks (Morgan Ervin, Ross A. Hendler, 2006)
American Idol (Simon Fuller, 2002–)
The Apprentice (Mark Burnett, 2004–2007)
Big Brother (Brian Smith, 2000–)
Fear Factor (Randall Einhorn, 2001–2006)
Survivor (Mark Burnett, 2000)

Game List

On-Line

World of Warcraft
EverQuest

Video Games

Halo 3
Guitar Hero III
Rock Band
Grand Thief Auto IV

Calvin Klein Underwear Ad

AFTER YOU READ: Analyze the Issues

1. What is the ad selling?
2. What is the main message?
3. Who is the audience?

AFTER YOU READ: Analyze the Rhetoric

1. Is the ad effective?
2. Why place the woman on top?

The Issues

In America and much of the Western World, we are overwhelmed by advertisements. Indeed, we even enjoy watching ads during the Super Bowl every year. Yet we also detest them even as we overbuy and overspend. Indeed, credit card companies love us. We don't seem to be in control. This chapter examines the various issues in our addiction to capitalism. Part of this addiction to capitalism is our addiction to fast food. We are much bigger in size than previous generations. Sadly, as our food products and restaurants go global, the rest of the world is joining the elite club of obesity and becoming as fat as we are.

Answers do await us. We can fight back and be more critical of what we see and read. Advertisers use a variety of rhetorical appeals to "reel" in their audiences. These appeals include logos, ethos, and pathos, in the form of sex, humor, famous people, and patriotism.

Ask the Right Questions

What should we ask when examining advertisements and when reading about them?

Logos

Do the statistics seem valid?
Is the ad logical and balanced?
Is enough evidence provided?
Does the ad use neutral colors?

Ethos

Does the ad use famous people?
Does the advertisement use scientific studies?
Is the ad directed at a certain age group?

Pathos

Does the ad have a catchy jingle that you can't get out of your mind?
Does the ad use sex appeal?
Does the ad use vibrant colors to affect your emotions?

Annotate the Text

When annotating the readings, keep in mind the following:

- Who is the writer's intended audience? Youth? Adults? Senior Citizens? Males? Females?
- Underline the main argument or summarize the key point in the margin.
- After reading a selection, write a brief overview commenting on the effectiveness of the organization of the message.
- Comment on the evidence provided. Was the evidence effective? Can you trust the source?
- Circle the weasel or buzz words such as *free, best, diet, healthy, pure, sale, discount, only,* and *last one.*

Comparing Ads: Obsession Ads

Examine the following spoof ads. One is for females and one is for males.

AS YOU READ: Annotate

1. Which rhetorical appeal is the ad using the most? Logos? Pathos? Ethos?
2. Does the lack of color affect your response to the ads?
3. Which ad appeals the most to you? Why?

"Obsession for Women"

(adbusters.com)

"Obsession for Men"

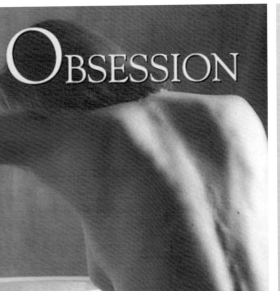

(adbusters.com)

AFTER YOU READ: Analyze the Issues

1. What is the main idea for each ad?
2. If the logo was not part of the ad(s), would you know what the ad(s) was about?
3. Who do you think the target audience is for the ad? How do you think people who are not part of the target audience would respond to it (them)?
4. What "values" does the ad(s) convey?

AFTER YOU READ: Analyze the Rhetoric

1. Give examples of how each ad uses *pathos, logos,* and *ethos.*
2. Evaluate the persuasive effect of each rhetorical appeal. In your view, is one more effective (or less effective) than the other two appeals? Why?

PERSUASION EXERCISE: Printed Advertisements

Pathos, Ethos, Logos

Look through magazines or search the Internet until you find three different advertisements: one which uses an appeal that is primarily pathos in nature, one that is primarily ethos and one that is primarily logos. Carefully cut or tear out the advertisements or print them out. On the back of each, write the following information with your name. Staple the three together and hand them in for next class period.

1. Name of product that uses **Pathos**:
   - What is the magazine or site name?
   - Who is the audience?
   - How does the ad use this appeal?
   - How are other appeals used?

2. Name of product that uses **Ethos:**
   - What is the magazine or site name?
   - Who is the audience?
   - How does the ad use this appeal?
   - How are other appeals used?

3. Name of product that uses **Logos:**
   - What is the magazine or site name?
   - Who is the audience?
   - How does the ad use this appeal?
   - How are other appeals used?

This assignment helps you become more familiar with the three types of persuasion appeals, and also helps you classify and analyze them. When your instructor takes up the exercise, he or she may hold up interesting advertisements and have the class determine which type of appeal the ad uses.

PERSUASION EXERCISE: Television Commercials

Pathos, Ethos, Logos

Find two examples of a television commercial which uses primarily one form of appeal. Choose pathos, ethos or logos. Bring a video copy of the two commercials to share with the class. Or find the commercials on-line and show them in the class if you have an Internet connection. On a separate sheet of paper, complete the following exercise:

1. **1st Commercial:** Name the Appeal: Ethos, Pathos or Logos.
   - What is the name of the commercial product?
   - What is the television show's name?
   - Who is the audience?
   - How does the commercial use this appeal?
   - Does it use any other?
   - Is it effective?

2. **2nd Commercial:** Name the Appeal: Ethos, Pathos or Logos.
   - What is the name of the commercial product?
   - What is the television show's name?
   - Who is the audience?
   - How does the commercial use this appeal?
   - Does it use any other?
   - Is it effective?

"A Backlash to Advertising in an Age of Anything Goes"

by Alexandra Marks

Christian Science Monitor *2/22/99 vol 91 Issue 59 p 1*

(Essay)

Alexandra Marks is staff writer for *The Christian Science Monitor*. She reports on important issues within many disciplines of science, including computer and natural science. Marks has covered such issues as computer tracking in airports, the invasion on American freedoms, the New York gridlock, and cloning.

AS YOU READ: Annotate

1. What does the title cause you to anticipate in the content of the article?
2. Does the information in the headnote indicate that the author is knowledgeable on the topic? Biased?
3. Annotate to describe the writing style of the author—highlight words and phrases that affect the style/tone, comment on sentence structure.
4. Read between the lines—Is the writing logical? Any fallacies?
5. Vocabulary. Circle the following words and any others you don't know, and write their meanings in the margins: *co-opted* and *malleability*.

The flap over latest Calvin Klein ads may be a response to commercial 'excesses'

Towering above Times Square, a huge billboard sits cloaked in white canvas. Behind the cover is a picture of two little children in their underwear, standing on a couch, grinning and clowning around.

It's the centerpiece of the ad campaign Calvin Klein pulled last week after critics complained it bordered on the pornographic and could encourage pedophilia.

On the surface, the controversy appeared to be a clash between outraged religious conservatives and the bold, edgy fashion designer who's known for pushing the bounds of sexuality and taste in *advertising*. But many social critics say the ad and ensuing controversy illustrate a deeper phenomenon: an increasingly aggressive commercialization.

From explicit sexual imagery to pictures that evoke tender emotions, such as happy kids at home romping around in their underwear, almost anything goes if it can help sell a product.

With the average American now exposed to 3,000 *advertising* images every day, ad designers perceive a need to shock, stand out, and grab consumers in new ways. Indeed, *advertising* executives have even co-opted the counter-culture, trying to capitalize on the spirit of the rebel and the nonconformist in their bid to sell products.

"It sounds like Calvin Klein is being scapegoated for the general excesses of our commercial culture," says Mark Crispin Miller, a professor of media studies at New York University. "I don't simply mean the near nudity or sexual innuendo; I mean the intensifying emphasis on shock value and the sheer omnipresence of *advertising*. What's immoral is not necessarily [*advertising's*] occasional lapse in taste, but its reduction of all of life to … pursuit of fulfillment in mere products."

The controversy prompted Mr. Klein to cancel the unveiling of the billboard in Times Square, and he decided not to send the children to a promotional appearance scheduled at Macy's last Thursday.

But he went ahead with an appearance by supermodel Christy Turlington. Many of the people waiting in line to get her autograph had seen the controversial ads the day before in *The New York Times* and several magazines.

While only one person agreed that the photos of the children verged on pornography, a few thought they were "creepy." But most people saw no problem with the pictures, thinking they were sweet and playful, and likening them to family snapshots.

Still, many of them also believed the pictures could be seen as questionable when viewed in the context of the larger *advertising* culture. "I can see how a concerned parent might see it as child pornography, considering what's going on the Internet and all," says Lolly Enriques, a student at Fordham Law School here. "But I'm not a pedophile, so I just see it as innocent children."

Selling to kids

What struck social critic Neil Postman was not that Calvin Klein was again possibly pushing the bounds of good taste, but that anyone would be trying to sell designer underwear to four—and five-year-olds.

"The general tendency to ignore the idea of childhood, and treat children as miniature adults, tends to destroy some of the ideas we used to associate with childhood —innocence and malleability and curiosity," says Professor Postman, author of the 1982 book *The Disappearance of Childhood*.

Calvin Klein contends this ad campaign was designed to celebrate just such attributes of childhood. Neither he nor his company returned repeated phone calls, but he did issue a statement that said the advertisements were designed simply to "show children smiling, laughing, and just being themselves."

But that innocent explanation didn't sit well with several advertising experts, given Klein's history of producing advertising that portrays young people as sex objects.

In fact, some suspect Klein consciously went ahead with what he knew would be a controversial campaign so he could pull it—and again reap lots of free media attention. To be sure, he did get lots of that, from New York Mayor Rudolph Giuliani to Rosie O'Donnell. CNN even dedicated a full segment of "Talk Back Live" to Klein's underwear ads.

"I can't believe this was done without the intent to cause controversy," says Diane Cook-Tench, director of the Ad Center at Virginia Commonwealth University in Richmond. "He's established a major brand based on controversy. He is the anti-establishment, and young people buy his clothes because he is anti-establishment. That's what he's selling—he's very savvy."

Intentional brouhaha?

Advertising critic Jean Kilbourne goes further. She believes he intentionally set up the controversy so that anyone who criticizes the ads will be characterized as a moralistic prude and he will be championed as a bold innovator.

"I wouldn't want him to get away with that. This is just about selling underwear —it's not about rebellion or being cool. This is a very cold-blooded marketing strategy," says Ms. Kilbourne. "And I refuse to be put in the so-called moralistic, antisex camp by the likes of Calvin Klein."

Others in the ad world were more generous, hoping that Klein and his ad executives wouldn't be that cynical. But they also believe his history helped prompt the controversy.

"Would this campaign have been OK if JC Penney had done it? I think maybe so," says David "Jelly" Helm of the Martin Agency in Richmond. "But if you associate it with someone who has surely capitalized on sexuality and pushing sexual bounds, then it is something that you want to ask questions about."

AFTER YOU READ: Analyze the Issues

1. What is the main idea?
2. Does the First Amendment give Calvin Klein the right to decide on advertising content?
3. What weaknesses does Marks's argument have?
4. What types of advertisements support her argument?

AFTER YOU READ: Analyze the Rhetoric

1. How does the vocabulary Marks uses persuade the audience? Does the vocabulary compromise her argument?
2. Marks's primary audience is comprised of Christians. How does the type of publication influence her approach to the argument?

Comparing Ads: War Posters

Examine the following military advertisements. One is for war bonds and the other for conserving fat.

AS YOU READ: Annotate

1. Which rhetorical appeal is the ad using the most? Logos? Pathos? Ethos?
2. Does the lack of color affect your response to the ads?
3. Which ad appeals the most to you? Why?

"I Gave a Man: War Bonds"

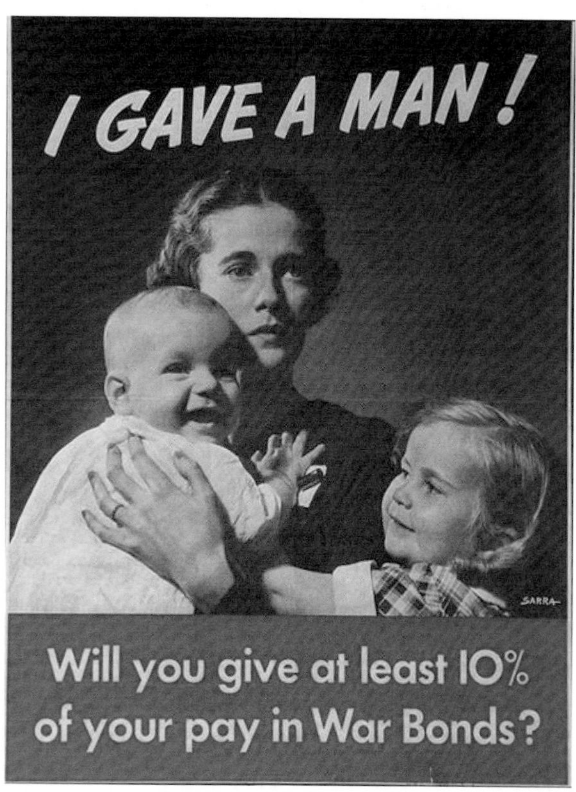

World War II Poster, 1941

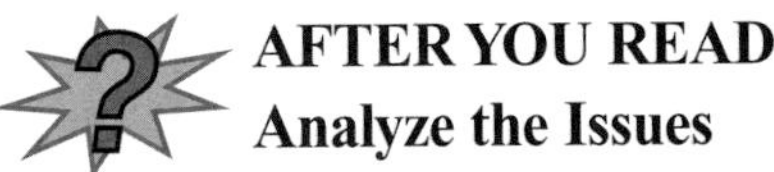

AFTER YOU READ: Analyze the Issues

1. What is the main idea of each poster?
2. If the logo was not part of the ad(s), would you know what the ad(s) was about?
3. Who do you think the target audience is for the ad? How do you think people who are not part of the target audience would respond to it (them)?
4. What patriotic "values" do the ad(s) convey?

AFTER YOU READ: Analyze the Rhetoric

1. Give examples of how each ad uses *pathos, logos,* and *ethos.*
2. Evaluate the persuasive effect of each rhetorical appeal. In your view, is one more effective (or less effective) than the other two appeals? Why?

"Save Waste Fats for Explosives"

World War II poster, 1943

"Californication"

by The Red Hot Chili Peppers
Warner Brothers 1999
(Lyrics)

The founding members, Anthony Keidis (singer) and Michael Balzary (bass) met at Fairfax High School in Los Angeles in 1983 and created this funk-rock band. They went on to become a popular band with a sordid twenty year history involving strange stage antics and drug use. One of the original members, Hillel Slovak, died of a heroin overdose. Visit their Web site at www.redhotchilipepers.com.

AS YOU READ OR LISTEN: Annotate

1. What does the title cause you to anticipate in the content of the song?
2. Does the information in the headnote indicate that the author is knowledgeable on the topic? Biased?
3. Annotate to describe the writing style of the author—highlight words and phrases that affect the style/tone.
4. Circle any words you don't know, and write their meanings in the margins.

Psychic spies from China
Try to steal your mind's elation
Little girls from Sweden
Dream of silver screen quotations
And if you want these kind of dreams
It's Californication

It's the edge of the world
And all of western civilization
The sun may rise in the East
At least it settles in the final location
It's understood that Hollywood
sells Californication

Pay your surgeon very well
To break the spell of aging
Celebrity skin is this your chin
Or is that war your waging

[Chorus:]
First born unicorn
Hard core soft porn
Dream of Californication
Dream of Californication

Marry me girl be my fairy to the world
Be my very own constellation
A teenage bride with a baby inside
Getting high on information
And buy me a star on the boulevard
It's Californication

Space may be the final frontier
But it's made in a Hollywood basement

Cobain can you hear the spheres
Singing songs off station to station
And Alderon's not far away
It's Californication

Born and raised by those who praise
Control of population everybody's been there
and
I don't mean on vacation

[Chorus]

Destruction leads to a very rough road
But it also breeds creation
And earthquakes are to a girl's guitar
They're just another good vibration
And tidal waves couldn't save the world
From Californication

Pay your surgeon very well
To break the spell of aging
Sicker than the rest
There is no test
But this is what you're craving

[Chorus]

AFTER YOU READ OR LISTEN: Analyze the Issues

1. What is the main idea?
2. According to the group, who is responsible for "Californication"?
3. What gender does the song target? Why does it work? Not work?
4. Why do you think the writer used the examples he used? What other examples can you think of that might be appropriate?

AFTER YOU READ OR LISTEN: Analyze the Rhetoric

1. Give examples of the song's use of *pathos* and *ethos.*
2. Evaluate the persuasive effect of each rhetorical appeal. In your view, is one more effective (or less effective) than the other two appeals? Why?
3. The title of the song "Californication" sends a message. How does the play on words compromise or support the message in the song?

"Super Size Me"

by Toothpick
(Lyrics)

Doug Ray (Toothpick) created these lyrics that capture the spirit of the documentary, *Super Size Me* (directed by Morgan Spurlock), the record of 30 days of eating only McDonalds food. If they ask Spurlock if he wanted to super-size-it, he would say yes. After the release of the film, McDonalds withdrew its super size it campaign. Toothpick has been influenced by a wide range of musical tastes from artists and groups like Cat Stevens to A Tribe Called Quest. Toothpick's music combines a variety of genres such as rap, rock, funk, folk, and blues. He is about to release his first solo effort "Time Travelin' Couch." Visit his Web site at toothpickmusic.com.

AS YOU READ: Annotate

1. Place a star by the stanza you like the most.
2. Write comments in the margins to explain why you like those sections.
3. If there is any humor, write the words "Ha Ha" in the margins.

Man:
[Right now you have the urge to eat something.
When it's through if you still want to eat, then you're probably really hungry.
Think about what I'm saying]

F.A.T.
That is me
But I didn't used to be
I was hot. I was hungry
I was loose. I was free
Then I waited in the line
For some burgers and some fries
Super size, that'd be nice
Take a bite and close your eyes

Round 2, what do I do
I can barely walk around
Jenny Craig, Richard Simmons
But I still lug the pounds
Hamburgers, coke cola
Getting gas from too much soda

Double double, chunky chunky
Hope this meal is never over
The world is round, and so am I
Big boys, big girls with real big thighs

(Chorus)
Super size, super size
The American way
Going down, throwing down
All day, every day
Super size, super size
The American way
Getting fat, getting broke
Either way you're gonna pay
Super size me
Super size me
Super size me
Super size me

Now I can't get out of bed
So I have to order in
I'm a triple fat fatty
And I have a triple chin
Who's the blame
Call the lawyer
Try to settle outta court
Get some cash
Spend it fast
Cos I'm staring at my fork

Cos it's sad and it's lonely
Ham and cheese with balogne
Large pies, stuff-crusted
Doggy bagels for a phony
I have lost the motivation
To inhibit the sensation
But I loathe the frustration
Birthday cake, I take my face in
Turkey club with double bacon's
got healthy connotations
Fast food has over-taken
And has super sized the nation

(Chorus)

[If I can keep up this progress, I'd have 25 pounds. 25 pounds!
That's a lot of weight.]

Kentucky fried, just fried
Chicken nuggets, dip it twice
Freeky fries and gelata
Philly cheese, drive-through diet
Pack more weight
Cardiac, heart attack
Back on track
Grow so fat, slim, fast, slim, slow
Touch your toes

Finger lickin'
Hit the border
Pull right up
And place your order
Yes sir, r'way
Right away
You deserve a break today!

Super size, super size
The American way
Going down, throwing down
All day, every day
Super size, super size
The American way
Getting fat, getting broke
Either way you're gonna pay
Super size me
Super size me
[Put something in your mouth]
Super size me
(Can I get extra cheese with that?)
Super size me
(Whatdaya mean 50 cents for extra cheese?)
Super size me
(I come here all the time!)
Super size me
(Hook your brother up!)
Super size me
(Ooh I'm a fan)
Super size me
(All you can eat all day)

Super size me
(Is that the biggest size you've got?)
Super size me
(I said I want it super-sized)
Super size me
(Can I get like, a bucket with a handle?)
Super size me
(2 for a dollar? I'll take it!)
Super size me
(All I need is 3 more forks)
Super size me
(And another seta hands)

[That's a pretty good idea]

AFTER YOU READ: Analyze the Issues

1. What do the lyrics refer to when they mention the American Way?
2. What is the main message of the song?
3. Do you agree with this message? Explain.
4. Why did the protagonist call a lawyer?

AFTER YOU READ: Analyze the Rhetoric

1. Read the lyrics silently, and then read them aloud or listen to the lyrics.
2. Discuss the arrangement of the song. Is there an introduction, body and conclusion? Comment.

"Why McDonald's Fries Taste Good"

by Eric Schlosser
(Essay)

Born in 1959, in New York City, Eric Schlosser became an award-winning journalist. He currently works for the *Atlantic Monthly*. His articles have appeared in a variety of periodicals: *Rolling Stone*, *Vanity Fair*, and *The New Yorker*. He also wrote *Reefer Madness: Sex, Drugs, and Cheap Labor in the American Black Market* in 2003. Schlosser is working on a book about the American prison system.

Excerpt from *Fast Food Nation: The Dark Side of the All-American Meal*. Houghton Mifflin Co, 2001. (120–132).

AS YOU READ: Annotate

1. Place stars by the sections you liked the most.
2. Write "Pathos" next to sections that are effective for this appeal.
3. Write "Smell" in the margin next to references to the nose.
4. Circle the following words and any you do not know, look up their meaning and write the definition in the margins: *palatable, volatile, olfactory, flavorist, evoke, indelible, spectrometers, ubiquitous,* and *brasserie.*

THE TASTE OF McDonald's french fries has long been praised by customers, competitors, and even food critics. James Beard loved McDonald's fries. Their distinctive taste does not stem from the type of potatoes that McDonald's buys, the technology that processes them, or the restaurant equipment that fries them. Other chains buy their french fries from the same large processing companies, use Russet Burbanks, and have similar fryers in their restaurant kitchens. The taste of a fast food fry is largely determined by the cooking oil. For decades, McDonald's cooked its french fries in a mixture of about 7 percent cottonseed oil and 93 percent beef tallow. The mix gave the fries their unique flavor—and more saturated beef fat per ounce than a McDonald's hamburger.

Amid a barrage of criticism over the amount of cholesterol in their fries, McDonald's switched to pure vegetable oil in 1990. The switch presented the company with an enormous challenge: how to make fries that subtly taste like beef without cooking them in tallow. A look at the ingredients now used in the preparation of McDonald's french fries suggests how the problem was solved. At the end of the list is a seemingly innocuous, yet oddly mysterious phrase: "natural flavor." That ingredient helps to explain not only why the fries taste so good, but also why most fast food—indeed, most of the food Americans eat today—tastes the way it does.

Open your refrigerator, your freezer, your kitchen cupboards, and look at the labels on your food. You'll find "natural flavor" or "artificial flavor" in just about every list of ingredients. The similarities between these two broad categories of flavor are far more significant than their differences. Both are man-made additives that give most processed food its taste. The initial purchase of a food item may be driven by its packaging or appearance, but subsequent purchases are determined mainly by its taste. About 90 percent of the money that Americans spend on food is used to buy processed food. But the canning, freezing, and dehydrating techniques used to process food destroy most of its flavor. Since the end of World War II, a vast industry has arisen in the United States to make processed food palatable. Without this flavor industry, today's fast food industry could not exist. The names of the leading American fast food chains and their best-selling menu items have become famous worldwide, embedded in our popular culture. Few people, however, can name the companies that manufacture fast food's taste.

The flavor industry is highly secretive. Its leading companies will not divulge the precise formulas of flavor compounds or the identities of clients. The secrecy is deemed essential for protecting the reputation of beloved brands. The fast food chains, understandably, would like the public to believe that the flavors of their food somehow originate in their restaurant kitchens, not in distant factories run by other firms.

The New Jersey Turnpike runs through the heart of the flavor industry, an industrial corridor dotted with refineries and chemical plants. International Flavors & Fragrances (IFF), the world's largest flavor company, has a manufacturing facility off Exit 8A in Dayton, New Jersey; Givaudan, the world's second-largest flavor company, has a plant in East Hanover. Haarmann & Reimer, the largest German flavor company, has a plant in Teterboro, as does Takasago, the largest Japanese flavor company. Flavor Dynamics has a plant in South Plainfield; Frutarom is in North Bergen; Elan Chemical is in Newark. Dozens of companies manufacture flavors in New Jersey industrial parks between Teaneck and South Brunswick. Indeed, the area produces about two-thirds of the flavor additives sold in the United States. …

In addition to being the world's largest flavor company, IFF manufactures the smell of six of the ten best-selling fine perfumes in the United States. It makes the smell of Estée Lauder's Beautiful, Clinique's Happy, Ralph Lauren's Polo, and Calvin Klein's Eternity. It also makes the smell of household products such as deodorant, dishwashing detergent, bath soap, shampoo, furniture polish, and floor wax. All of these aromas are made through the same basic process: the manipulation of volatile chemicals to create a particular smell. The basic science behind the scent of your shaving cream is the same as that governing the flavor of your TV dinner.

The aroma of a food can be responsible for as much as 90 percent of its flavor. Scientists now believe that human beings acquired the sense of taste as a way to avoid being poisoned. Edible plants generally taste sweet; deadly ones, bitter. Taste is supposed to help us differentiate food that's good for us from food that's not. The taste buds on our tongues can detect the presence of half a dozen or so basic tastes, including: sweet, sour, bitter, salty, astringent, and umami (a taste discovered by Japanese researchers, a rich and full sense of deliciousness triggered by amino acids in foods such as shellfish, mushrooms, potatoes, and seaweed). Taste buds offer a relatively limited means of detection, however, compared to the human olfactory system, which can perceive thousands of different chemical aromas. Indeed "flavor" is primarily the smell of gases being released by the chemicals you've just put in your mouth.

The act of drinking, sucking, or chewing a substance releases its volatile gases. They flow out of the mouth and up the nostrils, or up the passageway in the back of the mouth, to a thin layer of nerve cells called the olfactory epithelium, located at the base of the nose, right between the eyes. The brain combines the complex smell signals from the epithelium with the simple taste signals from the tongue, assigns a flavor to what's in your mouth, and decides if it's something you want to eat.

Babies like sweet tastes and reject bitter ones; we know this because scientists have rubbed various flavors inside the mouths of infants and then recorded their facial reactions. A person's food preferences, like his or her personality, are formed during the first few years of life, through a process of socialization. Toddlers can learn to enjoy hot and spicy food, bland health food, or fast food, depending upon what the people around them eat. The human sense of smell is still not fully understood and can be greatly affected by psychological factors and expectations. The color of a food can determine the perception of its taste. The mind filters out the overwhelming majority of chemical aromas that surround us, focusing intently on some, ignoring others. People can grow accustomed to bad smells or good smells; they stop noticing what once seemed overpowering. Aroma and memory are somehow inextricably linked. A smell can suddenly evoke a long-forgotten moment. The flavors of childhood foods seem to leave an indelible mark, and adults often return to them, without always knowing why. These "comfort foods" become a source of pleasure and reassurance, a fact that fast food chains work hard to promote. Childhood memories of Happy Meals can translate into frequent adult visits to McDonald's, like those of the chain's "heavy users," the customers who eat there four or five times a week.

The human craving for flavor has been a largely unacknowledged and unexamined force in history. Royal empires have been built, unexplored lands have been traversed, great religions and philosophies have been forever changed by the spice trade. In 1492 Christopher Columbus set sail to find seasoning. Today the influence of flavor in the world marketplace is no less decisive. The rise and fall of corporate empires—of soft drink companies, snack food companies, and fast food chains—is frequently determined by how their products taste…

The American flavor industry now has annual revenues of about $1.4 billion. Approximately ten thousand new processed food products are introduced every year in the United States. Almost all of them require flavor additives. And about nine out of every ten of these new food products fail. The latest flavor innovations and corporate realignments are heralded in publications such as *Food Chemical News, Food Engineering, Chemical Market Reporter,* and *Food Product Design.*

The growth of IFF has mirrored that of the flavor industry as a whole. IFF was formed in 1958, through the merger of two small companies. Its annual revenues have grown almost fifteenfold since the early 1970s, and it now has manufacturing facilities in twenty countries.

The quality that people seek most of all in a food, its flavor, is usually present in a quantity too infinitesimal to be measured by any traditional culinary terms such as ounces or teaspoons. Today's sophisticated spectrometers, gas chromatographs, and headspace vapor analyzers provide a detailed map of a food's flavor components, detecting chemical aromas in amounts as low as one part per billion. The human nose, however, is still more sensitive than any machine yet invented. A nose can detect aromas present in quantities of a few parts per trillion—an amount equivalent to 0.000000000003 percent. Complex aromas, like those of coffee or roasted meat, may be composed of volatile gases from nearly a thousand different chemicals. The smell of a strawberry arises from the interaction of at least 350 different chemicals that are present in minute amounts. The chemical that provides the dominant flavor of bell pepper can be tasted in amounts as low as .02 parts per billion; one drop is sufficient to add flavor to five average size swimming pools. The flavor additive usually comes last, or second to last, in a processed food's list of ingredients (chemicals that add color are frequently used in even smaller amounts). As a result, the flavor of a processed food often costs less than its packaging. Soft drinks contain a larger proportion of flavor additives than most products. The flavor in a twelve-ounce can of Coke costs about half a cent.

The Food and Drug Administration does not require flavor companies to disclose the ingredients of their additives, so long as all the chemicals are considered by the agency to be GRAS (Generally Regarded As Safe). This lack of public disclosure enables the companies to maintain the secrecy of their formulas. It also hides the fact that flavor compounds sometimes contain more ingredients than the foods being given their taste. The ubiquitous phrase "artificial strawberry flavor" gives little hint of the chemical wizardry and manufacturing skill that can make a highly processed food taste like a strawberry.

A typical artificial strawberry flavor, like the kind found in a Burger King strawberry milk shake, contains the following ingredients: amyl acetate, amyl butyrate, amyl valerate, anethol, anisyl formate, benzyl acetate, benzyl isobutyrate, butyric acid, cinnamyl isobutyrate, cinnamyl valerate, cognac essential oil, diacetyl, dipropyl ketone, ethyl acetate, ethyl amylketone, ethyl butyrate, ethyl cinnamate, ethyl heptanoate, ethyl heptylate, ethyl lactate, ethyl methylphenylglyci-date, ethyl nitrate, ethyl propionate, ethyl valerate, heliotropin, hydroxyphrenyl-2-butanone (10 percent solution in alcohol), ionone, isobutyl anthranilate, isobutyl butyrate, lemon essential oil, maltol, 4-methylacetophenone, methyl anthranilate, methyl benzoate, methyl cinnamate, methyl heptine carbonate, methyl naphthyl ketone, methyl salicylate, mint essential oil, neroli essential oil, nerolin, neryl isobutyrate, orris butter, phenethyl alcohol, rose, rum ether, undecalactone, vanillin, and solvent.

Although flavors usually arise from a mixture of many different volatile chemicals, a single compound often supplies the dominant aroma. Smelled alone, that chemical provides an unmistakable sense of the food. Ethyl-2-methyl butyrate, for example, smells just like an apple. Today's highly processed foods offer a blank palette: whatever chemicals you add to them will give them specific tastes. Adding methyl-2-peridylketone makes something taste like popcorn. Adding ethyl-3-hydroxybutanoate makes it taste like marshmallow. The possibilities are now almost limitless. Without affecting the appearance or nutritional value, processed foods could even be made with aroma chemicals such as hexanal (the smell of freshly cut grass) or 3-methyl butanoic acid (the smell of body odor)...

The flavorists with whom I spoke were charming, cosmopolitan, and ironic. They were also discreet, in keeping with the dictates of their trade. They were the sort of scientist who not only enjoyed fine wine, but could also tell you the chemicals that gave each vintage its unique aroma. One flavorist compared his work to composing music. A well-made flavor compound will have a "top note," followed by a "dry-down," and a "leveling-off," with different chemicals responsible for each stage. The taste of a food can be radically altered by minute changes in the flavoring mix. "A little odor goes a long way," one flavorist said....

Some of the most important advances in flavor manufacturing are now occurring in the field of biotechnology. Complex flavors are being made through fermentation, enzyme reactions, fungal cultures, and tissue cultures. All of the flavors being created through these methods—including the ones being synthesized by funguses—are considered natural flavors by the FDA. The new enzyme-based processes are responsible for extremely lifelike dairy flavors. One company now offers not just butter flavor, but also fresh creamy butter, cheesy butter, milky butter, savory melted butter, and super-concentrated butter flavor, in liquid or powder form. The development of new fermentation techniques, as well as new techniques for heating mixtures of sugar and amino acids, have led to the creation of much more realistic meat flavors. The McDonald's Corporation will not reveal the exact origin of the natural flavor added to its french fries. In response to inquiries from *Vegetarian Journal,* however, McDonald's did acknowledge that its fries derive some of their characteristic flavor from "animal products."

Other popular fast foods derive their flavor from unexpected sources. Wendy's Grilled Chicken Sandwich, for example, contains beef extracts. Burger King's BK Broiler Chicken Breast Patty contains "natural smoke flavor." A firm called Red Arrow Products Company specializes in smoke flavor, which is added to barbecue sauces and processed meats. Red Arrow manufactures natural smoke flavor by charring sawdust and capturing the aroma chemicals released into the air. The smoke is captured in water and then bottled, so that other companies can sell food which seems to have been cooked over a fire.

In a meeting room at IFF, Brian Grainger let me sample some of the company's flavors. It was an unusual taste test; there wasn't any food to taste. Grainger is a senior flavorist at IFF, a soft-spoken chemist with graying hair, an English accent, and a fondness for understatement. He could easily be mistaken for a British diplomat or the owner of a West End brasserie with two Michelin stars. Like many in the flavor industry, he has an Old World, old-fashioned sensibility which seems out of step with our brand-conscious, egocentric age. When I suggested that IFF should put its own logo on the products that contain its flavors—instead of allowing other brands to enjoy the consumer loyalty and affection inspired by those flavors—Grainger politely disagreed, assuring me such a thing would never be done. In the absence of public credit or acclaim, the small and secretive fraternity of flavor chemists praises one another's work. Grainger can often tell, by analyzing the flavor formula of a product, which of his counterparts at a rival firm devised it. And he enjoys walking down supermarket aisles, looking at the many products that contain his flavors, even if no one else knows it.

Grainger had brought a dozen small glass bottles from the lab. After he opened each bottle, I dipped a fragrance testing filter into it. The filters were long white strips of paper designed to absorb aroma chemicals without producing off-notes. Before placing the strips of paper before my nose, I closed my eyes. Then I inhaled deeply, and one food after another was conjured from the glass bottles. I smelled fresh cherries, black olives, sautéed onions, and shrimp. Grainger's most remarkable creation took me by surprise. After closing my eyes, I suddenly smelled a grilled hamburger. The aroma was uncanny, almost miraculous. It smelled like someone in the room was flipping burgers on a hot grill. But when I opened my eyes, there was just a narrow strip of white paper and a smiling flavorist.

AFTER YOU READ: Analyze the Issues

1. What is the significance of mentioning "umami"?
2. What is the main message of the essay?
3. What was the best section? Explain why.

AFTER YOU READ: Analyze the Rhetoric

1. Comment on whether the evidence or logos in this essay is presented objectively.
2. How effective was the author in describing smell?
3. Was the conclusion well written? Explain.

"The Selling Of Rebellion"

by John Leo
(Essay)

John Leo has numerous years experience in the journalism discipline. He has served as an associate editor, book editor, and deputy commissioner. He is most famous for his "Ralph & Wanda" dialogues, which are fictional conversations between a liberal feminist and her conservative husband. He has written for *Time*, *McCall's*, *The New York Times* and *Commonwealth*.

AS YOU READ: Annotate

1. What does the title cause you to anticipate in the content of the article?
2. Does the information in the headnote indicate that the author is knowledgeable on the topic? Biased?
3. Annotate to describe the writing style of the author—highlight words and phrases that affect the style/tone, comment on sentence structure.
4. Read between the lines—Is the writing logical? Any fallacies?
5. Circle the following words, and any others you don't know, and write their meanings in the margins: *postmodern, mantra,* and *pollster*.

U.S. News & Report, October 12, 1998.

Most TV viewers turn off their brains when the commercials come on. But they're worth paying attention to. Some of the worst cultural propaganda is jammed into those 60-second and 30-second spots.

Consider the recent ad for the Isuzu Rodeo. A grotesque giant in a business suit stomps into a beautiful field, startling a deer and jamming skyscrapers, factories, and signs into the ground. (I get it: Nature is good; civilization and business are bad.) One of the giant's signs says "Obey," but the narrator says, "The world has boundaries. Ignore them." Trying to trample the Rodeo, the hapless giant trips over his own fence. The Isuzu zips past him, toppling a huge sign that says "Rules."

Presumably we are meant to react to this ad with a wink and a nudge, because the message is unusually flat-footed and self-satirical. After all, Isuzus are not manufactured in serene fields by adorable lower mammals. The maddened giant makes them in his factories. He also hires hip ad writers and stuffs them in his skyscrapers, forcing them to write drivel all day, when they really should be working on novels and frolicking with deer.

But the central message here is very serious and strongly antisocial: We should all rebel against authority, social order, propriety, and rules of any kind. "Obey" and "Rules" are bad. Breaking rules, with or without your Isuzu, is good. Auto makers have been pushing this idea in various ways since "The Dodge *Rebellion*" of the mid-1960s. Isuzu has worked the theme especially hard, including a TV ad showing a bald and repressive grade-school teacher barking at kids to "stay within the lines" while coloring pictures, because "the lines are our friends."

Away with standards. A great many advertisers now routinely appeal to the so-called postmodern sensibility, which is heavy on irony (wink, nudge) and attuned to the message that rules, boundaries, standards, and authorities are either gone or should be gone. Foster Grant sunglasses has used the "no limits" refrain. So have Prince Matchabelli perfume ("Life without limits"), Showtime TV (its "No Limits" campaign) and AT&T's Olympics ads in 1996 ("Imagine a world without limits"). No Limits is an outdoor-adventure company, and No Limit is the name of a successful rap record label. Even the U.S. Army used the theme in a TV recruitment ad. "When I'm in this uniform I know no limits," says a soldier—a scary thought if you remember St. William Halley in Vietnam or the Serbian Army today.

Among the ads that have used "no boundaries" almost as a mantra are Ralph Lauren's Safari cologne, Johnnie Walker scotch ("It's not trespassing when you cross your own boundaries"), Merrill Lynch ("Know no boundaries"), and the movie *The English Patient* ("In love, there are no boundaries").

Some "no boundaries" ads are legitimate—the Internet and financial markets, after all, aim at crossing or erasing old boundaries. The antisocial message is clearer in most of the "no rules" and "antirules" ads, starting with Burger King's "Sometimes, you gotta break the rules." These include Outback Steakhouses ("No rules. Just right"), Don Q rum ("Break all the rules"), the theatrical troupe De La

Guardia ("No rules"), Newman Marcus ("No rules here"), Columbia House Music Club ("We broke the rules"), Comedy Central ("See comedy that breaks rules"), Red Camel cigarettes ("This baby don't play by the rules"), and even Woolite (wool used to be associated with decorum, but now "All the rules have changed," an ad says under a photo of a young woman groping or being groped by two guys). "No rules" also turns up as the name of a book and a CD and a tag line for an NFL video game ("no refs, no rules, no mercy"). The message is everywhere—"the rules are for breaking," says a Spice Girls lyric.

What is this all about? Why is the ad industry working so hard to use rule-breaking as a way of *selling* cars, steaks, and Woolite? In his book *The Conquest of Cool*, Thomas Frank points to the Sixties counterculture. He says it has become "a more or less permanent part of the American scene, a symbolic and musical language for the endless cycles of *rebellion* and transgression that make up so much of our mass culture ... *rebellion* is both the high—and mass-cultural motif of the age; order is its great bogeyman."

The pollster-analysts at Yankelovich Partners Inc. have a different view. In their book *Rocking the Ages: The Yankelovich Report on Generational Marketing*, J. Walker Smith and Ann Clurman say rule-breaking is simply a hallmark of the baby boom generation: "Boomers always have broken the rules... The drugs, sex, and rock 'n roll of the '60s and '70s only foreshadowed the really radical rule-breaking to come in the consumer marketplace of the '80s and '90s."

This may pass—Smith says the post-boomers of Generation X are much more likely to embrace traditional standards than boomers were at the same age. On the other hand, maybe it won't. Pop culture is dominated by in-your-face transgression now and the damage is severe. The peculiar thing is that so much of the rule-breaking propaganda is largely funded by businessmen who say they hate it, but can't resist promoting it in ads as a way of pushing their products. Isuzu, please come to your senses.

AFTER YOU READ: Analyze the Issues

1. What is the main idea?
2. Is rebellion a new phenomenon in the US culture? Why or why not?
3. What weaknesses does Leo's argument have?
4. What types of advertisements support his argument?
5. When and why might the rebellion approach backfire?

AFTER YOU READ: Analyze the Rhetoric

1. How does the vocabulary Leo uses "date" the article? Does this compromise his argument?
2. How do words such as "might" "should" and "perhaps" affect the argument?

"Some Hated Commercials Inspire Violent Fantasies"

by Dave Barry
(Essay)

Dave Barry writes for the *Miami Herald*. Mr. Barry has written several best sellers including: *Dave Barry in Cyberspace*; *Dave Barry Talks Back: Dave is from Mars and Venus*; *Big Trouble*; and *Dave Barry is Not Taking This Sitting Down*. The CBS television series *Dave's World* was based on two of his books, but the show was canceled.

AS YOU READ: Annotate

1. What does the title cause you to anticipate in the content of the article?
2. Does the information in the headnote indicate that the author is knowledgeable on the topic? Biased?
3. Annotate to describe the writing style of the author—highlight words and phrases that affect the style/tone, comment on sentence structure.
4. Read between the lines—Is the writing logical? Any fallacies?

Advertisers Beware: Most hated Commercial Inspire Viewers to Fantasize About Acts of Violence.

Whew! Do I have a headache! I think I'll take an Extra Strength Bufferin Advil Tylenol with proven city fighters, containing more of the lemon-freshened Borax that is recommended by doctors and plaque fighters for those days when I am feeling "not so fresh" in my personal region!

The reason I'm feeling this way is that I have just spent six straight days going through the thousands of letters you readers sent in when I asked you to tell me which advertisements you don't like.

It turns out that a lot of you really, REALLY hate certain advertisements, to the point where you fantasize about acts of violence. For example, quite a few people expressed a desire to kill the stuffed bear in the Snuggle fabric-softener commercial. "Die, Snuggle Bear! Die!" is how several put it.

Likewise, there was a great deal of hostility expressed, often by older readers, toward the relentlessly cheerful older couples depicted in the competing commercials for Ensure and Sustacal. These commercials strongly suggest that if you drink these products, you will feel "young," which, in these commercials, means "stupid." People were particularly offended by the commercial where the couple actually drinks a toast with Ensure. As Jamie Hagedorn described it: "One says, 'To your health,' and the other says, 'Uh-uh, to

OUR health,' and then for some reason they laugh like ninnies. I want to hit them both over the head with a hammer."

Some other commercial personalities who aroused great hostility were Sally Struthers; the little boy who lectures you incessantly about Welch's grape juice; the young people in the Mentos commercials (as Rob Spore put it, "Don't you think those kids should all be sent to military school?"); everybody in all Calvin Klein commercials ("I am sure they are what hell is really like," observed Robert E. Waller); the little girl in the Shake 'N Bake commercial—Southerners REALLY hate this little girl—who, for what seemed like hundreds of years, said "And I helped!" but pronounced it "An ah hayulpt!" (Louise Sigmund, in a typically restrained response, wrote, "Your mother shakes chickens in hell"); Kathie Lee Gifford (Shannon Saar wrote, "First person to push Kathie Lee overboard gets an all-you-can-eat buffet!"); the smug man in the Geritol commercial who said, "My wife… I think I'll keep her!" (the wife smiled, but you just know that one day she will put Liquid Drano in his Ensure); the bad actor pretending to be Dean Witter in the flagrantly fake "old film" commercial that's supposed to make us want to trust them with our money; the woman in the Pantene commercial who said, "Please don't hate me because I'm beautiful" (as many readers responded, "OK, how about if we just hate you because you're obnoxious?"); and of course the Pillsbury Doughboy ("I would sacrifice my microwave to watch him inside on high for 10 hours," wrote Gene Doerfler).

Also, they are none too fond of the giant Gen X dudes stomping all over the Rocky Mountains in the Coors Light ads. (Matt Scott asks: "Will they step on us if we don't buy their beer?" Scott McCullar asks: "What happens when they get a full bladder?")

Also, many people would like Candice Bergen to just shut up about the stupid dimes.

Also, I am pleased to report that I am not the only person who cannot stand the sight of the Infiniti Snot—you know, the guy with the dark clothes and the accent, talking about Infiniti cars as though they were Renaissance art. As Kathleen Schon, speaking for many, put it: "We hate him so much we wouldn't buy one of those even if we could afford it, which we can't, but we wouldn't buy one anyway."

Speaking of car commercials, here's a bulletin for the Nissan people: Nobody likes the creepy old man, OK? Everybody is afraid when the little boy winds up alone in the barn with him. This ad campaign does not make us want to purchase a Nissan. It makes us want to notify the police. Thank you.

And listen, Chevrolet: People didn't mind the first 389 million times they heard Bob Seger wail "Like a Rock!" But it's getting old. And some people wish to know what "genuine Chevrolet" means. As Don Charleston put it, "I intended to buy a genuine Chevy, but I couldn't tell the difference between the 'genuine' and all those counterfeit Chevys out there, so I bought a Ford."

But the car-related ads that people hate the most, judging from my survey, are the dealership commercials in which the announcer SHOUTS AT YOU AS THOUGH

YOU ARE AN IDIOT and then, in the last three seconds of the ad reads, in very muted tones, what sounds like the entire U.S. tax code. Hundreds and hundreds of people wrote to say they hate these commercials. I should note that one person defended them: His name is George Chapogas, and he is in—of all things—the advertising business. Perhaps by examining this actual excerpt from his letter, we can appreciate the thinking behind the shouting ads:

"I write, produce and VOICE those ads. Make a damn good living doing it, too. Maybe more than you even. And would you like to know why? Because they move metal, buddy."

Thanks, George! I understand now.

Well, I'm out of space. Tune in next week, and I'll tell you which commercial the readers hated the most; I'll also discuss repulsive bodily functions in detail. Be sure to read it! You'll lose weight without dieting, have whiter teeth in two weeks by actually growing your own hair on itching, flaking skin as your family enjoys this delicious meal in only minutes without getting soggy in milk! Although your mileage may vary. Ask a doctor! Or somebody who plays one on TV.

AFTER YOU READ: Analyze the Issues

1. What is the main idea?
2. This piece was published in 1997. Are Barry's and his readers' arguments relevant today?
3. What weaknesses does the argument have?
4. What other types of advertisements support his argument?

AFTER YOU READ: Analyze the Rhetoric

1. How does the sentence structure Barry uses affect the argument?
2. What tone does the article have? What words support this?
3. How does Barry rely on *ethos*, *logos*, or *pathos* for his argument?

Sample Student Papers

"Does This Ad Make Me Look Fat?"

by Sarah Bailey

AS YOU READ: Annotate

1. Place a star by the sections you like the most.
2. Place question marks by sections you have problems with or do not understand.
3. Place a [+] by sections that need to be developed more or that seem to be incomplete.
4. Write other comments in the margins as you see fit.

In today's information inundated culture, advertisements must grab our attention to make us slow down and, perhaps, buy the product. One very effective way to do this is by utilizing models that embody the "thin ideal." These are the super-skinny women and overly-muscled men that one sees frequently in today's advertisements. Everywhere one looks, models are featured in advertisements for products ranging from perfume to cars. Half-clothed, size-zero models may capture the attention of the viewer, but these images of highly idealized men and women can be hazardous to one's health. Exposure to the "thin ideal" in advertising lowers the level of the viewer's self-esteem.

Advertising is a strangely pervasive influence on today's society. One sees advertisements on the television and movie screens, in the newspapers and magazines, on highway billboards, and in innumerable other locations. It is not surprising, then, that the average person comes in contact with over four-hundred advertisements in a single day (Beray and Griffin 46). As many as thirty-six or more of these four-hundred advertisements have "a direct message about beauty" (Beray and Griffin 46). Many more of these advertisements, although they may not have a specific message about beauty, use beauty to sell a product. The sheer quantity of advertising only intensifies the dangerous effect of the "thin ideal."

The use of the "thin ideal" in advertising is nothing new. Advertisements with these types of models have been criticized and studied for almost as long as they have been in existence. James A. Kulik and Lily F. Lin conducted a scientific experiment measuring the effects of thin models in advertising and concluded that "[E]xposure to the thin peer did reduce body satisfaction and confidence… Exposure to an oversize peer produced no compensatory, elevating effects on body satisfaction and confidence. Such an asymmetric comparison effect may contribute to the high prevalence of body dissatisfaction reported among women" (115).

Despite such studies, some people argue that being exposed to the "thin ideal" can be a healthy experience. America today is one of the most obese nations on the planet. Even the children are more obese now than children in previous generations. Supporters of this view say that the "thin ideal" models give consumers an example of a healthy body to follow. Therefore, shouldn't seeing multitudes of thin models make overweight persons want to lose weight and give them a goal that they can try to attain?

At first glance, this proposition seems sound. Indeed, one study performed by Eaaron and Donna Henderson-King seems to support this viewpoint. They exposed thin women and overweight women to slides featuring ideally attractive models or to slides featuring no models at all and monitored the subjects' body satisfaction and self-esteem. "Bifurcating weight at its median revealed that thinner women, in the ideal image condition, felt more positive about their sexual attractiveness than did thinner women in the neutral condition. In comparison, heavier women felt less positive about their sexual attractiveness in the ideal image condition than in the neutral image condition" (Henderson-King 409). This conclusion indicates that, when exposed to the "thin ideal," heavier women feel worse about their bodies than do thinner women. Lowering their self-esteem might, in theory, motivate the women to lose weight.

Is lowering someone's self-esteem really the best way to induce that person to lose weight? It is not. It only makes people feel worse about themselves and renders them more susceptible to serious problems later on, including eating disorders such as anorexia and bulimia. "Although it is hard to demonstrate directly that increasing exposure to the thin ideal figure is related to an increase in the prevalence of eating disorders, there is experimental evidence showing that exposure to thin media models and eating disorder-related symptoms are positively related with each other" (de Vries and Jansen 209). The self-esteem lowering effect of the "thin ideal" is not healthy at all.

One interesting point discovered by the Henderson-Kings is that the thinner women felt more positive about their weight when exposed to images of the thin models. This seems to contradict the idea that exposure to such images lowers self-esteem. In theory, these women feel more positive about their weight in this situation because they more closely resemble the ideal presented to them. "Contemporary ideal images communicate that only slender women are viewed as sexually attractive" (Henderson-King 403). This can be a damaging message to anyone who is overweight, and even many who are not. Women whose self-esteems would be helped by such messages are a minority, indeed. Over half of today's adult women are considered overweight (Beray and Griffin 43), and so would, according to these results, most likely feel worse about their body.

Even those who are not overweight may still voice a desire to lose weight. When interviewing college students for her book, Sharlene Hesse-Biber discovered that ninety-five percent of women wanted to lose weight (61). Why do they feel the need to be thinner when they are already at a healthy weight? One of the root causes for this is, just as the Henderson-Kings said, the "thin ideals" glorified in today's media imagery. One hardly ever sees an average or overweight person in advertising. For many, this picture of thinness is an unattainable goal. "The 'right' female body is an amalgam of the impossible" (Hesse-Biber 53).

Obviously, not every person exposed to media models experiences serious effects like developing an eating disorder. Some people seem hardly affected by advertising at all. Perhaps advertisements only affect a certain portion of the population.

Many assume that women are the only people affected by the images of models in advertising, but this is not so. There is a male counterpart to the slender, beautiful female "thin ideal." He is handsome and, of course, very muscular and strong. "[M]odern society praises an increasingly muscular male body ideal… These trends parallel a rise in anabolic steroid use among men… and an apparently increasing prevalence of muscular dysmorphia, a disorder in which men become obsessed with muscularity. These observations suggest that the cultural ideal of hypermesomorphy may be just as dangerous to men as is the anorexic ideal to women" (Leit, Gray, and Pope 334).

Men are not only affected by the muscular ideal, but also by the thinness ideal presented to them. Although they are more secure about their body image than women, when interviewed, some of the male college students did express a desire to lose weight (Hesse-Biber 61). Unfortunately, most of the scientific studies conducted on advertising and self-esteem only involve female test subjects, so there is no strong indication of just how much the male "thin ideal" affects those men exposed to it.

Advertisements utilizing images of thin models are just as harmful to adolescents as they are to adults. Adolescents are just beginning to develop their own body image and self-esteem, and so are especially vulnerable to any influences, good or bad. One study found that advertising and the "thin ideal" increased "body dissatisfaction and schema activation in girls as young as 13 years old" (Hargreaves and Tiggerman 367). If advertising starts to affect people at such a young age, its influence on self-esteem could be more harmful than originally imagined. Adolescents influenced early might suffer from lowered self-esteem through their teenage years, and possibly into adulthood. Even children are affected by the "thin ideal." Faith McLellen says that "children inundated with commercialism" are likely to have "body-image and other emotional problems" (1001).

There was another interesting conclusion to Hargreaves's and Tiggerman's experiment. They also measured the body-satisfaction of the test subjects fifteen minutes after the subjects were exposed to the "thin ideal." Hargreaves and Triggerman found that feelings of dissatisfaction were still evident after this time. "[T]he brief, 15-min follow-up does not demonstrate the potential extent of the long-term effect. Nonetheless, this initial result shows that the negative effect of exposure to the thin ideal is not limited only to an immediate reaction, but can be maintained at least over a short period of time" (372).

Leit, Gray, and Pope echo this concern, stating that scientific studies cannot determine how a lifetime of being exposed to the "thin ideal" affects men. They continue, "[T]he real life effect of the media on body esteem in men may be far greater than that found under the relatively limited conditions of the present investigation" (337). The constant bombardment of idealized images of men and women only assists in further sustaining any negative effects such advertisements might have had in the first place.

Others argue that only those people who choose to think about the thin models in advertising end up suffering from low self-esteem. "[W]hen the beauty of a model is not consciously processed, the model has no effect on the mood, self-esteem and eating behavior of women" (de Vries and Jansen 215). This suggests that simple exposure to the "thin ideal" is not enough to lower someone's self-esteem. However, what happens if someone chooses to think about a model? His thinking about that model would lower their self-esteem. In a world where each person sees hundred of advertisements every day, many featuring super-skinny ideal models, it can only be expected that he would think about at least one. Totally ignoring the "thin ideal" is impossible.

But the most important confirmation that the "thin ideal" in advertising is harmful to the viewer's self esteem is the overwhelming amount of supportive scientific evidence. Many studies have been done on this subject, and many have found that exposure to the "thin ideal" is, indeed, harmful to the self-esteem of whoever sees that advertisement. "A woman's satisfaction with her body apparently can be undermined significantly" say Kulik and Lin, "by upward comparisons [comparison with 'exceptionally attractive media figures'] with multiple, ultra-thin fashion models" (120). "[E]xposure to muscular male figures in advertisements produces measurable body dissatisfaction in men" (Leit, Gray and Pope 337).

Why do advertising firms use these types of advertisements in the first place? There is plenty of evidence to indicate that, indeed, exposure to the "thin ideal" does lower one's self-esteem. Why do they continue to do this if they know the harmful effects their advertisements can have on people? Advertising firms say that they are only giving consumers what they want. Advertisements featuring "thin ideal" models boost sales, and consumers continue to buy products advertised in this way. "They [advertising industry] reach us not through the overt message—buy perfume—but through the value atmosphere they create—gorgeous-naked-Calvin-Klein-models-sure-are-pretty-and-are-having-a-terrific-time—and if I get some of that perfume, I'll be pretty too" (Scroth 60).

Advertisers may be giving consumers what they want, but is it what they really need? After exposure to these types of advertisements, the self-esteem of the consumer is lowered, which can conveniently and easily be remedied if he buys that product. Sadly, the "thin ideal" can have far more serious long-term effects. Lowered self-esteem and body-image are only the mildest and most immediate effects of the "thin ideal" in advertisements. Lowered self-esteem can lead to many other problems later in life.

Although consumers cannot totally stop the advertising industry from using such techniques, they can counteract their effects. One step to counteracting these effects might be to limit advertising, or to limit the use of unrealistically thin models in advertising. Adults can also teach adolescents and children that although advertising promises beauty, love, popularity, and many other things, it cannot deliver what it promises. Only they can achieve these things for themselves. Most importantly, adults can teach their children that despite what some advertisements may imply, their self-esteem is based on more than their appearance. It is based on who they really are—inside, not outside.

Works Cited

Beray, E.M., and J. Griffin, "A Modern Day Holy Anorexia? Religious Language in Advertising and Anorexia Nervosa in the West." *European Journal of Clinical Nutrition* 57 (2003): 43-51. EBSCOhost. Chambers Library, Edmond, OK. 26 Feb 2004 <http://www.epnet.com/login.html>.

de Vries, Maaike, and Anita Jansen. "Pre-attentive Exposure to the Thin Female Beauty Ideal Does Not Affect Women's Mood, Self-Esteem, and Eating Behavior." *European Eating Disorders Review* (2002): 208-217. EBSCOhost. Chambers Library, Edmond, OK. 17 Feb 2004 <http://www.epnet.com/ehost/login.html>.

Hargreaves, Duane, and Marika Tiggerman. "The Effect of 'Thin Ideal' Television Commercials on Body Dissatisfaction and Schema Activation During Early Adolescence." *Journal of Youth and Adolescence* 32 (October 2003): 367-373.

Henderson-King, Eaaron, and Donna Henderson-King. "Media Effects on Women's Body Esteem: Social and Individual Difference Factors." *Journal of Applied Social Psychology* 27 (1997): 399-417.

Hesse-Biber, Sharlene. *Am I Thin Enough Yet?* New York City: Oxford University Press, 1996.

Kulik, James A., and Lily F. Lin. "Social Comparison and Women's Body Satisfaction." *Basic and Applied Social Psychology* 24 (2002): 115-123. EBSCOhost. Chambers Library, Edmond, OK. 26 Feb 2004 <http://www.epnet.com/ehost/login.html>.

Leit, Richard A., James J. Gray, and Harrison G. Pope, Jr. "The Media's Representation of the Ideal Male Body: A Cause for Muscle Dysmorphia?" *International Journal of Eating Disorders* 31 (April 2003): 334-338 <http://ejournals.ebsco.com >.

McLellan, Faith. "Marketing and Advertising: Harmful to Children's Health." *The Lancet* 360(September 28, 2002): 1001. EBSCOhost. Chambers Library, Edmond, OK. 17 Feb 2004 <http://www.epnet.com/ehost/login.html.>.

Scroth, Raymond A. "Advertising is Harmful." *Mass Media: Opposing Viewpoints*. Ed. Byron L. Stay. San Diego: Greenhaven Press, Inc., 1999. 59-63.

PEER REVIEW OUTLINE

Directions. Asking the right questions: As you ask these questions and answer them, be specific in your comments so as to be more helpful to the author. Provide details.

1. **Logos.** Comment on the quality and amount of the evidence or research conducted. Is it balanced or enough? Does the author need more? Why or why

not? Is the paper too logical or not logical enough? What else can you say about logos?

2. **Pathos.** Comment on the emotional appeals used in the paper. What can the author do to improve this appeal? Should there be less, more, or no emotions? Explain.
3. **Ethos.** Does the author use enough quality sources to improve the impact of the ethos of the paper? Is there a human element in the paper? What does the author need to do to improve the character aspect? Should the author add a personal story? Is the paper too personal? Should it be more logical?
4. **Call for Improvement.** Which aspects in the paper need to be revised or improved? Explain in detail.

Advertising Sex: Company Bias

by Kimberly Williams

AS YOU READ: Annotate

1. Place a star by the sections you like the most.
2. Place question marks by sections you have problems with or do not understand.
3. Place a [+] by sections that need to be developed more or that seem to be incomplete.
4. Write other comments in the margins as you see fit.

The advertising industry uses many strategies to sell products, and individual consumers are usually drawn to a particular type of advertising that will stay in their minds. An advertisement that achieves its goal will catch the viewer's attention and help them remember that particular product. However, there are some groups of people that feel that some advertisements have become too sexual. They claim that some advertisements are pornographic. Yet, it is very possible that these same individuals are not upset by all controversial advertising. So, why are only particular companies being chastised when the majority of companies use sex as the main strategy for their advertisements? The answer to this question is that some companies have a well-known reputation for being "on the edge" and some companies maintain a wholesome family name.

A constant example of a controversial advertising is the underwear industry. It is virtually impossible to advertise undergarments and not offend somebody. Calvin Klein is constantly under fire for displaying underwear-clad people in his advertisements. The humorous part about him being controversial is that he is actually selling underwear. The probability of the merchandise actually appearing in the advertisement is expected. If consumers were never shown the product that was being advertised, in the advertisement, they would never be able to relate the product to the brand name. The only problem for this particular man is that he chooses to use very sexy models and provocative poses. However, this is particularly what he is trying to project on to his target market. It is very doubtful that Klein's target audience is children or older adults; he is trying to reach young men and women approximately ages twenty to thirty. This use of sex in advertising is supposed to make the buyer feel that they will be sexy if they buy Calvin Klein underwear. Calvin Klein had to pull an ad campaign that showed "children standing on a couch, grinning and clowning around" because critics complained that it was too sexy and could encourage pedophilia (Marks 716). What kind of people look at an advertisement of children and think about sex? That should be more controversial than the ad itself. Some people were asked what they thought about the ads and most agreed that they were "sweet and playful, and likening them to family snapshots" (Marks, 236). In contrast, companies such as Hanes are not considered to be controversial. However, they also have advertisements for undergarments, but because of the company name the half-naked models that are used in their advertisements do not offend critics. There was an advertisement done by Hanes that showed a man and a child, probably father and son, both playing in their underwear, yet there was probably not one critic that claimed this was encouraging sexual abuse or incest. An article in National Review says, "Calvin Klein had to yank a billboard from Times Square that showed toddlers romping in underwear. Coming from J.C. Penney, the ad would have seemed wholesome; coming from Klein, whose previous ad campaigns have featured young teens simulating heroin addiction and post-coital blues, it carried a whiff of degeneracy" ("Pedophilia"). This provides more evidence that only particular companies are being targeted in the accusations of being too sexy.

Calvin Klein has become an extremely well-known brand, and this is mostly because of his controversial ads. "By the end of the 1980's 'Calvin's' had become the generic term for sexy underwear" (Jobling). There are some critics that claim Klein's ad was a scheme to attract free publicity. "I can't believe this was done without the intent to cause controversy,'" says Diane Cook-Tench, director of the Ad Center at Virginia Commonwealth University in Richmond. Other critics claim that he wants to continue to be known for his controversy as a "bold innovator", and that he is trying to make it look like the critics are being narrow-minded prudes (Marks 237). This theory is probably true, as Klein's entire career is based on controversial ads. However, it could also be true that the children's underwear advertisement was not intended to be pornographic.

It is not just Calvin Klein that is catching media attention with the sexy advertising; there are many other companies that portray sex in just about every aspect of life. Victoria's Secret was unable to run an ad for cotton underwear because CBS claimed that "We see too much model and not enough underwear" (Seligmann). Herbal Essence shampoo has jumped onto the sexy advertising campaign with their "nearly orgasmic woman washing her hair." "Even Maidenform, a more conservative practitioner of underwear advertising, is expected to spice things up a bit when it introduces its first significant campaign in several years" (Sloan). Sex is everywhere in the marketing world and the trend seems to be on the rise. Critics of such advertisements need to be more aware of the current standards.

How can the advertising industry not portray such things as sex in their ads? People have become so accustomed to the sex that is shown on television programs that the advertising industry must now keep up to be able to compete. People choose to watch such programming knowing that the content is going to relate to sex, and marketers have to entice the viewers to relate their products to feeling sexy. "Marketers are merely taking a clue from the environment surrounding their ads" (Sloan). Even posters that are promoting breast-cancer research are resorting to using sex to promote their cause, yet no one "raised an eyebrow over Kenar model Linda Evangelista's stunningly bare poster" (Seligmann). This all just shows that people can be willing to accept sex in the advertisements; it just depends on which company is creating the ad.

Works Cited

Jobling, Paul. "Underexposed: Spectatorship and Pleasure in Men's Underwear Advertising in the Twentieth Century." *Paragraph.* Mar-Jul 2003. 147-62. *Academic Search Premier*. EBSCOhost. Chambers Library, Edmond, OK. 8 March 2005. <http://www.epnet.com>.

Marks, Alexandra. "Backlash to Advertising in Age of Anything Goes." *Stratagems*. Eds. Wayne Stein, et al. Texas: Fountainhead Press, 2007.

"Pedophilia Chic." *National Review*. April 1999. 14-16. *Academic Search Premier*. EBSCOhost. Chambers Library, Edmond, OK. 8 March 2005. <http://www.epnet.com>.

Seligmann, Jean and Jeanne Gordon. "Too Sexy for the Tube." *Newsweek.* July 1996. 65. *Academic Search Premier*. EBSCOhost. Chambers Library, Edmond, OK. 8 March 2005. <http://www.epnet.com>.

Sloan, Pat and Carol Krol. "Underwear Ads Caught in Bind Over Sex Appeal." *Advertising Age*. July 1996. 28. *Academic Search Premier*. EBSCOhost. Chambers Library, Edmond, OK. 8 March 2005. <http://www.epnet.com>.

PRO PEER REVIEW OUTLINE

Directions. Asking the right questions: As you ask these questions and answer them, be specific in your comments so as to be more helpful to the author. Provide details.

1. **Logos.** Comment on the quality and amount of the evidence or research conducted. Is it balanced or enough? Does the author need more? Why or why

not? Is the paper too logical or not logical enough? What else can you say about logos?

2. **Pathos.** Comment on the emotional appeals used in the paper. What can the author do to improve this appeal? Should there be less, more, or no emotions? Explain.
3. **Ethos.** Does the author use enough quality sources to improve the impact of the ethos of the paper? Is there a human element in the paper? What does the author need to do to improve the character aspect? Should the author add a personal story? Is the paper too personal? Should it be more logical?
4. **Call for Improvement.** Which aspects in the paper need to be revised or improved? Explain in detail.

Responding to Consumer and Capitalist Issues

Written Rhetoric: Opinion Papers, Arguments, and Research

1. Write a response to one of the essays in this section in which you argue the opposite point of view. Be sure to quote from the article.
2. Write an essay in which you explain how sexuality in advertising is ethical or unethical.
3. Super Bowl commercials are the most expensive commercials on television. Find out how much such commercials cost. Research whether these commercials are really worth it. Do company sales increase after showing the commercial? Are such commercials really so cost effective?
4. Beer commercials are some of the most entertaining commercials around. However, when we examine the ethical aspects of these commercials and the number of car accidents related to drinking and driving annually, should beer commercials be banned? Defend your point. Be sure to provide research.

Oral Rhetoric: Speeches, Lyrics, and Simulations

1. Is there a commercial that you hate or that you feel offended by? Write a protest speech to the creator of the ads. Try to use irony at certain points to emphasize your point. Be sure to describe aspects of the ad that you particularly dislike.
2. Watch an advertisement that uses a popular song. Write an essay on how the song enhances the advertisement.
3. In a *Truman Show*-like fashion, create a new reality television show examining the connection between our lives and advertising. Enact a moment from the show.

4. Create a drama where fictional characters from a beer commercial meet their counterparts in reality, e.g., someone from Mothers Against Drunk Drivers (MADD). As part of the simulation, show the original beer commercial/s where the characters come from.

Visual Rhetoric: Advertisement, Visuals, and Cinema

1. Go on the Internet and find a Super Bowl commercial that you like or dislike. Watch it several times. Describe what you liked about it and why it is a good or bad commercial.
2. Do advertisers today adhere to a code of ethics? Write an essay assessing the state of advertising today.
3. From the cinematic list, compare two similar films. What are some of the major similarities and some of the differences? Be sure to be specific.
4. Pick a film and write a parody of the film about consumerism or capitalism in a short story format.
5. The film *The Truman Show* was the ultimate reality television show which mixed truth and advertising in an ironic fashion. Watch the film and determine what its main argument or message is. Write a paper defending that argument. Research reality television shows and advertising associated with them.
6. Go to www.deviantart.com and search using the words "consumerism" and "advertisement." Save the images you find the most effective. Write an essay about the images. Include the images in your report.

WOVE Projects

1. Watch a film about consumerism or advertising, and write an essay about the main message of the film. How effective was the director? What were some of the weaknesses of the film? Then create a commercial spoof about the film and re-enact the commercial in front of the class. Or film the commercial and upload it to YouTube. Or create a radio ad of the commercial. Keep a blog recording the process of creating, enacting, and watching the commercial you created. Also interview students who watched the commercial and get their feedback. Finally, write an essay about your project.
2. Create your own WOVE project.

Electronic Rhetoric: The Emergent Media with Gaming

1. Go on the Internet and find a Super Bowl commercial that you like or dislike. Watch it several times. Describe what you liked about it and why it is a good or bad commercial.

2. Go to www.deviantart.com and search using the words "consumerism" and "advertisement." Save the images you find the most effective. Write an essay about the images. Include the images in your report.
3. How does the way we consume affect the environment? To find out, visit the online game **Consumer Consequences** at
   sustainability.publicradio.org/consumerconsequences
   What did you learn? Write a paper about your gaming experience and about how it made you think of the complexities of consumerism. What are some solutions that you can come up with?

Cinematic List

American Dreamz (2006, dir. Paul Weitz, 2006)
Battle Royale (Kinji Fukasaku, 2000)
Benny's Video (Michael Haneke, 1992)
Cache (Michael Haneke, 2005)
The Comeback (J. Clark Mathis, 2005)
Drawn Together (Dave Jeser, Matthew Silverstein, 2004)
Fast Food Nation (Richard Linklater, 2006)
Fight Club (David Fincher, 1999)
Games People Play (James Ronald Whitney, 2004)
The Insider (Michael Mann, 1999)
Man Bites Dog (Remy Balvaux, Andre Bonzel, Benoit Poelvoorde, 1993)
Nineteen Eighty-Four (Michael Radford, 1984)
Operation Good Guys (Ray Burdis, Dominic Anciano, 1997)
The Prize of Peril (Yves Boisset, 1983)
The Running Man (Paul Michael Glaser, 1987)
Series 7: The Contenders (Daniel Minihan, 2001)
Thank You for Smoking (Jason Reitman, 2005)
Tomb of the Werewolf (Fred Olen Ray, 2004)
The Truman Show (Peter Weir, 1998)
Wall Street (Oliver Stone, 1987)

Reality TV

American Idol (Simon Fuller, 2002)
The Apprentice (Mark Burnett, 2004)
Big Brother (Simon Hepworth, Helen Downing, 2000)
Queer Eye for the Straight Guy (David Collins, 2004)

"Welcome to the Suck"

From *Jarhead*

MOVIE POSTER APPEALS EXERCISE

"Leave No Man Behind"

from *Black Hawk Down*

"There Was a Time..."

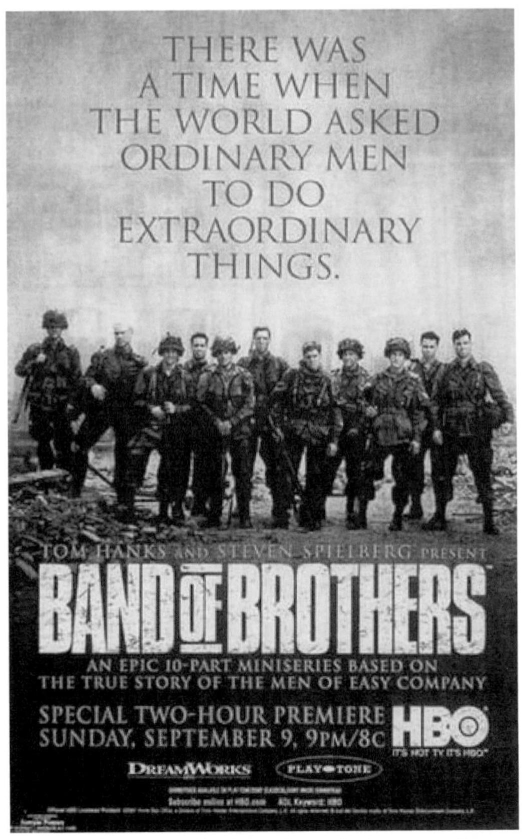

from *Band of Brothers (mini-series)*

Jarhead, Black Hawk Down, and Band of Brothers

Review the material on visual rhetoric. Look at the movie posters for *Jarhead*, *Black Hawk Down*, and *Band of Brothers*.

AFTER YOU READ: Analyze the Issues

1. Do these posters give you a positive or negative impression of war? What impressions are given of the soldiers?

2. If you have seen these films, discuss whether the poster reflects issues dealt with in the films. If you have not seen these films, discuss what you think the films will be about based on the poster.

AFTER YOU READ: Analyze the Rhetoric

1. How do the posters convey the appeals of ethos, pathos, and logos? Which are the stronger appeals that are used?
2. What are the common visual elements in these posters? What visual elements are different? How do these elements convey the theme and tone of the movies?
3. Are the images or text more persuasive? Balanced?

The Issues

As war remains a perennial issue, full of complexities, clashing nations continue to battle each other again and again. America, the greatest or currently the biggest military power, seems to find itself in military conflicts every couple of decades. What is the cost of such wars? The complexities of the issues of war can best be examined through a variety of perspectives: civilian, military, and political. Within the civilian viewpoints, movie posters are used to persuade people to see a film. What do such posters tell us about the film and about war in general? Do such posters glamorize violence and make the soldiers look heroic? Examine civilian viewpoints through graphic novels like *Maus* and *Barefoot Gen.* How does the visual representation match the textual narratives? How do lyrics tell the story of war? Is war simply about good over evil? Who is good and who is evil? Are the German and Japanese people to be blamed for World War II? Or do we blame the politicians? Or do we examine the historical realities? What are the real causes? Or do we focus on the effects of war?

When examining the voices of soldiers, what do they tell us? How is their perspective different? What did they sacrifice? How are they misunderstood? How do different writers examine different wars? Is each war different? What are some similarities? How does Tim O'Brien's approach differ from Anthony Swofford's telling of war, especially when one wrote about Vietnam and the other wrote about the Gulf War? How do politicians view the war differently?

More issues can be examined. Can wars be prevented? What can be learned from wars? Why are we doomed to repeat wars? What do wars tell us about ourselves? What religious factors contribute to war?

Ask the Right Questions

What should we ask when examining war and when reading about it?

Logos

What are some of the reasons for war?
How does one justify war?
Do these reasons change from war to war or are some of the reasons similar?
What type of evidence do authors use to prove their points?
Do the arguments seem logical?
What are some missing reasons?

Ethos

How does the voice change the message about war?
Is the message more important than who said it?
Do we value what generals and politicians say over what civilians and soldiers say?
Who do we believe the most?
Who is being protected?
Which sources are valid?
Does gender factor into voice?

Pathos

How do emotions play into the equation of war?
What emotions come to the top?
What types of sacrifice are allowed?
Is religion part of war?
What about morality?
Is war ever morally right?
Are there regrets about war?

Annotate the Text

In addition to paying attention to the text's use of logos, ethos, and pathos, annotate the readings as follows.

- Who is the writer's intended audience? Patriotic Americans? Non-violent Americans? All Americans? Others?
- Underline the main argument or summarize the key points in the margin.

- After reading a selection, write a brief overview commenting on the effectiveness of the organization of the message.
- Comment on the evidence provided. Was the evidence effective? Can you trust the source?
- Circle the weasel or buzz words such as *peace, brave, pride, manhood, honor, remember, blood, American, coward, nation, patriot, guilt,* and *aggression.*

Civilian Viewpoint

"Born in Hiroshima"

by Keiji Nakazawa (translated by Project Gen)
an excerpt from Barefoot Gen
(Graphic Novel)

Born in Hiroshima in 1939, Keiji Nakazawa wrote *Barefoot Gen*. Though a fictional manga (comic book) account, it is based on his own 1945 childhood experience of the nuclear bomb when he was seven. Everyone in his family died except his mother. In 1966, when his mother died and he returned to Hiroshima, he began to write about the effects of the A-bomb. One of his first works was "Struck by Black Rain." Publishers began to publish more of his works. Gen means "roots." Thus, the character is trying to understand the meanings or implications of Hiroshima. In 1983, it was made into an anime (animation.) In the following excerpt at one point, Mr. Pak carries Gen's mother to safety. The characters are just trying to survive the devastation when the reader is introduced to yet another complication.

AS YOU READ: Annotate

1. What is the main message of the narration?
2. Place a star by the panel that is the most effective.
3. Comment on the visual pathos in the margin.

COME ON, MAMA. LET'S GO-COME ON, MAMA -
No! No!
I'M GOING TO DIE WITH THEM!!
I'M GOING TO DIE WITH EVERYONE ELSE!!
CRACKLE
CRACKLE
W-W-WAAA! WA-A-A-A!! MAMA! MAMA!!

ROARRRR
CRRASH
RUN!
HELP!
A-A-A-G-H

RO~ARRRR

THANK YOU, MR. PAK....
I THINK WE'LL BE SAFE HERE. I'M GOING TO GO LOOK FOR MY FATHER.

......
I'M GLAD YOU'VE COME TO YOUR **SENSES**, MA'AM. YOU HAD ME **WORRIED**.

....
WHAT'LL WE DO **NOW**, MAMA?

NGH--!

UHHHHH... **IT HURTS**...!

MAMA! WHAT'S WRONG?
G-GEN... THE **BABY**... I'M **HAVING THE BABY**...

P-PAINS... L-LABOR PAINS--!
L-LABOR PAINS --?!

T-THERE'S NO DOCTOR ANYWHERE-- WHAT'LL WE DO?

AHHHHH... NGHH...

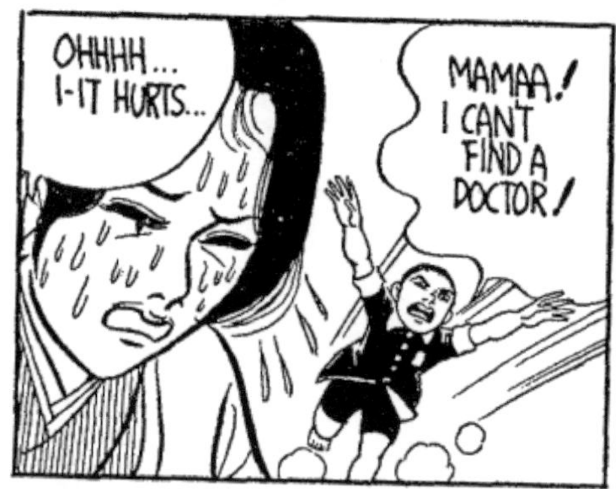
OHHHH... I-IT HURTS...
MAMAA! I CAN'T FIND A DOCTOR!

WHAT'LL WE DO?
I-IT'S NO WONDER, IN THIS CONFUSION...

GEN, YOU'LL HAVE TO DELIVER THE BABY...
M-ME? I CAN'T DO THAT!

PANT PANT
DO AS I SAY AND IT'LL BE ALL RIGHT.
GO GET SOME BEDDING, A BUCKET AND LOTS OF CLOTH FROM THOSE HOUSES OVER THERE...

F-FILL THE BUCKET FULL OF WATER, AND BRING SOME SCISSORS--

WHAT'RE THE SCISSORS FOR ?!
TO CUT THE UMBILICAL CORD. NOW HURRY!

G-G-GH
...

HANG ON, MAMA!
HANG ON!

AAAAA-AAAHHHH!

WAAAAAAH

PANT PANT

IT'S BORN!
THE BABY'S BORN, MAMA!

WAAHH! WAAHH!

PANT PANT!
HOLD THE BABY'S HEAD GENTLY AND WASH ITS BODY WITH WATER.
RIGHT!

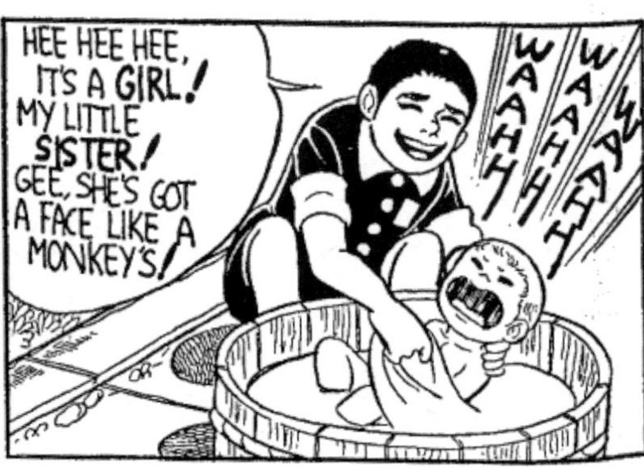
HEE HEE HEE, IT'S A GIRL! MY LITTLE SISTER! GEE, SHE'S GOT A FACE LIKE A MONKEY'S!
WAAHH
WAAHH

HEY THERE, TOMOKO! I JUST BROUGHT YOU INTO THE WORLD ALL BY MYSELF – I'M YOUR **BIG BROTHER**, SO YOU'D BETTER LISTEN TO ME...

WA-A WA-A
HURRY AND **GROW UP** SO WE CAN PLAY TOGETHER!

PAPA- EIKO- SHINJI- **LOOK!**
WE'VE GOT A NEW **LITTLE SISTER!!** SEE HOW HEALTHY SHE IS? SHE'S GOING TO BE BEAUTIFUL WHEN SHE GROWS UP... SHE'S...

SH- SHE'S...

W-A-A-A-A...

...Y-YOU'LL NEVER KNOW HER...

–LET ME HOLD HER, GEN...

REMEMBER THIS, TOMOKO! THIS IS WHAT TOOK YOUR FATHER, BROTHER AND SISTER FROM US... THIS IS WAR—

WHEN YOU GROW UP, YOU MUST NEVER LET THIS HAPPEN AGAIN!!

W-A-A-A...

AFTER YOU READ: Analyze the Issues

1. What does the birth of the baby symbolize?
2. How do the varied shapes of the word bubbles on different pages represent various states of pathos?

AFTER YOU READ: Analyze the Rhetoric

1. Is this graphic representation of Hiroshima too melodramatic? Explain.
2. Note the various sizes of the panels. What is the effect of having some panels larger than other panels?
3. Comment on the effectiveness or lack of effectiveness of the conclusion.

"Born in the U.S.A."

by Bruce Springsteen
(Lyrics)

Born in 1949, in Freehold, New Jersey, Bruce Springsteen is a famous singer, writer, and performer. He has won several Grammys during his career. He originally toured with the E Street band. He won an Academy Award for his song "Streets of Philadelphia" from the *Philadelphia* soundtrack. He continues to tour and record. Visit his site at www.brucespringsteen.net.

AS YOU READ: Annotate

1. Count in the margins the number of times the author uses the phrase "Born in the U.S.A."
2. Notice the use of rhyme. Draw lines and connect the words that rhyme.

Born down in a dead man's town
The first kick I took was when I hit the ground
You end up like a dog that's been beat too much
Till you spend half your life just covering up

Born in the U.S.A.
I was born in the U.S.A.
I was born in the U.S.A.
Born in the U.S.A.

Got in a little hometown jam
So they put a rifle in my hand
Sent me off to a foreign land
To go and kill the yellow man

Born in the U.S.A.
I was born in the U.S.A.
I was born in the U.S.A.
I was born in the U.S.A.
Born in the U.S.A.

Come back home to the refinery
Hiring man says "Son if it was up to me"
Went down to see my V.A. man
He said "Son, don't you understand"

I had a brother at Khe Sanh fighting off the Viet Cong
They're still there, he's all gone
He had a woman he loved in Saigon
I got a picture of him in her arms now

Down in the shadow of the penitentiary
Out by the gas fires of the refinery
I'm ten years burning down the road
Nowhere to run ain't got nowhere to go

Born in the U.S.A.
I was born in the U.S.A.
Born in the U.S.A.
I'm a long gone Daddy in the U.S.A.
Born in the U.S.A.
Born in the U.S.A.
Born in the U.S.A.
I'm a cool rocking Daddy in the U.S.A.

AFTER YOU READ OR LISTEN: Analyze the Issues

1. What is the main argument of the song?
2. Go on the Internet and look up the battle of Khe Sahn. When did it happen? Where is it located in the country?
3. Is the song anti-war, pro-war or neutral? Explain.

AFTER YOU READ OR LISTEN: Analyze the Rhetoric

1. How many times was the phrase, "Born in the U.S.A." mentioned? Why?
2. Comment on how the song is arranged.
3. If possible, listen to the song as Bruce Springsteen sings it. How does the music add to the meaning of the song? (Skip if you do not have access to the CD or an Internet version.)

"Dwight's Speech"

by Paul Lieberstein
(Teleplay from *The Office*)

Paul Lieberstein is an actor, writer and producer of the NBC comedy *The Office.* He portrays Toby Flenderson in the show. He has also been a producer and writer for *King of the Hill.* In this episode, co-worker Jim Halpert writes this speech for Dwight who has won Dunder-Mifflin Salesman of the Year. The speech is taken from a variety of revolutionary manifestoes by such figures as Karl Marx, Frederick Engels, Vladimir Lenin, and Benito Mussolini. Visually, Dwight looks like Hitler and Mussolini as he pounds his fists on the podium while delivering the following speech. By Paul Lieberstein, directed by Charles McDougall. *The Office*, Season 2, 17th episode, "Dwight's Speech" March 2, 2006.

AS YOU READ: Annotate

1. Place a star by the sections that are powerful.
2. Write "P" for pathos by those sections that are emotional.

> BLOOD ALONE MOVES THE WHEELS OF HISTORY! [pause]
>
> Have you ever asked yourselves in an hour of meditation—which everyone finds during the day —how long we have been striving for greatness? [bangs fist] Not only the years we've been at war—the war of work—but from the moment as a child, when we realize the world could be conquered. It has been a lifetime struggle [bangs fists again] a never-ending fight, I say to you [bangs again] and you will understand that it is a privilege to fight. WE ARE WARRIORS!

Salesmen of north-eastern Pennsylvania, I ask you once more rise and be worthy of this historical hour.

No revolution is worth anything unless it can defend itself. Some people will tell you salesman is a bad word. They'll conjure up images of used car dealers, and door to door charlatans. This is our duty to change their perception. I say, salesman—and women—of the world… unite! We must never acquiesce, for it is together… TOGETHER THAT WE PREVAIL. WE MUST NEVER CEDE CONTROL OF THE MOTHERLAND…

… FOR IT IS TOGETHER THAT WE PREVAIL!

AFTER YOU READ: Analyze the Issues

1. What is the key message of the speech?
2. Why is "blood" mentioned as part of the speech to salesmen?
3. What is your favorite section? Why?

AFTER YOU READ: Analyze the Rhetoric

1. Discuss the elements of humor in the speech.
2. How is the audience an important factor in the speech? Explain.
3. Why is banging the fist important for the speech?

"The War Prayer"

by Mark Twain
(Fiction)

Mark Twain or Samuel Langhorne Clemens was born in Florida, Missouri and became one of America's most famous writers. Though known for his humor, he was always critical of American politics. In 1905, Mark Twain (1835–1910) submitted this essay which was rejected by *Harper's Bazaar*. This satire stands as a protest against the Philippine-American Conflict (1899–1916). It was later published in 1923.

AS YOU READ: Annotate

1. Circle the following words, and any others you don't know, and write their meanings in the margins: *beseeching, fervid, supplication, benignant, ghastliness, smite,* and *contrite.*
2. Highlight and note the use of Biblical, or King James-like English. Circle words that could be found in a King James Bible.

It was a time of great and exalting excitement. The country was up in arms, the war was on, in every breast burned the holy fire of patriotism; the drums were beating, the bands playing, the toy pistols popping, the bunched firecrackers hissing and spluttering; on every hand and far down the receding and fading spread of roofs and balconies a fluttering wilderness of flags flashed in the sun; daily the young volunteers marched down the wide avenue gay and fine in their new uniforms, the proud fathers and mothers and sisters and sweethearts cheering them with voices choked with happy emotion as they swung by; nightly the packed mass meetings listened, panting, to patriot oratory which stirred the deepest deeps of their hearts, and which they interrupted at briefest intervals with cyclones of applause, the tears running down their cheeks the while; in the churches the pastors preached devotion to flag and country, and invoked the God of Battles beseeching His aid in our good cause in outpourings of fervid eloquence which moved every listener. It was indeed a glad and gracious time, and the half dozen rash spirits that ventured to disapprove of the war and cast a doubt upon its righteousness straightway got such a stern and angry warning that for their personal safety's sake they quickly shrank out of sight and offended no more in that way.

Sunday morning came—next day the battalions would leave for the front; the church was filled; the volunteers were there, their young faces alight with martial dreams—visions of the stern advance, the gathering momentum, the rushing charge, the flashing sabers, the flight of the foe, the tumult, the enveloping smoke, the fierce pursuit, the surrender! Then home from the war, bronzed heroes, welcomed, adored, submerged in golden seas of glory! With the volunteers sat their dear ones, proud, happy, and envied by the neighbors and friends who had no sons and brothers to send forth to the field of honor, there to win for the flag, or, failing, die the noblest of noble deaths. The service proceeded; a war chapter from the Old Testament was read; the first prayer was said; it was followed by an organ burst that shook the building, and with one impulse the house rose, with glowing eyes and beating hearts, and poured out that tremendous invocation

God the all-terrible! Thou who ordainest! Thunder thy clarion and lightning thy sword!

Then came the "long" prayer. None could remember the like of it for passionate pleading and moving and beautiful language. The burden of its supplication was, that an ever-merciful and benignant Father of us all would watch over our noble young soldiers, and aid, comfort, and encourage them in their patriotic work; bless them, shield them in the day of battle and the hour of peril, bear them in His mighty hand, make them strong and confident, invincible in the bloody onset; help them to crush the foe, grant to them and to their flag and country imperishable honor and glory—

An aged stranger entered and moved with slow and noiseless step up the main aisle, his eyes fixed upon the minister, his long body clothed in a robe that reached to his feet, his head bare, his white hair descending in a frothy cataract to his shoulders, his seamy face unnaturally pale, pale even to ghastliness. With all eyes following him and wondering, he made his silent way; without pausing, he ascended to the preacher's side and stood there waiting. With shut lids the preacher, unconscious of his presence, continued with his moving prayer, and at last finished it with the words, uttered in fervent appeal, "Bless our arms, grant us the victory, O Lord our God, Father and Protector of our land and flag!"

The stranger touched his arm, motioned him to step aside—which the startled minister did—and took his place. During some moments he surveyed the spellbound audience with solemn eyes, in which burned an uncanny light; then in a deep voice he said:

"I come from the Throne—bearing a message from Almighty God!" The words smote the house with a shock; if the stranger perceived it he gave no attention. "He has heard the prayer of His servant your shepherd, and will grant it if such shall be your desire after I, His messenger, shall have explained to you its import—that is to say, its full import. For it is like unto many of the prayers of men, in that it asks for more than he who utters it is aware of—except he pause and think.

"God's servant and yours has prayed his prayer. Has he paused and taken thought? Is it one prayer? No, it is two—one uttered, the other not. Both have reached the ear of Him Who heareth all supplications, the spoken and the unspoken. Ponder this—keep it in mind. If you would beseech a blessing upon yourself, beware! lest without intent you invoke a curse upon a neighbor at the same time. If you pray for the blessing of rain upon your crop which needs it, by that act you are possibly praying for a curse upon some neighbor's crop which may not need rain and can be injured by it.

"You have heard your servant's prayer—the uttered part of it. I am commissioned of God to put into words the other part of it—that part which the pastor—and also you in your hearts—fervently prayed silently. And ignorantly and unthinkingly? God grant that it was so! You heard these words: 'Grant us the victory, O Lord our God!' That is sufficient. The *whole* of the uttered prayer is compact into those pregnant words. Elaborations were not necessary. When you have prayed for victory you have prayed for many unmentioned results which follow victory—*must* follow it, cannot help but follow it. Upon the listening spirit of God fell also the unspoken part of the prayer. He commandeth me to put it into words. Listen!

"O Lord our Father, our young patriots, idols of our hearts, go forth to battle—be Thou near them! With them—in spirit—we also go forth from the sweet peace of our beloved firesides to smite the foe. O Lord our God, help us to tear their soldiers to bloody shreds with our shells; help us to cover their smiling fields with the pale forms of their patriot dead; help us to drown the thunder of the guns with the shrieks of their wounded, writhing in pain; help us to lay waste their humble homes with a hurricane of fire; help us to wring the hearts of their unoffending widows with unavailing grief; help us to turn them out roofless with little children to wander unfriended the wastes of their desolated land in rags and hunger and thirst, sports of the sun flames of summer and the icy winds of winter, broken in spirit, worn with travail, imploring Thee for the refuge of the grave and denied it—for our sakes who adore Thee, Lord, blast their hopes, blight their lives, protract their bitter pilgrimage, make heavy their steps, water their way with their tears, stain the white snow with the blood of their wounded feet! We ask it, in the spirit of love, of Him Who is the Source of Love, and Who is the ever-faithful refuge and friend of all that are sore beset and seek His aid with humble and contrite hearts. Amen.

(*After a pause.*) "Ye have prayed it; if ye still desire it, speak! The messenger of the Most High waits!"

It was believed afterward that the man was a lunatic, because there was no sense in what he said.

AFTER YOU READ: Analyze the Issues

1. What is the main message of the story?
2. How does the author support his message?
3. What effect does introducing the stranger have on the tale?
4. Do you agree that the man in the end was a lunatic?

AFTER YOU READ: Analyze the Rhetoric

1. What are some of the characteristics of Biblical English? Why is that important for this story?
2. The first paragraph is full of semi-colons. How many do you count in that first paragraph, and why does the writer use this technique throughout the story?
3. Note the repetition of "help us" used throughout the final war prayer. What is the effect of repetition here? Why do preachers often use such means of repetition?
4. The tone of the prayer changes drastically for the audience in the last section. How so?
5. What is satire? What does this story satirize?

"My Heart's Content: Thirty Years of One Man's Truth are Up for Reconsideration"

by Pat Conroy
(Memoir)

Pat Conroy was born in 1945. His father was a career military officer, and Conroy attended the Citadel in Charleston. His first novel, *The Great Santini*, was published in 1976 and later made into a film. Conroy is known for weaving personal experiences into his writing, and this novel explored his conflicted relationship with his father. *The Lords of Discipline* and *The Prince of Tides*, his next two novels, were also made into films. The excerpt below is from Conroy's memoir, *My Losing Season*, which was published in 2002 and explores the lives of his basketball teammates at the Citadel.

AS YOU READ: Annotate

1. This essay is a comparison between Pat Conroy's life and that of his classmate. As you read, start a list of Conroy's actions and a second list of Kroboth's actions.
2. As you read, highlight the connotative words. Make a note of what emotion the word makes you feel.
3. At the end of the essay, write the claim of the argument.

The true things always ambush me on the road and take me by surprise when I am drifting down the light of placid days, careless about flanks and rearguard actions. I was not looking for a true thing to come upon me in the state of New Jersey. Nothing has ever happened to me in New Jersey. But came it did, and it came to stay.

In the past four years I have been interviewing my teammates on the 1966-67 basketball team at the Citadel for a book I'm writing. For the most part, this has been like buying back a part of my past that I had mislaid or shut out of my life. At first I thought I was writing about being young and frisky and able to run up and down a court all day long, but lately I realized I came to this book because I needed to come to grips with being middle-aged and having ripened into a gray-haired man you could not trust to handle the ball on a fast break.

When I visited my old teammate Al Kroboth's house in New Jersey, I spent the first hours quizzing him about his memories of games and practices and the screams of coaches that had echoed in field houses more than 30 years before. Al had been a splendid forward-center for the Citadel; at 6 feet 5 inches and carrying 220 pounds, he played with indefatigable energy and enthusiasm. For most of his senior year, he led the nation in field-goal percentage, with UCLA center Lew Alcindor hot on his trail. Al was a battler and a brawler and a scrapper from the day he first stepped in as a Green Weenie as a sophomore to the day he graduated. After we talked basketball, we came to a subject I dreaded to bring up with Al, but which lay between us and would not lie still.

"Al, you know I was a draft dodger and antiwar demonstrator."

"That's what I heard, Conroy," Al said. "I have nothing against what you did, but I did what I thought was right."

"Tell me about Vietnam, big Al. Tell me what happened to you," I said.

On his seventh mission as a navigator in an A-6 for Major Leonard Robertson, Al was getting ready to deliver their payload when the fighter-bomber was hit by enemy fire. Though Al has no memory of it, he punched out somewhere in the middle of the ill-fated dive and lost consciousness. He doesn't know if he was unconscious for six hours or six days, nor does he know what happened to Major Robertson (whose name is engraved on the Wall in Washington and on the MIA bracelet Al wears).

When Al awoke, he couldn't move. A Viet Cong soldier held an AK-47 to his head. His back and his neck were broken, and he had shattered his left scapula in the fall. When he was well enough to get to his feet (he still can't recall how much time had passed), two armed Viet Cong led Al from the jungles of South Vietnam to a prison in Hanoi. The journey took three months. Al Kroboth walked barefooted through the most impassable terrain in Vietnam, and he did it sometimes in the dead of night. He bathed when it rained, and he slept in bomb craters with his two Viet Cong captors. As they moved farther north, infections began to erupt on his body, and his legs were covered with leeches picked up while crossing the rice paddies.

At the very time of Al's walk, I had a small role in organizing the only antiwar demonstration ever held in Beaufort, South Carolina, the home of Parris Island and the Marine Corps Air Station. In a Marine Corps town at that time, it was difficult to come up with a quorum of people who had even minor disagreements about the Vietnam War. But my small group managed to attract a crowd of about 150 to Beaufort's waterfront. With my mother and my wife on either side of me, we listened to the featured speaker, Dr. Howard Levy, suggest to the very few young enlisted marines present that if they get sent to Vietnam, here's how they can help end this war: Roll a grenade under your officer's bunk when he's asleep in his tent. It's called fragging and is becoming more and more popular with the ground troops who know this war is bullshit. I was enraged by the suggestion. At that very moment my father, a marine officer, was asleep in Vietnam. But in 1972, at the age of 27, I thought I was serving America's interests by pointing out what massive flaws and miscalculations and corruptions had led her to conduct a ground war in Southeast Asia.

In the meantime, Al and his captors had finally arrived in the North, and the Viet Cong traded him to North Vietnamese soldiers for the final leg of the trip to Hanoi. Many times when they stopped to rest for the night, the local villagers tried to kill him. His captors wired his hands behind his back at night, so he trained himself to sleep in the center of huts when the villagers began sticking knives and bayonets into the thin walls. Following the U.S. air raids, old women would come into the huts to excrete on him and yank out hunks of his hair. After the nightmare journey of his walk north, Al was relieved when his guards finally delivered him to the POW camp in Hanoi and the cell door locked behind him.

It was at the camp that Al began to die. He threw up every meal he ate and before long was misidentified as the oldest American soldier in the prison because his appearance was so gaunt and skeletal. But the extraordinary camaraderie among fellow prisoners that sprang up in all the POW camps caught fire in Al, and did so in time to save his life.

When I was demonstrating in America against Nixon and the Christmas bombings in Hanoi, Al and his fellow prisoners were holding hands under the full fury of those bombings, singing "God Bless America." It was those bombs that convinced Hanoi they would do well to release the American POWs, including my college teammate. When he told me about the C-141 landing in Hanoi to pick up the prisoners, Al said he felt no emotion, none at all, until he saw the giant American flag painted on the plane's tail. I stopped writing as Al wept over the memory of that flag on that plane, on that morning, during that time in the life of America.

It was that same long night, after listening to Al's story, that I began to make judgments about how I had conducted myself during the Vietnam War. In the darkness of the sleeping Kroboth household, lying in the third-floor guest bedroom, I began to assess my role as a citizen in the '60s, when my country called my name and I shot her the bird. Unlike the stupid boys who wrapped themselves in Viet Cong flags and burned the American one, I knew how to demonstrate against the war without flirting with treason or astonishingly bad taste. I had come directly from the warrior culture of this country and I knew how to act. But in the 25 years that have passed since South Vietnam fell, I have immersed myself in the study of totalitarianism during the unspeakable century we just left behind. I have questioned survivors of Auschwitz and Bergen-Belsen, talked to Italians who told me tales of the Nazi occupation, French partisans who had counted German tanks in the forests of Normandy, and officers who survived the Bataan Death March. I quiz journalists returning from wars in Bosnia, the Sudan, the Congo, Angola, Indonesia, Guatemala, San Salvador, Chile, Northern Ireland, Algeria. As I lay sleepless, I realized I'd done all this research to better understand my country. I now revere words like democracy, freedom, the right to vote, and the grandeur of the extraordinary vision of the founding fathers. Do I see America's flaws? Of course. But I now can honor her basic, incorruptible virtues, the ones that let me walk the streets screaming my ass off that my country had no idea what it was doing in South Vietnam. My country let me scream to my heart's content—the same country that produced both Al Kroboth and me.

Now, at this moment in New Jersey, I come to a conclusion about my actions as a young man when Vietnam was a dirty word to me. I wish I'd led a platoon of marines in Vietnam. I would like to think I would have trained my troops well and that the Viet Cong would have had their hands full if they entered a firefight with us. From the day of my birth, I was programmed to enter the Marine Corps. I was the son of a marine fighter pilot, and I had grown up on marine bases where I had watched the men of the corps perform simulated war games in the forests of my childhood. That a novelist and poet bloomed darkly in the house of Santini strikes me as a remarkable irony. My mother and father had raised me to be an Al Kroboth, and during the Vietnam era they watched in horror as I metamorphosed into another breed of fanatic entirely. I understand now that I should have protested the war after my return from Vietnam, after I had done my duty for my country. I have come to a conclusion about my country that I knew then in my bones but lacked the courage to act on: America is good enough to die for even when she is wrong.

I looked for some conclusion, a summation of this trip to my teammate's house. I wanted to come to the single right thing, a true thing that I may not like but that I could live with. After hearing Al Kroboth's story of his walk across Vietnam and his brutal imprisonment in the North, I found myself passing harrowing, remorseless judgment on myself. I had not turned out to be the man I had once envisioned myself to be. I thought I would be the kind of man that America could point to and say, "There. That's the guy. That's the one who got it right. The whole package. The one I can depend on." It had never once occurred to me that I would find myself in the position I did on that night in Al Kroboth's house in Roselle, New Jersey: an American coward spending the night with an American hero.

AFTER YOU READ: Analyze the Issues

1. What is a draft dodger? What are your feelings about draft dodgers? Does Al Kroboth's story change your feelings? Why or why not?
2. What is your definition of courage? Conroy wanted to be an example of American courage during the Vietnam War. Was he? Look at the list of actions you created. Do you agree with Conroy's judgment of his actions and Kroboth's?
3. How does time change how we view our actions? Can you think of something you did that you thought was right at the time, but now realize was wrong? What led you to act as you did? What might have led young men to become draft dodgers or volunteers?

AFTER YOU READ: Analyze the Rhetoric

1. What is the claim of the argument? What rhetorical devices does Conroy use to support his claim?
2. Look at the connotative words you highlighted. Does Conroy use connotative words to make you feel a specific way about his actions? About Kroboth's? How do these words contribute to the argument.
3. How does the organization of presenting Kroboth's experiences first affect your understanding of the claim? Would the essay have been effective if Conroy had given his experiences first?

"Time Flies"

by Art Spiegelman
excerpt from Maus II, A Survivor's Tale
(Graphic Novel)

Born in Stockholm, on February 15, 1948, Art Spiegelman grew up in Rego Park, New York. He worked for Topps Gum Company for nearly twenty years, illustrating cards and other products, such as Garbage Pail Kids and Wacky Packages. In 1979 he founded *RAW* magazine, an experimental graphic periodical. Episodes of *Maus* were printed in *RAW*. His *Maus* (1986) and *Maus II* (1991) defies categorization. Though it appears to be a comic book, its content and visual graphics concerning the holocaust have caused many readers to reevaluate what they define as comics. *Maus* is termed a graphic novel and even won a Pulitzer.

AS YOU READ: Annotate

1. Circle any words you don't know and write their meanings in the margins.
2. Place a star by the panels you think are effective.
3. Summarize the main points in the margins.

Time flies...

Vladek died of congestive heart failure on August 18, 1982...
Françoise and I stayed with him in the Catskills back in August 1979.

Vladek started working as a tinman in Auschwitz in the spring of 1944...
I started working on this page at the very end of February 1987.

In May 1987 Françoise and I are expecting a baby...
Between May 16, 1944, and May 24, 1944 over 100,000 Hungarian Jews were gassed in Auschwitz...

In September 1986, after 8 years of work, the first part of MAUS was published. It was a critical and commercial success.

At least fifteen foreign editions are coming out. I've gotten 4 serious offers to turn my book into a T.V. special or movie. (I don't wanna.)
In May 1968 my mother killed herself. (She left no note.)
Lately I've been feeling depressed.
Alright Mr. Spiegelman... We're ready to shoot!...

Tell our viewers what message you want them to get from your book?

a message? I dunno...

I-I never thought of reducing it to a message. I mean, I wasn't trying to CONVINCE anybody of anything. I just wanted—
Your book is being translated into German...

Many younger Germans have had it up to HERE with Holocaust stories. These things happened before they were even born. Why should THEY feel guilty?
Who am I to say?...

But a lot of the corporations that flourished in Nazi Germany are richer than ever. I dunno... Maybe EVERYONE has to feel guilty. EVERYONE! FOREVER!
Okay... Let's talk about Israel...

If your book was about ISRAELI Jews, what kind of animal would you draw?
I have no idea. ...porcupines?
Excuse me...

Artie, baby. Check out this licensing deal. You get 50% of the profits. We'll make a million. Your dad would be proud!
HUH?
MAUS
YOU'VE READ THE BOOK
NOW BUY THE VEST!

So, whaddya WANT— a bigger percentage? Hey, we can talk.
I want... ABSOLUTION. No... No... I want... I want... my MOMMY!

Could you tell our audience if drawing MAUS was cathartic? Do you feel better now?
WAH!

whew. they're gone.
Sometimes I just don't feel like a functioning adult.

I can't believe I'm gonna be a father in a couple of months.*
My father's ghost still hangs over me.
*NADJA MOULY SPIEGELMAN. BORN 5/13/87

It's 9:30 p.m. already. I've gotta head uptown for my appointment with Pavel.
Pavel is my shrink. He sees patients at night.

He's a Czech Jew, a survivor of Terezin and Auschwitz. I see him once a week.

His place is overrun with stray dogs and cats.
Hi Art. Come on in.
Can I mention this, or does it completely louse up my metaphor?

So, how are you feeling?
Completely messed up. I mean, things couldn't be going better with my "career," or at home, but mostly I feel like crying.

I can't work. My time is being sucked up by interviews and business propositions I can't deal with.

But even when I'm left alone I'm totally **BLOCKED.** Instead of working on my book I just lie on my couch for hours and stare at a small grease spot on the upholstery.

FRAMED PHOTO OF PET CAT. REALLY!

Somehow my arguments with my father have lost a little of their urgency... and Auschwitz just seems too scary to think about... so I just *LIE* there...

It sounds like you're feeling remorse-maybe you believe you exposed your father to ridicule.

Maybe. But I tried to be fair and still show how angry I felt.

Even so, EVERY boy when he's little, looks up to his father.

That sounds true, but its hard for me to remember..

Mainly I remember ARGUING with him... and being told that I couldn't do anything as well as he could.

And now that you're becoming successful, you feel bad about proving your father wrong.

No matter what I accomplish, it doesn't seem like much compared to surviving Auschwitz.

But you weren't in Auschwitz...you were in Rego Park.

Maybe your father needed to show that he was always right-that he could always SURVIVE-because he felt GUILTY about surviving.

maybe.

And he took his guilt out on YOU, where it was safe... on the REAL survivor.

um...Tell me, do YOU feel any guilt about surviving the camps?

No... just sadness.

AFTER YOU READ: Analyze the Issues

1. What did Spiegelman and Pavel say about guilt?
2. How does the author reply when asked if younger Germans should feel guilty about the Holocaust?
3. Why is the author wearing a mouse mask? Explain.

AFTER YOU READ: Analyze the Rhetoric

1. What effect does black and white have on "seeing" the Holocaust? Steven Spielberg also chose black and white for his film on the same topic, *Schindler's List.* If you have seen the film, compare the effects of using black and white to focus on a tragic moment in history.
2. This work is now considered a classic among graphic novels. What effect does using this medium have on the reader when compared to other mediums like film or literature?
3. In the story of Spiegelman's father in Auschwitz, the Jews are portrayed as mice and Nazi Germans are cats. Does this visual metaphor work? Why or why not?

Soldier's Viewpoint

"We Band of Brothers" St. Crispin's Day Speech

by William Shakespeare
excerpt from Henry V
(Drama)

Born in Stratford-upon-Avon, William Shakespeare (1564–1616) is considered the greatest dramatist in the English language. He was also a poet and actor who would marry Anne Hathaway. Not only was he successful as a dramatist, but Shakespeare was also a successful businessman who became one of the owners of the Globe theater. In this famous speech, the English are about to fight the French, who possess greater numbers at the Battle of Agincourt (1415). In the end, they would be victorious.

AS YOU READ: Annotate

1. Place a star by the section you like the most.
2. Circle any word you do not know and write their meanings in the margin, including *enow* and *covetous.*
3. Look up Saint Crispin and write who he is in the margins.

Enter the KING

WESTMORELAND
O that we now had here
But one ten thousand of those men in England
That do no work to-day!

KING HENRY V
What's he that wishes so?
My cousin Westmoreland? No, my fair cousin;
If we are mark'd to die, we are enow
To do our country loss; and if to live,
The fewer men, the greater share of honour.
God's will! I pray thee, wish not one man more.
By Jove, I am not covetous for gold,
Nor care I who doth feed upon my cost;
It yearns me not if men my garments wear;
Such outward things dwell not in my desires.
But if it be a sin to covet honour,
I am the most offending soul alive.
No, faith, my coz, wish not a man from England.
God's peace! I would not lose so great an honour
As one man more methinks would share from me
For the best hope I have. O, do not wish one more!
Rather proclaim it, Westmoreland, through my host,
That he which hath no stomach to this fight,
Let him depart; his passport shall be made,
And crowns for convoy put into his purse;
We would not die in that man's company
That fears his fellowship to die with us.
This day is call'd the feast of Crispian.
He that outlives this day, and comes safe home,
Will stand a tip-toe when this day is nam'd,
And rouse him at the name of Crispian.
He that shall live this day, and see old age,
Will yearly on the vigil feast his neighbours,

And say 'To-morrow is Saint Crispian.'
Then will he strip his sleeve and show his scars,
And say 'These wounds I had on Crispian's day.'
Old men forget; yet all shall be forgot,
But he'll remember, with advantages,
What feats he did that day. Then shall our names,
Familiar in his mouth as household words—
Harry the King, Bedford and Exeter,
Warwick and Talbot, Salisbury and Gloucester—
Be in their flowing cups freshly rememb'red.
This story shall the good man teach his son;
And Crispin Crispian shall ne'er go by,
From this day to the ending of the world,
But we in it shall be remembered—
We few, we happy few, we band of brothers;
For he to-day that sheds his blood with me
Shall be my brother; be he ne'er so vile,
This day shall gentle his condition;
And gentlemen in England now-a-bed
Shall think themselves accurs'd they were not here,
And hold their manhoods cheap whiles any speaks
That fought with us upon Saint Crispin's day.

AFTER YOU READ: Analyze the Issues

1. What does the line "I am the most offending soul alive" mean?
2. How does the speech build up its power?
3. How do the circumstances and the audience affect the power of the speech?

AFTER YOU READ OR LISTEN: Analyze the Rhetoric

1. Read the speech silently and aloud. Comment on the effect of reading it aloud. Watch a film version of the speech if you can and compare it to the textual or oral versions.
2. Why are references to religion so important to this speech?

General George S. Patton's "Blood and Guts Speech"

Somewhere in England, June 5th, 1944
(Speech)

Born in 1998 in San Gabriel, California, George S. Patton was raised in a military family and would graduate from West Point. He was a bigger than life figure wearing custom uniforms and an ivory handled pistol. He married Beatrice Ayer. He became an Olympic athlete. He was part of General John Pershing's military campaigns chasing "Pancho" Villa into Mexico. During World War I, he found success as part of the new Tank Corps. Once America entered World War II, Patton was prepared and would make his mark. George C. Scott would win an Academy Award for his portrayal of Patton in 1970. Be sure to compare the following speech with the opening rendition found in the film.

AS YOU READ: Annotate

1. Place a star by the section that is the most effective to you.
2. Write "P" for Pathos by those sections that are emotional.
3. Circle the following words and any other words you don't know and write their meaning in the margin: *bilious, treads, Huns*, and *goo.*

Be seated.

Now, I want you to remember that no bastard ever won a war by dying for his country. He won it by making the other poor dumb bastard die for his country. Men, all this stuff you've heard about America not wanting to fight, wanting to stay out of the war, is a lot of horse dung. Americans traditionally love to fight. All real Americans love the sting of battle. When you were kids, you all admired the champion marble shooter, the fastest runner, the big league ball player, the toughest boxer. Americans love a winner and will not tolerate a loser. Americans play to win all the time. I wouldn't give a hoot in hell for a man who lost and laughed. That's why Americans have never lost and will never lose a war. Because the very thought of losing is hateful to Americans.

Now, an Army is a team. It lives, eats, sleeps, fights as a team. This individuality stuff is a bunch of crap. The bilious bastards who wrote that stuff about individuality for the *Saturday Evening Post* don't know anything more about real battle than they do about fornicating.

We have the finest food and equipment, the best spirit and the best men in the world. You know, by God I actually pity those poor bastards we're going up against. By God, I do. We're not just going to shoot the bastards, we're going to cut out their living guts and use them to grease the treads of our tanks. We're going to murder those lousy Hun bastards by the bushel.

Now, some of you boys, I know, are wondering whether or not you'll chicken out under fire. Don't worry about it. I can assure you that you will all do your duty. The Nazis are the enemy. Wade into them. Spill their blood. Shoot them in the belly. When you put your hand into a bunch of goo that a moment before was your best friend's face, you'll know what to do.

Now there's another thing I want you to remember. I don't want to get any messages saying that we are holding our position. We're not holding anything. Let the Hun do that. We are advancing constantly and we're not interested in holding onto anything except the enemy. We're going to hold onto him by the nose and we're going to kick him in the ass. We're going to kick the hell out of him all the time and we're gonna go through him like crap through a goose.

There's one thing that you men will be able to say when you get back home. And you may thank God for it. Thirty years from now when you're sitting around your fireside with your grandson on your knee and he asks you what did you do in the great World War II, you won't have to say, "Well, I shoveled shit in Louisiana."

Alright now, you sons-of-bitches, you know how I feel. Oh, and I will be proud to lead you wonderful guys into battle—anytime, anywhere.

That's all.

AFTER YOU READ: Analyze the Issues

1. What is the main argument of the speech?
2. Was the speech effective?
3. Do you agree with the statement: "All Americans love the sting of battle"? Why or why not?

AFTER YOU READ: Analyze the Rhetoric

1. Who is the audience?
2. What about the language? Is it appropriate?
3. Why does the general call the audience "sons of bitches"?
4. Would this type of speech work today?

"The Things They Carried"

by Tim O'Brien
(Fiction)

Born in Austin, Texas on October 1, 1946, Tim O'Brien graduated in 1968 from Macalester College with a BA in political science. Drafted into the Vietnam War, he served in the war as a grunt and became disillusioned when he returned and started to write about his time there. He won the National Book Award in fiction for *Going After Cacciato*. "The Things They Carried" is often anthologized in readers.

AS YOU READ: Annotate

1. What does the title cause you to anticipate in the content of the article?
2. Does the information in the headnote indicate that the author is knowledgeable on the topic? Biased?
3. Annotate to describe the writing style of the author—highlight words and phrases that affect the style/tone.
4. Read between the lines—Is the writing logical? Any fallacies?
5. Circle the following words, and any others you don't know, and write their meanings in the margins: *topography, SOP, KIA*, and *grunt.*

First Lieutenant Jimmy Cross carried letters from a girl named Martha, a junior at Mount Sebastian College in New Jersey. They were not love letters, but Lieutenant Cross was hoping, so he kept them folded in plastic at the bottom of his rucksack. In the late afternoon, after a day's march, he would dig his foxhole, wash his hands under a canteen, unwrap the letters, hold them with the tips of his fingers, and spend the last hour of light pretending. He would imagine romantic camping trips into the White Mountain in New Hampshire. He would sometimes taste the envelope flaps, knowing her tongue had been there. More than anything, he wanted Martha to love him as he loved her, but the letters were mostly chatty; elusive on the matter of love. She was a virgin, he was almost sure. She was an English major at Mount Sebastian, and she wrote beautifully about her professors and roommates and midterm exams, about her respect for Chaucer and her great affection for Virginia Woolf. She often quoted lines of poetry; she never mentioned the war, except to say, Jimmy, take care of yourself. The letters weighed 10 ounces. They were signed Love, Martha, but Lieutenant Cross understood that Love was only a way of signing and did not mean what he sometimes pretended it meant. At dusk, he would carefully return the letters to his rucksack. Slowly, a bit distracted, he would get up and move among his men, checking the perimeter, then at full dark he would return to his hole and watch the night and wonder if Martha was a virgin.

The things they carried were largely determined by necessity. Among the necessities or near-necessities were P-38 can openers, pocket knives, heat tabs, wristwatches, dog tags, mosquito repellent, chewing gum, candy, cigarettes, salt tablets, packets of Kool-Aid lighters, matches, sewing kits, Military Payment Certificates, C rations, and two or three canteens of water. Together, these items weighed between 15 and 20 pounds, depending upon a man's habits or rate of metabolism. Henry Dobbins, who was a big man, carried extra rations; he was especially fond of canned peaches in heavy syrup over pound cake. Dave Jensen, who practiced field hygiene, carried a toothbrush, dental floss, and several hotel-sized bars of soap he'd stolen on R&R in Sydney, Australia. Ted Lavender, who was scared, carried tranquilizers until he was shot in the head outside the village of Than Khe in mid-April. By necessity, and because it was SOP, they all carried steel helmets that weighed 5 pounds including the liner and camouflage cover. They carried the standard fatigue jackets and trousers. Very few carried underwear. On their feet they carried jungle boots—2. 1 pounds—and Dave Jensen carried three pairs of socks and a can of Dr. Scholl's foot powder as a precaution against trench foot. Until he was shot, Ted Lavender carried six or seven ounces of premium dope, which for him was a necessity. Mitchell Sanders, the RTO, carried condoms. Norman Bowker carried a diary. Rat Kiley carried comic books. Kiowa, a devout Baptist, carried an illustrated New Testament that had been presented to him by his father, who taught Sunday school in Oklahoma City, Oklahoma. As a hedge against bad times, however, Kiowa also carried his grandmother's distrust of the white man, his grandfather's old hunting hatchet. Necessity dictated. Because the land was mined and booby-trapped, it was SOP for each man to carry a steel-centered, nylon-covered flak jacket, which weighed 6.7 pounds, but which on hot days seemed much heavier. Because you could die so quickly, each man carried at least one large compress bandage, usually in the helmet band for easy access. Because the nights were cold, and because the monsoons were wet, each carried a green plastic poncho that could be used as a raincoat or groundsheet or makeshift tent. With its quilted liner, the poncho weighed almost two pounds, but it was worth every ounce. In April, for instance, when Ted Lavender was shot, they used his poncho to wrap him up, then to carry him across the paddy, then to lift him into the chopper that took him away.

They were called legs or grunts.

To carry something was to "hump" it, as when Lieutenant Jimmy Cross humped his love for Martha up the hills and through the swamps. In its intransitive form, "to hump" meant "to walk," or "to march," but it implied burdens far beyond the intransitive.

Almost everyone humped photographs. In his wallet, Lieutenant Cross carried two photographs of Martha. The first was a Kodacolor snapshot signed "Love," though he knew better. She stood against a brick wall. Her eyes were gray and neutral, her lips slightly open as she stared straight-on at the camera. At night, sometimes,

Lieutenant Cross wondered who had taken the picture, because he knew she had boyfriends, because he loved her so much, and because he could see the shadow of the picture-taker spreading out against the brick wall. The second photograph had been clipped from the 1968 Mount Sebastian yearbook. It was an action shot—women's volleyball—and Martha was bent horizontal to the floor, reaching, the palms of her hands in sharp focus, the tongue taut, the expression frank and competitive. There was no visible sweat. She wore white gym shorts. Her legs, he thought, were almost certainly the legs of a virgin, dry and without hair, the left knee cocked and carrying her entire weight, which was just over one hundred pounds. Lieutenant Cross remembered touching that left knee. A dark theater, he remembered, and the movie was *Bonnie and Clyde*, and Martha wore a tweed skirt, and during the final scene, when he touched her knee, she turned and looked at him in a sad, sober way that made him pull his hand back, but he would always remember the feel of the tweed skirt and the knee beneath it and the sound of the gunfire that killed Bonnie and Clyde, how embarrassing it was, how slow and oppressive. He remembered kissing her good night at the dorm door. Right then, he thought, he should've done something brave. He should've carried her up the stairs to her room and tied her to the bed and touched that left knee all night long. He should've risked it. Whenever he looked at the photographs, he thought of new things he should've done.

What they carried was partly a function of rank, partly of field specialty.

As a first lieutenant and platoon leader, Jimmy Cross carried a compass, maps, code books, binoculars, and a .45-caliber pistol that weighed 2.9 pounds fully loaded. He carried a strobe light and the responsibility for the lives of his men.

As an RTO, Mitchell Sanders carried the PRC-25 radio, a killer, 26 pounds with its battery.

As a medic, Rat Kiley carried a canvas satchel filled with morphine and plasma and malaria tablets and surgical tape and comic books and all the things a medic must carry, including M&M's for especially bad wounds, for a total weight of nearly 20 pounds.

As a big man, therefore a machine gunner, Henry Dobbins carried the M-60, which weighed 23 pounds unloaded, but which was almost always loaded. In addition, Dobbins carried between 10 and 15 pounds of ammunition draped in belts across his chest and shoulders.

As PFCs or Spec 4s, most of them were common grunts and carried the standard M-16 gas-operated assault rifle. The weapon weighed 7.5 pounds unloaded, 8.2 pounds with its full 20-round magazine. Depending on numerous factors, such as topography and psychology, the riflemen carried anywhere from 12 to 20 magazines, usually in cloth bandoliers, adding on another 8.4 pounds at minimum, 14 pounds at maximum. When it was available, they also carried M-16 maintenance gear—rods and steel brushes and swabs and tubes of LSA oil—all of which weighed about a pound. Among the grunts, some carried the M-79 grenade launcher, 5.9

pounds unloaded, a reasonably light weapon except for the ammunition, which was heavy. A single round weighed 10 ounces. The typical load was 25 rounds. But Ted Lavender, who was scared, carried 34 rounds when he was shot and killed outside Than Khe, and he went down under an exceptional burden, more than 20 pounds of ammunition, plus the flak jacket and helmet and rations and water and toilet paper and tranquilizers and all the rest, plus the unweighed fear. He was dead weight. There was no twitching or flopping. Kiowa, who saw it happen, said it was like watching a rock fall, or a big sandbag or something—just boom, then down—not like the movies where the dead guy rolls around and does fancy spins and goes ass over teakettle—not like that, Kiowa said, the poor bastard just flat-fuck fell. Boom. Down. Nothing else. It was a bright morning in mid-April. Lieutenant Cross felt the pain. He blamed himself. They stripped off Lavender's canteens and ammo, all the heavy things, and Rat Kiley said the obvious, the guy's dead, and Mitchell Sanders used his radio to report one U.S. KIA and to request a chopper. Then they wrapped Lavender in his poncho. They carried him out to a dry paddy, established security, and sat smoking the dead man's dope until the chopper came. Lieutenant Cross kept to himself. He pictured Martha's smooth young face, thinking he loved her more than anything, more than his men, and now Ted Lavender was dead because he loved her so much and could not stop thinking about her. 'When the dustoff arrived, they carried Lavender aboard. Afterward they burned Than Khe. They marched until dusk, then dug their holes, and at night Kiowa kept explaining how you had to be there, how fast it was, how the poor guy just dropped like so much concrete. Boom-down, he said. Like cement.

In addition to the three standard weapons—the M-60, M-16, and M-79—they carried whatever presented itself, whatever seemed appropriate as a means of killing or staying alive. They carried catch-as-catch-can. At various times, in various situations, they carried M-44s and CAR-15s and Swedish Ks and grease guns and captured AK-47s and Chi-Coms and RPGs and Simonov carbines and black market Uzis and .38-caliber Smith & Wesson handguns and 66 mm LAWs and shotguns and silencers and blackjacks and bayonets and C-4 plastic explosives. Lee Strunk carried a slingshot; a weapon of last resort, he called it. Mitchell Sanders carried brass knuckles. Kiowa carried his grandfather's feathered hatchet. Every third or fourth man carried a Claymore antipersonnel mine—3.5 pounds with its firing device. They all carried fragmentation grenades—14 ounces each. They all carried at least one M-18 colored smoke grenade— 24 ounces. Some carried CS or tear gas grenades. Some carried white phosphorus grenades. They carried all they could bear, and then some, including a silent awe for the terrible power of the things they carried.

In the first week of April, before Lavender died, Lieutenant Jimmy Cross received a good-luck charm from Martha. It was a simple pebble, an ounce at most. Smooth to the touch, it was a milky white color with flecks of orange and violet, oval-shaped, like a miniature egg. In the accompanying letter, Martha wrote that she had found the pebble on the Jersey shoreline, precisely where the land touched water at high tide, where things came together but also separated. It was this separate-but-together quality, she wrote, that had inspired her to pick up the pebble and to carry it in her breast pocket for several days, where it seemed weightless, and then to send it through the mail by air, as a token of her truest feelings for him. Lieutenant Cross found this romantic. But he wondered what her truest feelings were, exactly, and what she meant by separate-but-together. He wondered how the tides and waves had come into play on that afternoon along the Jersey shoreline when Martha saw the pebble and bent down to rescue it from geology; He imagined bare feet. Martha was a poet, with the poet's sensibilities, and her feet would be brown and bare, the toenails unpainted, the eyes chilly and somber like the ocean in March, and though it was painful, he wondered who had been with her that afternoon. He imagined a pair of shadows moving along the strip of sand where things came together but also separated. It was phantom jealousy, he knew, but he couldn't help himself. He loved her so much. On the march, through the hot days of early April, he carried the pebble in his mouth, turning it with his tongue, tasting sea salt and moisture. His mind wandered. He had difficulty keeping his attention on the war. On occasion he would yell at his men to spread out the column, to keep their eyes open, but then he would slip away into daydreams, just pretending, walking barefoot along the Jersey shore, with Martha, carrying nothing. He would feel himself rising. Sun and waves and gentle winds, all love and lightness.

What they carried varied by mission.

When a mission took them to the mountains, they carried mosquito netting, machetes, canvas tarps, and extra bug juice.

If a mission seemed especially hazardous, or if it involved a place they knew to be bad, they carried everything they could. In certain heavily mined AOs, where the land was dense with Toe Poppers and Bouncing Betties, they took turns humping a 28-pound mine detector. With its headphones and big sensing plate, the equipment was a stress on the lower back and shoulders, awkward to handle, often useless because of the shrapnel in the earth, but they carry it anyway, partly for safety; partly for the illusion of safety.

On ambush, or other night missions, they carried peculiar little odds and ends.

Kiowa always took along his New Testament and a pair of moccasins for silence. Dave Jensen carried night-sight vitamins high in carotene. Lee Strunk carried his slingshot; ammo, he claimed, would never be a problem. Rat Kiley carried brandy and M&M's candy. Until he was shot, Ted Lavender carried the starlight scope, which weighed 6.3 pounds with its aluminum carrying case. Henry Dobbins carried his girlfriend's pantyhose wrapped around his neck as a comforter. They all carried ghosts. When dark came, they would move out single file across the meadows and paddies to their ambush coordinates, where they would quietly set up the Claymores and lie down and spend the night waiting.

Other missions were more complicated and required special equipment. In mid-April, it was their mission to search out and destroy the elaborate tunnel complexes in the Than Khe area south of Chu Lai. To blow the tunnels, they carried one-pound blocks of pentrite high explosives, four blocks to a man, 68 pounds in all. They carried wiring, detonators, and battery-powered clackers. Dave Jensen carried earplugs. Most often, before blowing the tunnels, they were ordered by higher command to search them, which was considered bad news, but by and large they just shrugged and carried out orders. Because he was a big man, Henry Dobbins was excused from tunnel duty. The others would draw numbers. Before Lavender died there were 17 men in the platoon, and whoever drew the number 17 would strip off his gear and crawl in headfirst with a flashlight and Lieutenant Cross's .45-caliber pistol. The rest of them would fan out as security. They would sit down or kneel, not facing the hole, listening to the ground beneath them, imagining cobwebs and ghosts, whatever was down there—the tunnel walls squeezing in—how the flashlight seemed impossibly heavy in the hand and how it was tunnel vision in the very strictest sense, compression in all ways, even time, and how you had to wiggle in—ass and elbows—a swallowed-up feeling—and how you found yourself worrying about odd things: Will your flashlight go dead? Do rats carry rabies? If you screamed, how far would the sound carry? Would your buddies hear it? Would they have the courage to drag you out? In some respects, though not many, the waiting was worse than the tunnel itself. Imagination was a killer.

On April 16, when Lee Strunk drew the number 17, he laughed and muttered something and went down quickly. The morning was hot and very still. Not good, Kiowa said. He looked at the tunnel opening, then out across a dry paddy toward the village of Than Khe. Nothing moved. No clouds or birds or people. As they waited, the men smoked and drank Kool-Aid, not talking much, feeling sympathy for Lee Strunk but also feeling the luck of the draw. You win some, you lose some, said Mitchell Sanders, and sometimes you settle for a rain check. It was a tired line and no one laughed.

Henry Dobbins ate a tropical chocolate bar. Ted Lavender popped a tranquilizer and went off to pee.

After five minutes, Lieutenant Jimmy Cross moved to the tunnel, leaned down, and examined the darkness. Trouble, he thought—a cave-in maybe. And then suddenly, without willing it, he was thinking about Martha. The stresses and fractures, the quick-collapse, the two of them buried alive under all that weight. Dense, crushing love. Kneeling, watching the hole, he tried to concentrate on Lee Strunk and the war, all the dangers, but his love was too much for him, he felt paralyzed, he wanted to sleep inside her lungs and breathe her blood and be smothered. He wanted her to be a virgin and not a virgin, all at once. He wanted to know her. Intimate secrets: 'Why poetry? Why so sad? Why that grayness in her eyes? Why so alone? Not lonely, just alone—riding her bike across campus or sitting off by herself in the cafeteria—even dancing, she danced alone—and it was the aloneness that filled him with love. He remembered telling her that one evening. How she nodded and looked away. And how, later, when he kissed her, she received the kiss without returning it, her eyes wide open, not afraid, not a virgin's eyes, just flat and uninvolved.

Lieutenant Cross gazed at the tunnel. But he was not there. He was buried with Martha under the white sand at the Jersey shore. They were pressed together, and the pebble in his mouth was her tongue. He was smiling. Vaguely, he was aware of how quiet the day was, the sullen paddies, yet he could not bring himself to worry about matters of security He was beyond that. He was just a kid at war, in love. He was twenty-four years old. He couldn't help it.

A few moments later Lee Strunk crawled out of the tunnel. He came up grinning, filthy but alive. Lieutenant Cross nodded and closed his eyes while the others clapped Strunk on the back and made jokes about rising from the dead.

Worms, Rat Kiley said. Right out of the grave. Fuckin' zombie.

The men laughed. They all felt great relief.

Spook City, said Mitchell Sanders.

Lee Strunk made a funny ghost sound, a kind of moaning, yet very happy, and right then, when Strunk made that high happy moaning sound, when he went *Ahhooooo*, right then Ted Lavender was shot in the head on his way back from peeing.

He lay with his mouth open. The teeth were broken. There was a swollen black bruise under his left eye. The cheekbone was gone. Oh shit, Rat Kiley said, the guy's dead. The guy's dead, he kept saying, which seemed profound—the guy's dead. I mean really.

The things they carried were determined to some extent by superstition. Lieutenant Cross carried his good-luck pebble. Dave Jensen carried a rabbit's foot. Norman Bowker, otherwise a very gentle person, carried a thumb that had been presented to him as a gift by Mitchell Sanders. The thumb was dark brown, rubbery to the touch, and weighed four ounces at most. It had been cut from a VC corpse, a boy of fifteen or sixteen. They'd found him at the bottom of an irrigation ditch, badly burned, flies in his mouth and eyes. The boy wore black shorts and sandals. At the time of his death he had been carrying a pouch of rice, a rifle, and three magazines of ammunition.

You want my opinion, Mitchell Sanders said, there's a definite moral here.

He put his hand on the dead boy's wrist. He was quiet for a time, as if counting a pulse, then he patted the stomach, almost affectionately, and used Kiowa's hunting hatchet to remove the thumb.

Henry Dobbins asked what the moral was.

Moral?

You know. *Moral.*

Sanders wrapped the thumb in toilet paper and handed it across to Norman Bowker. There was no blood. Smiling, he kicked the boy's head, watched the flies scatter, and said, It's like with that old TV show—*Paladin*. Have gun, will travel.

Henry Dobbins thought about it.

Yeah, well, he finally said. I don't see no moral.

There it *is*, man.

Fuck off.

They carried USO stationery and pencils and pens. They carried Sterno, safety pins, trip flares, signal flares, spools of wire, razor blades, chewing tobacco, liberated joss sticks and statuettes of the smiling Buddha, candles, grease pencils, *The Stars and Stripes*, fingernail clippers, Psy Ops leaflets, bush hats, bolos, and much more. Twice a week, when the resupply choppers came in, they carried hot chow in green mermite cans and large canvas bags filled with iced beer and soda pop. They carried plastic water containers, each with a two-gallon capacity; Mitchell Sanders carried a set of starched tiger fatigues for special occasions. Henry Dobbins carried Black Flag insecticide. Dave Jensen carried empty sandbags that could be filled at night for added protection. Lee Strunk carried tanning lotion. Some things they carried in common. Taking turns, they carried the big PRC-77 scrambler radio, which weighed 30 pounds with its battery. They shared the weight of memory. They took up what others could no longer bear. Often, they carried each other, the wounded or weak. They carried infections. They carried chess sets, basketballs, Vietnamese-English dictionaries, insignia of rank, Bronze Stars and Purple Hearts, plastic cards imprinted with the Code of Conduct. They carried diseases, among them malaria and dysentery. They carried lice and ringworm and leeches and paddy algae and various rots and molds. They carried the land itself—Vietnam, the place, the soil—a powdery orange-red dust that covered their boots and fatigues and faces. They carried the sky. The whole atmosphere, they carried it, the humidity; the monsoons, the stink of fungus and decay, all of it, they carried gravity. They moved like mules. By daylight they took sniper fire, at night they were mortared, but it was not battle, it was just the endless march, village to village, without purpose, nothing won or lost. They marched for the sake of the march. They plodded along slowly, dumbly, leaning forward against the heat, unthinking, all blood and bone, simple grunts, soldiering with their legs, toiling up the hills and down into the paddies and across the rivers and up again and down, just humping, one step and then the next and then another, but no volition, no will, because it was automatic, it was anatomy, and the war was entirely a matter of posture and carriage, the hump was everything, a kind of inertia, a kind of emptiness, a dullness of desire and intellect and conscience and hope and human sensibility. Their principles were in their feet. Their calculations were biological. They had no sense of strategy or mission. They searched the villages without knowing what to look for, not caring, kicking over jars of rice, frisking children and old men, blowing tunnels, sometimes setting fires and sometimes not, then forming up and moving on to the next village, then other villages, where it would always be the same. They carried their own lives. The pressures were enormous. In the heat of early afternoon, they would remove their helmets and flak jackets, walking bare, which was dangerous but which helped ease the strain. They would often discard things along the route of the march. Purely for comfort, they would throw away rations, blow their Claymores and grenades, no matter, because by nightfall the resupply choppers would arrive with more of the same, then a day or two later still more, fresh watermelons and crates of ammunition and sunglasses and woolen sweaters—the resources were stunning— sparklers for the Fourth of July, colored eggs for Easter—it was the great American war chest—the fruits of science, the smokestacks, the canneries, the arsenals at Hartford, the Minnesota forests, the machine shops, the vast fields of corn and wheat—they carried like freight trains; they carried it on their backs and shoulders—and for all the ambiguities of Vietnam, all the mysteries and unknowns, there was at least the single abiding certainty that they would never be at a loss for things to carry.

After the chopper took Lavender away, Lieutenant Jimmy Cross led his men into the village of Than Khe. They burned everything. They shot chickens and dogs, they trashed the village well, they called in artillery and watched the wreckage, then they marched for several hours through the hot afternoon, and then at dusk, while Kiowa explained how Lavender died, Lieutenant Cross found himself trembling.

He tried not to cry. With his entrenching tool, which weighed five pounds, he began digging a hole in the earth.

He felt shame. He hated himself. He had loved Martha more than his men, and as a consequence Lavender was now dead, and this was something he would have to carry like a stone in his stomach for the rest of the war.

All he could do was dig. He used his entrenching tool like an ax, slashing, feeling both love and hate, and then later, when it was full dark, he sat at the bottom of his foxhole and wept. It went on for a long while. In part, he was grieving for Ted Lavender, but mostly it was for Martha, and for himself, because she belonged to another world, which was not quite real, and because she was a junior at Mount Sebastian College in New Jersey, a poet and a virgin and uninvolved, and because he realized she did not love him and never would.

Like cement, Kiowa whispered in the dark. I swear to God—boom, down. Not a word.

I've heard this, said Norman Bowker.

A pisser, you know? Still zipping himself up. Zapped while zipping.

All right, fine. That's enough.

Yeah, but you had to see it, the guy just—

I *heard*, man. Cement. So why not shut the fuck *up*?

Kiowa shook his head sadly and glanced over at the hole where Lieutenant Jimmy Cross sat watching the night. The air was thick and wet. A warm dense fog had settled over the paddies and there was the stillness that precedes rain.

After a time Kiowa sighed.

One thing for sure, he said. The lieutenant's in some deep hurt. I mean that crying jag—the way he was carrying on—it wasn't fake or anything, it was real heavy-duty hurt. The man cares.

Sure, Norman Bowker said.

Say what you want, the man does care.

We all got problems.

Not Lavender.

No, I guess not, Bowker said. Do me a favor, though.

Shut up?

That's a smart Indian. Shut up.

Shrugging, Kiowa pulled off his boots. He wanted to say more, just to lighten up his sleep, but instead he opened his New Testament and arranged it beneath his head as a pillow. The fog made things seem hollow and unattached. He tried not to think about Ted Lavender, but then he was thinking how fast it was, no drama, down and dead, and how it was hard to feel anything except surprise. It seemed un-Christian. He wished he could find some great sadness, or even anger, but the emotion wasn't there and he couldn't make it happen. Mostly he felt pleased to be alive. He liked the smell of the New Testament under his cheek, the leather and ink and paper and glue, whatever the chemicals were. He liked hearing the sounds of night. Even his fatigue, it felt fine, the stiff muscles and the prickly awareness of his own body, a floating feeling. He enjoyed not being dead. Lying there, Kiowa admired Lieutenant Jimmy Cross's capacity for grief. He wanted to share the man's pain, he wanted to care as Jimmy Cross cared. And yet when he closed his eyes, all he could think was Boom-down, and all he could feel was the pleasure of having his boots off and the fog curling in around him and the damp soil and the Bible smells and the plush comfort of night.

After a moment Norman Bowker sat up in the dark.

What the hell, he said. You want to talk, *talk*. Tell it to me.

Forget it.

No, man, go on. One thing I hate, it's a silent Indian.

For the most part they carried themselves with poise, a kind of dignity now and then, however, there were times of panic, when they squealed or wanted to squeal but couldn't, when they twitched and made moaning sounds and covered their heads and said Dear Jesus and flopped around on the earth and fired their weapons blindly and cringed and sobbed and begged for the noise to stop and went wild and made stupid promises to themselves and to God and to their mothers and fathers, hoping not to die. In different ways, it happened to all of them. Afterward, when the firing ended, they would blink and peek up. They would touch their bodies, feeling shame, then quickly hiding it. They would force themselves to stand. As if in slow motion, frame by frame, the world would take on the old logic—absolute silence, then the wind, then sunlight, then voices. It was the burden of being alive. Awkwardly, the men would reassemble themselves, first in private, then in groups, becoming soldiers again. They would repair the leaks in their eyes. They would check for casualties, call in dustoffs, light cigarettes, try to smile, clear their throats and spit and begin cleaning their weapons. After a time someone would shake his head and say, No lie, I almost shit my pants, and someone else would laugh, which meant it was bad, yes, but the guy had obviously not shit his pants, it wasn't that bad, and in any case nobody would ever do such a thing and then go ahead and talk about it. They would squint into the dense, oppressive sunlight. For a few moments, perhaps, they would fall silent, lighting a joint and tracking its passage from man to man, inhaling, holding in the humiliation. Scary stuff, one of them might say. But then someone else would grin or flick his eyebrows and say, Roger-dodger, almost cut me a new asshole, *almost*.

There were numerous such poses. Some carried themselves with a sort of wistful resignation, others with pride or stiff soldierly discipline or good humor or macho zeal. They were afraid of dying but they were even more afraid to show it.

They found jokes to tell.

They used a hard vocabulary to contain the terrible softness. *Greased* they'd say. *Offed, lit up, zapped while zipping*. It wasn't cruelty, just stage presence. They were actors. When someone died, it wasn't quite dying, because in a curious way it seemed scripted, and because they had their lines mostly memorized, irony mixed with tragedy, and because they called it by other names, as if to encyst and destroy the reality of death itself. They kicked corpses. They cut off thumbs. They talked grunt lingo. They told stories about Ted Lavender's supply of tranquilizers, how the poor guy didn't feel a thing, how incredibly tranquil he was.

There's a moral here, said Mitchell Sanders.

They were waiting for Lavender's chopper, smoking the dead man's dope.

The moral's pretty obvious, Sanders said, and winked. Stay away from drugs. No joke, they'll ruin your day every time.

Cute, said Henry Dobbins.

Mind blower, get it? Talk about wiggy. Nothing left, just blood and brains.

They made themselves laugh.

There it is, they'd say. Over and over—there it is, my friend, there it is—as if the repetition itself were an act of poise, a balance between crazy and almost crazy, knowing without going, there it is, which meant be cool, let it ride, because Oh yeah, man, you can't change what can't be changed, there it is, there it absolutely and positively and fucking well *is*.

They were tough.

They carried all the emotional baggage of men who might die. Grief, terror, love, longing—these were intangibles, but the intangibles had their own mass and specific gravity, they had tangible weight. They carried shameful memories. They carried the common secret of cowardice barely restrained, the instinct to run or freeze or hide, and in many respects this was the heaviest burden of all, for it could never be put down, it required perfect balance and perfect posture. They carried their reputations. They carried the soldier's greatest fear, which was the fear of blushing. Men killed, and died, because they were embarrassed not to. It was what had brought them to the war in the first place, nothing positive, no dreams of glory or honor, just to avoid the blush of dishonor. They died so as not to die of embarrassment. They crawled into tunnels and walked point and advanced under fire. Each morning, despite the unknowns, they made their legs move. They endured. They kept humping. They did not submit to the obvious alternative, which was simply to close the eyes and fall. So easy, really. Go limp and tumble to the ground and let the muscles unwind and not speak and not budge until your buddies picked you up and lifted you into the chopper that would roar and dip its nose and carry you off to the world. A mere matter of falling, yet no one ever fell. It was not courage, exactly; the object was not valor. Rather, they were too frightened to be cowards.

By and large they carried these things inside, maintaining the masks of composure. They sneered at sick call. They spoke bitterly about guys who had found release by shooting off their own toes or fingers. Pussies, they'd say. Candy-asses. It was fierce, mocking talk, with only a trace of envy or awe, but even so the image played itself out behind their eyes.

They imagined the muzzle against flesh. So easy: squeeze the trigger and blow away a toe. They imagined it. They imagined the quick, sweet pain, then the evacuation to Japan, then a hospital with warm beds and cute geisha nurses.

And they dreamed of freedom birds.

At night, on guard, staring into the dark, they were carried away by jumbo jets. They felt the rush of takeoff. *Gone!* they yelled. And then velocity—wings and engines—a smiling stewardess—but it was more than a plane, it was a real bird, a big sleek silver bird with feathers and talons and high screeching. They were flying. The weights fell off; there was nothing to bear. They laughed and held on tight, feeling the cold slap of wind and altitude, soaring, thinking *It's over, I'm gone!*—they were naked, they were light and free—it was all lightness, bright and fast and buoyant, light as light, a helium buzz in the brain, a giddy bubbling in the lungs as they were taken up over the clouds and the war, beyond duty, beyond gravity and mortification and global entanglements—*Sin loi!* they yelled. *I'm sorry, motherfuckers, but I'm out of it, I'm goofed, I'm on a space cruise, I'm gone!*—and it was a restful, unencumbered sensation, just riding the light waves, sailing that big silver freedom bird over the mountains and oceans, over America, over the farms and great sleeping cities and cemeteries and highways and the golden arches of McDonald's, it was flight, a kind of fleeing, a kind of falling, falling higher and higher, spinning off the edge of the earth and beyond the sun and through the vast, silent vacuum where there were no burdens and where everything weighed exactly nothing—*Gone!* they screamed. *I'm sorry but I'm gone!*— and so at night, not quite dreaming, they gave themselves over to lightness, they were carried, they were purely borne.

On the morning after Ted Lavender died, First Lieutenant Jimmy Cross crouched at the bottom of his foxhole and burned Martha's letters. Then he burned the two photographs. There was a steady rain falling, which made it difficult, but he used heat tabs and Sterno to build a small fire, screening it with his body, holding the photographs over the tight blue flame with the tips of his fingers.

He realized it was only a gesture. Stupid, he thought. Sentimental, too, but mostly just stupid.

Lavender was dead. You couldn't burn the blame.

Besides, the letters were in his head. And even now, without photographs, Lieutenant Cross could see Martha playing volleyball in her white gym shorts and yellow T-shirt. He could see her moving in the rain.

When the fire died out, Lieutenant Cross pulled his poncho over his shoulders and ate breakfast from a can.

There was no great mystery; he decided.

In those burned letters Martha had never mentioned the war, except to say, Jimmy, take care of yourself. She wasn't involved. She signed the letters Love, but it wasn't love, and all the fine lines and technicalities did not matter. Virginity was no longer an issue. He hated her. Yes, he did. He hated her. Love, too, but it was a hard, hating kind of love.

The morning came up wet and blurry. Everything seemed part of everything else, the fog and Martha and the deepening rain.

He was a soldier, after all.

Half smiling, Lieutenant Jimmy Cross took out his maps. He shook his head hard, as if to clear it, then bent forward and began planning the day's march. In ten minutes, or maybe twenty, he would rouse the men and they would pack up and head west, where the maps showed the country to be green and inviting. They would do what they had always done. The rain might add some weight, but otherwise it would be one more day layered upon all the other days.

He was realistic about it. There was that new hardness in his stomach. He loved her but he hated her.

No more fantasies, he told himself.

Henceforth, when he thought about Martha, it would be only to think that she belonged elsewhere. He would shut down the daydreams. This was not Mount Sebastian, it was another world, where there were no pretty poems or mid-term exams, a place where men died because of carelessness and gross stupidity. Kiowa was right. Boom-down, and you were dead, never partly dead.

Briefly, in the rain, Lieutenant Cross saw Martha's gray eyes gazing back at him.

He understood.

It was very sad, he thought. The things men carried inside. The things men did or felt they had to do.

He almost nodded at her, but didn't.

Instead he went back to his maps. He was now determined to perform his duties firmly and without negligence. It wouldn't help Lavender, he knew that, but from this point on he would comport himself as an officer. He would dispose of his good-luck pebble. Swallow it, maybe, or use Lee trunk's slingshot, or just drop it along the trail. On the march he would impose strict field discipline. He would be careful to send out flank security, to prevent straggling or bunching up, to keep his troops moving at the proper pace and at the proper interval. He would insist on clean weapons. He would confiscate the remainder of Lavender's dope. Later in the day, perhaps, he would call the men together and speak to them plainly. He would accept the blame for what had happened to Ted Lavender. He would be a man about it. He would look them in the eyes, keeping his chin level, and he would issue the new SOPs in a calm, impersonal tone of voice, a lieutenant's voice, leaving no room for argument or discussion. Commencing immediately, he'd tell them, they would no longer abandon equipment along the route of march. They would police up their acts. They would get their shit together, and keep it together, and maintain it neatly and in good working order.

He would not tolerate laxity. He would show strength, distancing himself.

Among the men there would be grumbling, of course, and maybe worse, because their days would seem longer and their loads heavier, but Lieutenant Jimmy Cross reminded himself that his obligation was not to be loved but to lead. He would dispense with love; it was not now a factor. And if anyone quarreled or complained, he would simply tighten his lips and arrange his shoulders in the correct command posture. He might give a curt little nod. Or he might not. He might just shrug and say Carry on, then they would saddle up and form into a column and move out toward the villages west of Than Khe.

AFTER YOU READ: Analyze the Issues

1. What is the main idea?
2. Describe the main characters' response to their environment.
3. War is often romanticized. How does this story represent or disprove the romanticized ideas associated with war?

AFTER YOU READ: Analyze the Rhetoric

1. Discuss how the reading used *ethos.*
2. What are some examples of *pathos*?
3. Examine how the narration is organized.
4. Discuss the various burdens of the men in the platoon. What bearing does this have on the story?

"Why I Went to the War"

by Terry Farish
(Essay)

Novelist Terry Farish has spent the last forty years chronicling her time as a Red Cross volunteer in Vietnam. Her two novels *Flower Shadows* and *If The Tiger* both explore experiences in Cambodian refugee camps. Farish has an MA in writing and literature from Antioch College and an MLS from California State, Fullerton. This essay is posted on the PBS Web site as part of *The American Experience: Vietnam on Line*.

AS YOU READ: Annotate

1. Underline the reasons Farish went to the Vietnam War and note whether they were emotional, logical, or authoritarian reasons.
2. Beside each example/detail the author gives to support her argument, note whether it is a positive or negative example/detail.
3. At the end of the essay, write the claim of the argument in the margin.

I went to Vietnam because it was so much a part of the culture I lived in. I went to a women's college in Texas not far from the primary helicopter school at Fort Wolters. Angel, my friend, married a W.O.C., a warrant officer candidate. The W.O.C. I dated was later killed.

I went, also, because of my mother. Her brother brought home his war buddy—who became my father—from World War II. They had both won Purple Hearts and from that time my mother held military service in esteem. My most vivid childhood memory is of my mother crying in pride for Eisenhower at the Republican National Convention. The band's patriotic music gave her chills of excitement and passion. I remember the woman with the powerful voice who began the roll call of the states, and my mother said "Alabama" the way the woman said "Alabama." Later sometimes my mother would say the names of various states in the woman's voice when she was trying not to be sad.

My mother and my father tell his war stories together. My father says, "I was in Northern Africa in the war." And my mother says, "He was with Patton. You remember him." My mother thinks of war in conjunction with its protocols, the Geneva Convention and the respective roles of combatants and noncombatants.

When I said I was going to Vietnam, my father said he hoped I wasn't going to be hanging around with the officers like the Donut Dollies did in World War II. He grinned. When I left they were proud. They were the only parents in Houston they knew who could say their daughter was in Vietnam.

I went with my mother's passion for serving. I was at Cu Chi in an eight-girl unit and we took recreation programs out to fire support bases. I couldn't work enough. I took any run they'd give me, even Sunday runs if a unit called and said they had men in. We worked in pairs, traveling by chopper since the roads weren't secure, and were often stranded in a place because there was contact—fighting—or heavy rain and a chopper couldn't come back for us.

We spent so much time in the field. When I was brand new in country, I stayed ten hours on Meade, a fire support base in the center of an A.R.V.N. base camp (Armed Forces of Vietnam). It was all artillery. There were seven men to a gun and every guy had a dog or a monkey. We moved from gun to gun talking. One of the soldiers told me he was twenty-one that day. It wasn't uncommon to turn twenty-one over there, but I told the mess sergeant and he dug up a stubby candle and put it in a piece of cake and when the soldier came through the mess line we sang happy birthday to him. Soon I'd be seeing men we programmed to in 12th EVAC, the hospital, but it always took a while to remember which fire support base I knew him from, and which guy with the monkey or the puppy he was.

I learned the men's war, hanging out with them waiting for choppers. I listened to war stories. We girls seemed innocent to the soldiers and they were chivalrous and offered us their bunkers and candles if the choppers never came. Some men hated us for being there, we didn't have any business in this place. Some men were grateful. A lot of them wanted to talk. They were angry. They said they were only there as targets to bring Charlie out. And when Charlie came out they'd bring down artillery on him for the body count. I heard about fragging.

Later I got so angry. I didn't like General's Mess when we were required to get dressed up to go to on Sunday nights. My father didn't have to worry about my hanging out with the officers. The bravado over body count at General's Mess rang false to me, though the general was kind to us and talked about his family.

On Sunday mornings we had staff meetings. We'd still be in our bathrobes and our hair in curlers and we'd sit under the umbrella we ordered from Sears and sometimes we'd have to wait for a chopper to stop hovering above us to go on with the meeting. I remember hoping a unit would call and we could get clearance and go out.

The protocols of war were liquid in Vietnam. It wasn't my mother's war. It felt amorphous. It rained and rained. I didn't know at 21 what could happen to the W.O.C.s I'd dated back home in Texas, or how sorrow, for so many, could endure.

AFTER YOU READ: Analyze the Issues

1. Is this essay an argument for going to war, or for staying home?
2. Are any of the arguments ones that only a woman could/would make? Which ones?

3. Which reasons, emotional, logical or authoritarian, seemed most persuasive to you?
4. Were the male soldiers' feelings about the women being in Vietnam justified? Why would some be chivalrous and others angry?
5. What is the meaning of the final paragraph? Does it contradict or support the rest of the essay?

AFTER YOU READ: Analyze the Rhetoric

1. Which example/detail is the most memorable? Why?
2. What sense imagery does Farish use?
3. How does Farish organize her argument?

"Vietnam War Films as War Porn"

by Anthony Swofford
Excerpt from Jarhead: A Marine's Chronicle of the Gulf War and Other Battles
(Memoir)

Anthony Swofford served in the U.S. Marine Corps Surveillance and Target Acquisition/Scout-Sniper platoon during the Gulf War. After the war, he pursued his education at the University of California, Davis and the University of Iowa's Writer's Workshop. Swofford's memoir, *Jarhead*, was published in 2003 and explores his experiences in the 1990 Gulf War. The memoir was made into a movie in 2005. Swofford's fiction and non-fiction has appeared in *The New York Times*, *Harper's* and *The Iowa Review*.

AS YOU READ: Annotate

1. Note in the margins your impressions of the films Swofford lists that you have seen. Then match your comments with his impressions.
2. Put a star by any passages you find offensive.
3. Highlight the passages that affect you the most.

After hearing the news of imminent war in the Middle East, we march in a platoon formation to the base barber and get fresh high-and-tight haircuts. And no wonder we call ourselves jarheads—our heads look just like jars.

Then we send a few guys downtown to rent all of the war movies they can get their hands on. They also buy a hell of a lot of beer. For three days we sit in our rec room and drink all of the beer and watch all of those damn movies, and we yell *Semper fi* and we head-butt and beat the crap out of each other and we get off on the various visions of carnage and violence and deceit, the raping and killing and pillaging. We concentrate on the Vietnam films because it's the most recent war, and the successes and failures of that war helped write our training manuals. We rewind and review famous scenes, such as Rober Duvall and his helicopter gunships during *Apocalypse Now*, and in the same film Martin Sheen floating up the fake Vietnamese Congo; we watch as Willem Dafoe gets shot by a friend and left on the battlefield in *Platoon*; and we listen closely as Matthew Modine talks trash to a streetwalker in *Full Metal Jacket*. We watch again the ragged, tired, burnt-out fighters walking through the *villes* and the pretty native women smiling because if they don't smile the fighters might kill their pigs or burn their cache of rice. We rewind the rape scenes when American soldiers return from the bush after killing many VC to sip cool beers in a thatch bar while whores sit on their laps for a song or two (a song from the fifties when America was still sweet) before they retire to rooms and fuck the whores sweetly. The American boys, brutal, young farm boys or tough city boys, sweetly fuck the whores. Yes, somehow the films convinced us that these boys are sweet, even though we know we are much like these boys and that we are no longer sweet.

There is talk that many Vietnam films are antiwar, that the message is war is inhumane and look what happens when you train young American men to fight and kill, they turn their fighting and killing everywhere, they ignore their targets and desecrate the entire country, shooting fully automatic, forgetting they were trained to aim. But actually, Vietnam War films are all pro-war, no matter what the supposed message that Kubrick or Coppola or Stone intended. Mr. and Mrs. Johnson in Omaha or San Francisco or Manhattan will watch the films and weep and decide once and for all that war is inhumane and terrible, and they will tell their friends at church and their family this, but Corporal Johnson at Camp Pendleton and Sergeant Johnson at Travis Air Force Base and Seaman Johnson at Coronado Naval Station and Spec 4 Johnson at Fort Bragg and Lance Corporal Swofford at Twentynine Palms Marine Corps Base watch the same films and are excited by them, because the magic brutality of the films celebrates the terrible and despicable beauty of their fighting skills. Fight, rape, war, pillage, burn. Filmic images of death and carnage are pornography for the military man; with film you are stroking his cock, tickling his balls with the pink feather of history, getting him ready for his real First Fuck. It doesn't matter how many Mr. and Mrs. Johnsons are antiwar—the actual killers who know how to use the weapons are not.

We watch our films and drink our beer and occasionally someone begins weeping and exits the room to stand on the catwalk and stare at the Bullion Mountains, the treacherous, craggy range that borders our barracks. Once, this person is me. It's nearly midnight, the temperature still in the upper nineties, and the sky is wracked with stars. Moonlight spreads across the desert like a white fire. The door behind me remains open, and on the TV screen an ambush erupts on one of the famous murderous hills of Vietnam.

I reenter the room and look at the faces of my fellows. We are all afraid, but show this in various ways—violent indifference, fake ease, standard-issue bravura. We are afraid, but that doesn't mean we don't want to fight. It occurs to me that we will never be young again. I take my seat and return to the raging battle. The supposedly antiwar films have failed. Now is my time to step into the newest combat zone. And as a young man raised on the films of the Vietnam War, I want ammunition and alcohol and dope, I want to screw some whores and kill some Iraqi motherfuckers.

AFTER YOU READ: Analyze the Issues

1. Are Swofford's comments about the content of the Vietnam War movies correct? How many have you seen? How did they affect you?
2. Do you agree with Swofford's argument that war movies only excite soldiers to war? Why or why not?
3. Why does Swofford go outside to "weep and stare at the Bullion Mountains"? What is the significance of this act?
4. Does Swofford's prose offend you? Does it seem appropriate for his situation in life?

AFTER YOU READ: Analyze the Rhetoric

1. Which passages change your opinion of either war movies or soldiers? Was it the language or the images that influenced you the most?
2. What is the effect of repetition on the reader?
3. This is a section from a much longer memoir. How is it organized? Could you guess what went before or after? Is it able to effectively stand on its own?
4. Would you replace the offensive language and images?

Political Viewpoint

"America Should Not Enter the War"

by Charles Lindbergh
America First Committee, New York City, April 23, 1941
(Essay)

Charles Augustus Lindbergh, Jr. was born February 4, 1902 and died August 26, 1974. He is mainly known for being the first man to fly solo, non-stop across the Atlantic Ocean in 1927. Unfortunately, the kidnapping and murder of his infant son in 1939 and the oppressive media coverage of his family that followed drove Lindbergh to Europe on the eve of WWII. What he saw there, particularly in Germany, convinced him that America should not attempt to join the war. Back home in America, Lindbergh became the voice of the America First Movement that embraced the isolationist position. However, after the war began, Lindbergh flew more than 50 combat missions and served as an instructor for other pilots.

AS YOU READ: Annotate

1. Underline each of Lindbergh's arguments against the war.
2. Highlight connotative words.
3. In the margins, note arguments with which you agree and with which you disagree.

There are many viewpoints from which the issues of this war can be argued. Some are primarily idealistic. Some are primarily practical. One should, I believe, strive for a balance of both. But, since the subjects that can be covered in a single address are limited, tonight I shall discuss the war from a viewpoint, which is primarily practical. It is not that I believe ideals are unimportant, even among the realities of war; but if a nation is to survive in a hostile world, its ideals must be backed by the hard logic of military practicability. If the outcome of war depended upon ideals alone, this would be a different world than it is today.

I know I will be severely criticized by the interventionists in America when I say we should not enter a war unless we have a reasonable chance of winning. That, they will claim, is far too materialistic a viewpoint. They will advance again the same arguments that were used to persuade France to declare war against Germany in 1939. But I do not believe that our American ideals, and our way of life, will gain through an unsuccessful war. And I know that the United States is not prepared to wage war in Europe successfully at this time. We are no better prepared today than France was when the interventionists in Europe persuaded her to attack the Siegfried Line.

I have said before, and I will say again, that I believe it will be a tragedy to the entire world if the British Empire collapses. That is one of the main reasons why I opposed this war before it was declared, and why I have constantly advocated a negotiated peace. I did not feel that England and France had a reasonable chance of winning. France has now been defeated; and, despite the propaganda and confusion of recent months, it is now obvious that England is losing the war. I believe this is realized even by the British government. But they have one last desperate plan remaining. They hope that they may be able to persuade us to send another American Expeditionary Force to Europe, and to share with England militarily, as well as financially, the fiasco of this war.

I do not blame England for this hope, or for asking for our assistance. But we now know that she declared a war under circumstances which led to the defeat of every nation that sided with her from Poland to Greece. We know that in the desperation of war England promised to all these nations armed assistance that she could not send. We know that she misinformed them, as she has misinformed us, concerning her state of preparation, her military strength, and the progress of the war.

In time of war, truth is always replaced by propaganda. I do not believe we should be too quick to criticize the actions of a belligerent nation. There is always the question whether we, ourselves, would do better under similar circumstances. But we in this country have a right to think of the welfare of America first, just as the people in England thought first of their own country when they encouraged the smaller nations of Europe to fight against hopeless odds. When England asks us to enter this war, she is considering her own future, and that of her Empire. In making our reply, I believe we should consider the future of the United States and that of the Western Hemisphere.

It is not only our right, but it is our obligation as American citizens to look at this war objectively, and to weigh our chances for success if we should enter it. I have attempted to do this, especially from the standpoint of aviation; and I have been forced to the conclusion that we cannot win this war for England, regardless of how much assistance we extend.

I ask you to look at the map of Europe today and see if you can suggest any way in which we could win this war if we entered it. Suppose we had a large army in America, trained and equipped. Where would we send it to fight? The campaigns of the war show only too clearly how difficult it is to force a landing, or to maintain an army, on a hostile coast. Suppose we took our navy from the Pacific, and used it to convoy British shipping. That would not win the war for England. It would, at best, permit her to exist under the constant bombing of the German air fleet. Suppose we had an air force that we could send to Europe. Where could it operate? Some of our squadrons might be based in the British Isles; but it is physically impossible to base enough aircraft in the British Isles alone to equal in strength the aircraft that can be based on the continent of Europe.

I have asked these questions on the supposition that we had in existence an army and an air force large enough and well enough equipped to send to Europe; and that we would dare to remove our navy from the Pacific. Even on this basis, I do not see how we could invade the continent of Europe successfully as long as all of that continent and most of Asia is under Axis domination. But the fact is that none of these suppositions are correct. We have only a one-ocean navy. Our army is still untrained and inadequately equipped for foreign war. Our air force is deplorably lacking in modern fighting planes.

When these facts are cited, the interventionists shout that we are defeatists, that we are undermining the principles of Democracy, and that we are giving comfort to Germany by talking about our military weakness. But everything I mention here has been published in our newspapers, and in the reports of congressional hearings in Washington. Our military position is well known to the governments of Europe and Asia. Why, then, should it not be brought to the attention of our own people?

I say it is the interventionist in America, as it was in England and in France, who gives comfort to the enemy. I say it is they who are undermining the principles of Democracy when they demand that we take a course to which more than eighty percent of our citizens are opposed. I charge them with being the real defeatists, for their policy has led to the defeat of every country that followed their advice since this war began. There is no better way to give comfort to an enemy than to divide the people of a nation over the issue of foreign war. There is no shorter road to defeat than by entering a war with inadequate preparation. Every nation that has adopted the interventionist policy of depending on some one else for its own defense has met with nothing but defeat and failure.

When history is written, the responsibility for the downfall of the democracies of Europe will rest squarely upon the shoulders of the interventionists who led their nations into war uninformed and unprepared. With their shouts of defeatism, and their disdain of reality, they have already sent countless thousands of young men to death in Europe. From the campaign of Poland to that of Greece, their prophecies have been false and their policies have failed. Yet these are the people who are calling us defeatists in America today. And they have led this country, too, to the verge of war.

There are many such interventionists in America, but there are more people among us of a different type. That is why you and I are assembled here tonight. There is a policy open to this nation that will lead to success—a policy that leaves us free to follow our own way of life, and to develop our own civilization. It is not a new and untried idea. It was advocated by Washington. It was incorporated in the Monroe Doctrine. Under its guidance, the United States became the greatest nation in the world. It is based upon the belief that the security of a nation lies in the strength and character of its own people. It recommends the maintenance of armed forces sufficient to defend this hemisphere from attack by any combination of foreign powers. It demands faith in an independent American destiny. This is the policy of the America First Committee today. It is a policy not of isolation, but of independence; not of defeat, but of courage. It is a policy that led this nation to success during the most trying years of our history, and it is a policy that will lead us to success again.

We have weakened ourselves for many months, and still worse, we have divided our own people by this dabbling in Europe's wars. While we should have been concentrating on American defense, we have been forced to argue over foreign quarrels. We must turn our eyes and our faith back to our own country before it is too late. And when we do this, a different vista opens before us. Practically every difficulty we would face in invading Europe becomes an asset to us in defending America. Our enemy, and not we, would then have the problem of transporting millions of troops across the ocean and landing them on a hostile shore. They, and not we, would have to furnish the convoys to transport guns and trucks and munitions and fuel across three thousand miles of water. Our battleships and submarines would then be fighting close to their home bases. We would then do the bombing from the air, and the torpedoing at sea. And if any part of an enemy convoy should ever pass our navy and our air force, they would still be faced with the guns of our coast artillery, and behind them, the divisions of our army.

The United States is better situated from a military standpoint than any other nation in the world. Even in our present condition of unpreparedness, no foreign power is in a position to invade us today. If we concentrate on our own and build the strength that this nation should maintain, no foreign army will ever attempt to land on American shores.

War is not inevitable for this country. Such a claim is defeatism in the true sense. No one can make us fight abroad unless we ourselves are willing to do so. No one will attempt to fight us here if we arm ourselves as a great nation should be armed. Over a hundred million people in this nation are opposed to entering the war. If the principles of Democracy mean anything at all, that is reason enough for us to stay out. If we are forced into a war against the wishes of an overwhelming majority of our people, we will have proved Democracy such a failure at home that there will be little use fighting for it abroad.

The time has come when those of us who believe in an independent American destiny must band together, and organize for strength. We have been led toward war by a minority of our people. This minority has power. It has influence. It has a loud voice. But it does not represent the American people. During the last several years, I have travelled over this country, from one end to the other. I have talked to many hundreds of men and women, and I have had letters from tens of thousands more, who feel the same way as you and I. Most of these people have no influence or power. Most of them have no means of expressing their convictions, except by their vote which has always been against this war. They are the citizens who have had to work too hard at their daily jobs to organize political meetings. Hitherto, they have relied upon their vote to express their feelings; but now they find that it is hardly remembered except in the oratory of a political campaign. These people—the majority of hard-working American citizens are with us. They are the true strength of our country. And they are beginning to realize, as you and I, that there are times when we must sacrifice our normal interests in life in order to insure the safety and the welfare of our nation.

Such a time has come. Such a crisis is here. That is why the America First Committee has been formed—to give voice to the people who have no newspaper, or news reel, or radio station at their command; to the people who must do the paying, and the fighting, and the dying, if this country enters the war.

Whether or not we do enter the war, rests upon the shoulders of you in this audience, upon us here on this platform, upon meetings of this kind that are being held by Americans in every section of the United States today. It depends upon the action we take, and the courage we show at this time. If you believe in an independent destiny for America, if you believe that this country should not enter the war in Europe, we ask you to join the America First Committee in its stand. We ask you to share our faith in the ability of this nation to defend itself, to develop its own civilization, and to contribute to the progress of mankind in a more constructive and intelligent way than has yet been found by the warring nations of Europe. We need your support, and we need it now. The time to act is here.

AFTER YOU READ: Analyze the Issues

1. World War II has been so mythologized that it is hard to imagine that some of the populations were adamantly against joining the war. What positions in this argument surprised you?
2. Based on the evidence Lindbergh presents, did you agree or disagree with his arguments? Which arguments were the most persuasive?
3. What arguments might apply to Vietnam or Iraq? Make note of them in the margins so that you can find them later.

AFTER YOU READ: Analyze the Rhetoric

1. Looking back over your notes in the margin, were the arguments that persuade you logos, ethos, or pathos?
2. How is Lindbergh's argument organized? Is it similar or different from the organization of other speeches you've read? Does Lindbergh construct a deductive or inductive argument?
3. Look back over the connotative words you have highlighted. What feelings do they evoke?

"We Must Defeat Hitler"

by James B. Conant
(Essay)

Congressional Record, 76th Congress, 3d Session, June 7, 1940, LXXXVI, appendix, 3669-70

James Bryant Conant was born March 26, 1893 in Dorchester, Massachusetts. He earned a B.A. and Ph.D. from Harvard University where he became a chemistry professor. In 1933, Conant was made President of Harvard University where he served until 1953. He was chairman of the National Defense Research Committee and was responsible for the Manhattan Project, which developed the first nuclear weapons. An active member of the Committee to Defend America by Aiding the Allies, he was asked by its leader William Allen White, to give a speech on live radio as to what America should do after the report that the German armies had trapped the Allies at Dunkirk.

AS YOU READ: Annotate

1. Underline the claim of this speech. Highlight the main points.
2. Note in the margins the types of examples, historical, personal, etc., that Conant uses.
3. Circle connotative words that Conant uses to influence the way the reader views Germany.

…There is no need for me to dwell on the agonizing news of the last few days. Tonight the Germans stand on the shores of the English Channel and along the Somme. Tomorrow looms before us like a menacing question-mark. A total victory for German arms is now well within the range of possibility …

Let me ask you to visualize our future as a democratic free people in a world dominated by ruthless totalitarian states. There are those who argue that Hitler's war machine, when its task is done in Europe, will be converted to an instrument of peaceful industrial activity. I do not think so. There are those who imagine that a government which has broken promise after promise, which has scorned the democratic countries and all they stand for, which mocks and laughs at free institutions as a basis for civilization,—that such a government can live in a peaceful relationship with the United States. I do not think so.

To my mind a complete Nazi victory over France and England would be, by necessity, but a prelude to Hitler's attempt to dominate the world. If Germany were triumphant, at best there would result an armed truce. This country would be feverishly endeavoring to put itself into an impregnable position based on a highly militarized society. Our way of life would be endangered for years to come. If this be so, what should we do in these desperate, tragic hours?

We must rearm at once, that much is clear. The vision rises before us of the United States suddenly left alone and unprotected in a totalitarian and destructive world. It is obvious we are unprepared to meet an emergency of this nature. It is also obvious that our first aim must be to prepare with all rapidity. England's failure to listen to Winston Churchill, warning of approaching danger, is responsible for her plight. We must not make the same mistake. We are all agreed on that…

My purpose tonight is to urge another course of action equally important. I am advocating immediate aid to the Allies. I shall mince no words. *I believe the United States should take every action possible to insure the defeat of Hitler.* And let us face honestly the possible implications of such a policy. In a free state public opinion must guide the Government, and a wise public opinion on matters of foreign policy can result only if there is a continuous, clear-headed realistic discussion of all eventualities, including war.

At this moment, the entry of the United States into the war certainly does not seem necessary or wise….

What are then the actions that can be taken at once?

Let us state a few of them: first, the release to France and England of army and navy airplanes and other implements of war, without impairing our own security; second, repeal of the laws which prevent United States citizens from volunteering to serve in foreign armies; third, control of exports with the purpose of aiding the Allies by avoiding leaks to Germany and giving priority to France and England; four, the cooperation of our Maritime Commission with the Allies in every way possible under our present laws to expedite the sending of supplies and munitions. These steps, if promptly taken by our Government, would render effective aid which some experts believe might tip the scales in favor of an Allied victory. Furthermore, they would be of infinite value in strengthening the morale of the Allied nations and would serve notice to the world that our resources were now enlisted in the democratic cause.

I have purposely avoided the use of the words "moral issues." The younger generation in particular is highly suspicious of this phrase. Their feeling is chiefly due to the widespread misinterpretation of the reasons for America's participation in the war in 1914-1918. I have avoided this issue, not because I sympathize with those who proclaim that there is no fundamental difference between the actions and aims of the democracies on the one hand and the totalitarian powers on the other. Far from it. There is to my mind all the difference between piracy and peaceful trade, all the difference between ruthless tyranny and enlightened intercourse among free men.

But I am endeavoring to confine my argument this evening to a realistic appraisal of our foreign policy. Let me make this clear. I advocate no moral crusade to distant lands. If crusading were a proper policy, we should have had more than one provocation for war in the last dozen years. I am arguing that the changed military situation in Europe actually threatens our way of life.

At this moment, today, the war is in effect veering towards our shores. The issue before the United States is, I repeat, can we live as a free, peaceful, relatively unarmed people in a world dominated by the totalitarian states? Specifically, can we look with indifference as a nation (as a nation, mind you, not as individuals) on the possible subjugation of England by a Nazi Sate? If your answer is yes, then my words are in vain. If your answer is no, I urge you as a citizen to act.

Write or telegraph to the President of the United States, to your Congressman and your Senators, stating your belief that this nation must give immediate, effective aid to the Allies. Let your elected agents of Government have your thoughts. Urge that Congress stay in session to consider emergency legislation as may be necessary, and speed the process of rearmament.

Above all else, let us consider the situation boldly. This is no time for defeatism or despair. The allies may be expected to hold out if they have help from us and the promise of further help to come. The wrath of moral indignation is impotent in days like these. A struggle to the death is once again in progress on the fields of Western Europe. The British Isles are making ready to stand a siege… It is not too late but it is long past time to act. I urge you, let your voice be heard!

AFTER YOU READ: Analyze the Issues

1. Conant bases his argument that America cannot remain neutral on what fear? Is this an effective argument? Is this speech a foreshadowing of the policy of "spreading democracy"?
2. Why is Conant considered an "Interventionist"? Does history support the theory that America should be involved in world conflict? Give several examples to support your view.
3. In what ways does Conant agree with Lindbergh? In what ways does he differ?
4. Would this speech be effective today if we substituted Iran and terrorism for Germany and the Nazi state?

AFTER YOU READ: Analyze the Rhetoric

1. What types of examples did Conant use? Were they effective? Which ones were the most effective?
2. Were Conant's connotative words easy to find? Were they obvious? Did they help or hurt his argument?
3. Conant's conclusion is a fairly standard call to action. What elements does it contain? How is it similar to Lindbergh's call to action? Which is most effective?

"Why Iraq Was a Mistake"

by Lt. General Greg Newbold (Ret.)
(Essay)

General Newbold served in the Marine Corps for 32 years. He served as the warfare policy planner for the Joint Chiefs of Staff and commanded the 15th Marine Expeditionary Unit in Somalia. He retired as a three-star general in 2002. He has stated that his retirement was partially in opposition to the Iraq war. The article below appeared in the April 9, 2006 issue of *Time Magazine* and presents a dissenting opinion of the war from a military officer's point of view.

AS YOU READ: Annotate

1. Highlight any words that are "military-ese." Note their meanings in the margin.
2. Underline the claim of this essay. In the margin, note the underlying warrant.
3. Note in the margins the use of pathos, ethos, and logos. Keep count of how many of each type of example or argument Newbold uses.

In 1971, the rock group *The Who* released the antiwar anthem *Won't Get Fooled Again*. To most in my generation, the song conveyed a sense of betrayal by the nation's leaders, who had led our country into a costly and unnecessary war in Vietnam. To those of us who were truly counterculture—who became career members of the military during those rough times—the song conveyed a very different message. To us, its lyrics evoked a feeling that we must never again stand by quietly while those ignorant of and casual about war lead us into another one and then mismanage the conduct of it. Never again, we thought, would our military's senior leaders remain silent as American troops were marched off to an ill-considered engagement. It's 35 years later, and the judgment is in: *The Who* had it wrong. We have been fooled again.

From 2000 until October 2002, I was a Marine Corps lieutenant general and director of operations for the Joint Chiefs of Staff. After 9/11, I was a witness and therefore a party to the actions that led us to the invasion of Iraq—an unnecessary war. Inside the military family, I made no secret of my view that the zealots' rationale for war made no sense. And I think I was outspoken enough to make those senior to me uncomfortable. But I now regret that I did not more openly challenge those who were determined to invade a country whose actions were peripheral to the real threat—al-Qaeda. I retired from the military four months before the invasion, in part because of my opposition to those who had used 9/11's tragedy to hijack our security policy. Until now, I have resisted speaking out in public. I've been silent long enough.

I am driven to action now by the missteps and misjudgments of the White House and the Pentagon, and by my many painful visits to our military hospitals. In those places, I have been both inspired and shaken by the broken bodies but unbroken spirits of soldiers, Marines and corpsmen returning from this war. The cost of flawed leadership continues to be paid in blood. The willingness of our forces to shoulder such a load should make it a sacred obligation for civilian and military leaders to get our defense policy right. They must be absolutely sure that the commitment is for a cause as honorable as the sacrifice.

With the encouragement of some still in positions of military leadership, I offer a challenge to those still in uniform: a leader's responsibility is to give voice to those who can't—or don't have the opportunity to—speak. Enlisted members of the armed forces swear their oath to those appointed over them; an officer swears an oath not to a person but to the Constitution. The distinction is important.

Before the antiwar banners start to unfurl, however, let me make clear—I am not opposed to war. I would gladly have traded my general's stars for a captain's bars to lead our troops into Afghanistan to destroy the Taliban and al-Qaeda. And while I don't accept the stated rationale for invading Iraq, my view—at the moment—is that a precipitous withdrawal would be a mistake. It would send a signal, heard around the world, that would reinforce the jihadists' message that America can be defeated, and thus increase the chances of future conflicts. If, however, the Iraqis prove unable to govern, and there is open civil war, then I am prepared to change my position.

I will admit my own prejudice: my deep affection and respect are for those who volunteer to serve our nation and therefore shoulder, in those thin ranks, the nation's most sacred obligation of citizenship. To those of you who don't know, our country has never been served by a more competent and professional military. For that reason, Secretary of State Condoleezza Rice's recent statement that "we" made the "right strategic decisions" but made thousands of "tactical errors" is an outrage. It reflects an effort to obscure gross errors in strategy by shifting the blame for failure to those who have been resolute in fighting. The truth is, our forces are successful in spite of the strategic guidance they receive, not because of it.

What we are living with now is the consequences of successive policy failures. Some of the missteps include: the distortion of intelligence in the buildup to the war, McNamara-like micromanagement that kept our forces from having enough resources to do the job, the failure to retain and reconstitute the Iraqi military in time to help quell civil disorder, the initial denial that an insurgency was the heart of the opposition to occupation, alienation of allies who could have helped in a more robust way to rebuild Iraq, and the continuing failure of the other agencies of our government to commit assets to the same degree as the Defense Department. My sincere view is that the commitment of our forces to this fight was done with a casualness and swagger that are the special province of those who have never had to execute these missions—or bury the results.

Flaws in our civilians are one thing; the failure of the Pentagon's military leaders is quite another. Those are men who know the hard consequences of war but, with few exceptions, acted timidly when their voices urgently needed to be heard. When they knew the plan was flawed, saw intelligence distorted to justify a rationale for war, or witnessed arrogant micromanagement that at times crippled the military's effectiveness, many leaders who wore the uniform chose inaction. A few of the most senior officers actually supported the logic for war. Others were simply intimidated, while still others must have believed that the principle of obedience does not allow for respectful dissent. The consequence of the military's quiescence was that a fundamentally flawed plan was executed for an invented war, while pursuing the real enemy, al-Qaeda, became a secondary effort.

There have been exceptions, albeit uncommon, to the rule of silence among military leaders. Former Army Chief of Staff General Shinseki, when challenged to offer his professional opinion during prewar congressional testimony, suggested that more troops might be needed for the invasion's aftermath. The Secretary and Deputy Secretary of Defense castigated him in public and marginalized him in his remaining months in his post. Army General John Abizaid, head of Central Command, has been forceful in his views with appointed officials on strategy and micromanagement of the fight in Iraq—often with success. Marine Commandant General Mike Hagee steadfastly challenged plans to underfund, understaff and underequip his service as the Corps has struggled to sustain its fighting capability.

To be sure, the Bush Administration and senior military officials are not alone in their culpability. Members of Congress—from both parties—defaulted in fulfilling their constitutional responsibility for oversight. Many in the media saw the warning signs and heard cautionary tales before the invasion from wise observers like former Central Command chiefs Joe Hoar and Tony Zinni but gave insufficient weight to their views. These are the same news organizations that now downplay both the heroic and the constructive in Iraq.

So what is to be done? We need fresh ideas and fresh faces. That means, as a first step, replacing Rumsfeld and many others unwilling to fundamentally change their approach. The troops in the Middle East have performed their duty. Now we need people in Washington who can construct a unified strategy worthy of them. It is time to send a signal to our nation, our forces and the world that we are uncompromising on our security but are prepared to rethink how we achieve it. It is time for senior military leaders to discard caution in expressing their views and ensure that the President hears them clearly. And that we won't be fooled again.

AFTER YOU READ: Analyze the Issues

1. Is it somehow disloyal of Lt. General Newbold to make an argument against the military leadership? Why or why not?

2. Newbold says the distinction between whom the enlisted man is sworn to be loyal to and what the officer is sworn to be loyal to is important. Do you agree or disagree? Do the enlisted men actually fighting the war in Iraq have as much responsibility for the war as the officers who are planning it? Why or why not? Can you support the troops and not support the war? How?
3. Which of the policy failures and strategic errors that Newbold lists is most disturbing to you? Why?
4. Do you think that Newbold has called for the correct action in his conclusion? Why or why not?

AFTER YOU READ: Analyze the Rhetoric

1. Review your list of Newbold's use of pathos, logos, and ethos. Which arguments were most effective? How did Newbold's own ethos influence your acceptance of his arguments?
2. Did Newbold use a lot of "military-ese"? Why or why not?
3. What was Newbold's warrant? Do you believe the warrant?
4. What was the effect of Newbold's naming names? Did it make his argument more credible, or did it make his piece sound like it was written by someone trying to get even for being forced out of the military? Support your position with evidence from the essay.
5. Make note of the Introductory and Concluding devices Newbold uses. Brainstorm other devices that might have worked as well or better. List these in the margin.

"Our Troops Must Stay"

by Joe Lieberman

Joe Lieberman is best known for being the first Jewish candidate for vice-president of the United States when Al Gore chose him as his running mate in 2000. As a Democrat, he served as a U.S. Senator from Connecticut from 1988–2006. Lieberman graduated from Yale in 1964 and Yale Law School in 1967 and received an educational deferment and then a family deferment and did not serve in the military during the Vietnam war. Although Lieberman lost his reelection bid in August 2006, he has announced he would seek re-election as an independent. Lieberman has drawn criticism from his fellow Democrats because of his support of the Iraq war.

AS YOU READ: Annotate

1. Underline the word "progress" each time you read it.
2. In the margin, rewrite the claim of the essay.
3. Highlight any statistics that are used in the essay. Note in the margin if they influenced your opinion.

I have just returned from my fourth trip to Iraq in the last 17 months and can report real progress there. More work needs to be done, of course, but the Iraqi people are in reach of a watershed transformation from the primitive, killing tyranny of Saddam to modern, self-governing, self-securing nationhood unless the great American military that has given them and us this unexpected opportunity is prematurely withdrawn.

The progress in Iraq is visible and practical. In the Kurdish North, there is continuing security and growing prosperity. The primarily Shiite south remains largely free of terrorism, receives much more electric power and other public services than it did under Saddam, and is experiencing greater economic activity. The Sunni triangle, geographically defined by Baghdad on the East, Tikrit to the North, and Ramadi to the West, is where most of the terrorist enemy attacks occur. And yet here too, there is progress.

There are many more cars on the streets, satellite television dishes on the roofs, and literally millions more cell phones in Iraqi hands than before. All of that says the Iraqi economy is growing. And Sunni candidates are actively campaigning for seats in the National Assembly. People are working their way to a functioning society and economy in the midst of a very brutal, inhumane, sustained terrorist war against the civilian population and the Iraqi and American military there to protect it.

It is a war between 27 million and 10,000; 27 million Iraqis who want to live lives of freedom, opportunity, and prosperity and roughly 10,000 terrorists who are either Saddam "revengists," Iraqi Islamic extremists, or al-Qaeda foreign fighters, and know their wretched causes will be set back if Iraq becomes free and modern. They are intent on stopping this by instigating a civil war that will produce the chaos that will allow Iraq to replace Afghanistan as the base for their fanatical war-making in the Islamic world. We are fighting on the side of the 27 million because the outcome of this war is critically important to the security and freedom of America. If the terrorists win, they will be emboldened to strike us directly again and to further undermine the growing stability and progress in the Middle East, which has long been a major American national and economic security priority.

Before going to Iraq last week, I visited Israel and the Palestinian Authority. Israel has been the only genuine democracy in the region, but is now getting some welcome company from the Iraqis and Palestinians who are in the midst of robust national legislative election campaigns, the Lebanese who have risen up in proud, self-determination after the Hariri assassination to eject their Syrian occupiers (the Syrian—and Iranian-backed Hezbollah militias should be next), and the Kuwaitis, Egyptians, and Saudis who have taken steps to open up their governments more broadly to their people. In my meeting with the thoughtful prime minister of Iraq, Ibrahim al-Jaafari, he declared with justifiable pride that Iraq now has the most open, democratic political system in the Arab world. He is right.

In the face of terrorist threats and escalating violence, eight million Iraqis voted for their interim national government in January, almost 10 million participated in the referendum on their new Constitution in October, and even more than that are expected to vote in the elections for a full term government on Dec. 15. Every time the 27 million Iraqis have been given the chance since Saddam was overthrown, they vote for self-government and hope over the violence and hatred the 10,000 terrorists offer them. Most encouraging has been the behavior of the Sunni community which, when disappointed by the proposed Constitution, registered to vote and went to the polls instead of taking up arms and going to the streets. Last week, I was thrilled to see a vigorous political campaign going on in Iraq and a large number of independent television stations and newspapers covering it.

None of these remarkable changes in Iraq would have happened if Coalition Forces, led by the U.S., had not overthrown Saddam Hussein. And, I am convinced, almost all of the progress in Iraq and throughout the Middle East will be lost if those forces are withdrawn faster than the Iraqi military is capable of securing the country.

The leaders of Iraq's duly elected government understand this, and asked me for reassurance about America's commitment to Iraq. The question is whether the American people and enough of their representatives in Congress from both parties understand this. I am disappointed by Democrats who are more focused on how President Bush took America into the war in Iraq almost three years ago, and Republicans who are more worried about whether the war will bring them down in next November's elections, than they are concerned about how we continue the progress in Iraq in the months and years ahead.

Here is an ironic finding I brought back from Iraq. While public opinion polls in the U.S. show serious declines in support for the war and increasing pessimism about how it will end, polls conducted by Iraqis for Iraqi universities show increasing optimism. Two-thirds say they are better off than they were under Saddam and a resounding 82% are confident their lives in Iraq will be better a year from now than they are today. What a colossal mistake it would be for America's bipartisan political leadership to choose this moment in history to lose its will, and in the famous phrase, to seize defeat from the jaws of the coming victory.

The leaders of America's military and diplomatic forces in Iraq, Gen. George Casey and Ambassador Zal Khalilzad, have a clear vision of our mission there. It is to create the environment in which Iraqi democracy, security, and prosperity can take hold and the Iraqis themselves can defend their political progress against those ten thousand terrorists who would take it from them.

Does America have a good plan for doing this, a strategy for victory in Iraq? Yes we do. And it is important to make it clear to the American people that the plan has not remained stubbornly still but has changed over the years. Mistakes, some of them big, were made after Saddam was removed, and no one who supports the war should hesitate to admit that; but we have learned from those mistakes and, in characteristic American fashion, from what has worked and not worked on the ground in Iraq. The administration's recent use of the banner "clear, hold, and build" accurately describes the strategy as I saw it being implemented last week.

We are now embedding a core of Coalition Forces in every Iraqi fighting unit which makes each unit more effective and acts as a multiplier of our forces. Progress in "clearing" and "holding" is being made. The Sixth Infantry Division of the Iraqi Security Forces now controls and polices more than one-third of Baghdad on its own. Coalition and Iraqi forces have together cleared the previously terrorist controlled cities of Fallujah, Mosul, and Talafar and most of the border with Syria. Those areas are now being "held" secure by the Iraqi military themselves. Iraqi and Coalition Forces are now jointly carrying out a mission to clear Ramadi, now the most dangerous city in Al-Anbar province at the west end of the Sunni Triangle.

Nationwide, American military leaders estimate that about one-third of the approximately 100,000 members of the Iraqi military are able to "lead the fight" themselves with logistical support from the U.S. and that that number should double by next year. If that happens, American military forces could be able to begin to drawdown in numbers proportional to the increasing self-sufficiency of the Iraqi forces in 2006. If all goes well, I believe we can have a much smaller American military presence there by the end of 2006 or in 2007, but it is also likely that our presence will need to be significant in Iraq or nearby for years to come.

The economic reconstruction of Iraq has gone slower than it should have, and too much money has been wasted or stolen. Amb. Khalilzad is now implementing reform that has worked in Afghanistan—Provincial Reconstruction Teams composed of American economic and political experts working in partnership in each of Iraq's 18 provinces with its elected leadership, civil service, and the private sector. That is the "build" part of the "clear, hold, and build" strategy, and so is the work American and international teams are doing to professionalize national and provincial governmental agencies in Iraq.

These are new ideas that are working and changing the reality on the ground which is undoubtedly why the Iraqi people are optimistic about their future and why the American people should be too.

I cannot say enough about the U.S. Army and Marines who are carrying most of the fight for us in Iraq. They are courageous, smart, effective, innovative, very honorable and very proud. After a Thanksgiving meal with a great group of Marines at Camp Fallujah in western Iraq, I asked their commander whether the morale of his troops had been hurt by the growing public dissent in America over the war in Iraq. His answer was insightful, instructive, and inspirational: "I would guess that if the opposition and division at home go on a lot longer and get a lot deeper it might have some effect but, Senator, my Marines are motivated by their devotion to each other and the cause, not by political debates."

Thank you, General. That is a powerful, needed message for the rest of America and its political leadership at this critical moment in our nation's history. Semper Fi.

AFTER YOU READ: Analyze the Issues

1. In what areas does Lieberman claim we are making "progress" in Iraq? What evidence does he use to back up his claim? What types of things does he not mention?
2. According to Lieberman, why is the U.S. in the Iraq war? How does this compare to the reasons given in other articles?
3. Did Lieberman represent the feelings of the American people to the Iraqi government? Who did he represent? What would you say to the Iraqi government if you had the chance?
4. Does the fact that Lieberman was actually in Iraq help or hurt his argument?
5. How did the general's statement at the end of the article about why his Marines are fighting contribute to Lieberman's argument?

AFTER YOU READ: Analyze the Rhetoric

1. How does Lieberman use the word "progress"? How did the repetition of this word affect the argument?
2. How does Lieberman use statistics? Are they affective in advancing his argument? How do they relate to his claim that progress is being made?
3. What does Lieberman say to establish his ethos? Is it effective?
4. Look through the text for words that inspire a patriotic feeling. Does Lieberman rely heavily on pathos?

Sample Student Papers

Media and the Mind War

by Saad S. Muhammad

Saad Muhammad's essay is a thought provoking piece of writing of very high merit. His essay is an amalgam of efficient writing skills and strategies effectively employed to convey his thoughts and ideas. His adequate defense and support of the thesis throughout the essay shows his mastery of the language and writing techniques.

AS YOU READ: Annotate

1. Place a star by the sections you like the most.
2. Place question marks by sections you have problems with or do not understand.
3. Place a [+] by sections that need to be developed more or that seem to be incomplete.
4. Write other comments in the margins as you see fit.

Why is the media considered as one of the major powers in the elitist view of democracy, sharing the privileged place with the traditional power houses like business, military and political elites? The reason is pure and simple. No one would argue against the fact that the mind is the most important part of our bodies in terms of command and control. All the orders emanate from the brain and our body obeys these commands in order to perform simple tasks such as walking, speaking or listening. Hence, we can deduce that the mind controls the body. Now we are left with the question of who controls the mind. The answer to that is none other than the media in today's society. The role of the media in conducting a successful military operation is crucial, and the popular saying, "The pen is mightier than the sword" holds true to this day. The media's influence in shaping a war can never be over-estimated; whoever controls the media wins the war.

The mind is like a machine whose output is dependent upon its input. The input in this case is the environment. Our environs dictate our behavior, and so people in different surroundings behave differently. This is precisely what makes Americans, American, and Canadians, Canadian, that is, the influence of the environment or should we say media, on the people. Not only our place but also the time dictates our actions, and mass media is what helps give shape to time as well. That is why same people exhibit different behaviors at different times. A good example is the movie *The Green Berets* (1968) which extolled the Vietnam War, and *The Deer Hunter* (1978) which challenged its legitimacy ten years later. Media (input) is the single most important entity that influences our minds and shapes our behavior (output), and the war planners are very aware of the fact.

Noam Chomsky talks about the media in his book *Manufacturing Consent* as a highly sophisticated propaganda machine where issues and topics are chosen by elite consensus to the tune of the Government and certain vested interests. All this is sold daily as news. This tool is crucial for the Government to maintain steady support, especially when it comes to selling foreign wars to the public. Lydersen talks about the "embedded reporters, weapons of mass destruction and surgical strikes" in her article "An Army of Propaganda" and asserts:

> It's no coincidence that Americans, and others around the world, are echoing the exact same phrases and news-bites at the same times with near-military precision. It's the result of a slickly orchestrated public relations campaign on the part of the military and the US government that is borrowing the best practices of the corporate PR world. (1)

Lyderson quotes the *PR Week*, a trade publication of the PR industry as saying:

> The OGC, an office born out of post-September-11 efforts to combat anti-American news stories emerging from Arab countries, will be key in keeping all U.S. spokespeople on message. Each night, U.S. embassies around the world, along with all federal departments in DC, will receive a "Global Messenger" e-mail containing talking points and ready-to-use quotes. (1)

Kaufman talks about the role of the media in generating conflicts as well as countering propaganda to win a war. He tells about the war in Kosovo and how media was effectively employed to counter the threat posed by the Serbs:

> Biden said he learned many things about Milosevic and the Balkans during the visit, the most important thing being how media can be misused to start and feed religious, ethnic and racial, and regional conflicts. If the United States is to deal with these problems in the future, he concluded, we have to move beyond military, political and economic weapons. We must learn how to fight a media war. (116)

The media is instrumental in bringing about the desired outcome in any conflict situation, no matter what the scenario. Time and again, different governments, regimes and countries have used it as a tool to control the minds of the masses with this mass-media. The concept of psychological warfare is not new but the tool used to accomplish the same is (the media), programming and bombarding people's minds with readymade ideas to think and readymade opinions to hold.

Works Cited

Chomsky, Noam and Edward Herman. *Manufacturing Consent: The Political Economy of the Mass Media*. New York: Pantheon, 1988.

Kaufman, Edward. "A Broadcasting Strategy to Win Media Wars." *The Washington Quarterly.* 25.2 (2002): 115-127.

Lydersen, Kari. "An Army of Propaganda." *Alternet* 31 March 2003. 1 March 2003 <http://www.alternet.org>.

Sterritt, David. "War Stories." *Christian Science Monitor* 10 Aug. 2001. 8 April 2003 <http://csmonitor.com>.

PRO PEER REVIEW OUTLINE

Directions. Asking the right questions: As you ask these questions and answer them, be specific in your comments so as to be more helpful to the author. Provide details.

1. **Logos.** Comment on the quality and amount of the evidence or research conducted. Is it balanced or enough? Does the author need more? Why or why not? Is the paper too logical or not logical enough? What else can you say about logos?
2. **Pathos.** Comment on the emotional appeals used in the paper. What can the author do to improve this appeal? Should there be less, more, or no emotions? Explain.
3. **Ethos.** Does the author use enough quality sources to improve the impact of the ethos of the paper? Is there a human element in the paper? What does the author need to do to improve the character aspect? Should the author add a personal story? Is the paper too personal? Should it be more logical?
4. **Call for Improvement.** Which aspects in the paper need to be revised or improved? Explain in detail.

A Soldier's Manifesto

by Cory Washington

AS YOU READ: Annotate

1. Place a star by the sections you like the most.
2. Place question marks by sections you have problems with or do not understand.
3. Place a [+] by sections that need to be developed more or that seem to be incomplete.
4. Write other comments in the margins as you see fit.

I am an American Army soldier. I am sworn to defend my country and the freedoms that it possesses. I protect the constitution of the United States of America. I hold strict moral values and adhere to the seven-army values. These values include loyalty, duty, respect, self-less service, honor, integrity and personal courage, which help me learn leadership. I give commands to those below me and receive them from those appointed above me. I have signed my life away, knowing all the risks that I may endure in times to come. I live my life to the fullest and do not take it for granted. I love my family when I am with them and when I am not. I believe that having a preferred religion is necessary to be in this worldwide fraternity. Prayer keeps my fellow soldiers and I more aware, and it keeps us motivated. I am an American Army soldier.

Some of the civilians of the United States support what I do and how I do it. It helps me focus and stay motivated when they send their support to me through letters and goody boxes. If you see me walking through an airport with a uniform on, thank me for my service and dedication. I love to see those yellow ribbons on cars that say, "Support our troops." But what Americans do not realize is that they are the reason why I fight and that they are the people that I want to protect. I was once a civilian and still am when I am not working and doing my job. I respect the civilians and they respect me and that's what makes our nation strong. But for the people that don't support me, I disagree on their opinions. I think that those certain individuals should maybe move out of the country. They think of me as a force itching to fight, but that's not who I am. I am not the one who chooses war, I only choose to serve the country.

Allies can be very helpful to a soldier as well. They are in the battlefields with me and protect me as I do the same for them. Their medics help me when I am hurt if there are none of our medics around. They let me use their ammunition and weapons when I run low. They give me shelter, and they give me food. They instill hope and pride into me when my morale is low. They help me through the toughest times of battles and of war. I thank them for all that they risk as well. Maybe someday the world will understand that they or I do not intend to do bad in the world, but help correct the misdoings or wrongs. I will always help our allies, and I hope that they will return the favor.

The enemy looks down at me with an angry eye. They don't want me occupying their country and would rather see me dead. Fear and hate is their secret weapon against me. I trained to protect them in times of need, but they give me nothing in return. They used my weapons against me thinking that they can accept victory upon their half, and yet, all they receive is defeat. They follow none of the rules from the Geneva Convention or the rules of engagement. They don't think about the consequences of their actions and the repercussions that will haunt them for the rest of their lives. One day they shall find out how I intended good for the world and humanity. Lies and deceit help them win battles in war, but they are just hurting themselves because soon the people will find out. They are scattered around the world and never stay in the same place for a certain amount of time. I am like a hunter, and they are my prey. But will they ever go away? They will never go away unless I put an end to their existence.

In the end, I am an American Army soldier. I believe in myself, the civilians I live with and by, and my allies who are beside me. For those who oppose me, I hope you fear me and understand why I have signed the papers making me a soldier. Not to cause hate or make problems, but to defend my country, family, and friends.

PEER REVIEW OUTLINE

Directions. Asking the right questions: As you ask these questions and answer them, be specific in your comments so as to be more helpful to the author. Provide details.

1. **Logos.** Comment on the quality and amount of the evidence or research conducted. Is it balanced or enough? Does the author need more? Why or why not? Is the paper too logical or not logical enough? What else can you say about logos?
2. **Pathos.** Comment on the emotional appeals used in the paper. What can the author do to improve this appeal? Should there be less, more, or no emotions? Explain.
3. **Ethos.** Does the author use enough quality sources to improve the impact of the ethos of the paper? Is there a human element in the paper? What does the author need to do to improve the character aspect? Should the author add a personal story? Is the paper too personal? Should it be more logical?
4. **Call for Improvement.** Which aspects in the paper need to be revised or improved? Explain in detail.

Responding to War Issues

Written Rhetoric: Opinion Papers, Arguments, and Research

1. Write a response to one of the essays in this section in which you argue the opposite point of view. Be sure to quote from the article.
2. Compare and contrast a soldier's view of war with a politician's. Be sure to quote from specific articles.
3. Write a paper in which you analyze several of the arguments for going to war. Which are effective? Which are not? Are the best arguments based in ethos, logos, or pathos? Be sure to cite where you encountered that argument.
4. Research the effects that the media had on changing public attitudes against the Vietnam conflict. Should the media censor themselves and not show such graphic aspects of the war? Or is it the purpose of the media to show what really occurs in war in full details?
5. Research the Gulf War of 1990. What are historians now saying about this war? What did the media say about it when it happened? How has our view of the war changed over time?
6. Research official Democratic and Republican stands on the following wars: Korea, Operation Desert Storm, Afghanistan. Have Democrats always been against war? Are Republicans always pro war?

Oral Rhetoric: Speeches, Lyrics, and Simulations

1. This text contains several speeches given about war. Pick the one you think was the most effective as a speech, and write a paper explaining why it was effective. Be sure to mention the elements of oral argument.
2. Go to www.americanrhetoric.com/speeches and find the speeches George Bush and Tony Blair gave to the people of Iraq on April 10, 2003. Write a paper comparing the two speeches and stating which one was most effective and why.
3. Create the text for a 30-second commercial for or against war and then write an essay explaining your choices to use ethos, logos, or pathos.
4. Choose two or three songs about war and analyze their lyrics for use of ethos, logos or pathos. What rhetorical devices do song writers use to make their points? See the list of songs.
5. Propaganda or truth? As research, watch some war films that were made during the actual war compared to films made after the war. For example, *The Green Berets*, partially directed by John Wayne, was made during the Vietnam conflict, and *Platoon*, directed by Oliver Stone who fought in Vietnam, was made

after the war. In some ways, both films have aspects of propaganda and defend certain ideological or political stances. Create a simulation where characters from the films and the film directors debate their right to use propaganda in war films.

6. Create a simulation where a soldier, a general, a politician, and a conservative business man must argue for war to a war protestor, a minister, a frightened mother of a son, and an historian all of whom are against the war. Choose a war or conflict.

Visual Rhetoric: Advertisements, Visuals, and Cinema

1. Create a pictorial essay illustrating how war has affected your family or group of friends. Each picture should illustrate one of the main points you bring up in your text.
2. Based on an argument you discovered in the readings, record a 30-second commercial for or against the war and post it on YouTube. Be prepared either orally or in writing to discuss the argument you chose to illustrate.
3. Visit the Army, Air Force, and Marine Web sites to view their recruitment videos or take notes when the recruitment commercials appear on TV. Write a paper analyzing their effectiveness.
4. Compare war films made before the Vietnam conflict with war films made after the conflict. How did Vietnam change the way we view war in films? Be sure to mention specific films and specific scenes from those films.
5. Go to www.deviantart.com and search using the words "war" and "peace." Save the images you find the most effective. Write an essay about the images. Include the images in your report.

Electronic Rhetoric: Emergent Media and Gaming

1. There are 10 million registered players of *World of Warcraft*. Why is this game so popular? Find players who play this game and interview them about their character and what benefits they receive from playing the game. Write a paper in which you argue for or against joining a guild and playing the game.
2. Log on to www.worldofwarcraft.com and download the free 10 day trial. Construct a character and play the game until you think you have a sense of what the game is about. Then write a paper about how it feels to be in control of a character that commits violence to creatures and other characters. Does being an anonymous "character" make violence easier? Did any of the violence of the game spill into your real life? Try to argue for or against this type of game influencing real life violence.

WOVE Project

1. Create a blog about the current war in Iraq. Then imagine that you have been chosen to testify before congress about the effects of the war in Iraq. You must give a 90-second opening speech that should be illustrated with visuals. You also must submit a written document to congress to be published in the *Congressional Record*. Be prepared to turn in your written argument and present your opening speech.
2. Create your own WOVE project.

Song Lyrics

Civil War

"John Brown's Body"
"Battle Hymn of the Republic"

World War I

"Over There," George M. Cohan

World War II

"Hiroshima," Utopia
"Sally, Don't you Grieve," Woody Guthrie

Vietnam Conflict

"Ballad of the Green Berets," John Horton
"Blowin' in the Wind," Bob Dylan
"I Feel Like I'm Fixin' To Die," The Fish
"Give Peace a Chance," John Lennon

Middle East Conflicts

"Holiday," Green Day
"Devils & Dust," Bruce Springsteen
"Easy Silence," Dixie Chicks
"B.Y.O.B. (Bring Your Own Bombs)," System of a Down
"Courtesy of the Red, White, and Blue," Toby Keith

Cinematic List

World War II

Barefoot Gen (Mori Masaki, 1983)
The Bridge on the River Kwai (David Lean, 1957)
Catch-22 (Mike Nichols, 1970)
Das Boot (Wolfgang Petersen, 1981)
Fires on the Plain (Kon Ichikawa, 1959)
Flags of Our Fathers (Clint Eastwood, 2006)
Sands of Iwo Jima (Allan Dwan, 1949)
Saving Private Ryan (Steven Spielberg, 1998)
Shindler's List (Steven Spielberg, 1993)

Vietnam Conflict

Apocalypse Now (Francis Ford Coppola, 1979)
Born on the Fourth of July (Oliver Stone, 1989)
The Deer Hunter (Michael Cimino, 1978)
Full Metal Jacket (Stanley Kubric, 1987)
The Green Berets (John Wayne and Ray Kellogg, 1968)
R-Point (Su-chang Kong, 2004)
We Were Soldiers (Randall Wallace, 2002)

Middle East

Jarhead (Sam Mendes, 2005)
Three Kings (David O. Russell, 1999)
The Kite Runner (Marc Forster, 2006)
Rambo III (Peter MacDonald, 1988)

Video Games

Playstation3

Army of Two
Battlefield Bad Company
Call of Duty 4
God of War II
Metal Gear Solid 4: Guns of the Patriots

Xbox 360

Army of Two
BioShock

Call of Duty 4
F.E.A.R. (First Encounter Assault Recon)
Gears of War 2
Halo 3
Too Human

Wii

Call of Duty 4
House of Dead: Overkill

Online

World of Warcraft
Elfquest

"Plastic, again?!"

by John Pritchett

Plastic flotsam endangers sea birds.

AFTER YOU READ: Analyze the Issues

1. How does the lack of color add to the "bleakness" of the situation being argued?
2. What visual techniques are being used? Is this for entertainment? To inform?

AFTER YOU READ: Analyze the Rhetoric

1. What appeals does the cartoonist use to support his case?
2. How do the words at the bottom affect the argument of the cartoon?

The Issues

On the one hand, we are told that we are on a race against time with the environment falling apart faster than it can be restored. On the other hand, we are told that we have more time and that things are not as bad as they seem. Is the scientific data wrong? Who is right? Al Gore's *Inconvenient Truth* argues that the time to argue about this is over and that we need to act. Why do we seem not to be so fast to act? What is there about this issue that remains controversial and not self-evident? Are there other issues more important? Do we really have to act now?

Will more laws for the environment hurt our economy? Are we willing to make such sacrifices? Are we willing to pay more for a better environment?

What do Native Indians think about this? How does gender and race determine how we examine this issue?

Ask the Right Questions

What should we ask when examining the complex issues about the environment and when reading about it?

Logos

What factual data will prove that the environment is in danger?
What is wrong with that data?
What does the evidence say?
What are the underlying motives?

Ethos

Do we trust the evidence of scientists?
Do we trust the evidence of scientists hired by corporations?

How are we affected by the political voices in this issue?
Who is saying what and why?

Pathos

What emotions come to play in this issue?
Are we more emotional about such issues when it happens in our own back yard?
Should we be passionate about this issue?
Why do some not seem to care about this issue?

Annotate the Text

In addition to paying attention to the text's use of logos, ethos, and pathos, annotate the readings as follows.

- Who is the writer's intended audience? Conservatives? Liberals? Environmentalists? Capitalists?
- Underline the main argument or summarize the key points in the margin.
- After reading a selection, write a brief overview commenting on the effectiveness of the organization of the message.
- Comment on the evidence provided. Is the evidence effective? Can you trust the sources?
- Circle the weasel or buzz words such as *rights, prosperity,* and *nature*.

"Anywhere But Here"

by Rise Against
(Lyrics)

Rise Against is a hardcore/punk rock group from Chicago, Illinois consisting of four members, Tim McIlrath (vocals, lead guitar), Joe Principe (bass guitar), Brandon Barnes (drums), and Zach Blair (guitar). Rise Against has a liberal political stance which is seen in many of their songs such as "Blood Red White & Blue" and "State of the Union." The group members are vegetarians and active supporters of PETA. Their single "Ready to Fall" addresses environmental degradation and its effect on animals, as well as animal cruelty inherent to factory farming and sport hunting.

AS YOU READ: Annotate

1. Underline the adjectives used in the lyrics.
2. Put a star by the lines you find most powerful.

We've been alright up until now,
but the air that we breathe is about to run out.
We've rehearsed our lines clear and loud,
but the cue never came and the lights,
they never went down.
So we're passing the time,
while time passes us.
The fast lanes a term never applied to us.
Without a dime to my name,
or a prayer in the world.
I walk out the door.

Destination anywhere but here.
Away from you.

Now I'm on my way to the other side,
(On my way)
I'll forget everything I left behind.
(On my way)
These empty rooms,
(On my way)
are still filled with you.
(On my way)

So I dropped out of my own race,
a race with no finish line,
no first or last place.
These faces all rush right past me.
I turn and walk away,
cause we finally know now what our
time here's about, we were not meant to be
another face in the crowd.
We're a forest of lives,
but we grow tall and wide.
We'll never be cut down.

Destination anywhere but here.
Away from you.

Now I'm on my way to the other side,
(On my way)
I'll forget everything I left behind.
(On my way)
These empty rooms,
(On my way)

are still filled with you.
(On my way)

I'm so tired and turned around and scared.
I'm lying in empty beds again.
I'll wait for you to come
to your senses, barbed-wire fences
won't keep me from breaking through.
I swear I will to you.

Now I'm on my way to the other side,
(On my way)
I'll forget everything I left behind.
(On my way)
These empty rooms,
(On my way)
are still filled with you.
(On my way)

I'm so tired and turned around and scared.
I'm lying in empty beds again.
Away from you.

AFTER YOU READ: Analyze the Issues

1. What is the main argument of these lyrics? Provide evidence of your answer using the lyrics.
2. Cite lines that tell you, the reader, whom the singer is trying to avoid. Who is it and how do you know?
3. Who is "we" in the following lines:

   "We're a forest of lives
   But we grow tall and wide
   We'll never be cut down."

   And how does it affect the argument?

AFTER YOU READ: Analyze the Rhetoric

1. As you read, underline the words that are repeated (ignoring the words in the chorus). What is the importance of such repetition?
2. Watch a video or read aloud these lyrics. How does the video or reading aloud affect your understanding of the lyrics? Does it strengthen or weaken the lyric's argument?

I Heart Huckabees

by Jeff Baena
(Screenplay)

Jeff Baena was born in 1977 in Miami, Florida. *I Heart Huckabees* was produced and directed by David O. Russell, who co-wrote the screenplay with Jeff Baena.

AS YOU READ: Annotate

1. Underline the "facts" given by Dad and Tom.
2. Put a star by the lines you find most powerful.

INT. MR. NIMIERI'S HOME—DINING TABLE—NIGHT

MR. AND MRS. HOOTEN and their teen children CRICKET and BRET, plus Mr. Nimieri, Albert, and Tommy hold hands at dinner.

CRICKET
— for thine is the kingdom, the power, and the glory, forever and ever, amen.

Cut to everyone eating. Tommy glances at Albert.

ALBERT
How'd you end up working as a doorman, Steven?

MR. NIMIERI
It is part of our immigration agreement. We must work.

MRS. HOOTEN
The building supervisor who hired Steven is a member of our congregation.

BRET
He was so skinny when he moved in.

CRICKET (MURMERS CRYPTICALLY)
Skeleton man from Africaaaa.

Bret and Cricket giggle uncontrollably, Bret spits milk.

(CONTINUED)

MRS. HOOTEN
What did we say about that?

MR. HOOTEN
I don't want to hear it again. There will be no Internet tonight.

BRET
He didn't know what a can opener was. He opened cans with a big knife, like at the refugee camp.

MR. HOOTEN
Patience, Bret.

CRICKET
And there aren't lions roaming here, but there were in Sudan, and the orphan boys got chased, and a big alligator bit his friend's head off. He saw it.

BRET
Crocodile. There are no alligators in Africa.

CRICKET
He wanted to know where all the meat comes from since he doesn't see any cows around here.

MR. HOOTEN
That's enough, guys, Steven doesn't like to talk about that stuff.

Tommy looks at Steven with Empathy.

MRS. HOOTEN
What brought you to the philosophical club, Albert?

ALBERT
You mean the existential detectives?

MR. HOOTEN
Sounds like a support group.

CRICKET
Why can't he use the church?

(CONTINUED)

MRS. HOOTEN

Sometimes people have additional questions to explore.

CRICKET

Like what?

ALBERT

Well, for instance, if the forms of this world die, which is more real, the me that dies or the me that's infinite? Can I trust my habitual mind or do I try to look beneath those things?

MR. HOOTEN (CHUCKLES)

Sounds like we got a philosopher.

CRICKET

We don't have to ask those kinds of questions, do we, Mom?

MRS. HOOTEN

Oh, honey.

MR. HOOTEN

Ya know what happened to the cat, Albert?

ALBERT (TAKEN ABACK)

How do you know about my cat?

MR. HOOTEN (WINKS)

The cat was killed by curiosity.

ALBERT

Oh, that cat.

BRET

Do you have a job?

MRS. HOOTEN

Yes, Albert, tell us what you do.

ALBERT

I'm director of the Open Spaces Coalition. We fight suburban sprawl.

(CONTINUED)

CRICKET
What's suburban sprawl?

MR. HOOTEN
Ask Steven if they could have used a little suburban sprawl in Sudan.

MR. NIMIERI
Excuse me, dad?

MR. HOOTEN
Industry, houses, jobs, restaurants, medicine—

ALBERT
You can still preserve a lot of —

MR. HOOTEN
I beg your pardon, Albert. I wasn't finished.

ALBERT
Oh. I'm sorry, go ahead.

MR. HOOTEN
Clothes, videos, toys, cheeseburgers, cars, computer games, a functioning economy.

ALBERT
You can still have a functioning economy and preserve open spaces, with a little planning.

MRS. HOOTEN
Socialism. A complete disaster.

ALBERT (GROWING HEATED)
Then I guess Theodore Roosevelt was a socialist, and William Butler Yeats, and Elizabeth Bishop and Robinson Jeffers and Henry David Thoreau and the National Geographic Society —

CRICKET (WHISPERS)
Skeleton man from Africaaaa.

MRS. HOOTEN
You're talking about socialism.

(CONTINUED)

ALBERT (GETTING MORE HEATED)
I'm talking about not covering every square inch of populated America with strip malls and houses till people can't even remember what happens when you stand in a meadow at dusk.

BRET
What happens in the meadow at dusk?

ALBERT
Everything. Everything.

MRS. HOOTEN
Nothing. Nothing.

TOMMY CORN
It's beautiful

MR. HOOTEN (MAD)
I happen to work for an electrical engineering firm, son, and we do a great deal of commercial and residential contracts, so if development stops, so does my pay check, and then Steven couldn't be here as our guest, could he? So your ideas are hurting Steven, Albert.

ALBERT (HEATED)
I am not hurting Steven. That's an outrageous accusation.

MR. HOOTEN (VERY MAD)
Don't use that tone of voice in my house.

ALBERT
I think you started that tone, sir, and it's entirely possible for your engineering firm to have all kinds of contracts and still—

Albert suddenly stares at the table. He closes his eyes as everyone looks.

CRICKET
Why's he closing his eyes?

MRS. HOOTEN
Cricket.

MR. HOOTEN
Do you have a job, Tommy?

(CONTINUED)

TOMMY CORN
I'm a fireman.

MRS. HOOTEN
You're a hero, God bless you.

TOMMY CORN
I'm not a hero. We'd all be heroes if we quit using petroleum.

MR. HOOTEN
Excuse me?

TOMMY CORN
You say you're Christians living by Jesus' principles, but are you?

BRET
Of course we are.

CRICKET
Jesus is never mad at us if we live with him in our hearts.

TOMMY CORN
Well, I hate to break it to you, but he is, he most definitely is.

MRS. HOOTEN
Steven, you've brought blasphemous socialists into our house.

MR. NIMIERI
I'm sorry, Dad. I did not know.

MR. HOOTEN
Steve-O. I'm disappointed.

Steven looks down, ashamed.

MRS. HOOTEN
Now look, he's sad.

(CONTINUED)

MR. HOOTEN
I'm sorry, Steve-O. My bad, you didn't know.

TOMMY CORN
You should be ashamed of yourself.

MR. HOOTEN
I should be what?

TOMMY CORN
You should be ashamed of yourself.

MR. HOOTEN
And why is that? Why should I be ashamed of myself?

TOMMY CORN
You're a hypocrite. You're misleading these children.

MR. HOOTEN
I'm a what? How is that?

TOMMY CORN
'Cause you're the destroyer, man.

MR. HOOTEN
How am I the destroyer?

TOMMY CORN
I saw that SUV out there.

MR. HOOTEN
Oh my car's the destroyer? You want to know how many miles per gallon I get?

DIALOGUE CONTINUTES OFF SCREEN. CUT TO:

ALBERT
Steven, I really need to ask a question. It's why I came here. Why are autographs so important to you?

MR. NIMIERI
It is a pastime of this family which they have taught to me and which I can now carry on.

MRS. HOOTEN (O.S.)
It's just for fun, it's for entertainment. No games at the table, please.

(CONTINUED)

BRET (PLAYING COMPUTER GAME)
YESSS, 260, I reached the Omega Level.

MR. NIMIERI (SADLY)
I cannot achieve Omega level.

MR. HOOTEN
GOD GAVE US OIL! HE GAVE IT TO US!

TOMMY CORN
HE GAVE YOU A BRAIN, TOO.

MR. HOOTEN (TO ALBERT)
I want you sons of bitches out now.

TOMMY CORN
If Hitler were alive, he'd tell us NOT to think about oil.

MRS. HOOTEN (CRYING)
YOU'RE THE HITLER. I GAVE A SUDANESE REFUGEE A HOME.

TOMMY CORN
How did Sudan happen? Could it be related to dictatorships we support for some stupid reason?

MR. HOOTEN
YOU SHUT UP, YOU GET OUT.

TOMMY CORN
You shut up.

Tommy and Albert head to the door.

ALBERT
See you later, Steve.

TOMMY CORN
God bless you.

AFTER YOU READ: Analyze the Issues

1. Summarize Mr. Hooten's view on the environmental issues Tom develops.
2. Compare and contrast these views. How does the use of pathos, ethos, and logos support each view?
3. What fallacies are used by Mr. Hooten? Tom? Mrs. Hooten? How does this affect the scene?

AFTER YOU READ: Analyze the Rhetoric

1. Watch the movie, or read aloud in groups, specifically this scene. How does the dinner table affect the lines? How does the body language of each actor affect the lines?
2. What is the main argument of the scene? Support your response with specific lines from the scene.

"Environmental Illness"

by Todd Haynes
screenplay excerpt from Safe *1995*

Todd Haynes (1961–) was born in Los Angeles. In high school, he directed his first film *Suicide* (1978) about teenagers confronting the transformations of growing up. He recently completed a film about the life of Bob Dylan, *I'm Not Here* (2007). He attended Brown University. When he graduated, he made a controversial film, *Superstar: The Karen Carpenter Story* about anorexia using Barbie dolls as the stars. In 1991, he directed *Poison*, based on the works of the French writer, Jean Genet. *Safe* (1995) became his most critically acclaimed film, where the protagonist suffers from an illness that is misunderstood. Her struggles become a metaphor for AIDs.

"Environmental Illness" by Todd Haynes, *Far From Heaven, Safe, and Superstar: The Karen Carpenter Story, Three Screenplays.* © 2003 New York: Grove Press. 133–138.

AS YOU READ: Annotate

1. Place a star by the sections you feel are effective.
2. Circle all words or phrases that have negative references to the environment.
3. Write some questions in the margin that you want to ask the class.

Background for the film. The main protagonist of the film, Carol, lives the perfect life in San Fernando Valley, an elite, suburban California neighborhood. However, her health starts to fail her, but no one, not even doctors, can cure or solve the mystery to her illness. Even her husband, Greg, is starting to think that it may be in her head.

INT. WHITES' BEDROOM—NIGHT

Music spills over a slow track past articles in Carol's bedroom: some family photos, pictures of CAROL as a child, perfumes, souvenirs, a stuffed animal. Light is subdued so colors are rich. Over the track, we hear Carol's voice reading a letter she is in the process of writing.

CAROL(V.O.)
My name is Carol White and I live in Southern California. I saw your notice at the health center near my house and decided to write and tell you a little bit about myself. For some time now I have not been feeling up to par and was hoping your organization might be of some help. I'm originally from Texas, although I've lived in the L.A. area most of my life. I had asthma as a child but it never really got in the way of school or recreation. I've always thought of myself as someone with a pretty normal upbringing and as basically a healthy person. But for the past several months that has all started to change. Suddenly, I find myself feeling sick all the—

The track has brought us to CAROL, who sits in bed writing a letter on a Lucite clipboard. Beside her is the unfolded notice (DO YOU SMELL FUMES?). The shot concludes on a close-up of Carol's hand, at which point the light from an opening door spills in. We see a black drop of ink has seeped from her pen as music and voice-over stop.
She looks up.

GREG is at the door. Brief silence.

GREG
What's going on?—I've been calling you. I thought you were sleeping. Someone—Brenda—was calling about trading Thursday carpool for Wednesday or Saturday or something—she says you'll know what she means—

He stops, looking at her a moment.

GREG
Anyway…She says she'll call you back—I thought you were sleeping 'cause you weren't—… What're you doing?

CAROL stares at him in confusion. A sudden dizziness has completely fogged her mind.

(CONTINUED)

CAROL

I was writing this—

She looks down at her letter and back at GREG, anxiously.

CAROL (Half-smiles, to herself)

I don't even…

She nervously glances around the room, finds the mirror.
Her eyes fill.

CAROL(Under her breath)

Oh, God, what is this…

GREG

What?

CAROL (Quietly, not looking up)

Where am I? Right now.

GREG looks at her, frozen.

GREG (Also quietly)

We're in our house.

Her eyes dart to photos framed on the dresser. A wedding portrait.

GREG

Greg and Carol's house.

A tear rolls down her cheek.

Cut to:
The high-pitch intro tone of a videotape over

[Intertitle: CONTROL]

INT. COMMUNITY CENTER—DAY
Color bars on a TV monitor.

MODERATOR (O.S., over tone)

We're going to begin with a –introductory tape—

The tone and color bars abruptly end. There is a moment of black, a note of music, and the words: Q: WHO ARE YOU?

(CONTINUED)

VIDEO NARRATOR (V.O.)
Question: Who are you? Answer…

CAROL watches the tape in a community center auditorium. She sits among an audience of mostly white, middle-class women.

The screen dissolves to music and a montage of faces of different people "from all walks of life." Then it cuts to the VIDEO NARRATOR himself, a long faced white man seated at a desk addressing the camera.

VIDEO NARRATOR (V.O.)
You are of all ages and from all walks of life. But you find you all have one thing in common: strange, never-ending ailments. Suddenly, you can't cook dinner because the smell of gas from your stove makes you ill. Or if you take the freeway you feel as if you might choke on the fumes. Your family and friends tell you that you're overreacting, that it's "all in your head." But your symptoms worsen. Fatigue and depression turn to migraines, blackouts, even seizures.

THE MODERATOR, a bearded man in his early thirties, sits beside the monitor, watching. Many of the audience listeners show their recognition of the events being described.

VIDEO NARRATOR (V.O.)
Now, if this sounds familiar, you're not alone. What you most likely are is one of a vastly growing number of people who suffer from environmental illness. That means that for reasons not yet known certain people's natural tolerance of everyday substances is breaking down, usually as a result of some kind of chemical exposure. Today, there are sixty thousand chemicals in everyday use, yet only ten percent are tested for human toxicity. This is a disease that you catch from your environment…

The MODERATOR pauses the video.

MODERATOR
So are there any questions so far that I can—Yes?

MAN
Is it the same thing as total allergy syndrome?

(CONTINUED)

MODERATOR

Yes, it is. It's been called a lot of different things: total allergy syndrome, multiple chemical sensitivities. Sometimes just twentieth-century illness. Yes?

He points to a man in his late forties (JAKE) who raises a meticulously bandaged hand.

JAKE

I'm allergic to—chlorine—I, uh—

MODERATOR

Could you stand up? (He does so) What's your name?

JAKE

Jake—I'm an engineer and I used to—brush my teeth in the morning and get so—whacked-out I couldn't even find my way out of the bathroom…that's how bad it was. I'm much better now—So I just—I mean … are you saying there's nothing that you can do about it once you—once you get it—because with me—

MODERATOR

No there's a lot that you can do, there's a lot to be gained from early detection, and we'll get into that in a minute—

There are several hands up this time. CAROL looks around her as more questions are asked.

MODERATOR

Yes—over there?

SINGLE WOMAN

How do you know for sure if you—if this is what you—

MODERATOR

You test yourself. You begin to look for the possible sources of your symptoms and you test them out. You isolate them. "Control the environment, isolate the incident." Right? You have to know what's making you sick before you get any better.

CAROL listens with stony concentration as we slowly dissolve to:

EXT. WHITES' NEIGHBORHOOD—AFTERNOON

The view from the hood of Carol's car, heading home. It is late afternoon and long shadows sweep across the road as we climb the hill. Quiet music reminiscent of the opening credit sequence.

(CONTINUED)

We approach the Whites' house as the gate glides open and garage door sails up. The car pulls in.

Cut to:

INT. WHITES' HOUSE—AFTERNOON
CAROL enters the house through the garage door, walking through the kitchen and into the living room. It is dark and still inside. Somehow it all seems foreign, as if it belonged to somebody else.

CAROL
Fulvia!...Fulvia!

She walks through to the other end of the living room but there is no response.

CAROL(fainter)
Greg?

Silence. CAROL stands in the middle of the living room but there is no response. For ten seconds she is still.
She looks down at the books and crystal items on the coffee table. She looks over at the chair, the carpet, the walls, sensing, for the first time, their potential danger. A faint acid tone accompanies.

Suddenly—

GREG
Carol?

CAROL turns, gasping, startled.
GREG stands at the other end of the living room.

CAROL
You scared me.

GREG
Sorry.

CAROL
No—I was just—I'm sorry—

GREG
I just took Fulvia down. You just get home?

(CONTINUED)

CAROL

Yeah.

GREG

So how'd it go?

CAROL

What?

GREG

Your thing, this morning—What was it on?

CAROL

Oh it was just this thing on getting sick on fumes and bug sprays and stuff.

He stares at her a moment.

GREG

You mean on—like, pollution?

CAROL

Well, more just about people who get sick from chemicals and what it does to you.

GREG

Who told you to go to this?

CAROL

No, I just—at the health center I saw a flyer.

GREG

So you think this is what you've been—I mean—why you've been sick? Because of bug spray?

CAROL

No, I just—

Silence. They look at each other.

CAROL

I don't know why.

AFTER YOU READ: Analyze the Issues

1. Where was Carol originally from? Why would this be important?
2. What are some of the names of the illness she might have? What is in a name?
3. How is Carol's illness a metaphor for AIDs?
4. Discuss the ending. What does Carol mean by her answer to Greg?

AFTER YOU READ: Analyze the Rhetoric

1. What is the significance of Carol and Greg's last name?
2. How important is the narrative description from the dialogue?
3. Read the screenplay aloud with someone and discuss how it comes alive when spoken. How are screenplays different from other forms of fiction?

"Before They Got Thick"

by Percy Bigmouth
(ca early nineteenth century)
(to be read with the except from Winthrop, which immediately follows)
(Essay)

Percy Bigmouth was born in 1889 and suffered from tuberculosis of the spine or Pott's disease. This story is an excerpt from a series of Apache Tales. Bigmouth wrote them down in standard "Big Chief" legal pads. He wrote the stories for a young white teenage girl whom he befriended during 1939 while he was working as a ranger at the Mescalero Apache reservation near Ruidoso, New Mexico. He sent her the pads in 1949.

Bigmouth, Percy. "The white people who came in a boat." Originally published as "The white people who came in a boat." In M.E. Opler. *Memoirs of the American Folklore Society*, vol. 26., 1940.

AS YOU READ: Annotate

1. On a separate sheet of paper, list the adjectives associated with the land by Bigmouth and Winthrop.
2. Place a star by sections you like.

My grandmother used to tell this story; she told it to my mother. It was about the time when they lived near the gulf. She says that they lived in a place called "Beside the Smooth Water." They used to camp there on the sand. Sometimes a big wave would come up and then they would pick up many seashells. Sometimes they used to find water turtles. They used to find fish too and gather them and eat them.

One time they had a big wave. It was very bad. They thought the ocean was going to come right up. It came up a long way. Living thing from the water covered the bank, were washed up. Then, when the sun came out and it was hot all these things began to swell and swelled bad.

One day they looked over the big water. Then someone saw a little black dot over on the water. He came back and told that he had seen that strange thing. Others came out. They sat there and looked. It was getting larger. They waited. Pretty soon it came up. It was a boat. The boat came to the shore. The Indians went back to the big camp. All the Indians came over and watched. People were coming out. They looked at those people coming out. They saw that the people had blue eyes and were white. They thought these people might live in the water all the time.

They had a council that night. They were undecided whether they should let them live or kill them.

One leader said, "Well, they have a shape just like ours. The difference is that they have light skin and hair."

Another said, "Let's not kill them. They may be of help to us some day. Let's let them go and see what they'll do."

So the next day they watched them. "What shall we call them?" they asked…

Some still wanted to kill them. Others said no. So they decided to let them alone.

The Lipan went away. After a year they said, "Let's go back and see them."

They did so. Only a few were left. Many had starved to death. Some said, "Let's kill them now; they are so few." But others said, "No, let us be like brothers to them."

It was spring. The Lipan gave some pumpkin seed and seed corn and told them how to use it. The people took it and after that they got along all right. They raised a little corn and some pumpkins. They started a new life, later on the Lipan left for a while. When they returned, the white people were getting along very well. The Lipan gave them venison. They were getting along very well. After that, they began to get thick.

"The Indians Grew Very Inquisitive"

by John Winthrop
(Essay)

John Winthrop was one of the founders of the Massachusetts Bay Colony. After arriving in America aboard the *Arbella*, he was elected governor of the Colony and quickly established the center of government at Boston. Even though he was voted in and out of the governorship over the next 19 years, Winthrop's influence on the colony was substantial. He wrote many works over the course of those 19 years, including his famous *Journal*, from which the following passage comes.

Winthrop, John. "The Indians grew very inquisitive." In J.K. Hosmer (ed.), *Winthrop's Journal.* New York: Charles Scribner's Sons, 1908.

The Indians grew very inquisitive after knowledge both in things divine and also human, so as one of them, meeting with an honest plain Englishman, would need know of him, what were the first beginnings (which we call principles) of a commonwealth. The Englishman, being far short in the knowledge of such matters, yet ashamed that an Indian should find an Englishman ignorant of any thing, bethought himself what answer to give him, at last resolved upon this, viz. that the first principle of a commonwealth was salt, for (saith he) by means of salt we can keep out flesh and fist, to have it ready when we need it, whereas you lose much for want to it, and are some times ready to starve. A second principle is iron, for thereby we fell trees, build houses, till our land, etc. A third is, ships, by which we carry forth such commodities as we have to spare and fetch in such as we need, as cloth, wine. Alas! (saith the Indian) then I fear, we shall never have a commonwealth, for we can neither make salt, nor iron, nor ships.

AFTER YOU READ: Analyze the Issues

1. Compare and contrast the adjectives. What do you notice?
2. How does the use of adjectives demonstrate the polarized view of American lands during that time? How does the use of adjectives by Bigmouth and Winthrop inform our current view of American lands?

AFTER YOU READ: Analyze the Rhetoric

1. Bigmouth and Winthrop use different appeals to make their arguments. Determine which appeals each writer is using. Does that appeal(s) have the most influence on an audience that already agrees with the author or that might disagree? Why? Provide evidence.

2. How does Bigmouth's use of narrative support his rhetorical appeals? How does Winthrop's lack of narrative support his?
3. Read each piece aloud. Does the oral presentation change the tone of either or both pieces? Affect the content? Why would the oral tradition be more important to Bigmouth and the Native Americans than to Winthrop?

"How Can One Sell the Air? A Manifesto for the Earth"

by Chief Seattle
(Manifesto)

Chief Seattle was a famous warrior who maintained strong relations not only with local tribes but also with European settlers. The following speech was given in December 1854, when Chief Seattle was in his late fifties or early sixties. Many scholars question if Chief Seattle, though credited with the speech, actually gave the speech exactly as it is printed below. The only copy of the speech was recorded by Dr. Henry A. Smith, a settler and amateur writer, who could not speak or understand Chief Seattle's language. The rhetoric and style of the speech are common 19th Century European language strategies and sound more like other works from Smith.

AS YOU READ: Annotate

1. Underline the groups of words that create a rhythmic tone, a common strategy used in Native American oral tradition.
2. Put a star by any gaps or shifts in this rhythmic tone.

Yonder sky that has wept tears of compassion upon my people for centuries untold, and which to us appears changeless and eternal, may change. Today is fair. Tomorrow it may be overcast with clouds. My words are like the stars that never change. Whatever Seattle says, the great chief at Washington can rely upon with as much certainty as he can upon the return of the sun or the seasons. The white chief says that Big Chief at Washington sends us greetings of friendship and goodwill. This is kind of him for we know he has little need of our friendship in return. His people are many. They are like the grass that covers vast prairies. My people are few. They resemble the scattering trees of a storm-swept plain. The great, and I presume—good, White Chief sends us word that he wishes to buy our land but is willing to allow us enough to live comfortably. This indeed appears just, even generous, for the Red Man no longer has rights that he need respect, and the offer may be wise, also, as we are no longer in need of an extensive country.

There was a time when our people covered the land as the waves of a wind-ruffled sea cover its shell-paved floor, but that time long since passed away with the greatness of tribes that are now but a mournful memory. I will not dwell on, nor mourn over, our untimely decay, nor reproach my paleface brothers with hastening it, as we too may have been somewhat to blame.

Youth is impulsive. When our young men grow angry at some real or imaginary wrong, and disfigure their faces with black paint, it denotes that their hearts are black, and that they are often cruel and relentless, and our old men and old women are unable to restrain them. Thus it has ever been. Thus it was when the white man began to push our forefathers ever westward. But let us hope that the hostilities between us may never return. We would have everything to lose and nothing to gain. Revenge by young men is considered gain, even at the cost of their own lives, but old men who stay at home in times of war, and mothers who have sons to lose, know better.

Our good father in Washington—for I presume he is now our father as well as yours, since King George has moved his boundaries further north—our great and good father, I say, sends us word that if we do as he desires he will protect us. His brave warriors will be to us a bristling wall of strength, and his wonderful ships of war will fill our harbors, so that our ancient enemies far to the northward—the Haidas and Tsimshians—will cease to frighten our women, children, and old men. Then in reality he will be our father and we his children. But can that ever be? Your God is not our God! Your God loves your people and hates mine! He folds his strong protecting arms lovingly about the paleface and leads him by the hand as a father leads an infant son. But, He has forsaken His Red children, if they really are His. Our God, the Great Spirit, seems also to have forsaken us. Your God makes your people wax stronger every day. Soon they will fill all the land. Our people are ebbing away like a rapidly receding tide that will never return. The white man's God cannot love our people or He would protect them. They seem to be orphans who can look nowhere for help. How then can we be brothers? How can your God become our God and renew our prosperity and awaken in us dreams of returning greatness? If we have a common Heavenly Father, He must be partial, for He came to His paleface children. We never saw Him. He gave you laws but had no word for His red children whose teeming multitudes once filled this vast continent as stars fill the firmament. No, we are two distinct races with separate origins and separate destinies. There is little in common between us.

To us the ashes of our ancestors are sacred and their resting place is hallowed ground. You wander far from the graves of your ancestors and seemingly without regret. Your religion was written upon tablets of stone by the iron finger of your God so that you could not forget. The Red Man could never comprehend or remember it. Our religion is the traditions of our ancestors—the dreams of our old men, given them in solemn hours of the night by the Great Spirit; and the visions of our sachems, and is written in the hearts of our people.

Your dead cease to love you and the land of their nativity as soon as they pass the portals of the tomb and wander away beyond the stars. They are soon forgotten and never return. Our dead never forget this beautiful world that gave them being. They still love its verdant valleys, its murmuring rivers, its magnificent mountains, sequestered vales and verdant lined lakes and bays, and ever yearn in tender fond affection over the lonely hearted living, and often return from the happy hunting ground to visit, guide, console, and comfort them.

Day and night cannot dwell together. The Red Man has ever fled the approach of the White Man, as the morning mist flees before the morning sun. However, your proposition seems fair and I think that my people will accept it and will retire to the reservation you offer them. Then we will dwell apart in peace, for the words of the Great White Chief seem to be the words of nature speaking to my people out of dense darkness.

It matters little where we pass the remnant of our days. They will not be many. The Indian's night promises to be dark. Not a single star of hope hovers above his horizon. Sad-voiced winds moan in the distance. Grim fate seems to be on the Red Man's trail, and wherever he will hear the approaching footsteps of his fell destroyer and prepare stolidly to meet his doom, as does the wounded doe that hears the approaching footsteps of the hunter.

A few more moons, a few more winters, and not one of the descendants of the mighty hosts that once moved over this broad land or lived in happy homes, protected by the Great Spirit, will remain to mourn over the graves of a people once more powerful and hopeful than yours. But why should I mourn at the untimely fate of my people? Tribe follows tribe, and nation follows nation, like the waves of the sea. It is the order of nature, and regret is useless. Your time of decay may be distant, but it will surely come, for even the White Man whose God walked and talked with him as friend to friend, cannot be exempt from the common destiny. We may be brothers after all. We will see.

We will ponder your proposition and when we decide we will let you know. But should we accept it, I here and now make this condition that we will not be denied the privilege without molestation of visiting at any time the tombs of our ancestors, friends, and children. Every part of this soil is sacred in the estimation of my people. Every hillside, every valley, every plain and grove, has been hallowed by some sad or happy event in days long vanished. Even the rocks, which seem to be dumb and dead as they swelter in the sun along the silent shore, thrill with memories of stirring events connected with the lives of my people, and the very dust upon which you now stand responds more lovingly to their footsteps than yours, because it is rich with the blood of our ancestors, and our bare feet are conscious of the sympathetic touch. Our departed braves, fond mothers, glad, happy hearted maidens, and even the little children who lived here and rejoiced here for a brief season, will love these somber solitudes and at eventide they greet shadowy returning spirits. And when the last Red Man shall have perished, and the memory of my tribe shall have become a myth among the White Men, these shores will swarm with the invisible dead of my tribe, and when your children's children think themselves alone in the field, the store, the shop, upon the highway, or in the silence of the pathless woods, they will not be alone. In all the earth there is no place dedicated to solitude. At night when the streets of your cities and villages are silent and you think them deserted, they will throng with the returning hosts that once filled them and still love this beautiful land. The White Man will never be alone.

Let him be just and deal kindly with my people, for the dead are not altogether powerless.

AFTER YOU READ: Analyze the Issues

1. Look closely at the adjectives and language in the speech. Compare it with the short excerpts from Bigmouth and Winthrop. Does Chief Seattle's speech use the same strategies of either Bigmouth or Winthrop? How is the language similar? Different?
2. Does this speech use any of the advertising strategies discussed in chapter 5? If so, what are they? Are the strategies used to motivate? Provide evidence to support your answers.
3. Does this speech demonstrate the polarized views of the environment, as noted by Bigmouth and Winthrop? Provide evidence from the speech.

AFTER YOU READ: Analyze the Rhetoric

1. To whom is Chief Seattle directing this speech? His tribe? The European settlers? Both? Locate language that supports your assertion.
2. What rhetorical appeals are presented by Chief Seattle? Would different appeals be better suited for the argument? Provide evidence for your assertion.

"Mexican American Women Grassroots Community Activists: 'Mothers of East Los Angeles'"

by Mary Pardo

Mary Pardo is Professor of Chicana/o Studies at California State University, Northridge. She is the author of several articles and books on women and grassroots organizing and has been active in the Chicano Movement in Los Angeles for about twenty-five years.

AS YOU READ: Annotate

1. Underline the specific cultural references.
2. Circle any assertions you find particularly powerful or discerning.

The Community Context: East Los Angeles Resisting Siege

Political science theory often guides the political strategies used by local government to select the sites for undesirable projects. In 1984, the state of California commissioned a public relations firm to assess the political difficulties facing the construction of energy-producing waste incinerators. The report provided a "personality profile" of those residents most likely to organize effective opposition to projects:

> middle and upper socioeconomic strata possess better resources to effectuate their opposition. Middle and higher socioeconomic strata neighborhoods should not fall within the one-mile and five mile radii of the proposed site. Conversely, older people, people with a high school education or less are least likely to oppose a facility.

The state accordingly placed the plant in Commerce, a predominately Mexican American, low-income community. This pattern holds throughout the state and the country: three out of five Afro-Americans and Latinos live near toxic waste sites, and three of the five largest hazardous waste landfills are in communities with at least 80 percent minority population....

Prominent among the coalitions groups is "Mothers of East Los Angeles," a loosely knit group of over 400 Mexican American women. MELA initially coalesced to oppose the state prison construction but has since organized opposition to several other projects detrimental to the quality of life in the central city. Its second large target is a toxic waste incinerator proposed for Vernon, a small city adjacent to East Los Angeles. This incinerator would worsen the already debilitating air quality for the entire county and set a precedent dangerous for other communities throughout California. When MELA took up the fight against the toxic waste incinerator, it became more than a single-issue group and began working with environmental groups around the state. As a result of the community struggle, AB58 (Roybal-Allard), which provides all Californians with the minimum protection of an environmental impact report before the construction of hazardous waste incinerators, was signed into law. But the law's effectiveness relies on a watchful community network. Since its emergence, "Mothers of East Los Angeles" has become centrally important to just such a network of grassroots activists including a select number of Catholic priests and two Mexican American political representatives. Furthermore, the group's very formation, and its continued spirit and activism, fly in the face of the conventional political science beliefs regarding political participation.

Predictions by the "experts" attribute the low formal political participation (i.e., voting) of Mexican American people in the U.S. to a set of cultural "retardants" including primary kinship systems, fatalism, religious traditionalism, traditional cultural values, and mother country attachment. The core activists in MELA may appear to fit this description, as well as the state-commissioned profile of residents least likely to oppose toxic waste incinerator projects. All the women live in a low-income community. Furthermore, they identify themselves as active and committed participants in the Catholic Church; they claim an ethnic identity—Mexican American; their ages range from forty to sixty; and they have attainted at most high school educations. However, these women fail to conform to the predicted social apathy. Instead, they have transformed social identity—ethnic identity, class identity, and gender identity—into an impetus as well as a bias for activism. And, in transforming their existing social networks into grassroots political networks, they have also transformed themselves.

Transformation as a Dominant Theme

...First, women have transformed organizing experiences and social networks arising from gender-related responsibilities into political resources. When I asked the women about the first community, not necessarily "political," involvement they could recall, they discussed experiences that predated the formation of MELA....

Erlinda Robles recalled:

> I wanted my kids to go to Catholic school and from the time my oldest one went there, I was there every day. I used to take my two little ones with me and I helped one way or another. I used to question things they did. And the other mothers would just watch me. Later, they would ask me, "Why do you do that? They are going to take it out on your kids." I'd say, "They better not." And before you knew it, we had a big group of mothers that were very involved.

Part of a mother's "traditional" responsibilities includes overseeing her child's progress in school, interacting with school staff, and supporting school activities. In these processes, women meet other mothers and begin developing a network of acquaintanceships and friendships based on mutual concern for the welfare of their children.

...Women got men into the group by giving them a position they could manage. The men may have held the title of "president," but they were not making day-to-day decisions about work, nor were they dictating the direction of the group. Erlinda Robles laughed as she recalled an occasion when the president insisted, against the wishes of the women, on scheduling a parents' group fundraiser—a breakfast—on Mother's Day. On that morning, only the president and his wife were present to prepare breakfast. This should alert researchers against measuring power and influence by looking solely at who holds titles.

Each of the cofounders had a history of working with groups arising out of the responsibilities usually assumed by "mothers"—the education of children and the safety of the surrounding community. From these groups, they gained valuable experiences and networks that facilitated the formation of "Mothers of East Los Angeles."... MELA effectively linked up preexisting networks into a viable grassroots coalition.

Second, the process of activism also transformed previously "invisible" women, making them not only visible but the center of public attention. From a conventional perspective, political activism assumes a kind of gender neutrality. This means that anyone can participate, but men are the expected key actors. In accordance with this pattern, in winter 1986 an informal group of concerned businessmen in the community began lobbying and testifying against the prison at hearings in Sacramento. Working in conjunction with Assemblywoman Molina, they made many trips to Sacramento at their own expense. Residents who did not have the income to travel were unable to join them. Finally, Molina, commonly recognized as a forceful advocate for Latinas and the community, asked Frank Villalobos, an urban planner in the group, why there were no women coming up to speak in Sacramento against the prison. As he phrased it, "I was getting some heat from her because no women were going up there."

...The next juncture illustrates how perceptions of gender-specific behavior set in motion a sequence of events that brought women into the political limelight. Father Moretta decided to ask all the women to meet after mass. He told them about the prison site and called for their support. When I asked him about his rationale for selecting the women, he replied:

> I felt so strongly about the issue, and I knew in my heart what a terrible offense this was to the people. So, I was afraid that once we got into a demonstration situation we had to be very careful. I thought the women would be cooler and calmer than the men. The bottom line is that the men came anyway. The first times out the majority were women. Then they began to invite their husbands and their children, but originally it was just women.

Father Moretta also named the group. Quite moved by a film, *The Official Story*, about the courageous Argentine women who demonstrated for the return of their children who disappeared during a repressive right-wing military dictatorship, he transformed the name "Las Madres de la Plaza de Mayo" into "Mothers of East Los Angeles."

...Although the women played a key role in the mobilization, they emphasized the group's broad base of active supporters as well as the other organizations in the "Coalition Against the Prison." Their intent was to counter any notion that MELA was composed exclusively of women or mothers and to stress the "inclusiveness" of the group. All the women who assumed lead roles in the group had long histories of volunteer work in the Boyle Heights community; but formation of the group brought them out of the "private" margins and into the "public" light.

Third, the women in "Mothers of East L.A." have transformed the definition of mother to state-proposed projects they see as adverse to the quality of life in the community. Explaining how she discovered the issue, Aurora Castillo said,

> You know if one of your children's safety is jeopardized, the mother turns into a lioness. That's why Father John got the mothers. We have to have a well-organized, strong group of mothers to protect the community and oppose things that are detrimental to us. You know the governor is in the wrong and the mothers are in the right. After all, the mothers have to be right. Mothers are for the children's interest, not for self-interest; the governor is for his own political interest.

The women also have expanded the boundaries of "motherhood" to include social and political community activism and redefined the word to include women who are not biological "mothers." At one meeting a young Latina expressed her solidarity with the group and, almost apologetically, qualified herself as a "resident," not a "mother," of East Los Angeles. Erlinda Robles replied:

> When you are fighting for a better life for children and "doing" for them, isn't that what mothers do? So we're all mothers. You don't have to have children to be a "mother."

At critical points, grassroots community activism requires attending many meetings, phone calling, and door-to-door communications—all very labor intensive work. In order to keep harmony in the "domestic" sphere, the core activists must creatively integrate family members into their community activities. I asked Erlinda Robles how her husband felt about her activism, and she replied quite openly:

> My husband doesn't like getting involved, but he takes me because he knows I like it. Sometimes we would have two or three meetings a week. And my husband would say, "Why are you doing so much? It is really getting out of hand." But he is very supportive. Once he gets there, he enjoys it and he starts in arguing too! See, it's just that he is not used to it. He couldn't believe things happened the way that they do. He was in the Navy twenty years and they brainwashed him that none of the politicians could do wrong. So he has come a long way. Now he comes home and parks the car out front and asks me, "Well, where are we going tonight?"

When women explain their activism, they link family and community as one entity. Juana Gutierrez, a woman with extensive experience working on community and neighborhood issues, stated:

> ...As a mother and a resident of East L.A., I shall continue fighting tirelessly, so we will be respected. And I will do this with much affection for my community. I say "my community" because I am part of it. I love my "raza" [race] as part of my family; and if God allows, I will keep on fighting against all the governors that want to take advantage of us.

Like the other activists, she has expanded her responsibilities and legitimated militant opposition to abuse the community by representatives of the state.

Working-class women activists seldom opt to separate themselves from men and their families. In this particular struggle for the community quality of life, they are fighting for the family unit and thus are not competitive with men. Of course, this fact does not preclude different alignments in other contexts and situations.

Fourth, the story of MELA also shows the transformation of class and ethnic identity. Aurora Castillo told of an incident that illustrated her growing knowledge of the relationship of East Los Angeles to other communities and the basis necessary for coalition building:

> And do you know we have been approached by other groups? [She lowers her voice for emphasis.] You know that Pacific Palisades group asked for our backing. But what they did, they sent their powerful lobbyist that they pay thousands of dollars to get our support against the drilling in Pacific Palisades. So what we did was tell them to send their grassroots people, not their lobbyist. We're suspicious. We don't want to talk to a high-salaried lobbyist; we are humble people. We did our own lobbying. In one week we went to Sacramento twice.

The contrast between the often tedious and labor-intensive work of mobilizing people at the "grassroots" level and the paid work of a "high salaried lobbyist" represents a point of pride and integrity, not a deficiency or a source of shame. If the two groups were to construct a coalition, they must communicate on equal terms.

The women of MELA combine a willingness to assert opposition with a critical assessment of their own weaknesses. At one community meeting, for example, representatives of several oil companies attempted to gain support for placement of an oil pipeline through the center of East Los Angeles...The proposal was quickly defeated. But Auroral Castillo acknowledge that it was not solely their opposition that brought about the defeat:

> We won because the westside was opposed to it, so we united with them. You know there are a lot of attorneys who live there

> and they also questioned the representative. Believe me, no way is justice blind...We just don't want all this garbage thrown at us because we are low-income and Mexican American. We are lucky now that we have good representatives, which we didn't have before.

...the core activists typically tell stories illustrating personal change and a new sense of entitlement to speak for the community. They have transformed the unspoken sentiments of individuals into a collective community voice. Lucy Ramos related her initial apprehensions:

> I was afraid to get involved. I didn't know what was going to come out of this and I hesitated at first. Right after we started, Father John came up to me and told me, "I want you to be a spokesperson." I said, "Oh no, I don't know what I am going to say." I was nervous. I am surprised I didn't have a nervous breakdown then. Every time we used to get in front of the TV cameras and even interviews like this, I used to sit there and I could feel myself shaking. But as time went on, I started getting used to it.
>
> And this is what I have noticed with a lot of them. They were afraid to speak up and say anything. Now, with this prison issue, a lot of them have come out and come forward and given their opinions. Everybody used to be real "quietlike."

She also related a situation that brought all her fears to a climax, which she confronted and resolved as follows:

> When I first started working with the coalition, Channel 13 called me up and said they wanted to interview me and I said OK. Then I started getting nervous. So I called Father John and told him, "You better get over here right away." He said, "Don't worry, don't worry, you can handle it by yourself." Then Channel 13 called me back and said they were going to interview another person, someone I had never heard of, and asked if it was OK if he came to my house. And I said OK again. Then I began thinking, what if this guy is for the prison? What am I going to do? And I was so nervous and I thought, I know what I am going to do!

...People living in Third World countries as well as in minority communities in the United States face an increasingly degraded environment. Recognizing the threat to the well-being of their families, residents have mobilized at the neighborhood level to fight for "quality of life" issues. The common notion that environmental well-being is of concern solely to white middle-class and upper-class residents ignores the specific way working-class neighborhoods suffer from the fallout of the city "growth machine" geared for profit.

In Los Angeles, the culmination of postwar urban renewal policies, the growing Pacific Rim trade surplus and investment, and low-wage international labor migration from Third World countries are creating potentially volatile conditions. Literally palatial financial buildings swallow up the space previously occupied by modest, low-cost housing. Increasing density and development not matched by investment in social programs, services, and infrastructure erode the quality of life, beginning in the core of the city. Latinos, the majority of whom live close to the center of the city, must confront the distilled social consequences of development focused solely on profit. The Mexican American community in East Los Angeles, much like other minority working-class communities, has been a repository for prisons instead of new schools, hazardous industries instead of safe work sites, and one of the largest concentrations of freeway interchanges in the country, which transports much wealth past the community. And the concerns of residents in East Los Angeles may provide lessons for other minority as well as middle-class communities. Increasing environmental pollution resulting from inadequate waste disposal plans and an out-of-control "need" for penal institutions to contain the casualties created by the growing bipolar distribution of wages may not be limited to the Southwest. These conditions set the stage for new conflicts and new opportunities, to transform old relationships into coalitions that can challenge state agendas and create new community visions.

Mexican American women living east of downtown Los Angeles exemplify the tendency of women to enter into environmental struggles in defense of their community. Women have a rich historical legacy of community activism, partly reconstructed over the last two decades in social histories of women who contested other "quality of life issues," from the price of bread to "Demon Rum" (often representing domestic violence).

But something new is also happening. The issues "traditionally" addressed by women—health, housing, sanitation, and the urban environment—have moved to center stage as capitalist urbanization progresses. Environmental issues now fuel the fires of many political campaigns and drive citizens beyond the rather restricted, perfunctory political act of voting. Instances of political mobilization at the grassroots level, where women often play a central role, allow us to "see" abstract concepts like participatory democracy and social change as dynamic processes.

The existence of activities of "Mothers of East Los Angeles" attest to the dynamic nature of our gender, class, and ethnic identity. The story of MELA reveals, on the one hand, how individuals and groups can transform a seemingly "traditional" role such as "mother." On the other hand, it illustrates how such a role may also be a social agent drawing members of the community into the "political" arena. Studying women's contributions as well as men's will shed greater light on the networks dynamic of grassroots movements.

The work "Mothers of East Los Angeles" do to mobilize the community demonstrates that people's political involvement cannot be predicted by their cultural characteristics. These women have defied stereotypes of apathy and used ethnic, gender, and class identity as an impetus, a strength, a vehicle for political activism. They have expanded their—and our—understanding of the complexities of a political system, and they have reaffirmed the possibility of "doing something."

They also generously share the lessons they have learned. One of the women in "Mothers of East Los Angeles" told me, as I hesitated to set up an interview with another woman I hadn't yet met in person,

> You know, nothing ventured nothing lost. You should have seen how timid we were the first time we went to a public hearing. Now, forget it, I walk right up and make myself heard and that's what you have to do.

AFTER YOU READ: Analyze the Issues

1. Does the attitude of the MELA surprise you? How does it contradict the public stereotype of Hispanic families? How does it support it? Should this type of information impact the argument for immigration? How? Provide evidence for all assertions.
2. Locate the evidence Pardo provides to support her assertions. Can you categorize the evidence into several major topics? How does it impact her assertions?

AFTER YOU READ: Analyze the Rhetoric

1. Pardo's article tracks the history of the MELA. What does she argue persuades them to act and rally? Which rhetorical appeals does she use?
2. Why is this type of work seen as "women's work?" Will this attitude harm the cause? Help the cause? Will it impact the issue on a nation wide basis? How? Why? Provide evidence.

"The Dumping Ground: Big Utilities Look to Native Lands to House Nuclear Waste"

by Winona LaDuke

(Essay)

Winona LaDuke is a well known journalist, environmentalist, and activist from Minnesota. After attending Harvard and working with Jimmy Durham, another well known activist, she began publishing numerous articles and books about the environment and Native American lands. She was the recipient of the 1989 International Reebok Human Rights Award and in 1995 was named as one of "50 leaders" for the future by *Time Magazine*. Over the years she has testified at government hearings and was Ralph Nader's vice presidential running mate in the 1996 presidential election. Her latest book, *Recovering the Sacred: The Power of Naming and Claiming*, is a collection of essays based on research, including interviews, in which she argues for Native American rights to control and access sacred objects and sites.

AS YOU READ: Annotate

1. Underline the rhetorical devices used in the text and note if they are logos, pathos, or ethos.
2. Put a star next to the lines you find most convincing.
3. Circle the words you do not know.

On September 8, the Genesis satellite crashed into the Utah Test and Training Range, right next to the Skull Valley Goshute reservation. Although NASA had some pretty spectacular plans for a soft landing, the crash of that satellite might concern more than NASA. This same area, the Skull Valley Goshute reservation, is considering providing a repository for 40,000 tons of nuclear waste. NASA nosedives of the future might be more lethal.

The area looks a bit like a set for the movie *Mad Max and the Thunderdome*. Forty-five miles southwest of Salt Lake City, a small community of Goshutes live on an 18,600-acre reservation. For the past 40 years, the U.S. federal government has created and dumped toxic military wastes all around them. Less than 10 miles southwest is the Dugway Proving Grounds, where the government conducts tests of chemical and biological weapons. In 1968, chemical agents escaped from Dugway and killed over 6,000 sheep and other animals. More than 1,600 of these animals were buried on the reservation, leaving a toxic legacy in the ground. "My father had 30 head," Margene Bullcreek, a Goshute elder, remembers. "They buried them all here on the reservation, but no study was ever done on the effects of it." Fifteen miles east of the reservation is the Desert Chemical Depot., which stores more than 40 percent of the U.S. chemical weapons stockpile and is responsible for the incineration of many chemical munitions and nerve agents.

Thirty miles northwest of the reservation is the Envirocare Low Level Radioactive Disposal Site, a dump for radioactive waste that is trucked in from all over the country. Envirocare is in the business of dumps. The firm is exploring the possibility of developing a low level nuclear waste dump in the Iraqi desert to dispose of radioactive tanks and depleted uranium weapons. Hill Air Force Base, where the F-15s test and land, adjoins the company's area. Finally, north of the reservation is the Magnesium Corporation Plant, a large, toxic, magnesium production facility.

The Skull Valley Goshutes were never asked about the placement of any of these facilities. In many ways, the Goshute story is a microcosm of the impact of the military on Native people and how the nuclear industry can make what is a bad thing worse.

20-Year Lease, 250,000 Years Radioactive

Disposing of military waste is a massive problem confronting the United States. The General Accountability Office, the Congressional research agency, earlier this year concluded that removing unexploded munitions and hazardous waste from 15 closed military facilities could take more than 300 years. GAO estimates the clean up cost at $35 billion, and climbing rapidly. As the Goshutes know, lots of that waste is located near Native American lands.

But for the Goshutes, it looks like the toxic problems are getting still worse.

Enter Private Fuel Storage (PFS), a limited-liability consortium of eight commercial nuclear utilities led by Xcel Energy. PFS wants to construct a private, above-ground, "temporary" dump for 40,000 metric tons of high-level nuclear waste on the land of the Skull Valley Band of Goshute. "Limited liability" means that individual utility companies are protected from suit if there is an accident in shipping waste to Utah or at the facility itself.

Running out of nuclear waste storage space at its Prairie Island Nuclear Reactor, the Minnesota-based Xcel Energy created PFS and made overtures to the Skull Valley Goshute Tribal Council. On December 26, 1996, PFS secured an agreement from the three-member Tribal Council to lease 100 acres for construction of a nuclear waste dump.

However, in March 2003, the U.S. Nuclear Regulatory Commission's Atomic Safety and Licensing Board (ASLB) denied PFS its license to begin construction of the dump due to the risk of accidents involving F-16 fighter jets which routinely pass over Skull Valley en route from Hill Air Force Base to the nearby Utah Test and Training Range. "This [Skull Valley project] is the bridge to Yucca Mountain," explains Scott Northard, project manager for PFS. Yucca Mountain is the proposed site in Nevada for a permanent repository for U.S. nuclear waste. Many utilities realize that without an interim dump, and delays in construction of a permanent nuclear waste dump at Yucca Mountain, they will have to shut down their nuclear power plants.

Although the waste remains radioactive for 250,000 years, the Goshute's lease is for 20 years initially, with an option to renew the lease for an additional 20 years. The dump would be a parking lot for up to 40,000 metric tons of spent nuclear fuel sitting in 4,000 steel containers on a concrete pad outdoors.

The federal government has spent almost $2 billion and at least two decades trying to solve the dilemma of nuclear waste disposal. The nuclear utilities seem to believe that with a "limited liability corporation," they can solve the problem in less than a decade.

But many Goshutes do not think it is a solution at all. Xcel Energy "is just fortunate enough to have found a weak tribe that's going to put up with them and their partner utilities and their wastes," says Margene Bullcreek, a leader of a grassroots effort to oppose the dump.

Bullcreek is not alone. Since 1987, six other American Indian tribes have rejected proposals to site similar dumps on their land due to serious concerns over health, safety and environmental justice. Although the executive committee of the Skull Valley Goshute General Council accepted the deal in 1997, many members of the Skull Valley Band of Goshutes, as well as many indigenous organizations throughout the country, have actively opposed the agreement.

Ohngo Gaudadeh Devia Awareness (or OGDA, Goshute for "Timber Setting Community'"), a grassroots group of Skull Valley Goshute tribal members directed by Bullcreek, opposes the dump in an effort to protect tradition and the health and safety of the reservation's inhabitants. Throughout the process, OGDA has filed objections with the Nuclear Regulatory Commission, continues to engage allied organizations in opposition, and participates in lawsuits to oppose the dump.

In September 2001, a team of tribal members led by Sammy Blackbear of the Environmental Justice Foundation officially challenged the Skull Valley Goshute Tribal Council's Executive Committee for a leadership election over the nuclear waste issue. To this day, the results of that election are in dispute, demonstrating the lack of consensus on the reservation for a high-level nuclear dump as a development option. Outstanding lawsuits concerning improper agreements between the disputed tribal leadership and PFS remain unresolved. The dispute has raged for seven years.

Betrayal of Trust

The Bureau of Indian Affairs also faces some challenges. The BIA approved the lease just three days after the Tribal Council signed it. The issues of nuclear waste complicate trust responsibility, particularly when considering that the waste is lethal for 100,000 years or so. Federal law requires that the stipulations of the National Environmental Policy Act (NEPA) be met when Indian land is being considered for business lease or commercial development. Before 1970, it was acknowledged that the BIA's primary purpose in exercising lease approval authority was to preserve the Indian land base for the furtherance of Indian culture and values. In 1970, the Indian leasing statute was amended to broaden the list of factors that the Secretary must satisfy before approving a lease, requiring that "adequate consideration has been given to … the effect on the environment of the uses to which the leased lands will be subject."

The Nuclear Regulatory Commission (NRC), along with the Bureau of Indian Affairs, the Bureau of Land Management, and the Surface Transportation Board, issued a Draft Environmental Impact Statement (DEIS) in June 2000, and a final EIS in January 2002.

Critics say the BIA so narrowly defined the scope of its review in the DEIS that it has likely failed to meet its trust responsibilities. In the DEIS, the BIA states that "[a]s part of its government-to-government relationship with the Skull Valley Band, BIA's NEPA review is limited to the scope of the proposed lease negotiated between the parties, not evaluation of actions outside the lease (e.g., ultimate disposition of the Spent Nuclear Fuel)."

"The BIA cannot wish away this part of its trust responsibility," says Tom Goldtooth of the Indigenous Environmental Network which has been giving support to OGDA. "Ultimate disposition of nuclear waste is central to the question of whether the Indian land base will be preserved for the long term. The DEIS for PFS's proposal cannot satisfy the requirements of the law, because there can be no expectation that nuclear waste will be removed from the facility at the end of the lease period, which clearly creates a serious negative impact on the environment and potential endangerment to the survival of its Goshute Shoshone peoples. The BIA has basically relinquished to the NRC their fiduciary responsibility to ensure that the provisions of NEPA are followed for the Skull Valley radioactive waste dump."

"It's pretty clear that utilities are willing to spend billions to move it [the spent fuel] out of their back yard into ours," said then-Utah Governor Mike Leavitt, now director of the federal Environmental Protection Agency, when he was still answering to Utah constituents.

PFS continues to seek a permit for its dump. In August, the 10th Circuit Court of Appeals in Denver affirmed a 2002 district court decision that Utah state laws and regulations intended to block the PFS waste dump were unconstitutional, and that only the federal government has the authority to regulate the transportation and storage of spent nuclear fuel. August also brought three weeks of closed-door hearings for the Nuclear Regulatory Commission's Atomic Safety and Licensing Board to consider the license for the dump.

Amid all of these legal decisions, the Goshutes are pretty concerned.

"The real issue is not the money" the Goshutes would earn from hosting the dump, says Bullcreek. "The real issue is who we are as Native Americans and what we believe in. If we accept these wastes, we're going to lose our tradition and our need to keep the air, water and animals clean."

AFTER YOU READ: Analyze the Issues

1. To whom does LaDuke direct her article? How do you know? Locate three to six sentences that support your assertion.
2. Review the short excerpts from Bigmouth and Winthrop. Has the attitude toward the land changed? Does the polarized view of the lands still exist in this country? Provide evidence from resources outside of this book to support your assertions.

AFTER YOU READ: Analyze the Rhetoric

1. What rhetorical appeals does LaDuke use to make her arguments? Locate three sentences to support your assertions.
2. Comment on the effectiveness of the conclusion.

"The Eco-tist: Gore as Green"

by Ronald Bailey

Ronald Bailey is best known for his book called *ECOSCAM: The False Prophets of Ecological Apocalypse.* Published in 1993, *ECOSCAM* is Bailey's response to Al Gore's book *Earth in the Balance*. In this book, Bailey focuses on the agendas of radical environmentalists and attempts to expose their pseudo-scientific scare tactics. Currently, Bailey is the science correspondent for a monthly magazine, *Reason,* which focuses on politics and culture. He has produced several series and documentaries that were on PBS television and ABC News, and he is a member of the Society for Environmental Journalists.

AS YOU READ: Annotate

1. Underline the rhetorical devices used in the text and note if they are logos, pathos, or ethos.
2. Put a star next to the lines you find most convincing.
3. Circle the words you do not know and write down their meaning in the margin, including: *malleable, Neo-Luddite, depredation*, and *apocalypticism*.

Al Gore evidently believes that the world might come to an end if he's not elected president. How did he come to such an extraordinary conclusion?

The seeds of this conviction can he found at Harvard University. Back in the 1960s, when he was an underachieving— and intellectually malleable—student, Gore's two greatest pedagogical influences were oceanographer Roger Revelle and psychologist Erik Erikson. Revelle introduced Gore to the idea of the man-made "greenhouse effect"; Erikson's course taught Gore that Western civilization has been too "male" in its view of the world. Gore now apparently believes, combining the two perspectives, that what we need to save the planet is a woman's touch.

On the environment, especially, Gore is a creature of his times. In his 1992 manifesto *Earth in the Balance*, he reverently cites his mother's admiration for Rachel Carson's *Silent Spring*. The period of Gore's intellectual formation, the mid-1960s, was also the heyday of alarmist predictions (by, among others, the Paddocks in *Famine 1975*! and Paul Ehrlich in *The Population Bomb*) of imminent global famine owing to overpopulation. The early 1970s, when Gore was in graduate school, saw the oil crisis, as well as the publication of the Club of Rome's *Limits to Growth* and E. F. Schumacher's neo-Luddite *Small is Beautiful*.

It was against this background of cultural demoralization that Gore was elected to Congress in 1976. He was a part of that era's movement to control technological progress. He opposed deregulating natural gas, favored stringent controls on the nascent biotechnology industry, and supported the creation of the costly and slow Superfund waste-cleanup initiative. Just as the nuclear-freeze campaign was revving up in the early

1980s, Gore began studying the arcana of nuclear-deterrence theory. He writes in *Earth in the Balance* that studying nukes led him to "a deeper appreciation for the most horrifying fact in all our lives: Civilization is now capable of destroying itself." This realization caused Gore to think "about the course of our nation and our civilization … I also began to think about what role I might play in determining that course."

Gore's millenarian spark is expressed most clearly in this book, reissued for the election year. The book calls on Americans to "become partners in a bold effort to change the very foundation of our civilization" and to "make the rescue of the environment the central organizing principle of our civilization." Gore makes it clear that his crusade is not just to save the material world, but to save America's soul: "The more deeply I search for the roots of the global environmental crisis, the more I am convinced that it is an outer manifestation of our inner crisis that is, for lack of a better word, spiritual."

Gore cites the resurgence of religious fundamentalisms— and the rise of various New Age creeds—as evidence of "a spiritual crisis in modern civilization that seems to be based on an emptiness at its center and the absence of a larger spiritual purpose." Gore's response is to offer his own version of a New Age creed as a way to fill the spiritual void: the rescue of the natural world from humanity's depredations.

Gore has thus joined the long list of millenarians who hector the rest of us that the world will come to an end unless society does what they command. Political scientist Richard Hofstadter tagged this demagogic apocalypticism the "paranoid style" of politics; political paranoids, he wrote, believe that all of humanity's ills can be traced "to a single center and hence can be eliminated by some kind of final act of victory over the evil source." For Gore and many other environmentalists, the contemporary focus of evil is the alleged ecological crisis, and the source of the problem is, in Gore's words, "our dysfunctional civilization": "In psychological terms, our rapid and aggressive expansion into what remains of the wildness of the earth represents an effort to plunder from outside civilization what we cannot find inside … [It] is a willful expansion of our dysfunctional civilization into vulnerable parts of the natural world."

Hofstadter said that the political paranoid "traffics in the birth and death of whole worlds, whole political orders, whole systems of human values." Similarly, radical environmentalists believe themselves uniquely capable of seeing the impending catastrophe, while the rest of unrepentant humanity remains stubbornly blind to the danger. "There is a seduction in apocalyptic thinking," historian Eric Zencey writes. "If one lives in the Last Days, one's actions, one's very life, take on historical meaning and no small measure of poignance." The mission of rescuing the environment lends a richer meaning to Gore's life than the ordinary business of government possibly could.

Of course, part of being a true believer is brooking no opposition. Gore's staff apparently orchestrated a smear campaign against atmospheric scientist Fred Singer, having one of Roger Revelle's colleagues claim that Singer had manipulated Revelle (Gore's own mentor!) into writing that man-made global warming is "too uncertain to justify drastic action at this time." (Singer's attacker later apologized.) In another extraordinary episode, *Nightline* anchor Ted Koppel revealed that Gore had sent over reams of disparaging material in an effort to get the program to investigate the motives of prominent climatologists who are skeptical of the global-warming disaster scenario. *Nightline* did investigate—and concluded that the skeptics were sincere and had reasonable scientific arguments.

Many of Gore's specific policies have long been advocated by the radical environmental fringe. In *Earth in the Balance*, Gore proposes the creation of a "Strategic Environmental Initiative" that would focus on stabilizing the earth's population and atmosphere, and establish a United Nations Stewardship Council. This proposal echoes that of global-warming scaremonger Stephen Schneider, who, in *The Genesis Strategy* (1976), advocated the creation of "World Security Institutes" as "planning bodies considering environmental, political, economic, and social aspects of policy options from a global perspective."

Gore says one of our "strategic goal[s] should be the establishment of a cooperative plan for educating the world's citizens about our global environment… The ultimate goal of this effort would be to foster new patterns of thinking about the relationship of civilization to the environment." Compare this to Schneider's plan for a new fourth branch of government, which would broadcast the environmental agenda and lead the public to "question present value systems and adopt a new political consciousness." If Gore gets elected, Schneider might well get his wish.

The energy plan unveiled recently by the Gore campaign is also telling. It's largely a rehash of his old agenda: massive subsidies for alternative-energy technologies, and enforcement of energy conservation. Gore takes his energy policy cues from Amory Lovins, co-founder of the Rocky Mountain Institute, whose 1976 *Foreign Affairs* article "Energy Strategy: The Road Not Taken?" remains the environmentalists' bible on energy issues.

Gore's views are out of the mainstream, and they pose a new and unusual threat for America. When a president is motivated by cynicism or lust for power, he can do *some* damage—but when a president genuinely wants to turn the world upside down, he can do much more harm. A Gore presidency is a risk we just don't need.

AFTER YOU READ: Analyze the Issues

1. Does Bailey's "science correspondent" title give the article more validity or does it make you question his level of scientific evidence? Provide proof from the article to support your assertion.
2. What is the main message of the essay?

AFTER YOU READ: Analyze the Rhetoric

1. How effective is the arrangement?
2. Comment on the effectiveness of the conclusion.

An Inconvenient Truth: "The Politicization of Global Warming"

by Al Gore
pages 284–287 excerpt from An Inconvenient Truth
(Essay)

Perhaps symbolically, Al Gore, winner of the Nobel Prize (2007), was born in 1948, in Washington D.C. His father was a US Senator. He graduated from Harvard, served in Vietnam. He was a journalist for a brief period. He served in the US House of Representatives for Tennessee, and later he served in the US Senate. After being the 45th Vice President serving under Bill Clinton (1993–2001), he ran for President, winning the popular vote, but losing to a controversial Supreme Court decision (2000). Gore has long been an environmentalist.

AS YOU READ: Annotate

1. Write the word "Logos" (evidence) in the margin as the author presents his case.
2. Place a star by the paragraph that you like the most.
3. As you circle any words you do not know and write their meanings in the margins, be sure to circle and define the following words: *coalition, conglomerates, ludicrous,* and *belatedly.*

As I've traveled around the world giving my slide show, there are two questions I most often get— particularly in the United States—from people who already know how serious the crisis has become:

1. "Why do so many people still believe this crisis isn't real?" and
2. "Why is this a political issue at all?"

My response to the first question has been to try to make my slide show—and now this book—as clear and compelling as I can. As for why so many people still resist what the facts clearly show, I think, in part, the reason is that the truth about the climate crisis is an inconvenient one that means we are going to have to change the way we live our lives. Most of these changes will turn out to be for the better—things we really should do for other reasons anyway—but they are inconvenient nonetheless. Whether these changes involve something as minor as adjusting the thermostat and using different light bulbs, or as major as switching from oil and coal to renewable fuels, they will require effort.

But the answer to the first question is also linked to the second question. The truth about global warming is especially inconvenient and unwelcome to some powerful people and companies making enormous sums of money from activities they know full well will have to change dramatically in order to ensure the planet's livability.

These people—especially those at a few multinational companies with the most at stake—have been spending many millions of dollars every year in figuring out ways of sowing public confusion about global warming. They've been particularly effective in building a coalition with other groups who agree to support each other's interests, and that coalition has thus far managed to paralyze America's ability to respond to global warming. The Bush/Cheney administration has received strong support from this coalition and seems to be doing everything it can to satisfy their concerns.

For example, many scientists working on global warming research throughout the government have been ordered to watch what they say about the climate crisis and instructed not to talk to the news media. More important, all of America's policies related to global warming have been changed to reflect the unscientific view—the administration's view—that global warming is not a problem. Our negotiators in international forums dealing with global warming have been advised to try and stop any movement toward action that would inconvenience oil or coal companies, even if this means disrupting the diplomatic machinery in order to do it.

In addition, President Bush appointed the person in charge of the oil company disinformation campaign on global warming to head up all environmental policy in the White House. Even though this lawyer/lobbyist had no scientific training whatsoever, he was empowered by the president to edit and censor all warnings from the EPA and other governmental agencies about global warming.

Political leaders—especially the president—can have a major effect not only on public policy (especially when Congress is controlled by the president's party, is compliant, and does whatever the president wants it to) but also on public opinion, especially among those who count themselves followers of the president.

Consider this fact: Even as Americans in general have become increasingly concerned about global warming, opinion polls show members of the president's own party becoming less concerned, probably because they're naturally more inclined to give the president the benefit of the doubt.

The rationale offered by the so-called global warming skeptics for opposing any action to solve the climate crisis has changed several times over the years. At first, opponents argued that global warming was not occurring at all; they said it was just a myth. A few of them still say that today, but now there is so much undeniable evidence demolishing that assertion that, most naysayers have decided they need to change tactics. They now acknowledge that the globe is indeed warming, but in the very next breath, they claim it is just due to "natural causes."

President Bush himself still tried to take that position, asserting that even though it does seem the world is getting warmer, hey, there's no compelling evidence that human beings are responsible for it. And he seems to be particularly certain that the oil and coal companies that so strongly support him couldn't possibly have anything to do with it.

Another related argument used by the deniers is that yes, global warming does seem to be happening, but it will probably be good for us. Certainly any effort to stop it, they continue, would no doubt be bad for the economy.

But the latest—and in my opinion, most disgraceful—argument put forth by opponents of change is: Yes, it's happening, but there's nothing we can really do about it, so we might as well not even try. This faction favors the continued dumping of global-warming pollution into the atmosphere, even though they acknowledge that the crisis it's causing is real and harmful. Their philosophy seems to be "eat, drink, and be merry, for tomorrow our children will inherit the worst of this crisis; it's too inconvenient for us to be bothered."

All of these shifting rationales usually rely on the same underlying political tactic: Assert that the science is uncertain and that there is grave doubt about the underlying facts.

These groups emphasize uncertainty because they know that politics in America can be paralyzed by it. They understand that it is a politician's natural instinct to avoid taking any stand that seems controversial unless and until the voters demand it or conscience absolutely requires it. So if voters and the politicians who represent them can be convinced that scientists themselves disagree on fundamental issues concerning global warming, then the political process can be paralyzed indefinitely. That is exactly what has happened—at least until quite recently—and it is still unclear when the situation will really change.

Part of the problem has to do with a long-term structural change in the way America's marketplace of ideas now operates. The one-way nature of our dominant communications medium, television, has combined with the increasing concentration of ownership over the vast majority of media outlets by a smaller and smaller number of large conglomerates that mix entertainment values with journalism to seriously damage the role of objectivity in America's public forum. Today there are many fewer independent journalists with the freedom and stature to blow the whistle when important facts are consistently being distorted in order to deceive the public. The Internet offers the most hopeful opportunity to restore integrity to the public dialogue, but television is still dominant in shaping that dialogue. The "propaganda" techniques that emerged with the new film and broadcasting mass media of the 20th century prefigured the widespread use of related techniques for mass advertising and for political persuasion. And now, corporate lobbying efforts to influence and control public policy have been stepped up dramatically, which in turn is leading to the widespread and often cynical use of these same mass persuasion techniques to condition the public's thinking about important issues lest they begin to support solutions that will be inconvenient—and expensive—for particular industries.

One of the persistent techniques in the campaign to stop action against the climate crisis has been to repeatedly and persistently accuse the scientists trying to warn us about the crisis of being dishonest, greedy, and untrustworthy and of misrepresenting scientific facts in order to somehow beef up their research grants.

These charges are insulting and ludicrous, but they have been repeated often enough and loudly enough—through so many media megaphones—that many people do now wonder if the charges are true. And that is particularly ironic, given that so many of the skeptics actually do receive funding and support from self-interested groups financed by the corporations desperate to stop any action against global warming. Incredibly, the public has been hearing the discredited views of these skeptics as much as or more than they have heard the consensus view of the global scientific community. That disgraceful fact is a notable strain on the record of America's modern news media, and many leaders of journalism are belatedly taking steps to correct it.

But it is far from clear that the news media will be able to sustain a higher commitment to objectivity in the face of the intense pressures that increasingly erode it and render it shockingly vulnerable to this kind of organized propaganda. We have lost a lot of time that could have been spent solving the crisis, because the opponents of action have thus far successfully politicized the issue in the minds of many Americans.

We can't afford inaction any longer, and frankly, there's just no excuse for it. We all want the same thing: for our children and the generations after them to inherit a clean and beautiful planet capable of supporting a healthy human civilization. That goal should transcend politics.

Yes, the science is ongoing and always evolving, but there's already enough data, enough damage, to know without a question that we're in trouble. This isn't an ideological debate with two sides, pro and con. There is only one Earth, and all of us who live on it share a common future. Right now we are facing a planetary emergency, and it is time for action, not for more phony controversies designed to insure political paralysis.

AFTER YOU READ: Analyze the Issues

1. What is the main message of the essay?
2. Why does he mention President Bush?
3. How does he counter or refute the opposition? Give an example.

AFTER YOU READ: Analyze the Rhetoric

1. Note how he states his two main points that he will examine at the very start. Is that a good opening? Why or why not?
2. How does the author present evidence to prove his points? Is he specific enough?
3. Comment on the effectiveness of the conclusion.

"Better Living Through French Fries: Is Biodiesel the Fuel of the Future?"

by Hal Clifford
(Essay)

As the executive editor of *Orion* magazine, Hal Clifford's articles have appeared in numerous publications like *Business Week*, *National Geographic Adventure*, and *The New York Times Magazine*. He has also authored such books as *Downhill Slide* and *The Falling Season*. He lives in Colorado and often writes about ecology.

AS YOU READ: Annotate

1. Underline some of the most interesting adjectives.
2. Place stars by the most interesting paragraphs.
3. Circle the following words and any others you don't know, and write their meanings in the margin: *aka, coagulates,* and *retrofitted.*

***Grist Magazine.* 22 August 2003**

The Granola Ayatollah of Canola, aka Charris Ford, slides behind the wheel of his 1980 International Scout truck and turns the key. The truck burbles to life and off we go, cruising down the gravel roads that divide the aspen groves of southwestern Colorado's Horsefly Mesa. It would be just a standard evening joyride, except that Ford's truck doesn't run on gasoline. Or diesel. Or electricity, or even the sun. This truck is powered by grease, all of it drained from restaurant deep-fryers in the nearby resort town of Telluride.

The truck's top is off for the summer and the boxy, orange-and-black vehicle is in mint condition. Clean, vintage floor mats declare "Let's Boogie!" A small disco ball hangs from the rear-view mirror, and a five-inch Heinz A-1 cardboard air freshener, shaped like a ketchup bottle, dangles from the driver's sun visor.

"If you've got the french fry car, you've got to have the ketchup air freshener," Ford declares.

Does it actually smell like ketchup?

"Actually," he says a little sheepishly, "it smells like coconut."

The child of two Woodstock hippies, Ford, who is now 32, spent 10 years living a back-to-the-land existence on a remote Tennessee farm. He learned to farm from his Amish neighbors, logged trees with the help of two Belgian draft horses, and rode a bicycle that bore a sticker declaring "Friends Don't Let Friends Drive." Now, propelled by a commitment to "serve society," Ford is on a mission to save us from our petroleum addiction.

"If we made it through the ice age, we can make it through our energy crisis," he says.

Ford's truck runs on biodiesel, a fuel that can be made out of virgin oils from plants such as soybeans, corn, canola, coconuts, or peanuts, or by filtering and processing used vegetable oils, principally restaurant grease. Biodiesel is not new; indeed, when Rudolph Diesel first described plans for his engine in 1893, he thought he had designed something that farmers could fuel themselves using peanut oil. (Cheap petroleum hijacked his dream of rural self-sufficiency.)

But if biodiesel isn't new, it is newly popular: Production in the United States is growing fast, from about 15 million gallons last year to an expected 20-25 million gallons this year to as many as 40 million gallons next year. Still, biodiesel comprises just a tiny fraction of the 55 billion gallons of diesel fuel consumed annually in the United States, when it could account for a lot more: The U.S. Energy Department concluded last year that current soybean production and waste grease could produce about 6 billion gallons of biodiesel annually. Major oil companies such as BP and Gulf Oil are getting into the biodiesel business, and the fuel is already used in vehicle fleets across the country, including that of the U.S. Postal Service. (Retail biodiesel is hard to come by; only about 30 drive-up pumps exist nationwide.)

There are good reasons to welcome biodiesel's increasing popularity. In addition to being a renewable energy source, biodiesel is substantially cleaner than regular diesel. When the Berkeley, Calif., Ecology Center converted its recycling trucks from conventional diesel to biodiesel, particulate emissions dropped by 84 percent. According to Ecology Center Director Dave Williamson, biodiesel emits 78 percent less carbon dioxide than conventional diesel over its full life cycle, as well as 43 percent less carbon monoxide. He calculates that the daily waste grease of a single fast-food restaurant could fuel one of his trucks for its daily recycling collection rounds.

The fuel does have its drawbacks, however—principally expense. Currently, biodiesel costs about $2 per gallon, or almost twice the pump price of conventional diesel. In addition, biodiesel coagulates at cold temperatures, so vehicles must be retrofitted with a fuel-heating system. And although biodiesel vehicles are cleaner than regular diesel in many respects, they still emit about the same amount of nitrogen oxide, one of the main components of smog.

7-Eleven From Heaven

These problems aside, Ford thinks the biodiesel moment has come. "If we keep burning petroleum and just keep taking what The Man's got for us, we're not going to be making any big moves," says Ford, who is six feet tall and wiry. A fuzz of close-cropped brown hair covers his head and wraps around his face beneath intense blue eyes. "Biodiesel is a powerful message that we can send to oil companies and car companies and our fellow citizens. Alternative fuel is the wave of the future—if we're going to have a future."

Ford is charming, confident, and charismatic—so much so that his friend Howard Donner made a short film called *French Fries to Go* about Ford and his biodiesel passion. The 15-minute work premiered to popular acclaim at Telluride's Mountainfilm Festival in May, and since then the self-described Granola Ayatollah of Canola has been asked to introduce it at other festivals. Ford, who left Tennessee in 1998 and now works with his wife, Dulcie, as a caretaker on a 1,000-acre ranch outside Telluride, is only too happy to tell his story.

When a co-worker crashed Ford's previous, gas-powered truck in 1999, Ford decided to kick the petroleum habit. He found the Scout on the Internet, paid $8,000 for it, and drove it from Pennsylvania to Colorado. He switched out a few hoses—biodiesel will corrode natural rubber—and has been running it on recycled french fry grease ever since. With two partners, dentist Ken Hodges and builder Glen Harcourt, Ford collects used vegetable oil and refines it in Harcourt's barn in a simple process that removes the natural glycerin and leaves a petroleum-like fuel. Their $6,000 plant can produce up to 25 gallons of fuel a day, enough for all three men to run their biodiesel vehicles.

"My real commitment is to educate and inspire the nation's interest in biodiesel," Ford says with characteristic intensity, "and if I can do that, that's the job I'm interested in. My feeling is the people who are going to get rich off this are already rich."

Ford's larger goal is not simply to get us to buy renewable go-juice; he wants to reinvent the corner gas station. "I'm calling it the 7-Eleven from Heaven," he says of his vision for a 21st-century alternative to the modern, soul-destroying convenience store. "It would be the Hard Rock Cafe of alternative fueling stations," selling not only "Grassolean"—his catch-all term for biofuels—but health food, micro-brewed beers, and information on alternative medicine and energy-saving technologies.

It's hard for most of us to get excited about reinventing the gas station, but Ford is, deeply so. "I say, screw Exxon's green fueling station, where all they do is install a biodiesel pump," he says. "Let's have this be a grassroots thing. I want to create an icon. I want to give people a vision of what an incredible alternative energy station could be." He plans to have a promotional Web site (www.grassolean.com) up and running by the end of the summer. (In the meantime, more information on biodiesel is available on-line from the National Biodiesel Board, a Missouri consortium of soybean growers, and the Hawaii-based Pacific Biodiesel, which makes fuel from recycled vegetable oil.)

Ford's methods of getting the word out about biodiesel are refreshingly unconventional. "The first time I met Charris he had on this huge black wig and big sunglasses," says Ken Hodges, "and I thought, 'Oh no.' He got into rapping right away, and I knew this was something different."

By rapping, Hodges means *rapping*. When Run DMC released their first rap album, Ford was in high school in St. Petersburg, Fla., and he was taken with the way his African-American classmates would free-rap in the halls. A few years later, working alone in the fields of his Tennessee farm, he found the rap sound still stuck in his head, and he began making up verses about the world around him.

His first rap was about eating bugs; he tried it out on the Amish farm family down the road. "They liked it," he says. "They tend to frown on music, but this didn't have any instruments."

Today, Ford raps on request and to audiences at his speeches on biodiesel, accompanying himself by knee-pounding and various ad hoc instrumental-esque vocalizations:

We could get driven to extinction just for spinnin'
  our wheels
Up an offing ourselves with our
  automobiles
And like them dinosaurs that died out, that
  technology's old
And while they profit from pollution, we've been
  getting sold
Multi-national corporations lobby for
  their greed
And they can grease the palms of politicians at light speed
But think fast—that's just Big Brother and big business
  blowin' smoke up your ass
Brainwashin' us to believe the drama, bloodshed,
  and greed
That we keep on creatin' in the Middle East is
  completely removed
Oh yeah has nothin' to do with our out-and-out addiction
  to the flammable goo
Oil, that is
Well nice try, I hear it chirpin' but it just don't fly

People who've been around biodiesel vehicles frequently comment on their smell, often likened to french fries or popcorn, and I'd wanted to get a whiff ever since I introduced myself to Ford. Now, with evening settling in, he pulls the Scout over near a small guest house beside a spring, a place he sometimes stays when his ranch's California owner comes to visit. It is a beautiful spot.

I get out of Ford's truck, head to the tailpipe, and breathe deeply. It hardly smells like anything at all. It is, simply, clean.

AFTER YOU READ: Analyze the Issues

1. What is Charris Ford's nickname?
2. What did Rudolph Diesel want to originally do with the engine he developed in 1893?
3. How will Ford redo gas stations?

AFTER YOU READ: Analyze the Rhetoric

1. Note the use of numbers in the essay. What effect do such numbers have on enhancing the logos appeal to the audience?
2. Review the use of adjectives found in the essay. How does this help the essay? Did you like his use of these modifiers?

Sample Student Paper

Global Warming: Fact or Fiction?

by Lauren Kobernus

AS YOU READ: Annotate

1. Place a star by the sections you like the most.
2. Place question marks by sections you have problems with or do not understand.
3. Place a [+] by sections that need to be developed more or that seem to be incomplete.
4. Write other comments in the margins as you see fit.

Imagine waking up tomorrow and there being multiple natural disasters, mass animal and plant extinction, a large rise in sea level resulting in coastal flooding, and outbreaks of tropical disease. These are only some of the horrible predictions made by many scientists as to the eventual consequences of global warming. Global warming is the gradual warming of the Earth's atmosphere due to greenhouse gas emissions. This issue has been brought to the world's attention and has brought about many different opinions on this subject. Many people believe that this is a very serious problem that needs to be addressed immediately and others believe the exact opposite. They do not even believe that global warming exists or that it has any relation to human activities. There are many startling facts that should not be ignored. When something as important as our future on earth is at risk as many people should be informed as possible; global warming is a serious problem that is negatively affecting our planet's future in a very dramatic way.

Many people around the world need to consider what our atmosphere is and what is happening to cause its change. The greenhouse effect is a phenomenon that is produced naturally by gases surrounding the Earth. This effect holds in the heat that is reflected by the sun. This is what keeps the lower atmosphere warm (Tennesen 4). However, what causes this global warming is when more gases are put into this so called "blanket." The reason it is so easy for us to change the composition of our atmosphere is because it is so thin (Gore 24). Therefore, what we do has a direct affect on our environment. For example, atmospheric levels of carbon dioxide were 379 parts per million in 2005, higher than at any time in the past 650,000 years. Of the twelve warmest years on record, eleven occurred between 1995 and 2006 (Kluger 52).

These changes may seem insignificant, but this has already caused many problems around the world. Eskimos in Alaska are finding it almost impossible to hunt the main components of their diet which are seals and walruses. The warming is causing these animals to migrate earlier and earlier. In January 1995, a large section of ice broke away from the ice shelf of Antartica. This section was the size of the state of Rhode Island (Gelbspan 1). The extreme drought in China is causing many lakes to dry up and sand dunes to destroy much of the farming. This is the worst drought for China in a century (Lynas). Montana's Glacier National Park had 150 glaciers in 1910 and today there are fewer than thirty in the whole park. Eighty percent of the snow on Mount Kilimanjaro has melted (Clemmitt 74–5). Stronger storms are occurring due to the warming of the oceans. Florida was hit by four hurricanes that were incredibly strong in 2004 (Gore 80). More natural disasters are happening today that are caused by the weather. They are increasing three times faster than any other natural disasters such as earthquakes (Lean 21). These occurrences are not just hypothetical; they are happening now, they are real and becoming more and more common.

The main question on many people's minds today is what exactly is causing these effects and this warming of our planet. The answer to this question is the greenhouse gases that get trapped in the atmosphere. According to Richard Rickman Ph.D., Sr. Scientist Chemist for Halliburton, "We understand why certain gasses can facilitate global warming, it has to do with what wavelengths the molecules absorb or emit radiation, in this case it is in the infrared region." Some of these gases include carbon dioxide, methane, nitrous oxide, and chlorofluorocarbons. Each of these gases has a natural place and way in to the atmosphere and an unnatural way caused by our society's large gas emission life style. Either way these gases are making their way into our atmosphere it is causing more and more damage. There needs to be a solution to the amount of these gases being emitted.

Carbon dioxide is the main cause of global warming! Carbon dioxide is the most recognized of the heat trapping gases mainly because it has the longest life span. Carbon dioxide can stay in our atmosphere for more than 100 years, therefore, it causes the most damage. It comes from the burning of oil, coal, and gas (Tennesen 22-3). "Global carbon dioxide output last year approached a staggering thirty-two billion tons, with about twenty-five percent of that coming from the United States" (Kluger 53). Right now carbon dioxide is 33 percent higher than in the 19th century (Woodwell 39). According to Jon Russ, the Chair of the Chemistry Department at Rhodes College, "Humans are producing tons and tons of carbon dioxide everyday. It is a fact that the carbon dioxide concentration in our atmosphere has increased dramatically during the past century, due to burning of fossil fuels." If we stopped all carbon dioxide use right now it would keep affecting us for up to a century. This gas is very harmful to the atmosphere and many people realize these consequences and yet nothing dramatic is being done to remedy this problem. When thinking of a life span of 100 years and the amount of this gas being used each year the results will be devastating.

Methane is another component linked to global warming. It is twenty to thirty times more effective at keeping in heat than carbon dioxide, although its life span is only ten to twelve years. Naturally, methane is put out by the decomposition in swamps or wetlands. The other source is from the decomposition of bacteria such as in rice paddies, landfills, and in the guts of cattle and termites. When people cut down trees it becomes a breeding ground for bacteria and termites which also emit methane. There are also the man made sources of this gas which include emissions from oil drilling and coal mining (Tennesen 24). These are two prominent aspects of the United States economy, therefore, oil drilling and coal mining happen on a daily basis making this a very problematic issue. Methane is a serious problem in our atmosphere that needs to be addressed immediately.

Another contributor to this climate change is nitrous oxide. This is the gas that is emitted when fuel is burned. This gas is mainly released from industrial processes and from fertilizers. About twenty percent of nitrous oxide emissions come from power plants and transportation sources (Cooper 50). This causes a serious problem when there are over 500 million cars driving on the planet. Today our society is so accustomed to driving sport utility vehicles. These cars get very low gas mileage which in turn requires more burning of fuel and more nitrous oxide being put into the atmosphere

Another commonly used dangerous gas is chlorofluorocarbons. This gas is found primarily in refrigerants and in air conditioners. Many house holds today all over the planet have both of these devices which emit chlorofluorocarbons. These emissions go directly into the atmosphere and harm it in the same way as carbon dioxide. The other source for chlorofluorocarbons are aerosol propellants. These can be found in hair sprays and in household cleaning solvents. These emitters of chlorofluorocarbons are all normal items that the average individual probably has in their house at this moment. Therefore, making chlorofluorocarbons in excess amounts going straight into our atmosphere (Tennesen 25–6).

Now the question is what steps are being taken to fix this problem. In December 1997 a contract known as Kyoto Protocol was developed. This contract is a treaty among 150 countries that agree to reduce carbon dioxide and other greenhouse gas emissions. It calls for these countries to reduce these gases by five percent. The United States agreed to reduce their gas emissions by seven percent since they are the number one country for greenhouse gas pollution. This seems like a very good idea, however, not one industrialized country has actually come through with the promises of the Kyoto Protocol. This caused much unwanted attention toward the United States. They were then blamed for trying to avoid making any changes to their destructive life style regarding energy consumption. This Kyoto Protocol is a very good idea, but has not been very effective. Therefore, the greenhouse gas emissions are continuing to rise. It is clear that this treaty does not go nearly far enough; however, to help our planetary problem somewhat there should be an immediate ratification and implementation of this Kyoto Protocol (Cooper 41).

Many companies and corporations are doing all they can by their research and actions to help reduce their greenhouse gas emissions. According to Matt Blauch, the Principal Scientist for Halliburton, "There is no one single solution to this problem, it is not just a matter of switching from fossil fuel use. There needs to be a long term solution. I am working on a project for Halliburton in which we are taking the emissions, such as methane, from power plants and re-injecting them into the earth's geologic foundation where these gases can be permanently stored. This process is called geosequestration. Additional projects are already underway." Also, according to Richard Rickman, Ph.D., Sr. Scientist, Chemist for Halliburton, "Chemists can aid in the development of alternative fuel sources, for example, fuel cells, nuclear energy, more efficient photovoltaic cells, etc." This is only one of the many corporations that may be working on additional alternative solutions to this problem of global warming. This problem has been recognized by many and they are working in whatever way they can to help our planet's future.

Additional steps should also be taken by individuals daily. Many people in our society today are unaware of the harm they are causing. Each person should try to reduce their carbon footprint. This includes individuals taking steps such as using less heat in homes, driving less or more fuel efficient cars, and having a general understanding of how they can reduce their gas emissions. To start helping our planet there needs to be a reduction of fossil fuel use by sixty to eighty percent below the levels we have currently today (Lynas 128). According to Richard Rickman, Ph.D., Sr. Scientist, Chemist for Halliburton, " A paradigm shift in the way the general public views our ecosystem is going to have to occur before any meaningful change can take place" (Interview March 30 2007). Former Vice President Al Gore stated, "This will be a catastrophe, this is not a political issue. It is a moral, ethical, and spiritual issue. It is all of our responsibility to be good stewards, lest we destroy the habitability of this planet for those who come after us. This is the moral challenge of our lifetime" (qtd. in Sutter 4A).

In spite of all the evidence, many people in the world today still believe that global warming poses no serious threat. They may suggest that cold spells are still happening. Some may think of global warming just as heat waves and warming, therefore they believe these cold spells disprove the concept of global warming. This is a good point, but more information needs to be considered. For instance, according to Principal Scientist, Matt Blauch, "Global warming is not considered a theory any longer it is now considered a proven phenomenon. This problem is not just a warming effect, but it is a global climate change. This means that it is not just heat, it is extreme swings in storms and weather either hot or cold." Since global warming has now been proven, it seems that many minds may begin to change. This may help some people understand the true meaning of global warming.

Many may also believe that human activity has nothing to do with global warming. This has been a very arguable aspect of global warming. Some may say that this warming is just the natural course of our planet. This is also a very good arguable point, however, the earth's temperature has had what can be called a hockey stick curve. This is when earth's temperature has stayed the same over many centuries and then suddenly the temperature experiences a sudden increase (Greening Earth Society 43). This seems to have something to do with human influence due to more industrialization and the use of more fossil fuels. In 1995, the United Nations Intergovernmental Panel on Climate Change (IPCC) stated, "The balance of evidence suggests a discernible human influence on global climate." The most recent report on January 22, 2006 stated, "New and strong evidence that most of the observed warming of the last 50 years is attributable to human activities with 90 percent confidence" (Cooper 45).

If this problem continues without a solution very drastic consequences are in our future. It is estimated that global temperatures will inevitably rise. This change will be by about three to six degrees Fahrenheit by the end of this century. That will make it the hottest of anytime in human history. This increase will lead polar ice to melt, sea levels raising which will flood coastal areas, mass plant and animal extinction because they cannot handle the hotter conditions (Cooper 42-5). According to Matt Blauch, Principal Scientist, "In about 1,000 years time the Earth may actually go into a glaciation period." Through his research he has found that the effects of global warming can actually send us into another ice age. This is a frightening fact, but it is a reality that we may have to accept if no action is taken immediately.

Knowing that global warming is here and it is harmful is the first step. Knowing what exactly is causing this and how each individual can help are the following steps. This problem is just too important to ignore. It is a global emergency. It is so important because our future is in jeopardy. Not just our future, but our lives right now. We are already seeing the effects today. The results of our neglect are being seen now and are getting worse day by day. With so many advances being made in technology today it seems they should be able to find a reasonable response to this important global problem. Many people should wake up and realize that global warming is not going away without some change in our actions. The United States is the greatest carbon dioxide emitting country, yet, we will suffer the least from this issue. "We must abandon the old mindset that demands an oil-based economy, not just because it sparks wars and terrorism, but because the future of life on earth depends on leaving it behind" (Lynas 129).

Climate driven changes have been observed in five different continents. Millions are being left homeless and in great danger. We may be reaching the point of no return soon if no action is taken. Many people go by the saying, "Out of sight, out of mind." This happens when people refuse to accept the problem that they have caused. They try not to think about it and rely on someone else to think of a way out. This problem is almost impossible to keep out of sight or out of mind because the horrible consequences are happening right before our eyes. We must find a way to share more, consume less, and basically live more simply. We must wake up, accept the realization that this is happening, and think of how individually we can help.

Works Cited

Blauch, Matt. Personal Interview. 4 March 2007.

Clemmitt, Marcia. "Climate Change." *CQ Researcher* 16 (2006): 73-5.

Cooper, Mary. "Global Warming Treaty." *CQ Researcher* 6 (2001): 41-6.

Gelbspan, Ross. *The Heat Is On.* Reading: Addison-Wesley Publishing Company, Inc., 1997.

Gore, Al. *An Inconvenient Truth.* Emmaus: Rodale, 2006.

Greening Earth Society. *Many Scientists Do Not Agree That Global Warming Is a Human-Caused Problem*. Farmington Hills: Greenhaven Press, 2006.

Kluger, Jeffrey. "What Now?" *Time* 9 April 2007: 52-3.

Lean, Geoffrey. *Global Warming*. Farmington Hills: Greenhaven Press, 2006.

Lynas, Mark. *Humanity's Future*. Farmington Hills: Greenhaven Press, 2006.

Rickman, Richard. Internet Interview. 30 March 2007.

Russ, Jon. Internet Interview. 3 April 2007.

Sutter, John D. "Climate Ailing, Al Gore Warns OU Audience." *Daily Oklahoman* 2 March 2007, morning ed.: 4A.

Tennesen, Michael. *The Complete Idiot's Guide To Global Warming*. New York: Alpha, 2004.

Woodwell, George M. *The Environment*. Farmington Hills: Greenhaven Press, 2006.

PRO PEER REVIEW OUTLINE

Directions. Asking the right questions: As you ask these questions and answer them, be specific in your comments so as to be more helpful to the author. Provide details.

1. **Logos.** Comment on the quality and amount of the evidence or research conducted. Is it balanced or enough? Does the author need more? Why or why not? Is the paper too logical or not logical enough? What else can you say about logos?

2. **Pathos.** Comment on the emotional appeals used in the paper. What can the author do to improve this appeal? Should there be less, more, or no emotions? Explain.
3. **Ethos.** Does the author use enough quality sources to improve the impact of the ethos of the paper? Is there a human element in the paper? What does the author need to do to improve the character aspect? Should the author add a personal story? Is the paper too personal? Should it be more logical?
4. **Call for Improvement.** Which aspects in the paper need to be revised or improved? Explain in detail.

Responding to Environmental Issues

Written Rhetoric: Opinion Papers, Arguments, and Research

1. Write an essay where you argue that environmentalists or anti-environmentalists are most ethical in their persuasive strategies. Use the essays in the books or other resources to support your assertions.
2. Write a letter of appeal, as one of the tribal members from the Skull Valley Goshute Reservation, to the U.S. Government arguing that the government stop using the reservation as a dumping ground.
3. Write a letter of appeal, as a government official, to the Skull Valley Goshute reservation arguing why the government has the right to use reservation land for such dumping.
4. Conduct research, and write an essay using Pardo's article and the information from the chapter on conspiracy theory. Argue how and why these areas might be targeted for such harmful environmental waste.
5. Some claim that global warming is a hoax. Take a stand and research this.
6. For some people, there is no oil shortage. Research this and write an essay defending one side.

Oral Rhetoric: Speeches, Lyrics, and Simulations

1. Write an essay, as either a descendent of Chief Seattle or as a current resident of Seattle, Washington, that argues this speech was OR was not delivered by Chief Seattle exactly as it is written. Provide evidence from the speech to support your assertion.
2. Write a letter to the President of the United States about environmentalism and the changes you want. Write it as an oral speech and demand changes.

3. Create a simulation, with such characters as Bigmouth or as Winthrop, that demonstrate how current cultural views on land are similar or different, successful or unsuccessful, right or wrong. Remember to use adjectives to persuade the listeners.
4. Choose two authors from this chapter or two authors not in this book to meet in a debate about the environment. Be enthusiastic.

Visual Rhetoric: Advertisements, Visuals, and Cinema

1. Find advertisements or commercials that are green, emphasizing positive attributes for the environment. Analyze the effectiveness of such advertisements or commercials.
2. Watch a film based on the environment and write a report on the visual effects offered in the film.
3. Watch the documentary *An Inconvenient Truth* and read the critics that say some of the information is incorrect. Write a report discussing what is accurate and what is not.
4. Go to www.deviantart.com and search using the words "environment" and "global warming." Save the images you find the most effective. Write an essay about the images. Include the images in your report.

Electronic Rhetoric: Emergent Media and Gaming

Access YouTube.com and search for one (or more) of the following animations:

Award Winning Animation on Global Warming	by Grassrootinnovation
Global Warming PSA	by 359172
Global Warming (Read the Info)	by AndrewEdwardRoss
The Most Terrifying Video You'll Ever See	by Wonderingmind42

Tip: Search by the creator's name.

If you cannot find these animations, locate three on YouTube.com that focus on environmentalism.

Watch the video(s) closely. What rhetorical strategies are being used? How does the media format support the strategies? Compare and contrast the rhetorical strategies (specifically ethos, pathos, and logos) as developed in the oral, visual, and written presentations.

If possible, play one of the following games:

- *Civilization*
- *The Oregon Trail*
- *Sim Earth*
- *Sim City*
- *Harvest Moon*
- Games at WWF (World Wildlife Fund) at: http://www.panda.org/news_facts/multimedia/fun_games/index.cfm

WOVE Project

Create your own 60 second to 2 minute video or commercial about global warming or any other environmental issue. You may choose any side of the argument you want, but you must provide evidence to support it. Begin your project by first writing a script or speech. Transition the written script or speech to voice and add it to an electronic media (YouTube, PowerPoint, MySpace). Afterwards, evaluate how your strategies changed (or did not change) and why they changed (or did not change) as you moved from written to oral to visual to electronic.

Cinematic List

An Inconvenient Truth (Davis Guggenheim, 2006)
Baraka (Ron Fricke, 1992)
The Birds (Alfred Hitchcock, 1963)
The Day After Tomorrow (Roland Emmerich, 2004)
Erin Brockovich (Steven Soderbergh, 2000)
Ferngully: The Last Rainforest (Bill Kroyer, 1992)
Go Further: Your Guide to Leaving a Lighter Footprint (Ron Mann, 2003)
I Heart Huckabees (David O. Russell, 2004)
King Kong (Merian C. Cooper, Ernest B. Schoedsack, 1933; Peter Jackson, 2005)
Koyaanisqatsi (Godfrey Reggio, 1982)
The Life Aquatic with Steve Zissou (Wes Anderson, 2004)
Logan's Run (Michael Anderson, 1976)
Naqoyqatsi (Godfrey Reggio, 2002)
Never Cry Wolf (Carroll Ballard, 1983)
Powaqatis (Godfrey Reggio, 1988)
Princess Mononoke (Hayao Miyazaki, 1997)
Safe (Todd Haynes, 1995)
Silent Running (Douglas Trumbull, 1972)
Twister (Jan de Bont, 1996)

Television

The Lorax (Dr. Seuss)

Video Games

Civilization
The Oregon Trail
Sim Earth
Sim City
Harvest Moon

On-Line Games

Fun and Games

Save the Earth, Living Green, and Toxic Blaster

PowerUp, the Game. IBM.

www.powerupthegame.org
"Save Planet Helios from ecological devastation!"

"Nintendo Controls U.S.-Mexico Borders"

by Cary Stringfield

AFTER YOU READ: Analyze the Issues

1. What is the message of the cartoon?
2. Who is the audience?

AFTER YOU READ: Analyze the Rhetoric

1. Is the message effective?
2. How does the cartoon borrow from electronic games?

"Nuestro Himno" ("Star-Spangled Banner")

Versión por Francis Haffkine Snow

Amanece: ¿no veis, a la luz de la aurora,
Lo que tanto aclamamos la noche al caer?
Sus estrellas, sus barras flotaban ayer
En el fiero combate en señal de victoria,
Fulgor de cohetes, de bombas estruendo,
Por la noche decían: "!Se va defendiendo!"

Coro:
!Oh, decid! ¿Despliega aún su hermosura estrellada,
Sobre tierra de libres, la bandera sagrada?

En la costa lejana que apenas blanquea,
Donde yace nublada la hueste feroz
Sobre aquel precipicio que elévase atroz
¡Oh, decidme! ¿Qué es eso que en la brisa ondea?
Se oculta y flamea, en el alba luciendo,
Reflejada en la mar, donde va resplandeciendo

Coro:
!Aún allí desplegó su hermosura estrellada,
Sobre tierra de libres, la bandera sagrada!

¡Oh así sea siempre, en lealtad defendamos
Nuestra tierra natal contra el torpe invasor!
A Dios quien nos dio paz, libertad y honor,
Nos mantuvo nación, con fervor bendigamos.

Nuestra causa es el bien, y por eso triunfamos.
Siempre fue nuestro lema "¡En Dios confiamos!"

Coro:
!Y desplegará su hermosura estrellada,
Sobre tierra de libres, la bandera sagrada!

(Traducido, 1919)

AFTER YOU READ: Analyze the Issues

1. Who is the audience for this song?
2. Why would this version of the song anger some people?

AFTER YOU READ: Analyze the Rhetoric

1. Does the message of the song change when written in Spanish?
2. Is the message less or more effective in Spanish?

The Issues

How do you feel hearing the "The Star Spangled Banner" being sung in Spanish? In April 2006, British music producer Adam Kidron released "Nuestro Himno," or "Our Hymn," a Spanish version of the U.S. national anthem. Kidron asserted that he released the song to raise awareness of the plight of immigrants, but many were outraged by the translation. The main arguments revolved around people's attitudes about the issues in this chapter: immigration and acculturation.

Since the United States became a nation, people from around the world have been immigrating to this country. But should anyone be able to immigrate and become an American citizen? Who should be allowed to immigrate to this country, and who should be kept out? What policies should our nation have concerning immigration?

The question of who should be able to immigrate to our country remains an issue that concerns Americans, especially in light of the large numbers of illegal immigrants crossing our borders and in light of the possibility of foreign terrorists infiltrating our nation.

One group of immigrants that continues to grow in the United States is Hispanics. Some predict that in the future, people of Hispanic descent may, in fact, outnumber Caucasians in America.

Ask the Right Questions

Logos

In order to analyze issues concerning immigration and acculturation, you must seek to understand the complexity of the issues. Why do people immigrate? How does our nation benefit from immigrants? Do immigrants pose a threat to Americans? Do they take jobs away from Americans? What problems does a large immigrant population pose? Can you think of other dimensions of this issue? Take a moment to jot down your thoughts in the margin.

Ethos

If you were to research such issues discussed above, whom would you trust for valid information? Be aware as you read about immigration and acculturation that writers will cite all sorts of sources: teachers, immigrants, legislators, employers, individuals who have opinions about the subject, celebrities, clergymen, and government officials, just to cite a few. Always question the authority of the evidence presented.

Pathos

Immigration and acculturation are hot topics right now, and as with any hot topic, people are passionate about the subjects. Oftentimes, their passion stems from some fear, some need, or some other emotion. Writers will take advantage of emotional responses that they anticipate from their readers, so be on the lookout for such ploys. Answer the following questions in the margin to prepare to read about immigration and acculturation: Why are these topics hot right now? How do Americans fear immigrants will affect their lives? How might immigrants threaten Americans? Are any other emotions prevalent when people write about immigration and acculturation? As you read the essays in this chapter, pay particular attention to the emotional appeals the writers make.

Annotate the Text

In addition to paying attention to the text's use of logos, ethos, and pathos, annotate the readings as follows:

- Who is the writer's intended audience? Immigrants? Citizens? Both?
- Underline the thesis, or summarize the writer's main points in the margin.
- After reading a selection, jot down a description of the author's method of organizing his or her work. Is the writing organized purposefully? How so?
- Highlight the evidence the writer uses and, in the margin, comment on the effectiveness and trustworthiness of the evidence.
- Circle weasel words or buzz words. Some buzzwords we might find in articles on immigration and acculturation are *American values, patriotism, human rights*, and *terrorism*.

"It's My Yardman"

by John Branch

JOHN BRANCH, San Antonio Express-News

"Minute Men"

by Steve Breen

AFTER YOU READ: Analyze the Issues

1. What is the message of each cartoon?
2. Who is the audience for each cartoon?

AFTER YOU READ: Analyze the Rhetoric

1. Comment on the humor found in each cartoon.
2. Does the effectiveness of the humor depend on different audiences?

"The Vegetable"

by Marjane Satrapi
excerpted from Persepolis 2
(Graphic Novel)

Marjane Satrapi was born in Iran in 1969 and was raised during a transitional period in her country. In Tehran, she studied at the Lycee Francai until, at age 14, she went to Vienna to flee the regime of Iran's dictator, then to Strasbourg to study illustration. Although she returned to Iran briefly, she moved to Paris where she created her autobiographical graphic novels *Persepolis* and *Persepolis 2*. In addition to graphic novels, Satrapi also writes and illustrates children's books. Her illustrations appear regularly in French newspapers and magazines. An animated version of the graphic novels was released in 2007.

AS YOU READ: Annotate

1. In the margins, respond to Marjane's attempts to fit in with her friends in Vienna.
2. Place a star next to any illustrations you find particularly effective and comment on their effectiveness in the margins.
3. Count the number of panels on each page and write the number at the bottom of the page.

Background: Marjane, an Iranian girl, goes to high school in Vienna while her parents remain in Iran. The following chapter from *Persepolis 2* illustrates the problem of experiencing adolescence away from home.

THE VEGETABLE

MY HEAD ALSO CHANGED IN ITS OWN WAY. FIRST, MY FACE GOT LONGER.

THEN MY RIGHT EYE GREW,

FOLLOWED SWIFTLY BY MY CHIN WHICH DOUBLED IN LENGTH.

THEN IT WAS MY MOUTH,

MY RIGHT HAND,

MY LEFT FOOT.

(EVEN TODAY, IT'S HALF A SIZE BIGGER THAN MY RIGHT FOOT.)

OF COURSE MY NOSE TRIPLED ITS SIZE.

AND WAS DECORATED BY A LARGE BEAUTY MARK.

WHICH I THOUGHT HIDEOUS AT THE TIME.

THEN MY CHIN ADVANCED MAJESTICALLY,

ONLY TO RETREAT TO ITS ORIGINAL POSITION SEVERAL MONTHS LATER.

FINALLY MY CHEST DEVELOPED

AND MY CENTER OF GRAVITY WAS BALANCED OUT BY THE POUNDS ON MY BUTT.

IN SHORT, I WAS IN AN UGLY STAGE SEEMINGLY WITHOUT END.

AS IF MY NATURAL DEFORMITY WASN'T ENOUGH, I TRIED A FEW NEW HAIRCUTS. A LITTLE SNIP OF THE SCISSORS ON THE LEFT.

AND A WEEK LATER, A LITTLE SNIP OF THE SCISSORS ON THE RIGHT.

I LOOKED LIKE COSETTE IN "LES MISÉRABLES."

SO I COATED MY HAIR WITH GEL,

I ADDED A THICK LINE OF EYELINER,

A FEW SAFETY PINS,

WHICH WERE REPLACED BY A SCARF. IT SOFTENED THE LOOK.
IT WAS BEGINNING TO LOOK LIKE SOMETHING.

HAVE YOU SEEN HOW BEAUTIFUL SHE IS NOW?
...
UH ...

TO MY ENORMOUS SURPRISE, MY NEW LOOK EVEN PLEASED THE HALL MONITORS. IT SHOULD BE SAID THAT THEY WERE VERY YOUNG.
YOU CHANGE YOUR HAIRSTYLE EVERY DAY. WHO CUTS YOUR HAIR?
I DO.
IF I PAY YOU, WILL YOU CUT MY HAIR, TOO?

THAT'S HOW I BECAME THE SCHOOL'S OFFICIAL HAIRCUTTER.
IT HELPED ME EARN A LITTLE SPENDING MONEY.

MY RELATIONSHIP WITH THE SCHOOL'S LACKEYS DIDN'T PLEASE MY FRIENDS MUCH.
SO, YOU SEEM TO BE ON AWFULLY GOOD TERMS WITH THE PEONS.
NOT REALLY! I JUST CUT THEIR HAIR.

THAT'S NOT ALL YOU DO FOR THEM. YOU KISS THEIR ASSES FROM TIME TO TIME.
I DO NOT. I THINK THEY'RE NICE, THAT'S ALL.

PEONS, THEY'RE PEONS. THEY HAVE A FIXED PSYCHOLOGICAL PROFILE. THEY ARE THIRSTY FOR POWER AND ARE LOOKING TO CONTROL US.
YEAH, LIKE THE COPS.

EXACTLY! LIFE IS PAIN. PAIN IS EVERYTHING. EVERYTHING IS NOTHINGNESS. THEREFORE LIFE IS NOTHINGNESS. WHEN MAN RECOGNIZES THIS HOLE, HE CAN NO LONGER LIVE LIKE AN EARTHWORM, INVENTING GAMES OF LEADERS AND FOLLOWERS TO FORGET HIS FICKLENESS.

WHATEVER! EXISTENCE IS NOT ABSURD. THERE ARE PEOPLE WHO BELIEVE IN IT AND WHO GIVE THEIR LIVES FOR VALUES LIKE LIBERTY.
WHAT RUBBISH! EVEN THAT, IT'S A DISTRACTION FROM BOREDOM.

SO MY UNCLE DIED TO DISTRACT HIMSELF?
...
FOR MOMO, DEATH WAS THE ONLY DOMAIN WHERE MY KNOWLEDGE EXCEEDED HIS. ON THIS SUBJECT, I ALWAYS HAD THE LAST WORD.

NOBLE COMBAT, BLAH BLAH BLAH ...
OK! ARE WE GOING TO SMOKE A JOINT?
SURE!

IT WAS ALWAYS THIERRY WHO ROLLED THE JOINTS WHILE WE KEPT AN EYE OUT FOR THE MONITORS SO WE WOULDN'T BE CAUGHT BY SURPRISE.

HERE!
I DIDN'T LIKE TO SMOKE, BUT I DID IT OUT OF SOLIDARITY. AT THE TIME, TO ME, GRASS AND HEROIN WERE THE SAME THING.

EACH TIME I WAS OFFERED A JOINT, I REMEMBERED THIS CONVERSATION MY PARENTS HAD ABOUT MY COUSIN KAMRAN.

POOR BOY, HE'S STUCK HIMSELF SO MANY TIMES HE'S BEGUN TO LOOK LIKE A VEGETABLE.

THIS KIND OF THING ALWAYS HAPPENS TO THE MOST FRAGILE ONES.

BECOMING A VEGETABLE WAS OUT OF THE QUESTION.

SO I PRETENDED TO PARTICIPATE, BUT I NEVER INHALED THE SMOKE.

AND AS SOON AS MY FRIENDS' BACKS WERE TURNED, I STUCK MY FINGERS IN MY EYES TO MAKE THEM GOOD AND RED.

THEN, I IMITATED THEIR LAUGHTER.
I WAS QUITE BELIEVABLE.

THE HARDER I TRIED TO ASSIMILATE, THE MORE I HAD THE FEELING THAT I WAS DISTANCING MYSELF FROM MY CULTURE, BETRAYING MY PARENTS AND MY ORIGINS, THAT I WAS PLAYING A GAME BY SOMEBODY ELSE'S RULES.

EACH TELEPHONE CALL FROM MY PARENTS REMINDED ME OF MY COWARDICE AND MY BETRAYAL. I WAS AT ONCE HAPPY TO HEAR THEIR VOICES AND ASHAMED TO TALK TO THEM.

- YES, I'M DOING FINE. I'M GETTING GOOD GRADES.

- FRIENDS? OF COURSE, LOTS!

- DAD . . .

- DAD, I LOVE YOU!

- YOU HAVE SOME GOOD FRIENDS?

- THAT DOESN'T SURPRISE ME, YOU ALWAYS HAD A TALENT FOR COMMUNICATING WITH PEOPLE!

- EAT ORANGES. THEY'RE FULL OF VITAMIN C.

- US TOO, WE ADORE YOU. YOU'RE THE CHILD ALL PARENTS DREAM OF HAVING!

IF ONLY THEY KNEW . . . IF THEY KNEW THAT THEIR DAUGHTER WAS MADE UP LIKE A PUNK, THAT SHE SMOKED JOINTS TO MAKE A GOOD IMPRESSION, THAT SHE HAD SEEN MEN IN THEIR UNDERWEAR WHILE THEY WERE BEING BOMBED EVERY DAY, THEY WOULDN'T CALL ME THEIR DREAM CHILD.

I WANTED TO FORGET EVERYTHING, TO MAKE MY PAST DISAPPEAR, BUT MY UNCONSCIOUS CAUGHT UP WITH ME.

I EVEN MANAGED TO DENY MY NATIONALITY.

DURING A PARTY AT SCHOOL.
HI, I'M MARC. I GRADUATED LAST YEAR. YOU'RE NEW! WHAT'S YOUR NAME?
MARJANE. I'VE BEEN HERE A YEAR.

AND WHERE ARE YOU FROM MARIE-JEANNE?
I'M FRENCH.
OH REALLY? YOU HAVE A FUNNY ACCENT FOR A FRENCH GIRL.
OH! I HAVE TO FIND MY FRIENDS. BYE.

I SHOULD SAY THAT AT THE TIME, IRAN WAS THE EPITOME OF EVIL AND TO BE IRANIAN WAS A HEAVY BURDEN TO BEAR.
IT WAS EASIER TO LIE THAN TO ASSUME THAT BURDEN.

WHO'S THAT GUY?
MARC? HE'S ANNA'S BROTHER, THE GIRL IN THE STRIPED SWEATER. HE'S A JERK FROM BOURGE. YOU SHOULDN'T TALK TO THOSE PEOPLE.

AND WHEN I GOT BACK THAT NIGHT, I REMEMBERED THAT LINE MY GRANDMOTHER TOLD ME: "ALWAYS KEEP YOUR DIGNITY AND BE TRUE TO YOURSELF!"
OH GRANDMA ...

UNFORTUNATELY, IT ALL CAME OUT IN THE END. A FEW DAYS LATER IN A CAFÉ NEAR SCHOOL.
SHE TOLD MY BROTHER THAT SHE WAS FRENCH.
AND YOUR BROTHER BELIEVED HER?

WHAT DO YOU THINK? HAVE YOU HEARD THE WAY SHE TALKS?
HAVE YOU SEEN HER FACE?

BUT YOUR BROTHER WAS HITTING ON HER OR WHAT?
OF COURSE NOT!!
AH, THAT'S A RELIEF. CONSI-DERING HOW UGLY SHE IS, IT WOULD BE REALLY UNFAIR IF SHE GOT A GUY LIKE MARC.

HA, HA, HA! I WOULD COMMIT SUICIDE IF MY BROTHER WAS GOING OUT WITH A COW LIKE THAT!

I DON'T KNOW IF YOU'VE NOTICED, BUT SHE NEVER TALKS ABOUT EITHER HER COUNTRY OR HER PARENTS.
WELL, OF COURSE! SHE LIES WHEN SHE SAYS THAT SHE'S KNOWN WAR. IT'S ALL TO MAKE HERSELF SEEM INTERESTING.

ANYWAY, HER PARENTS CLEARLY DON'T CARE ABOUT HER, OR THEY WOULDN'T HAVE SENT HER ALONE.
THAT WAS TOO MUCH. I SAW RED.

YOU ARE GOING TO SHUT UP OR I AM GOING TO MAKE YOU!
I AM IRANIAN AND PROUD OF IT!

SHE IS COMPLETELY CRAZY.

I WANTED TO DIE.
CAFE
WHERE WERE MY PARENTS TO TAKE ME IN THEIR ARMS, TO REASSURE ME?

BUT REALLY, I HAD NOTHING TO CRY ABOUT.

I HAD JUST REDEEMED MYSELF.

FOR THE FIRST TIME IN A YEAR, I FELT PROUD.
I FINALLY UNDERSTOOD WHAT MY GRANDMOTHER MEANT. IF I WASN'T COMFORTABLE WITH MYSELF, I WOULD NEVER BE COMFORTABLE.

AFTER YOU READ: Analyze the Issues

1. Characterize Marjane's friends. Are they supportive? Explain.
2. In what ways do Marjane's problems appear to be those of a typical adolescent, and in what ways do they seem to be those of someone living outside of her culture?
3. How does Marjane cope with her physical problems? Her emotional problems? Are her methods of coping with these two types of problems similar or different?
4. Does Marjane have strong ethos? Explain.

AFTER YOU READ: Analyze the Rhetoric

1. Why is this chapter called "The Vegetable"? What other title(s) would be appropriate, or even better?
2. As you read, you counted the number of panels on a page. You probably noticed that the first page contains a series of small panels, while on other pages a large panel dominates the page. Explain how Satrapi uses the size of the panels that compose her novel.
3. The focus of this chapter constantly changes—from Marjane's physical transformation, to the responses of other students, to her friends, and so forth. What does Satrapi do to ensure coherence in her text?

"No Leniency for Illegal Aliens"

by Ian De Silva

Ian De Silva is an engineer who writes a great deal about both scientific topics and topics related to politics and history. De Silva regularly writes on the issue of immigration for *Human Events*, a weekly conservative journal.

AS YOU READ: Annotate

1. Note in the margin De Silva's use of pathos. Identify the fears and emotions he appeals to.
2. Note in the margin where De Silva works to build ethos.
3. Circle the following words, and any others you do not know, and write their definitions in the margins: *audacity, kowtow, formidable, indubitably,* and *decry.*

Posted Apr 05, 2006

The protests in some cities by thousands of illegal aliens are a stunning reminder of how shameless the lawless have become. It is bad enough that they came illegally and have no right to be here, but imagine their audacity to demand rights! What is even more troubling is that there are politicians who will kowtow to such brazen displays of impudence.

The protests are against the strict immigration bill that the House of Representatives passed last December. The bill, "Border Protection, Antiterrorism, and Illegal Immigration Control Act of 2005," has a myriad of measures against illegal immigration. It would, among other things, build a 700-mile fence along the U.S.-Mexico border, authorize local police to arrest illegal aliens, and make illegal presence a felony.

Needless to say, such a bill is sorely needed to address America's immigration crisis. Nevertheless, as the Senate debates immigration, it is clear that if some senators have their way, anarchy will not be too far away.

As a legal immigrant and naturalized American, I have earned the right to condemn illegal immigration. I got my green card by following the rules and waiting in line for years, and I view illegal aliens as line-jumpers who respect neither the law nor other immigrants. By coming illegally, their very first act in this country was to break the law. To legalize such people is to reward lawless behavior.

But liberal Democrats and a few so-called moderate Republicans are ready to surrender to illegal aliens by enacting an amnesty. They may call it a guest-worker plan, but any plan that legalizes those who came here illegally is an amnesty. It makes no sense to say we should legalize illegal aliens because they are here already. That is defeatism at its worst. By that standard, a burglar who breaks into your house, because he is already in your house, should now be treated as a guest!

Amnesties for illegal aliens have never worked. Consider what happened the last time, when the Congress amnestied illegal aliens in 1986. For that amnesty, politicians and pro-immigration groups bamboozled the public into believing that there were perhaps no more than 300,000 illegal aliens. Eventually, 10 times that number—3 million illegal aliens—got green cards under that amnesty.

The 1986 amnesty, designed mainly for Third World illegal aliens (mostly from Mexico and Central America), was a huge slap in the face to legal immigrants, including Third World legal immigrants. A Third World immigrant, I was here at that time on a temporary visa and badly needed a green card, since a green card allowed you to live here permanently and work for any employer. But, because I had come here legally, I was not eligible, and had to wait at the back of the line. Illegal aliens who could not speak a word of English were in the front of the line.

Back then, Americans were told it was a one-time leniency and that strict enforcement would follow. Twenty years later, today we have more than 10 million illegal aliens. And we are still waiting for strict enforcement.

Among today's most ardent supporters of another amnesty are those who got green cards under the 1986 amnesty and are now citizens with full political rights. If you think today's pro-amnesty groups are formidable, just imagine the enormous political and cultural consequences of legalizing ten million or more law-breakers.

Once they are legalized, they will indubitably use their political rights to further degrade immigration laws. Before long, immigration laws will cease to exist. And we will end up in a society where the lawless will dominate the lawful.

Anyone who doubts such a scenario is one who has turned a blind eye to the audacity of protests by illegal aliens.

In any case, a frequent refrain of amnesty supporters is that illegal aliens do the dirty jobs that nobody wants to do. Balderdash. Who did these jobs before the illegal aliens came? It was legal immigrants and Americans. What has happened is that illegal aliens have undercut wages so much that nobody else can afford to work at those wages. And if the illegal aliens leave, those jobs will once again pay a reasonable wage because employers will be forced to hire legal immigrants and Americans.

Some shameless critics make the ludicrous claim that whites who oppose illegal aliens do so out of racism. As a brown-skinned immigrant, I contend there is nothing wrong in requiring legal conduct from anyone. Rather, if there is racism on this issue, the guilty parties are amnesty-supporting whites, for it is they who seem to think that nonwhite immigrants are incapable of obeying the law and should not be held to high standards of conduct. How can such a low expectation be construed as anything but a bigoted condescension? After all, if nonwhite immigrants are held to high standards, then why not expect them to come legally?

Illegal immigration is not an irreversible problem. With strict, no-nonsense enforcement, we can send the illegal aliens back without having to deport every one of them. By relentless prosecution of employers of illegal aliens, and by requiring proof of legal presence before granting public services, illegal aliens will find themselves in trouble at every turn. Eventually, they will leave on their own. After all, it is a universal fact that law-breakers avoid places where the law is enforced.

Remember, the 10 million illegal aliens now here did not come overnight. They came over ten or twenty years. With strict enforcement, they will leave over ten or so years. It is like draining a bathtub—it sometimes takes about as long to drain it as it took to fill up.

As the Senate debates immigration, we the voters should decry proposals that offer leniency to illegal aliens. It was leniency that produced the 1986 amnesty and brought us the illegal immigration crisis of today.

We should not let them fool us again.

AFTER YOU READ: Analyze the Issues

1. What gives De Silva the authority to write on the issue of the treatment of illegal aliens?
2. De Silva compares creating a guest worker program to making a burglar a guest in your home. Is his comparison apt? Explain your response.
3. As you read, you noted De Silva's use of pathos. Are his appeals to his readers' emotions effective? Explain your response.
4. De Silva states, "Before long, immigration laws will cease to exist. And we will end up in a society where the lawless will dominate the lawful." Discuss the logic of this statement.
5. What is De Silva's plan for solving the illegal immigration problem? Do you agree or disagree with this plan? Why?

AFTER YOU READ: Analyze the Rhetoric

1. At what level of language does De Silva generally write? Do any words stand out as being from a different level? If so, what is the effect of using such words?
2. De Silva uses phrases such as "needless to say," "it is clear that," and "anyone who doubts such a scenario." Find these phrases in the text of this article. What is their effect on you, the reader?
3. Arguments generally end with a call to action. Does this argument do so?
4. If so, what action does De Silva want his readers to take? If not, write a call to action that would conclude this argument well.

"Conspiracy Against Assimilation"

by Robert J. Samuelson

(Essay)

Robert J. Samuelson earned a B.A. in government from Harvard University in 1967. He began his journalism career as a reporter on *The Washington Post's Business Desk*, and then became a freelance journalist. He has had articles published in such prestigious journals as *The Sunday Times (London)*, The *Los Angeles Times*, *The New Republic*, and *The Columbia Journalism Review*. Today he is a contributing editor to *Newsweek* and writes a biweekly column that appears in *The Washington Post*, *The Los Angeles Times*, *The Boston Globe* and other papers. Samuelson has earned many journalism awards, including the John Hancock Award for Best Business and Financial Columnist, the Gerald Loeb Award for Best Commentary, the National Headliner Award for Feature Column on a Single Subject, and a National Magazine Award.

AS YOU READ: Annotate

1. Write the main point of each body paragraph in the margin.
2. Samuelson uses many statistics in this article. Comment on some of these in the margin.
3. Highlight any phrasing that deliberately uses pathos and write the emotion the writer appeals to in the margin.

It's all about assimilation—or it should be. One of America's glories is that it has assimilated many waves of immigrants. Outsiders have become insiders. But it hasn't been easy. Every new group has struggled: Germans, Irish, Jews and Italians. All have encountered economic hardship, prejudice and discrimination. The story of U.S. immigration is often ugly. If today's wave of immigration does not end in assimilation, it will be a failure. By this standard, I think the major contending sides in the present bitter debate are leading us astray. Their proposals, if adopted, would frustrate assimilation.

On the one hand, we have the "cop" school. It adamantly opposes amnesty and would make being here illegally a felony, as opposed to a lesser crime. It toughens a variety of penalties against illegal immigrants. Elevating the seriousness of the crime would supposedly deprive them of jobs, and then illegal immigrants would return to Mexico, El Salvador or wherever. This is a pipe dream; the numbers are simply too large.

But it is a pipe dream that, if pursued, would inflict enormous social damage. The mere threat of a crackdown stigmatizes much of the Hispanic population—whether they're legal or illegal immigrants, or whether they've been here for generations. (In 2004 there were 40 million Hispanics, says the Pew Hispanic Center; about 55 percent were estimated to be native-born, 25 percent legal immigrants and 20 percent illegal immigrants.) People feel threatened and insulted. Who wouldn't?

On the other hand we have the "guest worker" advocates. They want 400,000 or more new foreign workers annually. This would supposedly curtail illegal immigration—people who now sneak into the country could get work permits—and also cure "shortages" of unskilled American workers. Everyone wins. Not really.

For starters, the term is a misnomer. Whatever the rules, most guest workers would not leave. The pull of U.S. wages (on average, almost five times what can be earned in Mexico) is too great. Moreover, there's no general shortage of unskilled workers. In March, the unemployment rate of high school dropouts 25 years and older was 7 percent; since 1996, it has been below 6 percent in only two months. By contrast, the unemployment rate of college graduates in March was 2.2 percent. Given the glut of unskilled workers relative to demand, their wages often lag inflation. From 2002 to 2004, consumer prices rose 5.5 percent. Median wages rose 4.8 percent for janitors, 4.3 percent for landscapers and not at all for waitresses.

Advocates of guest workers don't acknowledge that poor, unskilled immigrants—whether legal or illegal—create huge social costs. Every year the Census

Bureau issues a report on "Income, Poverty, and Health Insurance Coverage in the United States." Here's what the 2004 report shows:

- Since 1990 the number of Hispanics with incomes below the government's poverty line has risen 52 percent; that's almost all (92 percent) of the increase in poor people.
- Among children, disparities are greater. Over the same period, Hispanic children in poverty are up 43 percent; meanwhile, the numbers of black and non-Hispanic white children in poverty declined 16.9 percent and 18.5 percent, respectively.
- Hispanics account for most (61 percent) of the increase of Americans without health insurance since 1990. The overall increase was 11.1 million; Hispanics, 6.7 million.

By most studies, poor immigrants pay less in taxes than they use in government services. As these social costs have risen, so has the backlash. Already, there's a coalition of Mayors and County Executives for Immigration Reform. It includes 63 cities, counties and towns, headed by Republicans and Democrats, ranging from Cook County, Illinois (population: 5.3 million) to Gilliam County, Oregon (population: 1,817). Coalition members want the federal government to reimburse their extra costs.

We have a conspiracy against assimilation. One side would offend and ostracize much of the Hispanic community. The other would encourage mounting social and economic costs. Either way we get a more polarized society.

On immigration, I am an optimist. We are basically a decent, open and tolerant nation. Americans respect hard work and achievement. That's why assimilation has ultimately triumphed. But I am not a foolish optimist. Assimilation requires time and the right conditions. It cannot succeed if we constantly flood the country with new, poor immigrants or embark on a vendetta against those already here.

I have argued that our policies should recognize these realities. Curb illegal immigration with true border barriers. Provide legal status (call it amnesty or whatever)—first work permits, then citizenship—for most illegal immigrants already here. Remove the job lure by imposing harsh fines against employers who hire *new* illegal immigrants. Reject big guest-worker programs.

It's sometimes said that today's Hispanics will resemble yesterday's Italians. Although they won't advance as rapidly as some other groups of more skilled immigrants, they'll still move into the mainstream. Many have—and will. But the overall analogy is a stretch, according to a recent study, "Italians Then, Mexicans Now," by sociologist Joel Perlmann of Bard College. Since 1970 wages of Mexican immigrants compared with those of native whites have declined. By contrast, wages of Italians and Poles who arrived early in the last century rose over time. For the children of immigrants, gaps are also wide. Second-generation Italians and Poles typically earned 90 percent or more compared to native whites. For second-generation Mexican Americans, the similar figure is 75 percent.

One big difference between then and now: Immigration slowly halted during and after World War I. The Italians and Poles came mainly between 1890 and 1915.

Older immigrants didn't always have to compete with newcomers who beat down their wages. There was time for outsiders and insiders to adapt to each other. We should heed history's lesson.

AFTER YOU READ: Analyze the Issues

1. Look up the word "assimilation" in a dictionary. In what way is Samuelson writing about assimilation?
2. According to Samuelson, what's wrong with the argument that we must treat illegal immigration as a serious crime?
3. According to Samuelson, what's wrong with establishing a guest worker program?

AFTER YOU READ: Analyze the Rhetoric

1. Describe the organization of Samuelson's article.
2. Samuelson uses many statistics. Does he use too many? Does he use them well? Which statistic is most effective?
3. Samuelson compares the current immigration situation to past immigration situations. Does doing so further his argument? Explain your response.

"Immigration: 'Neither Preference Nor Prejudice'"

by Tim Kane and Kirk Johnson
(Essay)

Tim Kane, Ph.D., and Kirk Johnson, Ph.D., are economists in the Center for Data Analysis at the Heritage Foundation. Dr. Kane was a senior economist at the Joint Economic Committee of the U.S. Congress and a professor of economics at Occidental College and San Diego State University. He has appeared as a commentator on CBN, CBS, CNN, CNNfn, C-SPAN, Fox News, National Public Radio, and Bloomberg TV and radio. He also writes an editorial column that has appeared in such newspapers as *U.S.A. Today*, *The New York Times*, *The Los Angeles Times*, and *The San Diego Union-Tribune*. Dr. Johnson analyzes policies that affect low-income Americans. His commentary has been featured in such journals as *The Los Angeles Times*, *Investor's Business Daily*, *Forbes*, *Chicago Tribune*, *Washington Post*, *Miami Herald*, and *The Detroit Free Press*. He has worked at the Mackinac Center for Public Policy, the U.S. Census Bureau, and George Mason University.

AS YOU READ: Annotate

1. Underline the claim in this article.
2. Summarize the points of this argument in the margins.
3. Number the required steps of Kane and Johnson's proposal and highlight key words for each step.
4. Circle the following words and any others you do not know, and write their meanings in the margins: *flouting, benign* and *tenable*.

There's a difference between having an "open door" policy and having no doors at all.

The U.S. economy has been strengthened perpetually via its open doors. Free flows of immigration, trade and capital have fueled the wealthiest economy in history. But the continued success of this policy hinges on us knowing who is attempting to come through those doors—that is, on fostering community as well as growth.

Today America's exceptional status as a nation of immigrants is being challenged by globalization, a phenomenon that makes both migration and terrorism much easier. The favored approach of recent years—a policy of benign neglect regarding the immigration problem—is no longer tenable.

Successful immigration reform must be comprehensive. A lopsided, ideological approach is bound to fail, whether it focuses exclusively on border security while ignoring migrant workers or vice versa.

Just think through the numbers. Illegal immigration has reached massive proportions. The U.S. currently hosts more than 10 million undocumented aliens. When three out of every 100 people in America are undocumented (or documented with faked papers), we have a profound security problem.

And that's the point Congress should focus on. The real problem presented by illegal immigration is security, not a supposed threat to the economy.

Today the percentage of Americans who are foreign-born (12 percent) is the highest in decades. At the same time, the economy is strong, with higher total gross domestic product, higher GDP per person, higher productivity per worker and more Americans working than ever before. Immigration may not have caused this economic boom, but it is folly to blame immigrants for hurting the economy at a time when the economy simply isn't hurting.

Ironically, efforts to curtail the *economic* influx of migrants actually worsen the security dilemma by driving many migrant workers further underground, thereby encouraging the culture of illegality.

The real problem with accommodating a flood of undocumented workers is that it makes flouting the law the norm. And that makes the job of terrorists and drug traffickers infinitely easier. To solve that problem, we must develop a nationwide system that identifies all foreigners present within the U.S. A non-citizen guest-worker program is critical and would involve three steps.

First, all guest workers should be identified biometrically. A nationwide system of identification, such as fingerprints and retina scans, already has been developed for the US-VISIT program.

A sister "WORKER-VISIT" program is essential for enforcement efforts and would help American companies. Employers who want to hire guest workers would be required to verify electronically that the particular worker has registered with WORKER–VISIT and is eligible to work in the United States.

Second, a guest-worker program must not be amnesty. Potential guest workers should apply from *outside* the U.S. and be required to have a sponsoring employer. Documented migrant workers would enter with a new status: not citizen, not illegal, but rather temporary worker.

And third, the guest-worker program shouldn't be used as an excuse to create another large federal bureaucracy. Government should never micromanage migrant labor—or any labor, for that matter. Instead, the private sector ought to run the guest-worker visa process.

Incentives for employers and workers to comply should be written into the law, along with strict penalties for non-compliance. Guest-worker status should not be a path to citizenship or convey rights to U.S. social benefits. The guiding rule: Treat migrant workers with neither preference nor prejudice.

This century of globalization will see America either descend into timid isolation or affirm its openness. We can't afford to wait. Already China's economic power is ascending with openness, while western Europe declines into isolation.

Too many voices are saying that immigration reform is politically untenable. That supposes a false choice between openness and law. And it misreads the populist demand for a simple solution that's both obvious and true to our American heritage.

AFTER YOU READ: Analyze the Issues

1. What do Kane and Johnson contend is the real problem with illegal immigration?
2. Have they convinced you that illegal immigrants are not an economic threat? Explain your response.
3. Is "flouting the law" the norm in this country, as Kane and Johnson assert?
4. How would De Silva ("No Leniency for Illegal Aliens") respond to this article?

AFTER YOU READ: Analyze the Rhetoric

1. What fallacy do Kane and Johnson point out in the opposing side's argument? Is their own logic sound or does it contain any fallacy?
2. Identify the appeals in this article. In what way do these appeals rely on pathos?
3. How effective are the statistics in this article?

"Mexicans Begin Jogging"

by Gary Soto
(Poem)

Gary Soto is a native Californian who has written ten poetry collections. His *New and Selected Poems* was a 1995 finalist for both the Los Angeles Times Book Award and the National Book Award. His poems have appeared in *The Nation*, *Ploughshares*, *The Iowa Review*, and *Ontario Review*, as well as *Poetry*, which has honored him with the Bess Hokin Prize and the Levinson Award. Soto has received numerous awards including the U.S. Award of the International Poetry Forum, The California Library Association's John and Patricia Beatty Award [twice], the Silver Medal from The Commonwealth Club of California, the Tomás Rivera Prize, the Literature Award from the Hispanic Heritage Foundation, the Author-Illustrator Civil Rights Award from the National Education Association, and the PEN Center West Book Award. He has also received fellowships from the Guggenheim Foundation, the National Endowment for the Arts (twice), and the California Arts Council. He produced the film *The Pool Party*, which received the 1993 Andrew Carnegie Medal. Soto serves as Young People's Ambassador for the California Rural Legal Assistance (CRLA) and the United Farm Workers of America (UFW).

AS YOU READ: Annotate

1. Underline images that create a picture in your mind.
2. Put an exclamation mark (!) next to passages that add humor to this poem.
3. Comment on Soto's situation in the margins.

At the factory I worked
In the fleck of rubber, under the press
Of an oven yellow with flame,
Until the border patrol opened
Their vans and my boss waved for us to run.
"Over the fence, Soto," he shouted,
And I shouted that I was an American.
"No time for lies," he said, and passes
A dollar in my palm, hurrying me
Through the back door.

Since I was on his time, I ran
And became the wag to a short tail of Mexicans—

Ran past the amazed crowds that lined
The street and blurred like photographs, in rain.
I ran from that industrial road to the soft
Houses where people paled at the turn of an autumn sky.
What could I do but yell *vivas*
To baseball, milkshakes, and those sociologists
Who would clock me
As I jog into the next century
On the power of a great, silly grin.

AFTER YOU READ: Analyze the Issues

1. Why does the boss insist that Soto run with the other Mexicans even though Soto tells him he is an American? Why does he give him a dollar?
2. Why does Soto describe the houses as "soft"? Who most likely lives in those houses?
3. Why does Soto shout "*vivas*/To baseball, milkshakes, and those sociologists/ Who would clock me"? What is the signficance of the items in this list?
4. What does the poem say about the Mexican's place in American society?

AFTER YOU READ: Analyze the Rhetoric

1. When you think of illegal immigrants running from *la migra* (immigration officers), do you imagine them jogging? Why would Soto choose this word?
2. Some aspects of this poem are comic. How does Soto create a comic effect?
3. As you read, you noted images in the poem. Which is most effective? Why?

President Bush's Speech on Immigration Policy

January 7, 2004
(Speech)

Born on July 6, 1946, in New Haven, Connecticut, George W. Bush grew up in Texas. At one point, he was one of the owners of the Texas Rangers baseball franchise. He became the governor of Texas and later the 43rd president of America. Being governor in Texas, he developed strong opinions on immigration that interestingly often go against his party's viewpoints.

AS YOU READ: Annotate

1. Highlight the words "hard work," and any variations of those words, whenever you see them.
2. Underline words that Bush uses to describe America and its values.
3. Next to each paragraph of Bush's plan, write the objection Bush foresees and addresses.

Thanks for coming, thanks for the warm welcome, thanks for joining me as I make this important announcement—an announcement that I believe will make America a more compassionate and more humane and stronger country.

I appreciate members of my Cabinet who have joined me today, starting with our Secretary of State, Colin Powell. I'm honored that our Attorney General, John Ashcroft, has joined us. Secretary of Commerce, Don Evans. Secretary Tom Ridge, of the Department of Homeland Security. El Embajador of Mexico, Tony Garza. I thank all the other members of my administration who have joined us today.

I appreciate the members of Congress who have taken time to come: Senator Larry Craig, Congressman Chris Cannon, and Congressman Jeff Flake. I'm honored you all have joined us, thank you for coming.

I appreciate the members of citizen groups who have joined us today. Chairman of the Hispanic Alliance for Progress, Manny Lujan. Gil Moreno, the President and CEO of the Association for the Advancement of Mexican Americans. Roberto De Posada, the President of the Latino Coalition. And Hector Flores, the President of LULAC.

Thank you all for joining us.

Many of you here today are Americans by choice, and you have followed in the path of millions. And over the generations we have received energetic, ambitious, optimistic people from every part of the world. By tradition and conviction, our country is a welcoming society. America is a stronger and better nation because of the hard work and the faith and entrepreneurial spirit of immigrants.

Every generation of immigrants has reaffirmed the wisdom of remaining open to the talents and dreams of the world. And every generation of immigrants has reaffirmed our ability to assimilate newcomers—which is one of the defining strengths of our country.

During one great period of immigration—between 1891 and 1920—our nation received some 18 million men, women and children from other nations. The hard work of these immigrants helped make our economy the largest in the world. The children of immigrants put on the uniform and helped to liberate the lands of their ancestors. One of the primary reasons America became a great power in the 20th century is because we welcomed the talent and the character and the patriotism of immigrant families.

The contributions of immigrants to America continue. About 14 percent of our nation's civilian workforce is foreign-born. Most begin their working lives in America by taking hard jobs and clocking long hours in important industries. Many immigrants also start businesses, taking the familiar path from hired labor to ownership.

As a Texan, I have known many immigrant families, mainly from Mexico, and I have seen what they add to our country. They bring to America the values of faith in God, love of family, hard work and self reliance—the values that made us a great nation to begin with. We've all seen those values in action, through the service and sacrifice of more than 35,000 foreign-born men and women currently on active duty in the United States military. One of them is Master Gunnery Sergeant Guadalupe Denogean, an immigrant from Mexico who has served in the Marine Corps for 25 years and counting. Last year, I was honored and proud to witness Sergeant Denogean take the oath of citizenship in a hospital where he was recovering from wounds he received in Iraq. I'm honored to be his Commander-in-Chief, I'm proud to call him a fellow American.

As a nation that values immigration, and depends on immigration, we should have immigration laws that work and make us proud. Yet today we do not. Instead, we see many employers turning to the illegal labor market. We see millions of hard-working men and women condemned to fear and insecurity in a massive, undocumented economy. Illegal entry across our borders makes more difficult the urgent task of securing the homeland. The system is not working. Our nation needs an immigration system that serves the American economy, and reflects the American Dream.

Reform must begin by confronting a basic fact of life and economics: some of the jobs being generated in America's growing economy are jobs American citizens are not filling. Yet these jobs represent a tremendous opportunity for workers from abroad who want to work and fulfill their duties as a husband or a wife, a son or a daughter.

Their search for a better life is one of the most basic desires of human beings. Many undocumented workers have walked mile after mile, through the heat of the day and the cold of the night. Some have risked their lives in dangerous desert border crossings, or entrusted their lives to the brutal rings of heartless human smugglers. Workers who seek only to earn a living end up in the shadows of American life—fearful, often abused and exploited. When they are victimized by crime, they are afraid to call the police, or seek recourse in the legal system. They are cut off from their families far away, fearing if they leave our country to visit relatives back home, they might never be able to return to their jobs.

The situation I described is wrong. It is not the American way. Out of common sense and fairness, our laws should allow willing workers to enter our country and fill jobs that Americans are not filling. (Applause.) We must make our immigration laws more rational, and more humane. And I believe we can do so without jeopardizing the livelihoods of American citizens.

Our reforms should be guided by a few basic principles. First, America must control its borders. Following the attacks of September the 11th, 2001, this duty of the federal government has become even more urgent. And we're fulfilling that duty.

For the first time in our history, we have consolidated all border agencies under one roof to make sure they share information and the work is more effective. We're matching all visa applicants against an expanded screening list to identify terrorists and criminals and immigration violators. This month, we have begun using advanced technology to better record and track aliens who enter our country—and to make sure they leave as scheduled. We have deployed new gamma and x-ray systems to scan cargo and containers and shipments at ports of entry to America. We have significantly expanded the Border Patrol—with more than a thousand new agents on the borders, and 40 percent greater funding over the last two years. We're working closely with the Canadian and Mexican governments to increase border security. America is acting on a basic belief: our borders should be open to legal travel and honest trade; our borders should be shut and barred tight to criminals, to drug traders, to drug traffickers and to criminals, and to terrorists.

Second, new immigration laws should serve the economic needs of our country. If an American employer is offering a job that American citizens are not willing to take, we ought to welcome into our country a person who will fill that job.

Third, we should not give unfair rewards to illegal immigrants in the citizenship process or disadvantage those who came here lawfully, or hope to do so.

Fourth, new laws should provide incentives for temporary, foreign workers to return permanently to their home countries after their period of work in the United States has expired.

Today, I ask the Congress to join me in passing new immigration laws that reflect these principles, that meet America's economic needs, and live up to our highest ideals.

I propose a new temporary worker program that will match willing foreign workers with willing American employers, when no Americans can be found to fill the jobs. This program will offer legal status, as temporary workers, to the millions of undocumented men and women now employed in the United States, and to those in foreign countries who seek to participate in the program and have been offered employment here. This new system should be clear and efficient, so employers are able to find workers quickly and simply.

All who participate in the temporary worker program must have a job, or, if not living in the United States, a job offer. The legal status granted by this program will last three years and will be renewable—but it will have an end. Participants who do not remain employed, who do not follow the rules of the program, or who break the law will not be eligible for continued participation and will be required to return to their home.

Under my proposal, employers have key responsibilities. Employers who extend job offers must first make every reasonable effort to find an American worker for the job at hand. Our government will develop a quick and simple system for employers to search for American workers. Employers must not hire undocumented aliens or temporary workers whose legal status has expired. They must report to the government the temporary workers they hire, and who leave their employ, so that we can keep track of people in the program, and better enforce immigration laws. There must be strong workplace enforcement with tough penalties for anyone, for any employer violating these laws.

Undocumented workers now here will be required to pay a one-time fee to register for the temporary worker program. Those who seek to join the program from abroad, and have complied with our immigration laws, will not have to pay any fee. All participants will be issued a temporary worker card that will allow them to travel back and forth between their home and the United States without fear of being denied re-entry into our country.

This program expects temporary workers to return permanently to their home countries after their period of work in the United States has expired. And there should be financial incentives for them to do so. I will work with foreign governments on a plan to give temporary workers credit, when they enter their own nation's retirement system, for the time they have worked in America. I also support making it easier for temporary workers to contribute a portion of their earnings to tax-preferred savings accounts, money they can collect as they return to their native countries. After all, in many of those countries, a small nest egg is what is necessary to start their own business, or buy some land for their family.

Some temporary workers will make the decision to pursue American citizenship. Those who make this choice will be allowed to apply in the normal way. They will not be given unfair advantage over people who have followed legal procedures from the start. I oppose amnesty, placing undocumented workers on the automatic path to citizenship. Granting amnesty encourages the violation of our laws, and perpetuates illegal immigration. America is a welcoming country, but citizenship must not be the automatic reward for violating the laws of America.

The citizenship line, however, is too long, and our current limits on legal immigration are too low. My administration will work with the Congress to increase the annual number of green cards that can lead to citizenship. Those willing to take the difficult path of citizenship—the path of work, and patience, and assimilation—should be welcome in America, like generations of immigrants before them.

In the process of immigration reform, we must also set high expectations for what new citizens should know. An understanding of what it means to be an American is not a formality in the naturalization process, it is essential to full participation in our democracy. My administration will examine the standard of knowledge in the current citizenship test. We must ensure that new citizens know not only the facts of our history, but the ideals that have shaped our history. Every citizen of America has an obligation to learn the values that make us one nation: liberty and civic responsibility, equality under God, and tolerance for others.

This new temporary worker program will bring more than economic benefits to America. Our homeland will be more secure when we can better account for those who enter our country, instead of the current situation in which millions of people are unknown, unknown to the law. Law enforcement will face fewer problems with undocumented workers, and will be better able to focus on the true threats to our nation from criminals and terrorists. And when temporary workers can travel legally and freely, there will be more efficient management of our borders and more effective enforcement against those who pose a danger to our country.

This new system will be more compassionate. Decent, hard-working people will now be protected by labor laws, with the right to change jobs, earn fair wages, and enjoy the same working conditions that the law requires for American workers. Temporary workers will be able to establish their identities by obtaining the legal documents we all take for granted. And they will be able to talk openly to authorities, to report crimes when they are harmed, without the fear of being deported.

The best way, in the long run, to reduce the pressures that create illegal immigration in the first place is to expand economic opportunity among the countries in our neighborhood. In a few days I will go to Mexico for the Special Summit of the Americas, where we will discuss ways to advance free trade, and to fight corruption, and encourage the reforms that lead to prosperity. Real growth and real hope in the nations of our hemisphere will lessen the flow of new immigrants to America when more citizens of other countries are able to achieve their dreams at their own home. (Applause.)

Yet our country has always benefited from the dreams that others have brought here. By working hard for a better life, immigrants contribute to the life of our nation. The temporary worker program I am proposing today represents the best tradition of our society, a society that honors the law, and welcomes the newcomer. This plan will help return order and fairness to our immigration system, and in so doing we will honor our values, by showing our respect for those who work hard and share in the ideals of America.

May God bless you all.

AFTER YOU READ: Analyze the Issues

1. Summarize the main points of Bush's immigration plan.
2. How does Bush characterize immigrants? Americans? To what values does the president refer to link Americans and immigrants?
3. Does Bush convince you that his plan is a good one? Explain your response.

AFTER YOU READ: Analyze the Rhetoric

1. In this speech, President Bush is working to sell his immigration plan to the American people. What techniques does he use to sell his plan? Be specific. You should think about ethos, pathos, and logos to arrive at your answer.
2. Why does Bush discuss Master Gunnery Sergeant Guadalupe Denogean?
3. Explain the connection between the opening paragraph of the speech and the purpose of the speech.
4. In the news, Bush's plan is referred to as a "guest" worker plan, but Bush never uses this term. Instead, he uses the word "temporary" when referring to workers under his plan. Why? (You might refer to De Silva's article "No Leniency for Illegal Aliens" to arrive at your answer.) Along the same lines, Bush rarely uses the word "alien" when referring to immigrants. How does the language Bush chooses to use complement his purpose?

A Day Without a Mexican

by Sergio Arau
(Screenplay)

Born and raised in Mexico City , Sergio Arau received his MFA in film studies from the National School of Film in Mexico City. He began his career in journalism as a political cartoonist, later using his artistic skills to create animated films. He won the Coral De Plata award at the Havana Film Festival for his animated short *"El Muro"/"The Wall"* (2001). Arau is also an accomplished musician; in 1983 he formed the musical group Botellita De Jerez which blended humor and traditional Mexican music with rock 'n roll. Arau won MTV's Best Rock Video Award for directing the music video for his song "Alarma de Tos." Arau wrote and directed *A Day Without a Mexican*, a film based on his short by the same name, in 2004. His next film, *Plan B* (2007), is a documentary of his band Botellita de Jerez.

AS YOU READ: Annotate

1. Underline the reasons why people miss the Mexicans.
2. In the margins, comment on the reasons you underlined.
3. Identify techniques the director/screenwriter used to add satire to this film.

Film Synopsis: One day, the entire Latino population of California, about 14,000,000 Latinos, disappear, sending the state into chaos. Lela, a reporter who seems to be the only Latina left, agrees to do all she can to find out what happened to her people.

INT: EMPTY RESTAURANT — DAY

The RESTAURATEUR is sitting at a dining table alone.

RESTAURATEUR:

It's been an absolute fucking nightmare. Can I say fucking here? I had to call people that were in the black market, people from the '70's who used to do drugs, now they're selling fruits and vegetables. Had to risk my life to go there, and my car, for tomatoes, tomatoes! I uh, I uh, I didn't know whether they were prison people or people from an MTV video for God's sake. It was frightening. Then I came here, the place was a mess, I had to wash a dish… I am going to have to close my restaurant if they don't come back. I need these Mexican individuals.

(Title written over freeze frame of excited restaurateur—Every Hispanic on the West Coast is presumed to be missing).

CUT TO:

INT: Broadcast newsroom.

A live newscast.

FEMALE NEWSCASTER:

We now have Senator Abercrombie, our acting governor on the line. Go ahead Senator.

CUT TO:

INT: LELA's hospital room shown through camera's view, picture of SENATOR in corner.

SENATOR ABERCROMBIE (on the phone)

Hello, Lila, welcome to the team, it's good to meet you.

LELA

Thank you, and it's actually Lela, we met when I interviewed you for your last campaign, remember?

(CONTINUED)

CUT TO:

INT: Limo, SENATOR ABERCROMBIE is speaking on the phone as his assistant cheers him on.

SENATOR ABERCROMBIE

Of course, Ms. Rodriguez, in the name of California and the great nation we belong to, want to thank you for doing your duty as an American. You represent our hope, our future. (America the Beautiful plays in the background). I want to take this opportunity once more to ask the citizens of California not to panic; get back to your regular lives and the people close to the state border—do not attempt to cross the fog! (Assistant writes something down and Abercrombie pauses to look at it) More than ever, we need to be the great California familia and bring back our Hispanic brothers and sisters. (music swells) Let's go for the whole enchilada (music stops like needle being pulled off record player). Lela, we're with you every step of the way.

LELA (on television screen)

As we speak, Senator, I am signing my body over to science, to hopefully find out what happened to my people. Now, if I find them what should I tell them?

SENATOR ABERCROMBIE

Tell them, California needs them.

LELA

Okay, I wish they could have heard that before.

AFTER YOU READ: Analyze the Issues

1. In this film clip, why did the restaurateur and the senator miss the Mexicans?
2. Many argue that illegal Mexican immigrants are stealing jobs from Americans. How does this film respond to that argument?
3. Why does Senator Abercrombie show great respect for Lela? Do you think he is sincere? In what way does the film satirize politicians through Senator Abercrombie?

AFTER YOU READ: Analyze the Rhetoric

1. As you read, you identified techniques the director/writer used to add satire to this film. List some of these techniques.
2. Select one of the techniques you listed above and explain how it works to create satire.
3. In his discussion with Lela, Senator Abercrombie uses Spanish words. Why? How do you imagine Lela responded when he said, "Let's go for the whole *enchilada*"? Why?

Issues of Language

"Why Fear Spanish?"

by Carlos Alberto Montaner

(Essay)

Carlos Alberto Montaner was born in Havana in 1943 and has lived in Madrid since 1970. A former university professor, he is an acclaimed writer and journalist. He has served as an editor of Miami's *El Nuevo Herald*, and his syndicated column appears in newspapers in the United States, Latin America, and Spain.

Montaner, Carlos Alberto. "Why Fear Spanish." Taken from Rpt. *Language Loyalties*. Ed. James Crawford. Chicago: University of Chicago Press, 163–65. Originally from "Talk English—You Are in the United States ["Why Fear Spanish?]. *Miami Herald* 25 April 1988: 14A.

AS YOU READ: Annotate

1. Underline language you feel is well chosen.
2. Highlight memorable descriptive details in the text.

3. Agree or disagree with Montaner in the margins.
4. Circle the following words, and any others you do not know, and write their meanings in the margin: *monolingual, atavistic,* and *berated.*

I was walking quietly with my wife on a sidewalk in Miami Beach. We were speaking Spanish, of course, because that is our language. Suddenly, we were accosted by a spry little old lady, wearing a baseball cap and sneakers, who told us: "Talk English. You are in the United States." She continued on her way at once, without stopping to see our reaction. The expression on her face, curiously, was not that of somebody performing a rude action, but of somebody performing a sacred patriotic duty.

And the truth is that the lady in question was not an eccentric madwoman. Thousands, millions of monolingual Americans are mortified that in their country there is a vast minority that constantly speaks a language that they do not understand. It disturbs them to hear Spanish prattle in shops, at work, in restaurants. They are irritated when conversations that they do not understand are held in their presence. Indeed, they are upset to stumble across Spanish-language stations on their radio or television dial, or by the fact that the *Miami Herald* occasionally includes an unsolicited supplement in the language of Castile.

Actually, the old lady's attitude was natural. Miami Beach is, more or less, the United States. And the language of the United States is English. Moreover, one of the key elements in the configuration of a nation is its language. A monolingual American who suddenly finds himself on Miami's Calle Ocho or in San Francisco's Chinatown has the feeling that he is not in his own country. And when one is not in one's own country, one feels endangered. Not faced with any danger in particular, but subject to that diffuse and irrational fear caused by words, expressions, and traits different from our own.

Hostility to a foreign language on our own turf generally does not come from balanced reflection on the advantages or disadvantages of linguistic homogeneity but from an atavistic reaction that probably has been part of human nature for millions of years, when the differences between the groups that populated the planet might result in the death or destruction of the other. Much more recently, as far as the Greeks were concerned, barbarity flowed from ignorance of Greek. Since then—and, I fear, for all time—foreigners are inevitably considered barbarians.

All right, thus far, I have confined myself to a kindly comprehension of prejudice, but there are other factors that cannot be ignored in approaching this unhappy problem. A language is much more than a way to communicate. By one's own language—and on this Edward Sapir wrote much and well—one masters reality, one takes to oneself and understands all that exists. All history, interpersonal relations, the most intimate and definitive emotions. For example, anybody who learns to love in one language will never be able spontaneously to translate his expressions of affection into a language acquired later.

We quarrel, are jealous, love, and hate with certain words, with certain tones, with certain inflections of the voice learned in childhood and adapted to a given set of gestures that also cannot be transported into another language. And this matching of word and message comes solely in the mother tongue. "Language," said the Spanish writer Miguel Unamuno, "is the blood of the spirit." He was right. We cannot do without our own tongue without brutally mutilating our individual consciousness, without being left without blood.

If this is so, is it reasonable to ask millions of human beings to do without this fundamental part of their lives solely so that others are not inconvenienced, or in order to comply with a few debatable rules of urbanity? Is it not more sensible and less painful to explain to monolingual Americans that to live in places where various living tongues converge can have a certain enriching enchantment, because diversity is also an expression of cultural riches?

But, what is more, American society spends thousands of millions of dollars every year in attempting unavailingly to get high school and college students to learn Spanish, because it is assumed that mastery of a second language benefits the country. If this is the rationale, then why ask the bilingual citizens present in the nation to abandon their use of that other language so covetously sought in educational establishments?

Fear of Spanish and the desire that only English be spoken in the United States do not stand up to a calm analysis of reality. The United States is and will continue to be a fundamentally English-speaking nation, but it is a fortunate fact for the country that there are other languages and other marginal cultures capable of enriching the powerful current of the mainstream. This can be perfectly understood by any American, even a monolingual one, if he is capable of savoring a Mexican taco while listening to the Miami Sound Machine's Conga or reading a wonderful story by Isaac Bashevis Singer written in Yiddish—very near the spot where we were berated by the irate old lady in baseball cap and sneakers.

AFTER YOU READ: Analyze the Issues

1. Montaner suggests that Anglo Americans want Hispanics to abandon Spanish. Is this claim reasonable?
2. Is Montaner addressing those who want an English Language Amendment, or is he addressing some deeper prejudice in our society?
3. Why does Montaner tell us the woman who accosted him was wearing a baseball cap and sneakers? What is the purpose of using these details?
4. Montaner asserts that language is more than simply a way to communicate. Do you agree with him?

AFTER YOU READ: Analyze the Rhetoric

1. As you read, you underlined memorable descriptive details in the text. What did you underline? Why were these details memorable?
2. Who is Montaner's audience? How do you know?
3. How does Montaner build ethos for himself?

Sample Student Paper

Illegal Immigrants' Access to Medical Care

by Stephanie Egert

AS YOU READ: Annotate

1. Place a star by the sections you like the most.
2. Place question marks by sections you have problems with or do not understand.
3. Place a [+] by sections that need to be developed more or that seem to be incomplete.
4. Write other comments in the margins as you see fit.

The human body, in all its capacity, eventually breaks, malfunctions, has to fight an infection, or simply begins to deteriorate, and the need for medical care arises. The severity could range from a minor cut to a serious health concern such as cancer or injuries from a car accident. At one time or another, all people will need medical care that is vital to their life. Many people in the United States are fortunate enough to have access to medical care through their employer's health insurance benefits or government-funded programs that cover the cost of their treatment. However, there are people in the United States who do not have insurance and therefore cannot pay for the medical care that they require. Some of these people are illegal immigrants who entered the country unlawfully. But should they be provided with medical care? The number of illegal immigrants in the United States makes up a significant portion of the population, and that number is rising. It is definite that those people need medical care, but with costs that can reach into the billions, it is hard to provide. There are two distinct sides on the issue of whether or not illegal immigrants should be provided with medical care: a humanistic viewpoint and an economic viewpoint. Both sides must be considered when determining whether or not illegal immigrants should receive medical care and what the amount of that care should be. Although illegal immigrants in the United States may need medical care, the extent of that care must be limited because of economic reasons.

Immigrants move from one country to another for many reasons. Migration, both legal and illegal, is frequent around the world. Most commonly, people move from countries of lower standards of living (such as third world or developing countries) to countries that have a better standard of living. Immigrants that come to the U.S. may have come because they needed to find a better job or to simply find a job. They may have come because of the better economic opportunities that the U.S. presents. In some cases, they may be seeking escape from political oppression or because of war. No matter the reason for their coming, immigrants primarily want to better their lives.

The United States admits about 700,000 people into the country legally every year (Bilchik). But many more people enter the country. Between 5 and 8 million of the immigrants in the United States are in the country illegally (Dwyer 35). In California, almost 3 out of 5 children who are impoverished are illegal immigrants (Green and Martin 227). Immigrants come mainly from Mexico or other Latin American countries, but some also come from Asia.

Because immigrants live in the United States, when they do get sick or need medical care, they will most likely seek care from a hospital that is in the United States. According to the article, "Uncontrolled Immigration and the U.S. Health Care System," found in the *Journal of Social, Political and Economic Studies*, "more that 41 million Americans lack basic health insurance" (Green and Martin 227). In addition to that, more that 10 million immigrants also lack health insurance (Green and Martin 227). Illegal immigrants, because they do not have legal documentation to work in the U.S., may have a hard time finding a job legally. Because of this, they are forced to take jobs illegally. These jobs are low paying, no-benefit jobs that do not provide insurance. Often, when immigrants need medical care, they cannot pay for it.

Legislation surrounding medical care for illegal immigrants is extensive. In 1996, The Personal Responsibility and Work Opportunity Reconciliation Act (PRWORA) was passed. Under this piece of legislation, Medicaid was not available to legal immigrants until after their first 5 years in the country, and it was entirely unavailable to illegal immigrants. (This excludes emergency Medicaid that will pay for some medical care in emergency situations for both legal and illegal immigrants.) (Green and Martin 226)

Proposition 187 of California was approved by voters in California. Although it was never put into effect because it disagreed with other legislation, it does raise some valid questions. Preposition 187 "restricts the benefits of publicly-funded health care" (Ziv and Lo). This legislation regulates that if an illegal alien enters the emergency room, and the clerks determine that the person is illegal, then they must deny them care and report them to the Immigration and Naturalization Service and to state officials (Ziv and Lo). Proposition 187 raised significant questions about how illegal immigrants should be treated when entering emergency rooms when seeking emergency medical care. If this legislation were implemented, it would have given hospitals the role of border patrol. That responsibility would be out of its proper place. This could also deter illegal aliens from seeking care.

In 1985, EMTALA or, the Emergency Medical Treatment Act and Active Labor Act was passed, and in 2003, it was revised. Currently, EMTALA provides basic emergency care for anyone, regardless of immigration status, ability to pay, or proof of insurance, entering the emergency room or within 250 feet of the emergency room with a medical condition requiring immediate emergency care. EMTALA prohibits hospitals from asking about the immigration status of a patient (Bilchik). The hospital must at least stabilize the patient and provide for the patient's medical care within its ability. EMTALA also states that if the hospital is unable to treat the condition, then the hospital must transfer the individual to another facility that has the ability to stabilize the patient (Bittinger 348). Although the federal government requires that medical care be provided, they do not always reimburse hospitals for the costs of giving care. If any reimbursement is received, it is usually only a small amount and is insufficient to cover all the costs (Green and Martin 226).

The Illegal Immigration Reform and Immigrant Responsibility Act was passed in 1996. It stopped Medicaid from being given to any illegal immigrants. But it also approved that some money be sent to hospitals that had cared for illegal immigrants. Unfortunately, this program was never funded. In some cases, states have tried to sue the federal government for funds, but have been unsuccessful (Green and Martin 226).

For doctors and medical care providers, a certain code of ethics plays a defining role in their profession. Some have argued that denying healthcare "undermines professional ethics" (Ziv and Lo). The Hippocratic Oath states that as doctors or medical care providers, their job is to protect and promote the health of humans. By denying care to illegal immigrants, doctors are doing the very opposite of what they have vowed to do.

It has also been argued that all people have the right to be healthy and happy. This drive to live is an innate characteristic. The people who support giving care to illegal aliens point out that all people, regardless of a title that is put on them, calling them citizens or illegal aliens, still have a claim to these rights.

Most people arguing from the humanistic perspective point out that all people are human beings, and that there should not be a simple label on a name that determines whether or not a person gets the medical care that is crucial to their life or death. Illegal immigrant or citizen, it should not matter, they are both human beings with the same basic needs. Refusing someone the medical care that they need is inhumane and heartless. James Dwyer points out in his paper "Illegal Immigrants, Health Care and Social Responsibility," that there is a "common humanity [between] aliens and citizens," and that, "national borders can seem arbitrary" (38).

However, the government runs on limited resources. Because the distribution of medical care is largely determined by economic factors, availability of funds must be factored into deciding who receives medical care. It seems that even though Medicare and Medicaid provide a great deal of money for health care, there is still not enough even for the citizens.

Hospital closings are serious and numerous. Hospitals in California, Iowa, South Carolina, Pennsylvania, New Jersey, Illinois, Minnesota, New York, Tennessee, and North Carolina have had heavy financial burdens on them because of giving medical care to illegal aliens (Green and Martin 229-234). When federal or state money is not sufficient to pay the bills incurred from treating illegal aliens, the debt falls to the hospitals. "In some hospitals [in border states], as much as two thirds of total operating costs are for uncompensated care for illegal aliens" (Green and Martin 229). In Cochise County, Arizona, "a third of its [hospital's] budget [goes to] care for illegal aliens" (Green and Martin 226). Hospitals like Southeast Arizona Medical Center have been forced to file for bankruptcy (Green and Martin 230). As a state, California "provided and estimated $500 million in uncompensated care for illegal immigrants" (Fong). 60 hospitals in the previous ten years have closed in California due to the cost of care for illegal aliens (Green and Martin 231). In 2002, hospitals in Texas spent $393 million on illegal aliens (Green and Martin 231). This is a problem in the northern states also. "In 2002, Pennsylvania and New Jersey hospitals gave almost $2 billion in free emergency and short-term care to uninsured patients, a large share of who officials believe [were] illegal aliens" (Green and Martin 233). There are many more hospitals facing this same burden.

Congress has not ignored the problem of funding all together. In 1997, under the Balanced Budget Act, Congress made $25 million available to offset the costs of caring for illegal immigrants. The money was given to the 12 states with the most illegal immigrants (Bilchik). But in comparison to the total debt incurred by hospitals, this $25 million, divided between 12 states is miniscule compared to the financial need. The government, under the Medicare Modernization Act of 2003, provided $1 billion to emergency departments to offset the costs of providing care to illegal aliens. The money will be distributed over 4 years (Fong). But with 1.45 billion that hospitals spend each year for situations like this, $1 billion still leaves hospitals bitterly short.

The government has an obligation to protect the public. The article "Health of America's Newcomers" in the *Journal of Community Health Nursing* stated, "Infectious diseases, if left untreated, will invade our communities and threaten the health of U.S. citizens" (Smith 61). One infectious disease is Tuberculosis (TB). TB is common among immigrants. Immigrants who arrive here legally must first be screened for TB. But any immigrant who comes here illegally is not screened for TB, and therefore, there is a high possibility that they may bring it with them. The people who need medical care the most are exactly the ones who do not get it. This endangers the public health of the country as a whole because TB is very contagious. The infected people in the United States can give the disease to others in the community who could contract TB. Also, many immigrants have jobs that involve contact with food, cleaning homes, and caring for people (Smith 61). Because of this, it would be beneficial for everyone if the government made vaccinations available to anyone, including illegal aliens. In addition to TB, the Hepatitis B Virus (HBV) is also a problem. 14% to 20% of Indo-Chinese and 10% —15% of SE Asian refugees carry HBV. "Child-to-child transmission is a frequent occurrence," so vaccinations for children would also be beneficial (Smith 62). "Latino children with chronic illness face the highest…risk of being uninsured" (Smith). According to the U.S. Department of Health and Human Services, 34% of migrant children have "intestinal parasites, severe asthma, or chronic diarrhea" (U.S.).

There are some advantages of providing limited care to illegal aliens. All the illnesses listed in the above paragraph, if not treated in their preliminary stages, will only worsen. When these people do decide to seek care, most likely through emergency departments, the cost of treating an advanced case will exceed what treatment in the earlier stages might have cost. Early prevention through vaccinations or education could help keep costs low in the future by curing the problem before it develops into something more threatening to well being and more costly. The U.S. citizens that live, work, or come in contact with illegal aliens have a high risk of catching these communicable diseases. By providing some immunizations and some basic medical care to illegal aliens, the government is protecting the health of its citizens.

While the humanistic arguments cannot be ignored, the economics of the situation sadly force that a choice be made regarding who can receive medical care. Essentially, governments are established to protect, care for, and provide for their citizens. Yes, people are people; they are all humans, all needing medical care. But there is no way for the government to care for everyone. Therefore, the government must revert to its fundamental duty, that is, to protect its citizens first.

Because it is beneficial to the whole country to provide limited care to illegal immigrants, some provisions should be made. But, it is unreasonable that the government provides care that costs thousands of dollars. The *Journal of American Physicians and Surgeons* gives an example of one illegal immigrant family who is receiving government money. The family receives a monthly allowance totaling $12,000 per year solely to pay for the medical needs of their children. Another illegal immigrant received benefits that cost $30,000 per year (Cosman 7). In cases like these, too much money is being spent on illegal immigrants. "One Florida hospital spent $347,000 to treat [an] illegal alien" and send him home. In another case, $150,000 was spent on a "surgery for progressive curvature of the spine" (Green and Martin 234). The provisions that EMTALA makes are smart ones. Since some care ought to be provided, the emergency care that EMTALA provides finds a good balance between too much care and negligence.

The government could also encourage private organizations and charities to set up free or reduced-cost clinics that could treat illegal aliens without inquiring about their citizenship status. Some charities of this kind are already in place. According to an article in the *American Journal of Public Health*, some "clinics provide free or low-cost care, and schools, public health, social services, and religious organizations connect Latinos to the health care system" (Casey, Blewett, and Call 1709). Although this would not completely wipe out the problem, it would help in a small way. The citizens in the United States can put forth an effort to meet the needs of their neighbors (although they be illegal aliens), recognizing their common humanity.

It is easy to see how this issue can tear medical care providers apart. On one hand, they do want to serve and protect all people by bettering their health and quality of life. This is the main goal for health care workers. On the other hand, providing care to everyone is not a possibility. Resources are limited, and there is simply not enough money to go around. It is true that everyone should be able to enjoy healthy living and medical care when they need it. The Declaration of Independence grants Americans the right to "life, liberty, and the pursuit of happiness." This philosophy should be true for not only American citizens, but for all people. Sadly, the reality of the situation is that this is not possible.

Although these people are illegally in the country, one must accept that they are human beings. To turn away a person who is dying or severely injured from an emergency room is inhumane, but to fund their care when others die does not make sense either. To an extent, some care has to be provided for the people with whom we share our society. However, there should be no obligation to provide excessive or complete care. There is not even enough money to pay for the complete medical care for citizens of the United States, much less people who are not supposed to be here. Since some care will have to be provided, and some money will have to be spent, lawmakers should find ways to spend the money most effectively on the programs that will have the largest and most vital impact.

Works Cited

Bilchik, Gloria Shur. "No Easy Answers." *Hospitals & Health Networks* 1 May 2001:59. Academic Search Premier. EBSCOhost. Chambers Library. Edmond, OK 27 March 2006.

Bittinger, Ann M. "Changes to EMTALA Rules Affect Pediatric Emergency Departments." *Pediatric Emergency Care* 20.5 (2004): 347-354. Academic Search Premier EBSCOhost. Chambers Library. Edmond, OK 19 March 2006.

Casey, Michelle M., Lynn A. Blewett, and Kathleen T. Call. "Providing Health Care to Latino Immigrants: Community-Based Efforts in the Rural Midwest." *American Journal of Public Health* 94.10 (Oct. 2004): 1709-1711. Academic Search Premier EBSCOhost. Chambers Library. Edmond, OK 27 March 2006.

Cosman, Madeleine Pelner. "Illegal Aliens and American Medicine." *Journal of American Physicians and Surgeons* 10.1 (2005): 6-10. Academic Search Premier EBSCOhost. Chambers Library. Edmond, OK 27 March 2006

Dwyer, James. "Illegal Immigrants, Health Care and Social Responsibility." *Hastings Center Report* 34.1 (2004): 34-41. Academic Search Premier EBSCOhost. Chambers Library. Edmond, OK 29 Feb. 2006.

Fong, Tony. "Hospitals Get Some Back." *Modern Healthcare* 16 May 2005: 10. Academic Search Premier EBSCOhost. Chambers Library. Edmond, OK 17 March 2006.

Green, Alison, and Jack Martin. "Uncontrolled Immigration and the U.S. Health Care System." *Journal of Social, Political and Economic Studies* 29.2 (2004): 225-241. Academic Search Premier EBSCOhost. Chambers Library. Edmond, OK 27 March 2006.

Smith, Linda S. "Health of America's Newcomers." *Journal of Community Health Nursing* 18.1 (2001): 53-68. Academic Search Premier EBSCOhost. Chambers Library. Edmond, OK 6 April 2006.

The U.S. Department of Health and Human Services: "The Children's Health Initiative and Migrant and Seasonal Farmworker Children: The Current Situation and the Available Opportunities Migrant Health Program." Academic Search Premier EBSCOhost. Chambers Library. Edmond, OK 29 Feb. 2006.

Ziv, Tal Ann, and Berbard Lo. "Denial of Care to Illegal Immigrants—Proposition 187 in California." *New England Journal of Medicine* 332.16 (1995): 1095-1098. Academic Search Premier EBSCOhost. Chambers Library. Edmond, OL 29 Feb. 2006.

PEER REVIEW OUTLINE

Directions. Asking the right questions: As you ask these questions and answer them, be specific in your comments so as to be more helpful to the author. Provide details.

1. **Logos.** Comment on the quality and amount of the evidence or research conducted. Is it balanced or enough? Does the author need more? Why or why not? Is the paper too logical or not logical enough? What else can you say about logos?
2. **Pathos.** Comment on the emotional appeals used in the paper. What can the author do to improve this appeal? Should there be less, more, or no emotions? Explain.
3. **Ethos.** Does the author use enough quality sources to improve the impact of the ethos of the paper? Is there a human element in the paper? What does the author need to do to improve the character aspect? Should the author add a personal story? Is the paper too personal? Should it be more logical?
4. **Call for Improvement.** Which aspects in the paper need to be revised or improved? Explain in detail.

Responding to the Immigration and Acculturation Issues

Written Rhetoric: Opinion Papers, Arguments, and Research

1. This chapter contains essays with several points of view concerning the ethics of creating a guest worker program in the United States. Write an essay in which you argue for or against a guest worker program. Your audience is your state senator. Remember, if you reference any of the articles you have read, you must cite them.
2. Create a survey about U. S. immigration policy and get at least 25 people to respond. Then write an essay in which you analyze the information you receive from your survey. Be sure to draw a conclusion about the results.
3. Although America is, for the most part, a nation that derives from immigrants, immigration policy has been an issue since this nation's beginning. Research the history of immigration policy in the United States and write a paper to present your findings. Be sure to focus your essay on a clear thesis that grew out of your research.
4. One major issue in the immigration policy controversy is whether or not we should allow illegal immigrants who are currently in this country to gain legal status here. Do research to determine the complexities of this issue; then, write a paper in which you argue your position. You may argue for or against illegal immigrants gaining legal status, or you may propose a compromise.

Oral Rhetoric: Speeches, Lyrics, and Simulations

1. Convert your opinion paper on immigration into a speech. Be sure to identify your audience and write your speech so that listeners will clearly understand your points and be apt to agree with you. If possible, deliver this speech in order to receive feedback.
2. Search the Internet for a speech on immigration policy. After listening to the speech, write an analysis of it, explaining the techniques the speaker used to convince his or her audience to accept his or her point of view and why they were or were not effective.
3. Research the "Nuestro Himno" controversy. Then write a paper in which you present both sides of the issue and come to a reasoned conclusion about the translation.

4. Create a simulation in which bosses who employ illegal immigrants talk with politicians about their view on immigration policy. Be sure to include politicians with different viewpoints on this issue.

Visual Rhetoric: Advertisements, Visuals, and Cinema

1. The sign above appeared near our border with Mexico. While some find the sign amusing, immigrants find it quite offensive. Analyze the content of the sign to write an essay in which you explain its effects, and hypothesize why the sign would be posted.
2. Write an essay comparing the humor in the cartoons in this chapter.
3. Watch a film about the immigration experience (see the list at the end of this chapter) and research what others have written about the way in which this movie has portrayed immigrants. Then write an essay analyzing the way in which the film portrays immigrants. Be sure not to simply write a plot summary. Your goal should be to determine how effectively the director, actors, and screenplay writers presented the immigration experience.
4. Go to www.deviantart.com and search using the words "immigration" and "acculturation." Save the images you find the most effective. Write an essay about the photos. Include the images in your report.

Electronic Rhetoric: Emergent Media and Gaming

1. Find a video of "Nuestro Himno" on YouTube. After watching the video several times, write a paper in which you analyze the oral and visual aspects of the video as arguments for the validity of the translated version of the American national anthem.

2. Go to http://www.pbs.org/pov/pov2002/borders/games.html and play some of the immigrant games PBS has collected there. Do these games have arguments within them? Write a paper in which you explain what some of these games argue and how they present their argument in a gaming situation. You may compare and contrast the games to explain how they work to make their points.
3. "Iced!" is a video game that has players take on the personas of immigrants in the United States to experience their dilemmas. If this game, or a similar one, is available, play it until you feel you have a sense of the immigrant experience. Then write a paper in which you explain what you have learned. Be sure to refer to specific experiences you had playing the game to clarify your points.

WOVE Project

For this project, choose one aspect of our immigration and acculturation issues. Ask:

- Should we have a guest worker program?
- Should we allow illegal immigrants already in this country to gain legal status?
- Should English be the official language of the United States?

Thoroughly research the issue and write an opinion paper about the issue. Research should include listening to speeches available on the Internet and finding images that could enhance your presentation. Then decide on an electronic media through which to present your argument—a video, PowerPoint presentation, or any other electronic media with which you are familiar. As you plan your project, be sure to focus on the thesis of your opinion paper, decide on the appeals that will best reach your audience, and then script your presentation. You should include appropriate sound bites from the speeches you listened to and consider all aspects of visuals (color, arrangement, etc.) as you create an effective presentation of your argument.

Song Lyrics

"Coming to America," Neal Diamond
"Deportee," Woody Guthrie
"Help is Coming," Ayo
"Immigration Man," Davis Crosby and Graham Nash
"Immigration Song," Ozma
"Reggaeton," Don Omar
"Una Sangre (One Blood)," Lila Downs

Cinematic List

American Me (Edward James Olmos, 1992)
An American Tail (Don Bluth, 1986—animation)

Born in East LA (Cheech Martin, 1987)
Crossing Arizona (Joseph Mathew, 2005)
La Ciudad (David Riker, 1998)
A Day without a Mexican (Sergio Arau, 2004)
De Nadie (Tin Dirdamal, 2005)
Dirty Pretty Things (Steven Frears, 2003)
Everything is Illuminated (Liev Schreiber, 2005)
Game 6 (Michael Hoffman, 2005)
Gangs of New York (Martin Scorsese, 2002)
The Gatekeeper (John Carlos Frey, 2004)
God Grew Tired of Us (Christopher Quinn, 2006)
House of Sand and Fog (Vadim Perelman, 2003)
In America (Jim Sheridan, 2003)
In Between Days (So Yong Kim, 2006)
Living on Tokyo Time (Steven Okazaki, 1987)
Maria Full of Grace (Joshua Marston, 2004)
Men in Black (Barry Sonnenfeld, 1997)
Mi Vida Loca (Allison Anders, 1993)
A Million to Juan (Paul Rodriguez, 1994)
My Big Fat Greek Wedding (Joel Zwick, 2002)
The Namesake (Mira Nair, 2006)
Never Forever (Gina Kim, 2007)
Night of Henna (Hassin Zee, 2005)
El Norte (Gregory Nava, 1983)
Padre Nuestro (Christopher Zalla, 2007)
Persepolis (Vincent Paronnaud, Marjane Satrapi, 2007—animation)
Real Women Have Curves (Patricia Cardoso, 2003)
Romantico (Mark Becker, 2005)
Quinceanera (Wash Westmoreland, Richard Glatzer, 2005)
Saving Face (Nigel Cole, 2004)
Spanglish (James L. Brooks, 2004)
Stranger Than Paradise (Jim Jarmusch, 1984)
Sueno (Renee Chabria, 2005)
Sweet Land (Will Weaver, 2006)
The Three Burials of Melquiades Estrada (Tommy Lee Jones, 2005)
La Tragedia de Macario (Pablo Veliz, 2005)

Comix

Persepolis (Marjane Satrapi)
American Born Chinese (Gene Luen Yang)
One Hundred Demons (Lynda Barry)

GLOSSARY

Abstract
A summary of a paper highlighting the key aspects of that paper in a brief overview.

Abstract Visuals
Represent something that cannot actually take place; they represent actions that are not touchable or that you cannot see someone doing. For example, on your computer you can put electronic files in a recycle bin (on the PC) or trashcan (on the MAC) but you are not actually putting them in a physical trash can. You are imitating the action.

Analogous Colors
Colors that immediately follow one another on the color wheel. These colors are always in harmony, not having too much or too little contrast.

Annotation
The interaction with the text by writing critical commentaries in the margins.

APA (American Psychological Association)
Founded 1892, a scientific and professional organization that created its own style manual.

Appeals
Appeals are rhetorical strategies which improve the persuasive effectiveness of an argument. The three major types are ethos, pathos, and logos.

Avatar
A visual representation of a person in the virtual or gaming world. Originally, the term is from Hinduism meaning an incarnation that various deities are able to manifest. The term was popularized by Neal Stephenson (1959–) in his post-cyberpunk classic, *Snow Crash* (1992).

Backing
In the Toulman method, the evidence to support the warrant; i.e., the evidence that the audience does indeed hold the assumptions necessary for the warrant.

Bibliography
A list of sources an author used when writing a book, article or essay, found at the end of written works.

Boolean Logic
Developed by George Boole (1815-1864), a way to organize library searches.

Call Number
A combination of letters and numbers indicating a source's location in a library.

Citation
Information needed to locate an item; includes title, author, and publication information depending on item format.

Claim
The side of an issue about which the writer will argue.

Classical Canons of Rhetoric
The basic elements of rhetoric that allow for speakers, writers or creators to become meta-aware of how such aspects can effect change or be persuasive.

Classical Method
Developed by ancient Greek rhetoric and used in Roman rhetoric. It has remained one of the most popular ways to arrange an argument or paper throughout the ages. It is composed of five parts: introduction (with thesis), a statement of fact (narration), evidence (confirmation), refutation (with concessions), and summation.

Color Context
How colors look (bright, dark, dull) when placed on different backgrounds or when seen with different levels of light intensity. For example, if you want a red MP3 player to look big and bright, you would place it on a white background. If you want that same red MP3 player to look small and dull, you would place it on a gray background.

Color Harmony

Occurs when the colors on the page, in the visual, or on the screen are pleasing to the eye. The colors do not have too much contrast (differences) that prevent the eye from adjusting quickly to see the letters or picture and the background. The colors, also, do not have too little contrast, causing the eye to have difficulty in determining the difference in words or pictures, and the background, or any combination.

Complimentary Colors

Colors across the color wheel from each other. These colors are always in harmony, not having too much or too little contrast. Three pairs of complementary colors are: red and green, blue and orange, purple and yellow.

Concrete Visuals

Visuals of or that relate to an actual, specific thing or instance. For example, if a visual wants you to put your trash in a trash can, it would have a person putting trash in a trash can. The visual represents, exactly, what takes place.

Conspiracy Theory

Narratives or theories about critical events such as the Kennedy assassination, Area 51, 9/11 and so on developed by the public when a lack in confidence occurs in official investigative institutions either due to corruption and/or incompetency.

Counterclaim

The side of an issue the writer will not argue, but should consider as the argument is constructed.

Data

In the classical method, extrinsic proofs such as scientific evidence, survey results, or statistics. In the Toulman method, data is any evidence that supports the claim.

Database

An on-line index of articles, books, Web sites, or other media.

Deductive Appeal

An argument made up of a major premise, a minor premise and a conclusion. A deductive appeal argues from general to specific.

Documentation

Recognition of outside sources used by authors, often in the form of a works cited list or other reference list.

Ethos

By using the character of the writer or speaker or by using effective sources with writers of expertise, this appeal to ethos can make the discourse more appealing to the audience.

Evidence

The points presented to prove the claim. Evidence can be based on logos, pathos, or ethos.

Extrinsic Proof

Any evidence brought to the argument such as scientific evidence, survey results, or statistics.

Fields

Parts of a record: the author, title, periodical name, or abstract.

Format

The form in which information is presented, such as a book, CD, computer file, or journal.

Full Text

The complete electronic text of a source.

Gaming Model

Based on game theories and asks that arguments be played out as a game, not a winner take all or zero-sum game, but as a negotiation between players as a way to find solutions as joint collaborations: win-win games.

Gaming Senses

A super sensitivity to the audience, the game, and the plays or moves within a game that gamers must develop to be successful.

Index
A list of records searchable by various fields such as author or subject.

Inductive Appeal
An argument based on specific examples from which the writer draws a general conclusion.

Information Source
A material beyond one's own thoughts in nearly any format from book to Web site.

Interlibrary Loan
Refers to libraries borrowing materials from other libraries.

Invisible Web Sites
Web sites with restricted access, usually requiring a subscription; not searchable with public web searching tools.

Issue
An idea or belief about which there is debate.

Journal
Mostly scholarly periodicals but sometimes magazines and newspapers.

Library Catalog
A database that inventories all materials the library owns.

Logical Fallacy
Rational arguments that contain, weak, deceptive or false rhetorical patterns.

Logos
Using logic effectively to make the discourse seem more rational to the audience.

Marking up
Annotating by writing as a way of interacting with the text in a way to understand the text.

Meta-Awareness
A sensitive mindfulness of your own rhetorical processes. By overtly understanding how you write, you are able to identify weaknesses and effect positive change.

MLA (Modern Language Association)
Founded in 1883, a scholarly organization that promotes an annual conference, an extensive bibliography and a style manual.

Mock Advertisements
Fake (false) advertisements meant to mimic actual advertisements. Often mock advertisements treat the subject of the ad with contempt or ridicule. Sometimes mock advertisements seek to improve the message of an advertisement considered to be frivolous or dangerous. An example might be taking an advertisement for an oil company that has a picture of an oil pump set against a beautiful, natural background with flowers, trees, and animals and making it an oil pump set against a gray, drab background with oil covered birds, trees, and flowers. The first advertisment indicates that oil production and nature are in harmony; the second advertisement indicates that oil production destroys nature.

Natural Colors
Colors that occur together in nature. Examples of natural colors are white and light blue (as in the clouds in the sky) or orange, brown, and green (the color of fall leaves).

Nested Searching
Used in libraries or online queries, are provisions and/or phrases combined together in specific correlations using parentheses, quotation marks, and/or other symbols in order to make searches more effective.

Nonverbal Language
Refers to communication that does not derive from words. People communicate using their bodies—posture, gestures, and facial expressions; objects—clothing, hair styles, furnishings, or anything else people choose to surround themselves with; or even the nonverbal elements of speech—tone, emotional response such as crying, and the level of sound that accompanies their words.

Operators

Words used to connect ideas in Boolean Logic; **and**, **or**, and **not** are common.

Paraphrase

Rewording a quote from a source using different or original words instead of a verbatim word for word version.

Pathos

Creating elements within the text that move the emotions of the audience to make the discourse more appealing to the audience.

Peer-Reviewed or Refereed Journals

Journals containing articles reviewed and critiqued by noted experts ("peers") in the same profession.

The Penrose Triangle

Named after Roger Penrose (1931–) who made the tribar figure famous, and modeled on the Möbius strip, a mathematical geometrical circular fold symbolizing a continuous or indefinite plane where one can move along forever as it merges with its other side. M.C. Escher (1898–1972) used the mechanics of such a mathematical arrangement in his images to create the illusion of interconnectivity, infinity, or impossibility.

Periodicals

Journals, magazines, newspapers.

Persuasive Writing

The power to excite, engage, and arouse emotional, intellectual, or even moral awareness of an audience though textual discourse.

Plagiarism

The intentional or unintentional copying of text or ideas from another person or source and presenting them without due credit.

Popular Magazine

Publications for a general audience. Usually do not include Works Cited or references to other sources used.

Qualifier

In the Toulman method, the narrowing of the claim or warrant to be more specific or to limit the claim or warrant to a specific group of people.

Rebuttal

The point in the argument when the writer tries to refute or show as untrue the main points of the counterclaim.

Record

A description of a single source and often contains the necessary information to locate it.

Reference Page

A specific type of bibliography used by the American Psychological Association (APA).

Reference Work

Works with brief overviews of a topic, key ideas, important concepts, or tables of primary information.

Refutation

An important strategy for arguments, where you object to the main arguments presented by the opposition.

Rhetoric

Using the most effective means of influencing or persuading audiences.

Rhetorical Situation

A context involving a communicator, an issue, and an audience. The communicator (writer or speaker) will strive to use effective communication to discuss/analyze the issue so as to affect the audience in a specific way.

Rhythm (poem)

The regular or irregular pattern of beats or accents in a line of poetry.

Rogerian Method

Based on psychologist Carl Rogers (1902-1987), a type of argument that finds the middle ground of agreement instead of focusing on error and blame against the viewpoints of opponents.

Scholarly Journals
Journals published on an academic topic, assuming prior knowledge of the topic. Sometimes peer-reviewed but not always.

Social Bookmarking
Instead of simply recording the location of a site of personal interest, allows you to share those locations with others who value the same sites. Such sites became a virtual gathering of people who share the same interests where friends and acquaintances can be stimulated.

Social Network
Allows pictures, videos, words, music and a variety of information to be shared with friends, family, and anyone allowed access to the site. This virtual community grows in importance and extends the limits of how we define ourselves.

Sound (poem)
Has its own effect on those who hear it. An "s," for example, is soft and sensuous, while a "k" is harsh and crisp.

Source
The original document, person, or reference that a passage or idea is derived from when you are writing, speaking or creating a work.

Stasis Theory
A methodology of four questions developed by the ancient Greeks to discover the appropriate claim to argue for any given law case.

Stratagems
The art and the means of obtaining or maintaining a rhetorical command over a situation.

Subject Headings
A standardized list of terms representing particular topics. Library of Congress Subject Headings are commonly used, though not universally.

Syllogism
A way to build a proof by providing two true statements (a major premise and a minor premise) which then direct the listener or reader to a "logical" third statement or conclusion. The biggest problem with a syllogism remains that the conclusion is not always valid. "All A are B. All C are A. Therefore, all C are B."

Synonym
A word possessing the same meaning as another word.

Toulmin Method
A way to analyze an argument, breaking it into its parts so that we can judge how effective the argument is, how well the parts work together. Writers using the Toulmin method identify the claims, the reasons, and the evidence in order to determine whether or not the argument "works."

Trade Journals
Journals with content about a particular profession.

Truncation
A symbol added to the stem of a word, most often an asterisk (*) but sometimes a question mark (?), pound symbol (#), or exclamation point (!). A search with a truncated term finds that stem plus anything that comes after it.

Visible or Public Web Sites
Web sites accessed for free using search engines such as Google.

Visual Discourse
The way people communicate through visual cues and other aspects of seeing. For example, your mother might give you "the look," and you know exactly what that look means. In fact, we have grown accustomed to many forms of visual communications in the 21st century—film, posters, advertisements, the visual arts, and anything else around us that sends a visual message.

Warrant
In the Toulman method, any underlying assumption the audience would have about the issue being argued.

Weasel Words

Words that are ambiguous and not supported by facts. While their meaning may appear to be clear, in fact they tend to mislead readers into believing something that has no real proof.

Widgets

Allow information gathered at one site to be displayed or integrated into other sites. For example, the weather or time could be displayed at other sites. Music, art work, and other information can be shared at a variety of sites without the user being solely at that site.

Working Bibliography

A gathering of potential resources that a writer or speaker may use for a paper. Such a bibliography should have quality sources along with a larger quantity of sources or resources than are needed since many sources end up being un-useful to the paper. Developing a good working bibliography allows a writer to map out the research process and ascertain if more research is necessary.

Works Cited

When mentioning or quoting from sources, this type of bibliography is required for the Modern Language Association (MLA) format.

WOVE Approach

Created by Iowa State University's communication-across-the-curriculum initiative as a form of "multimodal communication" where "teachers provide all students with the kind of communication instruction that prepares them to communicate with expertise in multiple settings and with multiple media" <http://isucomm.iastate.edu/about>. Such an approach prepares students for today's working environment that incorporates the varieties of new media which are emerging.

Zero-Sum Situation

A gaming situation that is win or lose where the winner takes everything from the loser, like in the classic game of chess.

CITATIONS

Preface

Kelly, Travis. Cartoon. *Art by Travis Kelly*. 20 Jan. 2008. 15 July 2008 <http://www.traviskelly.com/cartoon/index.html>.

Chapter 1

"Joe Chemo Casket." *Adbusters.org*. 15 July 2008 <http://www.adbusters.org/gallery/spoofads/tobacco>.

Luckovich, Mike. Cartoon. *The Atlanta Constitution* 1995.

Wasserman, Dan. "The Nicotine or the Lying?" Cartoon. *Advocate* 29 June 1994.

Reed, Jerry. "Another Puff." 1971. *Thank You for Smoking Soundtrack*. Lakeshore Records, 2006.

Buckley, Christopher. *Thank You for Smoking*. New York: Random, 1994. 127-29.

Chapter 2

Parisi, Mark. Cartoon. *Off the Mark*. 3 Mar. 2004. 15 July 2008 <http://www.offthemark.com>.

Chapter 3

Harris, Sidney. Cartoon. *Science Cartoons Plus*. 15 July 2008 <http://www.sciencecartoonsplus.com/pages/gallery.php>.

Ford, Gerald R., and David W. Belin. "Kennedy Assassination: How About the Truth?" *Washington Post* 17 Dec. 1991: A21.

Chapter 4

Smith, Rob, Jr. Cartoon. *Cartoons by Rob Smith, Jr.* 25 Sept. 2007. 15 July 2008 <http://art.robsmithjr.com/gallery/4061059_6Sb8A#236512753_KCfpt>.

"The Kennedy/Nixon Presidential Debate." *Historical Background*. National Park Service, Special Collection. 4 Feb. 2004. 15 July 2008 <http://www.nps.gov/history/history/online_books/Presidents/intro.htm>.

Mali, Taylor. "How to Write a Political Poem." *Taylor Mali.com*. 2002. 15 July 2008 <http://www.taylormali.com/index.cfm?webid=16>.

The Kinks. "Give the People What They Want." *Give the People What They Want*. 1981. Velvel Records, 2004.

"Statement by the President in His Address to the Nation." *The White House.gov*. 11 Sept. 2001. 15 July 2008 <http://www.whitehouse.gov/news/releases/2001/09/20010911-16.html>.

Chapter 5

Davies, Ray. "Give the People What They Want." Lyrics. The Kinks.

Bush, George W. "911 Speech." Speech. 11 Sept. 2001.

"Inaugural Address of President John F. Kennedy." 20 Jan. 1961. *John F. Kennedy Presidential Library and Museum*. 15 July 2008 <http://www.jfklibrary.org/Historical+Resources/Archives/Reference+Desk/Speeches/JFK/003POF03Inaugural01201961.htm>.

Cochran, Johnnie. "Johnnie Cochran's Closing Arguments." Criminal Murder Case LA District Court. 27 Sept. 1995.

Parker, Trey, and Matt Stone. "Chewbacca Defense." Teleplay. Southpark, Season 2, Episode 14. "Chef Aid." 7 Oct. 1998.

LaGesse, David. "Richard Nixon Gets No Mercy from Camera During Debate with John Kennedy." *U.S. News and World Report*. 17 Jan. 2008. 15 July 2008 <http://www.usnews.com/articles/news/politics/2008/01/17/no-mercy-from-a-new-camera.html>.

"The CNN Democratic Presidential Debate in Texas." *CNN.com*. 21 Feb. 2008. 15 July 2008 <http://www.cnn.com/2008/POLITICS/02/21/debate.transcript/>.

"Closing Argument of Johnnie Cochran (Excerpts)." 27 Sept. 1995. University of Missouri-Kansas City School of Law (UMKC). 15 July 2008 <http://www.law.umkc.edu/faculty/projects/ftrials/Simpson/cochranclose.html>.

"Chef Aid." *South Park*. Comedy Central, 7 Oct. 1998.

"Chewbacca Defense" *South Park*. Comedy Central, 7 Oct. 1998.

Chapter 6

"CCP Heye for McDonald's (Austria)." *Adverblog.com*. 2 Aug. 2005. 15 July 2008 <http://www.adverblog.com/archives/001773.htm>.

Mitchell, Arnold. *Nine American Lifestyles: Who We Are and Where We're Going*. New York: Macmillan, 1983.

U.S. Army. Advertisement. 15 July 2008 <http://www.goarmy.com/strong/sniper.jsp?fl=false>.

Nike Women. Advertisement. Associated Press. 18 Aug. 2005. 15 July 2008 <http://www.msnbc.msn.com/id/8998863/>.

"Prozac." *Adbusters.org*. 15 July 2008 <http://www.adbusters.org/gallery/spoofads>.

"Absolut Impotence." *Adbusters.org*. 15 July 2008 <http://www.adbusters.org/gallery/spoofads/alcohol>.

"World War II Poster: Go Ahead, Please—Take Day Off!" *About.com*. National Archives and Records Administration. 15 July 2008 <http://history1900s.about.com/library/photos/blywwiip66.htm>.

Miller, J. Howard. "We Can Do It." *The National Archives*. 15 July 2008 <http://www.archives.gov/education/lessons/wwii-posters/>.

Hopps, H. R. "Destroy This Mad Brute." Harry Ransom Center: The University of Texas at Austin. 15 July 2008 <http://www.hrc.utexas.edu/collections/art/holdings/poster/index.html>.

The Golden Lamb. Advertisement. The Creative Department. 17 Apr. 2008. 15 July 2008 <http://blog.creativedepartment.com/2008/04/17/making-history-with-the-golden-lamb/>.

"Malboro: The New Frontier." *Adbusters.org*. 15 July 2008 <http://www.adbusters.org/gallery/spoofads>.

Fayaz (Minikaa be). FoXyAaz's Photostream. 19 Apr. 2008. 15 July 2008 <http://flickr.com/photos/fir3_101/2425317652/sizes/m>.

"In Pictures: Anna Nicole's Funeral." *BBCNews.com*. 3 Mar. 2007. 15 July 2008 <http://news.bbc.co.uk/2/hi/in_pictures/6414327.stm>.

"'Maamanithar' Title Only for Pro-Tiger MPs." *Asian Tribune*. 12 Nov. 2006. 15 July 2008 <http://www.asiantribune.com/index.php?q=node/3164>.

Napster. Advertisement. Napster.com. <http://www.napster.com>.

"A Look at the Record." Duke University Special Collections Library. Aug. 1996. 15 July 2008 <http://scriptorium.lib.duke.edu/americavotes/jfk.html>.

McCloud, Scott. *Understanding Comics*. New York: Harper Perennial, 1993. 28-33.

Block, Herbert L. Cartoon. *Washington Post* 11 Nov. 1986. Library of Congress. 15 July 2008 <http://www.loc.gov/rr/print/swann/herblock/images/s03287u.jpg>.

Glasbergen, Randy. Cartoon. *Glasbergen.com*. 2002. 15 July 2008 <http://www.glasbergen.com/images/mar12.gif>.

Student Film. *Sleeping Giant*. 2007.

"Utterfool." *Adbusters.org*. 15 July 2008 <http://www.adbusters.org/gallery/spoofads/tobacco>.

Chapter 7

Trudeau, G. B. *Doonesbury*. Cartoon. *Slate.com*. 9 Sept. 2007. 15 July 2008 <http://www.doonesbury.com/strip/dailydose/index.html?uc_full_date=20070909>.

Mashable Social Networking News. 15 July 2008 <http://mashable.com/social-networking/>.

"John Edwards—'Season' TV Ad." *YouTube.com*. 20 Dec. 2007. 15 July 2008 <http://www.youtube.com/watch?v=q4kBJGDkfq8>.

"John McCain: Courageous Service." *YouTube.com*. 29 Aug. 2007. 15 July 2008 <http://www.youtube.com/watch?v=vQsckD9trn4>.

"HuckChuckFacts." *YouTube.com*. 18 Nov. 2007. 15 July 2008 <http://www.youtube.com/watch?v=EjYv2YW6azE>.

"Mitt Romney Web Ad—Momentum." *YouTube.com*. 26 Feb. 2008. 15 July 2008 <http://www.youtube.com/watch?v=ZYHBtd9h5-g>.

"Fred Thompson TV Ad: 'Substance.'" *YouTube.com*. 26 Dec. 2007. 15 July 2008 <http://www.youtube.com/watch?v=lssb6gkjQa4>.

"Listen." *YouTube.com*. 11 Jan. 2008. 15 July 2008 <http://www.youtube.com/watch?v=Gg8PU_h3R-U>.

"No More Blood for Oil." *YouTube.com*. 3 June 2007. 15 July 2008 <http://www.youtube.com/watch?v=YRl4YLVW0b4>.

"Rudy Giuliani TV Ad, 'Freedom.'" *YouTube.com*. 27 Dec. 2007. 15 July 2008 <http://www.youtube.com/watch?v=I3tt8dniJXc>.

Rosenthal, Joe. *Raising the Flag on Iwo Jima*. 23 Feb. 1945.

"1984." *YouTube.com*. 6 Mar. 2007. 15 July 2008 <http://youtube.com/watch?v=cWvHbOoG3tI>.

Twitter.com. 15 July 2008 <http://twitter.com>.

Second Life.com. 15 July 2008 <http://secondlife.com>.

Writeboard.com. 15 July 2008 <http://writeboard.com>.

Wikipedia.org. 15 July 2008 <http://wikipedia.org>.

World of Warcraft: Wrath of the Lich King. Blizzard Entertainment. 15 July 2008 <http://www.worldofwarcraft.com/wrath/>.

EverQuest—Secrets of Faydwer. Sony. 15 July 2008 <http://everquest.station.sony.com/>.

"Halo 3." *Dual Monitor Backgrounds*. 15 July 2008 <http://www.dualmonitorbackgrounds.com/gaming/Halo3.jpg.html>.

Chriskrajci. "Halo 3 Movie Trailer (Oldboy)." *YouTube.com*. 23 Aug. 2007. 15 July 2008 <http://youtube.com/watch?v=5X58rG_Eajg>.

Guitar Hero III: Legends of Rock. Activision. 15 July 2008 <http://www.guitarherogame.com/gh3/>.

Rock Band. Harmonix Music Systems. 15 July 2008 <http://www.rockband.com>.

Super Mario Galaxy. Nintendo. 15 July 2008 <http://www.nintendo.com/sites/supermariogalaxy/>.

Chapter 8

Watterson, Bill. *Calvin and Hobbes*. Cartoon. *The Complete Calvin and Hobbes*. Riverside, NJ: Andrews McMeel, 2005.

Chapter 9

Kelly, Travis. "Killer Cell Phones." Cartoon. *Art by Travis Kelly*. 15 July 2008 <http://www.traviskelly.com/cartoon/editor.html>.

"Google Advanced Search." *Google.com*. 15 July 2008 <http://www.google.com/advanced_search?hl=en>.

Chapter 10

Modern Language Association. 15 July 2008 <http://www.mla.org>.

Kunkle, Abigail. "To Spank or Not to Spank: That Is the Question." Unpublished essay. 12 Apr. 2005.

Chapter 11

American Psychological Association. 15 July 2008 <http://www.apa.org>.

Nelson, Karen. "Waterproofing New Orleans." Unpublished essay. 15 Mar. 2008.

Chapter 12

Stringfield, Cary. *Captain Clark Comics.com*. 15 July 2008 <http://www.captainclarkcomics.com/captainclarkcomics_011.htm>.

Etienne, Kirk-Albert. *The Big Book of Conspiracies*. New York: Paradox, 1995. 63.

Stone, Oliver, and Zachary Sklar. *JFK: The Book of the Film*. New York: Applause, 1992.

Borgman, Jim. Cartoon. *Cincinnati Enquirer* 19 May 2006.

Stone, Oliver. "The JFK Assassination—What About the Evidence?" Letter. *Washington Post* 24 Dec. 1991: A13.

Robins, Robert S., and Jerrold M. Post. "Political Paranoia as Cinematic Motif: Stone's *JFK*." American Political Science Association. Washington, D.C. Aug./Sept. 1997. Rpt. by John Adams. *The Kennedy Assassination*. 15 July 2008 <http://mcadams.posc.mu.edu/robins.htm>.

Russell, Bertrand. "16 Questions on the Assassination." *The Minority of One* 6 Sept. 1964: 6-8. Rpt. at www.solstice.us. 15 July 2008 <http://www.solstice.us/russell/16questions.html>.

Orwell, George. *1984*. New York: Harcourt Brace, 2003. 309-23.

Clooney, George, and Grant Heslov. *Good Night, and Good Luck*. New York: Newmarket, 2006. 147-51.

Suu Kyi, Aung San. "Freedom from Fear." *Freedom from Fear and Other Writings*. Penguin, 1991. 180-85.

Wachowski, Andy, and Larry Wachowski. V for Vendetta*: From Script to Film*. Ed. Spencer Lamm and Sharon Bray. New York: Rizzoli, 2006. 35-42.

Moore, Alan, and David Lloyd. *V for Vendetta*. New York: DC Comics, 1988.

Coldwell, Jeff. "The Prince of Propaganda." Unpublished essay.

Chapter 13

Farzat, Ali. Cartoon. *A Pen of Damascus Steel: The Political Cartoons of an Arab Master*. Seattle: Cune, 2005. 103.

Brown, John Seely, and Douglas Thomas. "You Play *World of Warcraft*? You're Hired!" *Wired* Apr. 2006. 15 July 2008 <http://www.wired.com/wired/archive/14.04/learn.html>.

"Violence in Media Entertainment." *Media Awareness Network (MNet)*. 2008. 15 July 2008 <http://www.media-awareness.ca/english/issues/violence/violence_entertainment.cfm>.

Benedetti, Winda. "Were Video Games to Blame for Massacre?" *MSNBC.com*. 20 Apr. 2007. 15 July 2008 <http://www.msnbc.msn.com/id/18220228/>.

Jones, Gerard. "Violent Media Is Good for Kids." *Mother Jones.com*. 28 June 2000. 15 July 2008 <http://www.motherjones.com/commentary/columns/2000/06/violent_media.html>.

Knauss, Greg. "Dining with Cannibals." *Suck.com*. 24 June 1996. 15 July 2008 <http://www.suck.com/daily/96/06/24/>.

Fancher, Hampton, and David Webb Peoples. *Blade Runner*. 1982. 15 July 2008 <http://scribble.com/uwi/br/script_19810223.txt>.

Stephenson, Neal. *Snow Crash*. New York: Bantam Spectra, 1992. 1-10.

Waldrop, Will. "Fun vs. Family: Mind-Numbing Deviltry." Unpublished essay. 14 Feb. 2005.

Chapter 14

"Obsession for Women." *Adbusters.org*. 15 July 2008 <http://www.adbusters.org/gallery/spoofads>.

"Obsession for Men." *Adbusters.org*. 15 July 2008 <http://www.adbusters.org/gallery/spoofads>.

Marks, Alexandra. "A Backlash to Advertising in an Age of Anything Goes." *Christian Science Monitor* 22 Feb. 1999: 1+.

"I Gave a Man!" 1941. University of Maryland, College Park. 15 July 2008 <http://narademo.umiacs.umd.edu/cgi-bin/isadg/viewitem.pl?item=31569>.

Koerner, Henry. "Save Waste Fats for Explosives." 1943. National Archives and Records Administration. 15 July 2008 <http://www.archives.gov/exhibits/powers_of_persuasion/use_it_up/use_it_up.html>.

Red Hot Chili Peppers. "Californication." *Californication*. Warner Brothers, 1999.

Toothpick. "Super Size Me." 15 July 2008 <http://www.toothpickmusic.com>.

Schlosser, Eric. *Fast Food Nation: The Dark Side of the All-American Meal*. Boston: Houghton, 2001. 120-32.

Leo, John. "The Selling of Rebellion." *U.S. News and World Report* 12 Oct. 1998: 18.

Barry, Dave. "Some Hated Commercials Inspire Violent Fantasies." *SouthCoastToday.com*. 2 Feb. 1997. 15 July 2008 <http://archive.southcoasttoday.com/daily/02-97/02-02-97/e02li202.htm>.

Bailey, Sarah. "Does This Ad Make Me Look Fat?" Unpublished essay.

Williams, Kimberly. "Advertising Sex: Company Bias." Unpublished essay.

Chapter 15

"Jarhead." *Empire Design*. 2006. 15 July 2008 <http://www.empiredesign.com/main.html>.

"Black Hawk Down." 2001. *IMP Awards*. 15 July 2008 <http://www.impawards.com/2001/black_hawk_down_ver1.html>.

"Band of Brothers." 2001. *IMP Awards*. 15 July 2008 <http://www.impawards.com/tv/band_of_brothers.html>.

Nakazawa, Keiji. *Barefoot Gen: A Cartoon History of Hiroshima*. Trans. Project Gen. Philadelphia: New Society Publishers, 1987.

Springsteen, Bruce. "Born in the U.S.A." *Born in the U.S.A*. Columbia, 1984.

"Dwight's Speech." *The Office*. NBC, 2 Mar. 2006.

Twain, Mark. *The War Prayer*. 1905. New York: Harper Perennial, 1984.

Conroy, Pat. *My Losing Season*. New York: Nan A. Talese/Doubleday, 2002. 370-77.

Spiegelman, Art. *Maus II: A Survivor's Tale*. New York: Pantheon, 1995. 41-44.

Shakespeare, William. *Henry V. The Riverside Shakespeare: The Complete Works*. 2nd ed. Boston: Houghton, 1997. 979-1020.

Patton, George S. Speech. England. 5 June 1944.

O'Brien, Tim. *The Things They Carried*. Boston: Houghton, 1990. 3-25.

Farish, Terry. "Why I Went to War." *PBS.org*. 29 Mar. 2005. 15 July 2008 <http://www.pbs.org/wgbh/amex/vietnam/reflect/farish.html>.

Swofford, Anthony. *Jarhead: A Marine's Chronicle of the Gulf War and Other Battles*. New York: Scribner, 2003. 5-8.

Lindbergh, Charles. Address. America First Committee. New York. 23 Apr. 1941.

Conant, James B. "We Must Defeat Hitler." *Congressional Record* 7 June 1940. 3669-70.

Newbold, Greg. "Why Iraq Was a Mistake." *Time.com*. 9 Apr. 2006. 15 July 2008 <http://www.time.com/time/magazine/article/0,9171,1181629,00.html>.

Lieberman, Joe. "Our Troops Must Stay." *Wall Street Journal Online*. 29 Nov. 2005. 15 July 2008 <http://www.opinionjournal.com/editorial/feature.html?id=110007611>.

Muhammad, Saad S. "Media and the War Mind." Unpublished essay.

Washington, Cory. "A Soldier's Manifesto." Unpublished essay.

Chapter 16

Pritchett, John S. "Plastic Flotsam Endangers Sea Birds." Cartoon. *Pritchett Cartoons*. 15 July 2008 <http://www.pritchettcartoons.com/plastic.htm>.

Rise Against. "Anywhere but Here." *Siren Song of the Counter Culture*. Geffen, 2004.

Baena, Jeff. *I Heart Huckabees: The Shooting Script*. New York: Newmarket, 2004. 49-57.

Haynes, Todd. "Environmental Illness." *Far from Heaven, Safe, and Superstar: The Karen Carpenter Story: Three Screenplays.* New York: Grove, 2003. 133-38.

Bigmouth, Percy. "The White People Who Came in a Boat." *Memoirs of the American Folklore Society* 26 (1940).

Winthrop, John. "The Indians Grew Very Inquisitive." *Winthrop's Journal*. Ed. J. K. Hosmer. New York: Charles Scribner's Sons, 1908.

Chief Seattle. "How Can One Sell the Air?: A Manifesto for the Earth." Speech. Dec. 1854. *Chief Seattle Arts*. 8 Dec. 2006. 15 July 2008 <http://www.chiefseattle.com/history/chiefseattle/speech/speech.htm>.

Pardo, Mary. "Mexican American Women Grassroots Community Activists: 'Mothers of East Los Angeles.'" *Mexican American Women Activists: Identity and Resistance in Two Los Angeles Communities*. Philadelphia: Temple UP, 1998. Rpt. *Frontiers* 6 (2000): 1-5.

LaDuke, Winona. “The Dumping Ground: Big Utilities Look to Native Lands to House Nuclear Waste.” *Multinational Monitor* 25.11 (2004). 15 July 2008 <http://multinationalmonitor.org/mm2004/112004/laduke.html>.

Bailey, Ronald. “The Eco-tist: Gore as Green.” *National Review* 14 Aug. 2000: 25-27.

Gore, Al. *An Inconvenient Truth*. New York: Rodale, 2006. 284-87.

Clifford, Hal. “Better Living Through French Fries: Is Biodiesel the Fuel of the Future?” *Grist* 22 Aug. 2002. 15 July 2008 <http://www.grist.org/news/maindish/2002/08/22/better/>.

Kobernus, Lauren. “Global Warming: Fact or Fiction?” Unpublished essay.

Chapter 17

Stringfield, Cary. Unpublished cartoon.

Snow, Francis Haffkine. “Nuestro Himno (Star-Spangled Banner).” 1919. *Somos Americanos (We Are Americans)*. Urban Box Office, 2006.

Branch, John. Cartoon. *San Antonio Express-News*. 15 July 2008 <http://www2.mysanantonio.com/opinion/cartoonarchive/branch.cfm>.

Breen, Steve. Cartoon. *SignOnSanDiego.com*. 15 July 2008 <http://www.signonsandiego.com/news/features/breen/archiveindex.html>.

Satrapi, Marjane. “The Vegetable.” *Persepolis 2*. Trans. Anjali. New York: Pantheon, 2004. 35-43.

De Silva, Ian. “No Leniency for Illegal Aliens.” *Human Events* 5 Apr. 2006. 15 July 2008 <http://www.humanevents.com/article.php?id=13770>.

Samuelson, Robert J. “Conspiracy Against Assimilation.” *Washington Post* 20 Apr. 2006: A25. 15 July 2008 <http://www.washingtonpost.com/wpdyn/content/article/2006/04/19/AR2006041902483.htm>.

Kane, Tim, and Kirk Johnson. “Immigration: ‘Neither Preference nor Prejudice.’” *The Heritage Foundation*. 15 Mar. 2006. 15 July 2008 <http://www.heritage.org/Press/Commentary/ed031506b.cfm>.

Soto, Gary. “Mexicans Begin Jogging.” *Where Sparrows Work Hard*. Pittsburg: U of Pittsburg P, 1981. 51.

“President Bush Proposes New Temporary Worker Program.” *The White House.gov*. 7 Jan. 2004. 15 July 2008 <http://www.whitehouse.gov/news/releases/2004/01/20040107-3.html>.

Arau, Sergio. *A Day Without a Mexican*. Eye on the Ball Films, 2004.

Montaner, Carlos Alberto. “Talk English: You Are in the United States.” *Miami Herald* 25 Apr. 1988: 14A. Rpt. in *Language Loyalties*. Ed. James Crawford. Chicago: U of Chicago P, 1992. 163-65.

Egert, Stephanie. “Illegal Immigrants’ Access to Medical Care.” Unpublished essay.

AUTHOR INDEX

p. 604 Arau, Sergio. *A Day Without a Mexican*. Eye on the Ball Films, 2004.

p. 518 Baena, Jeff. *I Heart Huckabees: The Shooting Script*. New York: Newmarket, 2004. 49-57.

p. 552 Bailey, Ronald. "The Eco-tist: Gore as Green." *National Review* 14 Aug. 2000: 25-27.

p. 424 Bailey, Sarah. "Does This Ad Make Me Look Fat?" Unpublished essay.

p. 421 Barry, Dave. "Some Hated Commercials Inspire Violent Fantasies." *SouthCoastToday.com*. 2 Feb. 1997. 15 July 2008 <http://archive.southcoasttoday.com/daily/02-97/02-02-97/e02li202.htm>.

p. 366 Benedetti, Winda. "Were Video Games to Blame for Massacre?" *MSNBC.com*. 20 Apr. 2007. 15 July 2008 <http://www.msnbc.msn.com/id/18220228/>.

p. 533 Bigmouth, Percy. "The White People Who Came in a Boat." *Memoirs of the American Folklore Society* 26 (1940).

p. 123 Block, Herbert L. Cartoon. *Washington Post* 11 Nov. 1986. Library of Congress. 15 July 2008 <http://www.loc.gov/rr/print/swann/herblock/images/s03287u.jpg>.

p. 285 Borgman, Jim. Cartoon. *Cincinnati Enquirer* 19 May 2006.

p. 577 Branch, John. Cartoon. *San Antonio Express-News*. 15 July 2008 <http://www2.mysanantonio.com/opinion/cartoonarchive/branch.cfm>.

p. 577 Breen, Steve. Cartoon. *SignOnSanDiego.com*. 15 July 2008 <http://www.signonsandiego.com/news/features/breen/archiveindex.html>.

p. 356 Brown, John Seely, and Douglas Thomas. "You Play *World of Warcraft*? You're Hired!" *Wired* Apr. 2006. 15 July 2008 <http://www.wired.com/wired/archive/14.04/learn.html>.

p. 12 Buckley, Christopher. *Thank You for Smoking*. New York: Random, 1994. 127-29.

p. 66 Bush, George W. "911 Speech." Speech. 11 Sept. 2001.

p. 598 Bush, George W. "President Bush's Speech on Immigration Policy." Speech. 7 Jan 2004.

p. 536 Chief Seattle. "How Can One Sell the Air?: A Manifesto for the Earth." Speech. Dec. 1854. *Chief Seattle Arts*. 8 Dec. 2006. 15 July 2008 <http://www.chiefseattle.com/history/chiefseattle/speech/speech.htm>.

p. 559 Clifford, Hal. "Better Living Through French Fries: Is Biodiesel the Fuel of the Future?" *Grist* 22 Aug. 2002. 15 July 2008 <http://www.grist.org/news/maindish/2002/08/22/better/>.

p. 318 Clooney, George, and Grant Heslov. *Good Night, and Good Luck*. New York: Newmarket, 2006. 147-51.

p. 78 Cochran, Johnnie. "Johnnie Cochran's Closing Arguments." *Criminal Murder Case LA District Court*. 27 Sept. 1995.

p. 345 Coldwell, Jeff. "The Prince of Propaganda." Unpublished essay.

p. 492 Conant, James B. "We Must Defeat Hitler." *Congressional Record* 7 June 1940. 3669-70.

p. 454 Conroy, Pat. *My Losing Season*. New York: Nan A. Talese/Doubleday, 2002. 370-77.

p. 61 Davies, Ray. "Give the People What They Want." Lyrics. The Kinks.

p. 588 De Silva, Ian. "No Leniency for Illegal Aliens." *Human Events* 5 Apr. 2006. 15 July 2008 <http://www.humanevents.com/article.php?id=13770>.

p. 610 Egert, Stephanie. "Illegal Immigrants' Access to Medical Care." Unpublished essay.

p. 274 Etienne, Kirk-Albert. *The Big Book of Conspiracies*. New York: Paradox, 1995. 63.

p. 377 Fancher, Hampton, and David Webb Peoples. *Blade Runner*. 1982. 15 July 2008 <http://scribble.com/uwi/br/script_19810223.txt>.

p. 482 Farish, Terry. "Why I Went to War." *PBS.org*. 29 Mar. 2005. 15 July 2008 <http://www.pbs.org/wgbh/amex/vietnam/reflect/farish.html>.

p. 353 Farzat, Ali. Cartoon. *A Pen of Damascus Steel: The Political Cartoons of an Arab Master*. Seattle: Cune, 2005. 103.

p. 35 Ford, Gerald R., and David W. Belin. "Kennedy Assassination: How About the Truth?" *Washington Post* 17 Dec. 1991: A21.

p. 124 Glasbergen, Randy. Cartoon. *Glasbergen.com*. 2002. 15 July 2008 <http://www.glasbergen.com/images/mar12.gif>.

p. 555 Gore, Al. *An Inconvenient Truth*. New York: Rodale, 2006. 284-87.

p. 33 Harris, Sidney. Cartoon. *Science Cartoons Plus*. 15 July 2008 <http://www.sciencecartoonsplus.com/pages/gallery.php>.

p. 526 Haynes, Todd. "Environmental Illness." *Far from Heaven, Safe, and Superstar: The Karen Carpenter Story: Three Screenplays*. New York: Grove, 2003. 133-38.

p. 370 Jones, Gerard. "Violent Media Is Good for Kids." *Mother Jones.com*. 28 June 2000. 15 July 2008 <http://www.motherjones.com/commentary/columns/2000/06/violent_media.html>.

p. 594 Kane, Tim, and Kirk Johnson. "Immigration: 'Neither Preference nor Prejudice.'" *The Heritage Foundation*. 15 Mar. 2006. 15 July 2008 <http://www.heritage.org/Press/Commentary/ed031506b.cfm>.

p. xxiii Kelly, Travis. Cartoon. *Art by Travis Kelly*. 20 Jan. 2008. 15 July 2008 <http://www.traviskelly.com/cartoon/index.html>.

p. 185 Kelly, Travis. "Killer Cell Phones." Cartoon. *Art by Travis Kelly*. 15 July 2008 <http://www.traviskelly.com/cartoon/editor.html>.

p. 70 Kennedy, John F. "Inaugural Address of President John F. Kennedy." 20 Jan. 1961. *John F. Kennedy Presidential Library and Museum*. 15 July 2008 <http://www.jfklibrary.org/Historical+Resources/Archives/Reference+Desk/Speeches/JFK/003POF03Inaugural01201961.htm>.

p. 374 Knauss, Greg. "Dining with Cannibals." *Suck.com*. 24 June 1996. 15 July 2008 <http://www.suck.com/daily/96/06/24/>.

p. 563 Kobernus, Lauren. "Global Warming: Fact or Fiction?" Unpublished essay.

p. 547 LaDuke, Winona. "The Dumping Ground: Big Utilities Look to Native Lands to House Nuclear Waste." *Multinational Monitor* 25.11 (2004). 15 July 2008 <http://multinationalmonitor.org/mm2004/112004/laduke.html>.

p. 418 Leo, John. "The Selling of Rebellion." *U.S. News and World Report* 12 Oct. 1998: 18.

p. 498 Lieberman, Joe. "Our Troops Must Stay." *Wall Street Journal Online*. 29 Nov. 2005. 15 July 2008 <http://www.opinionjournal.com/editorial/feature.html?id=110007611>.

p. 487 Lindbergh, Charles. Address. America First Committee. New York. 23 Apr. 1941.

p. 8 Luckovich, Mike. Cartoon. *The Atlanta Constitution* 1995.

p. 58 Mali, Taylor. "How to Write a Political Poem." *Taylor Mali.com*. 2002. 15 July 2008 <http://www.taylormali.com/index.cfm?webid=16>.

p. 402 Marks, Alexandra. "A Backlash to Advertising in an Age of Anything Goes." *Christian Science Monitor* 22 Feb. 1999: 1+.

p. 116 McCloud, Scott. *Understanding Comics*. New York: Harper Perennial, 1993. 28-33.

p. 92 Mitchell, Arnold. *Nine American Lifestyles: Who We Are and Where We're Going*. New York: Macmillan, 1983.

p. 607 Montaner, Carlos Alberto. "Talk English: You Are in the United States." *Miami Herald* 25 Apr. 1988: 14A. Rpt. in *Language Loyalties*. Ed. James Crawford. Chicago: U of Chicago P, 1992. 163-65.

p. 338 Moore, Alan, and David Lloyd. *V for Vendetta*. New York: DC Comics, 1988.

p. 439 Nakazawa, Keiji. *Barefoot Gen: A Cartoon History of Hiroshima*. Trans. Project Gen. Philadelphia: New Society Publishers, 1987.

p. 495 Newbold, Greg. "Why Iraq Was a Mistake." *Time.com*. 9 Apr. 2006. 15 July 2008 <http://www.time.com/time/magazine/article/0,9171,1181629,00.html>.

p. 468 O'Brien, Tim. *The Things They Carried*. Boston: Houghton, 1990. 3-25.

p. 309 Orwell, George. *1984*. New York: Harcourt Brace, 2003. 309-23.

p. 540 Pardo, Mary. "Mexican American Women Grassroots Community Activists: 'Mothers of East Los Angeles.'" *Mexican American Women Activists: Identity and Resistance in Two Los Angeles Communities*. Philadelphia: Temple UP, 1998. Rpt. *Frontiers* 6 (2000): 1-5.

p. 17 Parisi, Mark. Cartoon. *Off the Mark*. 3 Mar. 2004. 15 July 2008 <http://www.offthemark.com>.

p 80 Parker, Trey, and Matt Stone. "Chewbacca Defense." Teleplay. *Southpark,* Season 2, Episode 14. "Chef Aid." 7 Oct. 1998.

p. 466 Patton, George S. Speech. England. 5 June 1944.

p. 513 Pritchett, John S. “Plastic Flotsam Endangers Sea Birds.” Cartoon. *Pritchett Cartoons*. 15 July 2008 <http://www.pritchettcartoons.com/plastic.htm>.

p. 10 Reed, Jerry. “Another Puff.” 1971. *Thank You for Smoking Soundtrack*. Lakeshore Records, 2006.

p. 292 Robins, Robert S., and Jerrold M. Post. “Political Paranoia as Cinematic Motif: Stone’s *JFK*.” American Political Science Association. Washington, D.C. Aug./Sept. 1997. Rpt. by John Adams. *The Kennedy Assassination*. 15 July 2008 <http://mcadams.posc.mu.edu/robins.htm>.

p. 300 Russell, Bertrand. “16 Questions on the Assassination.” *The Minority of One* 6 Sept. 1964: 6-8. Rpt. at www.solstice.us. 15 July 2008 <http://www.solstice.us/russell/16questions.html>.

p. 591 Samuelson, Robert J. “Conspiracy Against Assimilation.” *Washington Post* 20 Apr. 2006: A25. 15 July 2008 <http://www.washingtonpost.com/wpdyn/content/article/2006/04/19/AR2006041902483.htm>.

p. 578 Satrapi, Marjane. “The Vegetable.” *Persepolis 2*. Trans. Anjali. New York: Pantheon, 2004. 35-43.

p. 412 Schlosser, Eric. *Fast Food Nation: The Dark Side of the All-American Meal*. Boston: Houghton, 2001. 120-32.

p. 463 Shakespeare, William. *Henry V*. *The Riverside Shakespeare: The Complete Works*. 2nd ed. Boston: Houghton, 1997. 979-1020.

p. 43 Smith, Rob, Jr. Cartoon. *Cartoons by Rob Smith, Jr*. 25 Sept. 2007. 15 July 2008 <http://art.robsmithjr.com/gallery/4061059_6Sb8A#236512753_KCfpt>.

p. 574 Snow, Francis Haffkine. “Nuestro Himno (Star-Spangled Banner).” 1919. *Somos Americanos (We Are Americans)*. Urban Box Office, 2006.

p. 597 Soto, Gary. “Mexicans Begin Jogging.” *Where Sparrows Work Hard*. Pittsburg: U of Pittsburg P, 1981. 51.

p. 458 Spiegelman, Art. *Maus II: A Survivor’s Tale*. New York: Pantheon, 1995. 41-44.

p. 447 Springsteen, Bruce. “Born in the U.S.A.” *Born in the U.S.A*. Columbia, 1984.

p. 383 Stephenson, Neal. *Snow Crash*. New York: Bantam Spectra, 1992. 1-10.

p. 286 Stone, Oliver. “The JFK Assassination—What About the Evidence?” Letter. *Washington Post* 24 Dec. 1991: A13.

p. 280 Stone, Oliver, and Zachary Sklar. *JFK: The Book of the Film*. New York: Applause, 1992.

p. 574 Stringfield, Cary. *Captain Clark Comics.com*. 15 July 2008 <http://www.captainclarkcomics.com/captainclarkcomics_011.htm>.

p. 273 Stringfield, Cary. Unpublished cartoon.

p. 323 Suu Kyi, Aung San. "Freedom from Fear." *Freedom from Fear and Other Writings*. Penguin, 1991. 180-85.

p. 484 Swofford, Anthony. *Jarhead: A Marine's Chronicle of the Gulf War and Other Battles*. New York: Scribner, 2003. 5-8.

p. 132 Trudeau, G. B. *Doonesbury*. Cartoon. *Slate.com*. 9 Sept. 2007. 15 July 2008 <http://www.doonesbury.com/strip/dailydose/index.html?uc_full_date=20070909>.

p. 450 Twain, Mark. *The War Prayer*. 1905. New York: Harper Perennial, 1984.

p. 328 Wachowski, Andy, and Larry Wachowski. V for Vendetta*: From Script to Film*. Ed. Spencer Lamm and Sharon Bray. New York: Rizzoli, 2006. 35-42.

p. 391 Waldrop, Will. "Fun vs. Family: Mind-Numbing Deviltry." Unpublished essay. 14 Feb. 2005.

p. 506 Washington, Cory. "A Soldier's Manifesto." Unpublished essay.

p. 9 Wasserman, Dan. "The Nicotine or the Lying?" Cartoon. *Advocate* 29 June 1994.

p. 169 Watterson, Bill. *Calvin and Hobbes*. Cartoon. *The Complete Calvin and Hobbes*. Riverside, NJ: Andrews McMeel, 2005.

p. 429 Williams, Kimberly. "Advertising Sex: Company Bias." Unpublished essay.

p. 535 Winthrop, John. "The Indians Grew Very Inquisitive." *Winthrop's Journal*. Ed. J. K. Hosmer. New York: Charles Scribner's Sons, 1908.

INDEX

Abstract Visuals, 104
Abstract, 204
Abstract, 242
Ad Hominem, 30
Analogous Colors, 107
Annotation, 34
APA, 170
Appeals, 20
Avatar, 82
Backing, 49
Bandwagon Claim, 102
Bibliography, 186
Boolean Logic, 190
Call Number, 199
Chicken Fight, 156
Citation, 201
Claim, 18
Classical Canons of Rhetoric, 155
Classical Method, 19
Color Context, 108
Color Harmony, 106
Compliment the Consumer Claim, 101
Complimentary Colors, 108
Concrete Visuals, 105
Conspiracy Theory, 277
Counterclaim, 19
Cultural Preference, 22
Data, 48
Database, 190
Deductive Appeal, 24
Documentation, 206
Either-or, 30
Enargeia, 23
Endorsement or Testimonial Claim, 100
Ethos, 20
EverQuest, 161
Evidence, 20
Expert Testimony, 21
Extrinsic Proof, 27
Facebook, 138
False Authority, 30
False Cause, 30
False Dilemma Claim, 100
Fields, 203
Fonts, 109
Formal Quotations, 216
Format, 187
Gaming Model, 51
Gaming Senses, 155
Guitar Hero III, 164
Halo 3, 163
Hasty Generalization, 30
Honorific/Perjorative Language, 23
Incorporated Quotations, 217
Index, 198
Inductive Appeal, 26
Informal Quotations, 217
Information Source, 187
Interlibrary Loan, 201
In-text Citations, 215
Invisible Web Sites, 188
Issue, 18
Journal, 187
Library Catalog, 198
Logical Fallacy, 29
Logos, 21
Long Quotations, 246
Lyrics, 60
Marking Up, 34
Meaningless Words, 65
Meta-awareness, xiii
MLA, 170
Mock Advertisements, 126
My Space, 139
Nash Equilibrium, 158
Nested Searching, 190
Non Sequitur, 30
Nonverbal Aspects, 73
Nothing to Fear Claim, 101
Online Gaming, 153
Operators, 190
Paraphrase, 215
Parity Products or Ideas, 96
Pathos, 21
Patriotic Claim, 102
Peer-reviewed or Refereed Journals, 206
Penrose Triangle, xiii
Periodicals, 203
Personal Testimony, 22
Persuasive Writing, 44
Plagiarism, 182
Poem, 56
Popular Magazine, 206
Popular Testimony, 21
Prisoner's Dilemma, 156
Qualifier, 49
Rebuttal, 49
Record, 191
Red Herring, 30
Reference Page, 244
Reference Work, 187
Refutation, 51
Research Timeline, 175
Rhetoric, 6
Rhetorical Question, 65
Rhetorical Situation, 44
Rhythm, 57
Rock Band, 165
Rogerian Method, 50
Scholarly Journals, 206
Scientific and Statistical Language, 64
Second Life, 141
Sentence Outline, 172
Short Quotations, 245
Snob Claim, 102
Social Bookmarking, 134
Social Networks, 138
Sound, 56
Source, 178
Stacking the Deck, 30

Stag Hunt, 158
Stasis Theory, 19
Stating the Obvious, 63
Stratagems, xii
Subject Headings, 201
Syllogism, 48
Synonym, 192
Toulmin Method, 47
Trade Journal, 206
Traditional Wisdom Claim, 103
Truncation, 191
Twitter, 140
Unfinished Comparison, 63
Video Gaming, 153
Visible or Public Web Sites, 188
Visual Discourse, 90
Warrant, 48
Weasel Words, 62
Widgets, 134
Wii, 165
Wikipedia, 143
Wikis, 142
Working Bibliography, 178
Works Cited, 212
World of Warcraft, 161
WOVE Approach, 5
Writeboard, 143
xBox 360, 163
YouTube.com, 135
Zero-sum Situation, 157